Global History and Geography Regents Review

to accompany

McDougal Littell

WORLD HISTORY

PATTERNS OF INTERACTION

Reviewers:
Anne Kane
East High School
Rochester, New York

Lisa Kissinger
Shenendehowa High School
Department Administrator
Clifton Park, New York

McDougal Littell
A DIVISION OF HOUGHTON MIFFLIN COMPANY

Acknowledgments

Maps supplied by Mapping Specialists

Unit 1: 18 © Sonia Halliday Photographs; **23** Hirmer Verlag GmbH, Munich, Germany; **29** © Lowell Georgia/Corbis.

Unit 2: 52 Terra cotta tile with a musician (fifth century A.D.), Gupta period, central India. Photo © The British Museum; **56** Illustration by Peter Dennis; **60** © Archivo Iconografico, S.A./Corbis; **66** Sonia Halliday Photographs; **72** Museo Tesoro di San Pietro, Vatican State. Photo © Scala/Art Resource, New York; **78** Mary Evans Picture Library.

Unit 3: 87 Illustration by Peter Dennis; **90** Illustrations by Terry Gabbey; **93** James L. Stanfield/National Geographic Image Collection; **98** © North Carolina Museum of Art/Corbis; **104** Private collection; **110** MS français 6465, f. 212v. Bibliothèque Nationale, Paris. Photo by AKG London; **114** *Portrait of Niccolo Machiavelli,* Santi di Tito. Palazzo Vecchio, Florence, Italy. Photo © Scala/Art Resource, New York; **116** *Marriage of the Virgin* (1504), Raphael. Brera, Milan, Italy. Photo © Scala/Art Resource, New York; **120** *Portrait of Martin Luther* (1529) Lucas Cranach the Elder. Museo Poldi Pezzoli, Milan, Italy. Photo © The Bridgeman Art Library.

Unit 4: 131 Ming vase. Chinese School. Musée des Arts Asiatiques-Guimet, Paris, France. Photo © The Bridgeman Art Library; **135** *Suleiman the Magnificent.* Galleria degli Uffizi, Florence, Italy. Photo © Dagli Orti/The Art Archive; **139** Globe by Martin Behaim (about 1492). Bibliothèque Nationale, Paris. Photo © Giraudon/Art Resource, New York; **143** Quetzalcoatl (tenth century), Toltec, western Yucatan, Mexico. Photo © Dagli Orti/The Art Archive; **149** The Newberry Library, Chicago; **156** Louis XIV, King of France (1701), Hyacinthe Rigaud. Louvre, Paris. Photo © Erich Lessing/Art Resource, New York.

Unit 5: 167 Isaac Newton's reflecting telescope (1672). Photo by Eileen Tweedy/Royal Society/The Art Archive; **172** *Portrait of Francois-Dominique Toussaint*, known as Toussaint L'Ouverture, Anonymous. Musée des Arts d'Oceanie, Paris. Photo J.G. Berizzi © Réunion des Musées Nationaux/Art Resource, New York; **182** *Klemens Metternich, Austrian prince and statesman.* Museo Glauco, Lombardi, Parma, Italy. Photo © Dagli Orti/The Art Archive; **187** *Portrait of Porfirio Diaz.* Antochiw Collection, Mexico. Photo © Mireille Vautier/The Art Archive; **191** Hulton|Archive/Getty Images; **199** © Culver Pictures; **206** © Bettmann/Corbis; **211** The Granger Collection, New York.

Unit 6: 214 Popperfoto; **219** © Bettmann/Corbis; **223** © Bettmann/Corbis; **231** © UPI/Bettmann/Corbis.

Unit 7: 245 Tom Little/Nashville Tennessean; **250** Hulton|Archive/Getty Images; **255** © David Turnley/Corbis; **264** © Wally McNamee/Corbis, **270** © Peter Turnley/Corbis.

Unit 8: 281 © Reuters NewMedia Inc./Corbis; **286** © Peter Kornicker/Corbis.

Backmatter: 310 The Granger Collection, New York

Copyright © by McDougal Littell, a division of Houghton Mifflin Company.
All rights reserved.

Warning: No part of this work may be reproduced or transmitted in any form or by any means, electronic or mechanical, including photocopying and recording, or by any information storage or retrieval system without the prior written permission of McDougal Littell unless such copying is expressly permitted by federal copyright law. With the exception of not-for-profit transcription in Braille, McDougal Littell is not authorized to grant permission for further uses of copyrighted selections reprinted in this text without the permission of their owners. Permission must be obtained from the individual copyright owners as identified herein. Address inquiries to Supervisor, Rights and Permissions, McDougal Littell, P.O. Box 1667, Evanston, IL 60204.

ISBN-13 978-0-618-69698-7   ISBN-10 0-618-69698-9

Printed in the United States of America.

2 3 4 5 6 7 8 9 –VOM– 09 08 07

TABLE OF CONTENTS

Overview of McDougal Littell:
Global History and Geography Regents Review

McDougal Littell: Global History and Geography Regents Review has been created specifically for New York state educators and students to help prepare students for success on the Regents Examination in Global History and Geography. This book includes:

- test-taking strategies.
- a review of the content covered on the Regents Exam.
- practice Regents questions and tests that address both the multiple-choice and writing sections of the examination.
- an answer key, glossary, and index to help students master the content.

The Test-taking Strategies section of this book focuses on the types of questions and skills on the New York Regents Exam. Strategies are provided for answering multiple-choice questions, analyzing primary sources and political cartoons, interpreting charts and graphs, analyzing maps, writing thematic essays, and answering document-based questions. Basic test-taking strategies increase students' comfort and confidence as they approach the test.

The Content Review section of the book provides an overview of the topics covered on the Regents Exam. Its organization follows the eight content units of the Global History and Geography core curriculum: Ancient World—Civilizations and Religions, Expanding Zones of Exchange and Encounter, Global Interactions, The First Global Age, An Age of Revolution, A Half Century of Crisis and Achievement, The Twentieth Century Since 1945, and Global Connections and Interactions. The Content Review includes point-of-use study questions to focus students on the type of information typically covered on the examination.

Each unit of the Content Review also includes practice questions at the section level. The questions, which are drawn from past Regents Exams, focus on the section content. The multiple-choice questions have **"Analyze-the-Question"** tips to help students reinforce their test-taking skills. The thematic essay questions include the rubric for a level-5 essay. In addition, a **mini version** of the Regents Exam is included at the end of every unit. Like the section questions, these multiple-choice, thematic essay, and document-based questions are drawn from past Regents Exams. The topics of the question relate to the unit content.

McDougal Littell: Global History and Geography Regents Review also includes a full **Sample Regents Examination** in Global History and Geography. The questions cover content from the eight content units of the core curriculum. The **Answer Key** includes the answers to all point-of-use study questions and practice and sample multiple-choice questions. In addition, level-5 thematic and document-based rubrics are included. A glossary and index close out the book, making it easy for student to find the information they need to prepare for success on the Regents Examination in Global History and Geography.

Standard 1: History of the United States and New York

Students will use a variety of intellectual skills to demonstrate their understanding of major ideas, eras, themes, developments, and turning points in the history of the United States and New York.

Standard 2: World History

Students will use a variety of intellectual skills to demonstrate their understanding of major ideas, eras, themes, developments, and turning points in world history and examine the broad sweep of history from a variety of perspectives.

Standard 3: Geography

Students will use a variety of intellectual skills to demonstrate their understanding of the geography of the interdependent world in which we live—local, national, and global—including the distribution of people, places, and environments over the Earth's surface.

Standard 4: Economics

Students will use a variety of intellectual skills to demonstrate their understanding of how the United States and other societies develop economic systems and associated institutions to allocate scarce resources, how major decision-making units function in the U.S. and other national economies, and how an economy solves the scarcity problem through market and nonmarket mechanisms.

Standard 5: Civics, Citizenship, and Government

Students will use a variety of intellectual skills to demonstrate their understanding of the necessity for establishing governments; the governmental system of the U.S. and other nations; the U.S. Constitution; the basic civic values of American constitutional democracy; and the roles, rights, and responsibilities of citizenship, including avenues of participation.

Global History and Geography Concepts and Themes

The Regents Examination in Global History and Geography draws its content from the Global History and Geography core curriculum. To help students master the vast amount of information that is part of world history, the core curriculum emphasizes a variety of concepts and themes. Concepts and themes allow students to organize isolated facts and information about history into patterns across regions and through time. The Global History and Geography core curriculum emphasizes 24 concepts and themes. Following are their definitions.

HISTORY

Belief Systems are the established orderly ways that groups or individuals look at religious faith or philosophical tenets.

Change involves basic alterations in things, events, and ideas.

Conflict is a clash of ideas, interests, or wills that result from incompatible opposing forces.

Culture and Intellectual Life involves the patterns of human behavior—such as ideas, beliefs, values, artifacts, and ways of making a living—that any society transmits to succeeding generations to meet its fundamental needs.

Diversity refers to understanding and respecting others and oneself, including similarities and differences in language, gender, socioeconomic class, religion, and other human characteristics and traits.

Imperialism is the domination by one country of the political and/or economic life of another country or region.

Interdependence means reliance upon others in mutually beneficial interactions and exchanges.

Movement of People and Goods refers to the constant exchange of people, ideas, products, technologies, and institutions from one region or civilization to another that has existed throughout history.

Nationalism is the feeling of pride in and devotion to one's country or the desire of a people to control their own government, free from foreign interference or rule.

Urbanization is the movement of people from rural to urban areas.

GEOGRAPHY

Environment and Society refers to the ways in which the physical environment is modified by human activities, largely as a consequence of the ways in which human societies value and use Earth's natural resources. Human activities are also influenced by Earth's physical features and processes.

Human and Physical Geography refers to the human and physical systems. People are central to geography in that human activities help shape Earth's surface, human settlements and structures are part of Earth's surface, and humans compete for control of Earth's surface. Physical processes shape Earth's surface and interact with plant and animal life to create, sustain, and modify ecosystems.

ECONOMICS

Economic Systems include traditional, command, market, and mixed systems. Each must answer the three basic economic questions: What goods and services shall be produced and in what quantities? How shall these goods and services be produced? For whom shall goods and services be produced?

Factors of Production are human, natural, and capital resources, which when combined, become various goods and services (e.g., How land, labor, and capital inputs are used to produce food).

Needs and Wants refer to those goods and services that are essential, such as food, clothing, and shelter (needs), and those goods and services that people would like to have to improve the quality of their lives, (i.e., wants—education, security, health care, entertainment).

Scarcity means the conflict between unlimited needs and wants and limited natural and human resources.

Science and Technology means the tools and methods used by people to get what they need and want.

CIVICS, CITIZENSHIP, AND GOVERNMENT

Citizenship means membership in a community (neighborhood, school, region, state, nation, world) with its accompanying rights, responsibilities, and dispositions.

Decision Making means the processes used to monitor and influence public and civic life by working with others, clearly articulating ideals and interests, building coalitions, seeking consensus, negotiating compromise, and managing conflict.

Human Rights are those basic political, economic, and social rights that all human beings are entitled to, such as the right to life, liberty, and the security of person, and a standard of living adequate for the health and well-being of people and their families. Human rights are inalienable and expressed by various United Nations documents including the United Nations Charter and Universal Declaration of Human Rights.

Justice means the fair, equal, proportional, or appropriate treatment rendered to individuals in interpersonal, societal, or government interactions.

Nation State means a geographic/political organization uniting people by a common government.

Political Systems such as monarchies, dictatorships, and democracies address certain basic questions of government such as: What should a government have the power to do? What should a government not have the power to do? A political system also provides for ways that parts of that system interrelate and combine to perform specific functions of government.

Power refers to the ability of people to compel or influence the actions of others. "Legitimate power is called authority."

Source: Definitions are taken from *Social Studies Resource Guide with Core Curriculum*. New York State Education Department.

The Regents Examination in Global History and Geography for New York State has been developed to reflect the social studies content and intellectual skills described in the New York Social Studies Standards. This assessment provides students with multiple opportunities to demonstrate what they know and are able to do. Questions on this examination focus on the students' knowledge of commencement-level social studies skills and content emphasized in the *Social Studies Resource Guide with Core Curriculum* for Global History and Geography.

Items for this assessment have resulted from the collaborative efforts of New York State teachers, school districts, State Education Department staff, and the Educational Testing Service (ETS).

The multiple-choice questions are designed to assess both the students' understanding of the Global History and Geography content and their ability to apply the content understandings to the interpretation and analysis of reading passages, graphs, political cartoons, maps, and diagrams. Thematic essays require students to explore one of the major themes found in the Global History and Geography section of the *Social Studies Resource Guide with Core Curriculum*. Document-based questions require students to identify and explore events or issues by examining, analyzing, and evaluating textual and visual primary and secondary sources.

Each test is scaled, and all test forms equated, based on a standard-setting process. Students will benefit from having multiple opportunities to answer document-based questions and thematic essays. Test-taking strategies can be taught and students who have practiced answering these types of questions will be better prepared for this assessment.

You can improve your test-taking skills by practicing the strategies discussed in this section. First, read the tips on the left-hand page. Then apply them to the practice items on the right-hand page.

Multiple Choice

A multiple-choice question consists of a stem and a set of alternatives from which to select the right answer. The stem usually is in the form of a question or an incomplete sentence. One of the alternatives correctly answers the question or completes the sentence.

1. Read the stem carefully and try to answer the question or complete the sentence before looking at the alternatives.

2. Look for key words in the stem. They may direct you to the correct answer.

3. Read each alternative with the stem. Don't make your final decision on the correct answer until you have read all of the alternatives.

4. Eliminate alternatives that you know are wrong.

5. Look for modifiers to help you rule out incorrect alternatives.

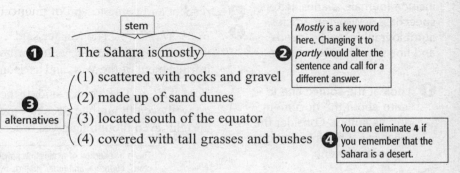

1. The Sahara is **mostly**

  (1) scattered with rocks and gravel

  (2) made up of sand dunes

  (3) located south of the equator

  (4) covered with tall grasses and bushes

stem

alternatives

Mostly is a key word here. Changing it to *partly* would alter the sentence and call for a different answer.

You can eliminate **4** if you remember that the Sahara is a desert.

2. Over hundreds of years, the Bantu people migrated from West Africa to

  (1) **all** of North Africa

  (2) East and South Africa

  (3) South and Southwest Asia

  (4) **every** continent except Antarctica

Absolute words, such as *all, never, always, every,* and *only,* often signal an incorrect alternative.

3. The traditional griots of West Africa passed on the histories of their people by

  (1) writing books

  (2) painting murals

  (3) telling stories

  (4) making sculptures

4. Ghana, Mali, and Songhai all were

  (1) conquered by the French

  (2) active in the Atlantic slave trade

  (3) part of the West African empire

  (4) involved in the gold-salt trade

answers: 1 (1); 2 (2); 3 (3); 4 (4)

Primary Sources

Primary sources are materials that have been written or made by people who were at historical events, either as observers or participants. Primary sources include journals, diaries, letters, speeches, newspaper articles, autobiographies, wills, deeds, and financial records.

❶ Look at the source line to learn about the document and its author. Consider the reliability of the information in the document.

❷ Skim the document to get an idea of what it is about. (This source includes three paragraphs that are distinct but address a related theme—rulers and moral behavior.)

❸ Note any special punctuation. Ellipses (. . .), for example, indicate that words or sentences have been removed from the original.

❹ Use active reading strategies. For instance, ask and answer questions on the content as you read.

❺ Use context clues to help you understand difficult or unfamiliar words. (From the context, you realize that *chastisements* means "punishments.")

❻ Before rereading the document, skim the questions. This will help you focus your reading and more easily locate answers.

Moral Rulers

Book II, 3. The Master said, Govern the people by regulations, keep order among them by chastisements, and they will flee **❺** from you, and lose all self-respect. Govern them by moral force, keep order among them by ritual and they will keep their self-respect and come to you of their own accord. . . . **❸**

Book XI, 23. . . . The Master said, . . . What I call a great minister is one who will only serve his prince while he can do so without infringement of the Way, and as soon as this is impossible, resigns. . . .

Book XIII, 6. The Master said, If the ruler himself is upright, all will go well even though he does not give orders. But if he himself is not upright, even though he gives orders, they will not be obeyed.

This is a collection of writings on government, ethics, literature, and other subjects by the ancient Chinese scholar and teacher Confucius. **❶**

—The Analects of Confucius

1 Which sentence best expresses the main idea shared by these paragraphs?

(1) Rules and regulations are hard to live by.

(2) Leaders should act morally in ruling the people.

(3) A leader's goodness is judged by the punishments he administers.

(4) Rulers should expect their people to obey them no matter what they say.

2 This advice from Confucius seems most appropriate for

(1) workers and farmers

(2) merchants and town artisans

(3) rulers and their advisers

(4) soldiers and priests

answers: 1 (2); 2 (3)

Political Cartoons

Political cartoons use a combination of words and images to express a point of view on political issues. They are useful primary sources, because they reflect the opinions of the time.

1 Identify the subject of the cartoon. Titles and captions often provide clues to the subject matter.

2 Use labels to help identify the people, places, and events represented in the cartoon.

3 Note where and when the cartoon was published for more information on people, places, and events.

4 Identify any important symbols—ideas or images that stand for something else—in the cartoon.

5 Analyze the point of view presented in the cartoon. The use of caricature—the exaggeration of physical features—often signals how the cartoonist feels.

6 Interpret the cartoonist's message.

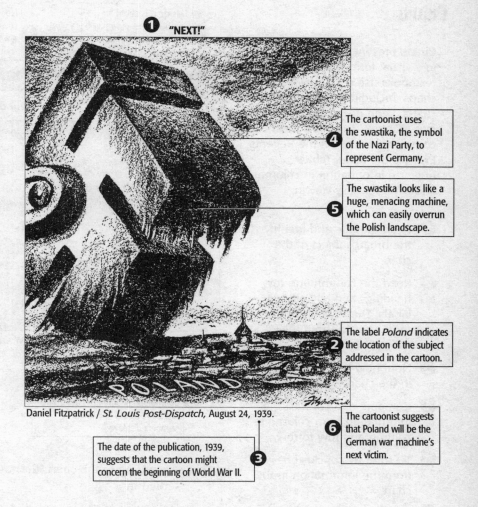

1 "NEXT!"

4 The cartoonist uses the swastika, the symbol of the Nazi Party, to represent Germany.

5 The swastika looks like a huge, menacing machine, which can easily overrun the Polish landscape.

2 The label *Poland* indicates the location of the subject addressed in the cartoon.

Daniel Fitzpatrick / *St. Louis Post-Dispatch,* August 24, 1939.

6 The cartoonist suggests that Poland will be the German war machine's next victim.

3 The date of the publication, 1939, suggests that the cartoon might concern the beginning of World War II.

1   The machine-like swastika in the cartoon represents

(1) Nazi Germany

(2) the Soviet Union

(3) Napoleon's empire

(4) the Polish military

2   Which sentence best summarizes the cartoonist's message?

(1) Germany must beware of Poland.

(2) Poland is in danger of civil war.

(3) Germany and Poland are military giants.

(4) Poland will be Germany's next victim.

answers: 1 (1); 2 (4)

Charts

Charts present information in a visual form. History textbooks use several types of charts, including tables, flow charts, Venn diagrams, and info-graphics. The chart most commonly found on the Regents Exam is the table. Tables organize information in columns and rows for easy viewing.

❶ Read the title and identify the broad subject of the chart.

❷ Read the column and row headings and any other labels. These will provide more details about the subject of the chart.

❸ Note how the information in the chart is organized.

❹ Compare and contrast the information from column to column and row to row.

❺ Try to draw conclusions from the information in the chart.

❻ Read the questions and then study the chart again.

❶ This chart is about the number of people who immigrated to different countries.

❹ Notice that the years covered in the table are not the same for all countries.

Immigration to Selected Countries

Country	Period	Number of Immigrants
Argentina	1856-1932	6,405,000
Australia	1861-1932	2,913,000
Brazil	1821-1932	4,431,000
British West Indies	1836-1932	1,587,000
Canada	1821-1932	5,206,000
Cuba	1901-1932	857,000
Mexico	1911-1931	226,000
New Zealand	1851-1932	594,000
South Africa	1881-1932	852,000
United States	1821-1932	34,244,000
Uruguay	1836-1932	713,000

Source: Alfred W. Crosby, Jr., *The Columbian Exchange: Biological and Cultural Consequences of 1492*

❸ This chart organizes the countries alphabetically. In some charts, information is organized according to years or the value of the numbers displayed.

❺ Think about what the countries with the highest number of immigrants have in common.

1 According to the chart, the vast majority of immigrants settled in

(1) Argentina
(2) Brazil
(3) Canada
(4) the United States

2 The Latin American country that received the most immigrants was

(1) Argentina
(2) Brazil
(3) Cuba
(4) Uruguay

answers: 1 (4); 2 (1)

Line and Bar Graphs

Graphs show statistics in a visual form. Line graphs are particularly useful for showing changes over time. Bar graphs make it easy to compare numbers or sets of numbers.

1 Read the title and identify the broad subject of the graph.

2 Study the labels on the vertical and horizontal axes to see the kinds of information presented in the graph. Note the intervals between amounts and between dates. This will help you read the graph more efficiently.

3 Look at the source line and evaluate the reliability of the information in the graph.

4 If the graph presents information over time, look for trends—generalizations you can make about changes over time.

5 Draw conclusions and make inferences based on information in the graph.

6 Read the questions carefully and then study the graph again.

1 Exports of English Manufactured Goods, 1699–1774

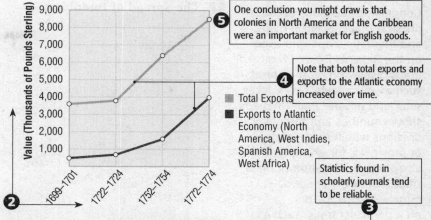

One conclusion you might draw is that colonies in North America and the Caribbean were an important market for English goods. **5**

Note that both total exports and exports to the Atlantic economy increased over time. **4**

Total Exports

Exports to Atlantic Economy (North America, West Indies, Spanish America, West Africa)

Statistics found in scholarly journals tend to be reliable. **3**

Source: R. Davis, "English Foreign Trade, 1700–1774, "*Economic History Review* (1962)

6 1 Which statement best describes the trend in total exports?

(1) They rose and fell.
(2) They remained unchanged.
(3) They grew over time.
(4) They decreased over time.

1 Nations with High Foreign Debt, 1998

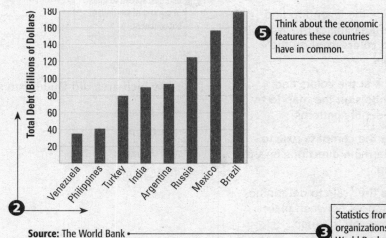

Think about the economic features these countries have in common. **5**

Source: The World Bank

Statistics from major organizations, such as the World Bank, tend to be reliable. **3**

6 2 Which nation has the largest foreign debt?

1 Venezuela
2 Brazil
3 Mexico
4 Russia

answers: 1 (3); 2 (2)

Maps

Generally, three kinds of maps—physical maps, political maps, and thematic maps—are used on the Regents Exam. Physical maps display physical features, such as mountains, rivers, lakes, seas, and oceans. Political maps show countries and the political divisions within them—states or provinces, for example. They also show the location of major cities. Thematic, or special-purpose, maps focus on a particular topic, such as population density, election results, or major battles in a war. The thematic map on this page shows the spread of Buddhism across South and East Asia.

❶ Read the title of the map to identify the area shown and the subject covered.

❷ Examine the labels on the map to find more information on the map's subject.

❸ Study the legend to find the meaning of the symbols and colors used on the map.

❹ Look at the colors and symbols on the map to try to identify patterns.

❺ Use the compass rose to determine directions on the map.

❻ Use the scale to determine distances between places shown on the map.

❼ Read the questions, and then carefully study the map to determine the answers.

❶ The Spread of Buddhism

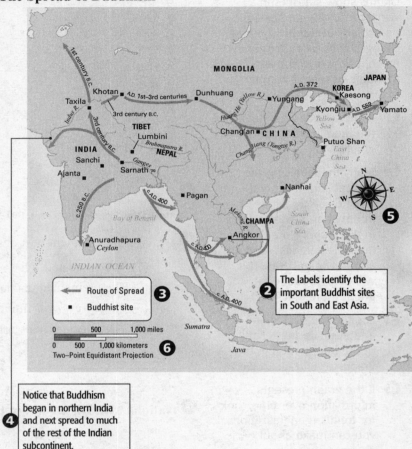

The labels identify the important Buddhist sites in South and East Asia.

Notice that Buddhism began in northern India and next spread to much of the rest of the Indian subcontinent.

1 To which area did Buddhism spread after A.D. 550?

(1) Java

(2) China

(3) Japan

(4) Champa

2 The routes tracing the spread of Buddhism reflect the cultural influence that China had on

(1) Mongolia and Vietnam

(2) Korea and Japan

(3) Vietnam and Korea

(4) India and Japan

answers: 1 (3); 2 (2)

Thematic Essay

Thematic-essay questions require you to write a well-thought-out essay on a specific theme. Belief systems, conflict, economic systems, human rights, imperialism, justice, migration, nationalism, power, social change, trade, and urbanization all are themes that might be addressed in thematic-essay questions on the Regents Exam.

1 Read the "Theme" section to find the broad focus of the question.

2 Read the "Task" section and note the action words. This will help you understand exactly what the essay question requires. The most frequently used action words in thematic essay questions are *define, discuss, describe, show, compare, contrast, explain, analyze,* and *evaluate.* Make sure that you understand the meaning of these words.

3 Jot down ideas about the essay theme. Then organize your ideas in an outline.

4 Use this outline to write your essay. Remember that the essay should consist of an introduction, two or more body paragraphs, and a conclusion. Make sure your essay shows a thorough understanding of the theme and addresses all aspects of the task.

Theme: Economic and Social Change

The Industrial Revolution brought major changes to the lives of workers.

1 This question focuses on the economic and social changes brought about by the Industrial Revolution.

2 **Task:**

- (Define) the term "Industrial Revolution"
- Identify and (describe) *two* inventions or developments associated with the Industrial Revolution
- (Discuss) the impact that these inventions or developments had on the lives of workers

2 Define means "give the meaning of"; describe means "give an account of" or "tell about"; discuss means "make observations using fact, reasoning, and argument" or "present in some detail."

You may use any of the inventions and developments from your study of global history. Some suggestions you might wish to consider include: mechanical reaper, steam engine, spinning mule, power loom, Macadam road, and locomotive.

You are *not* limited to these suggestions.

3 **4** **Sample Response** The best essays will point out that developments in agriculture reduced the need for labor on the land. Many farm workers left the country seeking work in factories in the cities. As a result, cities grew much larger. However, lack of sanitation and poor quality buildings made cities unhealthy, and sometimes dangerous, places to live. Life for factory workers was made worse because they worked long hours under dreadful conditions. Society split into clear social classes, with an upper class of landowners and aristocrats, a growing middle class of merchants and factory owners, and a large, generally poor lower class. Over the long term, though, working and living conditions improved somewhat for the working class, in part because factory-produced goods were cheaper.

Document-Based Questions

A document-based question (DBQ) requires you to analyze and interpret a variety of documents. These documents are accompanied by one or more short-answer questions. You use the answers to these questions, information from the documents, and your knowledge of global history to write an essay on a specified subject.

❶ Read the "Historical Context" section to get a sense of the issue addressed in the question.

❷ Read the "Task" section and note the action words. This will help you understand exactly what the essay question requires. (Here, *discuss* means "write about" or "give close examination or consideration to." *Evaluate* means "examine or judge carefully.")

❸ Study and analyze each document. Consider what connection the documents have to the essay question. Take notes on your ideas. (Document 1 establishes that Genghis Khan, who unified the Mongols, had a great passion for conquest.)

❹ Read and answer the short-answer questions for each document. Think about how these questions connect to the essay topic.

❶ Historical Context:
For hundreds of years, Mongol nomads lived in separate tribes, sometimes fighting among themselves. In the early 1200s, a new leader—Genghis Khan—united these tribes and turned the Mongols into a powerful fighting force.

❷ Task:
Using information from the documents and your knowledge of global history, answer the questions that follow each document in Part A. Your answers to these questions will help you write the Part B essay in which you will be asked to:

- (Discuss) how the Mongols achieved their conquest of Central and East Asia
- (Evaluate) the impact that the Mongol Empire had on Europeans

Part A: Short-Answer Questions

Directions: Study the documents and answer the short-answer questions that follow each document.

❸

Document 1: Genghis Khan

The Greatest Happiness is to scatter your enemy and drive him before you. To see his cities reduced to ashes. To see those who love him shrouded and in tears.

—Genghis Khan

The Granger Collection, New York

❹

1   What was Genghis Khan's attitude toward warfare and conquest? [1]

Warfare and conquest provided the "greatest happiness" for him.

❺ Document 2: Mongol Battle Tactics

The Mongols' sophisticated and devastating military tactics led to their overwhelming success. Organizing their campaigns at meetings held far in advance of their planned attack, they devised two- and three-flank operations. The invasion of Hungary, for example, was two-pronged: one division of their army arrived from Russia while the other moved through Poland and Germany. Perhaps half the population of Hungary perished in the assault as the Mongols, fighting mainly on horseback, with heavy lances and powerful bows and arrows whose shots traveled far and penetrated deeply, crushed the Hungarian army of mixed infantry and cavalry.

—Lynn Hunt, et al, *The Challenge of the West* (1995)

2   What military tactics did the Mongol armies use in their conquest of vast areas of Central and East Asia? [2]

They planned well ahead of time and used two- and three-pronged attacks, which enabled them to overrun enemy armies.

❻ Document 3: Mongol Warrior

3   What were the characteristics of Mongol soldiers? [2]

Mongol soldiers rode on horseback and were armed with bows and arrows.

❺ Use the following strategies to read secondary sources:

- Look at the title to preview the content of the passage.

- Skim the passage to locate the main idea.

- Read actively by asking and answering questions about the passage.

❻ To analyze a photograph, painting, or similar type of visual image, use these strategies:

- Study the image carefully, then jot down exactly what you see.

- Note any appropriate information you know about the person, period, or event shown in the image.

- Draw conclusions about the subject of the image.

Document 4: Kublai Khan's Wealth

Let me tell you further that several times a year a [command] goes forth through the towns that all those who have gems and pearls and gold and silver must bring them to the Great Khan's mint. This they do, and in such abundance that it is past all reckoning; and they are all paid in paper money. By this means the Great Khan acquires all the gold and silver and pearls and precious stones of all his territories. . . .

I have now told you how it comes about that the Great Khan must have, as indeed he has, more treasure than anyone else in the world. I may go further and affirm that all the world's great potentates put together have not such riches as belong to the Great Khan alone.

—Marco Polo, *The Travels of Marco Polo* (c. 1300)

4 Why did Marco Polo's descriptions of his travels encourage European interest in East Asia? [1]

Europeans were attracted by his descriptions of the great wealth.

❼ Part B: Essay

Directions:
- Write a well-organized essay that includes an introduction, several explanatory paragraphs, and a conclusion.
- Use evidence from at least *four* documents to support your response.
- Include additional related information.

Historical Context:
For hundreds of years, Mongol nomads lived in separate tribes, sometimes fighting among themselves. In the early 1200s, a new leader—Genghis Khan—united these tribes and turned the Mongols into a powerful fighting force.

Task:
Using information from the documents and your knowledge of global history, write an essay in which you:
- Discuss how the Mongols achieved their conquest of Central and East Asia
- Evaluate the impact that the Mongol Empire had on Europeans

❼ Carefully read the essay question. In particular, note the number of documents your are required to cite. Then write an outline for your essay.

❽ Write your essay. Be sure that it has an introductory paragraph that introduces your argument, main body paragraphs that explain it, and a concluding paragraph that restates your position. In your essay, include quotations or details from specific documents to support your ideas. Add other supporting facts or details that you know from your study of global history.

❽ **Sample Response** The best essays will link the Mongols' tactics, fierce will, and strong military organization to their successful conquest of vast areas in Central and East Asia (Documents 1, 2, 3, and 4). They will also note that rule over these vast lands brought a period of peace and united regions that had before then been separate. Essays should point out that this peace revived trade along the Silk Road (Document 4) and brought new inventions and ideas to Europe and that this revived trade. Further, accounts of the immense wealth in Mongol lands (Document 4) spurred Europeans' interest in tapping into that wealth.

UNIT 1

Ancient World—Civilizations and Religions
4000 B.C.–A.D. 500

Unit Overview

This unit traces the beginnings of civilization, from the appearance of the first humans through the rise and fall of the first great civilizations and empires. Along the way, it examines such turning points as the Neolithic Revolution, the rise of cities, the development of democracy, and the emergence and spread of the world's great belief systems.

Concepts and Themes

Among the concepts and themes explored in this unit are

- Belief Systems
- Citizenship
- Culture and Intellectual Life
- Human and Physical Geography
- Movement of People and Goods
- Needs and Wants
- Political Systems
- Power
- Science and Technology
- Urbanization

PREPARING FOR THE REGENTS: Building Thematic Essay Skills

Throughout time, the beliefs and achievements of individuals have helped shape global history. Many of these beliefs and achievements have had both positive and negative effects on society. As you read this unit, think about the beliefs and achievements of Hammurabi, Aristotle, Alexander the Great, Confucius, Muhammad, and the other people you encounter who have changed history. Use the following web diagram to organize information about the individuals. You can add additional boxes as needed.

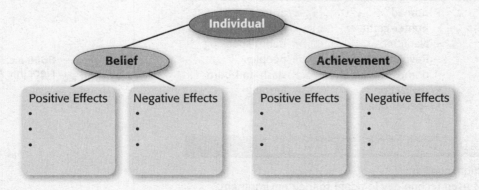

Early Peoples and the Rise of Civilization

Section Overview

What were the earliest humans like? Many people have asked this question. Because there are no written records of prehistoric peoples, scientists have to piece together information about the past. Teams of scientists use a variety of research methods to learn more about how, where, and when early humans developed.

Current evidence indicates that by about 40,000 years ago, human beings had become fully modern in their physical appearance. However, over the following thousands of years, the way of life of early humans underwent incredible changes. People developed new technology, artistic skills, and more importantly agriculture. Agriculture marked a dramatic turning point in how people lived together. They began dwelling in larger, more organized communities. From some of these settlements, cities gradually emerged, forming the backdrop of a more complex way of life—civilization.

A 9,000-year-old baked-clay figurine from Turkey

MAIN IDEAS

INTERACTION WITH ENVIRONMENT As early humans spread out over the world, they adapted to each environment they encountered. As time progressed, they learned to use natural resources.

SCIENCE AND TECHNOLOGY The earliest people came up with new ideas and inventions in order to survive. As people began to live in settlements, they continued to develop new technologies to control the environment.

ECONOMICS Early humans hunted animals and gathered wild plant foods for 3 to 4 million years. Then about 10,000 years ago, they learned to tame animals and plant crops. Gradually, more complex economies developed.

TERMS AND NAMES

- Paleolithic Age
- Neolithic Age
- artifact
- culture
- hominid
- *Homo sapiens*
- technology
- nomad
- hunter-gatherer
- Neolithic Revolution
- domestication
- civilization
- specialization
- artisan
- institution
- Bantu-speaking peoples
- slash-and-burn farming

TIME LINE

4,000,000 B.C.
First hominids appear in Africa.

2,500,000 B.C.
Paleolithic Age begins.

1,600,000 B.C.
Homo erectus appears.

40,000 B.C.
Cro-Magnons emerge.

8000 B.C.
Neolithic Age begins.

C. 3000 B.C.
First cities appear.

PREPARING FOR THE REGENTS

As you read this section, consider
- how early peoples used technology to adapt to their environment.
- why the introduction of agriculture was called the Neolithic Revolution.

Early Peoples

The invention of tools, mastery over fire, and the development of language are some of the most impressive achievements in human history. Scientists believe these occurred during the prehistoric period known as the Stone Age. The earlier and longer part of the Stone Age, called the Old Stone Age or **Paleolithic Age**, lasted from about 2.5 million to 8000 B.C. The New Stone Age, or **Neolithic Age**, began about 8000 B.C. in some areas.

Because there are no written records of prehistoric peoples, archaeologists, anthropologists, and paleontologists working in the field of anthropology have to piece together information about the past. Archaeologists excavate and study bones, artifacts, and other traces of early settlements. **Artifacts** are human-made objects, such as tools and jewelry. Anthropologists study artifacts to re-create a picture of early people's **culture**, or unique way of life. Paleontologists study fossils—evidence of early life preserved in rocks. These scientists work as a team to make new discoveries about early humans.

Human and Physical Geography About 1.6 million years ago, a new species of **hominids**, or creatures that walk upright, appeared in East Africa. This species is now known as *Homo erectus*, or "upright man." *Homo erectus* people used intelligence to develop **technology**—ways of applying knowledge, tools, and inventions to meet their needs. They gradually became skillful hunters and developed more sophisticated tools. According to scientists, they were the first to use fire and may have developed the beginnings of spoken language. These innovations gave them greater control over their environment.

Many scientists believe that *Homo erectus* eventually developed into ***Homo sapiens***—the species name for modern humans. About 40,000 years ago, a group of prehistoric humans called Cro-Magnons appeared. They made many new tools with specialized uses and developed advanced skills in spoken language. Cro-Magnons also planned their hunts. They studied animals' habits and stalked their prey. Eventually this allowed them to survive more easily.

Hunters and Gatherers and Their Tools For tens of thousands of years, men and women of the Old Stone Age were nomads. **Nomads** are highly mobile people who move from place to place foraging, or searching, for new sources of food. Nomadic groups whose food supply depends on hunting animals and collecting plant foods are called **hunter-gatherers**.

Prehistoric hunter-gatherers, such as the roving bands of Cro-Magnons, increased their food supply by inventing special spears and digging sticks. Spears enabled hunters to kill game at greater distances, and digging sticks helped gatherers pry plants loose at the roots. Early modern humans used stone, bone, and wood to fashion more than 100 different tools. These expanded tool kits included knives to kill and butcher game, and fish hooks and harpoons to catch fish. A chisel cutter was designed to make other tools. Cro-Magnons used bone needles to sew clothing made of animal hides.

Migration of Early Humans According to scientists, *Homo erectus* were the first hominids to migrate, or move, from Africa. Fossils and stone tools show that bands of *Homo erectus* hunters settled in India, China, Southeast Asia, and Europe. Cro-Magnons later migrated from North Africa to Europe and Asia. The picture of human origins in Africa and of the migration of early humans out of Africa is still sketchy, however. New findings continue to add to our knowledge, sometimes changing our views.

1.1 Preparing for the Regents

Human and Physical Geography In which field of study do people learn about the development of early human beings?

TAKING NOTES

Categorizing Use a diagram to list advances of each hominid group.

1.2 Preparing for the Regents

Human and Physical Geography What are the characteristics of hunter-gatherers?

Neolithic Revolution

For thousands and thousands of years, humans survived by hunting game and gathering edible plants. They lived in bands of 25 to 70 people. The men almost certainly did the hunting. The women gathered fruits, berries, roots, and grasses. Then about 10,000 years ago, some of the women may have scattered seeds near a regular campsite. When they returned the next season, they may have found new crops growing. This discovery would usher in the **Neolithic Revolution**, or agricultural revolution—the far-reaching changes in human life resulting from the beginning of farming. This shift from a food-gathering to a food-producing culture also included the **domestication**, or taming, of animals, such as horses, dogs, goats, and pigs.

Causes Scientists do not know exactly why the agricultural revolution occurred during the Neolithic Age. Change in climate was probably a key reason. Rising temperatures worldwide provided longer growing seasons and drier land for cultivating wild grasses. A rich supply of grain helped support a small population boom. As populations rose, hunter-gatherers felt pressure to find new food sources. Farming and the domestication of animals offered steady sources of food.

1.3 Preparing for the Regents

Human and Physical Geography What was an important result of the Neolithic Revolution?

Consequences The changeover from hunting and gathering to farming and herding took place not once but many times. Neolithic people in many parts of the world independently developed agriculture, especially in fertile river valleys. From these agricultural centers, farming spread to surrounding regions. Over the centuries, people settled in stable communities that were based on agriculture. Domesticated animals became more common. The invention of new tools and farming methods—hoes, sickles, plow sticks, and irrigation systems—made the task of farming easier. As people gradually developed the technology to control their natural environment, they reaped larger harvests. Food surpluses freed some villagers to pursue jobs other than farming. Some individuals became craftspeople, others became traders.

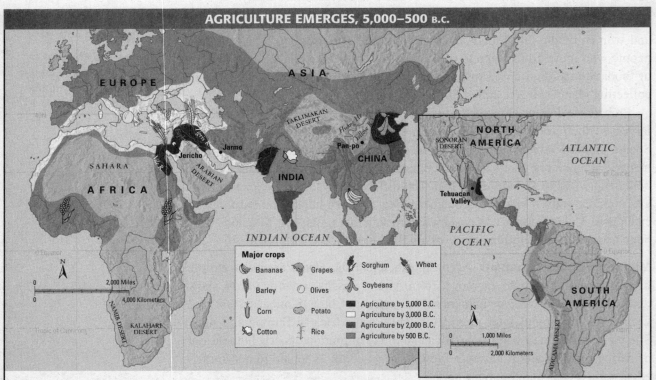

AGRICULTURE EMERGES, 5,000–500 B.C.

Major crops

Bananas   Grapes   Sorghum   Wheat

Barley   Olives   Soybeans

Corn   Potato   ■ Agriculture by 5,000 B.C.
□ Agriculture by 3,000 B.C.
Cotton   Rice   ■ Agriculture by 2,000 B.C.
▨ Agriculture by 500 B.C.

The Peopling of the World

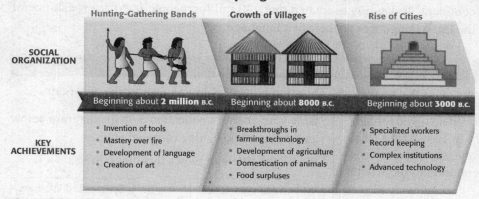

The Rise of Civilization

Over time farming communities grew into cities, and with the growth of cities came the first civilizations. A **civilization** is often defined as a complex culture with five characteristics: (1) advanced cities, (2) specialized workers, (3) complex institutions, (4) record keeping, and (5) advanced technology.

Ancient cities were centers of trade. Farmers, merchants, and traders brought goods to market in the cities. The city dwellers themselves produced a variety of goods for exchange. As cities grew, so did the need for more specialized workers. Food surpluses provided the opportunity for **specialization**—the development of skills in a specific kind of work. Some city dwellers became **artisans**—skilled workers who made goods by hand.

Soaring populations made government, or a system of ruling, necessary. In civilizations, leaders emerge to maintain order among people and to establish laws. Government is an example of an **institution**—a long lasting pattern of organization in a community. Religion and the economy are other examples of institutions that become more complex as civilizations advance. As government, religion, and the economy became more advanced, people recognized the need to keep records. Thus, most civilizations developed a system of writing. Civilizations also developed improved technologies, such as the ox-drawn plow, the potter's wheel, and new forms of metalworking.

Case Study: Bantu Migration

Beginning at least 2,000 years ago or earlier, small groups of **Bantu-speaking peoples** moved from the grassy plains in what is now southeastern Nigeria southward and eastward throughout southern Africa, spreading their language and culture. They were not one people, but rather a group of peoples who shared certain cultural traits.

The Bantu speakers were nomadic herders and farmers who practiced **slash-and-burn farming**. In this technique, a patch of forest or grassland is cut down and burned. The ashes are mixed with the soil to create a fertile garden area. When the soil loses its fertility, farmers move to another area. Anthropologists suggest that as the Bantus developed farming, their populations increased. Soon there was not enough land to farm. They could not go north in search of land, because the area was densely populated. So they moved southward.

The Bantu speakers brought their language, new techniques of agriculture, and the technology of ironworking to the lands they occupied. They also shared ideas about social and political organization. Some of these ideas still influence the political scene in southern and eastern Africa. Although the Bantu migration

TAKING NOTES

Summarizing Use a chart to summarize characteristics of the civilization.

Characteristics

1.
2.
3.
4.
5.

TAKING NOTES

Analyzing Causes and Recognizing Effects Identify causes and effects of specific events related to Bantu migration.

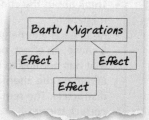

produced a great diversity of cultures, language had a unifying influence on the continent. Today it is estimated that 240 million people in Africa speak one of the Bantu languages as their first language.

Answer the following questions. Use the Analyze the Question hints to help you answer the questions.

1 "I am lucky enough to have been involved for half a century with work, mostly in East Africa, that very much belongs to everyone, since it concerns the human origins that are common to the whole human race."

— Mary Leakey, *Autobiography*

In this quotation, the author is implying that early humans

(1) migrated from Africa to Eurasia.
(2) first appeared in Africa.
(3) invented tools and mastered the use of fire.
(4) appeared shortly after the Neolithic Age.

ANALYZE THE QUESTION
- Read the question stem. You are being asked to indicate what Mary Leaky is saying about early humans.
- Look for key words like *East Africa* and *human origins* to determine her focus.
- Eliminate the alternatives that do not relate to the key words in her quotation.
- Select the alternative that would follow logically from her focus.

2 Which statement explains a cause rather than an effect of the Bantu migration?

(1) Techniques for herding and farming were spread to other peoples.
(2) Millions of people now speak a Bantu language.
(3) Trading cities developed along the coast of west Africa.
(4) Population growth increased the need for farmland.

ANALYZE THE QUESTION
- Read the question stem. You are being asked to identify the cause of Bantu migration.
- Think about the characteristics of the Bantu migration.
- Read each alternative and decide whether it is a cause, an effect, or a distracter (something that has nothing to do with Bantu migration).
- Eliminate the alternatives that are effects or distracters. The remaining alternative is the correct answer.

Base your answer to question 3 on the diagram below and on your knowledge of social studies.

3 Which title completes this diagram?

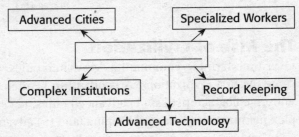

(1) Elements of a Civilization
(2) Features of a Nomadic Lifestyle
(3) Basic Components of the Paleolithic Age
(4) Human Life 50,000 Years Ago

ANALYZE THE QUESTION
- Read the question stem. You are being asked to select the best title for the diagram.
- Read the alternatives. Keywords such as *Elements, Features,* and *Basic Components* let you know that the surrounding boxes are characteristics.
- Determine the common theme of the characteristics.
- Select the alternative title that best fits the characteristics.

4 Early peoples who moved frequently as they searched for the food they needed for survival are called

(1) hunter-gatherers.
(2) village dwellers.
(3) subsistence farmers.
(4) guild members.

ANALYZE THE QUESTION
- Read the question stem. You are being asked to choose the term that matches the definition in the stem.
- Look for key words like *moved frequently* and *searched for food.*
- Think about how the people in each alternative live and how they obtain their food.
- Select the alternative that matches the keywords.

Early River Valley Civilizations

Section Overview

Civilizations first developed in the fertile river plains of Mesopotamia in modern Turkey, Iraq, and Syria; Egypt; the Indus Valley in modern India; and China. Some civilizations, like Mesopotamia, organized as city-states. Other civilizations, like Egypt, united into a single kingdom. All four civilizations had traditional economies. A **traditional economy** *is based on agriculture, with some people working at simple crafts, such as in manufacturing cloth or pottery. In a traditional economy, economic decisions are based on customs, beliefs, religion, and habits. Goods and services are often traded rather than exchanged for money. This is called* **barter***.*

Hammurabi, who instituted the first legal code.

MAIN IDEAS

INTERACTION WITH ENVIRONMENT   The earliest civilizations formed on the fertile river plains. These lands faced challenges, such as regional flooding and a limited growing area.

POWER AND AUTHORITY   Projects such as irrigation systems required leadership and laws—the beginning of organized government. In some societies, priests controlled the first governments. In others, military leaders and kings ruled.

SCIENCE AND TECHNOLOGY   Early civilizations developed bronze tools, the wheel, the sail, the plow, writing, and mathematics. These innovations spread through trade, wars, and the movement of people.

TIME LINE

3000 B.C.
City-states form in Sumer, Mesopotamia.

2600 B.C.
Egypt's Old Kingdom develops.

1792 B.C.
Hammurabi develops code of laws for Babylonian Empire.

1750 B.C.
Indus Valley civilization declines.

c. 1700 B.C.
Shang Dynasty forms in China.

TERMS AND NAMES

- traditional economy
- barter
- Fertile Crescent
- Mesopotamia
- city-state
- dynasty
- ziggurat
- polytheism
- cultural diffusion
- scribe
- cuneiform
- empire
- Hammurabi
- delta
- pharaoh
- theocracy
- pyramid
- mummification
- hieroglyphics
- papyrus
- subcontinent
- monsoon
- Harappan civilization
- loess

PREPARING FOR THE REGENTS

As you read this section, compare and contrast the following aspects of the early river civilizations:
- important ideas.
- social and cultural values.
- beliefs.
- traditions.

Present-day Persian Gulf

Tigris River
IRAQ
Euphrates River
IRAN
KUWAIT
Persian Gulf
SAUDI ARABIA

Mesopotamia

The Tigris (TY•grihs) and Euphrates (yoo•FRAY•teez) rivers flow from the mountains of what is now Turkey, down through Syria and Iraq, and finally southeastward to the Persian Gulf. Sometime before 4500 B.C., the waters of these two rivers allowed the formation of farming settlements in the area that scholars call the **Fertile Crescent**. This curve-shaped region included the lands facing the Mediterranean Sea and a plain that came to be called **Mesopotamia** (MEHS•uh•puh•TAY•mee•uh), which stretched from the mountains in what is now Turkey to the Persian Gulf. These early farming settlements eventually grew into the great cities of the Sumerians.

Human and Physical Geography The Sumerians arrived in Mesopotamia around 3300 B.C. They were attracted by the good soil created by the yearly flooding of the rivers. As the floodwater receded, it left a thick bed of mud called silt. Farmers could produce large quantities of wheat and barley in this rich, new soil. However, the region also presented challenges. The flooding was unpredictable and was combined with dry periods that sometimes turned the land almost to desert. The region also offered no natural barriers to protect villages and few building materials and other natural resources. The Sumerians responded to these challenges by digging irrigation ditches to carry river water to their fields, surrounding their cities with mud-brick walls, and trading with their neighbors for raw materials such as stone, wood, and metal.

Political and Belief Systems By 3000 B.C., the Sumerians had built several cities, each with their own governments and rulers. Each city and the surrounding land that it controlled formed a **city-state**. A city-state functioned much as an independent country does today. Sumer's earliest governments were controlled by temple priests. In times of war, however, the men of the city chose a military leader. Eventually, some military leaders became full-time rulers. These rulers usually passed their power on to their sons, who eventually passed it on to their own heirs. Such a series of rulers from a single family is called a **dynasty**. After 2500 B.C., many Sumerian city-states came under the rule of dynasties.

At the center of all Sumerian cities was a walled temple with a pyramid-shaped monument called a **ziggurat** (ZIHG•uh•RAT), which means "mountain of god." There the priests acted as go-betweens with the gods. The Sumerians practiced **polytheism** (PAHL•ee•thee•IHZ•umh)—the belief in more than one god. To keep the gods happy, the Sumerians built ziggurats for them and offered sacrifices of animals, food, and wine. However, they expected little help from their gods after death. Sumerians believed that the souls of the dead went to a gloomy "land of no return" between the earth's crust and the ancient sea.

Urbanization and Social Structure By 2500 B.C., new cities were arising all over the Fertile Crescent. Sumerians exchanged products and ideas, such as living in cities, with neighboring cultures. This process in which a new idea or a product spreads from one culture to another is called **cultural diffusion**.

The social structure in Sumerian cities consisted of several social classes. Kings, landholders, and some priests made up the highest level. Wealthy merchants ranked next. Then came the vast majority of ordinary Sumerians who worked with their hands in fields and workshops. At the lowest level of Sumerian society were the slaves. Slaves included foreigners captured in war and Sumerians sold into slavery to pay debts. Sumerian women enjoyed many rights. They could hold property and work as merchants, farmers, artisans, and priests.

TAKING NOTES

Identifying Problems and Solutions Use a chart to identify Sumer's environmental problems and their solutions.

Problems	Solutions
1.	1.
2.	2.
3.	3.

1.4 Preparing for the Regents

Culture and Intellectual Life What were the major characteristics of Mesopotamian society?

Cultural Achievements The Sumerians created many things to help them meet their needs and wants. Sumerian **scribes**—or professional record keepers—invented a writing system called **cuneiform** (KYOO•nee•uh•FAWRM). The Sumerians also created many architectural innovations and a number system in base 60. The Sumerians needed arithmetic and geometry in order to erect city walls and buildings, plan irrigation systems, and survey flooded fields. Historians believe that the Sumerians also invented the wheel, sail, and plow, and that they were the first to use bronze.

The Sumerian city-states eventually fell to outside attack. The civilization did not die, however. The new rulers adapted the basic ideas of Sumerian culture to meet their own needs. Sargon of Akkad, who conquered the city-states of Sumer around 2350 B.C., spread the culture through his conquests. By uniting both northern and southern Mesopotamia, Sargon created the first **empire**. An empire brings together several peoples, nations, or previously independent states under the control of one ruler.

The Amorites, nomadic warriors who invaded Mesopotamia in about 2000 B.C., also adopted and spread the region's culture through their establishment of the Babylonian Empire. The empire reached its height during the reign of Hammurabi (1792 B.C. to 1750 B.C.). **Hammurabi** is best remembered for establishing the Code of Hammurabi, a collection of 282 specific laws dealing with everything that affected the community. Hammurabi had the laws engraved in stone, and copies were placed throughout his lands for everyone to see. The code reinforced the principle that government had a responsibility for what happened in society.

Egypt

While Sumerian civilization was on the rise, a similar process was taking place along the banks of Nile River in Egypt. Rather than creating a collection of city-states, however, the Egyptians quickly united into a kingdom. During the dynasties of the Old and Middle Kingdoms, Egypt developed a rich civilization.

Human and Physical Geography The Nile River flows from the highlands of East Africa northward across Africa to the Mediterranean Sea. Egypt's settlements arose along the Nile on a narrow strip of land made fertile by yearly flooding. As in Mesopotamia, Egyptian farmers planted wheat and barley in the rich, wet soil before the sun could dry it out. They then used irrigation ditches to keep their crops watered. Egyptian farmers were luckier than those in Mesopotamia—the Nile's flooding was predictable. However, they still faced challenges. Thousands of people starved when too little flooding reduced the silt and water needed for crops. Houses, granaries, and precious seeds were washed away when the floodwaters were too high. In addition, the vast desert on either side of the Nile acted as a natural barrier between Egypt and other lands, but it also forced the Egyptians to live on a small portion of land.

Ancient Egyptians lived along the river from the mouth at the Mediterranean Sea well into the interior. River travel was possible from mouth to the First Cataract (KAT•uh•rakt), where boulders turned the river into churning rapids. The northern part of the river was called Lower Egypt. This area included the **delta** region—the broad, marshy, triangular area of land formed by silt deposits at the mouth of the river. The southern part was called Upper Egypt.

Political and Belief Systems Upper and Lower Egypt were originally two separate kingdoms. Eventually, the two kingdoms were united, possibly around 3000 B.C. The role of the king was one striking difference between Egypt and Mesopotamia. In Mesopotamia, kings were considered to be representatives of

1.5 Preparing for the Regents

Culture and Intellectual Life How did cuneiform contribute to recorded history?

1.6 Preparing for the Regents

Justice Why was the Code of Hammurabi an important development for society?

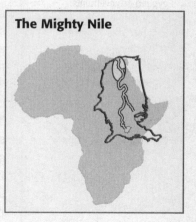

The Mighty Nile

1.7 Preparing for the Regents

Political and Belief Systems How were the political and belief systems of Mesopotamia and Egypt similar and different?

the gods. To the Egyptians, kings were gods. A government in which rule is based on religious authority is called a **theocracy**.

The Egyptian god-kings were called **pharaohs**. The pharaohs stood at the center of Egypt's religion as well as its government and army. Egyptians believed that the pharaoh caused the sun to rise, the Nile to flood, and the crops to grow. It was the pharaoh's duty to promote truth and justice. They also believed that the pharaoh's life force continued to rule even after death. Thus, they built immense structures called **pyramids** to serve as tombs and monuments. Like the Mesopotamians, the Egyptians were polytheistic. They built huge temples to honor their major deities. Unlike the Mesopotamians, the Egyptians believed that life continued after death and that they would be judged for their deeds after death. People of all classes prepared for their burials so that they might safely reach the Other World. Royal and elite Egyptians' bodies were preserved by **mummification**—which involves embalming and drying the corpse to prevent it from decaying.

Social Structure Like the grand monuments to the kings, Egyptian society formed a pyramid. The king, queen, and royal family stood at the top. Below them were other members of the upper class, including wealthy landowners, government officials, priests, and military commanders. Next came the middle class, which included merchants and artisans. At the base was the lower class, which consisted of peasant farmers and laborers. In the later periods of Egyptian history, the social structure also included slaves, who were generally captives from foreign wars. People were not locked into their social class. They could advance through marriage or success at their jobs. Even some slaves could earn their freedom. In addition, women had many of the same rights as men.

Cultural Achievements As in Mesopotamia, the development of writing was one of the keys to the growth of Egyptian civilization. Simple pictures were the earliest form of writing, but scribes quickly developed a more flexible writing system called **hieroglyphics** (HY•ur•uh•GLIHF•ihks). In hieroglyphics, pictures stood for sounds as well as ideas. At first hieroglyphics were written on stone and clay. The Egyptians soon invented a new writing surface—paperlike sheets made from **papyrus** (puh•PY•ruhs) reeds.

Practical needs led to many Egyptian inventions. For example, Egyptians developed a 365-day solar calendar to help them track floods and planting times. They also developed a system of written numbers for counting, adding, and subtracting that would have helped them assess and collect taxes. Scribes used an early form of geometry to survey and reset property boundaries following floods, and engineers and architects used mathematics in constructing pyramids and temples. Egyptian architects were the first to use stone columns in homes, palaces, and temples. Egyptian medicine was also famous in the ancient world. Doctors knew how to check a person's heart rate, set broken bones, treat wounds and fevers, and even use surgery to treat some conditions.

Indus Valley

Geographers often refer to the landmass that includes Indian, Pakistan, and Bangladesh as the Indian **subcontinent**. The Hindu Kush, Karakorum, and Himalayan mountain ranges separate this region from the rest of the Asian continent. These mountains guard the Indo-Ganges Plain, an enormous flat and fertile area formed by the Indus and Ganges (GAN•jeez) rivers. It was on this plain along the Indus River that the first Indian civilization appeared.

TAKING NOTES
Summarizing Use a web diagram to summarize Egyptian achievements.

Egyptian Achievements

1.8 Preparing for the Regents
Human and Physical Geography What geographic features had the greatest influence on Indus Valley civilization?

Human and Physical Geography The Indus and Ganges rivers carry not only water for irrigation, but also silt, which produces rich land for agriculture. Seasonal winds called **monsoons** dominate India's climate. Winter monsoons from the northeast blow dry air westward. In the summer, winds blow eastward from the southwest, carrying moisture from the ocean in great rain clouds. These storms bring so much rain that flooding often happens. When the summer rains fail to develop, droughts often cause crop disasters. The civilization that emerged along the Indus Valley had to deal with these challenges and with occasional shifts in the course of the rivers.

Urbanization Historians know less about the Indus civilization than those to the west. For example, no one is sure how human settlement began in the Indian subcontinent. It is known, however, that around 2500 B.C., people in the Indus Valley were laying bricks for India's first cities. Archaeologists have found the ruins of more than 100 settlements, including Mohenjo-Daro and Harappa. Because of the many archaeological discoveries made at Harappa, Indus Valley civilization is sometimes called the **Harappan civilization**.

Unlike cities in Mesopotamia, Harappan cities were laid out on a precise grid system. Buildings were constructed of oven-baked bricks cut in standard sizes, unlike the simpler, irregular, sun-dried mud bricks of the Mesopotamians. Engineers created sophisticated plumbing and sewage systems. They also constructed levees, or earthen walls, and built cities on human-made islands to protect against floodwaters.

Harappan Culture The Harappan civilization developed a written language, which consisted of about 400 symbols. However, no one has been able to decipher it. Instead, they rely on artifacts to help explain the culture. Artifacts suggest that social divisions in the society were not great, that conflict was limited, and that animals were an important part of the culture. Archaeologists think that the civilization was a theocracy, but no temple sites have been found. They know that the Harappans traded with distant peoples, including the Mesopotamians.

Indus Valley Culture Ends Around 1750 B.C., the quality of building in the Indus Valley declined. Gradually, the great cities fell into decay. Satellite evidence indicates that this was due in part to earthquakes and floods that altered the course of the Indus River. Archaeologists believe that some cities were destroyed and that agriculture and trade were disrupted.

Yellow River Civilization

The walls of China's first cities were built about 4,000 years ago. This was at least a thousand years after civilization developed in Mesopotamia, Egypt, and the Indus Valley. Unlike the other three river civilizations, the civilization that began along the Huang He (hwahng•HUH), or Yellow River, continues today.

Human and Physical Geography Natural barriers somewhat isolated ancient China from all other civilizations. To China's east lay the Yellow Sea, the East China Sea, and the Pacific Ocean. Mountain ranges and deserts dominate about two-thirds of China's landmass. Two major rivers flow from the mountainous west to the east coast. The Huang He is found in the north. In central China, the Chang Jiang (chang•jyhang), or Yangtze (yang•SEE), flows east to the Yellow Sea. The Huang He deposits huge amounts of yellow silt when it overflows its banks. This silt is actually fertile soil called **loess** (LOH•uhs), which is blown by the winds from deserts to the west and north.

Monsoon Winter

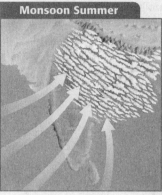
Monsoon Summer

TAKING NOTES

Drawing Conclusions
Use the graphic organizer to draw conclusions about Indus Valley civilizations.

Indus Valley	
Cities	fact
Language	fact
Trade	fact

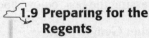

1.9 Preparing for the Regents

Human and Physical Geography Where did China's earliest civilizations develop? What geographic features encouraged their development?

Only about 10 percent of China's land is suitable for farming. Much of this land lies within the North China Plain between the Huang He and the Chang Jiang. It is here that China's first civilization took hold. Like the other river civilizations, this civilization faced many challenges. In addition to the effects of the Huang He's flooding, early settlers had to deal with China's relative geographic isolation. This meant that they had to supply their own goods rather than trade with outside peoples. It also meant that they developed a distinct culture.

1.10 Preparing for the Regents

Political and Belief Systems How did China's political and belief systems compare to those of Mesopotamia and Egypt?

Political System and Social Structure The Shang Dynasty, which lasted from around 1700 to 1027 B.C., was the dynasty to leave written records. The Shang kings built elaborate palaces and tombs. Like later Chinese societies, Shang society was sharply divided between nobles and peasants. A ruling class of warrior-nobles headed by a king governed the Shang. These noble families owned the land. They governed the scattered villages within the Shang lands and sent tribute, or payments, to the Shang ruler in exchange for local control.

Belief System The Shang worshipped a supreme god, Shang Di, as well as many lesser gods. Family was closely linked to religion. The Chinese believed that the spirits of family ancestors had the power to bring good fortune or disaster. Every family paid respect to the father's ancestors and made sacrifices in their honor.

Urbanization Among the oldest and most important Shang cities was Anyang (ahn•YAHNG). Unlike the cities in the Indus Valley or the Fertile Crescent, Anyang was built mainly of wood. The higher classes lived inside the city walls in timber-framed houses with walls of clay and straw. Peasants and craftspeople lived in huts outside the city. The city walls were made of packed earth.

Cultural Achievements Like the other river civilizations, the Chinese developed writing. In the Chinese method of writing, each character generally stood for one syllable or unit of language. There were practically no links between China's spoken language and its written language. Thus, one could read Chinese without being able to speak a word of it. This system of writing had one major advantage—people in all parts of China could learn the same system of writing, even if their spoken languages were very different. This helped unify the land.

PREPARING FOR THE REGENTS

On a separate sheet of paper, write a well-organized essay that includes an introduction, several paragraphs addressing the task below, and a conclusion. Before beginning, check the Score the Essay box for pointers.

Theme: Geography:
Geography features can positively or negatively affect the development of a region.

Task:
Select *one* geographic feature from your study of river valley civilizations.
- Explain how this geographic feature has had an effect on the historical development of two of the civilizations.

Be sure to include specific examples in your essay.

SCORE THE ESSAY To receive a score of 5 on your essay, you will need to:
- show a thorough understanding of the theme.
- address all aspects of the task.
- show an ability to compare and/or contrast the issues.
- richly support the theme with relevant facts, examples, and details.
- consistently demonstrate a logical and clear plan of organization.
- introduce the theme by establishing a framework that is beyond a simple restatement of the of the task and conclude with a summation of the theme.

Classical Civilizations and Empires

Ancient Chinese coins

Section Overview

The rise of classical civilizations and empires in China, Greece, Rome, India, and Mesoamerica transformed the world. These civilizations became wealthy and powerful through conquest and trade. In the process, they spread goods and ideas between cultures.

MAIN IDEAS

POWER AND AUTHORITY The early rulers in China introduced ideas about government and society that shaped Chinese civilization.
POWER AND AUTHORITY In the Greek city-state of Athens, democracy—a new form of government in which citizens exercised power—developed. Later, Alexander the Great spread Greek culture through much of Asia.
EMPIRE BUILDING Rome began as a republic, a government in which elected officials represented the people. Eventually absolute rulers called emperors seized power and expanded the empire. At its height, the Roman Empire touched Europe, Asia, and Africa.
POWER AND AUTHORITY The Mauryas established an empire, but could not unify India permanently.
RELIGIOUS AND ETHICAL SYSTEMS The Maya developed a highly complex civilization based on city-states and elaborate religious practices.
ECONOMICS Trading societies extended the development of civilizations.

TERMS AND NAMES

- feudalism
- Mandate of Heaven
- dynastic cycle
- Qin Dynasty
- Han Dynasty
- centralized government
- bureaucracy
- civil service
- polis
- monarchy
- aristocracy
- oligarchy
- tyrant
- democracy
- direct democracy

- classical art
- tragedy
- drama
- Peloponnesian War
- philosopher
- Socrates
- Plato
- Aristotle
- Macedonia
- Alexander the Great
- Hellenistic
- republic
- patrician
- plebeian
- tribune
- consul

- senate
- dictator
- *Pax Romana*
- Augustus
- inflation
- Greco-Roman culture
- aqueducts
- Mauryan Empire
- Asoka
- religious toleration
- maize
- glyph
- Silk Roads

TARGET THE REGENTS

As you read this section, consider
- what contributions the civilizations have made to the history of humankind.
- what forces caused the rise and fall of civilizations.
- what the status and role of women was in these civilizations.
- how contemporary democratic governments are rooted in classical traditions.

TIME LINE

1500 B.C.
Mycenaean culture thrives on Greek mainland.

1027 B.C.
Zhou Dynasty forms in China.

509 B.C.
Rome becomes a republic.

500 B.C.
Greek city-states flourish.

334 B.C.
Macedonia's Alexander the Great starts to build his empire.

321 B.C.
Chandragupta Maurya founds Mauryan Empire in India.

202 B.C.
Liu Bang establishes China's Han Dynasty.

A.D. 220
Han Dynasty falls.

A.D. 476
Western Roman Empire falls.

A.D. 900
Classic period of Maya civilization ends in Mesoamerica.

TAKING NOTES

Following Chronological Order On a time line, identify major events in early Chinese dynasties.

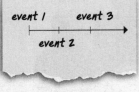

event 1   event 3

event 2

Around 1027 B.C., a people called the Zhou (joh) overthrew the Shang and established their own dynasty. The change in dynasty did not bring sweeping cultural change. Nevertheless, Zhou rule brought new ideas to Chinese civilization.

Human and Physical Geography Like the Shang, the Zhou settled in China's heartland—the area between the Huang He and the Chang Jiang. However, the Zhou controlled lands far beyond the Huang He in the north and the Chang Jiang in the south. To govern this vast area, the Zhou gave control over different regions to members of the royal family and other trusted nobles. This established a system called **feudalism**. Feudalism is a political system in which nobles, or lords, are granted the use of lands that legally belong to the king. In return, the nobles owe loyalty and military service to the king and protection to the people who live on their estates. Similar systems would arise centuries later in both Europe and Japan.

1.11 Preparing for the Regents

Political Systems What was the Mandate of Heaven?

Mandate of Heaven To justify their conquest, the Zhou leaders declared that the final Shang king had been such a poor ruler that the gods had taken away the Shang's rule and given it to the Zhou. This justification developed over time into a broader view that royal authority came from heaven. A just ruler had divine approval, known as the **Mandate of Heaven**. A wicked or foolish king could lose the Mandate of Heaven and so lose the right to rule. The Mandate of Heaven became central to the Chinese view of government. It was the explanation for rebellion, civil war, and the rise of a new dynasty. Historians describe the pattern of rise, decline, and replacement of dynasties as the **dynastic cycle**.

The Han Dynasty The Zhou Dynasty ruled from around 1027 to 256 B.C. By the later years of the Zhou, the lords of dependent territories began to think of themselves as independent kings. Their almost constant conflict, which is known as "the warring states period," led to the decline of the Zhou Dynasty. In the third century B.C., the **Qin Dynasty** (chihn) replaced the Zhou. The harsh dynasty lasted only a short time, however. Peasants rebelled just three years after the second Qin emperor took office. One of their leaders, a peasant from the land of Han, marched his troops into the capital city. By 202 B.C., the Qin Dynasty gave way to the Han Dynasty. The **Han Dynasty**, which ruled China for more than 400 years, is divided into two periods. The Former Han ruled for about two centuries, until A.D. 9. After a brief period when the Han were out of power, the Later Han ruled for almost another two centuries. The Han so influenced China that even today many Chinese call themselves "people of the Han."

Liu Bang, the Han's first emperor established a **centralized government**, in which a central authority controls the running of the state. Liu Bang's great-grandson, Wudi (woo•dee), continued the centralizing policies. His government employed more than 130,000 people. The **bureaucracy**—the agencies and departments formed to run the government—included 18 different levels of civil service jobs. **Civil service** jobs are government jobs that civilians obtain by taking examinations. Wudi reigned from 141 to 87 B.C., the longest of any Han emperor. During that time, he expanded China's empire through warfare. Among the enemies he had to fight were the Xiongnu (shee•UNG•noo), fierce nomads that roamed the steppes to the north and west of China. Wudi colonized the areas to the northeast now known as Manchuria and Korea and as far south as what is now Vietnam. By the end of his reign, the empire had expanded nearly to the bounds of present-day China.

1.12 Preparing for the Regents

Political Systems What were the main features of the Han government?

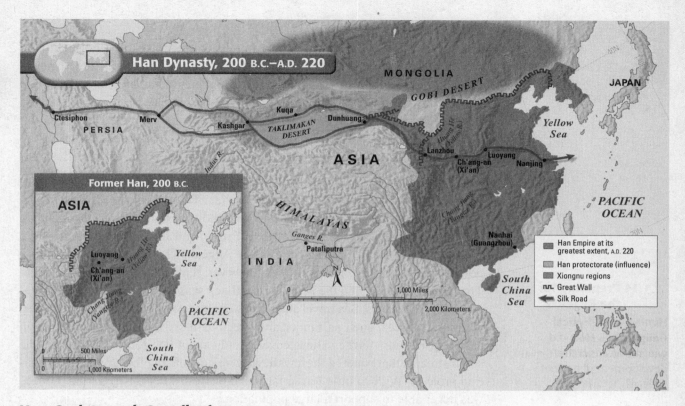

Han Dynasty, 200 B.C.–A.D. 220

MONGOLIA

GOBI DESERT

JAPAN

Ctesiphon Merv

PERSIA

Kashgar TAKLIMAKAN
DESERT

Kuqa

Dunhuang

ASIA

Lanzhou

Ch'ang-an
(Xi'an)

Luoyang

Nanjing

Yellow
Sea

PACIFIC
OCEAN

Indus R.

HIMALAYAS

Ganges R.

Pataliputra

INDIA

Nanhai
(Guangzhou)

South
China
Sea

Former Han, 200 B.C.

ASIA

Luoyang

Ch'ang-an
(Xi'an)

Yellow
Sea

Chang Jiang
(Yangtze R.)

PACIFIC
OCEAN

South
China
Sea

500 Miles

1,000 Kilometers

0   1,000 Miles

0   2,000 Kilometers

Han Empire at its greatest extent, A.D. 220
Han protectorate (influence)
Xiongnu regions
Great Wall
Silk Road

Han Society and Contributions Han society, like Han government, was highly structured. At the top was the emperor, who was considered semidivine. Next came the kings and governors, both appointed by the emperor. They governed with the help of state officials, nobles, and scholars. Then came peasant farmers, followed by artisans and merchants. Soldiers were near the bottom. At the very bottom were enslaved persons, who were usually conquered peoples. Most women of all classes led quiet lives at home, caring for their families. However, women in aristocratic and landowning families sometimes pursued education and culture. Some women ran small shops; still others practiced medicine.

The 400 years of Han rule saw great advances in technology. Paper was invented in A.D. 105. The Han also invented collar harnesses for horses, which made it easier for them to pull heavy loads. They perfected a plow, invented the wheelbarrow, and began using water mills to grind grain. The dynasty also made economic advances, increased foreign trade, and built roads to help with trade and transportation.

The Fall of the Han In spite of these gains, the Han emperors faced grave problems. One of the main problems was an economic imbalance caused by customs that allowed the rich to gain more wealth at the expense of the poor. According to custom, a family's land was divided equally among the father's male heirs. Unless a farmer could afford to buy more land, each generation inherited smaller plots. Thus, many farmers had a hard time raising enough food to sell or even to feed the family. Small farmers often had to borrow money from large landowners. If a farmer could not pay back the debt, the landowners took possession of the farmer's land. In addition, large landowners were not required to pay taxes, so when their landholdings increased, the amount of land that was left for the government to tax decreased. With less money coming in, the government pressed harder to collect money from small farmers. Eventually these economic imbalances helped bring about the fall of the Han. By A.D. 220, the Han Dynasty had disintegrated into three rival kingdoms.

1.13 Preparing for the Regents

Political Systems What led to the fall of the Han Dynasty?

The Greeks

In ancient times, Greece was not a united country. It was a collection of separate lands where Greek-speaking people lived. By 3000 B.C., the Minoans lived on the large Greek island of Crete. They created an elegant civilization that had great power in the Mediterranean world. The Minoans influenced the civilization of the Mycenaeans, Indo-Europeans peoples who settled on the Greek mainland around 2000 B.C. The Minoan-influenced culture of the Mycenaeans formed the core of Greek religious practice, art, politics, and literature.

Human and Physical Geography Ancient Greece consisted mainly of a mountainous peninsula jutting out into the Mediterranean Sea. It also included about 2,000 islands in the Aegean (ih•JEE•uhn) and Ionian (eye•OH•nee•uhn) seas and lands on the eastern edge of the Aegean. The moderate climate supported an outdoor life. It was the sea, however, that shaped Greek civilization. The Aegean, Ionian, and the neighboring Black seas were important transportation and trade routes. Sea travel and trade were important because Greece lacked natural resources, such as timber and precious metals. It also lacked enough usable farmland—fertile valleys covered only about one-fourth of Greece. The small streams that watered these valleys were not suitable for large-scale irrigation projects. With so little fertile farmland or freshwater for irrigation, Greece was never able to support a large population.

The rugged mountains that covered about three-fourths of ancient Greece ran mainly from the northwest to the southeast along the Balkan Peninsula. These mountains divided the land into a number of regions. This significantly influenced Greek political life. Instead of a single government, the Greeks developed small, independent communities within each valley and its surrounding mountains. Most Greeks gave their loyalty to these local communities.

The Rise of City-States—Athens and Sparta By 750 B.C., the city-state, or **polis**, was the fundamental political unit in ancient Greece. A polis was made up of a city and its surrounding countryside. Greek city-states had many different forms of government. **Monarchies** were run by kings, **aristocracies** by a small group of nobles, and **oligarchies** by a few powerful people. In many city-states, repeated clashes occurred between rulers and the common people. Powerful people, usually nobles or other wealthy citizens, sometimes seized control of the government by appealing to the common people for support. These rulers were called **tyrants**. Unlike today, tyrants generally were not considered cruel.

The idea of representative government also began to take root in some city-states, particularly Athens. Athenians avoided major political upheavals by moving toward **democracy**, rule by the people. In Athens, citizens participated directly in political decision making. Draco, a nobleman who took power in 621 B.C., took the first steps toward democracy with the development of a legal code based on the idea that all Athenians, both rich and poor, were equal under the law. Draco's code, however, upheld the practice of debt slavery, in which debtors worked as slaves to repay their debts. Solon (SO•luhn), who came to power in 594 B.C., outlawed debt slavery. Around 500 B.C., the Athenian leader Cleisthenes (KLYS•thuh•NEEZ) increased the power of the assembly by allowing all citizens to submit laws for debate. However, only free adult male property owners born in Athens were considered citizens. Women, slaves, and foreigners were excluded from citizenship and had few rights.

1.14 Preparing for the Regents

Human and Physical Geography How did geography affect the development of ancient Greece?

1.15 Preparing for the Regents

Human Rights How did the institution of slavery fit within the Athenian concept of democracy?

Sparta contrasted sharply with Athens. Instead of a democracy, Sparta built a military state. Spartan government was an oligarchy. An assembly, which was composed of all Spartan citizens, elected officials and voted on major issues. The Council of Elders, made up of 30 older citizens, proposed laws on which the assembly voted. Five elected officials carried out the laws passed by the assembly. In addition, two kings ruled over Sparta's military forces.

The Growth of Democracy Democracy in Athens grew under Pericles, who led the city-state from 461 to 429 B.C. To strengthen democracy, Pericles increased the number of public officials who were paid salaries. This meant that even the poorest citizens could afford to serve in the government. Consequently, Athens had more citizens engaged in self-government than any other city-state, making it one of the most democratic governments in history. Another important legacy of Periclean Athens was the introduction of **direct democracy**, a form of government in which citizens rule directly and not through representatives.

Contributions Pericles ruled during the Golden Age of Athens, a period in which Greek artists and architects created magnificent sculptures and buildings to glorify Athens. The 23,000-square-foot Parthenon, for instance, was built to honor Athena, the goddess of wisdom and the protector of Athens. Sculptors during this age developed values of harmony, order, balance, and proportion that became the standard of what is called **classical art**. Following in the great storytelling tradition of Homer, the Greeks also invented drama as an art form and built the first theaters in the West. The Greeks wrote two kinds of drama—tragedy and comedy. A **tragedy** was a serious drama about common themes such as love, hate, war, and betrayal. A **comedy** contained scenes filled with slapstick situations and crude humor. The Greeks also continued the long tradition of the Olympic games.

As Athens grew in wealth, prestige, and power, the other city-states grew hostile, especially Sparta. This led to the **Peloponnesian War**, which began in 431 B.C. By the time the fighting ended in 404 B.C., Athens had lost its wealth and power. Following the war, many Athenians lost confidence in democratic government and began to question their values. In this time of uncertainty, several great thinkers, or **philosophers**, appeared. These philosophers believed that the universe was put together in a logical way and subject to absolute and unchanging laws that could be understood through logic and reasoning. **Socrates** (SAHK•ruh•TEEZ) encouraged Greeks to question themselves and their moral character. His student, **Plato** (PLAY•toh), envisioned a perfectly governed society led by a philosopher king. Plato's student, **Aristotle** (AR•ih•STAHT•uhl), questioned the nature of the world and of human belief, thought, and knowledge. He invented a method for arguing according to rules of logic. He later applied his method to problems in psychology, physics, and biology. Aristotle's work provides the basis for the scientific method used today.

Alexander the Great and Hellenistic Culture One of Aristotle's most famous pupils was Alexander. He was son of King Philip II of **Macedonia**, a kingdom located just north of Greece. Macedonia defeated Greece in 338 B.C. Although the city-states of Greece retained self-government in local matters, they came under Macedonia's control. Alexander became king of Macedonia at the age of 20 upon his father's death in 336 B.C. Because of his accomplishments over the next 13 years, he became known as **Alexander the Great**. By the time he died at the age of 32 in 323 B.C., Alexander had conquered the Persian Empire and led his armies as far east as the Indus Valley.

1.16 Preparing for the Regents

Culture and Intellectual Life How did the characteristics of Spartan and Athenian society differ?

TAKING NOTES

Summarizing Use a web diagram to organize information about the Golden Age of Pericles

Golden Age

1.17 Preparing for the Regents

Culture and Intellectual Life What were the basic beliefs of the Greek philosophers?

TAKING NOTES

Outlining Use an outline to organize main ideas about the growth of Alexander's empire.

Alexander's Empire
I. Philip Builds Macedonian Power
  A.
  B.
II. Alexander Conquers Persia

Alexander started many new cities as administrative centers and outposts of Greek culture. In these cities, he actively sought to meld the conquered culture with that of the Greeks. As a result, a vibrant new culture emerged that blended Greek, Egyptian, Persian, and Indian influences. This blending became known as **Hellenistic** culture. Koine (koy•NAY), the popular spoken language used in Hellenistic cities, was a direct result of this blending. The language enabled educated people and traders from diverse backgrounds to communicate.

The Romans

While the great civilization of Greece was in decline, Rome—a new city to the west—was developing and increasing in power. In time, the Romans would build one of the most famous and influential empires in history.

Human and Physical Geography Rome was built on seven rolling hills at a curve on the Tiber River, midway between the Alps and Italy's southern tip and near the midpoint of the Mediterranean Sea. From about 1000 to 500 B.C., three groups—the Latins, the Greeks, and the Etruscans—settled in the region and battled for control. The Latins built the original settlement at Rome. Between 750 and 600 B.C., the Greeks established colonies along southern Italy and Sicily. These colonies brought Italy, including Rome, in closer contact with Greek civilization. The Etruscans influenced the development of Roman civilization through such elements as their alphabet and architecture.

The Early Republic About 600 B.C., an Etruscan became king of Rome. In the decades that followed, Rome grew from a collection of hilltop villages to a city that covered nearly 500 square miles. The last king of Rome was a harsh tyrant who was driven from power in 509 B.C. The Romans declared they would never again be ruled by a king. Instead, they established a **republic**, a form of government in which power rests with citizens who have the right to vote for their leaders. In Rome, citizenship with voting rights was granted only to freeborn male citizens.

In the early republic, the patricians and plebeians struggled for power. The **patricians** were wealthy landowners who inherited their power and social status. The **plebeians** were the common farmers, artisans, and merchants who made up the majority of the population. The plebeians were citizens with the right to vote. However, they were barred by law from holding most important government positions. In time, Rome's leaders allowed the plebeians to form the Tribal Assembly, which elected representatives called **tribunes**. Another important victory for the plebeians was to force the creation of a written law code. In 451 B.C., a group of ten officials began writing down Rome's laws. The laws were carved on twelve tablets, or tables, and hung for all to see. The Twelve Tables established the idea that all free citizens had a right to protection under the law.

The Romans believed that they had a government that balanced the best features of a monarchy (government by a king), an aristocracy (government by nobles), and a democracy (government by the people). Serving in place of a monarch, Rome had two officials called **consuls** who commanded the army and directed the government. However, their power was limited. One consul could overrule, or veto, the other's decisions. The **senate** was the aristocratic branch, although plebeians were eventually allowed in the senate. It had both legislative and administrative functions. The assemblies represented the more democratic side of government. In times of trouble, the republic could appoint a **dictator**—a leader who had absolute power to make laws and command the army.

1.18 Preparing for the Regents

Culture and Intellectual Life How did Alexander the Great contribute to the spread of Greek culture?

1.19 Preparing for the Regents

Justice In what ways were the Twelve Tables similar to the Code of Hammurabi?

1.20 Preparing for the Regents

Political Systems How was the government organized in the Roman Republic?

The Rise of the Roman Empire For hundreds of years after the founding of the republic, Rome sought to expand its territories through trade and conquest. As Rome enlarged its territory, its republican form of government grew increasingly unstable. Eventually, the Roman Republic gave way to a mighty dictator-ruled empire that continued to spread Rome's influence far and wide. Rome was at its peak of power from 27 B.C. to A.D. 180. For 207 years, peace reigned throughout the empire, except for some fighting with tribes along the border. This period of peace and prosperity is known as the ***Pax Romana***— "Roman peace." During this time, the Roman Empire included more than 3 million square miles. Its population numbered between 60 and 80 million people, with about 1 million people living in the city of Rome itself. Slaves may have accounted for as high as one-third of the population. Most slaves were conquered peoples and included men, women, and children.

Under the Roman Empire, hundreds of territories were knitted together into a single state. The Romans held their vast empire together in part through an efficient government and sound rulers. Each Roman province and city was governed in the same way. **Augustus**, who ruled the empire from 27 B.C. until A.D. 14, was Rome's ablest ruler. He stabilized the frontier, glorified Rome with splendid public buildings, and created a civil service to manage the affairs of government—a system that survived for centuries. Agriculture was the most important industry in the empire. About 90 percent of the people were engaged in farming. The empire also had a vast trading network that moved goods between Europe, Africa, and Asia. In addition, a complex set of roads linked the empire. These roads, many of which still exist, were originally built by the Roman army.

The Fall of the Western Roman Empire By the third century A.D., Rome faced many problems. Hostile tribes outside the boundaries of the empire and pirates on the Mediterranean Sea were disrupting trade. The economy was plagued by **inflation**, as the value of money dropped and prices rose. Harvests in western Europe were becoming increasingly meager, thanks to warfare and overworked soil. In addition, the military was in disarray.

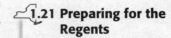

1.21 Preparing for the Regents

Political Systems What was the *Pax Romana*? How did the Romans hold their vast empire together?

TAKING NOTES

Comparing Use a chart to compare the fall of the Han and Roman empires.

Han	Roman
1.	1.
2	2
3	3

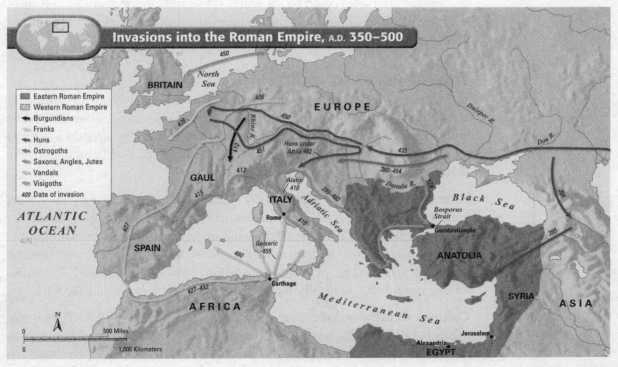

Invasions into the Roman Empire, A.D. 350–500

- ■ Eastern Roman Empire
- ▨ Western Roman Empire
- ← Burgundians
- ← Franks
- ← Huns
- ← Ostrogoths
- ← Saxons, Angles, Jutes
- ← Vandals
- ← Visigoths
- *409* Date of invasion

ATLANTIC OCEAN

BRITAIN
North Sea
EUROPE
GAUL
ITALY
Rome
SPAIN
AFRICA
Carthage
Mediterranean Sea
Adriatic Sea
Huns under Attila 452
Black Sea
Bosporus Strait
Constantinople
ANATOLIA
SYRIA
ASIA
Jerusalem
Alexandria
EGYPT

Rhine R.
Dnieper R.
Don R.
Danube R.

0 — 500 Miles
0 — 1,000 Kilometers

A series of emperors attempted reforms, including dividing the empire into two parts—the Greek-speaking East (Greece, Anatolia, Syria, and Egypt) and the Latin-speaking West (Italy, Gaul, Britain, and Spain). Then in A.D. 330, the emperor Constantine moved the capital of the empire from Rome to the Greek city of Byzantium (bih•ZAN•tshee•uhm), in what is now Turkey.

The decline of the Western Empire took place over many years. Its final collapse was the result of worsening internal problems, the separation of the Western Empire from the wealthier Eastern part, and outside invasion. The Huns, Mongol nomads from central Asia, moved into the region around A.D. 370. In an effort to flee the Huns, the Germanic peoples who lived on the empire's northern border pushed into Roman lands. The Western Empire was unable to field an army to stop them. Then, in 444, the Huns united under a chieftain named Attila, and invaded first the Eastern Empire and then the West. Although the Huns ceased to be a threat to the empire after Attila's death in 453, the German invasions continued. The last Roman emperor was ousted by German forces in 476, ending Roman power in the Western Empire.

Cultural Achievements The Romans borrowed and adapted cultural elements freely, especially from the Greek and Hellenistic cultures. This mixing of elements produced a new culture, called **Greco-Roman culture**. Roman artists, writers, and philosophers adapted Greek and Hellenistic models to convey Roman ideals of strength, permanence, and solidity. Latin, the language of the Romans, remained the language of learning in the West long after the fall of Rome. It was also adopted by different peoples and developed into French, Spanish, Italian, Portuguese, and Romanian. Roman architects and engineers used domes, arches, and concrete to create spectacular buildings, bridges, and **aqueducts**, which brought water into cities. Many awe-inspiring ruins still exist.

Rome's most lasting and widespread contribution, however, was its law. Romans believed that every person had the right to equal treatment under the law and that people were innocent until proven guilty. They also believed that a person should be punished only for actions, not thoughts, and that unreasonable or grossly unfair laws could be set aside. These and other principles of Roman law form the basis of legal systems in many European countries and other places influenced by Europe, including the United States of America.

The Mauryas in India

In 326 B.C., Alexander the Great brought the Indus Valley in the northwest corner of the Indian subcontinent under Macedonian control—but left almost immediately. Soon afterwards, a great military leader, Chandragupta Maurya (chuhn•druh•GUP•tuh MAH•oor•yuh), seized power and established the **Mauryan Empire**.

Human and Physical Geography Chandragupta Maurya may have been born in the kingdom of Magadha, centered on the Ganges River. In about 321 B.C., he gathered an army and killed the unpopular king. After claiming the throne, Chandragupta moved northwest, seizing all of the land from Magadha to the Indus. By 303 B.C., The Mauryan Empire stretched more than 2,000 miles, uniting north India politically for the first time. (See the map on page 53.)

Cultural Achievements Chandragupta relied on Kautilya (kow•TIHL•yuh), a member of a priestly caste, for advice on how to govern. Kautilya wrote a ruler's handbook that proposed tough-minded policies to hold the empire together,

1.22 Preparing for the Regents

Culture and Intellectual Life What were some of the cultural contributions made by the Roman Empire?

including spying and political assassination. Following Kautilya's advice, Chandragupta created a highly bureaucratic government that divided the empire into four provinces, each headed by a royal prince. Each province was then divided into local districts, whose officials assessed taxes and enforced laws.

The empire reached its greatest heights under **Asoka**, Chandragupta's grandson. Asoka is best remembered for his wise and humane edicts, or imperial decrees. Troubled by the number of people slain during a bloody war with a neighboring kingdom, Asoka decided to rule by the Buddhist teaching of "peace to all beings." Throughout the empire, Asoka erected huge stone pillars inscribed with his new policies. Some edicts guaranteed that Asoka would treat his subjects fairly and humanely. Others preached nonviolence. Still others urged **religious toleration**—acceptance of people who held different religious beliefs.

The Maya in Mesoamerica

While the Mauryan Empire was thriving in India, civilizations were also developing in the Americas in a region called **Mesoamerica**. Mesoamerica is an area that stretches south from central Mexico to northern Hondurus. A prime example were the Maya, who burst forth as a flourishing civilization by A.D. 250.

Human and Physical Geography The homeland of the Maya stretched from southern Mexico into northern Central America. This area includes a highland region to the south and a lowland region to the north. The lowlands include the dry scrub forest of the Yucatán (YOO•kuh•TAN) Peninsula and the dense, steamy jungles of southeastern Mexico and northern Guatemala. The highland mountains stretch from southern Mexico to El Salvador. (See the map on page 144.)

Maya City-States The period of A.D. 250 to 900 is known as the Classic Period of Maya civilization. During this time, the Maya built spectacular cities such as Tikal (tee•KAHL), a major center in northern Guatemala. Each Maya center was an independent city-state, ruled by a god-king and serving as a center for religious ceremonies and trade. Maya cities featured giant pyramids, temples, palaces, and elaborate stone carvings dedicated to the gods and to important rulers. Tens of thousands of people lived in residential areas surrounding the city center.

Farming, Trade, and Religion Although the Maya city-states were independent of each other, they were linked through alliances and trade. Cities exchanged local products such as salt, flint, honey, jade ornaments, and cotton textiles. Agriculture provided the basis for Maya life, particularly the growing of **maize**, or corn. The first steps toward agriculture had begun in Mesoamerica around 7000 B.C., when people began growing wild edible plants from seed. By 5000 B.C., many had begun to grow squashes, beans, and other plants. By 3400 B.C., early farmers were growing maize. This highly nourishing crop flourished in Mexico's tropical climate. In addition to slash-and-burn agriculture, the Maya also planted crops on raised beds above swamps and on hillside terraces.

Religion influenced most aspects of Maya life. The Maya believed in many gods. These gods could be good, evil, or both. The Maya believed that each day was a living god whose behavior could be predicted with the help of a system of calendars. The Maya worshipped their gods in variety of ways. They prayed and made offerings of food, flowers, incense, blood, and even human sacrifice.

Cultural Achievements Maya religious beliefs led to the development of the calendar, mathematics, and astronomy. The Maya developed a 260-day religious calendar and a 365-day solar calendar. The calendars were linked together like

1.23 Preparing for the Regents

Justice What were some of the topics addressed by Asoka's edicts?

TAKING NOTES

Summarizing Use a graphic organizer to note the major features of the Maya civilization.

1.24 Preparing for the Regents

Human and Physical Geography When did maize begin to be grown n Mesoamerica?

meshed gears so that any given day could be identified in both cycles. Maya astronomers and mathematicians calculated the solar year at 365.2420 days—only .0002 of a day short of the figure generally accepted today! They were able to attain such precision by using a math system that included the concept of zero. The Maya also developed the most advanced writing system in the ancient Americas, which included about 800 hieroglyphic symbols, or **glyphs**.

The Decline of the Maya The remarkable story of the Maya ended in mystery. In the late 800s, the Maya suddenly abandoned many of their cities. Invaders from the north moved into the lands occupied by the Maya, changing the culture.

The Growth of Global Trade

Just as trade was important to the Maya, it was important to ancient peoples in Europe, Asia, and Africa. Trade routes in ancient times connected the Mediterranean Sea with other centers of world commerce, such as South and East Asia. In addition to exchanging goods, traders carried ideas, religious beliefs, art, and ways of living, thereby helping the process of cultural diffusion.

The ancient seafaring traders along the Mediterranean, traded goods they got from other lands—wine, weapons, precious metals, ivory, and slaves. Two sea routes began by crossing the Arabian Sea to ports in the Persian Gulf and the Red Sea. From there, traders either went overland to Egypt, Syria, and the Mediterranean countries, or they continued to sail up the Red Sea. To sail across the Arabian Sea, sailors learned to make use of the monsoon winds. To widen the variety of exports, Indian traders used other monsoon winds to travel to Southeast Asia and Indonesia. Once there, they obtained spices and other products not native to India.

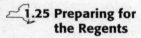

1.25 Preparing for the Regents

Interdependence Why were the Silk Roads and other routes important for trade and cultural diffusion?

Groups who invaded India after Mauryan rule ended helped to expand India's trade to new regions. Central Asian nomads told Indians of a vast network of caravan routes called the **Silk Roads**. They were called the Silk Roads because traders used them to bring silk and other goods from China to western Asia and then on to Rome. The Silk Roads also extended northeastward from China to Korea and by sea on to Japan, thereby spreading goods, religious ideas, and Chinese culture to the region. The trading networks of the Silk Roads helped the Han and Roman empires grow wealthy.

PREPARING FOR THE REGENTS

On a separate sheet of paper, write a well-organized essay that includes an introduction, several paragraphs addressing the task below, and a conclusion. Before beginning, check the Score the Essay box for pointers.

Theme: Turning Points
Political, economic, and social conditions have often led to turning points that have changed the course of history for peoples.

Task:
Identify *two* turning points from the civilizations you have studied in this section and for *each*:
- Describe the causes and key events that led to the turning point
- Explain how *each* changed the course of history for that civilization

SCORE THE ESSAY To receive a score of 5 on your essay, you will need to:
- thoroughly develop all aspects of the task evenly and in depth by describing the turning points and explaining how they changed the course of history.
- be more analytical than descriptive.
- richly support the theme with relevant facts, examples, and details.
- demonstrate a logical and clear plan of organization.

The Emergence and Spread of Belief Systems

Section Overview

Religion is defined as an organized system of beliefs, ceremonies, practices, and worship that center on one or more gods. Religion has had a significant impact on global history. Throughout the centuries, religion has guided the beliefs and actions of millions around the globe. It has brought people together. But it has also torn them apart. Religion continues to be a dominant force throughout the world, affecting everything from what people wear to how they behave.

MAIN IDEAS

RELIGIOUS AND ETHICAL SYSTEMS   The beliefs of the Verdic Age developed into Hinduism and Buddhism.

CULTURAL INTERACTION   Hinduism and Buddhism spread from India to other regions through trade.

RELIGIOUS AND ETHICAL SYSTEMS   The social disorder of warring states contributed to the development of three Chinese ethical systems.

RELIGIOUS AND ETHICAL SYSTEMS   The Hebrews maintained monotheistic religious beliefs that were unique in the ancient world.

RELIGIOUS AND ETHICAL SYSTEMS   Christianity arose in Roman-occupied Judea and spread throughout the Roman Empire.

RELIGIOUS AND ETHICAL SYSTEMS   Muhammad unified the Arab people both politically and through the religion of Islam.

TERMS AND NAMES

- animism
- Vedas
- Aryans
- reincarnation
- karma
- Brahma
- Vishnu
- Shiva
- Jainism
- Siddhartha Gautama
- enlightenment
- nirvana

- stupa
- Mahayana
- Theravada
- Confucius
- filial piety
- Daoism
- Legalism
- Shinto
- monotheism
- Torah
- Abraham
- covenant

- Moses
- Jesus
- apostle
- Paul
- Allah
- Muhammad
- Islam
- Muslim
- Hijrah
- mosque
- hajj
- Qur'an

TARGET THE REGENTS

As you read this section, consider
- in what ways the belief systems discussed here are similar and/or different.
- what individuals, groups, and holy books are associated with the major religions of the world.
- how the belief systems affect our lives today.
- what role missionaries, traders, and conquerors played in the spread of religion

TIME LINE

1300 to 1200 B.C.
Moses leads the Hebrews out of Egypt.

c. 599 B.C.
Mahavira, the founder of Jainism, is born.

c. 563 B.C.
Siddhartha Gautama, the future Buddha, is born.

551 B.C.
Confucius, the founder of Confucianism, is born.

c. 6 to 4 B.C.
Jesus is born.

c. A.D. 570
Muhammad is born.

Animism

1.26 Preparing for the Regents

Belief Systems   What is animism?

Traditional African peoples developed belief systems that helped them under-stand and organize information about their world. Nearly all of these local religions involved a belief in one creator, or god. They also included elements of **animism**, a religion in which spirits play an important role in regulating daily life. Animists belief that spirits are present in animals, plants, and other natural forces, and also take the form of the souls of their ancestors.

Hinduism

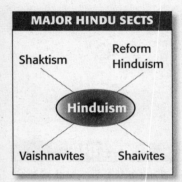

MAJOR HINDU SECTS

Shaktism

Reform Hinduism

Hinduism

Vaishnavites

Shaivites

Hinduism is a collection of religious beliefs that developed slowly over time. Unlike religions such as Buddhism, Christianity, or Islam, Hinduism cannot be traced back to one founder with a single set of ideas. However, Hindus share a common worldview. They see religion as a way of liberating the soul from the illusion, disappointments, and mistakes of everyday existence. Sometime between 750 and 550 B.C., Hindu teachers tried to interpret and explain the hymns in the **Vedas** (VAY•duhz), the sacred literature of the **Aryans**, the Indo-European people who settled in the Indus Valley around 1500 B.C. The teachers' comments were later written down as a dialogue between a student and his teacher and became known as the Upanishads (oo•PAHN•ih•shahdz).

1.27 Preparing for the Regents

Belief Systems   What are the basic beliefs of Hinduism?

The Upanishads explore how a person can achieve liberation from desires and suffering. This liberation is described as *moksha* (MOHK•shah), a state of perfect understanding of all things that brings a release from life in this world. *Moksha* is achieved by understanding the relationship between atman—the individual soul of a living being—and Brahman—the world soul that unites all atmans. This understanding does not usually come in one lifetime. By the process of **reincarnation** (rebirth), an individual soul or spirit is born again and again until *moksha* is achieved. A soul's **karma**—good or bad deeds—follows from one reincarnation to another.

Hinduism has undergone many changes over the last 2,500 years. The world soul, Brahman, is sometimes seen as having the personality of three gods: **Brahma** (BRAH•mah), the creator; **Vishnu** (VIHSH•noo), the preserver or protector; and **Shiva** (SHEE•vuh), the destroyer. Vishnu also takes on many forms or personali-ties, for example, as Krishna, the divine cowherder, and as Rama, the perfect king. Over the centuries, Brahma has gradually faded into the background, while the many forms of Devi, a great Mother Goddess, grew in importance.

Hindus today are free to choose the deity they worship or to choose none at all. Most, however, follow a family tradition that may go back centuries. They are also free to choose among three different paths for achieving *moksha*. These are the path of right thinking, the path of right action, or the path of religious devo-tion. Hinduism is the major religion of India. It also has followers in Indonesia, as well as in parts of Africa, Europe, and the Western Hemisphere.

Jainism

Jainism (JY•nihz•uhm) arose out of the same period of speculation reflected in the Upanishads. Mahavira, the founder of **Jainism**, was born about 599 B.C. and died in 527 B.C. Mahavira believed that everything in the universe has a soul and so should not be harmed. Jain monks carry the doctrine of nonviolence to its logical conclusion. For example, they sweep ants off their path. In keeping with this nonviolence, followers of Jainism look for occupations that will not harm any creatures. So they have a tradition of working in trade and commerce.

1.28 Preparing for the Regents

Belief Systems   What are the basic beliefs of Jainism?

Because of their business activities, Jains today make up one of the wealthiest communities in India. Jains have traditionally preached tolerance of all religions. As a result, they have made few efforts to convert followers of other faiths. Because of this tolerance, Jains have not sent out missionaries. So almost all of the nearly five million Jains in the world today live in India.

Buddhism

Buddhism developed out of the same period of religious questioning that shaped modern Hinduism and Jainism. The founder of Buddhism, **Siddhartha Gautama** (sidh•DAHR•tuh GOW•tuh•muh), was born around 563 B.C. into a noble family in Nepal. According to Buddhist legend, the baby exhibited the marks of a great man. A prophecy indicated that if the child stayed at home he was destined to become a world leader. If the child left home, however, he would become a universal spiritual leader. To make sure that the boy would be a great king and world ruler, his father isolated him in his palace.

Siddhartha never ceased thinking about the world outside. When he was 29, he ventured outside the palace four times. First he saw an old man, next a sick man, then a corpse, and finally a wandering holy man who seemed at peace with himself. Siddhartha understood these events to mean that every living thing experiences old age, sickness, and death and that only a religious life offers a refuge from this inevitable suffering. Siddhartha decided to spend his life searching for religious truth and an end to life's suffering.

Siddhartha wandered through the forests of India for six years seeking wisdom, or **enlightenment**. He tried many ways of reaching an enlightened state. He debated other religious leaders and fasted, but none of these methods brought him to the truth, and he continued to suffer. Finally, he sat in meditation under a large fig tree. After 49 days of meditation, he achieved an understanding of the cause of suffering in this world. From then on, he was known as the Buddha, meaning "the enlightened one."

The Buddha preached his first sermon to five companions who had accompanied him on his wanderings. That first sermon became a landmark in the history of the world's religions. In it, he laid out the four main ideas that he had come to understand in his enlightenment. He called these ideas the Four Noble Truths:

- **First Noble Truth** Life is filled with suffering and sorrow.
- **Second Noble Trut**h The cause of all suffering is people's selfish desire for the temporary pleasures of the world.
- **Third Noble Truth** The way to end all suffering is to end all desires.
- **Fourth Noble Truth** The way to overcome such desire and attain enlightenment is to follow the Eightfold Path, which is called the Middle Way between desires and self-denial.

The Eightfold Path consisted of right views, right resolve, right speech, right conduct, right livelihood, right effort, right mindfulness, and right concentration. By following the Eightfold Path, anyone could reach **nirvana**, the Buddhist word for release from selfishness and pain. The Buddha accepted the idea of reincarnation. He also accepted a cyclical, or repetitive, view of history, where the world is created and destroyed over and over again. However, he rejected the many gods of Hinduism.

Although there is no one scared book in Buddhism, the Buddha's teachings—the *dharma* of Buddhism—were written down after he died in 483 B.C. His followers developed many different interpretations of these teachings. Some

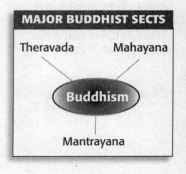

MAJOR BUDDHIST SECTS

Theravada   Mahayana

Buddhism

Mantrayana

1.29 Preparing for the Regents

Belief Systems According to Siddhartha Gautama—the Buddha—how can believers end personal suffering and reach nirvana?

TAKING NOTES

Comparing and Contrasting Use a Venn diagram to compare the beliefs and practices of Buddhism and Hinduism.

Buddhism only

both

Hinduism only

began to teach that Buddha was a god. Some also began to believe that many people could become Buddhas. These potential Buddhas, called bodhisattvas (BOH•dih•SUHT•vuhz), could choose to give up nirvana and work to save humanity through good works and self-sacrifice. The new ideas changed Buddhism from a religion that emphasized individual discipline to a mass religion that offered salvation to all and allowed popular worship. These new trends in Buddhism inspired Indian art. Artist carved huge statues of Buddha for people to worship. People also constructed **stupas**—mounded stone structures built over holy relics.

By the first century A.D., Buddhists had divided over the new doctrines. Those who accepted them belonged to the **Mahayana** (MAH•huh•YAH•nuh) sect. Those who held to Buddha's stricter, original teachings belonged to the **Theravada** (THEHR•uh•VAH•duh) sect. This is also called the Hinayana (HEE•nuh•YAH•nuh) sect, but Theravada is preferred.

Buddhism never gained a significant foothold in India, the country of its origin. However, in the centuries following the Buddha's death, missionaries were able to spread his faith over large parts of Asia. As important as missionaries were in the spread of Buddhism, traders played an even more crucial role. Along with their products, traders carried Buddhism to Sri Lanka, Burma, Thailand, the islands of Sumatra, and China. From China, Buddhism spread to Korea and from Korea to Japan. The movement of trade thus helped make Buddhism the most widespread religion in East Asia.

Chinese Philosophies

Toward the end of the Zhou Dynasty, China moved away from its ancient values of social order, harmony, and respect for authority. Chinese philosophers developed different solutions to restore these values.

Confucianism The philosopher **Confucius** (kuhn•FYOO•shuhs), who lived from 551 to 479 B.C., was China's most influential thinker. Confucius believed that social order, harmony, and good government could be restored in China if society was organized around five basic relationships: 1) ruler and subject, 2) father and son, 3) husband and wife, 4) older brother and younger brother, and 5) friend and friend. A code of proper conduct regulated each of these relationships. For example, rulers should practice kindness and virtuous living. In return, subjects should be loyal and law-abiding.

Three of Confucius's five relationships were based on family. Confucius stressed that children should practice **filial piety**, or respect for their parents and ancestors. Filial piety, according to Confucius, meant devoting oneself to one's parents during their lifetime. It also required honoring their memory after death through the performance of certain rituals. After serving for a brief time in the Zhou government, Confucius spent the remainder of his life teaching. His students later collected his words in a book called the *Analects*. A disciple named Mencius (MEHN•shee•uhs) also spread Confucius's ideas.

Confucianism was never a religion, but it was an ethical system, a systems based on accepted principles of right and wrong. It became the foundation for Chinese government and social order. In addition, the ideas of Confucius spread beyond China and influenced civilizations throughout East Asia.

Daoism For a Chinese thinker named Laozi (low•dzuh), who may have lived during the sixth century B.C., only the natural order was important. The natural order involves relations among all living things. His book *Dao De Jing* (*The Way of Virtue*) expressed Laozi's belief. He said that a universal force called the

1.30 Preparing for the Regents

Movement of People and Goods How did the ideas and customs of Buddhism spread to China and other parts of Asia?

1.31 Preparing for the Regents

Belief Systems According to Confucianism, how can harmony be achieved?

1.32 Preparing for the Regents

Belief Systems How can a child show filial piety?

Dao (dow), meaning "the Way," guides all things. Of all the creatures of nature, according to Laozi, only humans fail to follow the Dao. They argue about questions of right and wrong, good manners or bad. Laozi believed that when there was no desire, all things are at peace. His philosophy became known as **Daoism**. Its search for knowledge and understanding of nature led Daoism's followers to pursue scientific studies. Daoists made many important contributions to the sciences of alchemy, astronomy, and medicine.

Legalism In sharp contrast to the followers of Confucius and Laozi was a group of practical political thinkers called the Legalists, who were powerful during the Qin dynasty. They believed that a highly efficient and powerful government was the key to restoring order in society. They got their name from their belief that government should use the law to end civil disorder and restore harmony. Hanfeizi and Li Si were among the founders of **Legalism**. The Legalists taught that a ruler should provide rich rewards for people who carried out their duties well. Likewise, the disobedient should be harshly punished. The Legalists believed in controlling ideas as well as actions. They suggested that a ruler burn all writings that might encourage people to criticize government.

Shinto

Ancient Japan was not a united country. Instead, hundreds of clans controlled their own territories. Each clan worshipped its own nature gods and goddesses. In different parts of Japan, people honored thousands of local gods. Their varied customs and beliefs eventually combined to form Japan's earliest religion. This religion came to be called **Shinto** (SHIHN•toh), meaning "way of the gods." Shinto was based on respect for the forces of nature and on the worship of ancestors. Shinto worshipers believed in *kami*, divine spirits that dwelled in nature. Any unusual or especially beautiful tree, rock, waterfall, or mountain was considered the home of a *kami*.

Judaism

Judaism is the religion of more than 14 million Jewish people throughout the world. It had its origins among the Hebrews, later called the Jews. The Hebrews settled in Canaan (KAY•nuhn), which lay between the Jordan River and the Mediterranean Sea. Unlike the other groups around them, who were polytheists, the Hebrews practiced **monotheism** (MAHN•uh•thee•IHZ•uhm), a belief in a single god. The Hebrews proclaimed Yahweh as the one and only God. In their eyes, Yahweh had power over all peoples, everywhere. To the Hebrews, God was not a physical being, and no physical images were to be made of him.

Most of what we know about the early Hebrews comes from the **Torah** (TAWR•uh), the first five books of the Hebrew Bible. According to the Torah, Yahweh chose **Abraham** (AY•bruh•HAM), a shepherd who lived in the city of Ur in Mesopotamia, to be the "father" of the Hebrew people. Yahweh and Abraham entered into a **covenant** (KUHV•uh•nuhnt), or mutual promise. Yahweh would protect the Hebrew people. In return, the Hebrews would obey Yahweh. Around 1800 B.C., Abraham moved his family and herds to Canaan. Then around 1650 B.C., the descendents of Abraham moved to Egypt, where they were eventually forced into slavery. The Hebrews fled Egypt—perhaps between 1300 and 1200 B.C. Jews call this event "the Exodus," and they remember it every year during the festival of Passover. The Torah says that the man who led the Hebrews out of Egypt was named **Moses**.

1.33 Preparing for the Regents
Justice What views did the Legalist of the Qin Dynasty hold?

1.34 Preparing for the Regents
Belief Systems What belief do Shinto and animism share?

1.35 Preparing for the Regents
Justice What is monotheism?

TAKING NOTES
Following Chronological Order Use a time line to show major Hebrew leaders and one fact about each.

2000 B.C.
Abraham: father of Jewish people.

While the Hebrews were traveling across the Sinai (SY•ny) Peninsula, Moses climbed to the top of Mount Sinai to pray. The Bible says that he spoke with God. When Moses came down from Mount Sinai, he brought with him two stone tablets on which Yahweh had written the Ten Commandments:

1. I am the Lord thy God. . . . Thou shalt have no other gods before me.
2. Thou shalt not make unto thee any graven image. . . .
3. Thou shalt not take the name of the Lord thy God in vain. . . .
4. Remember the Sabbath day to keep it holy.
5. Honor thy father and thy mother. . . .
6. Thou shalt not kill.
7. Thou shalt not commit adultery.
8. Thou shalt not steal.
9. Thou shalt not bear false witness against thy neighbor.
10. Thou shalt not covet . . . anything that is thy neighbor's.

These commandments and the other teachings that Moses delivered to his people became the basis for the civil and religious code of laws of Judaism. The Hebrews believed that these laws formed a new covenant between the Hebrew people and God. God promised to protect the Hebrews. They promised to keep God's commandments.

In some ways, the Ten Commandments and the other laws delivered to Moses resembled Hammurabi's Code with its attitude of "an eye for an eye and a tooth for a tooth." However, the Jewish code's strict justice was softened by expressions of God's mercy. The code was later interpreted by religious teachers called prophets. These interpretations tended to emphasize greater equality before the law than did other codes of the time. The prophets taught that the Hebrews had a duty to worship God and live justly with one another. The goal was a moral life lived in accordance with God's laws. This emphasis on right conduct and the worship of one God is called ethical monotheism—a Hebrew idea that has influenced human behavior for thousands of years through Judaism, Christianity, and Islam.

Christianity

Around 63 B.C., Roman power spread to Judea, which was now the home of the Jews. In A.D. 6, Rome took control of the Jewish kingdom. A number of Jews, however, believed that they would once again be free. According to biblical tradition, God had promised that a savior known as the Messiah would arrive and restore the kingdom of the Jews. Roughly two decades after the beginning of Roman rule, many believed that a savior had arrived—a Jew named **Jesus**. Although the exact date is uncertain, historians believe that Jesus was born in Bethlehem in Judea sometime around 6 to 4 B.C. and raised in the Nazareth in northern Palestine.

At age 30, Jesus began his public ministry. For the next three years, he preached, taught, did good works, and reportedly performed miracles. His teachings contained many ideas from Jewish traditions, such as monotheism and the principles of the Ten Commandments. Jesus emphasized God's personal relationship to each human being. He stressed the importance of people's love for God, their neighbors, their enemies, and even themselves. He also taught that God would end wickedness in the world and would establish an eternal kingdom after death for people who sincerely repented their sins.

Historical records of the time mention very little about Jesus. The main source of information about his teachings are the Gospels, the first four books of the New Testament of the Bible. Some of the Gospels are thought to have been

MAJOR JEWISH SECTS

Reform   Orthodox

Judaism

Conservative

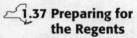

1.36 Preparing for the Regents

Justice   What common significance did the Ten Commandments, Hammurabi's Code, and the Twelve Tables of Rome have for their societies?

1.37 Preparing for the Regents

Belief Systems   How are Confucianism, Judaism, and Christianity similar in the way that they believe people should treat each other?

written by on or more of Jesus' disciples, or pupils. These 12 men later came to be called **apostles**.

As Jesus preached from town to town, his fame grew. His growing popularity concerned both Roman and Jewish leaders. When Jesus visited Jerusalem about A.D. 29, enthusiastic crowds greeted him as the Messiah, or king—the one whom the Bible had said would come to rescue the Jews. The chief priests of the Jews, however, denied that Jesus was the Messiah. The Roman governor Pontius Pilate accused Jesus of defying the authority of Rome. Pilate arrested Jesus and sentenced him to be crucified, or nailed to a large wooden cross to die. After Jesus' death, his body was placed in a tomb. According to the Gospels, three days later his body was gone, and a living Jesus began appearing to his followers. The Gospels go on to say that he then ascended into heaven. The apostles were more convinced than ever that Jesus was the Messiah. It was from this belief that Jesus came to be referred to as Jesus Christ. *Christos* is a Greek word meaning "messiah" or "savior." The name *Christianity* was derived from "Christ."

Strengthened by their conviction that he had triumphed over death, Jesus' followers continued to spread his ideas. Jesus' teaching did not contradict Jewish law, and many of his first followers were Jews. Soon, however, these followers began to create a new religion based on his messages. Despite political and religious opposition, the new religion of Christianity spread slowly but steadily through the Roman Empire. The spread of Christianity was helped by the P*ax Romana*, which made travel and the exchange of ideas fairly safe. Common languages—Latin and Greek—allowed the message to be easily understood.

One man, the apostle **Paul**, had an enormous influence on Christianity's development. He wrote influential letters, called Epistles, to groups of believers. In his teaching, Paul stressed that Jesus was the son of God who died for people's sins. He also declared that Christianity should welcome all converts, Jews or Gentiles (non-Jews). It was this attempt to be universal that enabled Christianity to become more than just a local religion. Through the centuries, it has been spread through trade, conquest, and missionary efforts. Today, Christianity is the largest religion in the world, with about 2 billion followers.

Islam

The Arabs were polytheists. However, the concept of belief in one God, called **Allah** (AL•luh) in Arabic, was known on the Arabian Peninsula. Many Christians and Jews lived there and practiced monotheism. **Muhammad** (mu•HAM•id), a member of a powerful Meccan clan, was born into this mixed religious environment around A.D. 570. Muhammad took great interest in religion and often spent time alone in prayer and meditation. At about the age of 40, Muhammad's life changed overnight when a voice called to him while he meditated in a cave outside of Mecca. According to Muslim belief, the voice was that of the angel Gabriel, who told Muhammad that he was a messenger of Allah. Muhammad became convinced that he was the last of the prophets. He began to teach that Allah was the one and only God and that all other gods must be abandoned. People who agreed to this basic principle of Islam were called Muslims. In Arabic, **Islam** (ihs•LAHM) means "submission to the will of Allah," and **Muslim** (MOOZ•lim) means "one who has submitted."

By 613, Muhammad had begun to preach publicly in Mecca, but he met with some hostility. After some of his followers had been attacked, Muhammad decided to leave Mecca in 622. He moved over 200 miles to the town of Yathrib, which was later renamed Medina. This migration, which became known as the

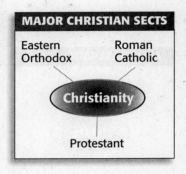

MAJOR CHRISTIAN SECTS

Eastern Orthodox

Roman Catholic

Christianity

Protestant

TAKING NOTES

Following Chronological Order Use a sequence graphic to show the events that led to the spread of Christianity .

Rome takes over Jewish kingdom.

TAKING NOTES

Synthesizing Use a diagram to list important aspects of Islam.

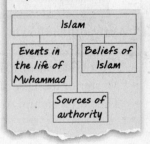

Islam

Events in the life of Muhammad

Beliefs of Islam

Sources of authority

Hijrah (hih•JEE•ruh), marked a turning point for Muhammad. Muhammad fashioned an agreement that joined his own people with the Arabs and Jews of Medina as a single community. These groups accepted Muhammad as a political leader. As a religious leader, he attracted many more devoted followers.

Muhammad also became a military leader in the growing hostilities between Medina and Mecca. He returned to Mecca with 10,000 followers in 630. Facing sure defeat, Mecca's leaders surrendered. Most Meccans pledged their loyalty to Muhammad, and many converted to Islam. Muhammad died two years later, at about the age of 62. By that time, he had taken great strides in unifying the Arabian Peninsula under Islam.

To be a Muslim, all believers must carry out five duties. These duties are known as the Five Pillars of Islam:

- **Faith** To become a Muslim, a person has to testify that "There is no God but Allah, and Muhammad is the Messenger of Allah."
- **Prayer** Five times a day, Muslims face toward Mecca to pray. They may assemble at a **mosque** (mahsk), an Islamic house of worship, or wherever they find themselves.
- **Alms** Muhammad taught that all Muslims have a responsibility to support the less fortunate. Muslims meet that social responsibility by giving alms, or money for the poor, through a special religious tax.
- **Fasting** During the Islamic holy month of Ramadan, Muslims fast between dawn and sunset. A simple meal is eaten at the end of the day. Fasting reminds Muslims that their spiritual needs are greater than their physical needs.
- **Pilgrimage** All Muslims who are physically and financially able perform the **hajj** (haj), or pilgrimage to Mecca, at least once.

The original source of authority for Muslims is Allah. According to Islamic belief, Allah expressed his will through the angel Gabriel, who revealed it to Muhammad. While Muhammad lived, his followers memorized and recited these revelations. After Muhammad's death, the revelations were collected in the **Qur'an** (kuh•RAN), the holy book of the Muslims.

Today, Muslims are concentrated from southwest to central Asia and parts of Africa. Islam also has many followers in Southeast Asia. This in part reflects the success of early Muslim military expansion and the effectiveness of Muslim traders.

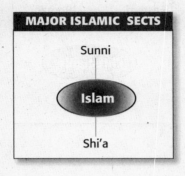

MAJOR ISLAMIC SECTS

Sunni

Islam

Shi'a

 1.38 Preparing for the Regents

Belief Systems What is one way in which Islam's Five Pillars of Faith and Buddhism's Eightfold Path are similar?

TARGET THE REGENTS

Answer the following question. Use the Analyze the Question hints to help you answer the question.

- "Most Gracious, Most Merciful;"
- "Master of the Day of Judgment."
- "Thee do worship, And Thine we seek."

Source: 'Abdullah Yusuf-Ali, trans.,
The Meaning of the Holy Qur'an,
Amana Publications (excerpted)

1 This translated quotation from the Qur'an [Koran] refers to

(1) Buddha   (3) Allah
(2) Shiva   (4) Muhammad

ANALYZE THE QUESTION
- Read the question stem. You are being asked to determine who is being referred to in the quotation.
- Read the source line. The source line and the question stem provide clues about which religious perspective is being discussed.
- Think about the beliefs and terminology of that religion while you read the alternatives. Chose the alternative that best matches that religion.

Ancient World–Civilizations and Religions
4000 B.C.–A.D. 500

Part I: MULTIPLE-CHOICE QUESTIONS

Directions (1–10): For each statement or question, write on a separate answer sheet the *number* of the word or expression that, of those given, best completes the statement or answers the questions.

1 Hammurabi's Code, the Ten Commandments, and the Twelve Tables were all significant to their societies because they established

(1) democratic governments
(2) official religions
(3) rules of behavior
(4) economic systems

2 The five relationships taught by Confucius encouraged people to

(1) improve their position in life
(2) maintain social and political order
(3) respect and worship nature
(4) serve the needs of religious leaders

3 Judaism, Islam, and Christianity share a belief in

(1) papal supremacy
(2) teachings of the Qur'an
(3) reincarnation and the Four Noble Truths
(4) an ethical code of conduct and monotheism

4 What was an important result of the Neolithic Revolution?

(1) Food supplies became more reliable.
(2) New sources of energy became available.
(3) People became more nomadic.
(4) Populations declined.

5 In a traditional economic system, which type of goods are most often produced?

(1) agricultural products
(2) heavy industrial machinery
(3) military supplies
(4) electronics and computers

6 The Han Dynasty and the Roman Empire were similar in that both grew wealthy because they

(1) developed extensive trade networks
(2) created classless societies
(3) encouraged democratic ideals
(4) established free-market economies

Base your answer to question 7 on the map below and on your knowledge of social studies.

**Movement of People
500 B.C. – A.D. 1500**

Source: Roger B. Beck et al., *World History: Patterns of Interaction*, McDougal Littell (adapted)

7 The routes shown on the map illustrate the

(1) spread of Christianity
(2) shift in European population
(3) expansion of apartheid
(4) patterns of Bantu migration

8 Olympic games, the poems of Homer, and Hellenistic culture are associated with which ancient civilization?

(1) Egyptian   (3) Roman
(2) Greek   (4) Phoenician

9 Which geographic feature was common to the development of civilizations in ancient Egypt, China, India, and Mesopotamia?

(1) river valleys   (3) rain forests
(2) deserts   (4) mountains

10 Shintoism and animism share a belief in the importance of

(1) reincarnation   (3) holy books
(2) spirits in nature (4) missionaries

In developing your answers to Parts II and III, be sure to keep these general definitions in mind:

(a) *explain* means "to make plain or understandable; to give reasons for or causes of; to show the logical development or relationship of"

(b) *discuss* means "to make observations about something using facts, reasoning, and argument; to present in some detail"

(c) *compare and contrast* means "to express similarities and differences"

Part II: THEMATIC ESSAY

Directions: Write a well-organized essay that includes an introduction, several paragraphs addressing the task below, and a conclusion.

Theme: Change [Individuals Who Have Changed History]

The beliefs and achievements of individuals have changed global history. These beliefs and achievements have had positive and negative effects on society.

Task:

Identify *two* individuals who have changed global history and for *each*:
- Explain *one* belief or achievement of that individual
- Discuss the positive *and/or* negative effects of the individual's belief or achievement

You may use any individual from your study of Unit One. The individuals you identify must have had a major role in shaping global history. Some individuals that you might consider include Hammurabi, Confucius, Aristotle, Alexander the Great, and Muhammad.

You are not limited to these suggestions.

Guidelines:

In your essay, be sure to
- Address all aspects of the *Task*
- Support the theme with relevant facts, examples, and details
- Use a logical and clear plan of organization
- Include an introduction and a conclusion that are beyond the simple restatement of the *Theme*

Part III: DOCUMENT-BASED QUESTION

This question is based on the accompanying documents (1–3). The question is designed to test your ability to work with historic documents. Some of these documents have been edited for the purpose of this question. As you analyze the documents, take into account both the source of each document and any point of view that may be presented in the document.

Historical Context:

Throughout history, social and political factors have influenced the roles of women in different societies. As a result, the roles of women have varied across time and in different places.

Task:

Using information from the documents and your knowledge of global history, answer the question that follows each document in Part A. Your answers to the questions will help you write the Part B essay, in which you will be asked to:

- Compare and contrast the role of women in different societies in the ancient world
- Discuss the impact of social or political factors on the status of women in these societies

Part A: Short Answer

Directions: Analyze the documents and answer the short-answer questions that follow in the space provided.

Document 1

A Manual of Polite Conduct

> If you are wise, look after your house; love your wife. . . . Be not brutal; tack will influence her better than violence; . . . behold to what she aspires [seeks], at what she aims, what she regards. It is that which fixes her in your house.

—Ptah-hotep, a sage during the 5th Dynasty, c. 2380 B.C.

1 How does Ptah-hotep think a wife should be treated?

_____

_____

Document 2

A Good Wife

> A good wife should be the mistress of her home, having under her care all that is within it, according to the rules we have laid down. . . . But in all other matters, let it be her aim to obey her husband; giving no heed to public affairs.

—Aristotle, Greek philosopher, c. 330 B.C.

2 According to Aristotle, what was the role of a good wife?

_____

_____

Document 3

Seven Feminine Virtues

> As a women, she should always be modest and respectful, should keep herself constantly in the background, whatever she does, should never speak of her own goodness or flinch [back away] from the performance of her assigned duties . . . and finally, should be able to endure all of the humiliations and insults, from wherever they come.

—Ban Zhao, a scholar and teacher during the Han Dynasty, 202 B.C.–A.D. 22

3 What was *one* rule women were expected to follow during the Han Dynasty?

_____

_____

Part B: Essay

Directions: Write a well-organized essay that includes an introduction, several paragraphs, and a conclusion. Use evidence from at least *two* documents in the body of the essay. Support your response with relevant facts, examples, and details. Include additional outside information.

Historical Context:
Throughout history, social and political factors have influenced the roles of women in different societies. As a result, the roles of women have varied across time and in different places.

Task:
Using information from the documents and your knowledge of global history, write an essay in which you:

- Compare and contrast the role of women in different societies in the ancient world
- Discuss the impact of social or political factors on the status of women in these societies

Guidelines:
In your essay, be sure to
- Address all aspects of the *Task* by accurately analyzing and interpreting at least **two** documents
- Incorporate information from the documents
- Incorporate relevant outside information
- Support the theme with relevant facts, examples, and details
- Use a logical and clear plan of organization
- Introduce the theme by establishing a framework that is beyond a simple statement of the *Task* or *Historical Context* and conclude with a summation of the theme

UNIT 2

Expanding Zones of Exchange and Encounter
500–1200

Unit Overview

This unit examines the Gupta Empire in India, the Tang and Song dynasties in China, and the Byzantine Empire and its impact on early Russia. It also looks at the growth of the Muslim world in the centuries following Muhammad's death and at life in Europe during the early Middle Ages and the Crusades.

Concepts and Themes

Among the concepts and themes explored in this unit are

- Belief Systems
- Conflict
- Culture and Intellectual Life
- Economic Systems
- Human and Physical Geography

- Justice
- Movement of People and Goods
- Political Systems
- Power
- Science and Technology

PREPARING FOR THE REGENTS: Building Thematic Essay Skills

Turning points are major events in history that have led to lasting change. The Neolithic Revolution, for example, was a major turning point in the development of civilization. The surplus food provided by farming and the domestication of animals allowed for increases in population, the growth of cities, and specialization among workers—all important elements in the growth of more complex societies. Knowing how to analyze critical turning points is an important skill to develop as you study global history. As you read this unit, think about how events such as the spread of Islam, European feudalism, and the Crusades produced lasting changes. Use the following chart to organize information about these events. You can add additional rows as needed.

Turning Point	Circumstances Surrounding the Turning Point	Changes Produced by the Turning Point

The Gupta Empire of India

Section Overview

The 500 years following the Mauryan Empire was a time of upheaval on the Indian subcontinent. Invaders poured into India, bringing new ideas and customs. In response, Indians began to change their own culture. A strong leader finally emerged in the northern Indian state of Magadha. His name was Chandra Gupta. The Gupta Empire that he founded in A.D. 320 lasted until 535. Under the Guptas, India entered a highly productive period in literature, art, science, and mathematics. This golden age continued until roughly A.D. 500.

Like earlier Indian societies, Gupta society was organized into strict social classes, or **castes** *(kasts). From top to bottom, the four castes were the Brahmins (priests), the Kshatriyas (rulers and warriors), the Vaishyas (peasants and traders), and Shudras (laborers). Outside the caste system were the "untouchables," those considered unclean because of the work they did. People were born into their caste for life. Their caste membership determined the work they did, the man or woman they could marry, and the people with whom they could eat.*

After Chandra Gupta II died in 415, new invaders threatened northern India. These fierce fighters were called the Hunas. They were related to the Huns who invaded the Roman Empire. Over the next 100 years, the Gupta Empire broke into small kingdoms. Many of these kingdoms were overrun by the Hunas or other Central Asian nomads.

Terra-cotta tile from the Gupta era

MAIN IDEAS

POWER AND AUTHORITY   The Guptas established empires, but could not unify India permanently.

CULTURAL INTERACTION   Indian religions, culture, and science evolved and spread to other regions through trade.

TERMS AND NAMES

- caste
- Tamil
- Gupta Empire
- patriarchal
- matriarchal
- Kalidasa

PREPARING FOR THE REGENTS

As you read this section, consider
- how the Gupta Empire contributed to human history.

TIME LINE

232 B.C.
Mauryan emperor Asoka dies.

A.D. 320
Gupta Empire forms in India.

A.D. 535
Gupta Empire ends.

Human and Physical Geography

The Mauryan emperor Asoka died in 232 B.C. His death left a power vacuum. In northern and central India, regional kings challenged the imperial government. The kingdoms of central India, which had only been loosely held in the Mauryan Empire, soon regained their independence. The Andhra (AHN•druh) Dynasty arose and dominated the region for hundreds of years. Because of their central position, the Andhras profited from the extensive trade between north and south India and also with Rome, Sri Lanka, and Southeast Asia.

At the same time, northern India had to absorb a flood of new people fleeing political instability in other parts of Asia. For 500 years, beginning about 185 B.C., wave after wave of Greeks, Persians, and Central Asians poured into northern India. These invaders disrupted Indian society. But they also introduced new languages and customs that added to the already-rich blend of Indian culture.

Southern India also experienced turmoil. It was home to three kingdoms that had never been conquered by the Mauryans. The people who lived in this region spoke the **Tamil** (TAM•uhl) language and are called the Tamil people. These three kingdoms were often at war with one another and with other states.

TAKING NOTES
Comparing Use a chart to compare the Mauryan and Gupta empires.

Mauryan	Gupta
1.	1.
2	2
3	3

The Guptas

After 500 years of invasion and turmoil, a strong leader again rose in the northern state of Magadha. His name was Chandra Gupta (GUP•tuh), but he was no relation to India's first emperor, Chandragupta Maurya. India's second empire, the **Gupta Empire**, oversaw a great flowering of Indian civilization, especially Hindu culture.

The first Gupta emperor came to power not through battle but by marrying a daughter of an influential royal family. After his marriage, Chandra Gupta I took the title "Great King of Kings" in A.D. 320. His empire included Magadha and the area north of it, with his power base along the Ganges River. His son, Samudra (suh•MU•druh) Gupta, became king in A.D. 335. Although a lover of the arts, Samudra had a warlike side. He expanded the empire through 40 years of conquest.

Indians revered the third emperor, Chandra Gupta II, for his heroic qualities. He defeated the Shakas—enemies to the west—and added their coastal territory to his empire. This allowed the Guptas to engage in profitable trade with the Mediterranean world. Chandra Gupta II also strengthened his empire through peaceful means by negotiating diplomatic and marriage alliances. He ruled from A.D. 375 to 415.

After Chandra Gupta II died, new invaders threatened northern India. These fierce fighters, called the Hunas, were related to the Huns who invaded the Roman Empire. Over the next 100 years, the Gupta Empire broke into small kingdoms. Many of these kingdoms were overrun by the Hunas or other Central Asian nomads. The empire ended about 535.

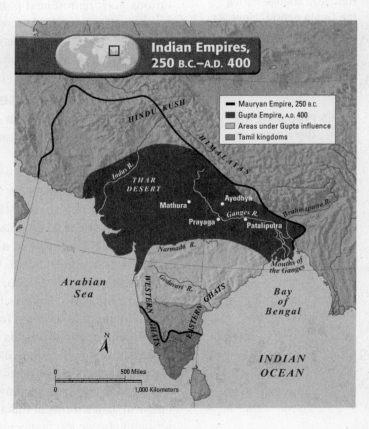

Indian Empires, 250 B.C.–A.D. 400

- ▬ Mauryan Empire, 250 B.C.
- ■ Gupta Empire, A.D. 400
- ▨ Areas under Gupta influence
- ■ Tamil kingdoms

HINDU KUSH
HIMALAYAS
Indus R.
THAR DESERT
Mathura
Ayodhya
Prayaga
Ganges R.
Pataliputra
Brahmaputra R.
Narmada R.
Arabian Sea
Godavari R.
WESTERN GHATS
EASTERN GHATS
Mouths of the Ganges
Bay of Bengal
INDIAN OCEAN

N

0   500 Miles
0   1,000 Kilometers

Social Organization

The Gupta period is the first period for which historians have much information about daily life in India. Like earlier Indian societies, the Gupta Empire had a rigid caste system. (See the Section Overview on page 52.) Most Indians lived in small villages. The majority were farmers, who walked daily from their homes to outlying fields. Craftspeople and merchants clustered in specific districts in the towns. They had shops on the street level and lived in the rooms above.

Most Indian families were **patriarchal**, headed by the eldest male. Parents, grandparents, uncles, aunts, and children all worked together to raise their crops. Because drought was common, farmers often had to irrigate their crops. There was a tax on water, and every month, people had to give a day's worth of labor to maintain wells, irrigation ditches, reservoirs, and dams. As in Mauryan times, farmers were required to give a large proportion of their earnings to the king. Southern India followed a different cultural pattern. Some Tamil groups were **matriarchal**, headed by the mother rather than the father. Property, and sometimes the throne, was passed through the female line.

A Hindu Rebirth

By 250 B.C., Hindu and Buddhism were India's two main religions. Over the centuries, both religions had become increasingly removed from the people. Hinduism became dominated by priests. By the time of the Mauryan Empire, Hinduism had developed a complex set of sacrifices that could be performed only by priests. Most people had less and less direct connection with the religion.

Gradually, though, the religion changed. Although the religion continued to embrace hundreds of gods, a trend towards monotheism was growing. Many people began to believe that there was only one divine force in the universe. The various gods represented parts of that force. The three most important Hindu gods were Brahma, Vishnu, and Shiva. Of the three, Vishnu and Shiva were by far the favorites. Many Indians began to devote themselves to these two gods. The Guptas created temples to honor the gods.

Cultural Achievements

Just as Hinduism underwent change, so did Indian culture and learning. India entered a golden age in literature, art, science, and mathematics that continued until roughly A.D. 500.

One of India's greatest writers was **Kalidasa** (KAH•lee•DAH•suh). He may have been the court poet for Chandra Gupta II. Kalidasa's most famous play is *Shakuntala*. It tells the story of a beautiful girl who falls in love with and marries a middle-aged king. After Shakuntala and her husband are separated, they suffer tragically because of a curse that prevents the king from recognizing his wife when they meet again. Generations of Indians have continued to admire Kalidasa's plays because they are skillfully written and emotionally stirring. Southern India also has a rich literary tradition. In the second century A.D., the city of Madurai in southern India became a site of writing academies. More than 2,000 Tamil poems from this period still exist.

In addition to literature, drama was very popular. In southern India, traveling troupes of actors put on performances in cities across the region. Women as well as men took part in these shows, which combined drama and dance. Many of the classical dance forms in India today are based on techniques explained in a book written between the first century B.C. and the first century A.D.

2.1 Preparing for the Regents

Culture and Intellectual Life What was daily life like for men and women living in the Gupta Empire?

2.2 Preparing for the Regents

Belief Systems How did Hinduism change during the Gupta period? How did people react to these changes?

2.3 Preparing for the Regents

Culture and Intellectual Life What are some of the accomplishments that occurred during India's golden age under the Guptas?

The expansion of trade spurred the advance of science in India. Because sailors on trading ships used the stars to help them figure their position at sea, knowledge of astronomy increased. From Greek invaders, Indians adapted Western methods of keeping time. They began to use a calendar based on the cycles of the sun rather than the moon. They also adopted a seven-day week and divided each day into hours. During the Gupta Empire, knowledge of astronomy increased further. Almost 1,000 years before Columbus, Indian astronomers proved that the earth was round by observing a lunar eclipse. During the eclipse, the earth's shadow fell across the face of the moon. The astronomers noted that the earth's shadow was curved, indicating that the earth itself was round.

Indian mathematics was among the most advanced in the world. Modern numerals, the zero, and the decimal system were invented in India. Around A.D. 500, an Indian named Aryabhata (AHR•yuh•BUHT•uh) calculated the value of pi (π) to four decimal places. He also calculated the length of the solar year as 365.3586805 days. This is very close to modern calculations made with an atomic clock. In medicine, two important medical guides were compiled. They described more than 1,000 diseases and more than 500 medicinal plants. Hindu physicians performed surgery—including plastic surgery—and possibly gave injections.

Increased trade led to the growth of banking in India. Commerce was quite profitable. Bankers were willing to lend money to merchants and charge them interest on the loans. Interest rates varied depending on how risky business was. During Mauryan times, the annual interest rate on loans used for overseas trade had been 240 percent! During the Gupta Empire, bankers no longer considered sea trade so dangerous, so they charged only 15 to 20 percent interest a year.

PREPARING FOR THE REGENTS

Answer the following question. Use the Analyze the Question hints to help you answer the question.

Base your answer to question 1 on the diagram below and on your knowledge of social studies.

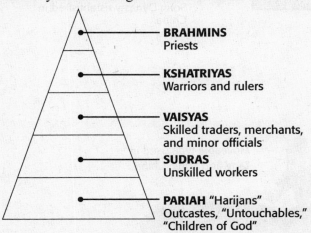

BRAHMINS
Priests

KSHATRIYAS
Warriors and rulers

VAISYAS
Skilled traders, merchants, and minor officials

SUDRAS
Unskilled workers

PARIAH "Harijans"
Outcastes, "Untouchables,"
"Children of God"

1 The diagram represents the rigid social class system of

   (1) colonial Latin America
   (2) traditional India
   (3) feudal Japan
   (4) dynastic China

ANALYZE THE QUESTION
- Read the question stem. You are being asked to indicate which society is represented by this diagram.
- Read the alternatives. Think about what you know about each society's class system.
- Select the alternative that fits the characteristics of the system illustrated in the diagram.

The Tang and Song Dynasties of China

Section Overview

After the Han Dynasty collapsed in A.D. 220, no emperor was strong enough to hold China together. Over the next 350 years, more than 30 local dynasties rose and fell. Finally, an emperor named Wendi united northern and southern China under the Sui Dynasty. Although the Sui Dynasty only lasted from 581 to 618, it laid the foundation for the next two dynasties, the Tang and the Song.

Under the Tang (618–907) and the Song (960–1279), China experienced a prolonged golden age. It became the richest, most powerful, and most advanced country in the world.

MAIN IDEAS

EMPIRE BUILDING   The Tang Dynasty built China into the most powerful and advanced empire in the world.
EMPIRE BUILDING   During the Tang and Song dynasties, China experienced an era of prosperity and technological innovation.

TERMS AND NAMES

- Tang Taizong
- Wu Zhao
- gentry
- movable type

PREPARING FOR THE REGENTS

As you read this section, consider
- how the Tang and Song dynasties contributed to human history

TIME LINE

678
Tang Dynasty begins 289-year rule in China.

850
Chinese invent gunpowder.

960
Song Dynasty established in China.

Moveable type used in Tang and Song, China

Human and Physical Geography

Wendi, the first emperor of the Sui (sway) Dynasty, came to power in 581. By 589 he had united northern and southern China for the first time since the fall of the Han Dynasty. The Sui's greatest accomplishment was the completion of the Grand Canal—a more than 1,000-mile waterway that connected the Huang He and the Chang Jiang. The canal provided a vital route for trade between the northern cities and the southern rice-producing region of the Chang delta. However, endless labor on state projects turned the people against the Sui Dynasty. Overworked and over-taxed, they finally revolted. In 618, a member of the imperial court assassinated the second Sui emperor, ending the dynasty. While short-lived, the Sui Dynasty built a strong foundation for the great achievements of the next dynasty, the Tang (tahng), which ruled for nearly 300 years (618–907).

TAKING NOTES

Comparing and Contrasting Use a Venn diagram to note the similarities and differences between the Tang and Song dynasties.

Tang only

Both

Song only

The Tang Dynasty

The great achievements of the Tang began under **Tang Taizong**, who reigned from 626 to 649. Taizong's armies reconquered the northern and western lands that China had lost since the decline of the Han Dynasty. By 668, China had extended its influence over Korea as well. The ruler during the Korean campaign was the empress **Wu Zhao** (woo jow). From about 660 on, she held the real power while weak emperors sat on the throne. Finally, in 690, Empress Wu assumed the title of emperor for herself—the only woman ever to do so in China.

Scholar-Officials Tang rulers strengthened the central government of China and expanded the network of roads and canals begun by the Sui. This helped to pull the empire together. To manage their large empire, the Tang rulers restored China's vast bureaucracy by reviving and expanding the civil service examination system begun by the Han. The relatively few candidates who passed the tough exams became part of an elite group of scholar-officials.

In theory, the exams were open to all men, even commoners. However, only the wealthy could afford the necessary years of education. Also, men with political connections could obtain high positions without taking the exams. Despite these flaws, the system created a remarkably intelligent and capable governing class in China. Before the Tang, a few noble families dominated the country. As the examination system grew in importance, talent and education became more important than noble birth in winning power. As a result, many moderately wealthy families shared in China's government.

The Tang Lose Power To meet the rising costs of government, Tang rulers imposed crushing taxes in the mid-700s. These brought hardship to the people but failed to cover the costs of military expansion and new building programs. Moreover, the Tang struggled to control their vast empire. In 751, Muslim armies soundly defeated the Chinese at the Battle of Talas. As a result, Central Asia passed out of Chinese control and into foreign hands. After this time, border attacks and internal rebellions steadily chipped away at the power of the imperial government. Finally, in 907, Chinese rebels sacked and burned the Tang capital at Ch'ang-an and murdered the last Tang emperor, a child.

The Song Dynasty

After the fall of the Tang Dynasty, rival warlords divided China into separate kingdoms. Then, in 960, an able general named Taizu reunited China and proclaimed himself the first Song (sung) emperor. The Song Dynasty, like the Tang, lasted

2.4 Preparing for the Regents

Political Systems How did the Tang strengthen the central government?

2.5 Preparing for the Regents

Political Systems How did the Tang fall from power?

about 300 years (960–1279). Although the Song ruled a smaller empire than either the Han or the Tang, China remained stable, powerful, and prosperous.

Song armies never regained the western lands lost after 751. Nor did they regain northern lands that had been lost to nomadic tribes during the Tang decline. For a time, Song emperors tried to buy peace with their northern enemies. They paid hefty annual tributes of silver, silk, and tea. This policy, however, ultimately failed to stop the threat from the north. In the early 1100s, a Manchurian people called the Jurchen conquered northern China and established the Jin Empire. The Jurchen forced the Song to retreat south across the Huang He. After 1127, the Song emperors ruled only southern China.

Social Organization

During Tang and Song times, the power of the old aristocratic families began to fade. A new, much larger upper class emerged, made up of scholar-officials and their families. Such a class of powerful, well-to-do people is called the **gentry**. The gentry attained their status through education and civil service positions rather than through land ownership. Below the gentry was an urban middle class. It included merchants, shopkeepers, skilled artisans, minor officials, and others. At the bottom of urban society were laborers, soldiers, and servants. In the countryside lived the largest class by far, the peasants. They toiled for wealthy landowners as they had for centuries.

Women had always been subservient to men in Chinese society. Their status further declined during the Tang and Song periods. This was especially true among the upper classes in cities, where a woman's work was deemed less important to the family's prosperity and status. Changing attitudes affected peasant women less, since they worked in the fields, helping produce their family's food and income.

One sign of the changing status of women was the new custom of binding the feet of upper-class girls. When a girl was very young, her feet were bound tightly with cloth, which eventually broke the arch and curled all but the big toe under. This produced what was admiringly called a "lily-foot." Women with bound feet were crippled for life. To others in society, such a woman reflected the wealth and prestige of her husband, who could afford such a beautiful but impractical wife.

Cultural Achievements

Artisans and scholars made important technological advances during the Tang and Song eras. Among the most important inventions were movable type and gunpowder. With **movable type**, a printer could arrange blocks of individual characters in a frame to make up a page for printing. Previously, printers had carved the words of a whole page into one large block. The development of gunpowder, in time, led to the creation of explosive weapons such as bombs, grenades, small rockets, and cannons. Other important inventions included porcelain, the mechanical clock, paper money, and the use of the magnetic compass for sailing. The Chinese also made advances in arithmetic and algebra. Ideas, such as using negative numbers, spread from China southward and westward.

The Tang and Song dynasties also nourished an age of artistic brilliance. The Tang Dynasty produced great poetry. Two of its most celebrated poets were Li Bo, who wrote about life's pleasures, and Tu Fu, who praised orderliness and Confucian virtues. Tu Fu also wrote critically about war and the hardships of soldiers. Chinese painting reached new heights of beauty during the Song

2.6 Preparing for the Regents

Power What was the status of women in Tang and Song society?

2.7 Preparing for the Regents

Culture and Intellectual Life What advances are associated with the Tang and Song dynasties?

Dynasty. Painting of this era shows Daoist influence. Artists emphasized the beauty of natural landscapes and objects such as a single branch or flower. The artists' favorite paint was black ink. Said one Song artist, "Black is ten colors."

Growth of Agriculture, Commerce, and Trade

China's population nearly doubled, soaring to 100 million, during the Tang and Song dynasties. By the Song era, China had at least ten cities with a population of 1 million each. This rapid growth resulted in part from advances in farming, especially the cultivation of rice. In about the year 1000, China imported a new variety of fast-ripening rice from Vietnam. This allowed farmers to harvest two rice crops each year rather than one, thereby producing more food to feed the expanding population.

Foreign trade also flourished. Ch'ang-an, the Tang capital, was located on a trade route. Tang armies guarded the Silk Roads, which linked China to the West. Eventually, however, China lost control over these routes during the long Tang decline. After this time, Chinese merchants relied increasingly on ocean trade. Chinese advances in sailing technology, including use of the magnetic compass, made it possible for sea trade to expand. Up and down China's long coastline, the largest port cities in the world bustled with international trade. Merchant ships carried trade goods to Korea and Japan. They sailed across the Indian Ocean to India, the Persian Gulf, and even the coast of Africa. Chinese merchants established trading colonies around Southeast Asia.

2.8 Preparing for the Regents
Movement of People and Goods What role did trade play in Tang society?

Chinese Influences on Korea and Japan

Chinese culture spread throughout East Asia through trade, travel, and migration. Koreans learned about centralized government, Confucianism, Buddhism, and writing from the Chinese. Through the Koreans, Buddhism spread to Japan. Japanese interest in Buddhist ideas soon grew into an enthusiasm for all things Chinese. The Japanese court sent missions to China to learn about Chinese culture firsthand. For a while, Japan even modeled its government on China's. In the late ninth century, however, Japan decided that it had learned enough from the Chinese and ended formal missions to the Tang Empire.

2.9 Preparing for the Regents
Culture and Intellectual Life How did Chinese influences spread to Korea and Japan?

PREPARING FOR THE REGENTS

Answer the following question. Use the Analyze the Question hints to help you answer the question.

1 The Age of Pericles in Athens, the Gupta Empire in India, and the Tang Dynasty in China all experienced a golden age with

   (1) advancements in the principles of democratic government
   (2) outstanding contributions in the arts and sciences
   (3) the end of foreign domination
   (4) the furthest expansion of their borders

ANALYZE THE QUESTION
- Read the question stem. You are being asked to indicate what achievements led the Age of Pericles, the Gupta Empire, and the Tang Dynasty to be considered golden ages.
- Think about the each society's achievements, then eliminate the alternatives that are not common to all three societies.
- Select the alternative that represents the common achievements.

The Byzantine Empire and Early Russia

Section Overview

The Western Roman Empire crumbled in the fifth century as it was overrun by invading Germanic tribes. By this time, however, the once great empire had already undergone significant changes. It had been divided into western and eastern empires, and its capital had moved east from Rome to the Greek city of Byzantium. The city would become known as Constantinople after the emperor Constantine, who made it the new capital in A.D. 330. The city stood on the Bosporus Strait, strategically located for trade and defense purposes on a crossroads between West and East. For nearly a thousand years after the collapse of the Western Empire, Byzantium and its flourishing capital would carry on the glory of Rome as the Byzantine Empire.

Like the last of the old Caesars, the Byzantine emperors ruled with absolute power. They headed not just the state but the church as well. They appointed and dismissed bishops at will. Their politics were brutal—and often deadly. Emperors lived under constant risk of assassination. Of the 88 Byzantine emperors, 29 died violently, and 13 abandoned the throne to live in monasteries.

Byzantium actively traded with its Slavic neighbors to the north. Because of this increased interaction, the Slavs began absorbing many Greek Byzantine ways. It was this blending of Slavic and Greek traditions that eventually produced Russian culture.

12th-century Russian icon of the Archangel Gabriel

MAIN IDEAS

RELIGIOUS AND ETHICAL SYSTEMS   After Rome split, the Eastern Empire, known as Byzantium, flourished for a thousand years.

CULTURAL INTERACTION   Byzantine influences inspired the growth of a unique Russian culture.

TERMS AND NAMES

- Justinian
- Justinian Code
- Hagia Sophia
- patriarch
- icon
- pope
- excommunication
- Slavs
- Cyrillic alphabet
- Vladimir
- Yaroslav the Wise

PREPARING FOR THE REGENTS

As you read this section, consider
- how the Byzantine Empire contributed to human history.
- how the Byzantine Empire affected the development of historical Russia.

TIME LINE

527
Justinian becomes ruler of the Byzantine Empire.

850s
Byzantine culture spreads to Russia.

980
Vladimir comes to the throne of Kievan Russia.

1054
Christian Church divides.

Human and Physical Geography

Roman leaders had divided the empire in 395, largely due to difficulties in communications between the eastern and the troubled western parts of the empire. Still, rulers in the East continued to see themselves as emperors for all of Rome.

In 527, **Justinian**, a high-ranking Byzantine nobleman, succeeded his uncle to the throne of the Eastern Empire. In an effort to regain Rome's fading glory, Justinian in 533 sent Belisarius (behl•uh•SAIR•ee•uhs), his best general, to recover North Africa from the invading Germanic tribes. Belisarius and his forces quickly succeeded. Two years later, Belisarius attacked Rome and seized it from a group known as the Ostrogoths. But the city faced repeated attacks by other Germanic tribes. Over the next 16 years, Rome changed hands six times. After numerous campaigns, Justinian's armies won nearly all of Italy and parts of Spain. Justinian now ruled almost all the territory that Rome had ever ruled. He could honestly call himself a new Caesar.

TAKING NOTES

Clarifying Use a cluster diagram to show Justinian's accomplishments as emperor of the New Rome.

Byzantine Achievements

A separate government and difficult communications with the West gave the Byzantine Empire its own character, different from that of the Western Empire. The citizens thought of themselves as sharing in the Roman tradition, but few spoke Latin anymore. Most Byzantines spoke Greek.

Political Structure Having unified the two empires, Justinian set up a panel of legal experts to regulate Byzantium's increasingly complex society. The panel combed through 400 years of Roman law. It found a number of laws that were outdated and contradictory. The panel created a single, uniform code known as the **Justinian Code**. After its completion, the code consisted of four works.

1. The *Code* contained nearly 5,000 Roman laws that were still considered useful for the Byzantine Empire.
2. The *Digest* quoted and summarized the opinions of Rome's greatest legal thinkers about the laws. This massive work ran to a total of 50 volumes.
3. The *Institutes* was a textbook that told law students how to use the laws.
4. The *Novellae* (New Laws) presented legislation passed after 534.

The Justinian Code decided legal questions that regulated whole areas of Byzantine life. Marriage, slavery, property, inheritance, women's rights, and criminal justice were just some of those areas. Although Justinian himself died in 565, his code served the Byzantine Empire for 900 years.

The Imperial City While his scholars were creating the legal code, Justinian launched the most ambitious public building program ever seen in the Roman world. He rebuilt the crumbling fortifications of Constantinople. Workers constructed a 14-mile stone wall along the city's coastline and repaired the fortifications along its western land border.

Church building, however, was the emperor's greatest passion. Justinian viewed churches as the most visible sign of the close connection between church and state in his empire. His crowning glory was **Hagia Sophia** (HAY•ee•uh soh•FEE•uh), which means "Holy

2.10 Preparing for the Regents

Justice What role did the Byzantine Empire play in the preservation and transmission of the Roman concept of law? What is one way that the Justinian Code is similar to the Twelve Tables and Hammurabi's Code?

Constantinople, A.D. 550

Wisdom" in Greek. A church of the same name had been destroyed in riots that swept Constantinople in 532. When Justinian rebuilt Hagia Sophia, many visitors hailed it as the most splendid church in the Christian world. As part of his building program, Justinian enlarged his palace into a vast complex. He also built baths, aqueducts, law courts, schools, and hospitals. By the time the emperor was finished, the city teemed with an almost visible excitement.

The main street running through Constantinople was the Mese (MEHS•ee), or "Middle Way." Merchant stalls lined the main street and filled the side streets. Constantinople's location on the Bosporus Strait made it a crossroads between the West and the East. Thus products from the most distant corners of Asia, Africa, and Europe passed through these stalls. Everywhere, food stands filled the air with the smell of their delicacies.

Meanwhile citizens could enjoy free entertainment at the Hippodrome, which offered wild chariot races and performance acts. The Hippodrome (from Greek words meaning "horse" and "racecourse") held 60,000 spectators. Fans of the different teams formed rowdy gangs named for the colors worn by their heroes.

Preserving Greco-Roman Culture Beneath such excitement of the city, a less obvious but vitally important activity took place: the preservation of Greco-Roman culture. Byzantine families valued classical learning. Basic courses for Byzantine students focused on Greek and Latin grammar, and philosophy. The classics of Greek and Roman literature served as textbooks. Students memorized Homer. They learned geometry from Euclid, history from Herodotus, and medicine from Galen. The modern world owes Byzantine scholars a huge debt for preserving many of the great works of Greece and Rome.

The Fall of Constantinople

After Justinian's death in 565, the empire suffered countless setbacks. There were street riots, religious quarrels, palace intrigues, and foreign dangers. Each time the empire moved to the edge of collapse, it found some way to revive— only to face another crisis.

The first crisis actually began before Justinian's death. It was a disease that resembled what we now know as the bubonic plague. This horrifying illness hit Constantinople in the later years of Justinian's reign. The plague probably arrived from India on ships infested with rats. Historians estimate that in 542, the worst year of the plague, 10,000 people were dying every day. The illness broke out repeatedly until around 700, when it finally faded. By that time, it had destroyed a huge percentage of the Byzantine population.

Byzantium also faced constant challenges from foreign enemies. Lombards overran Justinian's conquests in the west. Avars, Slavs, and Bulgars made frequent raids on the northern borders. The powerful Sassanid Persians attacked relentlessly in the east. The Persians and Avars struck against Constantinople itself in 626. With the rise of Islam, Arab armies attacked the city in 674 and once again in 717. Russians attempted invasions of the city three times between 860 and 1043. In the 11th century, the Turks took over the Muslim world and fought their way slowly into Byzantine territory.

The Byzantines used bribes, diplomacy, political marriages, and military power to keep their enemies at bay. In the seventh century, Emperor Heraclius reorganized the empire along military lines. Provinces became themes, or military districts. Each theme was run by a general who reported directly to the emperor. These strategies, however, could not work forever. Slowly, the

✎ **2.11 Preparing for the Regents**

Human and Physical Geography Why did Constantinople become the center of the Byzantine Empire?

✎ **2.12 Preparing for the Regents**

Culture and Intellectual Life What is the most important contribution that the Byzantine Empire made to later civilizations?

✎ **2.13 Preparing for the Regents**

Power What factors contributed to the fall of Constantinople?

Byzantine Empire shrank under the impact of foreign attacks. By 1350, it was reduced to the tip of Anatolia and a strip of the Balkans. Yet thanks to its walls, its fleet, and its strategic location, Constantinople held out for another 100 years. Finally, the city fell to the Ottoman Turks in 1453.

The Orthodox Christian Church

During the Byzantine Empire, Christianity underwent a dramatic development. Christianity had begun to develop differently in the Western and Eastern Roman Empires, due largely to the distance and lack of contact between the two regions. As the Eastern Empire became Byzantium and flourished, those differences grew and ultimately split apart the Church. Eastern Christianity built its heritage on the works of early Church fathers. One was Saint John Chrysostom (KRIHS•uhs•tuhm). As bishop of Constantinople from 398 to 404, Chrysostom was the **patriarch** (PAY•tree•AHRK), or leading bishop of the East. But even the patriarch bowed to the emperor.

A controversy that tested the emperor's authority over religious matters broke out in the eighth century. In 730, Emperor Leo III banned the use of **icons**, religious images used by Eastern Christians to aid their devotions. The emperor viewed the use of icons as idol worship. People responded with riots, and the clergy rebelled. In the West, the **pope**—the head of the Christian Church—became involved in this eastern dispute and supported the use of icons. One pope even ordered the **excommunication** of a Byzantine emperor—that is, he declared the emperor to be an outcast from the Church. In 843, more than 100 years after the controversy began, Empress Theodora—Justinian's wife—restored icons to Eastern churches.

Differences between the Eastern and Western churches, continued to grow. In 1054, matters came to a head when the pope and the patriarch excommunicated each other in a dispute over religious doctrine. Shortly afterward, Christianity officially split between the Roman Catholic Church in the West and the Orthodox Church in the East.

Byzantium's Impact on Russia and Eastern Europe

As West and East grew apart, the two traditions of Christianity competed for converts. Missionaries from the Orthodox Church, for example, took their form of Christianity to the **Slavs**, groups that inhabited the forests north of the Black Sea. Two of the most successful Eastern missionaries, Saint Methodius and Saint Cyril (SEER•uhl), worked among the Slavs in the ninth century. Cyril and Methodius invented an alphabet for the Slavic languages. With an alphabet, Slavs would be able to read the Bible in their own tongues. Many Slavic languages, including Russian, are now written in what is called the **Cyrillic** (suh•RIHL•ihk) **alphabet**.

Early Russia

In addition to sending its missionaries to the land, Byzantium actively traded with its neighbors to the north. Because of this increased interaction, the Slavs began absorbing many Greek Byzantine ways. It was this blending of Slavic and Greek traditions that eventually produced Russian culture.

Human and Physical Geography Russia's first unified territory originated west of the Ural Mountains in the region that runs from the Black Sea to the Baltic Sea. Hilly grasslands are found in the extreme south of that area. The

2.14 Preparing for the Regents

Belief Systems What challenges did the Greek Orthodox Church face during the Byzantine Empire?

2.15 Preparing for the Regents

Belief Systems What important contributions did the Byzantine Empire make to Russia?

2.16 Preparing for the Regents

Human and Physical Geography How did geography affect early Russia?

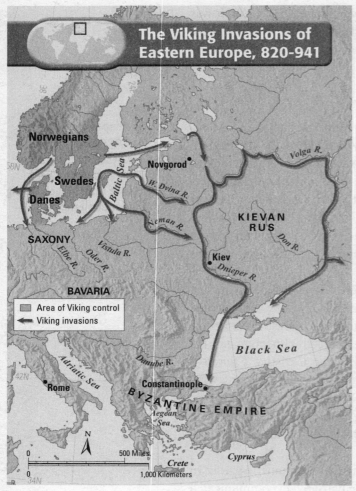

The Viking Invasions of Eastern Europe, 820-941

Norwegians

Swedes

Danes

SAXONY

Baltic Sea

Novgorod

W. Dvina R.

Neman R.

Vistula R.

Elbe R.

Oder R.

BAVARIA

KIEVAN RUS

Kiev

Dnieper R.

Volga R.

Don R.

Adriatic Sea

Rome

Danube R.

Constantinople

BYZANTINE EMPIRE

Aegean Sea

Black Sea

Cyprus

Crete

☐ Area of Viking control
← Viking invasions

N

0   500 Miles
0   1,000 Kilometers

north, however, is densely forested, flat, and swampy. Slow-moving, interconnecting rivers allow boat travel across these plains in almost any direction. Three great rivers, the Dnieper (NEE•puhr), the Don, and the Volga, run from the heart of the forests to the Black Sea or the Caspian Sea. In the early days of the Byzantine Empire, these forests were inhabited by tribes of Slavic farmers and traders. They spoke similar languages but had no political unity. Sometime in the 800s, small bands of adventurers came down among them from the north. These Varangians, or Rus as they were also called, were most likely Vikings. (The name "Russia" is taken from this group.) Eventually, these Vikings built forts along the rivers and settled among the Slavs.

Russian legends say the Slavs invited the Viking chief Rurik to be their king. So in 862, he founded Novgorod (NAHV•guh•rahd), Russia's first important city. That account is given in *The Primary Chronicle*, a history of Russia written by monks in the early 1100s. Around 880, a nobleman from Novgorod named Oleg moved south to Kiev (KEE•ehf), a city on the Dnieper River. From Kiev, the Vikings could sail by river and sea to Constantinople. There they could trade for products from distant lands.

Kiev grew into a principality, a small state ruled by a prince. As it did, the Viking nobles intermarried with their Slavic subjects and adopted many aspects of Slavic culture. Gradually, the line between Slavs and Vikings vanished.

Kievan Russia Thanks to its Byzantine ties, Kiev grew from a cluster of crude wooden forts to the glittering capital of a prosperous and educated people. The rise of Kiev marked the appearance of Russia's first important unified territory. **Vladimir** (VLAD•uh•meer), who came to the throne about 980, led the way in establishing Kiev's power. He expanded his state west into Poland and north almost to the Baltic Sea. He also fought off troublesome nomads from the steppes to the south.

In 1019, Vladimir's son **Yaroslav the Wise** came to the throne and led Kiev to even greater glory. Like the rulers of Byzantium, Yaroslav skillfully married off his daughters and sisters to the kings and princes of western Europe. Those marriages helped him to forge important trading alliances. At the same time, he created a legal code tailored to Kiev's commercial culture. Many of its rules dealt with crimes against property. Yaroslav also built the first library in Kiev.

The Kievan state started to decline after the death of Yaroslav in 1054. During his reign, Yaroslav had made what turned out to be a crucial error. He had divided his realm among his sons, instead of following the custom of passing on the throne to the eldest son. Upon their father's death, the sons tore the state apart fighting for the choicest territories. And because this system of dividing the kingdom among sons continued, each generation saw new struggles.

2.17 Preparing for the Regents

Power How did Vladimir and Yaroslav increase the power of Kievan Russia?

The Russian Orthodox Church In 957, Princess Olga, Vladimir's grandmother, paid a visit to Constantinople and publicly converted to Christianity. From 945 to 964, she governed Kiev until her son was old enough to rule. Her son resisted Christianity. However, Vladimir considered conversion to Christianity when he came to the throne. *The Primary Chronicle* reports that Vladimir sent out teams to observe the major religions of the times. Three of the teams returned with lukewarm accounts of Islam, Judaism, and Western Christianity. But the team from Byzantium told quite a different story. This report convinced Vladimir to convert to Byzantine Christianity and to make all his subjects convert, too.

In 989, a baptism of all the citizens of Kiev was held in the Dnieper River. Kiev, already linked to Byzantium by trade, now looked to the empire for religious guidance. Vladimir imported teachers to instruct the people in the new faith. All the beliefs and traditions of Orthodox Christianity flourished in Kiev. Vladimir appreciated the Byzantine idea of the emperor as supreme ruler of the Church. So the close link between Church and state took root in Russia as well. Under Yaroslav's rule, Christianity prospered. By the 12th century, Kiev was home to some 400 churches. Today, the Russian Orthodox Church is the largest religious group in Russia.

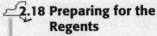

2.18 Preparing for the Regents

Belief Systems What role did the Russian Orthodox Church play in Kievan Russia?

PREPARING FOR THE REGENTS

Answer the following questions. Use the Analyze the Question hints to help you answer the questions.

1 The Eastern Orthodox Church and the Cyrillic alphabet originated in the Byzantine Empire. What does the practice of this religion and the use of this alphabet in Russia indicate?

(1) Russian was conquered by the Byzantine Empire.
(2) Russia's leaders eliminated the influence of the Mongols.
(3) Russia was influenced by cultural diffusion.
(4) Russia's geographic isolation led to cultural diversity.

ANALYZE THE QUESTION
- Read the question stem. You are being asked to indicate the significance of the fact that the Eastern Orthodox religion and the Cyrillic alphabet originated in the Byzantine Empire but were also a part of Russian culture.
- Think about the history of the interaction between the Byzantine Empire and Russia.
- Eliminate any alternatives that are untrue or that do not apply to Russia's practice of the Orthodox religion or its use of the alphabet.
- The remaining alternative is the correct answer.

2 What is a major contribution of the Byzantine Empire to global history?

(1) preservation of Greek and Roman culture
(2) construction of the pyramids
(3) expansion of equal rights
(4) invention of writing

ANALYZE THE QUESTION
- Read the question stem. You are being asked to determine the major contribution of the Byzantine Empire.
- Think about the contributions made by the Byzantines.
- Eliminate any alternative that was made by another civilization or that is uncharacteristic of the Byzantines.
- The remaining alternative is the correct answer.

The Spread of Islam

Section Overview

The cultures of the Arabian Peninsula were in constant contact with one another for centuries. Southwest Asia (often referred to as the Middle East) was a bridge between Africa, Asia, and Europe, where goods were traded and new ideas were shared. One set of shared ideas would become a powerful force for change in the world—the religion of Islam.

When Muhammad died in 632, the community faced a crisis. Muslims believed they had a duty to carry his word to the world. However, they lacked a clear way to choose a new leader. Eventually, the issue of leadership would divide the Muslim world into three groups—the Sunni, Shi'a, and Sufi.

The Abbasids (750–1258) governed during a prosperous period of Muslim history. Riches flowed into the empire from all over Europe, Asia, and Africa. Rulers could afford to build luxurious cities. They supported the scientists, mathematicians, and philosophers that those cities attracted. In the special atmosphere created by Islam, the scholars preserved existing knowledge and produced an enormous body of original learning.

A 13th-century miniature showing Arab traders navigating the Indian Ocean.

MAIN IDEAS

EMPIRE BUILDING   The leaders following Muhammad built a huge empire that by A.D. 750 included millions of people from diverse ethnic, language, and religious groups.

CULTURAL INTERACTION   Tolerance of conquered peoples and an emphasis on learning helped to blend the cultural traits of people under Muslim rule.

TERMS AND NAMES

- caliph
- Umayyads
- Shi'a
- Sunni

- Sufi
- Abbasids
- al-Andalus
- Fatimid

- Sunna
- shari'a
- House of Wisdom
- calligraphy

PREPARING FOR THE REGENTS

As you read this section, consider
· the vastness of the Muslim Empire.
· the ability of Islam to rule very diverse populations.
· the role of Islam in cultural innovation and trade.

TIME LINE

632
Abu-Bakr becomes first caliph.

750
Abbasids come to power.

800s
Al-Khwarizmi writes the first algebra book.

1000s
Muslim scholars, who preserved Greek medical works, share them with Europeans.

1100s
Muslim literature flourishes.

Human and Physical Geography

The Arabian Peninsula is a crossroads of three continents—Africa, Europe, and Asia. At its longest and widest points, the peninsula is about 1,200 miles from north to south and 1,300 miles from east to west. Only a tiny strip of fertile land in south Arabia and Oman and a few oases can support agriculture. The remainder of the land is desert, which in the past was inhabited by nomadic Arab herders.

On this desert, the Arab nomads, called Bedouins (BEHD•oo•ihnz), were organized into tribes and groups called clans. These clans provided security and support for a life made difficult by the extreme conditions of the desert. The areas with more fertile soil and the larger oases had enough water to support farming communities. Larger towns near the western coast of Arabia became market towns for local, regional, and long-distance trade goods.

By the early 600s, trade routes connected Arabia to the major ocean and land trade routes. Trade routes through Arabia ran from the extreme south of the peninsula to the Byzantine and Sassanid (Persian) empires to the north. Merchants from these two empires moved along the caravan routes, trading for goods from the Silk Roads of the East. They transported spices and incense from Yemen and other products to the West. They also carried information and ideas between Arabia and the outside world. It was from this setting that Islam would spread through Southwest and Central Asia and into parts of Africa and Europe.

Political Organization—The Caliphate

When Muhammad died in 632, his followers faced a crisis. Muslims, inspired by the message of Allah, believed they had a duty to carry his word to the world. However, they lacked a clear way to choose a new leader. Muhammad had not named a successor or instructed his followers how to choose one. Relying on ancient tribal custom, the Muslim community elected as their leader Abu-Bakr, a loyal friend of Muhammad. In 632, Abu-Bakr became the first **caliph** (KAY•lihf), a title that means "successor" or "deputy."

The "Rightly Guided" Caliphs Abu-Bakr and the next three elected caliphs—Umar, Uthman, and Ali—all had known the Prophet. They used the Qur'an and Muhammad's actions as guides to leadership. For this, they are known as the "rightly guided" caliphs. Their rule was called a caliphate (KAY•lih•FAYT).

Abu-Bakr had promised the Muslim community he would uphold what Muhammad stood for. Shortly after the Prophet's death, some tribes on the Arabian Peninsula abandoned Islam. Others refused to pay taxes, and a few individuals even declared themselves prophets. For the sake of Islam, Abu-Bakr invoked *jihad*. The word *jihad* means "striving" and can refer to the inner struggle against evil. However, the word is also used in the Qur'an to mean an armed struggle against unbelievers. For the next two years, Abu-Bakr applied this meaning of *jihad* to encourage and justify the expansion of Islam.

2.19 Preparing for the Regents

Human and Physical Geography How did geography affect life on the Arabian Peninsula?

TAKING NOTES

Summarizing Use a table to summarize developments that occurred in Islam during each ruler's period in power.

Rulers	Period of Rule	Developments in Islam
Rightly guided caliphs		
Umayyads		
Abbasids		

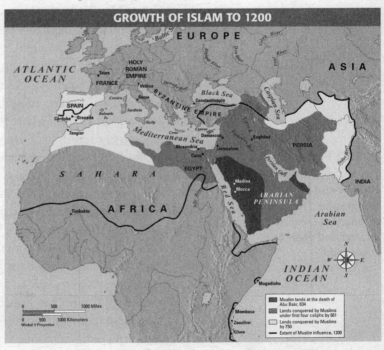

GROWTH OF ISLAM TO 1200

When Abu-Bakr died in 634, the Muslim state controlled all of Arabia. Under Umar, the second caliph, Muslim armies conquered Syria and lower Egypt, which were part of the Byzantine Empire. They also took parts of the Sassanid Empire. The next two caliphs, Uthman and Ali, continued to expand Muslim territory. By 750, the Muslim Empire stretched 6,000 miles from the Atlantic Ocean to the Indus River.

Internal Conflict and Crisis   Despite spectacular gains on the battlefield, the Muslim community had difficulty maintaining a unified rule. In 656, Uthman was murdered, starting a civil war in which various groups struggled for power. Ali, as Muhammad's cousin and son-in-law, was the natural choice as a successor to Uthman. However, his right to rule was challenged by Muawiya, a governor of Syria. Then, in 661, Ali, too, was assassinated. The elective system of choosing a caliph died with him.

A family known as the **Umayyads** (oo•MYE•yadz) then came to power. The Umayyads moved the Muslim capital to Damascus. This location, away from Mecca, made controlling conquered territories easier. However, the Arab Muslims felt it was too far away from their lands. In addition, the Umayyads abandoned the simple life of previous caliphs and began to surround themselves with wealth and ceremony similar to that of non-Muslim rulers. These actions, along with the leadership issue, gave rise to a fundamental division in the Muslim community.

2.21 **Preparing for the Regents**

Belief Systems   What led to the split between the Sunnis, Shi'a, and Sufi?

In the interest of peace, the majority of Muslims accepted the Umayyads' rule. However, a minority continued to resist. This group developed an alternate view of the office of caliph. In this view, the caliph needed to be a descendant of the Prophet. This group was called **Shi'a**, meaning the "party" of Ali. Members of this group are called Shi'ites. Those who did not outwardly resist the rule of the Umayyads later became known as **Sunni**, meaning followers of Muhammad's example. Another group, the **Sufi** (SOO•fee), rejected the luxurious life of the Umayyads. They pursued a life of poverty and devotion to a spiritual path.

Vigorous religious and political opposition to the Umayyad caliphate led to its downfall. Rebel groups overthrew the Umayyads in the year 750. The most powerful of those groups, the **Abbasids** (AB•uh•sihdz), took control of the empire.

The Abbasids   When the Abbasids came to power in 750, they ruthlessly murdered the remaining members of the Umayyad family. One prince named Abd al-Rahman escaped the slaughter and fled to Spain. There he set up an Umayyad caliphate. Spain had already been conquered and settled by Muslims from North Africa, who were known as Berbers. The Berber armies advanced north to within 200 miles of Paris before being halted at the Battle of Tours in 732. They then settled in southern Spain, where they helped form an extraordinary Muslim state in **al-Andalus** (al•an•duh•LUS).

2.22 **Preparing for the Regents**

Human and Physical Geography   What is one reason that cities such as Baghdad grew and succeeded?

To solidify power, the Abbasids moved the capital of the empire in 762 to a newly created city, Baghdad, in central Iraq. Its location on key trade routes gave the caliph access to trade goods, gold, and information about the far-flung empire. The Abbasids developed a strong bureaucracy to conduct the huge empire's affairs. A treasury kept track of the money flow. A special department managed the business of the army. Diplomats from the empire were sent to courts in Europe, Africa, and Asia to conduct imperial business. To support this bureaucracy, the Abbasids taxed land, imports and exports, and non-Muslims' wealth.

The Abbasid caliphate lasted from 750 to 1258. During that time, the Abbasids increased their authority by consulting religious leaders. But they failed to keep complete political control of the immense territory. Independent

Muslim states sprang up, and local leaders dominated many smaller regions. The **Fatimid** (FAT•uh•MIHD) caliphate was formed by Shi'a Muslims who claimed descent from Muhammad's daughter Fatima. The Fatimid caliphate began in North Africa and spread across the Red Sea to western Arabia and Syria. However, the Fatimids and other smaller states were still connected to the Abbasid caliphate through religion, language, trade, and the economy.

Islamic Trade

At this time, two major sea-trading networks existed—the Mediterranean Sea and the Indian Ocean. Through these networks, the Muslim Empire could engage in sea trade with the rest of the world. The land network connected the Silk Roads of China and India with Europe and Africa. Muslim merchants needed only a single language, Arabic, and a single currency, the Abbasid dinar, to travel in the empire.

To encourage the flow of trade, Muslim money changers set up banks in cities throughout the empire. Banks offered letters of credit, called *sakks*, to merchants. A merchant with a *sakk* from a bank in Baghdad could exchange it for cash at a bank in any other city in the empire. In Europe, *sakk* was pronounced "check." Thus, using checks dates back to the Muslim Empire.

2.23 Preparing for the Regents
Movement of People and Goods What role did Muslims play in world trade?

Muslim Society

Muslims believe that Muhammad's mission as a prophet was to receive the Qur'an and to demonstrate how to apply it in life. To them, the **Sunna** (SOON•uh), or Muhammad's example, is the best model for proper living. The guidance of the Qur'an and Sunna was assembled in a body of law known as **shari'a** (shah•REE•ah). This system of law regulates the family life, moral conduct, and business and community life of Muslims. The shari'a guided daily life under the Abbasids just as it guides the lives of devout Muslims today. Muslim society under the Abbasids had a sophistication matched at that time only by the Tang Empire of China. That cosmopolitan character was most evident in urban centers.

2.24 Preparing for the Regents
Belief Systems What are the Sunna and shari'a?

Muslim Cities Until the Abbasids constructed Baghdad, Damascus was the leading city. It was also the cultural center of Islamic learning. Other cities grew up around power centers, such as Cordoba (the Umayyad capital), Cairo (the Fatimid capital), and Jerusalem. Extensive planning went into Baghdad's distinctive circular design, formed by three circular protective walls. The caliph's palace of marble and stone sat in the innermost circle, along with the grand mosque. Originally, the main streets between the middle wall and the palace were lined with shops. Later, the marketplace moved to a district outside the walls. Baghdad's population approached one million at its peak.

Social Classes Muslim society was made up of four classes. The upper class included those who were Muslims at birth. Converts to Islam were in the second class. The third class consisted of the "protected people" and included Christians, Jews, and Zoroastrians. The lowest class was composed of slaves. Many slaves were prisoners of war, and all were non-Muslim. Slaves most frequently performed household work or fought in the military.

Because the Qur'an forbade forced conversion, Muslims allowed conquered peoples to follow their own religion. Shari'a law required Muslim leaders to extend religious tolerance to Christians and Jews. As "people of the book," they received special consideration. (Muslims refer to Christians and Jews as "people

2.25 Preparing for the Regents
Diversity Religious tolerance in Muslim Spain, for example, encouraged the growth of a rich and diverse culture. How was this tolerance rooted in Islamic law?

of the book" because each religion has a holy book with teachings similar to those of the Qur'an.) They paid a poll tax each year in exchange for exemption from military duties. However, Christians and Jews were also subject to various restrictions on their lives. For instance, although they could be officials, scholars, and bureaucrats, they were not allowed to spread their religion.

2.26 Preparing for the Regents

Justice   What was the status of women under Islamic law?

Role of Women   The Qur'an says, "Men are the managers of the affairs of women," and "Righteous women are therefore obedient." However, the Qur'an also declares that men and women, as believers, are equal. The shari'a gave Muslim women specific legal rights concerning marriage, family, and property. Thus, Muslim women had more economic and property rights than European, Indian, and Chinese women of the same time period. Nonetheless, Muslim women were still expected to submit to men. When a husband wanted to divorce his wife, all he had to do was repeat three times, "I dismiss thee." The divorce became final in three months.

Responsibilities of Muslim women varied with the income of their husbands. The wife of a poor man would often work in the fields with her husband. Wealthier women supervised the household and its servants. They had access to education, and among them were poets and scholars. Rich or poor, women were responsible for the raising of the children. In the early days of Islam, women could also participate in public life and gain an education. However, over time, Muslim women were forced to live increasingly isolated lives. When they did go out in public, they were expected to be veiled.

The Golden Age of Islam

The Abbasids governed during a prosperous period of Muslim history. Riches flowed into the empire from all over Europe, Asia, and Africa. In the special atmosphere created by Islam, the scholars preserved existing knowledge and produced an enormous body of original learning.

TAKING NOTES

Clarifying Use a web diagram to show the key elements of Muslim culture.

Preserving Greco-Roman Culture   After the fall of Rome in A.D. 476, Europe entered a period of upheaval and chaos, an era in which scholarship suffered. The scientific knowledge gained up to that time might have been lost if it were not for Muslim leaders and scholars. In the early 800s, Caliph al-Ma'mun opened in Baghdad a combination library, academy, and translation center called the **House of Wisdom**. There, scholars of different cultures and beliefs translated texts from Greece, India, Persia, and elsewhere into Arabic.

In addition to scientific works, scholars at the House of Wisdom translated works of Greek philosophers like Aristotle and Plato into Arabic. In the 1100s, Muslim philosopher Ibn Rushd (also known as Averroes), who lived in Cordoba, was criticized for trying to blend Aristotle's and Plato's views with those of Islam. However, Ibn Rushd argued that Greek philosophy and Islam both had the same goal: to find the truth.

Contributions in Literature, Art, and Architecture   Literature had been a strong tradition in Arabia even before Islam. Bedouin poets, reflecting the spirit of desert life, composed poems celebrating ideals such as bravery, love, generosity, and hospitality. Those themes continued to appear in poetry written after the rise of Islam. The Qur'an is the standard for all Arabic literature and poetry. Early Muslim poets sang the praises of the Prophet and of Islam and, later, of the caliphs and other patrons who supported them. During the age of the Abbasids, literary tastes expanded to include poems about nature and the pleasures of life and love.

As the Muslim Empire expanded, the Arabs entered regions that had rich artistic traditions. Muslims continued these traditions but often adapted them to suit Islamic beliefs and practices. For example, since Muslims believed that only Allah can create life, images of living beings were discouraged. Thus, many artists turned to **calligraphy**, or the art of beautiful handwriting, and to geometric designs. Others expressed themselves through the decorative arts, such as woodwork, glass, ceramics, cotton textiles, and woolen carpets.

It is in architecture that the greatest cultural blending of the Muslim world can be seen. To some extent, a building reflected the culture of people of the area. For example, the Great Mosque of Damascus was built on the site of a Christian church. In many ways, the huge dome and vaulted ceiling of the mosque blended Byzantine architecture with Muslim ideas. In Syrian areas, the architecture included features that were very Roman, including baths using Roman heating systems.

Contributions in Science Muslim contributions in the sciences were most recognizable in medicine, mathematics, and astronomy. A Persian scholar named al-Razi (Rhazes, according to the European pronunciation) was the greatest physician of the Muslim world, and more than likely, of world civilization, between A.D. 500 and 1500. He wrote an encyclopedia called the *Comprehensive Book* that drew on knowledge from Greek, Syrian, Arabic, and Indian sources as well as on his own experience. Al-Razi also wrote *Treatise on Smallpox and Measles,* which was translated into several languages.

Among the ideas that Muslim scholars introduced to modern math and science were the reliance on scientific observation and experimentation, and the ability to find mathematical solutions to old problems. Muslim scholars believed that mathematics was the basis of all knowledge. Al-Khwarizmi, a mathematician born in Baghdad in the late 700s, studied Indian rather than Greek sources. He wrote a textbook in the 800s explaining "the art of bringing together unknowns to match a known quantity." He called this technique *al jabr*—today called algebra.

Many of the advances in mathematics were related to the study of astronomy. Muslim observatories charted stars, comets, and planets. Ibn al-Haytham (Alhazen), a brilliant mathematician, produced a book called *Optics* that revolutionized ideas about vision. He showed that people see objects because rays pass from the objects to the eyes, not from the eyes to the objects as was commonly believed. His studies were used in developing lenses for telescopes and microscopes.

2.27 Preparing for the Regents

Culture and Intellectual Life How did Islamic art and architecture reflect a blend of many different cultures?

2.28 Preparing for the Regents

Culture and Intellectual Life Why do you think scholars refer to the Abbasid era as the golden age of Islam?

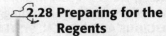

PREPARING FOR THE REGENTS

Answer the following question. Use the Analyze the Question hints to help you answer the question.

1 According to the map on page 67 and your knowledge of social studies, by A.D. 750 Islam had spread from

(1) Mecca to Asia
(2) Cairo to Cordoba
(3) Africa to India
(4) India to Cordoba

ANALYZE THE QUESTION
- Read the question stem. You are being asked to determine how far Islam spread by A.D. 750.
- Now look at the map on page 67. Read the title, legend, and labels to find the information that applies to the extent of Muslim lands by 750.
- Select the alternative that best matches the information on the map.

Medieval Europe

Section Overview

The gradual decline of the Roman Empire ushered in an era of European history called the **Middle Ages**, *or the medieval period. During this period, a feudal society emerged, one based on rights and obligations between kings, nobles, knights, and peasants.*

Amid the weak central governments in feudal Europe, the Church became a powerful institution. The Church was a stable force during an era of constant warfare and political turmoil. It provided Christians with a sense of security and of belonging to a religious community.

As the Church expanded its political role, rulers began to question the pope's authority. Dramatic power struggles unfolded in the Holy Roman Empire, the scene of mounting tensions between emperors and popes.

Pope's tiara

MAIN IDEAS

EMPIRE BUILDING   In western Europe, the Roman Empire had broken into many small kingdoms. During the Middle Ages, Charlemagne and Otto the Great tried to revive the idea of empire. Both allied with the Church.

POWER AND AUTHORITY   Weak rulers and the decline of central authority led to a feudal system in which local lords with large estates assumed power. This led to struggles over power with the Church.

RELIGIOUS AND ETHICAL SYSTEMS   During the Middle Ages, the Church was a unifying force. It shaped people's beliefs and guided their daily lives. Most Europeans at this time shared a common bond of faith.

TERMS AND NAMES

- Middle Ages
- Franks
- secular
- Carolingian Dynasty
- Charlemagne
- lord
- fief
- vassal
- knight
- serf
- manor
- tithe
- chivalry
- tournament
- clergy
- sacrament
- monastery
- canon law
- Holy Roman Empire
- lay investiture
- Gothic
- troubadour

PREPARING FOR THE REGENTS

As you read this section, consider
- what assumptions regarding power, authority, government, and law shaped the life of medieval Europe.
- what principles guided the decisions that were made about the use of scarce resources in medieval Europe.

TIME LINE

511
Clovis unites the Franks under Christian rule.

732
Charles Martel stops Muslim invasion at Tours.

800
Pope Leo III crowns the Frankish king Charlemagne emperor.

843
Treaty of Verdun divides Charlemagne's empire.

900s
Outside invasions spur growth of feudalism.

962
Otto the Great becomes emperor of the Holy Roman Empire.

1190
Holy Roman Empire weakens.

Human and Physical Geography

In the fifth century, Germanic invaders overran the western half of the Roman Empire. Repeated invasions and constant warfare led to a disruption in trade, the downfall of cities, and population shifts as people fled the cities for the countryside. These changes, in turn, altered the economy, government, and culture.

The Germanic invaders had a rich oral tradition of songs and legends, but they could not read or write. Among Romans themselves, the level of learning sank sharply as more families left for rural areas. Few people except church officials were literate. Knowledge of Greek was almost lost. As German-speaking peoples mixed with the Roman population, Latin changed. While it was still an official language, it was no longer understood. Different dialects developed as new words and phrases became part of everyday speech. By the 800s, French, Spanish, and other Roman-based languages had evolved from Latin.

The Frankish Empire

In the years of upheaval between 400 and 600, small Germanic kingdoms replaced Roman provinces. This caused the entire concept of government to change. Loyalty to public government and written law had unified Roman society. Family ties and personal loyalty, rather than citizenship in a public state, held Germanic society together. Unlike Romans, Germanic peoples lived in small communities that were governed by unwritten rules and traditions. Every Germanic chief led a band of warriors who had pledged their loyalty to him. These warriors felt no obligation to obey a king they did not even know. Nor would they obey an official sent to collect taxes or administer justice in the name of an emperor they had never met.

Clovis In the Roman province of Gaul (mainly what is now France and Switzerland), a Germanic people called the **Franks** held power. Their leader was Clovis (KLOH•vihs). He would bring Christianity to the region. According to legend, his wife, Clothilde, had urged him to convert to her faith, Christianity. In 496, Clovis led his warriors against another Germanic army. Fearing defeat, he appealed to the Christian God for help. The tide of the battle shifted and the Franks won. Afterward, Clovis and 3,000 of his warriors were baptized. The Church in Rome welcomed Clovis's conversion and supported his military campaigns against other Germanic peoples. By 511, Clovis had united the Franks into one kingdom.

The alliance between Clovis's kingdom and the Church marked the start of a partnership between two powerful forces. In 590, Gregory I, also called Gregory the Great, became pope. As head of the Church in Rome, Gregory broadened the authority of the papacy, or pope's office, beyond its spiritual role. The papacy also became a **secular**, or worldly, power involved in politics. This idea of a churchly kingdom, ruled by a pope, would be a central theme of the Middle Ages.

Charles Martel By 700, an official known as the *major domo*, or mayor of the palace, had become the most powerful person in the Frankish kingdom. Officially, he had charge of the royal household and estates. Unofficially, he led armies and made policy. In effect, he ruled the kingdom. The mayor of the palace in 719, Charles Martel (Charles the Hammer), held more power than the king. Charles Martel extended the Franks' reign to the north, south, and east. He also defeated Muslim raiders from Spain at the Battle of Tours in 732. This battle was highly significant for Christian Europeans. If the Muslims had won, western Europe might have become part of the Muslim Empire.

2.29 Preparing for the Regents

Human and Physical Geography What effect did the Germanic invasions have on society?

TAKING NOTES

Following Chronological Order Note important events in the unification of the Germanic kingdoms.

500

1200

2.30 Preparing for the Regents

Power How did Gregory I change the role of the Church?

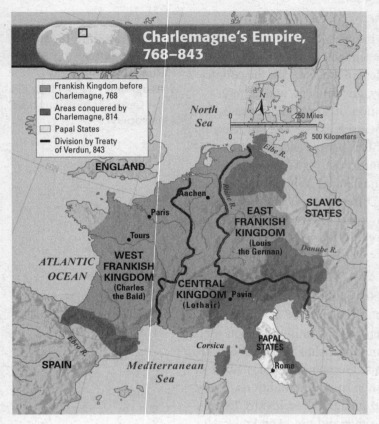

Charlemagne's Empire, 768–843

Legend:
- Frankish Kingdom before Charlemagne, 768
- Areas conquered by Charlemagne, 814
- Papal States
- Division by Treaty of Verdun, 843

North Sea

0 250 Miles
0 500 Kilometers

ENGLAND

Elbe R.

Aachen
Paris
Tours

Rhine R.

EAST FRANKISH KINGDOM (Louis the German)

SLAVIC STATES

Danube R.

ATLANTIC OCEAN

WEST FRANKISH KINGDOM (Charles the Bald)

CENTRAL KINGDOM (Lothair)

Pavia

Ebro R.

SPAIN

Mediterranean Sea

Corsica

PAPAL STATES

Rome

At his death, Charles Martel passed on his power to his son, Pepin the Short. Pepin wanted to be king, so he agreed to fight the Lombards, who had invaded central Italy and threatened Rome. In exchange, the pope anointed Pepin "king by the grace of God." Thus began the **Carolingian** (KAR•uh•LIHN•juhn) **Dynasty**, which ruled the Franks from 751 to 987.

Charlemagne Pepin died in 768. He left the kingdom to his two sons, Carloman and Charles. After Carloman died in 771, Charles, who was known as Charlemagne (SHAHR•luh•MAYN), or Charles the Great, ruled the kingdom. Charlemagne conquered new lands to both the south and the east. Through these conquests, he spread Christianity and reunited western Europe for the first time since the Roman Empire. By 800, Charlemagne's empire was larger than the Byzantine Empire. He had become the most powerful king in western Europe.

In 800, Charlemagne traveled to Rome to crush an unruly mob that had attacked the pope. In gratitude, Pope Leo III crowned him emperor. The coronation was historic. A pope had claimed the political right to confer the title "Roman Emperor" on a European king. This event signaled the joining of Germanic power, the Church, and the heritage of the Roman Empire.

A year before Charlemagne died in 814, he crowned his only surviving son, Louis the Pious, as emperor. Louis left the empire to his three sons: Lothair (loh•THAIR), Charles the Bald, and Louis the German. They fought one another for control of the empire. In 843, the brothers signed the Treaty of Verdun, dividing the empire into three kingdoms. As a result, Carolingian kings lost power and central authority broke down.

Feudalism

TAKING NOTES
Analyzing Causes and Recognizing Effects Use a web diagram to show the causes and effects of feudalism.

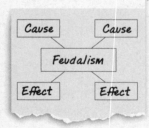

Cause   Cause
      Feudalism
Effect   Effect

As central authority broke down, Europe faced new waves of invaders. From the north came the fearsome Vikings, a Germanic people who set sail from Scandinavia (SKAN•duh•NAY•vee•uh) in Northern Europe. (The region is now the countries of Denmark, Norway, and Sweden.) From the east came the Magyars, a group of nomadic people from what is now Hungary. The Muslims struck from the south, invading first from their strongholds in North Africa.

The worst years of attacks spanned roughly 850 to 950. During this time, rulers in many parts of Europe granted warriors land in return for pledges of loyalty. This system of governing and landholding is called feudalism. A similar feudal system developed independently in China under the Zhou Dynasty (11th century B.C.–256 B.C.) and later arose in Japan (A.D. 1192–19th century).

Social Structure The feudal system was based on rights and obligations. In exchange for military protection and other services, a **lord**, or landowner, granted land called a **fief**. The person receiving a fief was called a **vassal**. Feudalism depended on the control of land.

The social-class structure of feudal society was much like a pyramid. At the peak reigned the king. Next came the most powerful vassals—wealthy landowners such as nobles and bishops. Serving beneath these vassals were **knights**, the mounted horsemen who pledged to defend their lords' lands in exchange for fiefs. At the base of the pyramid were landless peasants who toiled in the fields. The vast majority of people were peasants. Most peasants were serfs. **Serfs** were people who could not lawfully leave the place where they were born. Though bound to the land, serfs were not slaves. Their lords could not sell or buy them. But what their labor produced belonged to the lord.

Manorialism The **manor** was the lord's estate. During the Middle Ages, the manor system was the basic economic arrangement. It rested on a set of rights and obligations between a lord and his serfs. The lord provided the serfs with housing, farmland, and protection from bandits. In return, serfs tended the lord's lands, cared for his animals, and performed other tasks to maintain the estate. All peasants, whether free or serf, owed the lord certain duties. These included at least a few days of labor each week and a certain portion of their grain.

A manor usually covered only a few square miles of land. It typically consisted of the lord's manor house, a church, workshops, and a mill for grinding the grain. Generally, 15 to 30 families lived in the village on a manor. Fields, pastures, and woodlands surrounded the village. The manor was largely a self-sufficient community. The serfs and peasants raised or produced nearly everything that they and their lord needed for daily life—crops, milk and cheese, fuel, cloth, leather goods, and lumber. The only outside purchases were salt, iron, and a few unusual objects such as millstones. These were huge stones used to grind flour. Crops grown on the manor usually included grains, such as wheat, rye, barley, and oats, and vegetables, such as peas, beans, onions, and beets.

For the privilege of living on the lord's land, peasants paid a tax on all grain ground in the mill. They also paid a tax on marriage. In addition, peasant families owed the village priest a **tithe**, or church tax, of one-tenth of their income.

For most serfs, both men and women, life was work and more work. Their days revolved around raising crops and livestock and taking care of home and family. As soon as children were old enough, they were put to work in the fields or in the home. Many children did not survive to adulthood. Average life expectancy was about 35 years. Yet, despite the hardships they endured, serfs accepted their lot in life as part of the Church's teachings. They, like most Christians during medieval times, believed that God determined a person's place in society.

The Role of Knights Mounted knights were the most important part of a lord's army. As the lord's vassal, a knight's main obligation was to serve in battle. From his knights, a lord typically demanded about 40 days of combat a year. Knights' pastimes often revolved around training for war. .

Knights were expected to display courage in battle and loyalty to their lord. By the 1100s, the code of **chivalry** (SHIHV•uhl•ree), a complex set of ideals, demanded that a knight fight bravely in defense of three masters: his earthly feudal lord, his heavenly Lord, and his chosen lady. The chivalrous knight also protected the weak and the poor. The ideal knight was loyal, brave, and courteous. Most knights, though, failed to meet all of these high standards. For example, they treated the lower classes brutally.

At age 7, a noble boy would be sent off to the castle of another lord. As a page, he waited on his hosts and began to practice fighting skills. At around age 14, the page reached the rank of squire. A squire acted as a servant to a knight.

2.31 Preparing for the Regents

Culture and Intellectual Life What similar function did the feudal system in Europe and the caste system in India serve?

2.32 Preparing for the Regents

Economic Systems What were the features of manorialism?

2.33 Preparing for the Regents

Economic Systems How did the manor system affect the lives of serfs?

TAKING NOTES
Summarizing Identify the ideas associated with chivalry.

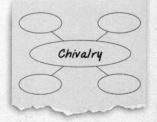

Chivalry

At around age 21, a squire became a full-fledged knight. The young knights gained experience fighting in local wars. Some took part in mock battles called **tournaments**. Tournaments combined recreation with combat training.

The Role of Women Most women in feudal society were powerless, just as most men were. But women had the added burden of being thought inferior to men. This was the view of the Church and was generally accepted in feudal society. Nonetheless, women played important roles in the lives of families.

A noblewoman could inherit an estate from her husband. Upon her lord's request, she could also send his knights to war. When her husband was off fighting, the lady of a medieval castle might act as military commander and a warrior. In reality, however, the lives of most noblewomen were limited. Females in noble families generally were confined to activities in the home or the convent, a religious community for women. Also, noblewomen held little property because lords passed down their fiefs to sons and not to daughters.

Peasant women performed endless labor around the home and often in the fields, bore children, and took care of their families. Young peasant girls learned practical household skills from their mother at an early age, unlike daughters in rich households who were educated by tutors. Females in peasant families were poor and powerless. Yet, the economic contribution they made was essential to the survival of the peasant household.

Role of the Church

Like feudalism, the Church had its own organization. Power was based on status. Church structure consisted of different ranks of **clergy**, or religious officials. The pope in Rome headed the Church. All clergy, including bishops and priests, fell under his authority. Bishops supervised priests, the lowest ranking members of the clergy. Bishops also settled disputes over Church teachings and practices. For most people, local priests served as the main contact with the Church.

The Church and Daily Life Shared beliefs in the teachings of the Church bonded people together and provided a sense of order and stability. Everyday life was harsh. Still everyone could follow the same path to salvation—everlasting life in heaven. Priests and other clergy administered the **sacraments**, or important religious ceremonies. These rites paved the way for achieving salvation. At the local level, the village church served as a religious and social center.

To adapt to rural conditions, the Church built religious communities called **monasteries**. There, Christian men called monks gave up their private possessions and devoted their lives to serving God. Women who followed this way of life were called nuns and lived in convents. Monks and nuns devoted their lives to prayer and good works. Monasteries became Europe's best-educated communities. Monks opened schools, maintained libraries, and copied books.

Church Authority The Church's authority was both religious and political. It provided a unifying set of spiritual beliefs and rituals. The Church also created a system of justice to guide people's conduct. All medieval Christians, kings and peasants alike, were subject to **canon law**, or Church law, in matters such as marriage and religious practices. The Church also established courts to try people accused of violating canon law. Two of the harshest punishments that offenders faced were excommunication—or banishment from the Church—and interdict. Under an interdict, many sacraments and religious services could not be performed in a king's lands.

2.34 Preparing for the Regents

Culture and Intellectual Life What roles did women play in feudal society?

2.35 Preparing for the Regents

Belief Systems What role did the Roman Catholic Church play in Europe during the Middle Ages?

Excommunication and the possible threat of an interdict forced Henry IV, emperor of the **Holy Roman Empire**, to submit to a pope's commands. The Holy Roman Empire had been created as the Roman Empire of the German Nation by Otto I, known as Otto the Great. Otto had been crowned emperor by the then pope in 962, after invading Italy on the pope's behalf. Henry and the Church clashed over the practice of **lay investiture**, a ceremony in which kings and nobles appointed church officials. Whoever controlled lay investiture held the real power in naming and controlling bishops. Church reformers felt that kings should not have that power. In 1075, Pope Gregory VII banned lay investiture.

With the approval of the German bishops he had appointed, the furious Henry ordered Gregory to step down from the papacy. Gregory then excommunicated Henry. After German bishops and princes sided with the pope, Henry asked for the pope's forgiveness to save his throne. Gregory ended Henry's excommunication. However, the fight over lay investiture continued until 1122. That year, representatives of the Church and the empire met in the German city of Worms (wurms) and reached a compromise known as the Concordat of Worms. By its terms, the Church alone could appoint a bishop, but the emperor had veto power.

TAKING NOTES
Following Chronological Order List the significant dates and events for the Holy Roman Empire.

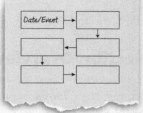

Architecture and the Arts

During the medieval period large churches called cathedrals were built in city areas. In the early 1100s, a new style of architecture, known as **Gothic**, evolved throughout medieval Europe. Gothic cathedrals thrust upward as if reaching toward heaven. Light streamed in through huge stained glass windows. Other arts of the medieval world were evident around or in the Gothic cathedral—sculpture, wood-carvings, and stained glass windows. All of these elements were meant to inspire the worshiper with the magnificence of God.

The themes of medieval literature idealized castle life and glorified knighthood, chivalry, tournaments, and real battles. Songs and poems about a knight's undying love for a lady were also very popular. Traveling poet-musicians called **troubadours** composed short verses and songs about the joys and sorrows of romantic love. Feudal lords and their ladies also enjoyed listening to epic poems. These poems recounted a hero's deeds and adventures. Many epics retold stories about legendary heroes such as Charlemagne.

2.36 Preparing for the Regents

Culture and Intellectual Life How did architecture and art reflect the views and structure of medieval society?

PREPARING FOR THE REGENTS

On a separate sheet of paper, write a well-organized essay that includes an introduction, several paragraphs addressing the task below, and a conclusion. Before beginning, check the Score the Essay box for pointers.

Theme: Economic Systems:
Societies have developed different economic systems for many reasons. One of these economic systems is manorialism.

Task:
Identify how manorialism was used in Europe and
- Discuss the historical circumstances surrounding the development of the economic system
- Describe *two* features of the economic system
- Evaluate the impact the economic system had on medieval European society

Be sure to include specific examples in your essay.

SCORE THE ESSAY To receive a score of 5 on your essay, you will need to:
- thoroughly develop all aspects of the task evenly and in depth by discussing the historical circumstances surrounding the development of manorialism in Europe, describing *two* features of the system, and evaluating the impact the system had on medieval society.
- be more analytical than descriptive.
- richly support the theme with relevant facts, examples, and details.
- demonstrate a logical and clear plan of organization.

The Crusades

Section Overview

Around the 900s, a new spirit invaded the Church. Filled with new energy, the Church began restructuring itself and started massive building programs to create new places of worship. A new age of religious feeling was born—the Age of Faith. The Age of Faith inspired wars of conquest. In 1093, the Byzantine emperor Alexius Comnenus appealed for help against the Muslim Turks, who were threatening to conquer his capital, Constantinople. Soon after, Pope Urban II issued a call for a "holy war," a Crusade for Christians to gain control of Palestine, the Holy Land. Over the next 300 years, a number of Crusades were launched.

European
Crusader

MAIN IDEAS

RELIGIOUS AND ETHICAL SYSTEMS In western Europe, the time period from 800 to 1500 is known as the Age of Faith. During this period, Christian beliefs inspired the Crusades.

TERMS AND NAMES

- Urban II
- Crusades
- Saladin
- Richard the Lion-Hearted
- Reconquista
- Inquisition

PREPARING FOR THE REGENTS

As you read this section, consider
- the causes and the consequences of the Crusades.
- how places like Jerusalem take on symbolic meaning.
- the different ways Muslims, Byzantines, and Christians viewed this period.

TIME LINE

1095
First Crusade begins.

1099
Crusaders capture Jerusalem.

1144
Edessa reconquered by the Turks.

1187
Jerusalem falls to Saladin.

1212
The Children's Crusade is launched.

Causes and Goals

In 1093, the Byzantine emperor Alexius Comnenus sent a letter to Robert, Count of Flanders, asking for help against the Muslim Turks. They were threatening to conquer his capital, Constantinople. Pope **Urban II** also read that letter. Shortly after this appeal, Urban issued a call for what he termed a "holy war," a **Crusade** to gain control of the Holy Land. Over the next 300 years, a number of such Crusades were launched.

The Crusades had economic, social, and political goals as well as religious motives. Muslims controlled Palestine (the Holy Land) and threatened Constantinople. The pope wanted to reclaim Palestine and reunite Christendom, which had split into Eastern and Western branches in 1054.

In addition, kings and the Church both saw the Crusades as an opportunity to get rid of quarrelsome knights who fought each other. These knights threatened the peace of the kingdoms, as well as Church property.

Others who participated in the Crusades were younger sons who, unlike eldest sons, did not stand to inherit their father's property. They were looking for land and a position in society, or for adventure. Still others joined the Crusades as a way to be released from feudal obligations or in the belief that participation would lead God to forgive them for their sins.

In the later Crusades, merchants profited by making cash loans to finance the journey. They also leased their ships to transport armies over the Mediterranean Sea. In addition, the merchants of Pisa, Genoa, and Venice hoped to win control of key Muslim trade routes to India, Southeast Asia, and China.

The Crusades

Pope Urban's call for a Crusade brought a tremendous outpouring of religious feeling and support. According to the pope, those who died on Crusade were assured of a place in heaven. With red crosses sewn on tunics worn over their armor and the battle cry of "God wills it!" on their lips, knights and commoners were fired by religious zeal and became Crusaders.

The First Crusade By early 1097, three armies of knights and people of all classes had gathered outside Constantinople. Most of the Crusaders were French, but Bohemians, Germans, Englishmen, Scots, Italians, and Spaniards came as well. The Crusaders were ill-prepared for war in this First Crusade. Many knew nothing of the geography, climate, or culture of the Holy Land. They had no grand strategy to capture Jerusalem. The nobles argued among themselves and could not agree on a leader. Finally an army of 12,000 (less than one-fourth of the original army) approached Jerusalem. The Crusaders besieged the city for over a month. On July 15, 1099, they captured the city.

All in all, the Crusaders had won a narrow strip of land. It stretched about 650 miles from Edessa in the north to Jerusalem in the south. Four feudal Crusader states were carved out of this territory, each ruled by a European noble.

The Second Crusade The Crusaders' states were extremely vulnerable to Muslim counterattack. In 1144, Edessa was reconquered by the Turks. The Second Crusade was organized to recapture the city. But its armies straggled home in defeat. In 1187, Europeans were shocked to learn that Jerusalem itself had fallen to a Kurdish warrior and Muslim leader **Saladin** (SAL•uh•dihn).

The Third Crusade The Third Crusade to recapture Jerusalem was led by three of Europe's most powerful monarchs. They were Philip II (Augustus) of France,

2.37 Preparing for the Regents

Belief Systems What was the major goal of the Christian Church during the Crusades?

2.38 Preparing for the Regents

Conflict What reasons did people have for joining the Crusades?

TAKING NOTES
Following Chronological Order Use a time line to note important events in the Crusades.

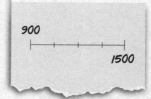

900

1500

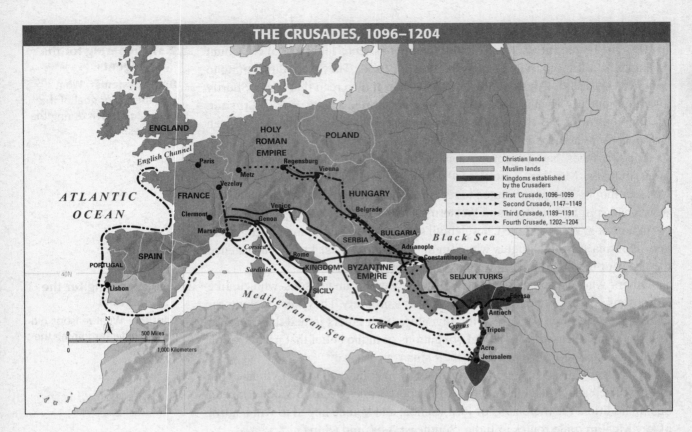

Christian lands
Muslim lands
Kingdoms established
by the Crusaders
→ First Crusade, 1096–1099
→ Second Crusade, 1147–1149
→ Third Crusade, 1189–1191
→ Fourth Crusade, 1202–1204

2.39 Preparing for the Regents

Conflict What compromise did Richard the Lion-Hearted and Saladin reach regarding Jerusalem?

the English king, **Richard the Lion-Hearted**, and German emperor Frederick I (Barbarossa). Philip argued with Richard and went home. Barbarossa drowned on the journey. So, Richard was left to lead the Crusaders in an attempt to regain the Holy Land from Saladin. Both Richard and Saladin were brilliant warriors. After many battles, the two agreed to a truce in 1192. Jerusalem remained under Muslim control. In return, Saladin promised that unarmed Christian pilgrims could freely visit the city's holy places.

The Crusading Spirit Dwindles In 1204, the Fourth Crusade to capture Jerusalem failed. The knights did not reach the Holy Land. Instead, they ended up looting the city of Constantinople. In the 1200s, four more Crusades to free the Holy Land were also unsuccessful. The religious spirit of the First Crusade faded, and the search for personal gain grew. In two later Crusades, armies marched not to the Holy Land but to Egypt. The Crusaders intended to weaken Muslim forces there before going to the Holy Land. But none of these attempts conquered much land.

The Children's Crusade The Children's Crusade took place in 1212. In two different movements, thousands of children set out to conquer Jerusalem. One group in France was led by 12-year-old Stephen of Cloyes. An estimated 30,000 children under 18 joined him. They were armed only with the belief that God would give them Jerusalem. On their march south to the Mediterranean, many died from cold and starvation. The rest drowned at sea or were sold into slavery.

In Germany, Nicholas of Cologne gathered about 20,000 children and young adults. They began marching toward Rome. Thousands died in the cold and treacherous crossing of the Alps. Those who survived the trip to Italy finally did meet the pope. He told them to go home and wait until they were older. About 2,000 survived the return trip to Germany. A few boarded a ship for the Holy Land and were never heard of again.

A Spanish Crusade In Spain, Muslims (called Moors) controlled most of the country until the 1100s. The **Reconquista** (ray•kawn•KEES•tuh) was a long effort by the Spanish to drive the Muslims out of Spain. By the late 1400s, the Muslims held only the tiny kingdom of Granada. In 1492, Granada finally fell to the Christian army of Ferdinand and Isabella, the Spanish monarchs.

To unify their country under Christianity and to increase their power, Isabella and Ferdinand made use of the **Inquisition**. This was a court held by the Church to suppress heresy. Heretics were people whose religious beliefs differed from the teachings of the Church. Many Jews and Muslims in Spain converted to Christianity during the late 1400s. Even so, the Inquisitors suspected these Jewish and Muslim converts of heresy. A person suspected of heresy might be questioned for weeks and even tortured. Once suspects confessed, they were often burned at the stake. In 1492, the monarchs expelled all practicing Jews and Muslims from Spain.

Impact of the Crusades

The Crusades are a forceful example of the power of the Church during the medieval period. The call to go to the Holy Land encouraged thousands to leave their homes for faraway lands. For those who stayed home, especially women, it meant a chance to manage affairs on the estates or to operate shops and inns.

European merchants who lived and traded in the Crusader states expanded trade between Europe and Southwest Asia (sometimes called the Middle East). The goods imported from Southwest Asia included spices, fruits, and cloth. This trade with the West benefited both Christians and Muslims.

However, the failure of later Crusades also lessened the power of the pope. The Crusades weakened the feudal nobility and increased the power of kings. Thousands of knights and other participants lost their lives and fortunes. The fall of Constantinople weakened the Byzantine Empire.

For Muslims, the intolerance and prejudice displayed by Christians in the Holy Land left behind a legacy of bitterness and hatred. This legacy continues to the present. For Christians and Jews who remained in the Muslim controlled region after the fall of the Crusader states, relations with the Muslim leadership worsened. For Jews in Europe, the Crusades were a time of increased persecution.

2.40 Preparing for the Regents

Religious Beliefs What were the Reconquista and Inquisition? What effect did they have on Muslims and Jews in Spain?

2.41 Preparing for the Regents

Movement of People and Goods What effect did the Crusades have on trade between Europe and Southwest Asia?

TARGET THE REGENTS

Answer the following questions. Use the Analyze the Question hints to help you answer the questions.

Base your answer to question 1 on the quotation below and on your knowledge of social studies.

"Come then, with all your people and give battle with all your strength, so that all this treasure shall not fall into the hands of the Turks. . . . Therefore act while there is still time lest the kingdom of Christians shall vanish from your sight. . . . And in your coming you will find your reward in heaven.

— Emperor Alexius Comnenus,
quoted in *The Dream and the Tomb*

1 Which event is referred to in this quotation?

(1) Enlightenment
(2) French Revolution
(3) Glorious Revolution
(4) Crusades

ANALYZE THE QUESTION
- Read the question stem and quotation. You are being asked to determine what event is being referred to in the quotation.
- Look for keywords like *Christians* and *Turks* in the quotation, and note the author of the quote.
- Select the alternative that matches the clues.

Expanding Zones of Exchange and Encounter (500–1200)

Part I: MULTIPLE-CHOICE QUESTIONS

Directions (1–10): For each statement or question, write on a separate answer sheet the *number* of the word or expression that, of those given, best completes the statement or answers the questions.

1 A major goal of the Christian Church during the Crusades (1096–1291) was to

(1) establish Christianity in western Europe
(2) capture the Holy Land from Islamic rulers
(3) unite warring Arab peoples
(4) strengthen English dominance in the Arab world

2 During the early Middle Ages, western European societies were most influenced by

(1) national monarchies
(2) the Roman Catholic Church
(3) elected parliaments
(4) the Byzantine emperors

3 Which heading best completes the partial outline below?

I. _____
   A. Development of medical encyclopedias
   B. Development of algebra and astronomical tables
   C. Production of cotton textiles and woolen carpets
   D. Production of literature, calligraphy, and geometric art

(1) Achievement of Feudal Societies
(2) Inventions During the Neolithic Revolution
(3) Issues of the Protestant Reformation
(4) Contributions of the Islamic Civilization

4 Which empire had the greatest influence on the development of early Russia?

(1) Roman   (3) Egyptian
(2) Byzantine   (4) British

5 Which empire introduced the Eastern Orthodox Church and the Cyrillic alphabet to Russia?

(1) Mongol   (3) British
(2) Byzantine   (4) Gupta

Base your answer to question 6 on the illustration below and your knowledge of social studies.

European Feudal System

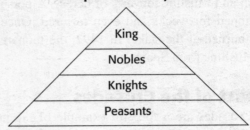

King
Nobles
Knights
Peasants

6 The illustration represents society based on

(1) social class
(2) educational achievement
(3) accumulated wealth
(4) political ability

7 One result of the Crusades was an increase in trade between the Middle East and

(1) East Asia   (3) North America
(2) Africa   (4) Europe

8 The phrase "from southern Spain, across northern Africa, occupying the Arabian peninsula to Southeast Asia" once described the extent of the

(1) Aztec Empire   (3) Gupta Empire
(2) Pax Romana   (4) Muslim world

9 One reason for the growth and success of ninth-century cities such as Baghdad, Constantinople, and Ch'ang-an (Xian) was that they

(1) were part of the Roman Empire
(2) tolerated religious diversity
(3) traded only with people in immediate region
(4) were located on major trade routes

10 After the Western Roman Empire fell, the eastern part eventually became known as the

(1) Byzantine Empire
(2) Carthaginian Empire
(3) Islamic Empire
(4) Persian Empire

In developing your answers to Parts II and III, be sure to keep these general definitions in mind:

(a) *describe* means "to illustrate something in words or tell about it"

(b) *explain* means "to make plain or understandable; to give reasons for or causes of; to show the logical development or relationships of"

(c) *discuss* means "to make observations about something using facts, reasoning, and argument, to present in some detail"

Part II: THEMATIC ESSAY

Directions: Write a well-organized essay that includes an introduction, several paragraphs addressing the task below, and a conclusion.

Theme: Turning Points

Turning points are major events that have led to lasting change.

Task:

Identify *two* major turning points in global history and for *each*:
* Describe the historical circumstances surrounding the turning point
* Explain how *each* turning point changed the course of history

You may use any example from your study of Unit Two. Some suggestions you might wish to consider include the spread of Islam, European feudalism, and the Crusades.

You are not limited to these suggestions.
Do *not* use any turning points in United States history.

Guidelines:

In your essay, be sure to
* Address all aspects of the *Task*
* Support the theme with relevant facts, examples, and details
* Use a logical and clear plan of organization, including an introduction and a conclusion that are beyond the simple restatement of the *Theme*

Part III: DOCUMENT-BASED QUESTION

This question is based on the accompanying documents (1–3). The question is designed to test your ability to work with historic documents. Some of these documents have been edited for the purpose of this question. As you analyze the documents, take into account both the source of each document and any point of view that may be presented in the document.

Historical Context:

Throughout global history, people have migrated as a result of political, social, and economic conditions.

Task:

Using information from the documents and your knowledge of global history, answer the question that follows each document in Part A. Your answers to the questions will help you write the Part B essay, in which you will be asked to:

> • Discuss the political, social, and/or economic reasons for the mass movement of people during the early Middle Ages in Europe

Part A: Short Answer

Directions: Analyze the documents and answer the short-answer questions that follow in the space provided.

Document 1

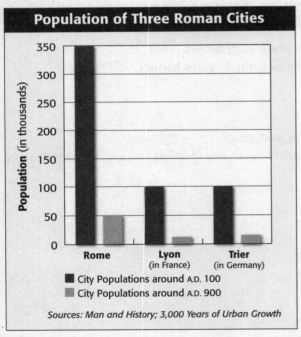

Population of Three Roman Cities

■ City Populations around A.D. 100
■ City Populations around A.D. 900

Sources: Man and History; 3,000 Years of Urban Growth

Document 2

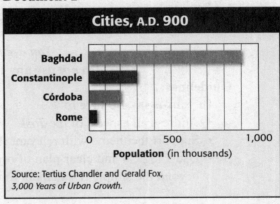

Cities, A.D. 900

Source: Tertius Chandler and Gerald Fox, *3,000 Years of Urban Growth.*

1 According to Document 1, what was the drop in Rome's population between 100 and 900?

_____

2 According to Document 2, what was the population of Baghdad in 900?

_____

Document 3

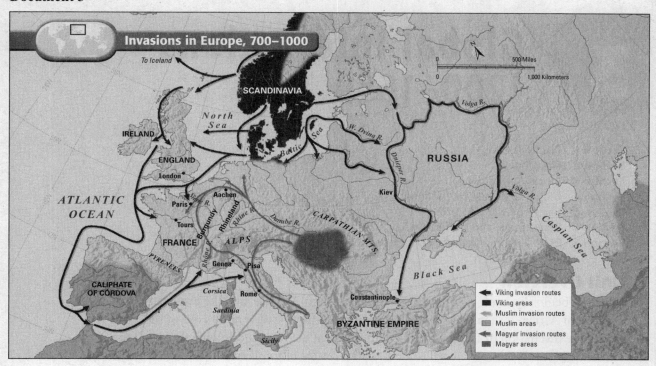

Invasions in Europe, 700–1000

3 According to the map, what groups invaded Europe between 700 and 1000?

_____

_____

Part B: Essay

Directions: Write a well-organized essay that includes an introduction, several paragraphs, and a conclusion. Use evidence from at least *two* documents to support your response.

Historical Context: Throughout history, people have migrated as a result of political, social, and economic conditions.

Task: Using information from the documents and your knowledge of global history, write an essay in which you:

> • Discuss the political, social, and/or economic reasons for the mass movement of people during the early Middle Ages in Europe

Guidelines:

In your essay, be sure to
• Address all aspects of the *Task* by accurately analyzing and interpreting at least **two** documents
• Incorporate information from the documents
• Incorporate relevant outside information
• Support the theme with relevant facts, examples, and details
• Use a logical and clear plan of organization
• Introduce the theme by establishing a framework that is beyond a simple statement of the *Task* or *Historical Context* and conclude with a summation of the theme

Global Interactions
1200–1650

Unit Overview

This unit begins by exploring feudal Japan, the Mongol Empire, and the city-states and empires of Africa. It then turns to an examination of Europe as it moves out of the Middle Ages. The discussion of Europe begins with a look at the impact of global trade and the bubonic plague. It then reviews the rise of nation-states in England and France. The unit closes with a look at the causes and consequences of the Renaissance, as well as the Protestant and Catholic Reformations.

Concepts and Themes

Among the concepts and themes explored in this unit are

- Belief Systems
- Conflict
- Culture and Intellectual Life
- Economic Systems
- Human and Physical Geography
- Movement of People and Goods
- Nation States/Nationalism
- Political Systems
- Science and Technology
- Urbanization

PREPARING FOR THE REGENTS: Building Thematic Essay Skills

Science and technology play a critical role in shaping the course of human history. Scientific and technological advances are often born of the need to solve specific problems. Knowing how to identify the factors that spark scientific and technological innovation and knowing how to analyze the short-term and long-term effects of those innovations are important history skills. As you read this unit, think about the scientific and/or technological advances that contributed to the societies under discussion. Try to identify what problems or needs these advances were meant to address and what short- and long-tern effects they had. Use the following web diagram to organize information about the advances. You can add additional boxes as needed.

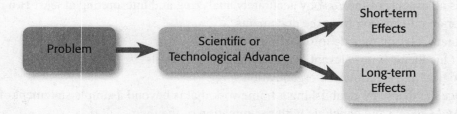

Feudal Japan

Section Overview

Japan lies east of China, in the direction of the sunrise. In fact, the name Japan comes from the Chinese word ri-ben, *which means "origin of the sun" or "land of the rising sun." From ancient times, Japan borrowed ideas, institutions, and culture from the Chinese. Japan's genius was its ability to take in new ideas and make them uniquely Japanese. The Japanese tea ceremony, for instance, developed out of a blending of the people's love for tea and Buddhist practices, both cultural elements adopted from the Chinese.*

Early Japan was home to hundreds of clans that controlled their own territories. Slowly the rule of emperors emerged, but real power still rested with the clans. In the 11th century, an early form of feudalism developed in Japan. However, this original system was shattered by civil war in the mid-1400s. The new form of feudalism that emerged more closely resembled European feudalism.

In the early 1600, the Tokugawa Shogunate came to power and unified Japan. Their rule, which lasted until 1867, brought order and stability to the country.

Samurai warrior

MAIN IDEAS

RELIGIOUS AND ETHICAL SYSTEMS   Japanese civilization was shaped by cultural borrowing from China and the rise of feudalism and military leaders.

ECONOMICS   The Tokugawa regime unified Japan and began 250 years of isolation, autocracy, and economic growth.

TERMS AND NAMES

- samurai
- Bushido
- shogun
- daimyo
- Oda Nobunaga
- Toyotomi Hideyoshi
- Tokugawa Shogunate
- haiku
- kabuki

PREPARING FOR THE REGENTS

As you read this section, consider
- how location impacted Japanese history.
- how Japanese and European feudalism were both similar and different.

TIME LINE

794
Heian period begins in Japan.

1192
Kamakura Shogunate rules Japan.

1603
Tokugawa Shogunate rules Japan.

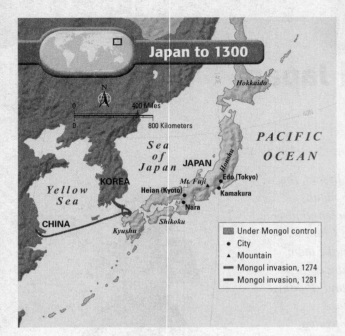

Japan to 1300

Human and Physical Geography

Japan is an archipelago (AHR•kuh•PEHL•uh•GOH), or island group, made up of about 4,000 islands. It extends in an arc more than 1,200 miles long. Historically, most Japanese people have lived on the four largest islands: Hokkaido (hah•KY•doh), Honshu (HAHN•shoo), Shikoku (shee•KAW•koo), and Kyushu (kee•OO•shoo).

Japan's geography has both advantages and disadvantages. Southern Japan enjoys a mild climate with plenty of rainfall. However, the country is so mountainous that only about 12 percent of the land is suitable for farming. Natural resources such as coal, oil, and iron are in short supply. During the late summer and early fall, strong tropical storms called typhoons occur. Earthquakes and tsunamis, or tidal waves, are also threats.

3.1 Preparing for the Regents

Human and Physical Geography What are the advantages and disadvantages of Japan's geography?

TAKING NOTES

Following Chronological Order Use a time line to record the main periods and events in Japanese history from 300 to 1300.

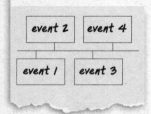

3.2 Preparing for the Regents

Belief Systems How did Buddhism spread to Japan?

Japanese Traditions and Culture

The first historic mention of Japan comes from Chinese writings of the first century B.C. Japan was not a united country at that time. Hundreds of clans controlled their own territories. Each clan worshiped its own nature gods and goddesses. The clans' varied customs and beliefs eventually combined to form Shinto, Japan's earliest religion. Shinto is based on respect for the forces of nature and on the worship of ancestors.

By A.D. 400s, the Yamato clan had established itself as the leading clan. By the seventh century, the Yamato chiefs called themselves the emperors of Japan. These early emperors did not control the entire country, or even much of it, but the Japanese gradually accepted the idea of an emperor.

Although many of the Yamato rulers lacked real power, the dynasty was never overthrown. When rival clans fought for power, the winning clan claimed control of the emperor and then ruled in the emperor's name. Japan had both an emperor who served as a figurehead and a ruling power who reigned behind the throne. This dual structure became an enduring characteristic of Japanese government.

During the 400s, the Japanese began to have more and more contact with mainland Asia. They soon came under the influence of Chinese ideas and customs, which they first learned about from Korean travelers.

The Koreans Bring Buddhism One of the most important influences brought by Korean travelers was Buddhism. In the mid-700s, the Japanese imperial court officially accepted Buddhism. By the eighth or ninth century, Buddhist ideas and worship had spread through Japanese society. The Japanese, however, did not give up their Shinto beliefs. Some Buddhist rituals became Shinto rituals, and some Shinto gods and goddesses were worshiped in Buddhist temples.

The form of Buddhism that had the greatest impact on Japan was Zen Buddhism. Zen Buddhism sought spiritual enlightenment through meditation. Strict discipline of mind and body was the Zen path to wisdom. Zen monks would sit in meditation for hours. If they showed signs of losing concentration, a Zen master might shout at them or hit them with a stick.

Cultural Borrowings from China Interest in Buddhist ideas soon grew into an enthusiasm for all things Chinese. The Japanese adopted the Chinese system of writing and interest in calligraphy, the art of beautiful handwriting. Japanese artists painted landscapes in the Chinese manner. The Japanese also followed Chinese styles in cooking, gardening, drinking tea, and hairdressing. For a time, Japan even modeled its government on China's. They tried to introduce China's civil-service system. However, this attempt failed. In Japan, noble birth remained the key to winning a powerful position. Unlike China, Japan continued to be a country where a few great families held power.

Life in the Heian Period In the late 700s, the imperial court moved its capital from Nara to Heian (HAY•ahn), the modern Kyoto (kee•OH•toh). Many of Japan's noble families also moved to Heian. Among the upper class in Heian, a highly refined court society arose. This era in Japanese history, from 794 to 1185, is called the Heian period. Gentlemen and ladies of the court filled their days with elaborate ritual and artistic pursuits. Rules dictated every aspect of court life—from the length of swords to the color of official robes.

Feudalism in Japan

For most of the Heian period, the rich Fujiwara family held the real power. By about the middle of the 11th century, however, the power of the central government and the Fujiwaras began to slip. Large landowners living away from the capital set up private armies. The countryside became lawless and dangerous. Armed soldiers on horseback preyed on farmers and travelers, and pirates took control of the seas. For safety, farmers and small landowners traded parts of their land to strong warlords in exchange for protection. This marked the beginning of a feudal system of localized rule like that of ancient China and medieval Europe. As in Europe, feudalism provided social stability in troubled times.

Early Feudalism Since wars between rival lords were commonplace, each lord surrounded himself with a bodyguard of loyal warriors called **samurai** (SAM•uh•RY). (*Samurai* means "one who serves.") Samurai lived according to a demanding code of behavior called **Bushido** (BUSH•ih•DOH), or "the way of the warrior." A samurai was expected to show reckless courage, reverence for the gods, fairness, and generosity toward those weaker than himself. Dying an honorable death was judged more important than living a long life.

During the late 1100s, Japan's two most powerful clans fought for power. After almost 30 years of war, the Minamoto family emerged victorious. In 1192, the emperor gave a Minamoto leader named Yoritomo the title of **shogun**, or "supreme general of the emperor's army." In effect, the shogun had the powers of a military dictator. Following tradition, the emperor still reigned from Kyoto. (Kyoto was rebuilt on the ruins of Heian, which had been destroyed in war.) However, the real center of power was at the shogun's military headquarters at Kamakura (KAHM•uh•KUR•uh). The 1200s are known in Japanese history as the Kamakura shogunate. The pattern of government in which shoguns ruled through puppet emperors lasted in Japan until 1868.

The Kamakura shoguns were strong enough to turn back the two naval invasions sent by the great Mongol ruler Kublai Khan in 1274 and 1281. However, the Japanese victory over the Mongols drained the shoguns' treasury. Loyal samurai were bitter when the government failed to pay them. The Kamakura shoguns lost prestige and power. Samurai attached themselves more closely to their local lords, who soon fought one another as fiercely as they had fought the Mongols.

3.3 Preparing for the Regents

Culture and Intellectual Life What were some of the cultural elements of early Japan?

3.4 Preparing for the Regents

Culture and Intellectual Life How was the code of Bushido similar to the code of chivalry in medieval Europe?

Political Systems How were the causes and characteristics of feudalism similar in Japan and Europe?

A New Feudalism In 1467, civil war shattered Japan's old feudal system. The country collapsed into chaos. Centralized rule ended. A violent era of disorder followed. This time in Japanese history, which lasted from 1467 to 1568, is known as the Sengoku, or "Warring States," period. Powerful samurai seized control of old feudal estates. They offered peasants and others protection in return for loyalty. These warrior-chieftains, called **daimyo** (DYE•mee•oh), became lords in a new kind of Japanese feudalism. Under this system, security came from these powerful warlords. The emperor became a figurehead, with no real power.

The new Japanese feudalism resembled European feudalism in many ways. The daimyo built fortified castles and created small armies of samurai on horses. Later they added foot soldiers with muskets (guns) to their ranks. Rival daimyo often fought each other for territory. This led to disorder throughout the land.

A number of ambitious daimyo hoped to gather enough power to take control of the entire country. One, **Oda Nobunaga** (oh•dah noh•boo•nah•gah), seized the imperial capital Kyoto in 1568. Nobunaga then sought to eliminate his enemies. In 1575, Nobunaga's 3,000 soldiers armed with muskets crushed an enemy force of samurai cavalry. This was the first time firearms had been used effectively in battle in Japan. However, Nobunaga was not able to unify Japan. He committed *seppuku*, the ritual suicide of a samurai, in 1582.

Nohunaga's mission was continued by **Toyatomi Hideyoshi** (toh•you•toh•mee hee•deh•yoh•shee), his best general. Hideyoshi set out to destroy the daimyo that remained hostile. By 1590, he controlled most of the country. Hideyoshi did not stop with Japan. With the idea of eventually conquering China, he invaded Korea in 1592 and began a long campaign against the Koreans and their Chinese allies. When Hideyoshi died in 1598, his troops withdrew from Korea.

Japanese Feudalism

Emperor

Daimyo

Daimyo

Samurai

Samurai

Artisans

Peasants

Merchants

European Feudalism

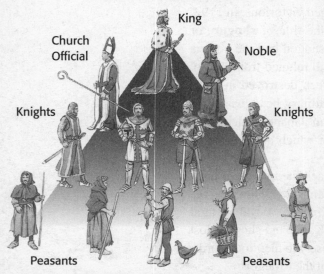

King

Church Official

Noble

Knights

Knights

Peasants

Peasants

Tokugawa Shogunate

One of Hideyoshi's strongest allies, Tokugawa Ieyasu (toh•koo•gah•wah ee•yeh•yah•soo), completed the unification of Japan. In 1600, Ieyasu defeated his rivals at the Battle of Sekigahara. His victory earned him the loyalty of daimyo throughout Japan. Three years later, Ieyasu became the sole ruler, or shogun. He then moved Japan's capital to his power base at Edo, a small fishing village that would later become the city of Tokyo. The **Tokugawa Shogunate** would hold power until 1867.

Japan was unified, but the daimyo still governed at the local level. To keep them from rebelling, Ieyasu required that they spend every other year in the capital. Even when they returned to their lands, they had to leave their families behind as hostages in Edo. Through this "alternate attendance policy" and other restrictions, Ieyasu tamed the daimyo. This was a major step toward restoring centralized government. As a result, the rule of law overcame the rule of the sword.

Life in Tokugawa Japan Tokugawa society was very structured. The emperor had the top rank but was just a figurehead. The actual ruler was the shogun, who was the supreme military commander. Below him were the daimyo. Samurai warriors came next. The peasants and artisans followed them. Peasants made up about four-fifths of the population. Merchants were at the bottom, but they gradually became more important as the Japanese economy expanded.

In Japan, as in China, Confucian values influenced ideas about society. According to Confucius, the ideal society depended on agriculture, not commerce. Farmers, not merchants, made ideal citizens. In the real world of Tokugawa Japan, however, peasant farmers bore the main tax burden and faced more difficulties than other classes. Many abandoned farm life and headed for the expanding towns and cities. There, they mixed with samurai, artisans, and merchants.

By the mid-1700s, Japan began to shift from a rural to an urban society. Edo had grown from a small village in 1600 to a city of more than one million. The rise of large commercial centers increased employment opportunities for women. Women found jobs in entertainment, textile manufacturing, and publishing. Still, the majority of Japanese women led sheltered and restricted lives as peasant wives. They worked in the fields, managed the household, cared for the children, and obeyed their husband without question.

Traditional culture continued to thrive. Samurai attended ceremonial noh dramas, which were based on tragic themes, and read tales of ancient warriors and their courage in battle. But traditional entertainment faced competition in the cities from new styles of literature and drama. Townspeople read a new type of fiction—realistic stories about self-made merchants or the hardships of life. The people also read **haiku** (HI•koo), 5-7-5-syllable, 3-line verse poetry that presented images rather than ideas. Townspeople also attended **kabuki** theater. Actors in elaborate costumes, using music, dance, and mime, performed skits about modern life.

Contact Between Europe and Japan

Europeans began coming to Japan in the 16th century, during the Warring States period. The Japanese first encountered Europeans in 1543, when shipwrecked Portuguese sailors washed up on the shores of southern Japan. Portuguese merchants soon followed. They hoped to involve themselves in Japan's trade with China and Southeast Asia. The Portuguese brought clocks, eyeglasses, tobacco, firearms, and other unfamiliar items from Europe. Japanese merchants, eager to expand their markets, were happy to receive the newcomers and their goods.

Weapons of War The daimyo, too, welcomed the strangers. They were particularly interested in the Portuguese muskets and cannons, because every daimyo sought an advantage over his rivals. The Japanese purchased weapons from the Portuguese and soon began their own production. Firearms forever changed the time-honored tradition of the Japanese warrior, whose principal weapon had been the sword. Some daimyo recruited and trained corps of peasants to use muskets. Many samurai, who retained the sword as their principal weapon, would lose their lives to musket fire in future combat.

The cannon also had a huge impact on warfare and life in Japan. Daimyo had to build fortified castles to withstand the destructive force of cannonballs. The castles attracted merchants, artisans, and others to surrounding lands. Many of these lands were to grow into the towns and cities of modern Japan, including Edo (Tokyo), Osaka, Himeji, and Nagoya.

3.6 Preparing for the Regents

Culture and Intellectual Life   What were some of the cultural elements of Tokugawa Japan?

3.7 Preparing for the Regents

Movement of People and Goods   Why did the Japanese at first welcome the Europeans?

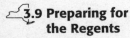

3.8 Preparing for the Regents

Belief Systems What role did missionaries play in the spread of Christianity to Japan? How did missionaries contribute to the closing of Japan?

Christian Missionaries In 1549, Christian missionaries began arriving in Japan. The Japanese accepted the missionaries in part because they associated them with the muskets and other European goods that they wanted to purchase. However, the religious orders of Jesuits, Franciscans, and Dominicans came to convert the Japanese. Francis Xavier, a Jesuit, led the first mission to Japan. He baptized about a hundred converts before he left Japan. By the year 1600, other European missionaries had converted about 300,000 Japanese to Christianity.

The success of the missionaries upset Tokugawa Ieyasu. The missionaries scorned traditional Japanese beliefs and sometimes involved themselves in local politics. At first, Ieyasu did not take any action, fearing that he would drive off the European traders who spurred Japan's economy. By 1612, however, the shogun had come to fear religious uprisings more. He banned Christianity and focused on ridding his country of all Christians.

Ieyasu died in 1616, but repression of Christianity continued off and on for the next two decades. In 1637, the issue came to a head. An uprising in southern Japan of some 30,000 peasants, led by dissatisfied samurai, shook the Tokugawa shogunate. Because so many of the rebels were Christian, the shogun decided that Christianity was at the root of the rebellion. After that, the shoguns ruthlessly persecuted Christians. European missionaries were killed or driven out of Japan. All Japanese were forced to demonstrate faithfulness to some branch of Buddhism. These policies eventually eliminated Christianity in Japan.

The Closed Country Policy

3.9 Preparing for the Regents

Change What was Japan's "closed country policy?" Why did Japan establish the policy?

The persecution of Christians was part of an attempt to control foreign ideas. The Tokugawa shoguns did not like the introduction of European ideas and ways, but they valued European trade. As time passed, they realized that they could safely exclude both the missionaries and the merchants. By 1639, they had sealed Japan's borders and instituted a "closed country policy." Most commercial contacts with Europeans ended. One port, Nagasaki, remained open to foreign traders. But only Dutch and Chinese merchants were allowed into the port. Since the Tokugawa shoguns controlled Nagasaki, they now had a monopoly on foreign trade, which continued to be profitable.

PREPARING FOR THE REGENTS

Answer the following question. Use the Analyze the Question hints to help you answer the question.

1 Which fact relating to early Japan was the result of the other three?

(1) Japan experienced earthquakes and volcanic eruptions.
(2) The Japanese developed a nature-based belief called Shinto.
(3) Tsunamis and typhoons sometimes destroyed coastal Japanese villages.
(4) Mountains are found throughout the islands of Japan.

ANALYZE THE QUESTION
- Read the question stem. You are being asked to choose which alternative statement is the *result* of the other three.
- Read each alternative against each other alternative to determine whether there is a cause–effect relationship.
- The alternative that is the effect in every pairing is the correct answer.

The Mongols

Section Overview

The Mongols of the Asian steppe lived their lives on the move. They prided themselves on their skill on horseback, their discipline, their ruthlessness, and their courage in battle. They also wanted the wealth and glory that came with conquering mighty empires. This desire soon exploded into violent conflict that transformed Asia and Europe forever.

Around 1200, a Mongol clan leader named Temujin sought to unify the Mongols under his leadership. He fought and defeated his rivals one by one. In 1206, Temujin accepted the title Genghis Khan, or "universal ruler" of the Mongol clans. Over the next 21 years, Genghis led the Mongols in conquering much of Asia.

Kublai Khan, the grandson of Genghis Khan, assumed the title Great Khan in 1260. In theory, the Great Khan ruled the entire Mongol Empire. In reality, the empire had split into four khanates. Other descendants of Genghis ruled Central Asia, Persia, and Russia as semi-independent states. So, Kublai focused instead on extending the power and range of his own khanate, which already included Mongolia, Korea, Tibet, and northern China. As his first step, however, he fulfilled the goal of his grandfather to conquer all of China.

Genghis Khan (1162?–1227)

MAIN IDEAS

EMPIRE BUILDING The Mongols, a nomadic people from the steppe, conquered settled societies across much of Asia.
CULTURAL INTERACTION As emperor of China, Kublai Khan encouraged foreign trade.

TERMS AND NAMES

- pastoralists
- Genghis Khan
- Kublai Khan
- Pax Mongolica
- Marco Polo

PREPARING FOR THE REGENTS

As you read this section, consider
- how a nomadic people conquered more advanced civilizations.
- the global significance and great diversity of the Mongol Empire.
- the importance of cities as centers of trade and culture.

TIME LINE

1206
Mongol leader Temujin accepts the title Genghis Khan.

1227
Genghis Khan dies.

1260
Kublai Khan assumes the title Great Khan.

1279
Kublai Khan conquers China.

1294
Kublai Khan dies

Human and Physical Geography

A vast belt of dry grassland, called the steppe, stretches across the landmass of Eurasia. The significance of the steppe to neighboring civilizations was twofold. First, it served as a land trade route connecting the East and the West. Second, it was home to nomadic peoples who frequently swept down on their neighbors to plunder, loot, and conquer.

The Physical Geography There are two main expanses of the Eurasian steppe. The western steppe runs from Central Asia to eastern Europe. It was the original home of ancient invaders such as the Hittites. The eastern steppe, covering the area of present-day Mongolia, was the first home of the Huns, the Turks, and the Mongols. Very little rain falls on the steppe, but the dry, windswept plain supports short, hardy grasses. Seasonal temperature changes can be dramatic. Temperatures in Mongolia, for example, range from –57°F in winter to 96°F in the summer. Rainfall is somewhat more plentiful and the climate milder in the west than in the east. For this reason, movements of people have historically tended to be toward the west and the south.

The People The nomadic peoples of the steppe were **pastoralists**—that is, they herded domesticated animals. They were constantly on the move, searching for good pasture to feed their herds. But they did not wander. Rather, they followed a familiar seasonal pattern and returned on a regular basis to the same campsites. Keeping claim to land that was not permanently occupied was difficult. Battles frequently arose among nomadic groups over grassland and water rights.

Asian nomads practically lived on horseback as they followed their huge herds over the steppe. They depended on their animals for food, clothing, and housing. Their diet consisted of meat and mare's milk. They wore clothing made of skins and wool, and they lived in portable felt tents called yurts.

Steppe nomads traveled together in clans. The members of each clan claimed to be descended from a common ancestor. Different clans sometimes came together when they needed a large force to attack a common enemy or raid their settled neighbors.

The differing ways of life of nomadic and settled peoples resulted in constant interaction between them. Often, they engaged in peaceful trade. The nomads exchanged horses, for example, for basic items they lacked, such as grain, metal, cloth, and tea. Nomads were accustomed to scarcity and hardship. However, they were sometimes tempted by the rich land and relative wealth of townspeople and took what they wanted by force. Time and again in history, nomadic peoples rode out of the steppe to invade border towns and villages. When a state or empire was strong and organized, it could protect its frontier. If the state or empire became divided and weak, the nomads could increase their attacks and gain more plunder. Occasionally, a powerful nomadic group was able to conquer a whole empire and become its rulers. Over generations, these nomadic rulers often became part of the civilization they conquered.

The Mongol Empire

For centuries, the Mongol people had roamed the eastern steppe in loosely organized clans. It took a military and political genius to unite the Mongols into a force with a single purpose—conquest.

☙3.10 Preparing for the Regents

Human and Physical Geography What are the geographic characteristics of the steppe?

☙3.11 Preparing for the Regents

Human and Physical Geography How did the people of the steppe adapt to their physical environment?

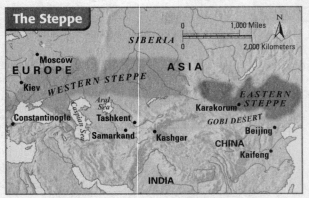

The Steppe

Genghis Khan and the Rise of the Mongols Around 1200, a Mongol clan leader named Temujin sought to unify the Mongols under his leadership. He fought and defeated his rivals one by one. In 1206, Temujin accepted the title **Genghis Khan** (JEHNG•gihs KAHN), or "universal ruler" of the Mongol clans.

Over the next 21 years, Genghis led the Mongols in conquering much of Asia. His first goal was China. After invading the northern Jin Empire in 1211, however, his attention turned to the Islamic region west of Mongolia. Angered by the murder of Mongol traders and an ambassador at the hands of the Muslims, Genghis launched a campaign of terror across Central Asia. By 1225, Central Asia was under Mongol control.

Genghis Khan died in 1227. After his death, his sons and grandsons continued the campaign of conquest. Armies under their leadership drove south, east, and west out of inner Asia. They completed their conquest of northern China and invaded Korea. They leveled the Russian city of Kiev and reached the banks of the Adriatic Sea. The cities of Venice and Vienna were within their grasp. However, in the 1250s the Mongols halted their westward campaign and turned their attention to Persia. By 1260, the Mongols had divided their huge empire into four regions, or khanates. These were the Khanate of the Great Khan (Mongolia and China), the Khanate of Chagatai (Central Asia), the Ilkhanate (Persia), and the Khanate of the Golden Horde (Russia). A descendant of Genghis ruled each khanate.

The Mongols in Russia The Mongols attacked and demolished Kiev in 1240. They rode under the leadership of Batu Khan, Genghis's grandson. So many inhabitants were slaughtered, a Russian historian reported, that "no eye remained to weep." After the fall of Kiev, Mongols ruled all of southern Russia for 200 years. The empire's official name was the "Khanate of the Golden Horde"— *Khanate* from the Mongol word for "kingdom," *Golden* because gold was the royal color of the Mongols, and *Horde* from the Mongol word for "camp."

Under Mongol rule, the Russians could follow all their usual customs, as long as they made no attempts to rebel. As fierce as they were, the Mongols tolerated all the religions in their realms. The Church, in fact, often acted as a mediator between the Russian people and their Mongol rulers. The Mongols demanded just two things from Russians: absolute obedience and massive amounts of tribute, or payments. However, Mongol rule isolated the Russians more than ever from their neighbors in Western Europe. This meant that among other things, the Russians had little access to many new ideas and inventions.

Kublai Khan and the Yang Dynasty Genghis Khan's grandson **Kublai Khan** assumed the title of Great Khan in 1260. Kublai focused on extending the power and range of his khanate, which already included Mongolia, Korea, Tibet, and northern China. To begin, however, he had to fulfill the goal of his grandfather to conquer all of China. The Chinese held off Kublai's attacks for several years. However, his armies finally overwhelmed them in 1279.

As China's new emperor, Kublai Khan founded a new dynasty called the Yuan (yoo•AHN) Dynasty. It lasted less than a century, until 1368, when it was overthrown. However, the Yuan era was an important period in Chinese history for several reasons. First, Kublai Khan united China for the first time in more than 300 years. For this he is considered one of China's great emperors. Second, the control imposed by the Mongols across all of Asia opened China to greater foreign contacts and trade. Finally, Kublai and his successors tolerated Chinese culture and made few changes to the system of government.

TAKING NOTES
Following Chronological Order Use a chart to list the series of events leading to the creation of the Mongol Empire.

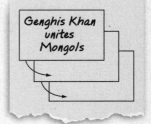

Genghis Khan
unites
Mongols

3.12 Preparing for the Regents

Diversity What evidence supports the claim that diversity was an important characteristic of the Mongol Empire?

3.13 Preparing for the Regents

Power What was one of the effects on Russia of the Mongol invasions?

3.14 Preparing for the Regents

Power Why is Kublai Khan considered one of China's greatest emperors?

⌁**3.15 Preparing for the Regents**

Conflict What happen to the Mongols when they tried to invade Japan in 1281?

After conquering China, Kublai Khan tried to extend his rule to Japan. In 1274 and again in 1281, he sent huge fleets against Japan. The Mongols forced Koreans to build, sail, and provide provisions for the boats, a costly task that almost ruined Korea. Both times the Japanese turned back the Mongol fleets. In 1281, the Mongol fleet was actually destroyed by a typhoon before the ship could escape.

The Mongols in China

Unlike his Mongol ancestors, Kublai abandoned the Mongolian steppes for China. He did not share his ancestors' dislike of the settled life. He maintained a beautiful summer palace at Shangdu, on the border between Mongolia and China. He also built a new square-walled capital at the site of modern Beijing. Previously, the Great Khans had ruled their empire from Mongolia. Moving the capital from Mongolia to China was a sign that Kublai intended to make his mark as emperor of China.

Kublai and the other Mongol rulers had little in common with their Chinese subjects. Mongols lived apart from the Chinese and obeyed different laws. They kept the Chinese out of high government offices, although they retained as many Chinese officials as possible to serve on the local level. Most of the highest government posts went to Mongols or to foreigners. The Mongols believed that foreigners were more trustworthy since they had no local loyalties.

Despite his differences with the Chinese, Kublai Khan was an able leader. He restored the Grand Canal and extended it 135 miles north to Beijing. Along its banks he built a paved highway that ran some 1,100 miles, from Hangzhou to Beijing. These land and water routes ensured the north a steady supply of grain and other goods from the southern heartland.

⌁**3.16 Preparing for the Regents**

Movement of People and Goods Why did foreign trade increase under Kublai Khan?

Foreign trade increased under Kublai Khan. This was largely due to the Mongol Peace—the **Pax Mongolica**—that imposed stability and law and order across much of Eurasia. The Pax Mongolica made the caravan routes across Central Asia safe for missionaries, travelers, and traders. Traders transported Chinese silk and porcelain, which were greatly valued in Europe and western Asia, over the Silk Roads and other routes. These traders also carried with them such Chinese products and inventions as printing, gunpowder, the compass, paper currency, and playing cards. Kublai further encouraged trade by inviting foreign merchants to visit China. Most of them were Muslims from India, Central Asia, and Persia. Many European traders and travelers, including Christian missionaries, also reached China.

The most famous European to visit China in these years was a young Venetian trader, **Marco Polo**. He traveled by caravan on the Silk Roads with his father and uncle, arriving at Kublai Khan's court around 1275. Polo had learned several Asian languages in his travels, and Kublai Khan sent him to various Chinese cities on government missions. Polo served the Great Khan well for 17 years. In 1292, the Polos left China and made the long journey back to Venice.

Decline of the Mongols

Kublai Khan died in 1294. After his death, the Yuan Dynasty began to fade. Family members continually argued over who would rule. Rebellions broke out in many parts of China in the 1300s. The Chinese had long resented their Mongol rulers, and the Mongol humiliation of the Chinese only increased under Kublai Khan's successors. The rebellions were also fueled by years of famine, flood,

⌁**3.18 Preparing for the Regents**

Power What factors contributed to the decline of the Mongols?

and disease, along with growing economic problems and official corruption. In 1368, Chinese rebels finally overthrew the Mongols.

Many of the areas invaded by the Mongols never recovered. The populations of some cities were wiped out. In addition, the Mongols destroyed ancient irrigation systems in areas such as the Tigris and Euphrates valleys. Thus, the land could no longer support resettlement. By the time of the collapse of the Yuan Dynasty, the entire Mongol Empire had disintegrated. The government of the Ilkhanate in Persia fell apart in the 1330s. The Chagatai khans ruled Central Asia until the 1370s. Only the Golden Horde in Russia stayed in power. The Golden Horde ruled Russia for 250 years until Ivan III finally led Russia to independence in 1480.

PREPARING FOR THE REGENTS

Answer the following question. Use the Analyze the Question hints to help you answer the question. Base your answer to question 1 on the map below and your knowledge of social studies.

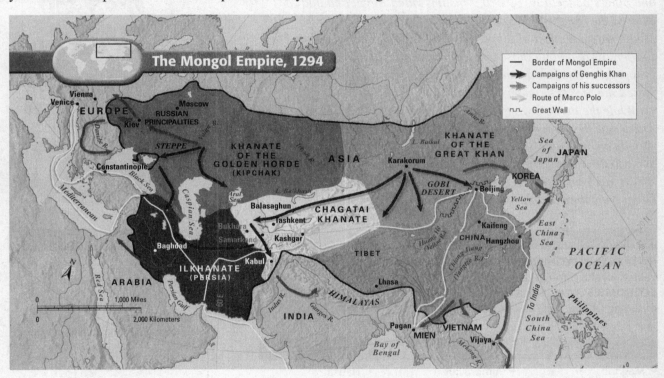

1 The map shows that the Mongol empire stretched across

(1) Africa and Southeast Asia
(2) North America and Europe
(3) Europe and Asia
(4) South America and Asia

ANALYZE THE QUESTION
- Read the question stem. You are being asked to determine how far the Mongol Empire stretched.
- Look at the map. Read the title, legend, and labels to find the information that applies to the extent of Mongol Empire.
- Select the alternative that best matches the information on the map.

African Civilizations

Section Overview

Arab peoples crossed the Red Sea into Africa perhaps as early as 1000 B.C. There they intermarried with Kushite herders and farmers. This blended group of Africans and Arabs would form the basis of a new and powerful trading kingdom—Aksum.

*Aksum's power was eventually ended by the spread of Islam. After Muhammad's death in 632, Muslims swept across the northwest part of the continent. They converted many by conquest and others peacefully. By 670, Muslims ruled Egypt and had entered the **Maghrib**, the part of North Africa that is today the Mediterranean coast of Libya, Tunisia, Algeria, and Morocco. The Berbers were among those who converted to Islam. Two Berber groups, the Almoravids and the Almohads, founded empires that united the Maghrib under Muslim rule.*

While the Berbers were building empires in North Africa, West Africa saw the flourishing of Ghana, Mali, and Songhai. These ancient African empires grew strong by controlling trade. West Africa was also home to the Hausa city-states, the Yoruba kingdoms, and Benin. In East Africa, such city-states as Kilwa thrived, while in southern Africa first Great Zimbabwe and then the Mutapa Empire grew powerful.

Yoruba crown from West Africa

MAIN IDEAS

INTERACTION WITH ENVIRONMENT   African city-states and empires gained wealth through developing and trading resources.
ECONOMICS   West Africa contained several rich and powerful states, including Ghana, Mali, and Songhai.

TERMS AND NAMES

- Maghrib
- Sahara
- Sahel
- savanna
- Aksum
- Ezana
- Adulis
- terraces

- Almoravids
- Almohads
- Ghana
- Mali
- Sundiata
- Mansa Musa
- Ibn Battuta
- Songhai

- Hausa
- Yoruba
- Benin
- Swahili
- Great Zimbabwe
- Mutapa

PREPARING FOR THE REGENTS

As you read this section, consider
- how the rise and fall of African kingdoms compared to the rise and fall of other empires.
- what role the kingdoms played in trade.
- what impact Islam had on African kingdoms.

TIME LINE

320
King Ezana rules Aksum.

800
Empire of Ghana thrives on trade.

1000
Hausa city-states begin to emerge.

1100
Yoruba kingdom of Ife is established.

1235
Sundiata founds Mali Empire.

1324
Mali king Mansa Musa goes on hajj to Mecca.

1464
Sunni Ali begins Songhai Empire.

Human and Physical Geography

Africa stretches 4,600 miles from east to west and 5,000 miles from north to south, occupying about one-fifth of Earth's land surface. Narrow coastlines (50 to 100 miles) lie on either side of a central plateau. Waterfalls and rapids often form as rivers drop down to the coast from the plateau, making navigation impossible to or from the coast. Africa's coastline has few harbors, ports, or inlets.

The deserts are largely unsuitable for human life and also hamper people's movement to more welcoming climates. The largest deserts are the **Sahara** in the north and the Kalahari (kahl•uh•HAHR•ee) in the south. Stretching from the Atlantic Ocean to the Red Sea, the Sahara covers an area roughly the size of the United States. Only a small part of the Sahara consists of sand dunes. The rest is mostly a flat, gray wasteland of scattered rocks and gravel. Each year the desert takes over more and more of the land at the southern edge of the Sahara Desert, the **Sahel** (suh•HAYL).

Africa's rain forest produces mahogany and teak trees up to 150 feet tall. Their leaves and branches form a dense canopy that keeps sunlight from reaching the forest floor. The tsetse (TSET•see) fly is found in the rain forest. Its presence prevented Africans from using cattle, donkeys, and horses to farm near the rain forests. This deadly insect also prevented invaders—especially Europeans—from colonizing fly-infested territories.

The northern coast and the southern tip of Africa have fertile soils and welcoming Mediterranean-type climates. Because these coastal areas are so fertile, they are densely populated with farmers and herders.

Most people in Africa live on the **savannas**, or grassy plains. Africa's savannas include mountainous highlands and swampy tropical stretches. Covered with tall grasses and dotted with trees, the savannas cover over 40 percent of the continent. Dry seasons alternate with rainy seasons—often, two of each a year. Unfortunately, the topsoil throughout Africa is thin, and heavy rains strip away minerals. In most years, however, the savannas support abundant agricultural production.

Aksum

The ancient kingdom of **Aksum** (AHK•soom) arose on a rugged plateau on the Red Sea, in what are now the countries of Eritrea and Ethiopia. Arab traders from across the Red Sea established trading settlements that eventually became colonies of traders and farmers. The first mention of Aksum was in a Greek guidebook written around A.D. 100. It describes Zoskales (ZAHS•kuh•leez), thought to be the first king of Aksum. Under Zoskales and other rulers, Aksum seized areas along the Red Sea and the Blue Nile in Africa and took control of lands on the southwestern Arabian Peninsula. Askum reached its height between A.D. 325 and 360, during the reign of **Ezana** (AY•zah•nah).

Aksum's location and expansion made it a hub for caravan routes to Egypt and Meroë. Access to sea trade on the Mediterranean Sea and Indian Ocean helped Aksum become an international trading power. Traders from Egypt, Arabia, Persia, India, and the Roman Empire crowded Aksum's chief seaport, **Adulis** (AHD•uh•luhs), near present-day Massawa. Aksumite merchants traded necessities such as salt and luxuries such as rhinoceros horns, tortoise shells, ivory, emeralds, and gold. In return, they chose from items such as imported cloth, glass, olive oil, wine, brass, iron, and copper.

Merchants exchanged ideas as well as raw materials and finished goods in Aksum. One of these ideas was Christianity. Under Ezana, Christianity

3.19 Preparing for the Regents

Human and Physical Environment How has Africa's physical environment affected migration? How might this affect cultural diversity and economic development?

3.20 Preparing for the Regents

Movement of People and Goods Why did Aksum experience economic prosperity?

became the kingdom's official religion. The establishment of Christianity was the longest lasting achievement of the Aksumites. Today, the land of Ethiopia, where Aksum was located, is home to millions of Christians.

Aside from Egypt and Meroë, Aksum was the only ancient African kingdom known to have developed a written language. The language, Ge'ez (GEE•ehz), was brought to Aksum by its early Arab inhabitants. It was also the first state south of the Sahara to mint its own coins. The Aksumites constructed **terraces**, or steplike ridges, on the mountain slopes to help them farm their hilly land. The terraces helped the soil retain water and prevented its being washed downhill in heavy rains. The Aksumites dug canals to channel water from mountain streams into the fields and built dams and cisterns, or holding tanks, to store water.

Aksum lasted for 800 years. The kingdom finally declined, however, under Islamic invaders. In 710 they destroyed Adulis. This conquest cut Aksum off from the major ports along both the Red Sea and the Mediterranean. To escape the advancing wave of Islam, Aksum's rulers moved their capital over the mountains into what is now northern Ethiopia. Aksum's new geographic isolation—along with depletion of the forests and soil erosion—led to its decline as a world trading power.

Muslim States

3.21 Preparing for the Regents

Belief Systems What role did the Berbers play in the spread of Islam?

As Islam spread, some African rulers converted. Among the converts were the Berbers. Fiercely independent desert and mountain dwellers, the Berbers were the original inhabitants of North Africa. In the 11th century, Muslim reformers founded the Almoravid (al•muh•RAHV•uhd) Empire. Its members came from a Berber group living in the western Sahara in what is today Mauritania. The movement began after devout Berber Muslims made a hajj, or pilgrimage, to Mecca. On their journey home, they convinced a Muslim scholar from Morocco named Abd Allah Ibn Yasin to return with them to teach their people about Islam. Ibn Yasin's teachings soon attracted followers, and he founded a strict religious brotherhood, known as the **Almoravids**.

In the 1050s, Ibn Yasin led the Almoravids in an effort to spread Islam through conquest. After Ibn Yasin's death in 1059, the Almoravids went on to take Morocco and to found Marrakech, which became their capital. The Almoravids also captured parts of southern Spain, where they were called Moors.

In the mid-1100s, the **Almohads** (AL•moh•HADZ), another group of Berber Muslim reformers, seized power from the Almoravids. The Almohads followed the teachings of Ibn Tumart. After a pilgrimage to Mecca, Ibn Tumart criticized the later Almoravid rulers for moving away from the traditional practice of Islam. The Almohads fought the Almoravids and by 1148 controlled most of Morocco. By the end of the 12th century, they had also conquered much of southern Spain. In Africa, their territory stretched from Marrakech to Tripoli and Tunis on the Mediterranean. While the Almohad Empire lasted just over 100 years, it united the Maghrib under one rule for the first time.

Ghana

TAKING NOTES

Comparing and Contrasting Use a Venn diagram to compare and contrast information about the Mali and Ghana empires.

By A.D. 200, trade across the Sahara had existed for centuries. However, it remained infrequent and irregular because pack animals such as oxen, donkeys, and horses could not travel far in the hot, dry Sahara without rest or water. Then, in the third century A.D., Berber nomads began using camels. The camel could cover as much as 60 miles in a day and go more than ten days without water. With the camel, nomads blazed new routes across the desert and trade increased.

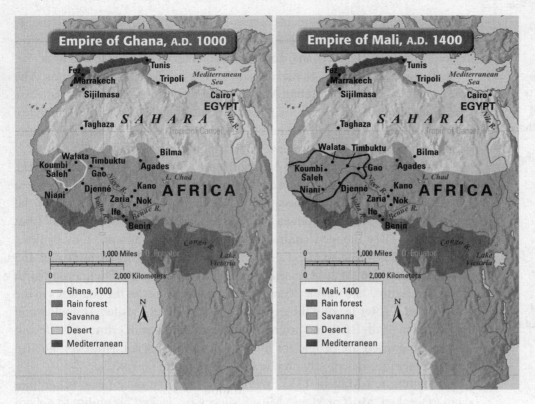

Empire of Ghana, A.D. 1000

Empire of Mali, A.D. 1400

The trade routes crossed the savanna through the region farmed by the Soninke (soh•NIHN•keh) people. The Soninke people called their ruler ghana, or war chief. Muslim traders began to use the word to refer to the Soninke region. By the 700s, **Ghana** was a kingdom, and its rulers were growing rich by taxing the goods that traders carried through their territory.

The two most important trade items were gold and salt. Gold came from a forest region south of the savanna between the Niger (NY•juhr) and Senegal (SEHN•ih•GAWL) rivers. Although rich in gold, West Africa's savanna and forests lacked salt, a material essential to human life. Arab and Berber traders crossed the desert with camel caravans loaded down with salt. Meanwhile, African traders brought gold north from the forest regions. Merchants met in trading cities, where they exchanged goods under the watchful eye of the king's tax collector. By the year 800, Ghana had become an empire.

While Islam spread through North Africa by conquest, it spread south of the Sahara through trade. Ghana's African rulers eventually accepted Islam. Many people in the empire, however, clung to their animistic beliefs and practices and never converted. In 1076 the Muslim Almoravids conquered Ghana. Although the Almoravids eventually withdrew, the war had badly disrupted the gold-salt trade. As a result, Ghana never regained its power.

Mali

By 1235 the kingdom of **Mali** had emerged. Its founders were Mande-speaking people, who lived south of Ghana. Mali's wealth, like Ghana's, was built on gold. Miners found new gold deposits farther east. This caused the most important trade routes to shift eastward, making it possible for Mali to seize power.

Mali's first leader was **Sundiata** (sun•JAHT•ah). After crushing a cruel, unpopular leader, Sundiata became Mali's *mansa*, or emperor. Through a series of military victories, he took over the kingdom of Ghana and the trading cities of Kumbi and Walata. A period of peace, prosperity, and artistic creativity followed.

3.22 Preparing for the Regents

Belief Systems Through what process did Islam spread to Ghana and Mali?

TAKING NOTES

Comparing and Contrasting Use a Venn diagram to compare and contrast information about the Mali and Songhai empires.

Mali

both

Songhai

Sundiata put able administrators in charge of Mali's finances, defense, and foreign affairs. From his new capital at Niani, he promoted agriculture and reestablished the gold-salt trade. Niani became an important center of commerce and trade.

Sundiata died in 1255. Some of Mali's next rulers became Muslims. The most famous of them was **Mansa Musa** (MAHN•sah moo•SAH). Mansa Musa ruled from about 1312 to 1332. Under his leadership, the empire expanded to roughly twice the size of the Ghana Empire. To govern his far-reaching empire, Mansa Musa divided it into provinces and appointed governors.

Mansa Musa went on a hajj to Mecca from 1324 to 1325. When he returned, he ordered the building of new mosques at the trading cities of Gao and Timbuktu (TIHM•buhk•TOO). Timbuktu became one of the most important cities of the empire. It attracted Muslim judges, doctors, religious leaders, and scholars from far and wide. They attended Timbuktu's outstanding mosques and universities.

In 1352, one of Mansa Musa's successors prepared to receive a traveler and historian named **Ibn Battuta** (IHB•uhn ba•TOO•tah). A native of Tangier in North Africa, Ibn Battuta had traveled for 27 years, visiting most of the countries in the Islamic world. After leaving the royal palace, Ibn Battuta visited Timbuktu and other cities in Mali. He found he could travel without fear of crime. As a devout Muslim, he praised the people for their study of the Qur'an. However, he also criticized them for not strictly practicing Islam's moral code.

Ibn Battuta left Mali in 1353. Within 50 years, the once-powerful empire began to weaken. Most of Mansa Musa's successors lacked his ability to govern well. In addition, the gold trade that had been the basis of Mali's wealth shifted eastward as new goldfields were developed elsewhere.

Songhai

As Mali declined in the 1400s, people who had been under its control began to break away. Among them were the **Songhai** (SAWNG•HY) people to the east. They extended their territory to the large bend in the Niger River near Gao and gained control of the all-important trade routes. Gao was the empire's capital.

The Songhai had two extraordinary rulers, both Muslims. One was Sunni Ali, who built a vast empire by military conquest. His rule began in 1464 and lasted almost 30 years. He built a professional army that had a river fleet of war canoes and a mobile fighting force on horseback.

After Sunni Ali's death in 1492, his son succeeded him as ruler. Almost at once, the son faced a major revolt by Muslims who were angry that he did not practice their religion faithfully. A devout Muslim named Askia Muhammad replaced him. During his 37-year rule, Askia Muhammad proved to be an excellent administrator. He set up an efficient tax system and chose able officials.

Despite its wealth and learning, the empire lacked modern weapons. In 1591, a Moroccan fighting force equipped with gunpowder and cannons crossed the Sahara and invaded Songhai. The Moroccan troops quickly defeated the Songhai warriors, who were armed only with swords and spears. The collapse of the Songhai Empire ended a 1,000-year period in which powerful kingdoms and empires ruled the central region of West Africa.

3.23 Preparing for the Regents

Culture and Intellectual Life What evidence is there to support the idea that Mansa Musa's ruled during Mali golden age?

3.24 Preparing for the Regents

Culture and Intellectual Life Who was Ibn Battuta?

3.25 Preparing for the Regents

Movement of People and Goods Why did Songhai experience economic prosperity?

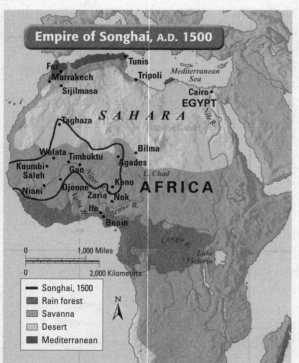

Empire of Songhai, A.D. 1500

Fez
Marrakech
Sijilmasa
Tunis
Tripoli
Mediterranean Sea
Cairo
EGYPT
SAHARA
Taghaza
Welata
Timbuktu
Bilma
Koumbi Saleh
Gao
Agades
Niani
Djenne
Kano
Zaria
Nok
AFRICA
Ife
Benin
L. Chad

0   1,000 Miles
0   2,000 Kilometers

— Songhai, 1500
▪ Rain forest
▪ Savanna
▫ Desert
▪ Mediterranean

N

Other Kingdoms of Africa

While the Ghana, Mali, and Songhai empires rose and fell, city-states developed in other parts of West Africa. The **Hausa** (HOW•suh) profited greatly from supplying the needs of the caravans. Some of the Hausa city-states also conducted a vigorous trade in enslaved persons. The **Yoruba** (YAWR•uh•buh) kingdoms, particularly Ife (EE•fay) and Oyo, were large urban centers where traders and craftspeople live. The Ife were gifted artists who carved in wood and ivory, sculpted in terra cotta, and cast in metal. The people in the kingdom of **Benin** (buh•NIHN) were also gifted artists. The Benin carved in ivory and created brass heads of the royal family, copper figurines, and brass plaques that showed Benin legends, history, and deeds of the rulers.

In East Africa, city-states thrived because of Indian Ocean trade. Many Muslim and Arab traders settled in East African port cities. Arabic blended with the Bantu language to create the **Swahili** (swah•HEE•lee) language. Along with luxury goods and gold, Muslim traders exported enslaved persons from the East African coast. By 1300, more than 35 trading cities dotted the coast from Mogadishu in the north to Kilwa and Sofala in the south. Kilwa grew rich and powerful because it was as far south on the coast as a ship from India could sail in one monsoon season. Therefore, trade goods from southerly regions had to funnel into Kilwa, so Asian merchants could buy them. In addition, Kilwa controlled the port city of Sofala, which was a trading center for gold mined inland. This allowed Kilwa to control the overseas gold trade from southern Africa.

The gold and ivory that helped the coastal city-states grow rich came from the interior of southern Africa. In southeastern Africa the Shona people established a city called **Great Zimbabwe** (zihm•BAHB•way), which grew into an empire built on the gold trade. But by 1450, Great Zimbabwe was abandoned. No one knows for sure why. According to Shona oral tradition, a man named Mutota left Great Zimbabwe about 1420 to find a new source of salt. Traveling north, he founded a new state to replace Great Zimbabwe. It grew into the **Mutapa** Empire.

3.26 Preparing for the Regents

Movement of People and Goods What role did trade play in the city-states of West and East Africa?

PREPARING FOR THE REGENTS

Answer the following question. Use the Analyze the Question hints to help you answer the question.

1 Which term best completes the partial outline below

> I. Rise of civilizations of Ghana and Mali
> A. _____
> B. Spread of Islam
> C. Development of centers of learning

(1) Use of gunpowder
(2) Trade of gold and salt
(3) Development of Hammurabi's Code
(4) Distribution of printing press

ANALYZE THE QUESTION
- Read the question stem. You are being asked to choose which alternative statement will complete the outline about Mali and Ghana.
- Think about what you know about each empire. Rule out any alternative that does not apply to both empires.
- The remaining alternative is the correct answer.

Global Trade and Interactions

Section Overview

Between 1000 and 1300, agriculture, trade, and finance made significant advances in medieval Europe. Towns and cities grew. People were no longer content with their old feudal existence on manors or in tiny villages. Even though legally bound to their lord's manor, many serfs ran away. According to custom, a serf could now become free by living within a town for a year and a day. A saying of the time went, "Town air makes you free."

The growth of cities was linked to the Commercial Revolution, an expansion of trade and finance that changed the way people lived and worked. The merchants and craftspeople who lived in the towns and cities did not fit into the old feudal order. They organized into guilds to control wages and prices. As trade expanded, the merchant-class town dwellers demanded and won new privileges, including the right to govern the towns.

Trade was at the center of the Commercial Revolution. But trade routes brought more than goods. They also brought the dreaded bubonic plague. In the 1300s, the deadly epidemic claimed millions of lives. Unlike catastrophes that pull communities together, this epidemic was so terrifying that it ripped apart the very fabric of society.

The plague brought death to millions in Europe, Asia, and North Africa in the 1300s.

MAIN IDEAS

ECONOMICS   The feudal system declined as agriculture, trade, finance, and towns developed.
CULTURAL INTERACTION   In the 1300s, the bubonic plague struck Europe, Asia, and North Africa.

TERMS AND NAMES

- capitalism
- factors of production
- three-field system
- guild
- Commercial Revolution
- burgher
- Bartolomeu Dias
- Vasco da Gama
- bubonic plague

TIME LINE

1347
Bubonic plague strikes Europe.

1488
Bartolomeu Dias of Portugal sails round tip of Africa

1498
Vasco da Gama of Portugal sails to Calicut, India

PREPARING FOR THE REGENTS

As you read this section, consider
- how the capitalism of the Commercial Revolution was made possible by changes within the European economic system.
- how the Commercial Revolution changed the way men and women worked.
- the role that the bubonic plague played in major demographic and social shifts in Europe, Asia, and North Africa.

Resurgence of Europe

Between 1000 and 1300, Europe's population and economy grew significantly. One aspect of this growth was the rise of **capitalism**. Capitalism is an economic system based on private ownership and the investment of resources, such as money, for profit. The resources needed to produce goods and services for profit are known as **factors of production**. They include land, labor, and capital (money). No longer were governments the sole owners of great wealth. Many merchants had become wealthy through trade. These merchants continued to invest in trade. They also used their profits to invest in other enterprises. As a result, businesses across Europe grew and flourished. The feudal order was giving way to a new economic and social order.

Advances in Agriculture Europe's economic changes would have been impossible without an increased food supply. A warmer climate, which lasted from about 800 to 1200, allowed farmers to cultivate lands in regions once too cold to grow crops. Farmers also developed new methods to take advantage of more available land. One new method was the use of horses rather than oxen to plow fields. A team of horses could plow three times as much land in a day as a team of oxen. Before farmers could use horses, however, they needed a better harness. Sometime before 900, farmers in Europe began using a harness that fitted across the horse's chest, enabling it to pull a plow. As a result, horses gradually replaced oxen for plowing and for pulling wagons.

Another new method, which occurred sometime around 800, was the organization of farmland into three fields instead of two. Two of the fields were planted and the other lay fallow (resting) for a year. Under this new **three-field system**, farmers could grow crops on two-thirds of their land each year, not just on half of it. As a result, food production increased. Well-fed people, especially children, could better resist disease and live longer, and as a result the European population grew dramatically.

Medieval Guilds Another important factor in Europe's economic change was the development of the guild. A **guild** was an organization of individuals in the same business or occupation working to improve the economic and social conditions of its members. The first guilds were merchant guilds. Merchants banded together to control the number of goods being traded and to keep prices up. They also provided security in trading and reduced losses. About the same time, skilled artisans, such as wheelwrights, glassmakers, winemakers, tailors, and druggists, began craft guilds. In most crafts, both husband and wife worked at the family trade. In a few crafts, especially for cloth making, women formed the majority. The guilds set standards for quality of work, wages, and working conditions.

By the 1000s, people were manufacturing goods by hand for local and long-distance trade. More and better products were now available to buyers. Because of the wealth they generated, guilds became powerful political and economic forces.

The Commercial Revolution Just as agriculture was expanding and craftsmanship changing, so were trade and finance. Increased availability of trade goods and new ways of doing business changed life in Europe. Taken together, this expansion of trade and business is called the **Commercial Revolution.**

Most trade took place in towns. Peasants from nearby manors traveled to town on fair days, hauling items to trade. Great fairs were held several times a year, usually during religious festivals, when many people would be in town. People visited the stalls set up by merchants from all parts of Europe. Cloth was

TAKING NOTES
Determining Main Ideas
Use a diagram to identify changes in medieval society.

Changes in Medieval Society

3.27 Preparing for the Regents
Science and Technology What impact did new farming technologies have on Europe during the Middle Ages?

3.28 Preparing for the Regents
Economic Systems What factors contributed to the start of the Commercial Revolution?

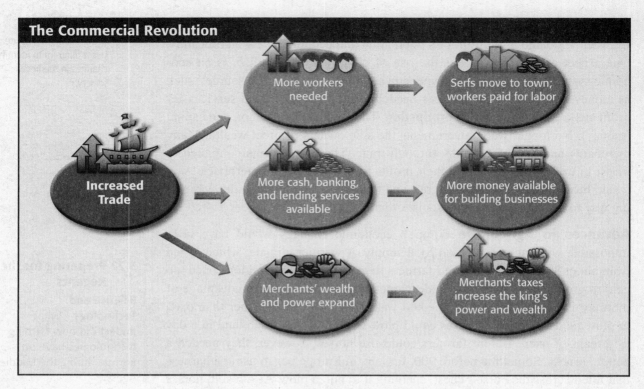

the most common trade item. Other items included bacon, salt, honey, cheese, wine, leather, dyes, knives, and ropes. These markets met all the needs of daily life for a small community. No longer was everything produced on the manor.

More foreign goods became available. Trade routes spread across Europe from Flanders to Italy. Italian merchant ships traveled the Mediterranean to ports such as Constantinople. They also traveled to Muslim ports along the North African coast. Trade routes were opened to Asia, in part by the Crusades.

As traders moved from fair to fair, they needed large amounts of cash or credit and ways to exchange many types of currencies. Enterprising merchants created bills of exchange that established exchange rates between different coinage systems. They also used letters of credit that eliminated the need to carry large amounts of cash and made trading easier. Trading firms and associations formed to offer these services to their groups. Since the Church forbade Christians from lending money at interest, a sin called usury, money lending and banking became the occupation of many of Europe's Jews. Over time, the Church relaxed its rule on usury and Christians entered the banking business. Banking became an important business, especially in Italy.

The Growth of Cities

One of the changes brought about by the Commercial Revolution was where people lived. Scholars estimate that between 1000 and 1150, western Europe's population rose from around 30 million to about 42 million. Towns grew and flourished. Compared to great cities like Constantinople, European towns were unsophisticated and tiny. Europe's largest city, Paris, probably had no more than 60,000 people by the year 1200. A typical medieval town had only about 1,500 to 2,500 people. Even so, towns became a powerful force for change in Europe.

By the later Middle Ages, trade was the very lifeblood of the new towns, which sprung up at ports and crossroads, on hilltops, and along rivers. As trade grew, towns all over Europe swelled with people, drawn by the excitement and bustle. But there were some drawbacks to living in a medieval town. Streets

3.29 Preparing for the Regents

Human and Physical Geography During the Commercial Revolution, where did trading centers most often develop?

were narrow. With no sewers, most people dumped household and human waste into the street in front of the house. Most people never bathed, and their houses lacked fresh air, light, and clean water. Because houses were built of wood with thatched roofs, they were a constant fire hazard.

The Growing Power of the Merchant Class The merchants and crafts-people of medieval towns did not fit into the traditional medieval social order of noble, clergy, and peasant. At first, towns came under the authority of feudal lords, who used their authority to levy fees, taxes, and rents. As trade expanded, the **burghers**, or merchant-class town dwellers, resented this interference in their trade and commerce. They organized themselves and demanded privileges. These included freedom from certain kinds of tolls and the right to govern the town. At times they fought against their landlords and won these rights by force.

Italian City-States and the Hanseatic League European trade was con-trolled by the Italians in the south and the Germans in the north. Overseas trade, spurred by the Crusades, had led to the growth of large city-states in north-ern Italy. A wealthy merchant class developed in each Italian city-state. These merchants dominated politics. Unlike nobles, merchants did not inherit social rank. To succeed in business, they used their wits. As a result, many merchants believed they deserved power and wealth because of their individual merit.

3.30 Preparing for the Regents

Urbanization What effect did the growth of overseas trade have on Italian city-states?

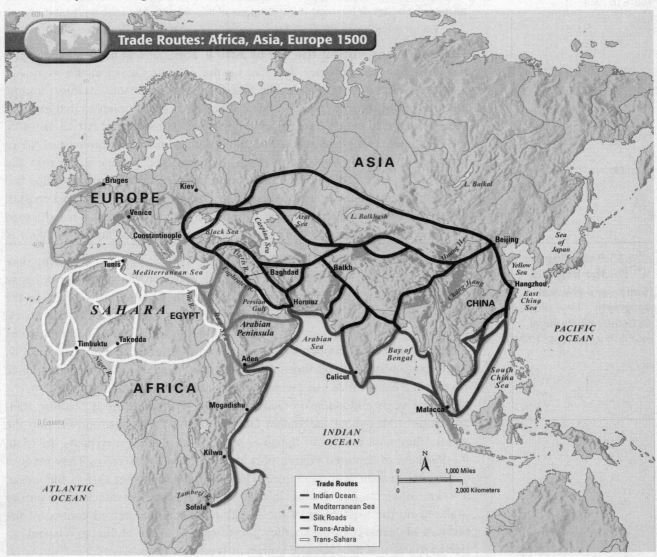

Trade Routes: Africa, Asia, Europe 1500

Trade Routes
— Indian Ocean
— Mediterranean Sea
— Silk Roads
— Trans-Arabia
— Trans-Sahara

3.31 Preparing for the Regents

Movement of People and Goods What was the purpose of the Hanseatic League?

The German trading towns were organized into the Hanseatic League. The purpose of the league was to protect the trading interests of the member towns. Like the Italian city-states of Venice, Pisa, Naples, and Genoa, the major Hanseatic League towns such as Lübeck, Hamburg, Bremen, and Bruges were accessible by water. This allowed them to grow into major centers for sea trade.

Expansion of Portuguese Spice Trade

The Italians and the Muslims controlled Asian trade. Muslims sold Asian goods to Italian merchants, who controlled trade across the land routes of the Mediterranean region. The Italian merchants resold the items at increased prices to merchants throughout Europe. By the 1400s, European merchants—as well as the new monarchs of England, Spain, Portugal, and France—sought to bypass the Italian merchants. This meant finding a sea route directly to Asia. A sea route would allow Europeans to reach such world trade centers as Mogadishu in East Africa, Calicut in India, and Nanjing in China.

3.32 Preparing for the Regents

Science and Technology What new technologies helped Europeans find a sea route to Asia?

During the 1200s, it would have been nearly impossible for a European sea captain to cross 3,000 miles of ocean and return again. European ships could not sail against the wind. Then, in the 1400s, shipbuilders designed a new, sturdier vessel, the caravel. Triangular sails adopted from the Arabs allowed it to sail effectively against the wind. Europeans also improved their navigational techniques. To better determine their location at sea, sailors used the astrolabe, which the Muslims had perfected, and the magnetic compass, a Chinese invention.

Portugal Goes Round the Tip of Africa Portugal was the leader in applying these new technologies. Located on the Atlantic Ocean at the southwest corner of Europe, Portugal was the first European country to establish trading outposts along the west coast of Africa. The Portuguese believed that to reach Asia by sea, they would have to sail around the southern tip of Africa. In 1488, the Portuguese explorer **Bartolomeu Dias** ventured far down the coast of Africa until he and his crew reached the tip. As they arrived, a huge storm rose and battered the fleet for days. When the storm ended, Dias realized his ships had been blown around the tip to the other side. Dias explored the southeast coast of Africa and then considered sailing to India. However, his crew was exhausted and food supplies were low. As a result, the captain returned home.

3.33 Preparing for the Regents

Human and Physical Geography How did Vasco da Gama help Portugal establish a sea route to Asia?

Portugal Reaches Asia With the tip of Africa finally rounded, the Portuguese continued pushing east. In 1497, Portuguese explorer **Vasco da Gama** began exploring the east African coast. In 1498, he reached the port of Calicut, on the southwestern coast of India. Da Gama and his crew were amazed by the spices, rare silks, and precious gems that filled Calicut's shops. They filled their ships with such spices as pepper and cinnamon and returned to Portugal in 1499. Their cargo was worth 60 times the cost of the voyage. Da Gama's remarkable voyage of 27,000 miles had given Portugal a direct sea route to India.

In the years following da Gama's voyage, Portugal built a bustling trading empire throughout the Indian Ocean. As the Portuguese moved into the region, they took control of the spice trade from Muslim merchants. In 1510, the Portuguese captured Goa, a port city on India's west coast. They made it the capital of their trading empire. They then sailed farther east to Indonesia, also known as the East Indies. In 1511, a Portuguese fleet attacked the city of Malacca on the west coast of the Malay Peninsula and seized control of the Strait of Malacca. In doing so, they gained control of the Moluccas—islands so rich in spices that they became known as the Spice Islands.

The Plague

Trade routes carried more than goods. They also carried the deadly disease known as the **bubonic plague**, or Black Death. It got the name from the purplish or blackish spots it produced on the skin. During the 1300s an epidemic struck parts of Asia, North Africa, and Europe. Approximately one-third of the population of Europe died.

The plague began in Asia and traveled the trade routes. In 1347, a fleet of Genoese merchant ships arrived in Sicily carrying plague. The disease swept through Italy. From there it followed trade routes to Spain, France, Germany, England, and other parts of Europe and North Africa.

The bubonic plague took about four years to reach almost every corner of Europe. Some communities escaped unharmed, but in others, approximately two-thirds to three-quarters of those who caught the disease died. Before the bubonic plague ran its course, it killed almost 25 million Europeans and many more millions in Asia and North Africa.

The plague returned every few years, though it never struck as severely as in the first outbreak. However, the periodic attacks further reduced the population. The economic and social effects were enormous. The prestige of the Church suffered when prayer failed to end the plague and priests abandoned their duties. Because there were fewer laborers, survivors could demand higher wages. The old manorial system began to crumble as serfs left the manor in search of higher wages. Nobles fiercely resisted demands for higher wages, causing peasant revolts in England, France, Italy, and Belgium. Trade declined, and prices rose. All over Europe, Jews were blamed for bringing the plague. They were driven from their homes, or worse, massacred. The bubonic plague and its aftermath disrupted medieval society, hastening changes that were already in the making.

Death Tolls, 1300s

Western Europe	☠☠☠☠☠☠	20–25 million
China, India, other Asians	☠☠☠☠☠☠	25 million
	☠ = 4 million	

3.34 Preparing for the Regents

Movement of People and Goods   How did the Black Death spread?

3.35 Preparing for the Regents

Change   What effect did the plague have on the population of Europe?

PREPARING FOR THE REGENTS

Answer the following questions. Use the Analyze the Question hints to help you answer the questions.

1 Which development led to shortages of labor in 14th century Europe?

   (1) rise of nation-states
   (2) outbreak of the Black Death
   (3) fall of Constantinople
   (4) introduction of new military technologies

   ANALYZE THE QUESTION
   - Read the question stem. You are being asked to determine what caused labor shortages in Europe during the 1300s.
   - Think about the focus and time frame of each alternative.
   - Rule out the alternatives that do not fit the time frame or would not have a significant effect on the labor pool. The remaining alternative is the correct answer.

2 Look at the map on page 107. Which economic practice developed as a result of the growth of the trade routes shown on the map?

   (1) capitalism of the Commercial Revolution
   (2) hunting and gathering
   (3) subsistence farming
   (4) manorialism

   ANALYZE THE QUESTION
   - Read the question stem. You are being asked to determine which economic practice developed because of the trade routes shown on the map.
   - Study the map to determine the types and extent of the trade routes.
   - Select the alternative that would be a logical outgrowth of such routes.

European Nation-States

Section Overview

By the early 800s, small Anglo-Saxon kingdoms covered the former Roman province of Britain. In Europe, the decline of the Carolingian Empire in the 900s left a patchwork of feudal states controlled by local lords. Gradually, the growth of towns and villages, and the breakup of the feudal system were leading to more centralized government and the development of nations. The earliest nations in Europe to develop a strong unified government were England and France.

When a nation has its own independent government, it becomes a **nation-state**. *A nation-state defends the nation's territory and way of life. In establishing nation-states, England and France took the first steps along the road to nationalism.* **Nationalism** *is the belief that people's greatest loyalty should not be to a king or empire but to a group of people who share a common culture and history.*

In establishing nation-states, England and France also took the first steps toward a democratic tradition. This tradition rested on setting up a centralized government that would be able to govern widespread lands. The creation of common law and court systems was a first step toward increased central government power. Including commoners in the decision-making process of government was also an important step in the direction of democratic rule.

Coronation of Philip II of France

MAIN IDEAS

RELIGIOUS AND ETHICAL SYSTEMS As the kingdoms of England and France began to develop into nations, certain democratic traditions evolved.

RELIGIOUS AND ETHICAL SYSTEMS In the 1300s, Europe was torn apart by religious strife and the Hundred Years' War.

TERMS AND NAMES

- nation-state
- nationalism
- William the Conqueror
- Henry II
- common law
- Magna Carta
- parliament
- Hugh Capet
- Phillip II
- Estates-General
- Hundred Years' War

PREPARING FOR THE REGENTS

As you read this section, consider
- what forces led to the rise of nation-states.
- the relationship between the rise of strong central governments and nationalism.
- what forces opposed the absolute power of monarchs.
- how the establishment of nation-states led to conflict between secular and church powers.

TIME LINE

987
Capetian dynasty begins in France.

1066
Norman invasion of England.

1215
King John approves Magna Carta.

1453
Hundred Years' War ends with French victory.

England

For centuries, invaders from various regions in Europe landed on English shores. The Angles and the Saxons—two Germanic tribes—stayed, bringing their own ways and creating an Anglo-Saxon culture. In the 800s, Britain was battered by fierce raids of Danish Vikings. Only Alfred the Great, Anglo-Saxon king from 871 to 899, managed to turn back the invaders. Gradually he and his successors united the kingdom under one rule, calling it England, "land of the Angles." In 1016, the Danish king Canute (kuh•NOOT) conquered England, molding Anglo-Saxons and Vikings into one people.

Forces Leading to the Rise of the Nation-State In January 1066, King Edward the Confessor died without an heir. A struggle for the throne erupted, leading to one last invasion. The invader was William, duke of Normandy—**William the Conqueror**. Normandy is a region in the north of France that had been conquered by the Vikings. Its name comes from the French term for the Vikings—North men, or Norman. The Normans were descended from the Vikings, but they were French in language and in culture. As King Edward's cousin, William claimed the English crown and invaded England with a Norman army.

William's rival was Harold Godwinson, the Anglo-Saxon who claimed the throne. On October 14, 1066, Normans and Anglo-Saxons faced off in the Battle of Hastings. The Normans won a decisive victory, changing the course of English history. After his victory, William declared all England his personal property. He kept about one-fifth of England for himself. The English lords who supported Harold lost their lands. William gave their lands to about 200 Norman lords who swore oaths of loyalty to him personally. By doing this, William unified control of the lands and laid the foundation for centralized government in England.

Over the next centuries, English kings tried to achieve two goals—hold and add to their French lands and strengthen their power over the nobles and the Church. One such king was **Henry II**. He added to England's French holdings by marrying Eleanor of Aquitaine from France. The marriage brought Henry a large territory in France called Aquitaine. Because Henry held lands in France, he was a vassal to the French king. But he was also a king in his own right.

The Development of Centralized Government Henry ruled England from 1154 to 1189. He strengthened the royal courts of justice by sending royal judges to every part of England at least once a year. They collected taxes, settled lawsuits, and punished crimes. Henry also introduced the use of the jury in English courts. A jury in medieval England was a group of loyal people—usually 12 neighbors of the accused—who answered a royal judge's questions about the facts of a case. Jury trials became a popular means of settling disputes. Only the king's courts were allowed to conduct them. Over the centuries, case by case, the rulings of England's royal judges formed a unified body of law that became known as **common law**. Today the principles of English common law are the basis for law in many English-speaking countries, including the United States.

Henry was succeeded first by his son Richard the Lion-Hearted. When Richard died, his younger brother John took the throne. John, who ruled from 1199 to 1216, was cruel to his subjects and tried to squeeze money out of them. He alienated the Church and threatened to take away town charters guaranteeing self-government. John raised taxes to an all-time high to finance his wars. After he lost Normandy and all his lands in northern France to the French, his nobles revolted. On June 15, 1215, they forced John to agree to the most celebrated document in English history, the **Magna Carta** (Great Charter).

TAKING NOTES
Clarifying Identify major steps toward democratic government in England.

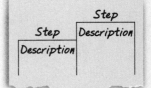

3.36 Preparing for the Regents

Nation State What forces led to the rise of the English nation-state?

3.37 Preparing for the Regents

Power How did the rise of the nation-state affect the power of nobles?

3.38 Preparing for the Regents

Nationalism How might nationalism support a strong central government?

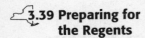
The Magna Carta guaranteed certain basic political rights. The nobles wanted to safeguard their own feudal rights and limit the king's powers. In later years, however, English people of all classes argued that certain clauses in the Magna Carta applied to every citizen. Guaranteed rights included no taxation without representation, a jury trial, and the protection of the law. The Magna Carta guaranteed what are now considered basic legal rights both in England and in the United States.

Another important step toward democratic government came during the rule of England's next king, Edward I. Edward needed to raise taxes for a war. In 1295, Edward summoned two burgesses (citizens of wealth and property) from every borough (self-governing town) and two knights from every county to serve as a **parliament**, or legislative group. In November 1295, knights, burgesses, bishops, and lords met together at Westminster in London. This is now called the Model Parliament because its new makeup (commoners, or non-nobles, as well as lords) served as a model for later kings.

Over the next century, from 1300 to 1400, the king called the knights and burgesses whenever a new tax was needed. In Parliament, these two groups gradually formed an assembly of their own called the House of Commons. Nobles and bishops met separately as the House of Lords. Under Edward I, Parliament was in part a royal tool that weakened the great lords. As time went by, Parliament became strong. Like the Magna Carta, it provided a check on royal power.

France

The kings of France, like those of England, looked for ways to increase their power. After the breakup of Charlemagne's empire, French counts and dukes ruled their lands independently under the feudal system. In 987, the last member of the Carolingian family—Louis the Sluggard—died. **Hugh Capet** (kuh•PAY), an undistinguished duke from the middle of France, succeeded him. Hugh Capet began the Capetian dynasty of French kings that ruled France from 987 to 1328.

Forces Leading to the Rise of the Nation-State
The Capetian territory, though small, included Paris and sat astride important trade routes in northern France. For 300 years, Capetian kings tightened their grip on this strategic area. The power of the king gradually spread outward from Paris. Eventually, the growth of royal power would unite France.

One of the most powerful Capetians was **Philip II**, who ruled from 1180 to 1223. As a child, Philip had watched his father lose land to King Henry II of England. When Philip became king at the age of 15, he set out to weaken the power of the English kings in France. Philip had little success against Henry II or Richard the Lion-Hearted. However, when King John gained the English throne, it was another matter. Philip seized Normandy and other lands from John. By the end of Philip's reign, he had tripled the lands under his direct control. For the first time, a French king had become more powerful than any of his vassals.

The Development of Centralized Government
Philip II not only wanted more land, he also wanted a stronger central government. He established royal officials called bailiffs. They were sent from Paris to every district in the kingdom to preside over the king's courts and to collect the king's taxes.

France's central government became even stronger during the reign of Philip's grandson, Louis IX, who ruled from 1226 to 1270. Louis created a French appeals court, which could overturn the decisions of local courts. These royal courts of France strengthened the monarchy while weakening feudal ties.

TAKING NOTES

Clarifying Identify major steps toward democratic government in France.

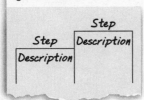

3.40 Preparing for the Regents

Nation State What forces led to the rise of the French nation-state?

Philip IV, who ruled France from 1285 to 1314, took another step toward strengthening the central government. In 1302, Philip was involved in a quarrel with Pope Boniface VIII. The pope refused to allow priests to pay taxes to the king. Philip disputed the right of the pope to control Church affairs in his kingdom. As in England, the French king usually called a meeting of his lords and bishops when he needed support for his policies. To win wider support against the pope, Philip IV decided to include commoners in the meeting.

In France, the Church leaders were known as the First Estate, and the great lords as the Second Estate. The commoners, wealthy landholders or merchants, that Philip invited to participate in the council became known as the Third Estate. The whole meeting was called the **Estates-General**. Like the English Parliament in its early years, the Estates-General helped to increase royal power against the nobility. Unlike Parliament, however, it did not become an independent force that limited the king's power.

Philip's confrontation with the pope had another consequence—it weakened the Church's secular power. When Philip asserted his authority over French bishops, Boniface responded with an official document stating that kings must always obey popes. Instead of obeying, Philip had the pope held prisoner. The king planned to bring him to France for trial. The elderly pope was rescued, but died a month later. Never again would a pope be able to force monarchs to obey him.

The Hundred Years' War

English attempts to hold their French lands often led to conflict. When the last Capetian king died without a successor, England's Edward III, as grandson of Philip IV, claimed the French throne. The war that this launched continued on and off from 1337 to 1453. It became known as the **Hundred Years' War**. Victory passed back and forth between the two countries. Finally, between 1421 and 1453, the French rallied and drove the English out of France entirely, except Calais.

One of the consequences of the Hundred Years' War was the feeling of nationalism that emerged in England and France. Now people thought of the king as a national leader, fighting for the glory of the country, not simply as a feudal lord. Some historians consider the end of the war in 1453 as the end of the Middle Ages. The twin pillars of the medieval world, religious devotion and the code of chivalry, both crumbled. Chivalry died on the battlefields of the war. The Age of Faith died slowly as the Church's authority was challenged.

3.41 Preparing for the Regents

Power How did the rise of the French nation-state lead to conflict with the Church?

3.42 Preparing for the Regents

Nationalism How did the Hundred Years War contribute to feelings of nationalism?

PREPARING FOR THE REGENTS

On a separate sheet of paper, write a well-organized essay that includes an introduction, several paragraphs addressing the task below, and a conclusion. Before beginning, check the Score the Essay box for pointers.

Theme: Nationalism
Nationalism is a powerful force that can have positive and negative effects on nations and regions.

Task:
• Define the term *nationalism*
• Discuss the positive and negative effects that the rise of nationalism had on England and France

Be sure to include specific examples in your essay.

SCORE THE ESSAY To receive a score of 5 on your essay, you will need to:
• thoroughly develop all aspects of the task evenly and in depth by describing both the positive and negative effects that the rise of nationalism had on England and France.
• be more analytical than descriptive.
• richly support the theme with relevant facts, examples, and details.
• demonstrate a logical and clear plan of organization.

Renaissance and Humanism

SECTION 6

Section Overview

During the late Middle Ages, Europe suffered from both plague and war. Those who survived wanted to celebrate life and the human spirit. They began to question institutions of the Middle Ages, which had been unable to relieve suffering brought by the plague or to prevent war. Some people questioned the Church, which taught Christians to endure suffering while they awaited their rewards in heaven. In northern Italy, writers and artists began to express this new spirit and to experiment with different styles. This movement became known as the Renaissance.

The Renaissance produced extraordinary achievements in many different forms of art, including painting, architecture, sculpture, and drawing. These art forms where used by talented artists to express important ideas and attitudes of the age. The work of such artists as Leonardo da Vinci, Michelangelo, and Raphael showed the Renaissance spirit. All three artists demonstrated an interest in classical culture, a curiosity about the world, and a belief in human potential.

Humanist writers expanded ideas about individuality. The Renaissance belief in the dignity of the individual played a key role in the gradual rise of democratic ideas. Furthermore, the impact of the movable-type printing press was tremendous. Some historians have suggested that its effects were even more dramatic than the arrival of personal computers in the 20th century.

Renaissance writer Niccolò Machiavelli, author of *The Prince* (1513)

MAIN IDEAS

CULTURAL INTERACTION Trade with the East and the rediscovery of ancient manuscripts caused Europeans to develop new ideas about culture and art. The period was called the "Renaissance," which means rebirth.
REVOLUTION The invention of the printing press allowed books and pamphlets to be made faster and more cheaply. This new technology helped spread the revolutionary ideas of the Renaissance.

TERMS AND NAMES

- Renaissance
- humanism
- patron
- perspective
- vernacular
- utopia
- William Shakespeare
- Johann Gutenberg

PREPARING FOR THE REGENTS

As you read this section, consider
- in what ways the Renaissance period was like the medieval period and how it was different.

TIME LINE

1300
The Renaissance begins in Italian city-states such as Florence, Milan, and Mantua.

1434
Medici family takes control of Florence.

1455
Gutenberg Bible printed in Mainz.

Human and Physical Geography

From approximately 1300 to 1600, Europe experienced an explosion of creativity in art, writing, and thought. This artistic and intellectual movement began in northern Italy and eventually spread to the rest of Europe. Historians call this period the **Renaissance** (REHN•ih•SAHNS), which means rebirth. In this context, it refers to a revival of art and learning. The educated men and women of Italy hoped to bring back to life the culture of classical Greece and Rome. Yet in striving to revive the past, the people of the Renaissance created something new.

Italy had three advantages that made it the birthplace of the Renaissance. First, overseas trade had led to the growth of large city-states in northern Italy. The region also had many sizable towns. Thus, northern Italy was urban while the rest of Europe was still mostly rural. Since cities are often places where people exchange ideas, they were an ideal breeding ground for an intellectual revolution.

Second, a wealthy merchant class developed in each Italian city-state. In the 1300s, the bubonic plague struck these cities hard, killing up to 60 percent of the population. This brought economic changes. Because there were fewer laborers, survivors could demand higher wages. With few opportunities to expand business, merchants began to pursue other interests, such as art.

Third, Renaissance scholars looked down on the art and literature of the Middle Ages. Instead, they wanted to return to the learning of the Greeks and Romans. They achieved this in several ways. The artists, architects, and scholars of Italy drew inspiration from the ruins of Rome that surrounded them. Scholars also studied ancient Latin manuscripts that had been preserved in monasteries and Greek manuscripts that had been brought to Rome when Christian scholars fled Constantinople as it fell to the Turks in 1453.

A Shift in Worldview—the Birth of Humanism

The study of classical texts helped scholars develop a new outlook on life and art. This led to **humanism**, an intellectual movement that focused on human potential and achievements. Instead of trying to make classical texts agree with Christian teaching as medieval scholars had, humanists studied them to understand ancient Greek values. Humanists influenced artists and architects to carry on classical traditions. Also, humanists popularized the study of subjects common to classical education, such as history, literature, and philosophy. These subjects are called the humanities.

In the Middle Ages, some people had demonstrated their piety by wearing rough clothing and eating plain foods. Humanists suggested that a person might enjoy life without offending God. In Renaissance Italy, the wealthy enjoyed material luxuries, good music, and fine foods. Most people remained devout Catholics. However, the basic spirit of Renaissance society was secular—worldly rather than spiritual and concerned with the here and now. Even church leaders became more worldly. Some lived in beautiful mansions and wore expensive clothes.

Church leaders, successful merchants, and wealthy families became **patrons** of the arts by financially supporting artists. Church leaders beautified Rome and other cities by spending huge amounts of money on art. The wealthy demonstrated their own importance by having their portraits painted or by donating art to the city to place in public squares. Among the most influential of the wealthy patrons was the Medici (MEHD•ih•chee) family, a powerful banking family that eventually took political control of Florence in 1434.

TAKING NOTES

Outlining Use an outline to organize main ideas and details.

Italian Renaissance
I. Italy's advantages
    A.
    B.
II. Classical and worldly values

3.43 Preparing for the Regents

Environment and Society What were the main reasons that the Renaissance began in Italy?

3.44 Preparing for the Regents

Culture and Intellectual Life What was humanism? How was humanism influenced by ancient Greek thought?

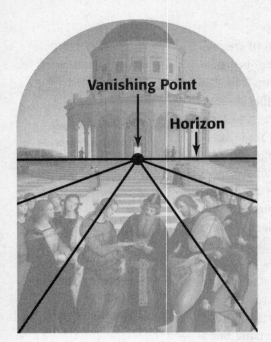

Vanishing Point

Horizon

▲ Perspective is based on an optical illusion. As parallel lines stretch away from the viewer, they seem to draw together, until they meet at a spot on the horizon called the vanishing point.

Renaissance writers introduced the idea that all educated people were expected to create art. In fact, the ideal individual strove to master almost every area of study. A man who excelled in many fields was praised as a "universal man." Later ages called such people "Renaissance men." To learn how to become such a person, Renaissance men could turn to *The Courtier* (1528), a book by Baldassare Castiglione (KAHS•teel•YOH•nay). According to the book, a young man should be charming, witty, and well educated in the classics. The book advised upper-class women to know the classics and be charming. Yet women were not expected to seek fame. They were expected to inspire art but rarely to create it.

Renaissance Art and Architecture

As the Renaissance advanced, artistic styles changed. Medieval artists had used religious subjects to convey a spiritual ideal. Renaissance artists often portrayed religious subjects, but they used a realistic style copied from classical models. Greek and Roman subjects also became popular. Renaissance painters used the technique of **perspective**, which shows three dimensions on a flat surface. Classical artists had used perspective, but medieval artists had abandoned the technique.

Michelangelo and Donatello Artists such as the sculptor, poet, architect, and painter Michelangelo (MY•kuhl•AN•juh•LOH) Buonarroti used a realistic style when depicting the human body. Among Michelangelo's achievements are the paintings on the ceiling of the Sistine Chapel. Donatello (DAHN•uh•TEHL•oh) made sculpture more realistic by carving natural postures and expressions that reveal personality. He revived a classical form in his statue of David, a boy who, according to the Bible, became a great king. It was the first European sculpture of a large, free-standing nude since ancient times. For sculptors of the period, including Michelangelo, David was a favorite subject.

🗽 **3.45 Preparing for the Regents**

Culture and Intellectual Life What are some of the characteristics of Italian Renaissance art?

Leonardo and Raphael Painter, sculptor, inventor, and scientist Leonardo da Vinci (LAY•uh•NAHR•doh duh•VIHN•chee) was a true "Renaissance man." He was interested in how things worked. He filled his notebooks with observations and sketches. Then he incorporated his findings in his art. Among his many masterpieces was the *Mona Lisa*. The woman in the portrait seems so real that many writers have tried to explain the thoughts behind her smile. Raphael (RAHF•ee•uhl) Sanzio was younger than Michelangelo and Leonardo. He learned from studying their works. He was famous for his use of perspective. One of his paintings, *School of Athens*, conveys the classical influence on the Renaissance.

Anguissola and Gentileschi Renaissance society generally restricted the roles of women. However, a few Italian women became notable painters. Sofonisba Anguissola (ahng•GWEES•soh•lah) was the first woman artist to gain an international reputation. Artemisia Gentileschi (JAYN•tee•LEHS•kee) was another accomplished artist. She trained with her painter father and helped with his work. In her own paintings, Gentileschi painted pictures of strong, heroic women.

Flemish Painters By 1450 the population of northern Europe, which had declined due to bubonic plague, was beginning to grow. When the Hundred Years' War between France and England ended in 1453, many cities grew rapidly. Urban merchants became wealthy enough to sponsor artists. This happened first in Flanders, which was rich from long-distance trade and the cloth industry.

The first great Flemish Renaissance painter was Jan van Eyck (yahn van YK). Van Eyck used recently developed oil-based paints to develop techniques that painters still use. Van Eyck's paintings display unusually realistic details and reveal the personality of their subjects. Flemish painting reached its peak after 1550 with the work of Pieter Bruegel (BROY•guhl) the Elder. Bruegel was also interested in realistic details and individual people. He captured scenes from everyday peasant life such as weddings, dances, and harvests.

German Painters Northern European artists who studied in Italy carried Renaissance ideas back to their homelands. Perhaps the most famous person to do this was the German artist Albrecht Dürer (DYUR•uhr). He traveled to Italy to study in 1494. After returning to Germany, Dürer produced woodcuts and engravings. The popularity of Dürer's work helped to spread Renaissance styles. Dürer's emphasis upon realism influenced the work of another German artist, Hans Holbein (HOHL•byn) the Younger. Holbein specialized in painting portraits that are almost photographic in detail.

Architecture The Italians looked to ancient Greece and Rome for inspiration in architecture but created a style that was very much their own. The principles of Renaissance architecture were laid out in a book by Leon Battista Alberti (ahl•BEHR•tee), first printed in 1485. In the book, Alberti defined in mathematical detail the elements and strict proportions of the new architecture. He also discussed construction methods and even gave advice on city planning. Among the greatest of Renaissance buildings was St. Peter's in Rome, with its massive dome designed by Michelangelo. The building, which was initially designed by architect Donato Bramante (brah•MAHN•tay), took 120 years to complete. Over that time, many people worked on it, including Raphael and Michelangelo.

Renaissance Writers

Renaissance writers produced works that reflected their time, but they also used techniques that writers rely on today. Some followed the example of the medieval writer Dante, who wrote in the **vernacular**, his native language, instead of Latin. In addition, Renaissance writers wrote either for self-expression or to portray the individuality of their subjects.

Petrarch and Boccaccio Francesco Petrarch (PEE•trahrk) was one of the earliest and most influential humanists. Some have called him the father of Renaissance humanism. He was also a great poet. Petrarch wrote both in Italian and in Latin. In Italian, he wrote sonnets—14 line poems. They were about a mysterious woman named Laura, who was his ideal.

The Italian writer Boccaccio (boh•KAH•chee•oh) is best known for the *Decameron*, a series of realistic, sometimes off-color stories. The stories are supposedly told by a group of worldly young people waiting in a rural villa to avoid the plague sweeping through Florence. Boccaccio presents his characters in all their individuality and all their folly.

Machiavelli *The Prince* (1513), by the Italian writer Niccolò Machiavelli (MAK•ee• uh•VEHL•ee), also explores the imperfect conduct of human beings. In the book, Machiavelli examines how a ruler can gain power and keep it in spite of his enemies. In answering this question, Machiavelli begins with the idea that most people are selfish, fickle, and corrupt. To succeed in such a wicked world, Machiavelli said, a prince must be strong as a lion and shrewd as a fox. He might have to trick his enemies and even his own people for the good of the state. In

3.46 Preparing for the Regents
Culture and Intellectual Life What are some of the characteristics of the art created by the Flemish and German artists of the Northern Renaissance?

3.47 Preparing for the Regents
Culture and Intellectual Life What is vernacular? Why do you think some Renaissance writers began publishing books in the vernacular?

3.48 Preparing for the Regents
Political Systems According to Niccolò Machiavelli's book *The Prince*, what does a wise ruler do?

The Prince, Machiavelli was not concerned with what was morally right, but with what was politically effective.

Vittoria Colonna The women writers who gained fame during the Renaissance usually wrote about personal subjects, not politics. Yet, some of them had great influence. Vittoria Colonna (1492–1547), who was born of a noble family, exchanged sonnets with Michelangelo and helped Castiglione publish *The Courtier*. Her own poems expressed personal emotions.

3.49 Preparing for the Regents
Belief Systems How did the views of Christian humanists differ from medieval Christian views?

Christian Humanists When the Italian humanist ideas reached the north, people used them to examine the traditional teachings of the Church. The northern humanists were critical of the failure of the Christian Church to inspire people to live a Christian life. This criticism produced a new movement known as Christian humanism. The focus of Christian humanism was the reform of society. Of particular importance to humanists was education. The humanists promoted the education of women and founded schools attended by both boys and girls.

The best known of the Christian humanists were Desiderius Erasmus (DEHZ•ih•DEER•ee•uhs ih•RAZ•muhs) of Holland and Thomas More of England. The two were close friends. In 1509, Erasmus wrote his most famous work, *The Praise of Folly*. This book poked fun at greedy merchants, heartsick lovers, quarrelsome scholars, and pompous priests. Erasmus believed in a Christianity of the heart, not one of ceremonies or rules. He thought that in order to improve society, all people should study the Bible.

Thomas More tried to show a better model of society. In 1516, he wrote the book *Utopia*. In Greek, **utopia** means "no place." In English it has come to mean an ideal place as depicted in More's book. The book is about an imaginary land where greed, corruption, and war have been weeded out.

Christine de Pizan Christine de Pizan was one of the first women to earn a living as a writer. Writing in French, she produced many books, including short stories, biographies, novels, and manuals on military techniques. She frequently wrote about the objections men had to educating women and was one of the first European writers to question different treatment of boys and girls.

3.50 Preparing for the Regents
Culture and Intellectual Life What was the Elizabethan Age?

Shakespeare and the Elizabethan Age The Renaissance spread to England in the mid-1500s. The period was known as the Elizabethan Age, after Queen Elizabeth I, who reigned from 1558 to 1603. Elizabeth was well educated and spoke French, Italian, Latin, and Greek. She also wrote poetry and music. As queen she did much to support the development of English art and literature.

The most famous writer of the period was **William Shakespeare**, born in 1564. Many people regard him as the greatest playwright of all time. Like many Renaissance writers, Shakespeare revered the classics and drew on them for inspiration and plots. His works display a masterful command of the English language and a deep understanding of human beings. Shakespeare's most famous plays include the tragedies *Macbeth, Hamlet, Romeo and Juliet,* and *King Lear*, and the comedies *A Midsummer Night's Dream* and *The Taming of the Shrew*.

Innovations in Science and Technology

Renaissance achievements were not limited to art, architecture, and writing. The Renaissance was also a period of innovation in science and technology. This innovation was driven in part by practical needs. The feudal system and the Black Death had produced labor shortages. Thus, people had an incentive to develop labor-saving machines and to find alternatives to human power.

Innovations in Sea Travel The 1400s bought innovations in shipbuilding and navigation. The caravel, with its triangular sails and sturdy design, could travel to distant ports and back. Sailors were aided by navigational tools such as the magnetic compass, first developed by the Chinese, and the astrolabe, which the Muslims had perfected. The astrolabe was a brass circle with carefully adjusted rings marked off in degrees. Using the rings to sight the stars, a sea captain could calculate latitude, or how far north or south of the equator the ship was. Sailors were also aided by the rediscovery and translation of *Geography*, a text written by Ptolemy, the second-century geographer, mathematician, and astronomer from Alexandria. Although not entirely accurate, the maps created from the information in Ptolemy's text presented a more realistic view of the known world than medieval maps. Renaissance mapmakers built on these maps over time.

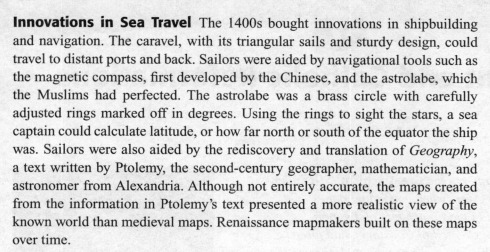

3.51 Preparing for the Regents

Human and Physical Geography How did the rediscovery of Ptolemy's *Geography* assist sea travel?

Gutenberg Improves the Printing Press Ptolemy's text might not have had the impact that it did if it were not for advances in printing that allowed it to be widely distributed. During the 13th century, block-printed items reached Europe from China, where block printing was invented. In block printing, a printer carved words or letters on a wooden block, inked the block, and then used it to print on paper. European printers began using block printing to create whole pages that were then bound into books. However, this process was too slow to satisfy the Renaissance demand for knowledge, information, and books.

Around 1440 **Johann Gutenberg**, a craftsman from Mainz, Germany, developed a screw-type printing press that was an adaptation of an Asian olive-oil press. The press used movable metal type, or a separate piece of type for each letter. The letters could be put together in any fashion and reused. (The Chinese had invented wooden moveable type around 1045, but it proved impractical because of the thousands of characters in the Chinese language.) Gutenberg's process made it possible to produce books quickly and cheaply. Using this improved process, Gutenberg printed a complete Bible, the Gutenberg Bible, in about 1455. It was the first full-sized book printed with movable type. The printing press enabled a printer to produce hundreds of copies of a single work. For the first time, books were cheap enough that many people could buy them.

3.52 Preparing for the Regents

Science and Technology What impact did Gutenberg's printing press have on Renaissance society, and how did it change the course of history?

PREPARING FOR THE REGENTS

On a separate sheet of paper, write a well-organized essay that includes an introduction, several paragraphs addressing the task below, and a conclusion. Before beginning, check the Score the Essay box for pointers.

Theme: Turning Points

Turning points are major events in history that have led to lasting change. The Renaissance is one of those turning points.

Task:

- Describe the historical circumstances surrounding the Renaissance
- Explain how the Renaissance changed the course of history

Be sure to include specific examples in your essay.

SCORE THE ESSAY To receive a score of 5 on your essay, you will need to:

- thoroughly develop all aspects of the task evenly and in depth by describing the historical circumstances surrounding the Renaissance and explaining how the Renaissance changed the course of history.
- be more analytical than descriptive.
- richly support the theme with relevant facts, examples, and details.
- demonstrate a logical and clear plan of organization.

Protestant and Catholic Reformations

Section Overview

The Catholic Church had weathered the **Great Schism** *(SIHZ•uhm),
or division, during the Middle Ages, when competing popes
were established in Rome and in the French city of Avignon
(av•vee•NYAWN). In 1417, the Council of Constance had forced
the rival popes to resign and had chosen a new pope. However, the
papacy had been left greatly weakened. By 1500, the Church faced
growing criticism. Prompted by the actions of one man—Martin
Luther—that criticism would lead to religious reform that gave rise
to a new branch of Christianity—Protestantism.*

*Martin Luther launched Protestantism in northern Germany,
but reformers were soon at work in other countries. In Switzerland,
another major branch of Protestantism emerged. Based mainly
on the teachings of John Calvin, a French follower of Luther, it
promoted unique ideas about the relationship between people and
God. Under the leadership of Queen Elizabeth I, the Anglican
Church, though Protestant, remained similar to the Catholic
Church in many of its doctrines and ceremonies. Prompted by the
growth of Protestantism, the Catholic Church made reforms.*

Martin Luther (1483–1546),
leader of the Protestant Reformation

MAIN IDEAS

RELIGIOUS AND ETHICAL SYSTEMS Martin Luther began a movement to
reform practices in the Catholic Church that he believed were wrong. That
movement, the Reformation, led to the founding of non-Catholic churches.
RELIGIOUS AND ETHICAL SYSTEMS As Protestant reformers divided
over beliefs, the Catholic Church made reforms.

TERMS AND NAMES

- Great Schism
- indulgence
- Reformation
- Lutheran
- Protestant
- Peace of Augsburg

- annul
- Anglican
- predestination
- Calvinism
- theocracy
- Presbyterian

- Anabaptist
- Catholic
  Reformation
- Jesuits
- Council of Trent

TIME LINE

1517
Martin Luther begins the
Reformation in Wittenberg.

1534
English king Henry VIII starts the
Church of England.

1563
Council of Trent mandates reforms
in Catholic Church.

PREPARING FOR THE REGENTS

As you read this section, consider
- how the Reformation challenged the traditional power and authority of
  the Roman Catholic Church,
- how religious reform led to conflict.
- to what extent the conflict was resolved.

Human and Physical Geography

By 1500, the Church faced growing criticism. The Renaissance emphasis on the secular and the individual challenged Church authority. The printing press spread these secular ideas. In addition, some rulers began to challenge the Church's political power, and northern merchants resented paying church taxes to Rome. Critics of the Church claimed that its leaders were corrupt. The popes who ruled during the Renaissance patronized the arts, spent extravagantly on personal pleasure, and fought wars. Many popes were too busy pursuing worldly affairs to have much time for spiritual duties. The lower clergy had problems as well. Many priests and monks were so poorly educated that they could scarcely read, let alone teach people. Others broke their priestly vows by marrying, and some drank to excess or gambled.

Prompted by reformers, people had come to expect higher standards of conduct from priests and church leaders. In the late 1300s and early 1400s, John Wycliffe (WIHK•lihf) of England and Jan Hus of Bohemia (now part of the Czech Republic) had advocated Church reform. They denied that the pope had the right to worldly power. They also taught that the Bible had more authority than Church leaders did. In the 1500s, Christian humanists like Desiderius Erasmus and Thomas More added their criticisms. In addition, many Europeans were reading religious works and forming their own opinions about the Church. The atmosphere in Europe was ripe for reform. Prompted by the actions of one man—Martin Luther—calls for reform would lead to a religious revolution.

3.53 Preparing for the Regents

Belief Systems   Why were some people critical of the Catholic Church?

Martin Luther

Martin Luther was a monk and a teacher. From 1512 until his death, he taught scripture at the University of Wittenberg in the German state of Saxony.

The 95 Theses In 1517, Luther decided to take a public stand against the actions of Johann Tetzel, a friar who was selling indulgences to raise money for the Church. An **indulgence** was a pardon. It released a sinner from performing the penalty that a priest imposed for sins. Indulgences were not supposed to affect God's right to judge. Unfortunately, Tetzel gave people the impression that they could buy their way into heaven with indulgences.

Troubled by Tetzel's tactics, Luther wrote 95 Theses, or formal statements, attacking the "pardon-merchants." On October 31, 1517, he posted these statements on the door of the castle church in Wittenberg and invited other scholars to debate him. Someone copied Luther's words and took them to a printer. Quickly, Luther's name became known all over Germany. His actions began the **Reformation**, a movement for religious reform. It led to the founding of Christian churches that did not accept the pope's authority.

Soon Luther went beyond criticizing indulgences. He wanted full reform of the Church. His teachings rested on three main ideas: 1) People could win salvation only by faith in God's gift of forgiveness. The Church taught that faith and "good works" were needed for salvation. 2) All Church teachings should be clearly based on the words of the Bible. Both the pope and Church traditions were false authorities. 3) All people with faith were equal. Therefore, people did not need priests to interpret the Bible for them.

The Response to Luther Initially, Church officials in Rome viewed Luther simply as a rebellious monk who needed to be punished by his superiors. However, as Luther's ideas became more popular, the pope realized that Luther was a serious threat. In 1520, Pope Leo X issued a decree threatening Luther with

3.54 Preparing for the Regents

Belief Systems   Why is Martin Luther's posting of the 95 Theses considered by many to be a turning point in history?

TAKING NOTES
Recognizing Effects
Use a chart to identify the effects of Martin Luther's protests.

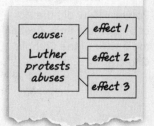

excommunication unless he took back his statements. When Luther responded by burning the decree, Leo excommunicated him.

Holy Roman Emperor Charles V, a devout Catholic, also opposed Luther's teaching. Charles controlled a vast empire, including the German states. He summoned Luther to the town of Worms (vawrmz) in 1521 to stand trial. Told to recant, or take back his statements, Luther refused. A month later, Charles issued an imperial order, the Edict of Worms. It declared Luther an outlaw and a heretic.

Luther returned to Wittenberg in 1522. There he discovered that many of his ideas were already being put into practice. Instead of continuing to seek reforms in the Catholic Church, Luther and his followers had become a separate religious group, called **Lutherans**.

Many northern German princes supported Lutheranism. While some princes genuinely shared Luther's beliefs, others liked Luther's ideas for selfish reasons. They saw his teachings as a good excuse to seize Church property and to assert their independence from Charles V. In 1529, German princes who remained loyal to the pope agreed to join forces against Luther's ideas. Those princes who supported Luther signed a protest against that agreement. These protesting princes came to be known as Protestants. Eventually, the term **Protestant** was applied to Christians who belonged to non-Catholic churches.

Still determined that his subjects should remain Catholic, Charles V went to war against the Protestant princes. Even though he defeated them in 1547, he failed to force them back into the Catholic Church. In 1555, Charles, weary of fighting, ordered all German princes, both Protestant and Catholic, to assemble in the city of Augsburg. There the princes agreed that each ruler would decide the religion of his state. This agreement is known as the **Peace of Augsburg**.

Henry VIII and the English Reformation

The Catholic Church soon faced another great challenge to its authority, this time in England. When Henry VIII became king of England in 1509, he was a devout Catholic. Political needs, however, soon tested his religious loyalty. He needed a male heir. Henry and his wife, Catherine of Aragon, had one living child— a daughter, Mary—but no woman had ever successfully claimed the English throne. Convinced that the 42-year old Catherine would have no more children, he wanted to divorce her and take a younger queen. Church law did not allow divorce. However, the pope could **annul**, or set aside, the marriage. In 1527, Henry asked the pope to annul his marriage. The pope turned him down, not wanting to offend Catherine's nephew, the Holy Roman Emperor Charles V.

The Reformation Parliament In 1529, Henry called Parliament into session and asked it to pass a set of laws that ended the pope's power in England. This Parliament is known as the Reformation Parliament. In 1533, Henry secretly married Anne Boleyn (BUL•ihn), who was in her twenties. Shortly after, Parliament legalized Henry's divorce from Catherine. In 1534, Henry's break with the pope was completed when Parliament approved the Act of Supremacy. This called on people to take an oath recognizing the divorce and accepting Henry, not the pope, as the official head of England's Church.

Consequences of Henry's Changes Henry did not immediately get the male heir he sought. After Anne Boleyn gave birth to a daughter, Elizabeth, she fell out of Henry's favor. Eventually, she was charged with treason and beheaded in 1536. Almost at once, Henry took a third wife, Jane Seymour. In 1537, she gave him a son named Edward. Henry's happiness was tempered by his wife's

≈3.56 **Preparing for the Regents**

Power How did the Act of Supremacy help weaken the power of the Catholic Church?

death just two weeks later. Henry married three more times. None of these marriages, produced children.

After Henry's death in 1547, each of his three children ruled England in turn. This created religious turmoil. Henry's son, Edward, became king when he was just nine years old. Too young to rule alone, Edward VI was guided by adult advisers who introduced Protestant reforms to the English Church. Almost constantly in ill health, Edward reigned for just six years. When Mary, Catherine's daughter, took the throne in 1553, she returned the English Church to the rule of the pope. Her efforts met with considerable resistance, and she had many Protestants executed.

When Mary died in 1558, Elizabeth, Anne Boleyn's daughter, inherited the throne. Elizabeth I was determined to return her kingdom to Protestantism. In 1559, Parliament followed Elizabeth's wishes and set up the Church of England, or **Anglican** Church, with Elizabeth as its head. This was to be the only legal church in England. Elizabeth decided to establish a state church that moderate Catholics and moderate Protestants might both accept. To please Protestants, priests in the Church of England were allowed to marry. They could deliver sermons in English, not Latin. To please Catholics, the Church of England kept some of the trappings of the Catholic service such as rich robes. In addition, church services were revised to be somewhat more acceptable to Catholics. By taking this moderate approach, Elizabeth brought a level of religious peace to England. Religion, however, remained a problem. Some Protestants pushed for Elizabeth to make more far-reaching church reforms. At the same time, some Catholics tried to overthrow Elizabeth and replace her with her cousin, the Catholic Mary Queen of Scots.

Calvin and Other Reformers

Religious reform in Switzerland was begun by Huldrych Zwingli (HUL•drykh ZWIHNG•lee), a Catholic priest in Zurich. He called for a return to the more personal faith of early Christianity. He also wanted believers to have more control over the Church. Zwingli's reforms were adopted in Zurich and other cities. In 1531, a bitter war between Swiss Protestants and Catholics broke out. During the fighting, Zwingli met his death. Meanwhile, John Calvin, then a young law student in France with a growing interest in Church doctrine, was beginning to clarify his religious beliefs.

Calvinism In 1536, John Calvin published *Institutes of the Christian Religion*. It was a summary of Protestant theology, or religious beliefs. Calvin wrote that men and women are sinful by nature. Taking Luther's idea that humans cannot earn salvation, Calvin went on to say that God chooses a very few people to save. Calvin called these few the "elect." He believed that God has known since the beginning of time who will be saved. This doctrine is called **predestination**. The religion based on Calvin's teachings is called **Calvinism**.

Spread of Protestantism

Spread of Religion
- ← Lutheran
- ← Anglican
- ← Calvinist

3.57 Preparing for the Regents

Belief Systems What role did Elizabeth I play in the English Reformation?

TAKING NOTES

Comparing Use a chart to compare the ideas of the reformers who came after Luther.

Reformers	Ideas
Zwingli	
Calvin	
Anabaptists	
Catholic Reformers	

3.58 Preparing for the Regents

Power How did the Calvin's *Institutes of the Christian Religion* help weaken the power of the Catholic Church?

Calvin believed that the ideal government was a **theocracy**, a government controlled by religious leaders. In 1541, Protestants in Geneva, Switzerland, asked Calvin to lead their city. He and his followers ran the city according to strict rules. Everyone attended religion class. No one wore bright clothing or played card games. Authorities would imprison, excommunicate, or banish those who broke such rules. Anyone who preached different doctrines might be burned at the stake. Yet, to many Protestants, Calvin's Geneva was a model city.

One admiring visitor to Geneva was a Scottish preacher named John Knox. When he returned to Scotland in 1559, Knox put Calvin's ideas to work. Each community church was governed by a group of laymen called elders or presbyters (PREHZ•buh•tuhrs). Knox's followers became known as **Presbyterians**. In the 1560s, Protestant nobles led by Knox made Calvinism Scotland's official religion. They also deposed their Catholic ruler, Mary Queen of Scots, in favor of her infant son, James. Elsewhere, Swiss, Dutch, and French reformers adopted the Calvinist form of church organization. One reason Calvin is considered so influential is that many Protestant churches today trace their roots to Calvin. Over the years, however, many of them have softened Calvin's strict teachings.

In France, Calvin's followers were called Huguenots. Hatred between Catholics and Huguenots frequently led to violence. The most violent clash occurred in Paris on August 24, 1572—the Catholic feast of St. Bartholomew's Day. At dawn, Catholic mobs began hunting for Protestants and murdering them. The massacres spread to other cities and lasted six months.

Other Protestant Reformers As Christians interpreted the Bible for themselves, new Protestant groups formed over differences in belief. One group only baptized those who were old enough to decide to be Christian. They said that persons who had been baptized as children should be rebaptized as adults. These believers were called **Anabaptists**, from a Greek word meaning "baptize again." The Anabaptists also shared their possessions, refused to fight in wars, and taught that church and state should be separate. Viewed as radicals, both Catholics and Protestants persecuted them. But the Anabaptists survived and became the forerunners of the Mennonites and the Amish. Their teaching influenced the later Quakers and Baptists, groups who split from the Anglican Church.

The Catholic Reformation

While Protestant churches won many followers, millions of people remained true to Catholicism. Helping Catholics to remain loyal was a movement within the Catholic Church to reform itself. This movement is now known as the **Catholic Reformation**. It was once referred to it as the Counter Reformation.

One important reformer was Ignatius (ihg•NAY•shuhs) of Loyola. In 1522, Ignatius began writing a book called *Spiritual Exercises* that laid out a day-by-day plan of meditation, prayer, and study. For the next 18 years, he gathered followers. In 1540, Pope Paul III created a religious order for his followers called the Society of Jesus. Members were called **Jesuits** (JEHZH•u•ihts). The Jesuits focused on three activities: teaching, the conversion of non-Christians to Catholicism, and stopping the spread of Protestantism. The zeal of the Jesuits overcame the drift toward Protestantism in Poland and southern Germany.

Two popes took the lead in reforming the Catholic Church. In addition to creating the Jesuits, Paul III, pope from 1534 to 1549, directed a council of cardinals to investigate indulgence selling and other abuses in the Church. He also used the Inquisition to seek out heresy in papal territory. (The Inquisition

3.43 Preparing for the Regents

Belief Systems What were the major goals of the Catholic Reformation?

in Spain, for example, prevented the introduction of Protestantism to that nation during the 1500s.) Most importantly, he called the **Council of Trent**, which met in Trent in northern Italy from 1545 to 1563. The council agreed on several doctrines: 1) The Church's interpretation of the Bible was final. Any Christian who substituted his or her own interpretation was a heretic. 2) Christians needed faith and good works for salvation. They were not saved by faith alone, as Luther argued. 3) The Bible and Church tradition were equally powerful authorities for guiding Christian life. 4) Indulgences were valid expressions of faith. But the false selling of indulgences was banned.

The next pope, Paul IV, vigorously carried out the council's decrees. In 1559, he had officials draw up a list of books considered dangerous to the Catholic faith. This list was known as the Index of Forbidden Books. Catholic bishops throughout Europe were ordered to gather up the offensive books (including Protestant Bibles) and burn them in bonfires.

The Legacy of the Reformation

The Reformation had an enduring impact. Through its religious, social, and political effects, the Reformation set the stage for the modern world. It also ended the Christian unity of Europe and left it culturally divided. Despite religious wars and persecutions, Protestant churches flourished and new denominations developed. The Roman Catholic Church itself became more unified as a result of the reforms started at the Council of Trent. Both Catholics and Protestants gave more emphasis to the role of education in promoting their beliefs. This led to the founding of parish schools and new colleges and universities throughout Europe.

Some women reformers had hoped to see the status of women in the church and society improve as a result of the Reformation. But it remained much the same both under Protestantism and Roman Catholicism. Women were still mainly limited to the concerns of home and family.

As the Catholic Church's moral and political authority declined, individual monarchs and states gained power. This led to the development of modern nation-states. In the 1600s, rulers of nation-states would seek more power for themselves and their countries through warfare, exploration, and expansion.

3.60 Preparing for the Regents

Power How did the Protestant Reformation affect the power of the Catholic Church? How did it affect the power of European monarchies?

PREPARING FOR THE REGENTS

On a separate sheet of paper, write a well-organized essay that includes an introduction, several paragraphs addressing the task below, and a conclusion. Before beginning, check the Score the Essay box for pointers.

Theme: Change
Individuals have brought about great change in history. These individuals have had positive and/or negative effects.

Task:
Choose *two* individuals from your study of the Protestant and Catholic Reformations and for *each* individual chosen:

• Discuss *two* specific changes made by the individual

• Evaluate whether these changes have had a positive or negative effect

SCORE THE ESSAY To receive a score of 5 on your essay, you will need to:
• thoroughly develop all aspects of the task evenly and in depth by discussing the changes and evaluating their positive and/or negative effects.
• be more analytical than descriptive.
• richly support the theme with relevant facts, examples, and details.
• demonstrate a logical and clear plan of organization.

Global Interactions
(1200–1650)

Part I: MULTIPLE-CHOICE QUESTIONS

Directions (1–10): For each statement or question, write on a separate answer sheet the *number* of the word or expression that, of those given, best completes the statement or answers the questions.

1 The rise of the West African kingdoms of Ghana, Mali, and Songhai can be attributed to

(1) their emphasis on nationalism
(2) the spread of Christianity
(3) the rise of European imperialism
(4) their location near the trans-Sahara trade routes

2 Prior to the Protestant Reformation, the medieval church in western Europe was criticized for

(1) sponsoring explorations to the Middle East
(2) allowing the Bible to be printed and distributed to people
(3) being too concerned with worldly power and riches
(4) refusing to sell indulgences to peasants

3 Which statement concerning the Renaissance is based on opinion rather than on fact?

(1) Literature began to appear in languages other than Latin.
(2) The art of the Northern Renaissance was superior to that of the Italian Renaissance.
(3) Art reflected the ideas of humanism and individualism.
(4) Art produced during the Renaissance had religious as well as secular themes.

4 One way that Martin Luther, Henry VIII, and John Calvin were similar is that they all were

(1) Latin American revolutionary leaders
(2) Reformation leaders
(3) Imperialist painters
(4) divine right monarchs

5 The feudal system in both medieval Europe and early Japan were characterized by

(1) a decentralized political system
(2) religious diversity
(3) an increased emphasis on education
(4) the development of a wealthy middle class

Base your answers to questions 6 and 7 on the statement below:

"The pope is no judge of matters pertaining to God's word and faith; the true Christian must examine and judge for himself."

6 Who is the most likely author of this statement?

(1) Martin Luther   (3) John Locke
(2) Socrates   (4) Adam Smith

7 Which historic era was based on the spirit of this statement?

(1) *Pax Romana*   (3) Enlightenment
(2) Crusades   (4) Reformation

8 Which historical events are in correct chronological order?

(1) Crusades → Renaissance → Neolithic Revolution → Roman Empire
(2) Roman Empire → Neolithic Revolution → Crusades → Renaissance
(3) Renaissance → Neolithic Revolution → Crusades → Roman Empire
(4) Neolithic Revolution → Roman Empire → Crusades → Renaissance

9 The travels are Marco Polo and Ibn Battuta were similar in that these travels

(1) led to national movements
(2) helped to spread the ideas of religious leaders
(3) stimulated the expansion of trade
(4) supported democratic forms of government

10 Which factor contributed to the success of the vast empire created by the Mongols?

(1) avoiding contact with the West
(2) paying monetary tribute to local rulers
(3) employing superior military skills
(4) converting conquered peoples to Confucianism

In developing your answers to Parts II and III, be sure to keep these general definitions in mind:

(a) *discuss* means "to make observations about something using facts, reasoning, and argument; to present in some detail"

(b) *explain* means "to make plain or understandable; to give reasons for or causes of; to show the logical development or relationships of"

(c) *analyze* means "to determine the nature and relationships of the component elements"

Part II: THEMATIC ESSAY

Directions: Write a well-organized essay that includes an introduction, several paragraphs addressing the task below, and a conclusion.

Theme: Science and Technology

> Science and technology have played a critical role in altering the course of human history

Task:

> - Identify *two* scientific or technological advances that had a major impact on global history
> - Explain the relationship between the scientific or technological advance and a specific historical event or period in history
> - Analyze how these advances changed the course of history

You may use any scientific or technological advance from your study of Unit Three. Some suggestions you might wish to consider include the astrolabe and the printing press.

You are not limited to these suggestions.
Do *not* use any turning points in United States history.

Guidelines:

In your essay, be sure to
- Address all aspects of the *Task*
- Support the theme with relevant facts, examples, and details
- Use a logical and clear plan of organization, including an introduction and a conclusion that are beyond the simple restatement of the *Theme*

Part III: DOCUMENT-BASED QUESTION

This question is based on the accompanying documents (1–3). The question is designed to test your ability to work with historic documents. Some of these documents have been edited for the purpose of this question. As you analyze the documents, take into account both the source of each document and any point of view that may be presented in the document.

Historical Context:

Throughout global history, rapidly spreading epidemics such as the Black Death, or bubonic plague, of the 14th century have had significant effects on societies.

Task:

Using information from the documents and your knowledge of global history, answer the question that follows each document in Part A. Your answers to the questions will help you write the Part B essay, in which you will be asked to:

- Explain why the Black Death spread
- Discuss the effects of the epidemic on a specific society or societies

Part A: Short Answer

Directions: Analyze the documents and answer the short-answer questions that follow in the space provided.

Document 1

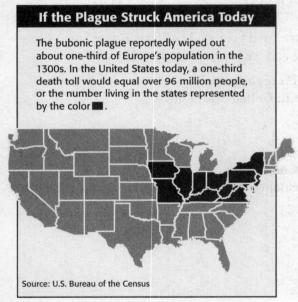

If the Plague Struck America Today

The bubonic plague reportedly wiped out about one-third of Europe's population in the 1300s. In the United States today, a one-third death toll would equal over 96 million people, or the number living in the states represented by the color ■.

Source: U.S. Bureau of the Census

Document 2

Oh, what great palaces, how many fair houses and noble dwellings, once filled with attendants and nobles and ladies, were emptied to the meanest servant! How many famous names and vast possessions and renowned estates were left without an heir! How many gallant men and fair ladies and handsome youth, whom Galen, Hippocrates and Æsculapius themselves would have said were in perfect health, at noon dined with their relatives and friends, and at night supped with their ancestors in the next world! . . .

—Giovanni Boccaccio, *The Decameron*

1 According to Document 1, how many people would a one-third death toll equal in the United States?

_____

2 According to Document 2, what was *one* impact of the Black Death on European society?

_____

_____

Document 3

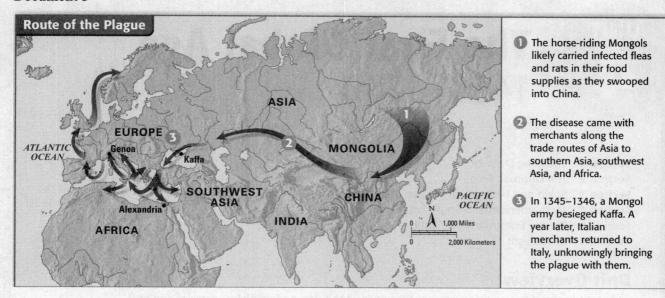

Route of the Plague

1. The horse-riding Mongols likely carried infected fleas and rats in their food supplies as they swooped into China.

2. The disease came with merchants along the trade routes of Asia to southern Asia, southwest Asia, and Africa.

3. In 1345–1346, a Mongol army besieged Kaffa. A year later, Italian merchants returned to Italy, unknowingly bringing the plague with them.

3 According to Document 3, how did the plague reach Europe?

_____

_____

Part B: Essay

Directions: Write a well-organized essay that includes an introduction, several paragraphs, and a conclusion. Use evidence from at least *two* documents to support your response.

Historical Context: Throughout global history, rapidly spreading epidemics such as the Black Death, or bubonic plague, of the 14th century have had significant effects on societies.

Task: Using information from the documents and your knowledge of global history, write an essay in which you:

- Explain why the Black Death spread
- Discuss the effects of the epidemic on a specific society or societies

Guidelines:

In your essay, be sure to

- Address all aspects of the *Task* by accurately analyzing and interpreting at least **two** documents
- Incorporate information from the documents
- Incorporate relevant outside information
- Support the theme with relevant facts, examples, and details
- Use a logical and clear plan of organization
- Introduce the theme by establishing a framework that is beyond a simple statement of the *Task* or *Historical Context* and conclude with a summation of the theme

UNIT 4
The First Global Age
1450–1700

Unit Overview

This unit looks at the causes and consequences of the first age of global exploration and expansion from 1450–1700. It begins by examining the Ming Dynasty in China and the rise and spread of the Ottoman Empire. It then turns to European exploration and expansion. After looking at Portugal, Spain, Mesoamerica, and South America on the eve of encounter, it examines the effects of European expansion on the Americas, Africa, Asia, and Europe. The unit closes by examining the absolute authority of monarchies and challenges to that authority.

Concepts and Themes

Among the concepts and themes explored in this unit are

- Belief Systems
- Change
- Citizenship
- Conflict
- Culture and Intellectual Life

- Economic Systems
- Human and Physical Geography
- Movement of People and Goods
- Political Systems
- Power

PREPARING FOR THE REGENTS: Building Thematic Essay Skills

Throughout time, the beliefs and achievements of individuals have helped shape global history. Many of these beliefs and achievements have had both positive and negative effects on society. As you read this unit, think about the beliefs and achievements of Suleyman, Queen Isabella, Christopher Columbus, Hernando Cortés, Francisco Pizarro, Philip II, Peter the Great, Louis XIV, Charles I, Oliver Cromwell, and the other people you encounter who have changed history. Use the following web diagram to organize information about the individuals. You can add additional boxes as needed.

The Ming Dynasty

Section Overview

Hongwu, the son of a Chinese peasant, led a rebel army that drove the Mongols from China in 1368. The Ming dynasty that he founded ruled China until 1644. When Hongwu's son, Yonglo, came to power, he launched seven voyages of exploration to impress the world with China's power and riches. Some of the voyages sailed as far east as the Arabian Peninsula and the eastern coast of Africa. The voyages made China the greatest sea power of its time. Yet, following the seventh voyage in 1433, China withdrew into isolation.

China became the dominant power in Asia under the Ming. Vassal states from Korea to Southeast Asia paid the Ming regular tribute. When Europeans arrived to trade with the Chinese, the Ming expected them to do the same. China's rulers were not going to allow outsiders from distant lands to threaten the peace and prosperity the Ming had brought to China when they ended Mongol rule.

Ming porcelain vase

MAIN IDEAS

CULTURAL INTERACTION Advances under the Ming Dynasty left China uninterested in European contact.

TERMS AND NAMES

- Hongwu
- Ming dynasty
- Yonglo
- Zheng Ze
- Manchus
- Qing dynasty

PREPARING FOR THE REGENTS

As you read this section, consider
- what impact China's self-concept of the Middle Kingdom had on political, economic, and cultural relationships with other societies in Eastern and Western Asia.
- to what extent Europe was more interested in trade with China than China was interested in trade with Europe.

TIME LINE

1368
Ming dynasty begins.

1405
Zheng He takes first voyage.

1433
Zheng He takes last voyage.

1644
Ming dynasty collapses.

Human and Physical Geography

During the last years of Kublai Khan's reign, weaknesses began to appear in Mongol rule. Heavy spending on fruitless wars, on public works, and on the luxuries of the Yuan court burdened the treasury and created resentment among the overtaxed Chinese. This presented problems that Kublai's less able successors could not resolve. Rebellions broke out in many parts of China in the 1300s.

The Rise of the Ming A peasant's son, **Hongwu**, commanded the rebel army that finally drove the Mongols out of China in 1368. That same year, he became the first emperor of the **Ming dynasty** (1368–1644). Hongwu continued to rule from the former Yuan capital of Nanjing in the south. He began reforms designed to restore agricultural lands devastated by war, erase all traces of the Mongol past, and promote China's power and prosperity. Hongwu's agricultural reforms increased rice production and improved irrigation. He also encouraged fish farming and growing commercial crops, such as cotton and sugar cane.

Hongwu used respected traditions and institutions to bring stability to China. For example, he encouraged a return to Confucian moral standards. He improved imperial administration by restoring the merit-based civil service examination system. Later in his rule, however, when problems developed, Hongwu became a ruthless tyrant. Suspecting plots against his rule everywhere, he conducted purges of the government, killing thousands of officials.

Hongwu's death in 1398 led to a power struggle. His son **Yonglo** (yung•lu) emerged victorious. Yonglo had a far-ranging curiosity about the outside world. In 1405, before Europeans began to sail beyond their borders, he launched the first of seven voyages of exploration. He hoped they would impress the world with the power and splendor of Ming China. He also wanted to expand China's tribute system.

The Voyages of Zheng He A Chinese Muslim admiral named **Zheng He** (jung huh) led all of the seven voyages. His expeditions were remarkable for their size. Everything about them was large—distances traveled, fleet size, and ship measurements. The voyages ranged from Southeast Asia to eastern Africa (see the map on page 134). From 40 to 300 ships sailed in each expedition. Among them were fighting ships, storage vessels, and huge "treasure" ships measuring more than 400 feet long. The fleet's crews numbered over 27,000 on some voyages. They included sailors, soldiers, carpenters, interpreters, accountants, doctors, and religious leaders. Like a huge floating city, the fleet sailed from port to port along the Indian Ocean.

Everywhere Zheng He went, he distributed gifts including silver and silk to show Chinese superiority. As a result, more than 16 countries sent tribute to the Ming court. Even so, Chinese scholar-officials complained that the voyages wasted valuable resources that could be used to defend against barbarians' attacks on the northern frontier. After the seventh voyage, in 1433, China withdrew into isolation.

China's Relationship with the West

China's official trade policies in the 1500s reflected its isolation. To the Chinese, their country—called the Middle Kingdom—had been the cultural center of the universe for 2,000 years. If foreign states wished to trade with China, they would have to follow Chinese rules. To keep the influence of outsiders to a minimum, only the government was to conduct foreign trade, and only through three

TAKING NOTES

Summarizing Use a chart to summarize relevant facts about Hongwu, Yonglo, and Zheng He.

Person	Facts
1.	1.
2.	2.
3.	3.

4.1 Preparing for the Regents

Human and Physical Geography Why did China undertake voyages of exploration?

4.2 Preparing for the Regents

Movement of People and Goods What effect do you think voyages like Zheng He's might have on global trade?

coastal ports, Canton, Macao, and Ningbo. In reality, trade flourished up and down the coast. Profit-minded merchants smuggled silk, porcelain, and other valuable goods out of the country into the eager hands of European merchants.

Demand for Chinese goods had a ripple effect on the economy. Industries such as silk-making and ceramics grew rapidly. Manufacturing and commerce increased. But China did not become highly industrialized for two main reasons. First, the idea of commerce offended China's Confucian beliefs. Merchants, it was said, made their money "supporting foreigners and robbery." Second, Chinese economic policies traditionally favored agriculture. Taxes on agriculture stayed low. Taxes on manufacturing and trade skyrocketed.

Christian missionaries accompanied European traders into China. They brought Christianity and knowledge of European science and technology, such as the clock. The first missionary to have an impact was an Italian Jesuit named Matteo Ricci. He gained special favor at the Ming court through his intelligence and fluency in Chinese. Still, many educated Chinese opposed the European and Christian presence.

4.3 Preparing for the Regents

Culture and Intellectual Life How might China's concept of the Middle Kingdom have influenced is relations with other nations?

China's Impact on East and Southeast Asia

China became the dominant power in Asia under the Ming dynasty. The dynasty reaffirmed control of lands in the southwest that the Mongols had brought under China's control. They also invaded Mongolia and Vietnam. Vassal states from Korea to Southeast Asia paid their Ming overlords regular tribute in acknowledgment of their submission to China's power.

In 1592, the Japanese emperor Toyotomi Hideyoshi invaded Korea, with the intent of eventually conquering China. The Ming came to Korea's defense. Raising the huge armies needed to fight the Japanese was costly for the Ming. By 1600, the dynasty was weakening. The government was out of money, the rulers were ineffectual, and the officials were corrupt. Higher taxes and bad harvests pushed millions of peasants toward starvation. Civil strife and rebellion followed. In 1644, invaders from Manchuria called the **Manchus** (MAN•chooz) swept the Ming from power. As the Mongols had done in the 1300s, the Manchus took a Chinese name for their dynasty, the **Qing** (chihng) **dynasty**. They would rule for more than 260 years and expand China's borders to include Taiwan, Chinese Central Asia, Mongolia, and Tibet.

4.4 Preparing for the Regents

Power How did the tribute system demonstrate China's supremacy and strength?

Cultural Achievements

The Ming dynasty's nearly 300-year rule was a time of many achievements. Among these was Yonglo's construction of a new capital at Beijing. Under his orders, workers built a great palace complex to symbolize his power and might. Construction took 14 years, from 1406 to 1420. Red walls 35 feet in height surrounded the complex, which had dozens of buildings, including palaces and temples. The complex became known as the Forbidden City because commoners and foreigners where not allowed to enter. To supply the Forbidden City, Yonglo had the Grand Canal extended. Fearing that the Mongols might try to reclaim China, Yonglo also undertook the engineering feat of rebuilding the Great Wall. The Great Wall, a defensive wall that stretched from the Yellow Sea in the east to the Gobi Desert in the west, had originally been built by the Qin in the third century B.C. Watch towers arose every 200 to 300 yards along the wall.

The arts flourished under the Ming. Most artists of the time painted in traditional styles, which valued technique over creativity. In pottery, technical skill

4.5 Preparing for the Regents

Culture and Intellectual Life What were some of the Ming's achievements?

as well as experimentation led to the production of high-quality ceramics, including porcelain. Drama was a popular entertainment, especially in rural China where literacy rates were low. Plays that presented Chinese history and cultural heroes entertained and also helped unify Chinese society by creating a national culture.

Answer the following question. Use the Analyze the Question hints to help you answer the question. Base your answer to question 1 on the map below and your knowledge of social studies.

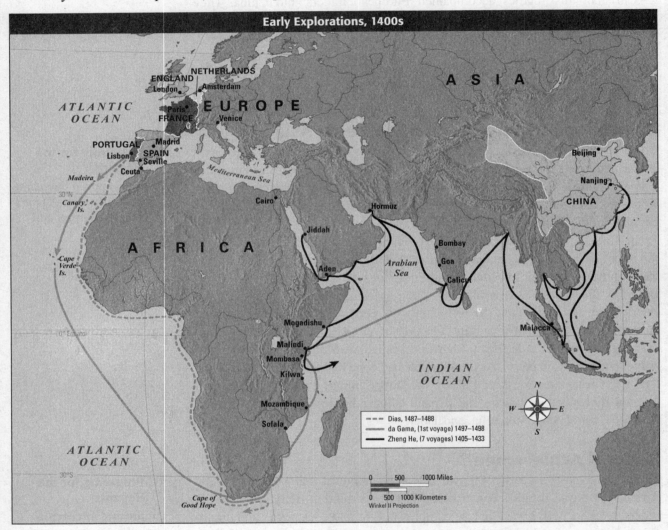

Early Explorations, 1400s

Legend:
- Dias, 1487–1488
- da Gama, (1st voyage) 1497–1498
- Zheng He, (7 voyages) 1405–1433

0   500   1000 Miles
0   500   1000 Kilometers
Winkel II Projection

1 The map shows that on his voyages, Zheng He explored

(1) both the Pacific and the Atlantic Oceans
(2) at the same time as the Spanish explorers
(3) lands in the Western Hemisphere
(4) Arabia and the east coast of Africa

ANALYZE THE QUESTION
- Read the question stem. You are being asked to determine what area of the world Zheng He explored.
- Look at the map. Read the legend to determine which information on the map is about Zheng He. Then trace his voyages, noting the areas he came a shore.
- Choose the alternative that best matches the information on the map.

The Ottoman Empire

Section Overview

By 1300, the Byzantine Empire was declining, and the Mongols had destroyed the Turkish Seljuk kingdom of Rum. Anatolia was inhabited mostly by the descendants of nomadic Turks. These militaristic people had a long history of invading other countries. Loyal to their own groups, they were not united by a strong central power. A small Turkish state occupied land between the Byzantine Empire and that of other Muslim groups. From this place, a strong leader named Osman emerged to unite the Turks into what eventually would become the Ottoman Empire. By the 1500s, the Ottoman Empire stretch across three continents.

Suleyman the Lawgiver

MAIN IDEAS

EMPIRE BUILDING   The Ottomans established a Muslim empire that combined many cultures and lasted for more than 600 years.

TERMS AND NAMES

- Anatolia
- ghazi
- Ottoman
- sultan
- Timur the Lame
- Mehmed II
- Suleyman the Lawgiver
- *devshirme*
- janissary

TIME LINE

1300
Osman founds the Ottoman state.

1402
Timur the Lame defeats the Ottomans in the Battle of Ankara.

1453
Ottomans capture Constantinople.

PREPARING FOR THE REGENTS

As you read this section, consider
- what factors led to the rise and decline of the Ottomans.
- how Suleyman compares to other absolute rulers.
- what impact Ottoman domination had on eastern Europe.
- the long-term impacts of the Ottomans on global history.

Anatolia (AN•uh•TOH•lee•uh), also called Asia Minor, is a huge peninsula in modern-day Turkey that juts out into the Black and Mediterranean seas. Anatolia is a high, rocky plateau, rich in timber and agriculture. Nearby mountains hold important mineral deposits. By the 1300s, Anatolia was inhabited mostly by the descendents of nomadic Turks. Many Anatolian Turks saw themselves as **ghazis** (GAH•zees), or warriors for Islam. They formed military societies under the leadership of an emir, a chief commander, and followed a strict Islamic code of conduct. They raided the territories of the "infidels," or people who didn't believe in Islam. These infidels lived on the frontiers of the Byzantine Empire.

Rise of the Ottomans

The most successful ghazi was Osman. People in the West called him Othman and named his followers **Ottomans**. Osman built a small Muslim state in Anatolia between 1300 and 1326. His successors expanded it through land purchases, alliances, and conquest. The Ottomans' military success was largely based on the use of gunpowder. They replaced their archers on horseback with musket-carrying foot soldiers. They also were among the first people to use cannons as offensive weapons. Even heavily walled cities fell to an all-out attack by the Turks.

The second Ottoman leader, Orkhan I, was Osman's son. He felt strong enough to declare himself **sultan**, meaning "overlord" or "one with power." In 1361, the Ottomans captured Adrianople (ay•dree•uh•NOH•puhl), the second most important Byzantine city. A new Turkish empire was on the rise.

That rise was briefly halted in the early 1400s by a conqueror from Samarkand in Central Asia. Permanently injured by an arrow in the leg, he was called Timur-i-Lang, or **Timur the Lame** (or Tamerlane by Europeans). Timur crushed the Ottomans at the Battle of Ankara in 1402. When Timur turned his attention to China, war broke out among the sultan's four sons. Mehmed I defeated his brothers and took the throne. His son, Murad II, was the first of four powerful sultans who led the expansion of the Ottoman Empire through 1566.

Ottomans Take Constantinople Murad's son **Mehmed II** achieved the most dramatic feat in Ottoman history—the capture of Constantinople. By the time Mehmed took power in 1451, Constantinople had shrunk from a population of a million to a mere 50,000. Although it controlled no territory outside its walls, it still dominated the Bosporus Strait. Controlling this waterway meant that it could choke off traffic between the Ottomans' territories in Asia and in the Balkans.

In 1453, Mehmed II decided to face the situation head-on. His forces began firing on the city walls with mighty cannons. But a chain across the Golden Horn between the Bosporus Strait and the Sea of Marmara kept the Turkish fleet out of the city's harbor. In response, Mehmed's army dragged 70 ships over a hill on greased runners from the Bosporus to the harbor. Now Mehmed's army could attack Constantinople from two sides. The city held out for over seven weeks, but the Turks finally found a break in the wall and entered the city.

Mehmed the Conqueror, as he was now called, proved to be an able ruler as well as a magnificent warrior. He opened Constantinople to new citizens of many religions and backgrounds—Jews, Christians, and Muslims, Turks and non-Turks. They helped rebuild the city, which was now called Istanbul.

One of the consequences of the fall of Constantinople for Europeans was that they were now cut off from land routes to Asia. This helped spur efforts by Portugal and Spain to find a sea route to the East.

TAKING NOTES

Comparing List the main rulers of the Ottoman Empire and their successes.

Rulers	Successes

4.6 Preparing for the Regents

Human and Physical Geography How did the Ottomans create their vast empire? How might Anatolia's location between Europe and Asia have helped the Ottomans expand their empire?

4.7 Preparing for the Regents

Movement of People and Goods What did the fall of Constantinople prompt Spain and Portugal to do?

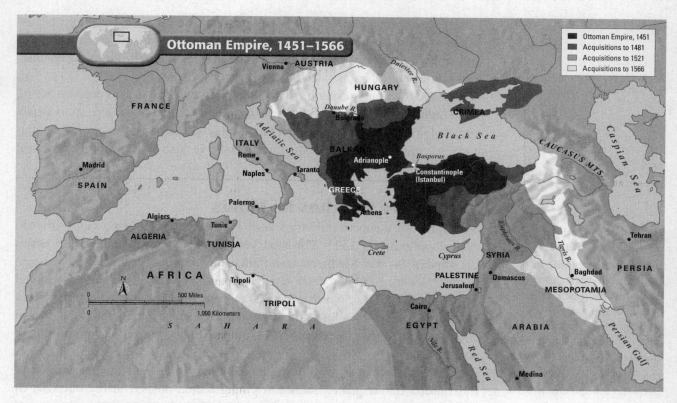

Ottoman Empire, 1451–1566

Legend:
- Ottoman Empire, 1451
- Acquisitions to 1481
- Acquisitions to 1521
- Acquisitions to 1566

Ottomans Take Islam's Holy Cities Mehmed's grandson, Selim the Grim, came to power in 1512. In 1514, he defeated the Safavids (suh•FAH•vihdz) of Persia at the Battle of Chaldiran, then he swept south through Syria and Palestine and into North Africa. Selim captured Mecca and Medina, the holiest cities of Islam. Finally he took Cairo, the intellectual center of the Muslim world. The once-great civilization of Egypt had become just another province in the empire.

Suleyman the Lawgiver

The Ottoman Empire didn't reach its peak size and grandeur until the reign of Selim's son, Suleyman I (SOO•lay•mahn). Suleyman came to the throne in 1520 and ruled for 46 years. His own people called him **Suleyman the Lawgiver**. He was known in the West, though, as Suleyman the Magnificent. This title was a tribute to the splendor of his court and to his cultural achievements.

Social Organization Creating an efficient government structure and social organization for the Ottoman Empire was Suleyman's crowning achievement. Suleyman created a law code to handle both criminal and civil actions. He also simplified the system of taxation and reduced government bureaucracy. These changes bettered the daily life of almost every citizen and helped earn Suleyman the title of Lawgiver. Nevertheless, Suleyman ruled with complete power.

The sultan's 20,000 personal slaves staffed the palace bureaucracy. The slaves were acquired as part of a policy called *devshirme* (dehv•SHEER•meh). Under the **devshirme** system, the sultan's army drafted boys from conquered Christian territories. The army educated them, converted them to Islam, and trained them as soldiers. An elite force of 30,000 soldiers known as **janissaries** was trained to be loyal to the sultan only. Their superb discipline made them the heart of the Ottoman war machine.

Cultural Achievements Suleyman had broad interests, which contributed to the cultural achievements of the empire. He found time to study poetry,

> **4.8 Preparing for the Regents**
>
> **Justice** Why was Suleyman called the Lawgiver?

history, geography, astronomy, mathematics, and architecture. He employed one of the world's finest architects, Sinan, to construct the Mosque of Suleyman in Istanbul, an immense complex topped with domes and half domes. It includes four schools, a library, a bath, and a hospital.

Art and literature also flourished under Suleyman's rule. This creative period was similar to the European Renaissance. Painters and poets looked to Persia and Arabia for models. The works that they produced used these foreign influences to express original Ottoman ideas in the Turkish style. They are excellent examples of cultural blending.

The Empire Reaches Its Limits

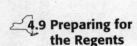

4.9 Preparing for the Regents

Movement of People and Goods What effect do you think the Ottoman Empire's control of the eastern Mediterranean and the North African coast had on global trade routes?

Suleyman was a superb military leader. He conquered the important European city of Belgrade in 1521. The next year, Turkish forces captured the island of Rhodes in the Mediterranean and now dominated the whole eastern Mediterranean. Applying their immense naval power, the Ottomans captured Tripoli on the coast of North Africa. They continued conquering peoples along the North African coastline. Although the Ottomans occupied only the coastal cities of North Africa, they managed to control trade routes to the interior of the continent.

In 1526, Suleyman advanced into Hungary and Austria, throwing central Europe into a panic. Suleyman's armies then pushed to the outskirts of Vienna, Austria. Reigning from Istanbul, Suleyman had waged war with central Europeans, North Africans, and Central Asians. He had become the most powerful monarch on earth. Only Charles V, head of the Hapsburg Empire in Europe, came close to rivaling his power.

Despite Suleyman's achievements, the Ottoman Empire was losing ground. Suleyman killed his ablest son and drove another into exile. His third son, the incompetent Selim II, inherited the throne. Suleyman set the pattern for later sultans to gain and hold power. It became customary for each new sultan to have his brothers strangled. The sultan would then keep his sons prisoner in the harem, cutting them off from education or contact with the world. This practice produced a long line of weak sultans who eventually brought ruin on the empire. However, the Ottoman Empire continued to influence the world into the early 20th century.

PREPARING FOR THE REGENTS

Answer the following question. Use the Analyze the Question hints to help you answer the question.

1 Look at the map on page 137. Which generalization is best supported by the information in this map?

   (1) The Ottoman Empire controlled the largest amount of territory by 1451.

   (2) The Ottoman Empire controlled Constantinople by 1451.

   (3) By the 1500s, the Ottoman Empire controlled parts of the Middle East, North Africa, and eastern Europe.

   (4) The Mediterranean Sea served as a cultural barrier between Asia Minor and North Africa.

ANALYZE THE QUESTION
- Read the question stem. You are being asked to determine which of the alternatives is best supported by the information on the map on page 137.
- Look at the map's legend and labels, then find the information on the map that is relevant to each alternative.
- Rule out alternatives that are not supported by information on the map.
- The remaining alternative is the correct answer.

Spain and Portugal on the Eve of Encounter

Section Overview

Europeans had not been completely isolated from the rest of the world before the 1400s. Beginning around 1100, European Crusaders battled Muslims for control of the Holy Lands in Southwest Asia. In 1275, the Italian trader Marco Polo reached the court of Kublai Khan in China. For the most part, however, Europeans had neither the interest nor the ability to explore foreign lands. That changed by the early 1400s. The desire to grow rich through trade and to spread Christianity, coupled with advances in sailing technology, spurred an age of European exploration.

Portugal and Spain led the way. Both nations were eager to find a sea route to Asia. Portugal sought a western route. The Portuguese believed that to reach Asia by sea, they would have to sail around the tip of Africa. Bartolomeu Dias rounded the tip of Africa in 1488 and in 1498 Vasco da Gama sailed all the way to Calicut, India. By 1511, Portugal had control of the Molaccas in the East Indies. Influenced by the views of Christopher Columbus, Spain sought an eastern route. Columbus set sail in 1492. When he reached land in October, he mistakenly thought that he had reached the East Indies. He was actually in the Caribbean. But his voyage would open the way for European colonization of the Americas—a process that would forever change the world.

Globe, c. 1492

MAIN IDEAS

SCIENCE AND TECHNOLOGY Advances in sailing technology enabled Europeans to explore other parts of the world.

ECONOMICS The desire for wealth was a driving force behind the European exploration of the East. Europeans wanted to control trade with Asia.

EMPIRE BUILDING The voyages of Columbus prompted the Spanish to establish colonies in the Americas.

TERMS AND NAMES

- Prince Henry
- Christopher Columbus
- colony
- Treaty of Tordesillas
- Ferdinand Magellan

PREPARING FOR THE REGENTS

As you read this section, consider
- what Spain and Portugal were like on the eve of encounter.
- what forces came together in the mid-1400s that made the age of European exploration possible.

TIME LINE

1419
Prince Henry founds navigation school.

1488
Bartolomeu Dias sails round tip of Africa.

1492
Columbus makes first voyage.

1494
Spain and Portugal sign Treaty of Tordesillas.

1498
Vasco da Gama sails to Calicut, India.

Human and Physical Geography

By the early 1400s, Europeans were ready to explore the world beyond their borders. The Renaissance encouraged, among other things, a new spirit of adventure and curiosity. However, the Europeans' main motives for exploration were their desires to develop new sources of wealth and to spread Christianity.

Through overseas exploration, merchants and traders hoped ultimately to benefit from what had become a profitable business in Europe: the trade of spices and other luxury goods from Asia. The people of Europe had been introduced to these items during the Crusades. After the Crusades ended, Europeans continued to demand such spices as nutmeg, ginger, cinnamon, and pepper, all of which added flavor to the bland foods of Europe. Because demand for these goods was greater than the supply, merchants could charge high prices and thus make great profits. Merchants faced a problem, however. The Muslims and the Italians controlled Asian trade. Italian merchants bought Asian goods from Muslim traders and then resold them to other European merchants at increased prices. Paying such high prices to the Italians severely cut into a merchant's profits. The solution was to bypass the Italians. This meant finding a sea route directly to Asia.

The desire to spread Christianity also motivated Europeans to explore. The Crusades had left Europeans with a taste for spices, but more significantly with feelings of hostility toward Muslims. European countries believed that they had a sacred duty not only to continue fighting Muslims, but also to convert non-Christians throughout the world.

Exploration was made possible by the development of the caravel and a variety of improved navigational tools and techniques. The design of the caravel was well suited for exploration. The ship had triangular sails for maneuverability and square sails for power. The large cargo area could hold the numerous supplies needed for long voyages. The ship's shallow draft—the depth of the ships keel under the water—allowed it to explore close to shore. Navigational tools such as the astrolabe and magnetic compass helped explorers more accurately determine their location at sea. In the 1500s, navigation was further improved by a new map projection developed by Gerardus Mercator. The Mercator projection allowed sailors to plot a straight line between two points on a map. Thanks to the printing press, new navigational and geographical information could be quickly shared.

Portugal Leads the Way

The leader in developing and applying these sailing innovations was Portugal. Portugal took the lead in part due to strong government support. The nation's most enthusiastic supporter of exploration was **Prince Henry**, the son of Portugal's king. Henry's dreams of overseas exploration began in 1415 when he helped conquer the Muslim city of Ceuta in North Africa. There, he had his first glimpse of the dazzling wealth that lay beyond Europe. In Ceuta, the Portuguese invaders found exotic stores filled with pepper, cinnamon, cloves, and other spices. In addition, they encountered large supplies of gold, silver, and jewels.

Henry returned to Portugal determined to reach the source of these treasures in the East. The prince also wished to spread the Christian faith. In 1419, Henry founded a navigation school on the southwestern coast of Portugal. Mapmakers, instrument makers, shipbuilders, scientists, and sea captains gathered there to perfect their trade.

Within several years, Portuguese ships began sailing down the western coast of Africa. By the time Henry died in 1460, the Portuguese had established a

TAKING NOTES

Following Chronological Order On a time line, note the important events in the European voyages of exploration.

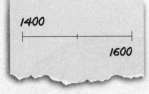

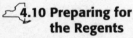

4.10 Preparing for the Regents

Science and Technology What technological advances contributed to the European exploration and expansion?

4.11 Preparing for the Regents

Human and Physical Geography In what ways did Portugal lead the way for the European age of exploration?

series of trading posts along western Africa's shores. There, they traded with Africans for such profitable items as gold and ivory. Eventually, they traded for African captives to be used as slaves. Having established their presence along the African coast, Portuguese explorers plotted their next move. They would attempt to find a sea route to Asia by sailing round the southern tip of Africa. By 1488, Bartolomeu Dias had rounded the tip Africa. Vasco da Gama began exploring the east African coast in 1497, then sailed across the Indian Ocean to the port of Calicut on the southwestern coast of India in 1498. By 1511, the Portuguese had sailed all the way to the East Indies and taken control of the Moluccas—the Spice Islands. In the process, they broke the old Muslim-Italian domination on trade from the East, much to the delight of European consumers. Portuguese merchants brought back goods from Asia at about one-fifth of what they cost when purchased through the Arabs and Italians.

Spain Also Makes Claims

As the Portuguese were establishing trading posts along the west coast of Africa, Spain watched with increasing envy. In 1492, the Spanish monarchs, Ferdinand and Isabella, completed the Reconquista—their long effort to drive the Moors from Spain. With the help of the Inquisition, they also unified their country under Christianity. They were now free to turn their attention to finding a direct sea route to Asia.

Christopher Columbus, an Italian sea captain, convinced the monarchs to finance a bold plan: finding a route to Asia by sailing west across the Atlantic Ocean. The monarchs agreed to fund the voyage. Columbus's ships—the *Niña*, *Pinta*, and *Santa María*—sailed out of a Spanish port around dawn on August 3, 1492. In a matter of months, Columbus's fleet would reach the shores of what Europeans saw as an astonishing new world.

The Voyages of Christopher Columbus In the early hours of October 12, 1492, the long-awaited cry came. A lookout aboard the *Pinta* caught sight of a shoreline in the distance. *"Tierra! Tierra!"* he shouted. "Land! Land!" By dawn, Columbus and his crew were ashore. Thinking he had successfully reached the East Indies, Columbus called the surprised inhabitants who greeted him, *los indios*. The term translated into "Indian," a word mistakenly applied to all the native peoples of the Americas. Columbus had miscalculated where he was. He had not reached the East Indies. Scholars believe he landed instead on an island in the Bahamas in the Caribbean Sea. The natives there were not Indians, but a group who called themselves the Taino. Nonetheless, Columbus claimed the island for Spain. He named it San Salvador, or "Holy Savior." Columbus, like other explorers, was interested in gold. Finding none on San Salvador, he explored other islands, staking his claim to each one.

In early 1493, Columbus returned to Spain. The reports he relayed about his journey delighted the Spanish monarchs. Spain's rulers agreed to finance three more trips. Columbus embarked on his second voyage to the Americas in September of 1493. He journeyed no longer as an explorer, but as an empire builder. He commanded a fleet of some 17 ships that carried over 1,000 soldiers, crewmen, and colonists. The Spanish intended to transform the islands of the Caribbean into **colonies**, or lands that are controlled by another nation.

The Treaty of Tordesillas Columbus's first voyage opened the way for colonization and forever changed the world. The immediate impact of the voyage, however, was to increase tensions between Spain and Portugal. At first,

4.12 Preparing for the Regents
Human and Physical Geography In what way was 1492 a turning point in global history?

🗽 **4.13 Preparing for the Regents**

Nationalism Why did Columbus's first voyage cause tension between Spain and Portugal?

the Portuguese believed that Columbus had indeed reached Asia. Portugal suspected that Columbus had claimed for Spain lands that Portuguese sailors might have reached first. The rivalry between Spain and Portugal grew more tense. In 1493, Pope Alexander VI stepped in to keep peace between the two nations. He suggested an imaginary dividing line, drawn north to south, through the Atlantic Ocean. All lands to the west of the line, known as the Line of Demarcation, would be Spain's. These lands included most of the Americas. All lands to the east of the line would belong to Portugal.

Portugal complained that the line gave too much to Spain. So it was moved farther west to include parts of modern-day Brazil for the Portuguese. In 1494, Spain and Portugal signed the **Treaty of Tordesillas**, in which they agreed to honor the line. The era of exploration and colonization was about to begin in earnest.

Exploration and Overseas Expansion

In 1500, the Portuguese explorer Pedro Álvares Cabral reached the shores of modern-day Brazil and claimed the land for his country. A year later, Amerigo Vespucci (vehs•POO•chee), an Italian in the service of Portugal, also traveled along the eastern coast of South America. Upon his return to Europe, he claimed that the land was not part of Asia, but a "new" world. In 1507, a German mapmaker named the new continent "America" in honor of Amerigo Vespucci.

In 1519, Portuguese explorer Ferdinand Magellan led the boldest exploration yet. Several years earlier, Spanish explorer Vasco Núñez de Balboa had marched through modern-day Panama and had become the first European to gaze upon the Pacific Ocean. Soon after, Magellan convinced the king of Spain to fund his voyage into the newly discovered ocean.

🗽 **4.14 Preparing for the Regents**

Human and Physical Geography How did Ferdinand Magellan contribute to the European age of exploration?

With about 250 men and five ships, Magellan sailed around the southern end of South America and into the waters of the Pacific. The fleet sailed for months without seeing land, except for some small islands. Food supplies soon ran out. After exploring the island of Guam, Magellan and his crew eventually reached the Philippines, which they claimed for Spain. Unfortunately, Magellan became involved in a local war there and was killed. His crew, greatly reduced by disease and starvation, continued sailing west toward home. Out of Magellan's original crew, only 18 men and one ship arrived back in Spain in 1522, nearly three years after they had left. They were the first persons to circumnavigate, or sail around, the world.

🗽 **PREPARING FOR THE REGENTS**

Answer the following question. Use the Analyze the Question hints to help you answer the question.

1 • Invention of the compass and astrolabe
   • European dependence on spices from Asia
   • Rise of nation-states in Europe

These developments influenced the start of the

(1) Crusades
(2) Renaissance
(3) Reformation
(4) Age of Exploration

ANALYZE THE QUESTION
• Read the question stem. You are being asked to match the listed developments with one of the four alternatives.
• Think about the characteristics of each alternative.
• Rule out the alternatives that could not have been spurred by all three developments.
• The remaining alternative is the correct answer.

Mesoamerican and South American Empires

Section Overview

While the Maya were developing their civilization on the Yucatán Peninsula, other high cultures were evolving in central Mexico. Some of the most important developments took place in and around the Valley of Mexico. This valley, where modern Mexico City is located, eventually became the site of the greatest empire of Mesoamerica, the Aztec. The Aztec arrived in the area around A.D. 1200. At its height, their empire covered some 80,000 square miles, stretching from central Mexico to the Atlantic and Pacific coasts and south into Oaxaca.

While the Aztecs ruled in the Valley of Mexico, another people— the Inca—created an equally powerful state in South America. By the A.D. 1200s, the Inca had established a small kingdom in southern Peru. From there, they spread outward in all directions, bringing various Andean peoples under their control. By 1500, the Incan Empire stretched from Ecuador in the north to Chile in the south. It was the largest empire ever seen in the Americas.

Mesoamerican god, Quetzalcoatl

MAIN IDEAS

POWER AND AUTHORITY Through alliances and conquest, the Aztec created a powerful empire in Mexico.

POWER AND AUTHORITY The Inca built a vast empire supported by taxes, governed by a bureaucracy, and linked by extensive road systems.

TERMS AND NAMES

- Triple Alliance
- Quetzalcoatl
- Montezuma II
- Pachacuti
- ayllu
- mita
- quipu
- Atahualpa

PREPARING FOR THE REGENTS

As you read this section, consider
- how the Aztec and Inca empires compare to earlier Afro-Eurasian classical civilizations in terms of organization and achievement.
- the characteristics of Aztec and Incan trade.

TIME LINE

1325
Aztecs build Tenochtitlán.

1438
Pachacuti becomes Incan emperor.

1502
Montezuma II crowned Aztec emperor.

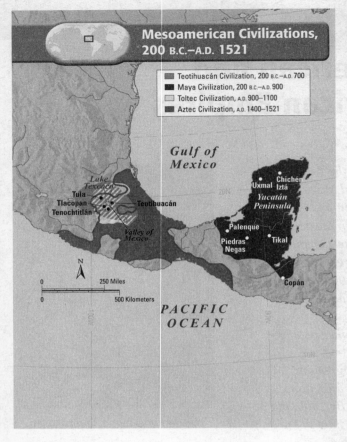

Mesoamerican Civilizations, 200 B.C.–A.D. 1521

- Teotihuacán Civilization, 200 B.C.–A.D. 700
- Maya Civilization, 200 B.C.–A.D. 900
- Toltec Civilization, A.D. 900–1100
- Aztec Civilization, A.D. 1400–1521

Gulf of Mexico

Lake Texcoco
Tula
Tlacopan
Tenochtitlán
Teotihuacán
Valley of Mexico

Chichén Itzá
Uxmal
Yucatán Peninsula
Palenque
Piedras Negas
Tikal
Copán

N

0   250 Miles
0   500 Kilometers

PACIFIC OCEAN

Aztec Empire

The Valley of Mexico, where modern Mexico City is located, was home to the Aztec, the greatest empire of Mesoamerica. The Aztecs were preceded by two other important civilizations—Teotihuacán (TAY•oh•TEE•wah•KAHN) and the Toltecs.

Human and Physical Geography
The Valley of Mexico is a mountain basin about 7,500 feet above sea level. The Aztecs, like the Teotihuacán and the Toltecs before them, were attracted by the valley's several large, shallow lakes, accessible resources, and fertile soil. The Aztecs arrived in the Valley of Mexico around A.D. 1200. The area contained a number of small city-states that had survived the collapse of Toltec rule. The Aztecs, who were then called the Mexica, were a poor, nomadic people from the harsh deserts of northern Mexico. Fierce and ambitious, they soon adapted to local ways, finding work as soldiers-for-hire to local rulers.

According to Aztec legend, Huitzilopochtli (wee•tsee•loh•POHCH•tlee), the god of the sun and warfare, told the Aztec to found a city of their own. He said to look for a place where an eagle perched on a cactus, holding a snake in its mouth. They found such a place on a small island in Lake Texcoco. There, in 1325, they founded their city, Tenochtitlán (teh•NOCH•tee•TLAHN).

Social and Political Organization
In 1428, the Aztec joined with two other city-states—Texcoco and Tlacopan—to form the **Triple Alliance**. This alliance became the leading power in the Valley of Mexico and soon gained control over neighboring regions. By the early 1500s, they controlled a vast empire that covered some 80,000 square miles stretching from central Mexico to the Atlantic and Pacific coasts and south into Oaxaca. This empire was divided into 38 provinces. It had an estimated population of between 5 and 15 million people.

The Aztecs generally exercised loose control over the empire, often letting local rulers govern their own regions. The Aztecs did demand tribute, however, in the form of gold, maize, cacao beans, cotton, jade, and other products. If local rulers failed to pay tribute, or offered any resistance, the Aztecs responded brutally, destroying the rebellious villages and capturing or slaughtering the inhabitants.

At the height of the Aztec Empire, military leaders held great power in Aztec society. Along with government officials and priests, these military leaders made up the noble class. Many nobles owned vast estates, which they ruled over like lords. There were two other broad classes in Aztec society, commoners and enslaved persons. Commoners included merchants, artisans, soldiers, and farmers who owned their own land. The merchants formed a special elite. They often traveled widely, acting as spies for the emperor and gaining great wealth for themselves. The lowest class, enslaved persons, were captives who did many different jobs. The emperor sat atop the Aztec social pyramid. Although he sometimes consulted with top generals or officials, his power was absolute.

TAKING NOTES
Following Chronological Order Use a "chain of events" diagram to list events in the establishment and growth of the Aztec Empire.

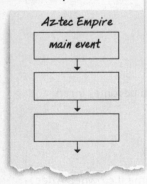

Aztec Empire

main event

↓

↓

↓

⬛ **4.15 Preparing for the Regents**

Culture and Intellectual Life How was the Aztec society structured?

Religious Life Religion played a major role in Aztec society. Tenochtitlán contained hundreds of temples and religious structures dedicated to the approximately 1,000 gods that the Aztecs worshiped. The Aztecs adopted many of their gods and religious practices from other Mesoamerican peoples. For example, they worshiped the Toltec god **Quetzalcoatl** (keht•SAHL•koh•AHT•uhl) in many forms. The Aztecs pictured Quetzalcoatl not only as a feathered serpent, but also as a pale-skinned man with a beard.

The most important Aztec religious rituals involved Huitzilopochtli. According to Aztec belief, Huitzilopochtli made the sun rise every day. When the sun set, he had to battle the forces of evil to get to the next day. To make sure that he was strong enough for this ordeal, he needed the nourishment of human blood. Without regular blood offerings, Huitzilopochtli would be too weak to fight and all life would perish. For this reason, Aztec priests practiced human sacrifice on a massive scale. Each year, thousands of victims had their hearts carved out atop Tenochtitlán's Great Temple.

Sacrificial victims included enslaved persons, criminals, and people offered as tribute by conquered provinces. Prisoners of war, however, were the preferred victims. As a result, the Aztecs often went to war not to conquer new lands, but simply to capture prisoners for sacrifice.

Cultural Achievements and Trade By the early 1500s, Tenochtitlán had become an extraordinary urban center. With a population of between 200,000 and 400,000 people, it was larger than any European capital of the time. The city remained on its original island site. To connect the island to the mainland, Aztec engineers built three raised roads, called causeways, over the water and marshland. Other smaller cities ringed the lake, creating a dense concentration of people.

Streets and broad avenues connected the city center with outlying residential districts. The canals that intersected with these roadways allowed canoes to bring people and goods directly into the city center. The economic heart of the city was the huge market of Tlatelolco (TLAH•tehl•AWL•koh). Visitors to the market found a great deal of local agricultural produce on display, including avocados, beans, chili peppers, corn, squash, and tomatoes. Most of the fruits and vegetables sold at the market were grown on *chinampas*, farm plots built on the marshy fringes of the lake. These plots, sometimes called "floating gardens," were extremely productive, providing the food needed for a huge urban population.

Among the many accomplishments of the Aztecs was an intricate calendar system, which archaeologists believe the Aztec derived from the Maya system. The Aztecs followed two main calendars: a sacred one with 13 months of 20 days and an agricultural or solar one with 18 months of 20 days. Notice that the solar calendar comes to 360 days. The Aztec then had an unlucky five-day period known as the *nemontemi*, making their solar calendar 365 days long.

Problems in the Empire In 1502, **Montezuma II** (MAHN•tih•ZOO•muh) was crowned emperor. Under Montezuma, the Aztec Empire began to weaken. For nearly a century, the Aztecs had been demanding tribute and sacrificial victims from the provinces under their control. Montezuma called for even more tribute and sacrifice. A number of provinces rose up against Aztec oppression. This began a period of unrest and rebellion, which the military struggled to put down. Many Aztecs began to predict that terrible things were about to happen. They saw bad omens in every unusual occurrence—lightning striking a temple in Tenochtitlán, or a partial eclipse of the sun, for example. For many, however, the most worrying event was the arrival of the Spanish from across the sea.

4.16 Preparing for the Regents

Belief Systems What role did religion play in Aztec society?

4.17 Preparing for the Regents

Human and Physical Geography Why can *chinampas* be viewed as an example of how the Aztec adapted to their physical environment?

4.18 Preparing for the Regents

Conflict What factors led to conflict in the Aztec Empire?

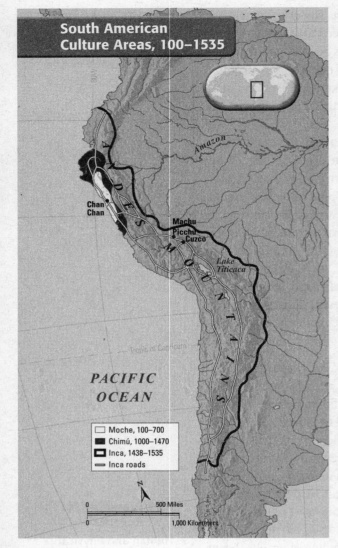

PACIFIC OCEAN

Chan Chan

Machu Picchu
Cuzco

Lake Titicaca

☐ Moche, 100–700
■ Chimú, 1000–1470
▢ Inca, 1438–1535
— Inca roads

0   500 Miles
0   1,000 Kilometers

4.19 Preparing for the Regents

Human and Physical Environment What environmental challenges did the Inca face in establishing their empire?

TAKING NOTES

Categorizing Use a web diagram to identify the methods the Inca used to build their vast, unified empire.

The Inca built a vast empire.

Incan Empire

While the Aztecs ruled in Mesoamerica, the Inca created an equally powerful state in South America. From Cuzco, their capital in southern Peru, the Inca built an empire that stretched from Ecuador in the north to Chile in the south. By 1500, it was the largest empire ever seen in the Americas. Like the Aztecs, the Inca built their empire on the cultural foundations of older civilizations, such as Chavín (sha•VEEN), Moche (MO•chay), Nazca, and Chimú.

Human and Physical Geography The Andes Mountains stretches about 4,500 miles down the western edge of South America, from Columbia in the north to Chile in the south. After the Himalayas in southern Asia, the Andes is the next highest mountain range in the world, with a number of peaks over 20,000 feet in elevation. The area is a harsh place to develop a civilization. The Andes are steep and rocky, with generally poor soil. Ice and snow cover the highest elevations year-round. Overland travel often is difficult. The climate is also severe: hot and dry during the day, and often freezing at night. Between the mountains and the Pacific Ocean lies a narrow coastal plain. Most of this plain is harsh desert where rain seldom falls. In some places, however, rivers cross the desert on their path from the mountains to the sea.

The Rise of the Inca The Inca originally lived in a high plateau of the Andes. After wandering the highlands for years, the Inca finally settled on fertile lands in the Valley of Cuzco. By the 1200s, they had established their own small kingdom in the valley. During this early period, the Inca developed traditions and beliefs that helped launch and unify their empire. One of these traditions was the belief that the Incan ruler was descended from the sun god, Inti, who would bring prosperity and greatness to the Incan state. Only men from one of 11 noble lineages believed to be descendants of the sun god could be selected as Incan leaders.

At first the Incan kingdom grew slowly. In 1438, however, a powerful and ambitious ruler, **Pachacuti** (PAH•chah•KOO•tee), took the throne. Under his leadership, the Inca conquered all of Peru and then moved into neighboring lands. By 1500, the Inca ruled an empire that stretched 2,500 miles along the western coast of South America. It included about 80 provinces and was home to as many as 16 million people.

Pachacuti and his successors accomplished this feat of conquest through a combination of diplomacy and military force. The Inca had a powerful military but used force only when necessary. They were also clever diplomats. Before attacking, they typically offered enemy states the option of keeping their own customs and rulers in exchange for loyalty to the Incan state. Because of this treatment, many states gave up without resisting. Even when force was used, the Inca made every effort to gain the conquered people's loyalty.

Social and Political Organization and Trade To control the huge empire, the rulers divided their territory and its people into manageable units, governed by a central bureaucracy, and created an extensive road system to tie the empire together. They also imposed a single official language, Quechua (KEHCH•wuh), and founded schools to teach Incan ways. The Incan state exercised almost total control over economic and social life. Unlike the Maya and the Aztecs, the Inca allowed little private commerce or trade.

The Incan social system was based on an age-old form of community cooperation—the ayllu (EYE•loo). The **ayllu**, or extended family group, undertook tasks too big for a single family. These tasks included building irrigation canals or cutting agricultural terraces into steep hillsides. The ayllu also stored food and other supplies to distribute among members during hard times.

The Inca incorporated the ayllu structure into a governing system based on the decimal system. They divided families into groups of 10, 100, 1,000, and 10,000. A chief led each group. He was part of a chain of command. That chain stretched from the community and regional levels all the way to Cuzco, where the Incan ruler and his council of state held court. In general, local administration was left in the hands of local rulers, and villages were allowed to continue their traditional ways. If a community resisted Incan control, however, the Inca might relocate the whole group to a different territory and place them under the control of government-appointed rulers.

The main demand the Incan state placed on its subjects was for tribute, usually in the form of labor. The labor tribute was known as **mita** (MEE•tuh). It required all able-bodied citizens to work for the state a certain number of days every year. Mita workers might labor on state farmlands, produce craft goods for state warehouses, or help with public works projects. Historians have compared the Incan system to a type of socialism or a modern welfare state. Citizens were expected to work for the state and were cared for in return. For example, the aged and disabled were often supported by the state, and the government distributed freeze-dried potatoes, called *chuño*, in times of food shortages.

Cultural Achievements To exercise control over their empire, the Inca built many cities in conquered areas. The architecture of government buildings was the same all over the empire, making the presence of the government apparent. As in Rome, all roads led to the capital, Cuzco. The heart of the Incan empire, Cuzco was a splendid city of temples, plazas, and palaces. Like the Romans, the Inca were masterful engineers and stonemasons. Though they had no iron tools and did not use the wheel, Incan builders carved and transported huge blocks of stone, fitting them together perfectly without mortar.

The Inca had an ambitious public works program. The most spectacular project was the Incan road system. A marvel of engineering, this road system symbolized the power of the Incan state. The 14,000-mile-long network of roads and bridges spanned the empire, traversing rugged mountains and harsh deserts. The roads ranged from paved stone to simple paths. A system of runners, known as *chasquis* (SHAH•skeys), traveled these roads as a kind of postal service, carrying messages from one end of the empire to the other. The road system also allowed the easy movement of troops when necessary.

The Inca never developed a writing system. History and literature were memorized as part of an oral tradition. For numerical information, the Inca created an accounting device known as the **quipu**, a set of knotted strings that could be used to record data. The knots and their position on the string indicated

4.20 Preparing for the Regents
Human and Physical Geography Why can terrace farming be viewed as an example of how the Inca adapted to their physical environment?

4.21 Preparing for the Regents
Culture and Intellectual Life What were some of the cultural achievements of the Inca?

numbers. Additionally, the colors of the strings represented different categories of information important to the government. For example, red strings were used to count warriors; yellow strings were used to count gold. However, the meanings of the colors changed depending on the general purpose of the quipu.

4.22 Preparing for the Regents

Belief Systems What role did religion play in Incan society?

Religious Life As with the Aztecs, religion was important to the Inca and helped reinforce the power of the state. The Inca worshiped fewer gods than the Aztecs. Chief of the Incan gods was a creator god called Viracocha. Next in importance was the sun god, Inti. Because the Incan ruler was considered a descendant of Inti, sun worship amounted to worship of the king. Sacrifice of llamas and exchange of goods were a part of the religious activities. The goods were distributed by the priests to the people as gifts from the gods.

The Temple of the Sun in Cuzco was the most sacred of all Incan shrines. It was heavily decorated in gold, a metal the Inca referred to as "sweat of the sun." While Cuzco was the religious capital of the Incan Empire, other Incan cities also may have served a ceremonial purpose. Like Cuzco, Machu Picchu also had a sun temple, public buildings, and a central plaza.

4.23 Preparing for the Regents

Conflict What events led to conflict in the Incan Empire?

Problems in the Incan Empire The Incan Empire reached its height in the early 1500s during the reign of Huayna Capac. Trouble was brewing, however. In the 1520s, Huayna Capac undertook a tour of Ecuador, a newly conquered area of the empire. In the city of Quito, he received a gift box. When he opened it, out flew butterflies and moths, considered an evil omen. A few weeks later, while still in Quito, Huayna Capac died of disease—probably smallpox. After his death, the empire was split between his sons, **Atahualpa** (ah•tah•WAHL•pah) and Huascar (WAHS•kahr). Atahualpa received Ecuador, about one-fifth of the empire. The rest went to Huascar. At first, this system of dual emperors worked. Soon, however, Atahualpa laid claim to the whole of the empire. A bitter civil war followed. Atahualpa eventually won, but the war tore apart the empire.

PREPARING FOR THE REGENTS

Answer the following questions. Use the Analyze the Question hints to help you answer the questions.

1 The archaeological evidence found at Tenochtitlán and Machu Picchu suggests that these societies

(1) consisted of hunters and gatherers
(2) were highly developed and organized cultures
(3) practiced monotheistic religions
(4) followed a democratic system

ANALYZE THE QUESTION
- Read the question stem. You are being asked to determine which alternative is supported by the archaeological evidence from Tenochtitlán and Machu Picchu.
- Think about what you know about each society. Rule out the alternatives that are not characteristic of both the Aztec and the Inca.
- The remaining alternative is the correct answer.

2 Look at the map on page 146. Which conclusion about Incan society could be drawn from this map?

(1) An extensive road system connected all parts of the empire.
(2) Their trade depended on many seaports.
(3) Tropical climatic conditions existed throughout the empire.
(4) A similar language unified the Incan Empire.

ANALYZE THE QUESTION
- Read the question stem. You are being asked to determine what conclusion about Incan society can be drawn from the map.
- Look at the map's legend and labels to determine what the map shows.
- Rule out the alternatives that are not supported by information on the map.
- The remaining alternative is the correct answer.

Europe Encounters the World

Section Overview

*Competition for wealth in Asia among European nations was
fierce. The voyages of Christopher Columbus launched that same
competition in the Americas. Spain was the first nation to establish
American colonies. The Portuguese, French, and British were soon
building their own empires in the Americas.*

*Wealth from the Americas was built in part on agriculture. Sugar
plantations and tobacco farms required a large supply of workers to
make them profitable for their owners. European owners had planned
to use Native Americans as a source of cheap labor. But millions of
Native Americans died from disease, warfare, and brutal treatment.
Therefore, the Europeans turned to Africa for workers. This demand
for cheap labor resulted in the brutalities of the slave trade.*

*The colonization of the Americas dramatically changed the
world. It prompted both voluntary and forced migration of millions
of people. It led to the establishment of new and powerful societies.
Other effects of European settlement of the Americas were less
noticeable but equally important. Colonization resulted in the
exchange of new items that greatly influenced the lives of people
throughout the world. The new wealth from the Americas resulted in
new business and trade practices in Europe.*

Diagram of British slave ship

MAIN IDEAS

EMPIRE BUILDING   Over the span of several centuries, Europeans
conquered the Americas' native inhabitants and built powerful American
empires.

ECONOMICS   The vast wealth to be had from colonizing the Americas
sealed the fate of millions of Native Americans and Africans who were
forced to work in the mines and on plantations.

CULTURAL INTERACTION   The voyages of Columbus prompted a
worldwide exchange of everything from religious and political ideas to
new foods and plants.

TIME LINE

1521
Cortés conquers Aztec Empire.

1533
Pizarro conquers Incan Empire.

1607
English found Jamestown.

1608
Champlain claims Quebec for
France.

1619
Dutch open trade with Java.

1650
The number of Africans toiling in
Spanish America reaches 300,000.

TERMS AND NAMES

- Dutch East India
  Company
- Hernando Cortés
- conquistadors
- Francisco Pizarro

- mestizo
- *encomienda*
- Atlantic slave trade
- triangular trade
- middle passage

- Columbian Exchange
- joint-stock company
- mercantilism
- favorable balance of
  trade

PREPARING FOR THE REGENTS

As you read this section, consider
- how life changed as a result of the encounter.
- how the standard of living in Europe changed as a result of the encounter.

Human and Physical Geography— The Extent of European Expansion

The attempts by Portugal and Spain to find a sea route to Asia in the late 1400 set the European age of exploration in full motion. Portugal's success in Asia attracted the attention of other European nations. Beginning around 1600, the English and Dutch began to challenge Portugal's dominance over the Indian Ocean trade. The Dutch had the largest fleet of ships in the world—20,000 vessels. Pressure from Dutch and English fleets eventually eroded Portuguese control. The Dutch and English then battled one another for dominance of the area, with the Dutch finally winning.

Spain held claim to the Philippines and began settling the islands in 1565. Spain's main efforts, however, were in the Americas, where it sought to establish colonies. Spain's success in the Americas did not go unnoticed. Other European nations soon became interested in obtaining their own valuable colonies. The Treaty of Tordesillas, signed in 1494, had divided the newly discovered lands between Spain and Portugal. However, other European countries ignored the treaty.

Magellan's voyage showed that ships could reach Asia by way of the Pacific Ocean. Spain claimed the route around the southern tip of South America. Other European countries hoped to find an easier and more direct route to the Pacific. If it existed, a northwest trade route through North America to Asia would become highly profitable. Not finding the route, the French, English, and Dutch instead established colonies in North America. As the map on this page shows, by 1700 the Europeans had laid claim to large areas of the Americas.

4.24 Preparing for the Regents

Imperialism What was the extent of European claims in the Americas by 1700?

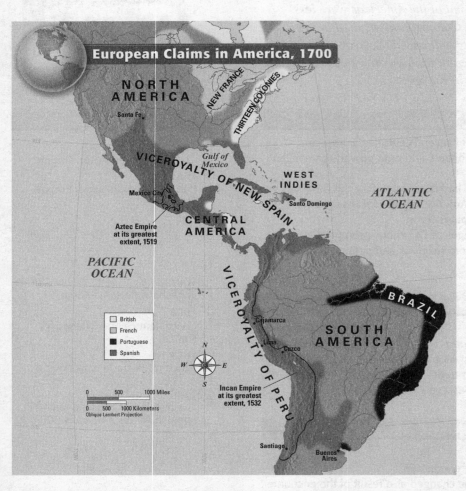

European Claims in America, 1700

- ☐ British
- ☐ French
- ■ Portuguese
- ☐ Spanish

Dutch East Indies

The Dutch formed the **Dutch East India Company** in 1602 to direct trade throughout Asia. The company had the power to mint money, make treaties, and even raise its own army.

In 1619, the Dutch established their trading headquarters at Batavia on the island of Java. From there, they expanded west to conquer nearby islands. In addition, the Dutch seized Malacca from the Portuguese and fought the British and Javanese for control of Java. The discovery of oil and tin on the islands and the desire for more rubber plantations prompted the Dutch to gradually expand their control over Sumatra, part of Borneo, Celebes, the Moluccas, and Bali. Eventually, the Dutch ruled the whole island chain of Indonesia, then called the Dutch East Indies.

Spanish America

In 1519, a Spaniard named <u>**Hernando Cortés**</u> landed on the shores of Mexico. After colonizing several Caribbean islands, the Spanish had turned their attention to the American mainland. Cortés marched inland, looking to claim new lands for Spain. Cortés and the many other Spanish explorers who followed him were known as **conquistadors** (conquerors). Lured by rumors of vast lands filled with gold and silver, conquistadors carved out colonies in regions that would become Mexico, South America, and the United States. The Spanish were the first European settlers in the Americas. As a result of their colonization, the Spanish greatly enriched their empire and left a mark on the cultures of North and South America that exists today.

Cortés Conquers the Aztecs   Soon after landing in Mexico, Cortés learned of the vast and wealthy Aztec Empire in the region's interior. Cortés and his force of roughly 600 men finally reached the magnificent Aztec capital of Tenochtitlán. The Aztec emperor, Montezuma II, was convinced at first that Cortés was a god wearing armor. He agreed to give the Spanish explorer a share of the empire's existing gold supply. The conquistador was not satisfied.

In the late spring of 1520, some of Cortés's men killed many Aztec warriors and chiefs while they were celebrating a religious festival. In June of 1520, the Aztecs rebelled against the Spanish intruders and drove out Cortés's forces. The Spaniards, however, struck back. Despite being greatly outnumbered, Cortés and his men conquered the Aztecs in 1521.

Several factors played a key role in the victory. First, the Spanish had the advantage of superior technology. Aztec arrows were no match for the Spaniards' muskets and cannons. Second, Cortés was able to enlist the help of various native groups who resented the Aztecs. Finally, the Aztecs could do little to stop the invisible warrior that marched alongside the Spaniards—disease. Measles, mumps, smallpox, and typhus were just some of the diseases Europeans brought to the Americas. Native Americans had never been exposed to these diseases. Thus, they had developed no natural immunity to them. By the time Cortés launched his counterattack, the Aztec population had been greatly reduced by smallpox and measles. In time, European disease would kill millions of natives of Central Mexico.

Pizarro Subdues the Inca   In 1532, <u>**Francisco Pizarro**</u>, another conquistador, conquered the Incan Empire. Pizarro and his army of about 200 met the Incan ruler, Atahualpa, near the city of Cajamarca. Atahualpa, who commanded a force of about 30,000, brought several thousand mostly unarmed men for the meeting. The Spaniards waited in ambush, crushed the Incan force, and kidnapped Atahualpa. Atahualpa offered to fill a room once with gold and twice with silver in exchange for his release. However, after receiving the ransom, the Spanish strangled the Incan king. Demoralized by their leader's death, the remaining Incan force retreated from Cajamarca. Pizarro then marched on the Incan capital, Cuzco. He captured it without a struggle in 1533.

Spain's Patterns of Conquest   In building their new American empire, the Spaniards drew from techniques used during the Reconquista of Spain. When conquering the Muslims, the Spanish lived among them and imposed their culture upon them. The Spanish settlers to the Americas, known as *peninsulares*, were mostly men. As a result, relationships between Spanish settlers and native women were common. These relationships created a large <u>**mestizo**</u>—or mixed Spanish and Native American—population.

TAKING NOTES

Following Chronological Order Use a diagram to trace the major events in the establishment of Spain's empire in the Americas.

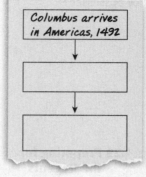

Columbus arrives in Americas, 1492

4.25 Preparing for the Regents

Conflict   What factors contributed to Hernando Cortés's ability to conquer the Aztecs?

4.26 Preparing for the Regents

Conflict   How did Francisco Pizarro defeat the Incan Empire?

4.27 Preparing for the Regents

Diversity   Who were the mestizos?

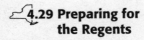

Although the Spanish conquerors lived among the native people, they also oppressed them. In their effort to exploit the land for its precious resources, the Spanish forced Native Americans to work within a system known as **encomienda** (ehng•kaw•MYEHN•dah). Under this system, natives farmed, ranched, or mined for Spanish landlords. These landlords had received the rights to the natives' labor from Spanish authorities. The holders of *encomiendas* promised the Spanish rulers that they would act fairly and respect the workers. However, many abused the natives and worked many laborers to death, especially inside dangerous mines.

Spanish priests pushed for better treatment of Native Americans. In particular, they criticized the harsh pattern of labor that emerged under the *encomienda* system. "There is nothing more detestable or more cruel," Dominican monk Bartolomé de Las Casas wrote, "than the tyranny which the Spaniards use toward the Indians for the getting of pearl [riches]."

The Slave Trade

The Spanish government abolished the *encomienda* system in 1542. To meet the colonies' need for labor, Las Casas suggested Africans. The priest later changed his view and denounced African slavery. However, others promoted it.

4.29 Preparing for the Regents

Factors of Production How did the abolition of the *encomienda* system contribute to the rise of the Atlantic slave trade?

The Atlantic Slave Trade In time, the buying and selling of Africans for work in the Americas—known as the **Atlantic slave trade**—became a massive enterprise. Between 1500 and 1600, nearly 300,000 Africans were transported to the Americas. During the next century, that number climbed to almost 1.3 million. By the time the Atlantic slave trade ended around 1870, Europeans had imported about 9.5 million Africans to the Americas.

Many African rulers and merchants played a willing role in the Atlantic slave trade. Most European traders, rather than travel inland, waited in ports along the coasts of Africa. African merchants, with the help of local rulers, captured Africans to be enslaved. They then delivered them to the Europeans in exchange for gold, guns, and other goods.

As the slave trade grew, some African rulers voiced their opposition to the practice. Nonetheless, the slave trade steadily grew. Lured by its profits, many African rulers continued to participate. African merchants developed new trade routes to avoid rulers who refused to cooperate.

4.30 Preparing for the Regents

Economic Systems Study the map on page 153, which shows the triangular trade that supported mercantilism. What role did the slave trade play in the system?

The Triangular Trade After being captured, African men and women were shipped to the Americas as part of a profitable trade network. Along the way, millions of Africans died. Africans transported to the Americas were part of a transatlantic trading network known as the **triangular trade**. Over one trade route, Europeans transported manufactured goods to the west coast of Africa. There, traders exchanged these goods for captured Africans. The Africans were then transported across the Atlantic and sold in the West Indies. Merchants bought sugar, coffee, and tobacco in the West Indies and sailed to Europe with these products.

On another triangular route, merchants carried rum and other goods from the New England colonies to Africa. There they exchanged their merchandise for Africans. The traders transported the Africans to the West Indies and sold them for sugar and molasses. They then sold these goods to rum producers in New England. Various other transatlantic routes existed. The "triangular" trade encompassed a network of trade routes crisscrossing the northern and southern colonies, the West Indies, England, Europe, and Africa. The network carried a variety of traded goods.

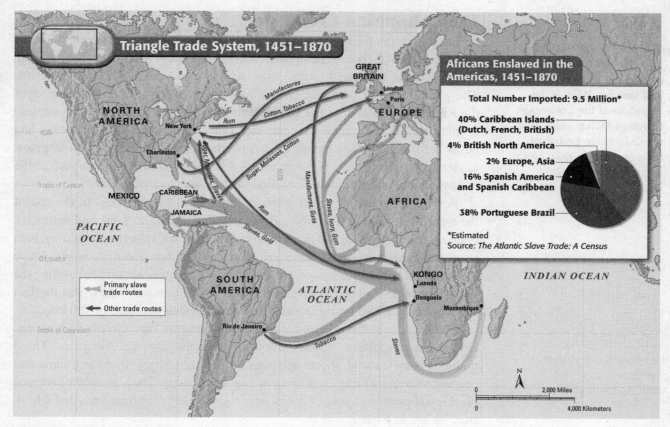

Triangle Trade System, 1451–1870

NORTH AMERICA
New York
Charleston
MEXICO
CARIBBEAN
JAMAICA
PACIFIC OCEAN
SOUTH AMERICA
Rio de Janeiro

GREAT BRITAIN
London
Paris
EUROPE
AFRICA
ATLANTIC OCEAN
KONGO
Luanda
Benguela
Mozambique
INDIAN OCEAN

Manufactures
Cotton, Tobacco
Rum
Sugar, Molasses, Cotton
Sugar, Molasses, Slaves
Rum
Slaves, Gold
Manufactures, Guns
Slaves, Ivory, Gum
Tobacco
Slaves

Primary slave trade routes
Other trade routes

Africans Enslaved in the Americas, 1451–1870

Total Number Imported: 9.5 Million*

40% Caribbean Islands (Dutch, French, British)
4% British North America
2% Europe, Asia
16% Spanish America and Spanish Caribbean
38% Portuguese Brazil

*Estimated
Source: *The Atlantic Slave Trade: A Census*

0   2,000 Miles
0   4,000 Kilometers

The Middle Passage The voyage that brought captured Africans to the West Indies and later to North and South America was known as the **middle passage**. It was considered the middle leg of the transatlantic trade triangle. Sickening cruelty characterized this journey. In African ports, European traders packed Africans into the dark holds of large ships. On board, Africans endured whippings and beatings from merchants, as well as diseases that swept through the vessel. Numerous Africans died from disease or physical abuse aboard the slave ships. Many others committed suicide by drowning. Scholars estimate that roughly 20 percent of the Africans aboard each slave ship perished during the brutal trip.

Consequences of the Slave Trade The Atlantic slave trade had a profound impact on both Africa and the Americas. In Africa, numerous cultures lost generations of their fittest members—their young and able—to European traders and plantation owners. In addition, countless African families were torn apart. Many of them were never reunited. The slave trade devastated African societies in another way: by introducing guns into the continent.

While they were unwilling participants in the growth of the colonies, African slaves contributed greatly to the economic and cultural development of the Americas. Their greatest contribution was their labor. Without their back-breaking work, colonies such as those on Haiti and Barbados may not have survived. In addition to their muscle, enslaved Africans brought their expertise, especially in agriculture. They also brought their culture. Their art, music, religion, and food continue to influence American societies.

The influx of so many Africans to the Americas also has left its mark on the very population itself. From the United States to Brazil, many of the nations of the Western Hemisphere today have substantial African-American populations. Many Latin American countries have sizable mixed-race populations.

4.31 Preparing for the Regents

Movement of People and Goods What was the voyage that brought captured Africans from West Africa to the Americas called?

TAKING NOTES

Recognizing Effects Use a diagram like the one below to list effects of the Atlantic slave trade.

Consequences of the slave trade
I. in Africa
  A.
  B.
II. in the Americas
  A.
  B.

The Columbian Exchange

4.32 Preparing for the Regents

Movement of People and Goods   What is the definition of the Columbian Exchange? What impact did the Columbian Exchange have on Europe, Asia, Africa, and the Americas?

Africans were not the only cargo transported across the Atlantic during the colonization of the Americas. The settlement of the Americas resulted in the exchange of many items between Europe, Asia, Africa, and North and South America. The global transfer of foods, plants, and animals during the colonization of the Americas is known as the **Columbian Exchange**. Ships from the Americas brought back a wide array of items that Europeans, Asians, and Africans had never before seen. They included such plants as tomatoes, squash, pineapples, tobacco, and cacao beans (for chocolate). And they included animals such as the turkey, which became a source of food in the Eastern Hemisphere.

Perhaps the most important items to travel from the Americas to the rest of the world were corn and potatoes. Both were inexpensive to grow and nutritious. Potatoes, especially, supplied many essential vitamins and minerals. Over time, both crops became an important and steady part of diets throughout the world. These foods helped people live longer. Thus they played a significant role in boosting the world's population. The planting of the first white potato in Ireland and the first sweet potato in China probably changed more lives than the deeds of 100 kings.

Traffic across the Atlantic did not flow in just one direction, however. Europeans introduced various livestock animals into the Americas. These included horses, cattle, sheep, and pigs. Foods from Africa (including some that originated in Asia) migrated west in European ships. They included bananas, black-eyed peas, and yams. Grains introduced to the Americas included wheat, rice, barley, and oats.

Some aspects of the Columbian Exchange had a tragic impact on many Native Americans. Disease was just as much a part of the Columbian Exchange as goods and food. The diseases Europeans brought with them, which included smallpox and measles, led to the deaths of millions of Native Americans.

Global Trade and Mercantilism

The establishment of colonial empires in the Americas influenced the nations of Europe in still other ways. New wealth from the Americas was coupled with a dramatic growth in overseas trade. The two factors together prompted the growth of capitalism and gave rise to a wave of new business and trade practices in Europe during the 16th and 17th centuries. These practices, many of which served as the root of today's financial dealings, dramatically changed the economic atmosphere of Europe.

4.33 Preparing for the Regents

Economic Systems   How did joint-stock companies contribute to the rise of capitalism?

Joint-Stock Companies   One business venture that developed during this period was known as the **joint-stock company**. The joint-stock company worked much like the modern-day corporation, with investors buying shares of stock in a company. It involved a number of people combining their wealth for a common purpose.

In Europe during the 1500s and 1600s, that common purpose was American colonization. It took large amounts of money to establish overseas colonies. Moreover, while profits may have been great, so were risks. Many ships, for instance, never completed the long and dangerous ocean voyage. Because joint-stock companies involved numerous investors, the individual members paid only a fraction of the total colonization cost. If the colony failed, investors lost only their small share. If the colony thrived, the investors shared in the profits. It was a joint-stock company that was responsible for establishing Jamestown, England's first North American colony.

Mercantilism During this time, the nations of Europe adopted a new economic policy known as **mercantilism**. The theory of mercantilism held that a country's power depended mainly on its wealth. Wealth, after all, allowed nations to build strong navies and purchase vital goods. As a result, the goal of every nation became the attainment of as much wealth as possible.

According to the theory of mercantilism, a nation could increase its wealth and power in two ways. First, it could obtain as much gold and silver as possible. Second, it could establish a **favorable balance of trade**, in which it sold more goods than it bought. A nation's ultimate goal under mercantilism was to become self-sufficient, not dependent on other countries for goods.

Mercantilism went hand in hand with colonization, for colonies played a vital role in this new economic practice. Aside from providing silver and gold, colonies provided raw materials that could not be found in the home country, such as wood or furs. In addition to playing the role of supplier, the colonies also provided a market. The home country could sell its goods to its colonies.

Changes in European Society The economic changes that swept through much of Europe during the age of American colonization also led to changes in European society. The economic revolution spurred the growth of towns and the rise of a class of merchants who controlled great wealth. The changes in European society, however, only went so far. While towns and cities grew in size, much of Europe's population continued to live in rural areas. And although merchants and traders enjoyed social mobility, the majority of Europeans remained poor. More than anything else, the economic revolution increased the wealth of European nations. In addition, mercantilism contributed to the creation of a national identity and the expansion of the power of European monarchs.

4.34 Preparing for the Regents

Economic Systems What are the basic principles of mercantilism? How was mercantilism related to the triangular trade?

4.35 Preparing for the Regents

Economic Systems What impact did mercantilism have on European society?

PREPARING FOR THE REGENTS

Answer the following questions. Use the Analyze the Question hints to help you answer the questions.

1 Look at the map on page 150. Which conclusion regarding early European settlements is best supported by the information on the map?

 (1) Portugal became the dominant colonial power in South America by 1700.
 (2) Geography made the interior of South America easy to explore.
 (3) Neither the Spanish nor the Portuguese developed major urban centers in Latin America.
 (4) In 1700, most of the land in South America was not settled by Europeans.

> **ANALYZE THE QUESTION**
> • Read the question stem. You are being asked to determine what conclusion about early European settlement can be drawn from the map.
> • Look at the map's legend and labels to determine what the map shows.
> • Select the alternative that is supported by the information on the map.

2 Look at the graph, Africans Enslaved in the Americas, 1451–1810, on page 153. Which idea is best supported by this graph?

 (1) Slavery had its greatest effect on Europe and Asia.
 (2) Slavery was more important in North America than it was in South America.
 (3) The Portuguese made early efforts to outlaw the slave trade.
 (4) Many slaves were transported to the Caribbean islands.

> **ANALYZE THE QUESTION**
> • Read the question stem. You are being asked to determine what the graph shows.
> • Look at the graph's title and labels to determine what the graph shows.
> • Select the alternative that is supported by the information in the graph.

Absolutism

Section Overview

The 17th century was a period of great upheaval in Europe. Religious and territorial conflicts between states led to almost continuous warfare. This caused governments to build huge armies and to levy even heavier taxes on an already suffering population. These pressures in turn brought about widespread unrest. Sometimes peasants revolted.

In response to these crises, monarchs tried to impose order by increasing their own power. As absolute rulers, they regulated everything from religious worship to social gatherings. They created new government bureaucracies to control their countries' economic life. Their goal was to free themselves from the limitations imposed by the nobility and by representative bodies such as Parliament. Only with such freedom could they rule absolutely, as did the most famous monarch of his time, Louis XIV of France.

In Great Britain, the unchecked power of monarchs led to revolution and reform. Absolute rulers were overthrown. A constitutional monarchy was established, which placed limits on the ruler's power. As British monarchs lost power, the power of Parliament grew.

Louis XIV of France
(1638–1715)

MAIN IDEAS

POWER AND AUTHORITY   As feudalism declined, stronger national kingdoms developed in Europe.

ECONOMICS   Absolute rulers wanted to control their countries' economies so that they could free themselves from limitations imposed by the nobility. In France, Louis XIV's unrestrained spending left his country with huge debts.

REVOLUTION   In Great Britain, people challenged the monarch's authority. The overthrow of the king led to important political changes.

TERMS AND NAMES

- absolute monarch
- divine right
- social contract
- Philip II
- Louis XIV
- intendant
- Ivan the Terrible

- boyar
- Peter the Great
- westernization
- Charles I
- English Civil War
- Oliver Cromwell
- Restoration

- *habeas corpus*
- Glorious Revolution
- constitutional monarchy
- cabinet

PREPARING FOR THE REGENTS

As you read this section, consider
- how absolutism in Europe compared to absolutism in Asia and Africa.

TIME LINE

1520
Suleyman begins to rule the Ottoman Empire.

1556
Akbar begins to rule the Mughal Empire. Philip II begins to rule Spain.

1643
Louis XIV begins to rule France.

1649
Puritans under Oliver Cromwell execute English king Charles I.

1696
Peter the Great becomes sole czar of Russia.

Human and Physical Geography

As Europe emerged from the Middle Ages, monarchs grew increasingly powerful. The decline of feudalism, the weakening of Church authority, the rise of cities, and the growth of national kingdoms all helped to centralize authority. In addition, the growing middle class usually backed monarchs, because they promised a peaceful, supportive climate for business. Monarchs used the wealth of colonies to pay for their ambitions.

Crises during the 17th century further increased the power of monarchs. Religious and territorial conflicts between states led to almost continuous warfare. In response, governments built huge armies, which they paid for through heavy taxes. These pressures in turn brought about widespread unrest and sometimes even peasant revolts. Monarchs in Spain, France, Austria, England, Prussia, and Russia tried to impose order by increasing their own power. They regulated everything from religious worship to social gatherings. They created new government bureaucracies to control their countries' economic life. Their goal was to free themselves from the limitations imposed by the nobility and by representative bodies such as Parliament. These rulers wanted to be **absolute monarchs**, kings or queens who held all of the power within their states' boundaries.

Theories of Absolutism

The goal of absolute monarchs was to control every aspect of society. Absolute monarchs believed in **divine right**, the idea that God created the monarchy and that the monarch acted as God's representative on earth. An absolute monarch answered only to God, not to his or her subjects. One vocal supporter of this view was Jacques Bossuet (baw•soo•eh), a French bishop.

The English political thinker Thomas Hobbes also supported strong rulers. In a work called *Leviathan* (1651), Hobbes argued that without governments to keep order, there would be "war . . . of every man against every man," and life would be "solitary, poor, nasty, brutish, and short." To escape such a bleak life, people had to hand over their rights to a strong ruler. In exchange, they gained law and order. Hobbes called this agreement by which people created a government the **social contract**. Because people acted in their own self-interest, Hobbes said, the ruler needed total power to keep citizens under control. In Hobbes's view, such a government was an absolute monarchy.

Absolute Rulers

Although practiced by several monarchs in Europe during the 16th through 18th centuries, absolutism has been used in many regions throughout history. In ancient times, Shi Huangdi in China, Darius in Persia, and the Roman caesars were all absolute rulers. As you have already learned, from 1520 to 1566, Suleyman I exercised great power as sultan of the Ottoman Empire. Similarly, Akbar, who ruled the Mughal Empire in India from 1556 to 1605, also held great power. Among European monarchs of the same time period, the Hapsburg king Charles V ruled with almost as much power. When his son, **Philip II**, came to power in 1556, he continued to rule with a strong hand.

Philip II Charles V divided his vast empire between his brother, Ferdinand, and Philip. Philip received Spain, the Spanish Netherlands, and the American colonies. In 1580, he added Portugal with all of its possessions. Philip's empire provided him with incredible wealth. With this wealth, Spain was able to support a large standing army of about 50,000 soldiers.

4.36 Preparing for the Regents

Power Why did some monarchs argue that they should have absolute power?

4.37 Preparing for the Regents

Power How did Jacques Bossuet view absolute monarchs?

4.38 Preparing for the Regents

Political Systems How is Thomas Hobbes similar to Niccoló Machiavelli in his view of the proper power of rulers?

TAKING NOTES

Clarifying Use a chart to list the conditions that allowed European monarchs to gain power.

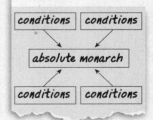

4.39 Preparing for the Regents

Power Why can Philip II be considered an absolute monarch?

When Philip assumed the throne, Europe was experiencing religious wars caused by the Reformation. Philip believed it was his duty to defend Catholicism against the Muslims of the Ottoman Empire and the Protestants of Europe. In 1571, he battled a large Ottoman fleet in a fierce battle near Lepanto and won. He was not as lucky against the Protestants. In 1588, Philip launched the Spanish Armada in an attempt to punish Protestant England and its queen, Elizabeth I, who had supported Protestant subjects who had rebelled against Philip. However, his fleet was defeated. He also failed in his attempts to bring the Protestants in the Spanish Netherlands under control. In 1579, the seven northern provinces of the Netherlands, which were largely Protestant, united and declared their independence from Spain. They became the United Provinces of the Netherlands. The ten southern provinces (present-day Belgium) were Catholic and remained under Spanish control.

4.40 Preparing for the Regents

Power Why can Louis XIV be considered an absolute monarch?

Louis XIV Even though Philip II lost his Dutch possessions, he was a forceful ruler in many ways. He tried to control every aspect of his empire's affairs. **Louis XIV**, who ruled France from 1643 to 1715, was even more forceful. In Louis's view, he and the state were one and the same. He reportedly boasted, *"L'état, c'est moi,"* meaning "I am the state."

Although Louis XIV became the strongest king of his time, he was only a four-year-old boy when he began his reign. The true ruler of the country was Cardinal Mazarin (MAZ•uh•RAN). Many people in France, particularly the nobles, hated Mazarin because he increased taxes and strengthened the central government. From 1648 to 1653, violent anti-Mazarin riots tore France apart. At times, the nobles who led the riots threatened the young king's life. Even after the violence was over, Louis never forgot his fear or his anger at the nobility. He determined to become so strong that they could never threaten him again.

When Cardinal Mazarin died in 1661, the 22-year-old Louis took control of the government himself. He weakened the power of the nobles by excluding them from his councils. In contrast, he increased the power of the government agents called **intendants**, who collected taxes and administered justice. To keep power under central control, he regularly communicated with local officials.

4.41 Preparing for the Regents

Power Why can Ivan the Terrible be considered an absolute monarch?

Ivan the Terrible Ivan IV, called **Ivan the Terrible**, came to the throne of Russia in 1533 when he was only three years old. His young life was disrupted by struggles for power among Russia's landowning nobles, known as **boyars**. The boyars fought to control young Ivan. When he was 16, Ivan seized power and had himself crowned czar. This title meant "caesar," and Ivan was the first Russian ruler to use it officially.

The years from 1547 to 1560 are often called Ivan's "good period." He won great victories, added lands to Russia, gave Russia a code of laws, and ruled justly. Ivan's "bad period" began in 1560 after his wife, Anastasia, died. Accusing the boyars of poisoning his wife, Ivan turned against them. He organized his own police force, whose chief duty was to hunt down and murder people Ivan considered traitors. Using these secret police, Ivan executed many boyars, their families, and the peasants who worked their lands. Thousands of people died. Ivan seized the boyars' estates and gave them to a new class of nobles, who had to remain loyal to him or lose their land.

Following the death of Ivan and then his son, Russia experienced a period of turmoil known as the Time of Troubles. Finally, in 1613, representatives from many Russian cities met to choose the next czar. Their choice was Michael Romanov, grandnephew of Ivan the Terrible's wife, Anastasia.

Peter the Great Over time, the Romanovs restored order to Russia. They strengthened government by passing a law code and putting down a revolt. This paved the way for the absolute rule of Czar Peter I. At first, Peter shared the throne with his half-brother. However, in 1696, Peter became sole ruler of Russia. He is known to history as **Peter the Great**, because he was one of Russia's greatest reformers. He also continued the trend of increasing the czar's power.

When Peter I came to power, Russia was still a land of boyars and serfs. Serfdom in Russia lasted into the mid-1800s, much longer than it did in western Europe. Most boyars knew little of western Europe. In the Middle Ages, Russia had looked to Constantinople, not to Rome, for leadership. Then Mongol rule had cut Russia off from the Renaissance and the Age of Exploration. Geographic barriers also isolated Russia. Its only seaport, Archangel in northern Russia, was choked with ice much of the year.

Peter was 24 years old when he became the sole ruler of Russia. In 1697, just one year later, he embarked on the "Grand Embassy," a long visit to western Europe. One of Peter's goals was to learn about European customs and manufacturing techniques. Inspired by his trip to the West, Peter resolved that Russia would compete with Europe on both military and commercial terms. Peter's goal of **westernization**, of using western Europe as a model for change, was not an end in itself. Peter saw it as a way to make Russia stronger.

Although Peter believed Russia needed to change, he knew that many of his people disagreed. To force change upon his state, Peter increased his powers as an absolute ruler. Peter brought the Russian Orthodox Church under state control. He abolished the office of patriarch, head of the Church. He set up a group called the Holy Synod to run the Church under his direction. Like Ivan the Terrible, Peter reduced the power of the great landowners. He recruited men from lower-ranking families. He then promoted them to positions of authority and rewarded them with grants of land. Peter also hired European officers to help him modernize the army. By the time of Peter's death, the Russian army numbered 200,000 men. To pay for this huge army, Peter imposed heavy taxes.

Peter also instituted many reforms, however. He introduced potatoes into the Russia diet, started Russia's first newspaper, raised the status of women, ordered nobles to wear western clothes, and improved education. In addition, Peter built a new seaport city—St. Petersburg—on the Baltic coast on land won from Sweden. From St. Petersburg, ships could sail down the Neva River into the Baltic Sea and on to western Europe.

Responses to Absolutism in England

During her reign, Queen Elizabeth I of England had frequent conflicts with Parliament. Many of the arguments were over money, because the treasury did not have enough funds to pay the queen's expenses. By the time Elizabeth died in 1603, she had left a huge debt for her successor to deal with. Parliament's financial power was one obstacle to English rulers' becoming absolute monarchs. The resulting struggle between Parliament and the monarchy would have serious consequences for England.

The Stuarts and the Divine Right of Monarchy Elizabeth had no child, and her nearest relative was her cousin, James Stuart. Already king of Scotland, James Stuart became King James I of England in 1603. James inherited the unsettled issues of Elizabeth's reign. His worst struggles with Parliament were over money and his refusal to reform the English church.

4.42 Preparing for the Regents

Power Why can Peter the Great be considered an absolute monarch?

TAKING NOTES
Summarizing Use a cluster diagram to list the important events of Peter the Great's reign.

Peter the Great

4.43 Preparing for the Regents

Change What steps did Peter the Great take to westernize Russia?

4.44 Preparing for the Regents

Power Why can Charles I be considered an absolute monarch?

In 1625, James I died. **Charles I**, his son, took the throne. Charles always needed money, in part because he was at war with both Spain and France. Several times when Parliament refused to give him funds, he dissolved it. By 1628, Charles was forced to call Parliament again. This time it refused to grant him any money until he signed a document that is known as the Petition of Right. In this petition, the king agreed to four points: 1) He would not imprison subjects without due cause. 2) He would not levy taxes without Parliament's consent. 3) He would not house soldiers in private homes. 4) He would not impose martial law in peacetime. After agreeing to the petition, Charles ignored it. Even so, the petition was important. It set forth the idea that the law was higher than the king. This idea contradicted theories of absolute monarchy. In 1629, Charles dissolved Parliament and refused to call it back into session.

4.45 Preparing for the Regents

Conflict What factors led to the English Civil War?

Oliver Cromwell—the English Civil War Charles offended Puritans by upholding the rituals of the Anglican Church. In addition, in 1637, Charles tried to force the Presbyterian Scots to accept a version of the Anglican prayer book. He wanted both his kingdoms to follow one religion. The Scots rebelled, assembled a huge army, and threatened to invade England. To meet this danger, Charles needed money—money he could get only by calling Parliament into session. This gave Parliament a chance to oppose him.

During the autumn of 1641, Parliament passed laws to limit royal power. Furious, Charles tried to arrest Parliament's leaders in January 1642, but they escaped. Equally furious, a mob of Londoners raged outside the palace. Charles fled London and raised an army in the north of England, where people were loyal to him. From 1642 to 1649, supporters and opponents of King Charles fought the **English Civil War**. At first neither side could gain a lasting advantage. The tide turned in favor of the Puritans when **Oliver Cromwell** became their general. In 1649, the Puritans brought Charles to trial for treason against Parliament. They found him guilty and sentenced him to death. His execution was revolutionary. Never before had a reigning monarch faced a public trial and execution.

Cromwell now held the reins of power. In 1649, he abolished the monarchy and the House of Lords. He established a commonwealth, a republican form of government. In 1653, Cromwell sent home the remaining members of Parliament. Cromwell's associate John Lambert drafted a constitution, the first written constitution of any modern European state. However, Cromwell eventually tore up the document and became a military dictator

The Glorious Revolution Cromwell ruled until his death in 1658. Shortly afterward, the government he had established collapsed, and a new Parliament was selected. In 1659, Parliament voted to ask Charles II, the older son of Charles I, to rule England. Because he restored the monarchy, the period of Charles II's rule is called the **Restoration**.

4.46 Preparing for the Regents

Justice During whose reign was *habeas corpus* passed? How did *habeas corpus* contribute to the growth of legal rights and to the development of a constitutional monarchy?

During Charles II's reign, Parliament passed an important guarantee of freedom, ***habeas corpus***. *Habeas corpus* is Latin meaning "to have the body." This 1679 law gave every prisoner the right to obtain a writ or document ordering that the prisoner be brought before a judge to specify the charges against the prisoner. The judge would decide whether the prisoner should be tried or set free. Because of the Habeas Corpus Act, a monarch could not put someone in jail simply for opposing the ruler, and prisoners could not be held indefinitely without trials.

In addition, Parliament debated who should inherit Charles's throne. Charles's heir was his brother James, who was Catholic. When Charles died in 1685, James II became king. James soon offended his subjects by displaying his Catholicism. Violating English law, he appointed several Catholics to high office. When Parliament protested, James dissolved it. In 1688, James's second wife gave birth to a son. English Protestants were terrified at the prospect of a line of Catholic kings.

James had an older daughter, Mary, who was Protestant. She was also the wife of William of Orange, a prince of the Netherlands. Seven members of Parliament invited William and Mary to overthrow James for the sake of Protestantism. When William led his army to London in 1688, James fled to France. This bloodless overthrow of King James II is called the **Glorious Revolution**.

The English Bill of Rights At their coronation, William and Mary vowed to recognize Parliament as their partner in governing. England had become not an absolute monarchy but a **constitutional monarchy**, where laws limited the ruler's power. To make clear the limits of royal power, Parliament drafted a Bill of Rights in 1689. Building on the democratic principles first outlined in the Magna Carta, this document listed many things that a ruler could not do. For example, a ruler could not suspend Parliament's laws, levy taxes without a specific grant from Parliament, interfere with freedom of speech in Parliament, or penalize a citizen who petitions the king about grievances. William and Mary consented to these and other limits on their royal power.

After 1688, no British monarch could rule without the consent of Parliament. At the same time, Parliament could not rule without the consent of the monarch. If the two disagreed, government came to a standstill. During the 1700s, this potential problem was remedied by the development of a group of government ministers, or officials, called the **cabinet**. These ministers acted in the ruler's name but in reality represented the major party of Parliament. Therefore, they became the link between the monarch and the majority party in Parliament.

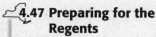
4.47 Preparing for the Regents

Political Systems
What was the result of the Glorious Revolution? How did it contribute to the development of parliamentary democracy?

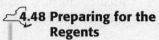
4.48 Preparing for the Regents

Political Systems
How did the English Bill of Rights contribute to the development of parliamentary democracy and a constitutional monarchy?

PREPARING FOR THE REGENTS

Answer the following questions. Use the Analyze the Question hints to help you answer the questions. Base your answers to questions 1 and 2 on the excerpt below and on your knowledge of social studies.

> ". . . The person of the King is sacred, and to attack him in any way is an attack on religion itself. Kings represent the divine majesty and have been appointed by him to carry out His purposes. Serving God and respecting kings are bound together."
>
> —Bishop Jacques Bossuet

1 This statement describes the philosophy that existed during the

(1) Enlightenment
(2) Age of Absolutism
(3) Renaissance
(4) Industrial Revolution

ANALYZE THE QUESTION
- Read the quotation and the question stem. You are being asked to determine the time period to which the quotation refers.
- Look for key words like *kings* and *divine majesty* to help you determine the subject of the quotation.
- Select the alternative time period that best matches the subject of the quotation.

2 Which person would most agree with this statement?

(1) John Locke
(2) Karl Marx
(3) Elizabeth II
(4) Louis XIV

ANALYZE THE QUESTION
- Read the question stem. You are being asked to determine which of the people listed would most agree with the quotation.
- Read the alternatives and think about the views of each person.
- Select the person who would be most likely to agree with the statement.

Part I: MULTIPLE-CHOICE QUESTIONS

Directions (1–10): For each statement or question, write on a separate answer sheet the *number* of the word or expression that, of those given, best completes the statement or answers the questions.

1 The ability of the Ottoman Empire to expand its borders depended on

(1) military assistance from western Europe
(2) extensive trade with the Americas
(3) alliances formed during World War I
(4) strategic location between Europe and Asia

2 One result of the voyages of Zheng He was that

(1) Chinese merchants began trading with Africa
(2) Christian missionaries arrived in China
(3) Indian artisans showed the Chinese how to make Ming porcelain
(4) China set up colonies in Europe

3 Which statement explains the long-term significance of the travels of Columbus?

(1) His interactions with the indigenous peoples served as a model for fair treatment of minorities.
(2) His ships were the first to complete an around the world voyage and prove the Earth was round.
(3) His calculations of the distance between Europe and Asia became the basis for our modern maps.
(4) His voyages started a vast cultural exchange between two hemispheres.

4 One similarity of the Aztec, Maya, and Incan empires is that they

(1) developed in fertile river valleys
(2) maintained democratic political systems
(3) coexisted peacefully with neighboring empires
(4) created complex civilizations

5 The economic policy of mercantilism first developed during the

(1) Age of Exploration   (3) Cold War
(2) Enlightenment   (4) Green Revolution

6 • Magna Carta signed by King John
• Habeas Corpus Act passed during the rule of Charles II
• Bill of Rights agreed to by William and Mary

These events in English history were similar in that they all

(1) promoted religious freedom
(2) limited the power of the monarch
(3) provided universal suffrage
(4) supported divine right theory

7 During the 1500s, technological advances in navigation, naval engineering, and mapmaking contributed directly to the start of the

(1) Gupta Empire   (3) Age of Exploration
(2) Mongol Empire   (4) medieval guilds

8 The success of the triangular trade system depended on increasing the

(1) political independence of the Caribbean nations
(2) emphasis on free trade in European nations
(3) slave trade in the Western Hemisphere
(4) industrialization of South American colonies

9 The fall of the Byzantine Empire to the Ottoman Turks (1453) prompted Spain and Portugal to

(1) seek new trade routes to East Asia
(2) extend religious tolerance to Muslim peoples
(3) reform their political systems
(4) expand the Catholic Inquisition into the Middle East

10 Inca terrace farming and Aztec floating gardens are examples of

(1) the ability of civilizations to adapt to their region's physical geography
(2) slash-and-burn farming techniques
(3) Mesoamerican art forms symbolizing the importance of agriculture
(4) colonial economic policies that harmed Latin American civilizations.

In developing your answers to Parts II and III, be sure to keep these general definitions in mind:

(a) *discuss* means "to make observations about something using facts, reasoning, and argument; to present in some detail"

(b) *explain* means "to make plain or understandable; to give reasons for or causes of; to show the logical development or relationships of"

(c) *evaluate* means "to examine and judge the significance, worth, or condition of; to determine the value of"

Part II: THEMATIC ESSAY

Directions: Write a well-organized essay that includes an introduction, several paragraphs addressing the task below, and a conclusion.

Theme: Change [Individuals Who Have Changed History]

> The beliefs and achievements of individuals have changed global history. These beliefs and achievements have had positive and negative effects on history.

Task:

> Identify *two* individuals who have changed global history and for *each*:
> * Explain one belief or achievement of that individual
> * Discuss the positive and/or negative effects of the individual's belief or achievement

You may use any individual from your study of Unit Four. The individuals you identify must have had a major role in shaping global history. Some individuals that you might consider include Suleyman, Queen Isabella, Christopher Columbus, Hernando Cortés, Francisco Pizarro, Philip II, Peter the Great, Louis XIV, Charles I, and Oliver Cromwell.

You are not limited to these suggestions.

Guidelines:

In your essay, be sure to
* Address all aspects of the *Task*
* Support the theme with relevant facts, examples, and details
* Use a logical and clear plan of organization
* Include an introduction and a conclusion that are beyond the simple restatement of the *Theme*

Part III: DOCUMENT-BASED QUESTION

This question is based on the accompanying documents (1–3). The question is designed to test your ability to work with historic documents. Some of these documents have been edited for the purpose of this question. As you analyze the documents, take into account both the source of each document and any point of view that may be presented in the document.

Historical Context:

A *turning point* is defined as a period in history when a significant change occurs. One of these turning points was the ***Age of Exploration***.

Task:

Using information from the documents and your knowledge of global history, answer the question that follows each document in Part A. Your answers to the questions will help you write the Part B essay, in which you will be asked to:

> • Explain why the Age of Exploration is considered a turning point
> • Evaluate whether the impact of the turning point has been positive or negative

Part A: Short Answer

Directions: Analyze the document and answer the short-answer questions that follow in the space provided.

Document 1

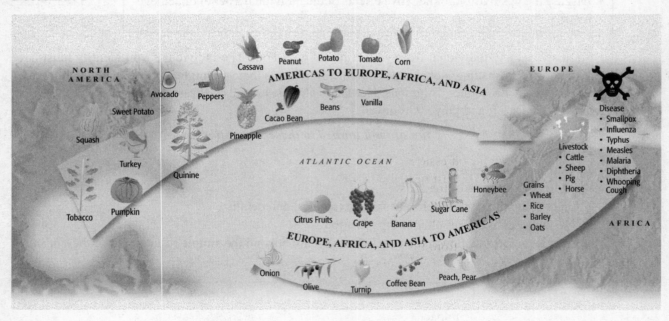

1 According to Document 1, what elements were exchanged between the continents?

_____

_____

Document 2

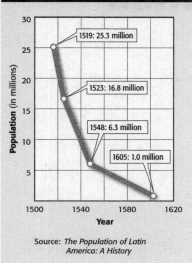

Native Population of Central Mexico, 1500–1620

- 1519: 25.3 million
- 1523: 16.8 million
- 1548: 6.3 million
- 1605: 1.0 million

Population (in millions) / Year

Source: *The Population of Latin America: A History*

Document 3

I was immediately handled and tossed up to see if I were sound, by some of the crew, and I was now persuaded that I had gotten into a world of bad spirits, and that they were going to kill me. Their complexions, too, differing so much from ours, their long hair, and the language they spoke . . . united to confirm me in this belief. . . . The closeness of the place and the heat of the climate, added to the number in the ship, which was so crowded that each had scarcely room to turn himself, almost suffocated us.

—Olaudah Equiano, former African slave

2 According to Document 2, by approximately how many million people did the population of Central Mexico decline between 1519 and 1605?

_____

3 What is the author in Document 3 describing?

_____

Part B: Essay

Directions: Write a well-organized essay that includes an introduction, several paragraphs, and a conclusion. Use evidence from at least *two* documents to support your response.

Historical Context: A *turning point* is defined as a period in history when a significant change occurs. One of these turning points was the *Age of Exploration*.

Task: Using information from the documents and your knowledge of global history, write an essay in which you:

- Explain why the Age of Exploration is considered a turning point
- Evaluate whether the impact of the turning point has been positive or negative

Guidelines:

In your essay, be sure to
- Address all aspects of the *Task* by accurately analyzing and interpreting at least *two* documents
- Incorporate information from the documents
- Incorporate relevant outside information
- Support the theme with relevant facts, examples, and details
- Use a logical and clear plan of organization
- Introduce the theme by establishing a framework that is beyond a simple statement of the *Task* or *Historical Context* and conclude with a summation of the theme

UNIT 5
An Age of Revolution
1450–1914

Unit Overview

This unit looks at the causes and consequences of revolutions in science, thought, politics, and economics. It begins by examining the Scientific Revolution and the Enlightenment. It then looks at the impact of the Enlightenment on political thought and action in the 1700s and 1800s, focusing on the American, French, and Latin American revolutions and the rise of nationalism as a movement. It also looks at conservative reactions to these political changes and at the challenges faced by Latin America after independence. The unit closes by examining the causes and consequences of industrialization and imperialism in Europe and Japan.

Concepts and Themes

Among the concepts and themes explored in this unit are

- Change
- Citizenship
- Conflict
- Culture and Intellectual Life
- Economic Systems
- Factors of Production
- Imperialism
- Nationalism/Nation State
- Political Systems
- Power
- Science and Technology
- Urbanization

PREPARING FOR THE REGENTS: Building Thematic Essay Skills

Throughout history, societies have developed various economic systems. One of these systems is capitalism. In capitalism, the factors of production are privately owned and money is invested in business ventures to make a profit. Capitalism was the driving force in the Industrial Revolution that began in Great Britain in the mid-1700s. As you read about the Industrial Revolution, use the following chart to organize information about the historical circumstances surrounding the development of capitalism, capitalism's major features, and the impact of capitalism on Western Europe. You can add additional rows as needed.

Development	Features	Impact on Western Europe

The Scientific Revolution and the Enlightenment

Section Overview

The Scientific Revolution, which began in the mid-1500s, permanently changed the way people thought about the natural world. A combination of discoveries and circumstances led to this new way of thinking and helped spread its impact. As European explorers traveled to Africa, Asia, and the Americas, they encountered peoples and animals previously unknown in Europe. These discoveries opened Europeans to the possibility that there were new truths to be found. The invention of the printing press helped spread challenging ideas. European exploration also fueled a great deal of scientific research, especially in astronomy and mathematics. Navigators needed better instruments and geographic measurements, for example, to determine their location in the open sea. As scientists began to look more closely at the world around them, they made observations that did not match the ancient beliefs.

In the wake of the Scientific Revolution, and the new ways of thinking it prompted, scholars and philosophers began to reevaluate old notions about other aspects of society. They sought new insight into the underlying beliefs regarding government, religion, economics, and education. Their efforts spurred the Enlightenment, a new intellectual movement that stressed reason and thought and the power of individuals to solve problems. Known also as the Age of Reason, the movement reached its height in the mid-1700s and brought great change to many aspects of Western civilization.

Early telescope like the one used by Galileo (1564–1642)

MAIN IDEAS

SCIENCE AND TECHNOLOGY   The Scientific Revolution began when astronomers questioned how the universe operates. By shattering long-held views, these astronomers opened a new world of discovery.
POWER AND AUTHORITY   The thinkers of the Enlightenment challenged old ideas about power and authority.

TERMS AND NAMES

- geocentric theory
- Scientific Revolution
- heliocentric theory
- Galileo Galilei
- Isaac Newton

- scientific method
- Enlightenment
- John Locke
- philosophe
- Voltaire

- Montesquieu
- Rousseau
- enlightened despot
- Catherine the Great

PREPARING FOR THE REGENTS

As you read this section, consider
- to what extent the Scientific Revolution and the Enlightenment are related.

TIME LINE

1543
Copernicus publishes the heliocentric theory.

1609
Galileo observes heavens through a telescope.

1687
Newton publishes treatise on law of gravity.

1748
Montesquieu publishes *On the Spirit of Laws.*

1751
Diderot publishes first volumes of *Encyclopedia.*

1762
Rousseau publishes *The Social Contract.*

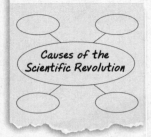

Causes of the
Scientific Revolution

5.1 Preparing for the Regents

Culture and Intellectual Life To what extent can the Scientific Revolution be seen as a rejection of traditional authority?

5.2 Preparing for the Regents

Science and Technology What is heliocentric theory? Who developed the theory?

5.3 Preparing for the Regents

Belief System Why did Galileo's findings frighten religious leaders?

The Scientific Revolution

During the Middle Ages, most scholars believed that the moon, the sun, and the planets all moved in perfectly circular paths around an immovable earth. This earth-centered view of the universe was called the **geocentric theory**. The idea came from Aristotle, the Greek philosopher of the fourth century B.C. The Greek astronomer Ptolemy (TOL•a•mee) expanded the theory in the second century A.D. In addition, Christianity taught that God had deliberately placed the earth at the center of the universe.

Beginning in the mid-1500s, a few scholars published works that challenged the ideas of the ancient thinkers and the church. As these scholars replaced old assumptions with new theories, they launched a change in European thought that historians call the **Scientific Revolution**. The Scientific Revolution was a new way of thinking about the natural world. That way was based upon careful observation and a willingness to question accepted beliefs.

Nicolaus Copernicus An early challenge to accepted scientific thinking came in the field of astronomy. The fact that geocentric theory did not accurately explain the movements of the sun, moon, and planets troubled a Polish cleric and astronomer named Nicolaus Copernicus (koh•PUR•nuh•kuhs). In the early 1500s, Copernicus became interested in an old Greek idea that the sun stood at the center of the universe. After studying planetary movements for more than 25 years, Copernicus reasoned that indeed, the stars, the earth, and the other planets revolved around the sun. In 1543, Copernicus published his findings in *On the Revolutions of Heavenly Bodies*.

Copernicus's **heliocentric**, or sun-centered, **theory** did not completely explain why the planets orbited the way they did. Other scientists would build on the foundation laid by Copernicus. In the early 1600s, for instance, Johannes Kepler concluded that certain mathematical laws govern planetary motion. One of these laws showed that the planets revolve around the sun in elliptical orbits instead of circles, as was previously thought.

Galileo Galilei An Italian scientist named **Galileo Galilei** built on the new theories about astronomy. As a young man, Galileo learned that a Dutch lens maker had built an instrument that could enlarge far-off objects. Galileo built his own telescope and used it to study the heavens in 1609. Then, in 1610, he published a small book called *Starry Messenger*, which described his astonishing observations. Galileo announced that Jupiter had four moons and that the sun had dark spots. He also noted that the earth's moon had a rough, uneven surface. This shattered Aristotle's theory that the moon and stars were made of a pure, perfect substance. Galileo's observations, as well as his laws of motion, also clearly supported the theories of Copernicus.

Galileo's findings frightened both Catholic and Protestant leaders because they went against church teaching and authority. If people believed the church could be wrong about this, they could question other church teachings as well. In 1616, the Catholic Church warned Galileo not to defend the ideas of Copernicus.

Although Galileo remained publicly silent, he continued his studies. Then, in 1632, he published *Dialogue Concerning the Two Chief World Systems*. This book presented the ideas of both Copernicus and Ptolemy, but it clearly showed that Galileo supported the Copernican theory. Galileo was ordered to stand trial before the Inquisition in 1633. Under the threat of torture, he knelt before Catholic leaders and read aloud a signed confession. In it, he agreed that the ideas of Copernicus were false. Galileo spent the remainder of his life under house arrest.

Isaac Newton The English scientist <u>Isaac Newton</u> helped to bring together the breakthroughs of Copernicus, Kepler, and Galileo under a single theory of motion. Newton's great discovery was that the same force ruled motion of the planets and all matter on earth and in space. The key idea that linked motion in the heavens with motion on the earth was the law of universal gravitation. According to this law, every object in the universe attracts every other object. The degree of attraction depends on the mass of the objects and the distance between them. Newton published his ideas in *The Mathematical Principles of Natural Philosophy* (1687), one of the most important scientific books ever written. The universe he described was like a giant clock. Its parts all worked together perfectly in ways that could be expressed mathematically. Newton believed that God was the creator of this orderly universe, the clockmaker who had set everything in motion.

The Scientific Method The revolution in scientific thinking eventually developed into a new approach to science called the **scientific method**. This method is a logical procedure for gathering and testing ideas. It begins with a problem or question arising from an observation. Scientists next form a hypothesis, or unproved assumption. The hypothesis is then tested in an experiment or on the basis of data. In the final step, scientists analyze and interpret their data to reach a new conclusion. That conclusion either confirms or disproves the hypothesis.

The work of 15th-century thinkers Francis Bacon of England and René Descartes (day•KAHRT) of France helped to advance the scientific method. Bacon urged scientists to experiment and then draw conclusions. This approach is called empiricism, or the experimental method. Descartes developed analytical geometry, which linked algebra and geometry. Rather than using experimentation as Bacon did, Descartes relied on mathematics and logic. He believed that everything should be doubted until proved by reason. The only thing he knew for certain was that he existed—because, as he wrote, "I think, therefore I am." From this starting point, he followed a train of strict reasoning to arrive at other basic truths.

The Enlightenment

In the wake of the Scientific Revolution, scholars and philosophers began to reevaluate old notions about other aspects of society. They sought new insight into the underlying beliefs regarding government, religion, economics, and education. Their efforts spurred the **Enlightenment**, a new intellectual movement that stressed reason and thought and the power of individuals to solve problems. Known also as the Age of Reason, the movement reached its height in the mid-1700s and brought great change to many aspects of Western civilization.

The Enlightenment started from some key ideas put forth by two English political thinkers of the 1600s, Thomas Hobbes—whom you have already read about—and John Locke. Both men experienced the political turmoil of England early in that century. However, they came to very different conclusions.

Thomas Hobbes supported an absolute monarchy. The horrors of the English Civil War convinced him that all humans were naturally selfish and wicked. The only answer was for people to enter a social contract in which they handed over their rights to a strong ruler with absolute power in exchange for law and order. The philosopher **John Locke** held a different, more positive, view of human nature. He favored self-government. According to Locke, all people are born free and equal, with three natural rights—life, liberty, and property. The purpose of government, said Locke, is to protect these rights. If a government fails to do so, citizens have a right to overthrow it.

5.4 Preparing for the Regents

Science and Technology What is the scientific method? How does the work of Galileo, Newton, and Descartes illustrate elements of the scientific method?

TAKING NOTES

Summarizing Use a web diagram to list key information about Enlightenment ideas.

5.5 Preparing for the Regents

Political Systems John Locke believed that individuals entered into a social contract with each other to create society and government. Thus, power rested with the people. How is this different from the view held by Thomas Hobbes?

Core Concepts of the Philosophes
Reason Truth can be discovered through reason or logical thinking.
Nature What is natural is also good and reasonable.
Happiness People should seek well-being on earth, rather than find joy in the hereafter.
Progress Society and humankind can improve.
Liberty The liberties won in England's Glorious Revolution and Bill of Rights should be extended to everyone.

Enlightenment Writers The Enlightenment reached its height in France in the mid-1700s. Paris became the meeting place for people who wanted to discuss politics and ideas. The social critics of this period in France were known as **philosophes** (FIHL•uh•SAHFS), the French word for philosophers. The philosophes believed that people could apply reason to all aspects of life, just as Isaac Newton had applied reason to science.

Probably the most brilliant and influential of the philosophes was François Marie Arouet. Using the pen name **Voltaire**, he published more than 70 books of political essays, philosophy, and drama. Although he made powerful enemies, Voltaire never stopped fighting for tolerance, reason, freedom of religious belief, and freedom of speech.

Baron de **Montesquieu** (MAHN•tuh•skyoo) was another influential French philosophe. Montesquieu believed that Britain was the most politically balanced and best-governed country of his own day. The British king and his ministers held executive power. They carried out the laws of the state. The members of Parliament held legislative power. They made the laws. The judges of the English courts held judicial power. They interpreted the laws to see how each applied to a specific case. Montesquieu called this division of power among different branches separation of powers. Montesquieu oversimplified the British system. It did not actually separate powers this way. His idea, however, became a part of his most famous book, *On the Spirit of Laws* (1748). In his book, Montesquieu proposed that separation of powers would keep any individual or group from gaining total control of the government. "Power," he wrote, "should be a check to power." This idea later would be called checks and balances.

A third great philosophe was Jean Jacques **Rousseau** (roo•SOH). Rousseau believed that the only good government was one that was freely formed by the people and guided by the "general will" of society—a direct democracy. As he explained in his book, *The Social Contract* (1762), under such a government, people agree to give up some of their freedom in favor of the common good. Rousseau's view of the social contract differed greatly from that of Hobbes. For Hobbes, the social contract was an agreement between a society and its government. For Rousseau, it was an agreement among free individuals to create a society and a government.

Another leading philosophe, Denis Diderot (DEE•duh•r oh), created a large set of books to which many leading scholars of Europe contributed articles and essays. He called it *Encyclopedia* and began publishing the first volumes in 1751. The Enlightenment views expressed in the articles soon angered both the French government and the Catholic Church. Their censors banned the work. Nonetheless, Diderot continued publishing his *Encyclopedia*.

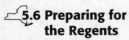

5.6 Preparing for the Regents

Political Systems Why did Montesquieu belief that the separation of powers was a good idea?

5.7 Preparing for the Regents

Political Systems What effect did Enlightenment thought have on political reform?

The Impact of the Enlightenment Enlightenment writers challenged long-held ideas about society. They examined such principles as the divine right of monarchs, the union of church and state, and the existence of unequal social classes. They held these beliefs up to the light of reason and found them in need of reform. The theories they popularized eventually inspired the American and French revolutions and other revolutionary movements in the 1800s.

Enlightenment thinking produced three other long-term effects that helped shape Western civilization. The first effect was a belief in progress. Galileo, Newton, and others had discovered the key for unlocking the mysteries of nature in the 1500s and 1600s. With the door thus opened, the growth of scientific knowledge seemed to quicken in the 1700s. A second outcome was the rise of a more secular, or non-religious, outlook. Before the Scientific Revolution, people accepted the mysteries of the universe as the workings of God. One by one, scientists discovered that these mysteries could be explained mathematically. Faith in science and in progress produced a third outcome, the rise of individualism. The philosophes encouraged people to use their own ability to reason in order to judge what was right or wrong. They also emphasized the importance of the individual in society. Government, they argued, was formed by individuals to promote their welfare.

Enlightenment and the Monarchy Many philosophes, including Voltaire, believed that the best form of government was a monarchy in which the ruler respected the people's rights. The philosophes tried to convince monarchs to rule justly. Some monarchs embraced the new ideas and made reforms that reflected the Enlightenment spirit. They became known as **enlightened despots**. Despot means "absolute ruler." The enlightened despots supported the philosophes' ideas. But they also had no intention of giving up any power. The changes they made were motivated by two desires: they wanted to make their countries stronger and their own rule more effective. The foremost of Europe's enlightened despots were Frederick II of Prussia, Holy Roman Emperor Joseph II of Austria, and Catherine II of Russia.

Frederick II, known as Frederick the Great, granted many religious freedoms, reduced censorship, improved education, reformed the justice system, and abolished the use of torture. Frederick's most important contribution, however, was his attitude toward being king. He called himself "the first servant of the state." Joseph II, the son and successor of Maria Theresa, introduced legal reforms, freedom of the press, and freedom of worship. In his most radical reform, he abolished serfdom. The abolition of serfdom, like many of Joseph's reforms, was undone after his death. Catherine II, known as **Catherine the Great**, was the ruler most admired by the philosophes. She ruled with absolute authority but also sought to reform Russia. Few of her proposed reforms were carried out, however.

5.8 Preparing for the Regents

Political Systems Why were some monarchs called enlightened despots?

PREPARING FOR THE REGENTS

Answer the following questions. Use the Analyze the Question hints to help you answer the questions.

1 One similarity of the Scientific Revolution and the Enlightenment is that both

(1) had the support of the Roman Catholic Church
(2) placed great value on traditional beliefs
(3) emphasized the value of human reasoning
(4) contributed to the end of feudalism

> **ANALYZE THE QUESTION**
> - Read the question stem. You are being asked to determine one characteristic that the Scientific Revolution and the Enlightenment shared.
> - Think about the characteristics of each movement.
> - Rule out the alternatives that are not characteristic of both movements. The remaining alternative is the correct answer.

2 The writings of Jean Jacques Rousseau, Baron de Montesquieu, and John Locke were similar in that each supported the principles of

(1) a military dictatorship
(2) an autocracy
(3) a theocratic society
(4) a democratic republic

> **ANALYZE THE QUESTION**
> - Read the question stem. You are being asked to determine which principle Rousseau, Montesquieu, and Locke supported in their writings.
> - Rule out the alternatives that have characteristics that are not consistent with the writers' views. The remaining alternative is the correct answer.

Political Revolutions and Reactions

Section Overview

The Enlightenment thinkers were not active revolutionaries. However, their theories had a profound influence on political thought. The ideas of government by popular consent and the right to rebel against unjust rulers helped inspire struggles for liberty in the Americas and in Europe. In Europe, conservatives tried to restore the old monarchies and territorial divisions that existed before the French Revolution and Napoleon. On an international level, this attempt to turn back history succeeded. For the next century, European countries seldom turned to war to solve their differences. Within countries, however, the effort failed, and Europe experienced widespread political uprising in the 1830s and in 1848.

Toussaint L'Ouverture (c. 1743–1803), leader of the Haitian Revolution

MAIN IDEAS

REVOLUTION   Enlightenment ideas helped spur the American colonies to shed British rule and create a new nation. Driven by the example of the American Revolution and such Enlightenment ideas as liberty, equality, and democracy, the French ousted the government of Louis XVI and established a new political order.

POWER AND AUTHORITY   After seizing power in 1799, Napoleon created a huge empire that included much of Western Europe. His attempt to conquer Russia, however, led to his downfall.

REVOLUTION   Spurred by discontent and Enlightenment ideas, peoples in Latin America fought colonial rule.

POWER AND AUTHORITY   After exiling Napoleon, European leaders at the Congress of Vienna tried to restore order and reestablish peace.

TIME LINE

1776
American colonies declare independence.

1789
Storming of the Bastille ignites the French Revolution.

1804
Napoleon declares himself emperor of France and begins to create a vast European empire.
1804
Haiti wins freedom from France.

1810
Padre Hidalgo calls for Mexican independence.

1815
Napoleon defeated at the Battle of Waterloo.

TERMS AND NAMES

- Declaration of Independence
- Thomas Jefferson
- checks and balances
- Bill of Rights
- Old Regime
- estates
- Louis XVI
- Marie Antoinette
- National Assembly
- Great Fear
- Legislative Assembly

- guillotine
- Maximilien Robespierre
- Reign of Terror
- Napoleon Bonaparte
- Napoleonic Code
- Continental System
- Hundred Days
- Toussaint L'Ouverture
- creoles
- Simón Bolívar

- José de San Martín
- Congress of Vienna
- Klemens von Metternich
- balance of power
- legitimacy
- Conservative
- Liberal
- Radical
- Alexander II

PREPARING FOR THE REGENTS

As you read this section, consider
- what role the Enlightenment had on the revolutions of the period.
- to what extent the stages of the American, French, and Latin American revolutions are similar or different.
- why these revolutions were turning points in global history.

Human and Physical Geography of Revolutions

A revolution is a sudden or significant change in the old ways of doing things. Revolutions can occur in many areas, such as government, technology, art, and ideas. The Enlightenment is an example of a revolution in ideas. In the late 1700s and the 1800s, Enlightenment ideas about the proper role of government inspired people in the Americas and Europe to launch political revolutions that led to major governmental, social, and economic changes. In the Americas, people sought freedom from colonial rule. In Europe, first France and then other nations attempted to break free of the absolute control of monarchs. These rebellions changed the maps of Europe and the Americas and usher in a new age of politics and nationalism.

The American Revolution

Between 1754 and 1763, the English and the French squared off in North America in the French and Indian War. Britain and its colonies were victorious, but the war left Great Britain with a huge debt. Because the American colonies benefited from the victory, Britain expected the colonists to help pay the costs of the war. Beginning in 1765, Parliament passed a series of tax acts that required the colonists to pay taxes directly to the British government—something they had never had to do before. Colonial lawyers argued that these taxes violated colonists' natural rights, and they accused the government of "taxation without representation." In Britain, citizens consented to taxes through their representatives in Parliament. The colonists, however, had no representation in Parliament. Thus, they argued they could not be taxed.

Impact of the Enlightenment Over the next decade, hostilities between the two sides increased. Some colonial leaders favored independence from Britain. These leaders used Enlightenment ideas to justify their calls for independence. The colonists had asked for the same political rights as people in Britain, they said, but the king had stubbornly refused. Therefore, the colonists were justified in rebelling against a tyrant who had broken the social contract.

In July 1776, the Americans issued the **Declaration of Independence**. This document, written by political leader **Thomas Jefferson**, was firmly based on the ideas of John Locke and the Enlightenment. Since Locke had asserted that people had the right to rebel against an unjust ruler, the Declaration of Independence included a long list of George III's abuses. The document ended by declaring the colonies' separation from Britain.

The British were not about to let their colonies leave without a fight. Shortly after the publication of the Declaration of Independence, the two sides went to war. At first glance, the colonists seemed destined to go down in quick defeat. In the end, however, the Americans won their war for independence.

Americans Create a Republic In 1781, all 13 states ratified the Articles of Confederation, which established the United States as a republic, a government in which citizens rule through elected representatives. The Articles deliberately created a weak national government that consisted only of a Congress. Congress could declare war, enter into treaties, and coin money. It had no power, however, to collect taxes or regulate trade. Passing new laws was difficult because laws needed the approval of 9 of the 13 states.

Colonial leaders eventually recognized the need for a strong national government. In February 1787, Congress approved a Constitutional Convention to revise the Articles of Confederation. Using the political ideas of the Enlightenment,

5.9 Preparing for the Regents

Change What factors contributed to the beginning of the American Revolution?

5.10 Preparing for the Regents

Culture and Intellectual Life How does the Declaration of Independence show the influence of John Locke?

TAKING NOTES

Identifying Problems and Solutions Use a chart to list the problems American colonists faced in shaping their republic and solutions they found.

Problem	Solution
1.	1.
2.	2.
3.	3.

the delegates created a new federal system of government. Like Montesquieu, the delegates distrusted a powerful central government controlled by one person or group. They therefore established three separate branches—legislative, executive, and judicial. This setup provided a built-in system of **checks and balances**, with each branch checking the actions of the other two.

The delegates signed the new Constitution on September 17, 1787. In order to become law, however, the Constitution required approval by conventions in at least 9 of the 13 states. Supporters of the Constitution were called Federalists. Their opponents, the Antifederalists, feared that the Constitution gave the central government too much power. They also wanted a bill of rights to protect the rights of individual citizens. The Federalists agreed, and the Constitution was ratified. Congress formally added the **Bill of Rights** as the first ten amendments to the Constitution. The amendments protected such basic rights as freedom of speech, press, assembly, and religion. Many of these rights had been advocated by Voltaire, Rousseau, and Locke.

Impact of the American Revolution The American Revolution inspired the growing number of French people who sought reform in their own country. They saw the new government of the United States as the fulfillment of Enlightenment ideals, and longed for such a government in France.

The Declaration of Independence was widely circulated and admired in France. In addition, the Constitution and the Bills of Rights marked a turning point in people's ideas about government. Both documents put Enlightenment ideas into practice. They expressed an optimistic view that reason and reform could prevail and that progress was inevitable. Such optimism swept across the Atlantic to France. Less than a decade after the American Revolution ended, an armed struggle to topple the government would begin in France.

The French Revolution

In the 1700s, France was considered the most advanced country of Europe. It had a large population and a prosperous foreign trade. It was the center of the Enlightenment, and France's culture was widely praised and imitated by the rest of the world. However, the appearance of success was deceiving. There was great unrest in France, caused by bad harvests, high prices, high taxes, and disturbing questions raised by the Enlightenment ideas of Locke, Rousseau, and Voltaire.

Causes of the Revolution In the 1770s, the social and political system of France—the **Old Regime**—remained in place. Under this system, the people of France were divided into three large social classes, or **estates**. Power rested in the hands of the First Estate—the Roman Catholic clergy—and the Second Estate—the nobility. The majority of people in these estates scorned Enlightenment ideas. The Third Estate included the bankers, factory owners, merchants, professionals, and skilled artisans who made up the bourgeoisie (BUR•zhwah•ZEE), or middle class; the tradespeople, apprentices, laborers, and domestic servants of the urban lower class; and peasant farmers. These people had no power to influence government. The Third Estate resented the First and Second Estates and embraced Enlightenment ideals. The heavily taxed (see the charts on this page) and discontented Third Estate was ready for change.

Serious economic problems also helped to generate a desire for change. By the 1780s, France's economy was in decline. This caused alarm, particularly among the Third Estate's bourgeoisie. The heavy burden of taxes

5.11 Preparing for the Regents

Political Systems Why was the American Revolution a turning point in history?

TAKING NOTES

Analyzing Causes
Use a web diagram to identify the causes of the French Revolution.

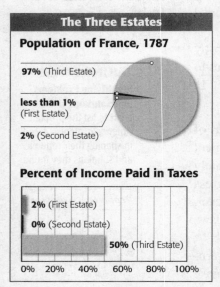

Causes of Revolution

The Three Estates

Population of France, 1787

97% (Third Estate)

less than 1% (First Estate)

2% (Second Estate)

Percent of Income Paid in Taxes

2% (First Estate)

0% (Second Estate)

50% (Third Estate)

0%   20%   40%   60%   80%   100%

made it almost impossible to conduct business profitably within France. Further, the cost of living was rising sharply. In addition, bad weather in the 1780s caused widespread crop failures, resulting in a severe shortage of grain. The price of bread doubled in 1789, and many people faced starvation. To make matters worse, the government was deeply in debt, thanks in part to the extravagant spending of **Louis XVI** and his queen, **Marie Antoinette**. Louis also inherited a considerable debt from previous kings. And he borrowed heavily in order to help the American revolutionaries in their war against Great Britain, France's chief rival.

Strong leadership might have solved these and other problems. Louis XVI, however, was indecisive and allowed matters to drift until he was almost out of money. His solution was to impose taxes on the nobility. The Second Estate forced him to call a meeting of the Estates-General—an assembly of representatives from all three estates—to approve this new tax. The meeting, the first in 175 years, was held on May 5, 1789, at Versailles.

Louis XVI and the Revolution Under the assembly's medieval rules, each estate's delegates met in a separate hall to vote, and each estate had one vote. The two privileged estates could always outvote the Third Estate. Eager to make changes in the government, the Third Estate delegates insisted that all three estates meet together and that each delegate have a vote. This would give the advantage to the Third Estate, which had many more delegates.

Siding with the nobles, the king ordered the Estates-General to follow the medieval rules. This only made the Third Estate more determined. On June 17, 1789, the Third Estate delegates voted to establish the **National Assembly**, in effect proclaiming the end of absolute monarchy and the beginning of representative government. This vote was the first deliberate act of revolution. Three days later, the Third Estate delegates found themselves locked out of their meeting room. They broke down a door to an indoor tennis court, pledging to stay until they had drawn up a new constitution. Soon after, nobles and members of the clergy who favored reform joined the Third Estate delegates. In response to these events, Louis stationed his mercenary army of Swiss guards around Versailles.

In Paris, rumors flew. Some people suggested that Louis was intent on using military force to dismiss the National Assembly. Others charged that the foreign troops were coming to Paris to massacre French citizens. People began to gather weapons in order to defend the city against attack. On July 14, a mob searching for gunpowder and arms stormed the Bastille, a Paris prison, and seized the building. Before long, rebellion spread from Paris into the countryside. A wave of senseless panic called the **Great Fear** rolled through France.

The Old Regime died on August 4, 1789. On that day, motivated more by fear than idealism, noblemen joined with other members of the National Assembly to sweep away the feudal privileges of the First and Second Estates, thus making commoners equal to the nobles and the clergy. Three weeks later, the National Assembly adopted a statement of revolutionary ideals, the Declaration of the Rights of Man and of the Citizen. Reflecting the influence of the Declaration of Independence, the document stated that "men are born and remain free and equal in rights." These rights included "liberty, property, security, and resistance to oppression." The document also guaranteed citizens equal justice, freedom of speech, and freedom of religion.

In September 1791, the National Assembly completed France's new constitution, which Louis reluctantly approved. The constitution created a limited constitutional monarchy. It stripped the king of much of his authority. It also created a new legislative body—the **Legislative Assembly**. This body had the

5.12 Preparing for the Regents

Change What factors contributed to the beginning of the French Revolution?

5.13 Preparing for the Regents

Political Systems Why was the establishment of the National Assembly significant?

5.14 Preparing for the Regents

Culture and Intellectual Life How did the Declaration of the Rights of Man and the Citizen reflect Enlightenment ideals?

TAKING NOTES

Recognizing Effects
Use a flow chart to
identify the major events
that followed the
creation of the
Constitution of 1791.

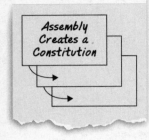

Assembly
Creates a
Constitution

power to create laws and to approve or reject declarations of war. However, the king still held the executive power to enforce laws. The Legislative Assembly was split into three political factions. Radicals opposed the idea of a monarchy and wanted sweeping changes in the way the government was run. Moderates wanted some changes in government, but not as many as the radicals. Conservatives upheld the idea of a limited monarchy and wanted few changes in government.

Monarchs and nobles in many European countries watched the changes taking place in France with alarm. They feared that similar revolts might break out in their own countries. When Austria and Prussia urged the French to restore Louis to his position as an absolute monarch, the Legislative Assembly responded by declaring war in April 1792. The war began badly for the French. By the summer of 1792, Prussian forces were advancing on Paris. The Prussian commander threatened to destroy Paris if the revolutionaries harmed any member of the royal family. This enraged the Parisians. On August 10, about 20,000 men and women invaded the Tuileries, the palace where the royal family was staying. The mob massacred the royal guards and imprisoned Louis, Marie Antoinette, and their children.

Under pressure from radicals, the Legislative Assembly set aside the Constitution of 1791. It declared the king deposed, dissolved the assembly, and called for the election of a new legislature. This new governing body, the National Convention, took office on September 21. It quickly abolished the monarchy and declared France a republic. Adult male citizens were granted the right to vote and hold office. Despite the important part they had already played in the Revolution, women were not given the vote.

5.15 Preparing for the Regents

Justice How was Louis XVI put to death?

Robespierre and the Reign of Terror   The National Convention had reduced Louis XVI's role from that of a king to that of a common citizen and prisoner. Now, guided by a radical political organization, the Jacobin (JAK•uh•bihn) Club, the Convention found Louis guilty of treason, and, by a very close vote, sentenced him to death. On January 21, 1793, the former king was beheaded by a machine called the **guillotine**. His queen, Marie Antoinette, eventually met the same fate, as did thousands of others who the Jacobins considered enemies.

In the early months of 1793, one Jacobin leader, **Maximilien Robespierre** (ROHBZ•peer), slowly gained power. Robespierre and his supporters set out to build a "republic of virtue" by wiping out every trace of France's past. In July 1793, Robespierre became leader of the Committee of Public Safety. For the next year, he governed France virtually as a dictator, and the period of his rule became known as the **Reign of Terror**. The Committee of Public Safety's chief task was to protect the Revolution from its enemies, including any radicals who challenged Robespierre's leadership. In 1793 and 1794, many of those who had led the Revolution received death sentences. In July 1794, fearing for their own safety, some members of the National Convention turned on Robespierre. They demanded his arrest and execution. The Reign of Terror, the radical phase of the French Revolution, ended on July 28, 1794, when Robespierre was beheaded.

5.16 Preparing for the Regents

Power What was the Reign of Terror? When did it end?

People of all classes were weary of the Terror and of skyrocketing prices. In 1795, moderate leaders in the National Convention drafted a new plan of government, the third since 1789. It placed power firmly in the hands of the upper middle class and called for a two-house legislature and an executive body of five men, known as the Directory. These five were moderates, not revolutionary idealists. Some of them were corrupt and made themselves rich at the country's expense. Even so, they gave their troubled country a period of order. They also found the right general to command France's armies—Napoleon Bonaparte.

The Rise and Fall of Napoleon

In October 1795, fate handed **Napoleon Bonaparte** a chance for glory. When royalist rebels marched on the National Convention, a government official told Napoleon to defend the delegates. Napoleon and his gunners greeted the thousands of royalists with a cannonade. Within minutes, the attackers fled in panic. Napoleon Bonaparte became the hero of the hour.

Napoleon Seizes Power By 1799, the Directory had lost control of the political situation and the confidence of the French people. In early November 1799, Napoleon moved to seize power. Troops under his command surrounded the national legislature and drove out most of its members. The lawmakers who remained voted to dissolve the Directory. In its place, they established a group of three consuls, one of whom was Napoleon. Napoleon quickly took the title of first consul and assumed the powers of a dictator.

Napoleon did not try to return the nation to the days of Louis XVI. In general, he supported laws that would both strengthen the central government and achieve some of the goals of the Revolution. He also took steps to put the economy back on a solid footing and end corruption and inefficiency in government. Napoleon thought that his greatest work was his comprehensive system of laws, known as the **Napoleonic Code**. This gave the country a uniform set of laws and eliminated many injustices. However, it actually limited liberty and promoted order and authority over individual rights. For example, freedom of speech and of the press, established during the Revolution, were restricted under the code. The code also restored slavery in the French colonies of the Caribbean.

Napoleon Creates an Empire In 1804, Napoleon decided to make himself emperor, and the French voters supported him. Not content simply to be master of France, Napoleon wanted to control the rest of Europe. He had already annexed the Austrian Netherlands and parts of Italy to France and set up a puppet government in Switzerland. Now he looked to expand his influence further. Fearful of his ambitions, the British persuaded Russia, Austria, and Sweden to join them against France. Napoleon met this challenge with his usual boldness. In a series of brilliant battles, he crushed the opposition. By 1812, the only areas of Europe free from Napoleon's control were Britain, Portugal, Sweden, and the Ottoman Empire.

Napoleon's Empire Collapses The French Empire was huge but unstable. Napoleon was only able to maintain it at its greatest extent from 1807 to 1812. Then it quickly fell to pieces. Its sudden collapse was caused in part by Napoleon's actions. In his attempt to extend the French Empire and crush Great Britain, Napoleon made three disastrous mistakes. In 1806, he instituted the **Continental System**, which banned trade and communication between Europe and Great Britain. To enforce the system, Napoleon set up a blockade—a forcible closing of ports. The British responded with a much more effective blockade that prevented neutral ships from reaching European ports. Then, in 1808, in an attempt to force Portugal to accept the Continental System, Napoleon sent an invasion force through Spain. When Spain protested, he removed the Spanish king and put his own brother, Joseph, on the throne. This led to the Peninsular War, which cost Napoleon about 300,000 men. His most disastrous mistake of all came in 1812, when he invaded Russia. Out of a force of more than 420,000 soldiers, only about 10,000 survived the unsuccessful campaign.

Napoleon's enemies were quick to take advantage of his weakness. Soon all of the main powers of Europe were at war with France. Napoleon managed

---

TAKING NOTES

Following Chronological Order On a time line, note the events that led to Napoleon's crowning as emperor of France.

1789		1804

French Revolution breaks out.   Napoleon crowned emperor.

5.17 Preparing for the Regents

Nationalism What were the only areas of Europe that were not under Napoleon's control by 1812?

TAKING NOTES

Recognizing Effects Use a chart to identify Napoleon's three mistakes and the impact they had on the French Empire.

Napoleon's Mistakes	Effect on Empire

to raise another army. However, since most of his troops were untrained and ill prepared for battle, they were easily defeated. In April 1814, Napoleon accepted terms of surrender and gave up his throne. The victors gave Napoleon a small pension and exiled, or banished, him to Elba, a tiny island off the Italian coast. The allies expected no further trouble from Napoleon, but they were wrong.

Louis XVI's brother assumed the French throne as Louis XVIII. (The executed king's son, Louis XVII, had died in prison in 1795.) When word reached Napoleon that the new king was unpopular, he escaped from Elba and returned to France on March 1, 1815. Within days, Napoleon was again emperor of France.

In response, the European allies quickly marshaled their armies. The British army prepared for battle near the village of Waterloo in Belgium. On June 18, 1815, Napoleon attacked. The British army defended its ground all day. Late in the afternoon, the Prussian army arrived. Together, the British and the Prussian forces attacked the French. Two days later, Napoleon's exhausted troops gave way, and the British and Prussian forces chased them from the field. This defeat ended Napoleon's last bid for power, called the **Hundred Days**.

Independence Movements in Latin America

Ideas of liberty, equality, and democratic rule found their way across the seas to Europe's colonies. In Latin America, most of the population resented the domination of European colonial powers. The time seemed right for the people who lived there to sweep away old colonial masters and gain control of the land.

Revolution in Haiti The French colony called Saint Domingue was the first Latin American territory to free itself from European rule. The colony, now known as Haiti, occupied the western third of the island of Hispaniola in the Caribbean Sea. The nearly 500,000 enslaved Africans worked on French plantations dramatically outnumbered their masters. In August 1791, 100,000 enslaved Africans rose in revolt. The formerly enslaved **Toussaint L'Ouverture** (too•SAN loo•vair•TOOR) soon emerged as a leader. By 1801, Toussaint had taken control of the entire island and freed all the enslaved Africans.

Toussaint was seized by French troops in May 1802 and sent to prison in the French Alps, where he died in April 1803. Toussaint's lieutenant, Jean-Jacques Dessalines (zhahn•ZHAHK day•sah•LEEN), took up the fight for freedom. On January 1, 1804, General Dessalines declared the colony an independent country. It was the first black colony to free itself from European control. Dessalines called the country Haiti.

Revolutions in South America Napoleon's conquest of Spain in 1808 triggered revolts in the Spanish colonies in the South American. These revolts were led by **creoles**, Spaniards born in Latin America. Many creoles might have supported a Spanish king. However, they felt no loyalty to a king imposed by the French. Recalling Locke's idea of the consent of the governed, creoles argued that when the real king was removed, power shifted to the people. The South American wars of independence rested on the achievements of two brilliant creole generals—**Simón Bolívar** (see•MAWN boh•LEE•vahr), a wealthy Venezuelan, and **José de San Martín** (hoh•SAY day san mahr•TEEN), an Argentinian.

By 1821, Bolívar had won Venezuela's independence. San Martín's Argentina had declared its independence in 1816. However, Spanish forces in nearby Chile and Peru still posed a threat. In 1817, San Martín led an army on a grueling march across the Andes to Chile. He was joined there by forces led by Bernardo O'Higgins, son of a former viceroy of Peru. With O'Higgins's help, San Martín freed Chile.

TAKING NOTES

Clarifying Identify details about Latin American independence movements.

Who	Where
When	Why

5.18 Preparing for the Regents

Power Read the following quotation by Simón Bolívar. What is he suggesting by comparing people in the Spanish colonies to medieval serfs?

"Americans today, and perhaps to a greater extend than ever before, who live within the Spanish system, occupy a position in society no better than that of serfs destined for labor."

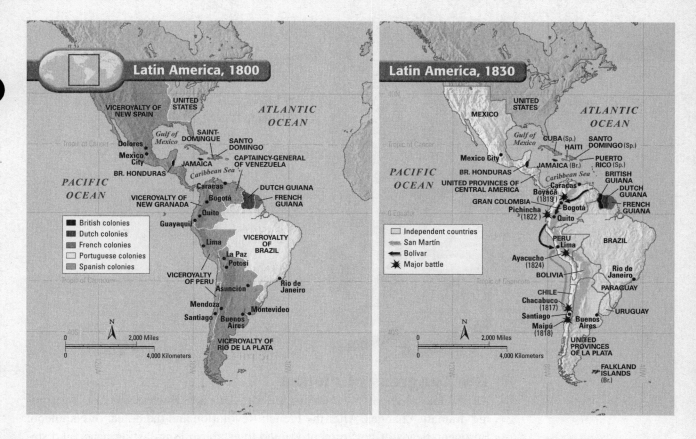

Latin America, 1800

VICEROYALTY OF NEW SPAIN
UNITED STATES
ATLANTIC OCEAN
Tropic of Cancer
Dolores
Gulf of Mexico
SAINT-DOMINGUE
SANTO DOMINGO
Mexico City
JAMAICA
CAPTAINCY-GENERAL OF VENEZUELA
BR. HONDURAS
Caribbean Sea
PACIFIC OCEAN
Caracas
DUTCH GUIANA
FRENCH GUIANA
VICEROYALTY OF NEW GRANADA
Bogotá
Quito
Guayaquil
■ British colonies
■ Dutch colonies
■ French colonies
□ Portuguese colonies
▨ Spanish colonies
Lima
La Paz
Potosí
VICEROYALTY OF BRAZIL
VICEROYALTY OF PERU
Asunción
Rio de Janeiro
Mendoza
Santiago
Buenos Aires
Montevideo
N
2,000 Miles
4,000 Kilometers
VICEROYALTY OF RÍO DE LA PLATA

Latin America, 1830

UNITED STATES
MEXICO
ATLANTIC OCEAN
Tropic of Cancer
Gulf of Mexico
CUBA (Sp.)
HAITI
SANTO DOMINGO (Sp.)
Mexico City
BR. HONDURAS
JAMAICA (Br.)
PUERTO RICO (Sp.)
UNITED PROVINCES OF CENTRAL AMERICA
Caribbean Sea
BRITISH GUIANA
PACIFIC OCEAN
Caracas
Boyacá (1819)
DUTCH GUIANA
GRAN COLOMBIA
Bogotá
FRENCH GUIANA
Pichincha (1822)
Quito
□ Independent countries
➤ San Martín
← Bolívar
✷ Major battle
PERU
Lima
Ayacucho (1824)
BRAZIL
BOLIVIA
Rio de Janeiro
PARAGUAY
CHILE
Chacabuco (1817)
Santiago
Maipú (1818)
Buenos Aires
URUGUAY
N
2,000 Miles
4,000 Kilometers
UNITED PROVINCES OF LA PLATA
FALKLAND ISLANDS (Br.)

In 1821, San Martín planned to drive the remaining Spanish forces out of Lima, Peru. But to do so, he needed a much larger force. To solve the problem, San Martín left his army for Bolívar to command. With unified revolutionary forces, Bolívar's army went on to defeat the Spanish at the Battle of Ayacucho (Peru) on December 9, 1824. In this last major battle of the war for independence, the Spanish colonies in Latin America won their freedom. The future countries of Venezuela, Colombia, Panama, and Ecuador were united into a country called Gran Colombia.

Brazil's quest for independence was unique in this period of Latin American history because it occurred without violent upheavals or widespread bloodshed. When Napoleon's armies invaded Portugal in 1807, Prince John (later King John VI) moved the Portuguese government to Portugal's largest colony, Brazil. After Napoleon's defeat, King John and the Portuguese government returned to Portugal. Dom Pedro, King John's son, remained in Brazil. King John intended to once again make Brazil a colony. However, many Brazilians could not accept a return to colonial status. In 1822, creoles demanded Brazil's independence from Portugal. Eight thousand Brazilians signed a petition asking Dom Pedro to rule. He agreed. On September 7, 1822, he officially declared Brazil's independence.

Mexican Independence In Mexico, Indians and mestizos, not creoles, played the leading role in revolt. First under Padre Miguel Hidalgo (mee•GEHL ee•THAHL•goh) and then under Padre José María Morelos (moh•RAY•lohs), Indian and mestizo forces fought for independence. Both leaders were defeated by the Spanish army. Then, in 1820, events took a turn when a revolution in Spain put liberals in power there. Mexico's creoles, fearing the loss of their privileges in the Spanish-controlled colony, united in support of Mexico's independence. Ironically, Agustín de Iturbide (ah•goos•TEEN day ee•toor•BEE•day)—the man who had defeated the rebel Padre Morelos—proclaimed independence in 1821.

5.19 Preparing for the Regents

Change Examine the two maps above. Based on a comparison of the two maps, what conclusion can be drawn about political changes in Latin America between 1800 and 1830? What two people are closely associated with the changes indicated on the maps?

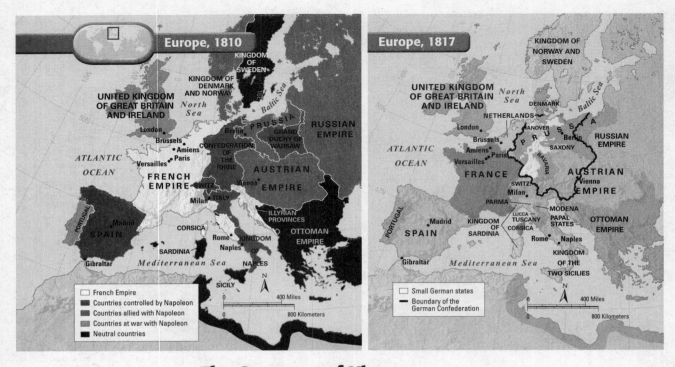

Europe, 1810

KINGDOM OF SWEDEN

UNITED KINGDOM OF GREAT BRITAIN AND IRELAND

North Sea

KINGDOM OF DENMARK AND NORWAY

Baltic Sea

ATLANTIC OCEAN

London

Brussels
Amiens
Paris
Versailles

FRENCH EMPIRE

PRUSSIA

Berlin

GRAND DUCHY OF WARSAW

CONFEDERATION OF THE RHINE

SWITZ.

Vienna

AUSTRIAN EMPIRE

RUSSIAN EMPIRE

Milan
ITALY

PORTUGAL

Madrid

SPAIN

CORSICA

Rome
Naples

KINGDOM OF NAPLES

SARDINIA

Gibraltar

ILLYRIAN PROVINCES

OTTOMAN EMPIRE

Mediterranean Sea

SICILY

N

0   400 Miles
0   800 Kilometers

☐ French Empire
■ Countries controlled by Napoleon
■ Countries allied with Napoleon
■ Countries at war with Napoleon
■ Neutral countries

Europe, 1817

KINGDOM OF NORWAY AND SWEDEN

UNITED KINGDOM OF GREAT BRITAIN AND IRELAND

North Sea

DENMARK

Baltic Sea

NETHERLANDS

London

Brussels
Amiens
Paris
Versailles

FRANCE

HANOVER

PRUSSIA

Berlin

SAXONY

BAVARIA

SWITZ.

Milan

Vienna

AUSTRIAN EMPIRE

RUSSIAN EMPIRE

ATLANTIC OCEAN

PARMA

MODENA

LUCCA
TUSCANY

CORSICA

PAPAL STATES

KINGDOM OF SARDINIA

Rome   Naples

PORTUGAL

Madrid

SPAIN

Gibraltar

Mediterranean Sea

KINGDOM OF THE TWO SICILIES

OTTOMAN EMPIRE

N

0   400 Miles
0   800 Kilometers

☐ Small German states
— Boundary of the German Confederation

The Congress of Vienna

As revolutions shook the colonies in Latin America, Europe was also undergoing dramatic changes. After the French Revolution and the defeat of Napoleon, European heads of government wanted to establish long-lasting peace and stability on the continent. In 1814–1815, a series of meetings in Vienna, known as the **Congress of Vienna**, were called to set up policies to achieve this goal. Most of the decisions made in Vienna were made in secret among representatives of the five "Great Powers"—Russia, Prussia, Austria, Great Britain, and France. By far the most influential of these representatives was the foreign minister of Austria, Prince **Klemens von Metternich** (MEHT•uhr•nihk).

Metternich had three goals at the Congress of Vienna. First, he wanted to prevent future French aggression by surrounding France with strong countries. The Congress took the following steps to make the weak countries around France stronger: 1) The former Austrian Netherlands and Dutch Republic were united to form the Kingdom of the Netherlands. 2) A group of 39 German states were loosely joined as the newly created German Confederation, dominated by Austria. 3) Switzerland was recognized as an independent nation. 4) The Kingdom of Sardinia in Italy was strengthened by the addition of Genoa. Second, Metternich wanted to restore a **balance of power**, so that no country would be a threat to others. Third, he wanted to restore Europe's royal families to the thrones they had held before Napoleon's conquests, thereby affirming the principle of **legitimacy**, the hereditary right of a monarch to rule.

Revolutions of the 1830s and 1848

The French Revolution had given Europe its first experiment in democratic government. Although the experiment had failed, it set new political ideas in motion. Three schools of political thought struggled for supremacy in European society. **Conservatives** argued for protecting the traditional monarchies. **Liberals** wanted to give more power to elected parliaments, but only the educated and the landowners would vote. **Radicals** still held to the ideals of the French Revolution and favored drastic change to extend democracy to all people. Added to this was a

TAKING NOTES

Recognizing Effects
Use a chart to show how the three goals of Metternich's plan at the Congress of Vienna solved a political problem.

Metternich's Plan	
Problem	Solution

5.20 Preparing for the Regents

Political Systems
What effect did the French Revolution have on political ideas and actions in Europe?

growing nationalist movement that stressed that people's greatest loyalty should not be to a king or an empire but to a nation of people who share a common culture and history. This explosive mixture of ideas and factions would contribute directly to revolutions in the 1830s and in 1848.

By the 1830s, the old order, carefully arranged at the Congress of Vienna was breaking down. Throughout Europe, liberals and nationalists were openly revolting against conservative governments. In October 1830, the Belgians declared their independence from Dutch rule. Conservatives were able to crush nationalist uprisings on the Italian peninsula and in Poland. By the mid-1830s, the old order seemed to have reestablished itself. But the appearance of stability did not last long. In 1848, ethnic uprising erupted throughout Europe. European politics continued to seesaw. Many liberal gains were lost to conservatives within a year. In one country after another, the revolutionaries failed to unite themselves or their nations. By 1849, Europe had practically returned to the conservatism that had controlled governments before 1848.

Russian Absolutism

Russia also faced calls for reform in the 1800s. Unlike the rest of Europe, Russia still operated under a feudal system. Serfs were bound to the nobles whose land they worked. By the 1820s, many Russians believed that serfdom must end. In their eyes, the system was morally wrong. It also prevented the empire from advancing economically.

When the lack of industrial development led to Russia's defeat in the Crimean War, **Alexander II** decided to move the country toward modernization and social change. Alexander's first and boldest reform was freeing the serfs in 1861. The abolition of serfdom, however, went only halfway. Peasant communities—rather than individual peasants—received about half the farmland in the country. Each peasant community had 49 years to pay the government for the land. So, while the serfs were technically free, the debt still tied them to the land.

Reform ground to a halt when terrorists assassinated Alexander II in 1881. His successor, Alexander III, tightened czarist control over the country.

> **5.21 Preparing for the Regents**
> **Political Systems** In what way was Alexander II like Catherine the Great?

PREPARING THE REGENTS

On a separate sheet of paper, write a well-organized essay that includes an introduction, several paragraphs addressing the task below, and a conclusion. Before beginning, check the Score the Essay box for pointers.

Theme: Change
Political revolutions had many causes. These revolutions affected society and led to many changes. The changes may or may not have resolved the problems that caused the revolution.

Task:
Choose one revolution from this section and:
- Explain the causes of the revolution
- Describe the effects this political revolution had on society
- Evaluate whether the changes that resulted from the political revolution resolved the problems that caused it

SCORE THE ESSAY To receive a score of 5 on your essay, you will need to:
- thoroughly develop all aspects of the task evenly and in depth by describing both the causes and effects of the revolution and whether the changes that resulted from it resolved the problems that caused it..
- be more analytical than descriptive.
- richly support the theme with relevant facts, examples, and details.
- demonstrate a logical and clear plan of organization.

Global Nationalism

Section Overview

Nationalism was the most powerful idea of the 1800s. Its influence stretched throughout Europe, the Americas, Asia, North Africa, and the Middle East. It shaped countries by creating new ones or breaking up old ones. In Europe, it also upset the balance of power set up at the Congress of Vienna in 1815, affecting the lives of millions. Empires in Europe were made up of many different groups of people. Nationalism fed the desire of most of those groups to be free of the rule of empires and govern themselves in their traditional lands.

Under the direction of Prince Clemens von Metternich of Austria, the Congress of Vienna had established five Great Powers in Europe—Britain, France, Austria, Prussia, and Russia. In 1815, the Great Powers were nearly equal in strength. The wars of the mid-1800s greatly strengthened one of the Great Powers, as Prussia joined with other German states to form Germany. By 1871, Britain and Germany were clearly the most powerful, both militarily and economically. Austria and Russia lagged far behind. France struggled along somewhere in the middle. The European balance of power had broken down.

Prince Clemens von Metternich (1773–1859) of Austria

MAIN IDEAS

POWER AND AUTHORITY   Nationalism contributed to the formation of two new nations and a new political order in Europe.

TERMS AND NAMES

- Camillo di Cavour
- Giuseppe Garibaldi
- Junkers
- Otto von Bismarck
- realpolitik
- kaiser
- the Balkans
- geopolitics
- Crimean War
- Zionism

PREPARING FOR THE REGENTS

As you read this section, consider
- what role nationalism played in Europe, Eastern Europe, Asia, and the Middle East.
- what role nationalism plays in these regions today.

TIME LINE

1830
Greece achieves independence.

1853
Camillo di Cavour becomes prime minister of Sardinia.

1862
Otto von Bismarck becomes prime minister of Prussia.

1870
Italy unites.

1871
Wilhelm I crowned Kaiser of united Germany.

Human and Physical Geography

Nationalism—the belief that people should be loyal to their nation—was not widespread until the 1800s. The rise of modern nationalism is tied to the spread of democratic ideas and the growth of an educated middle class. People wanted to decide how they were governed, instead of having monarchs impose government on them.

Most of the people who believed in nationalism were either liberals or radicals. In most cases, the liberal middle class—teachers, lawyers, and businesspeople—led the struggle for constitutional government and the formation of nation-states. (As you learned in Unit 3, Section 5, a nation becomes a nation-state when it has its own independent government.) In Europe in 1815, only France, England, and Spain could be called nation-states. But that would soon change as nationalism fueled efforts to build nation-states. In Germany, for example, liberals wanted to gather the many different German states into a single nation-state. Other liberals in large empires, such as the Hungarians in the Austrian Empire, wanted to split away and establish self-rule.

Nationalists were not loyal to kings, but to people—to those who shared common bonds. They believed that people of a single "nationality," or ancestry, should unite under a single government. In contrast, people who wanted to restore the old order from before the French Revolution saw nationalism as a force for disunity. Gradually, however, authoritarian rulers began to see that nationalism could also unify masses of people. They soon began to use nationalist feelings for their own purposes. They built nation-states in areas where they remained firmly in control.

A Force for Unity and Self-Determination

While nationalism destroyed empires, it also built nations. Italy and Germany were two European nation-states to achieve unity in the mid-1800s.

Italy Between 1815 and 1848, fewer and fewer Italians were content to live under foreign rulers. Italian nationalists looked for leadership from the kingdom of Piedmont-Sardinia, the largest and most powerful of the Italian states. The kingdom had adopted a liberal constitution in 1848. So, to the liberal Italian middle classes, unification under Piedmont-Sardinia seemed a good plan.

Sardinia's king, Victor Emmanuel II, named Count **Camillo di Cavour** (kuh•VOOR) as his prime minister in 1853. Cavour set about gaining control of northern Italy for Sardinia. He realized that the greatest roadblock to annexing northern Italy was Austria. In 1858, the French agreed to help drive Austria out of the northern Italian provinces. Cavour then provoked a war with the Austrians in which Sardinia succeeded in taking all of northern Italy, except Venetia.

As Cavour was uniting northern Italy, he secretly started helping nationalist rebels in southern Italy. In May 1860, a small army of Italian nationalists led by **Giuseppe Garibaldi** (gar•uh•BAWL•dee) captured Sicily. From Sicily, Garibaldi and his rebel forces

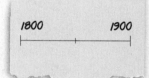

5.22 Preparing for the Regents

Nationalism Why can nationalism be seen as having both positive and negative effects?

TAKING NOTES

Following Chronological Order List major events in the unification of Italy and of Germany.

1800   1900

The Unification of Italy, 1858–1870

FRANCE

SWITZERLAND

ALPS

AUSTRIAN EMPIRE

SAVOY

To France, 1860

Milan

LOMBARDY

Turin

VENETIA

Venice

PIEDMONT

PARMA

Genoa

MODENA

NICE

LUCCA

Florence

Pisa

TUSCANY

PAPAL STATES

CORSICA (Fr.)

Rome

Mediterranean Sea

SARDINIA

Naples

Tyrrhenian Sea

KINGDOM OF THE TWO SICILIES

Palermo

SICILY

Drava R.

Sava R.

Danube R.

Adriatic Sea

OTTOMAN EMPIRE

Loire R.

Rhône R.

■ Kingdom of Sardinia, 1858
■ Added to Sardinia, 1859–1860
☐ Added to Italy, 1866
■ Added to Italy, 1870
– Papal States

0   200 Miles
0   400 Kilometers

Nationalism Why can the following quotation by Camillo di Cavour be seen as an expression of Italy's desire for self-determination?

"We ardently wish to free Italy from foreign rule. We agree that we must put aside all petty differences in order to gain this most important goal."

crossed to the Italian mainland and marched north. Eventually, Garibaldi agreed to unite the southern areas he had conquered with the kingdom of Piedmont-Sardinia and let King Victor Emmanuel II rule.

In 1866, the Austrian province of Venetia, which included the city of Venice, became part of Italy. Then, in 1870, Italian forces took over the last part of a territory known as the Papal States. With this victory, the city of Rome came under Italian control. Soon after, Rome became the capital of the united kingdom of Italy. The pope, however, would continue to govern a section of Rome known as Vatican City.

Germany Like Italy, Germany also achieved national unity in the mid-1800s. Beginning in 1815, 39 German states formed a loose grouping called the German Confederation. The Austrian Empire dominated the confederation. However, Prussia was ready to unify all the German states.

Prussia enjoyed several advantages that would eventually help it forge a strong German state. First of all, unlike the Austro-Hungarian Empire, Prussia had a mainly German population. As a result, nationalism actually unified Prussia. In contrast, ethnic groups in Austria-Hungary tore the empire apart. Moreover, Prussia's army was by far the most powerful in central Europe. In 1848, Berlin rioters forced a constitutional convention to write up a liberal constitution for the kingdom, paving the way for unification.

In 1861, Wilhelm I succeeded Frederick William to the throne. The liberal parliament refused him money for reforms that would double the strength of the army. Wilhelm saw the parliament's refusal as a major challenge to his authority. He was supported in his view by the **Junkers** (YUNG•kuhrz), strongly conservative members of Prussia's wealthy landowning class. In 1862, Wilhelm chose a conservative Junker named **Otto von Bismarck** as his prime minister. Bismarck was a master of what came to be known as **realpolitik**. This German term means "the politics of reality." The term is used to describe tough power politics with no room for idealism.

In 1864, Bismarck took the first step toward molding an empire. Prussia and Austria formed an alliance and went to war against Denmark to win two border provinces, Schleswig and Holstein. A quick victory increased national pride among Prussians. It also won new respect from other Germans and lent support for Prussia as head of a unified Germany. After the victory, Prussia governed Schleswig, while Austria controlled Holstein.

Bismarck purposely stirred up border conflicts with Austria over Schleswig and Holstein, provoking Austria to declare war in 1866. The Seven Weeks' War was a humiliating defeat for Austria. The Austrians lost Venetia, which was given to Italy, and had to accept Prussian annexation of more German territory. Prussia took control of northern Germany. For the first time, the eastern and western parts of the Prussian kingdom were joined. In 1867, the remaining states of the north joined the North German Confederation, which Prussia dominated.

The Unification of Germany, 1865–1871

Prussia, 1865
Annexed by Prussia, 1866
Joined Prussia in North German Confederation, 1867
South German States (joined Prussia to form German Empire, 1871)
Conquered from France, 1871
German Empire, 1871

By 1867, a few southern German states remained independent of Prussian control. The majority of southern Germans were Catholics, and many resisted domination by a Protestant Prussia. However, Bismarck felt he could win the support of southerners if they faced a threat from outside. He reasoned that a war with France would rally the south. Bismarck was an expert at manufacturing "incidents" to gain his ends. The resulting conflict—the Franco-Prussian War—was the final stage in German unification. People in southern Germany finally accepted Prussian leadership. On January 18, 1871, King Wilhelm I of Prussia was crowned **kaiser** (KY•zuhr), or emperor. Germans called their empire the Second Reich. (The Holy Roman Empire was the first.)

India Nationalist movements were not limited to Europe. Nationalist feelings started to surface in India in the 1800s. At that time, India was part of the British colonial system. Indians hated this system, which made them second-class citizens in their own country. They were barred from top posts in the Indian Civil Service. Those who managed to get middle-level jobs were paid less than Europeans. A British engineer on the East India Railway, for example, made nearly 20 times as much money as an Indian engineer. This growing nationalism led to the founding of two nationalist groups, the Indian National Congress in 1885 and the Muslim League in 1906. At first, such groups concentrated on specific concerns for Indians. By the early 1900s, however, they were calling for self-government.

Turkey and the Young Turks By the early 1900s, the Ottoman Empire was in rapid decline. Fueled by nationalist feelings, many subject groups had succeeded in breaking away from their Turkish rulers (see below). Nationalist feelings, however, were not limited to the Ottomans' subject peoples. There was also a growing nationalist movement among Ottoman Turks. This movement came to a head in 1908, when a group known as the Young Turks staged a series of revolts that led the sultan to restore a liberal constitution that had been granted in 1876 but later withdrawn. The Young Turks helped push through many reforms. The sultan lost much of his power, parliamentary elections were instituted, and the secret police and censorship were dismantled. The Young Turks also supported improvements in women's rights. However, when conservatives staged a counter-revolution, the Young Turks seized power and ruled as virtual dictators.

A Force for Conflict

Nationalism often served as a source of conflict, as groups struggled to break free from the empires that had absorbed them. This was particularly true for groups under Ottoman control.

The Balkans In the early 1800s, the Ottoman Empire controlled most of **the Balkans**. This mountainous peninsula in the southeastern corner of Europe includes all or part of present-day Greece, Albania, Bulgaria, Romania, Turkey, and the former Yugoslavia. In 1830, Greece gained its independence, and Serbia gained self-rule. By early 1914, other groups had succeeded in breaking away from Turkish rule. These peoples had formed new nations, including Bulgaria, Montenegro, and Romania. Nationalism was a powerful force in these countries. Each group longed to extend its borders. Serbia, for example, had a large Slavic population. It hoped to absorb all the Slavs on the Balkan Peninsula. Russia, itself a mostly Slavic nation, supported Serbian nationalism. However, Serbia's powerful northern neighbor, Austria-Hungary, opposed such an effort. Austria feared that efforts to create a Slavic state would stir rebellion among its Slavic population.

5.25 Preparing for the Regents

Nationalism How does the following quotation by Otto von Bismarck illustrate the tactic he used to unify Germany?

"Not by democracy or liberal standards will our goal be achieved but by blood and iron. Then we will be successful, no nation is born without the traumatic experience of war."

5.26 Preparing for the Regents

Nationalism When did Indians first begin calling for self-government?

5.27 Preparing for the Regents

Change Why can the Young Turks be seen as having both a positive and negative effect?

5.28 Preparing for the Regents

Nationalism Why did Austria-Hungary oppose Serbia's desire to create a Slavic state?

In 1908, Austria annexed, or took over, Bosnia and Herzegovina. These were two Balkan areas with large Slavic populations. Serbian leaders, who had sought to rule these provinces, were outraged. In the years that followed, tensions between Serbia and Austria steadily rose. The Serbs continually vowed to take Bosnia and Herzegovina away from Austria. In response, Austria-Hungary vowed to crush any Serbian effort to undermine its authority in the Balkans.

The Ottoman Empire Nationalists efforts often caused tensions in the empire. For example, in response to nationalism in Armenia, the Ottomans massacred and deported Armenians from 1894 to 1896 and again in 1915.

The Ottomans also faced problems with European powers. As the empire weakened, the Europeans began to look for ways to take control of Ottoman lands. **Geopolitics**, an interest in or taking of land for its strategic location or products, played an important role in the fate of the Ottoman Empire. World powers were attracted to its strategic location. The Ottomans controlled access to the Mediterranean and the Atlantic sea trade.

The Ottomans became a pawn in the game of European geopolitics. In 1853, for instance, the Russians started the **Crimean War** with the Ottomans in an effort to secure a warm-weather port on the Black Sea. Fearful that Russia would gain control of additional Ottoman lands, Britain and France entered the war on the side of the Ottoman Empire. The combined forces defeated Russia. However, the war revealed the Ottoman Empire's military weakness. Despite the help of Britain and France, the Ottoman Empire continued to lose lands in Europe and Africa. By the beginning of World War I, the Ottoman Empire was reduced in size and in deep decline.

Zionism

Many Jewish people also embraced nationalism. After being forced out of Palestine during the second century, the Jewish people were not able to establish their own state and lived in different countries throughout the world. The global dispersal of the Jews is known as the Diaspora. For many Jews, the long history of exile and persecution convinced them to work for a homeland in Palestine. In the 1890s, a movement known as **Zionism** developed to pursue this goal. Its leader was Theodor Herzl (HEHRT•suhl), a writer in Vienna. It took many years, however, before the state of Israel was established.

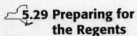

5.29 Preparing for the Regents

Power Why can the Ottoman Empire be seen as a pawn of the European powers?

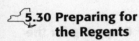

5.30 Preparing for the Regents

Nationalism Why is the Zionist movement an example of nationalism?

PREPARING THE REGENTS

On a separate sheet of paper, write a well-organized essay that includes an introduction, several paragraphs addressing the task below, and a conclusion. Before beginning, check the Score the Essay box for pointers.

Theme: Nationalism
Nationalism is a powerful force that can have positive and negative effects on nations and regions.

Task:
• Define the term *nationalism*.
• Discuss the positive and negative effects of nationalism in the late 1800s and early 1900s.

Be sure to include specific examples in your essay.

> **SCORE THE ESSAY** To receive a score of 5 on your essay, you will need to:
> • thoroughly develop all aspects of the task evenly and in depth by describing both the positive and negative effects of nationalism in the 1800s and early 1900s.
> • be more analytical than descriptive.
> • richly support the theme with relevant facts, examples, and details.
> • demonstrate a logical and clear plan of organization.

Latin America After Independence

Section Overview

Latin America's long struggle to gain independence from colonial domination left the new nations in shambles. Farm fields had been neglected and were overrun with weeds. Buildings in many cities bore the scars of battle. Some cities had been left in ruins. The new nations of Latin America faced a struggle for economic and political recovery that was every bit as difficult as their struggle for independence had been.

Mexico, like other Latin American nations, faced many problems. In 1910, Francisco Madero called for an armed revolution against the then president, Porfirio Díaz. "Pancho" Villa, Emiliano Zapata, and others raised armies to fight against Díaz. By 1911, they were able to force him from power.

Mexican leader Porfirio Díaz
(1830–1915)

MAIN IDEAS

REVOLUTION   Political, economic, and social inequalities in Mexico triggered a period of revolution and reform.

TERMS AND NAMES

- caudillo
- Porfirio Díaz
- Francisco Madero
- "Pancho" Villa
- Emiliano Zapata

PREPARING FOR THE REGENTS

As you read this section, consider
- what forces led to the failure of democracy in Latin America in the 19th century.
- what the perspectives of various social classes were on the revolutions in Latin America.
- what role nationalism played in the Mexican Revolution.

TIME LINE

1821
Mexico declares independence from Spain.

1910
Mexican Revolution begins.

1917
Mexican constitution adopted.

Human and Physical Geography

Political independence meant little for most citizens of the new Latin American nations. The majority remained poor laborers caught up in a cycle of poverty. Independence also did not bring democracy and political stability. Many Latin American army leaders had gained fame and power during their long struggle for independence. They often continued to assert their power. They controlled the new nations as military dictators, or **caudillos** (kow•DEE•yohz). They were able to hold on to power because they were backed by the military. By the mid-1800s, nearly all the countries of Latin America were ruled by caudillos. The Church also played a major role in government. Given its huge landholdings and its influence with the people, the Church was able to exert considerable power.

Reform governments did occasionally come to power. In Argentina, for example, Domingo Sarmiento made a strong commitment to improving education during his presidency. Between 1868 and 1874, the number of students in Argentina doubled. But such reformers did not stay in office for long. More often than not, a caudillo, supported by the army, seized control of the government.

The caudillos faced little opposition. The wealthy landowners usually supported them because they opposed giving power to the lower classes. In addition, Latin Americans had gained little experience with democracy under European colonial rule. So, the dictatorship of a caudillo did not seem unusual to them. But even when caudillos where not in power, most Latin Americans still lacked a voice in government. Voting rights—and with them, political power—were restricted to the relatively few members of the upper and middle classes who owned property and could read.

Social Classes in Latin America

In Latin American colonial society, class dictated people's place in society and jobs. At the top of Spanish-American society were the *peninsulares*, people who had been born in Spain. They formed a tiny percentage of the population. Only *peninsulares* could hold high office in Spanish colonial government. Creoles, Spaniards born in Latin America, were below the *peninsulares* in rank. Creoles could not hold high-level political office, but they could rise as officers in Spanish colonial armies. Together these two groups controlled land, wealth, and power in the Spanish colonies. Below the *peninsulares* and creoles came the mestizos, persons of mixed European and Indian ancestry. Next were the mulattos, persons of mixed European and African ancestry, and enslaved Africans. Indians were at the bottom of the social ladder.

Things did not really change after independence. Both before and after independence, most Latin Americans worked for large landowners. The employers paid their workers with vouchers that could be used only at their own supply stores. Since wages were low and prices were high, workers went into debt. Their debt accumulated and passed from one generation to the next. In this system known as peonage, "free" workers were little better than slaves.

Landowners, on the other hand, only got wealthier after independence. Many new Latin American governments took over the lands owned by native peoples and by the Catholic Church. Then they put those lands up for sale. Wealthy landowners were the only people who could afford to buy them, and they snapped them up. But as one Argentinean newspaper reported, "Their greed for land does not equal their ability to use it intelligently." The unequal distribution of land

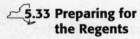

5.31 Preparing for the Regents

Political Systems Who were the caudillos? Why were the able to gain power?

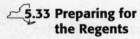

5.32 Preparing for the Regents

Power What social classes existing in Latin American society? Who held the power?

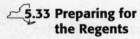

5.33 Preparing for the Regents

Power In what way was the peonage like serfdom in medieval Europe?

and the landowners' inability to use it effectively combined to prevent social and economic development in Latin America.

The Economy

When colonial rule ended in Latin America in the early 1800s, Britain and, later, the United States, became Latin America's main trading partners. Latin America's economies continued to depend on exports. As during the colonial era, each country concentrated on one or two profitable crops, known as cash crops. With advances in technology, however, Latin America's exports grew. The development of the steamship and the building of railroads in the 19th century, for example, greatly increased Latin American trade. Toward the end of the century, the invention of refrigeration helped increase Latin America's exports. The sale of beef, fruits and vegetables, and other perishable goods soared.

But foreign nations benefited far more from the increased trade than Latin America did. In exchange for their exports, Latin Americans imported European and North American manufactured goods. As a result, they had little reason to develop their own manufacturing industries. And as long as Latin America remained unindustrialized, it could not be a leading player in the world economy.

Furthermore, Latin American countries used little of their export income to build roads, schools, or hospitals. Nor did they fund programs that would help them become self-sufficient. Instead, they often borrowed money at high interest rates to develop facilities for their export industries. Countries such as Britain, France, the United States, and Germany were willing lenders. The Latin American countries often were unable to pay back their loans, however. In response, foreign lenders sometimes threatened to collect the debt by force. At other times, they threatened to take over the facilities they had funded. In this way, foreign companies gained control of many Latin American industries. This began a new age of economic colonialism in Latin America.

The Mexican Revolution and Civil War

The legacy of colonialism and long-term political instability that plagued the other Latin American nations caused problems for Mexico as well. In the 1876, a new caudillo, __Díaz__, came to power. Díaz was an Indian from Oaxaca. He had the support of the military. He also had the support of Indians and small land-holders, because they thought he would work for more radical land reform.

During the Díaz years, elections became meaningless. Díaz offered land, power, or political favors to anyone who supported him. He terrorized many who refused to support him, ordering them to be beaten or put in jail. Using such strong-arm methods, Díaz managed to remain in power until 1911.

In the early 1900s, Mexicans from many walks of life began to protest Díaz's harsh rule. Idealistic liberals hungered for liberty. Farm laborers hungered for land. Workers hungered for fairer wages and better working conditions. Even some of Díaz's handpicked political allies spoke out for reform. A variety of political parties opposed to Díaz began to form. Among the most powerful was a party led by **Francisco Madero**.

Madero Begins the Revolution Born into one of Mexico's ten richest families, Francisco Madero was educated in the United States and France. He believed in democracy and wanted to strengthen its hold in Mexico. Madero announced his candidacy for president of Mexico early in 1910. Soon afterward,

5.34 Preparing for the Regents

Movement of People and Goods Who were Latin America's major trading partners after independence?

5.35 Preparing for the Regents

Economic Systems In what ways did Latin America fail to become economically self-sufficient following independence?

5.36 Preparing for the Regents

Conflict What factors led to the Mexican Revolution?

TAKING NOTES

Comparing Use a chart to compare the major accomplishments of the Mexican leaders discussed in this section.

Leader	Major Accomplishment

Díaz had him arrested. From exile in the United States, Madero called for an armed revolution against Díaz.

The Mexican Revolution began slowly. Leaders arose in different parts of Mexico and gathered their own armies. In the north, Francisco **"Pancho" Villa** became immensely popular. He had a bold Robin Hood policy of taking money from the rich and giving it to the poor. South of Mexico City, another strong, popular leader, **Emiliano Zapata**, raised a powerful revolutionary army. Like Villa, Zapata came from a poor family. He was determined to see that land was returned to peasants and small farmers. He wanted the laws reformed to protect their rights. Villa, Zapata, and other armed revolutionaries won important victories against Díaz's army. By the spring of 1911, Díaz agreed to step down. He called for new elections.

Mexican Leaders Struggle for Power Madero was elected president in November 1911. However, his policies were seen as too liberal by some and not revolutionary enough by others. Villa, Zapata, and others took up arms against him. In 1913, realizing that he could not hold on to power, Madero resigned. The military leader General Victoriano Huerta then took over the presidency.

Huerta was unpopular with many people, including Villa and Zapata. They joined forces with Venustiano Carranza to overthrow Huerta 15 months after he came to power. Carranza took control of the government and then turned his army on his former revolutionary allies. Both Villa and Zapata continued to fight. In 1919, however, Carranza lured Zapata into a trap and murdered him. With Zapata's death, the civil war also came to an end. More than a million Mexicans had lost their lives.

The New Mexican Constitution Carranza began a revision of Mexico's constitution. It was adopted in 1917. A revolutionary document, that constitution is still in effect today. It promoted education, land reforms, and workers' rights. Carranza did not support the final version of the constitution, however, and in 1920, he was overthrown by one of his generals, Alvaro Obregón. Although Obregón seized power violently, he did not remain a dictator. Instead, he supported the reforms the constitution called for, particularly land reform. He also promoted public education. Mexican public schools taught a common language—Spanish—and stressed nationalism. In this way, his policies helped unite the various regions and peoples of the country. Nevertheless, Obregón was assassinated in 1928. The next year, a new political party, the Institutional Revolutionary Party (PRI), arose. Although the PRI did not tolerate opposition, it initiated an ongoing period of peace and political stability in Mexico.

5.37 Preparing for the Regents

Conflict What role did peasants play in the Mexican Revolution?

5.38 Preparing for the Regents

Nationalism What role did nationalism play in the Mexican Revolution and its aftermath?

PREPARING FOR THE REGENTS

Answer the following question. Use the Analyze the Question hints to help you answer the question.

1 A lasting result of colonial rule in many Latin American nations has been the

(1) elimination of national debt
(2) control of power by wealthy landowners
(3) decrease in power of the Catholic Church
(4) creation of industrial economies

ANALYZE THE QUESTION
- Read the question stem. You are being asked to determine a legacy of colonial rule.
- Think about the characteristics of Latin American society following independence.
- Rule out the alternatives that do not match those characteristics. The remaining alternative is the correct answer.

Economic and Social Revolutions

Section Overview

Between 1700 and 1900, revolutions in agriculture, production, transportation, and communication changed the lives of people in Western Europe and the United States. Industrialization gave Europe tremendous economic power. In contrast, the economies of Asia and Africa were still based on agriculture and small workshops. Industrialization revolutionized every aspect of society, from daily life to life expectancy. Despite the hardships early urban workers suffered, population, health, and wealth eventually rose dramatically in all industrialized countries. The development of a middle class created great opportunities for education and democratic participation. Greater democratic participation, in turn, fueled a powerful movement for social reform.

George Stephenson's steam locomotive, the *Rocket* (1829)

MAIN IDEAS

SCIENCE AND TECHNOLOGY The Industrial Revolution started in England and soon spread to other countries.

ECONOMICS The factory system changed the way people lived and worked, introducing a variety of problems.

ECONOMICS The Industrial Revolution led to economic, social, and political reforms.

TERMS AND NAMES

- Industrial Revolution
- industrialization
- factors of production
- enclosure
- crop rotation
- factory
- factory system

- entrepreneur
- urbanization
- middle class
- laissez faire
- Adam Smith
- capitalism
- utilitarianism

- socialism
- Karl Marx
- communism
- union
- strike
- suffrage
- Chartist movement

 PREPARING FOR THE REGENTS

As you read this section, consider
- what geographic factors explain why industrialization began in Great Britain.
- to what extent the Industrial Revolution led to greater urbanization.
- how social class impacted the way in which various groups looked at the Industrial Revolution.
- what role the Industrial Revolution played in the changing role of men and women.
- how the abuses of the Industrial Revolution led to the ideologies of utilitarianism, socialism, and communism.
- what impact the Industrial Revolution had on the expansion of suffrage.

TIME LINE

1701
Jethro Tull invents seed drill.

1765
James Watt builds steam engine.

1825
First railroad opens in Great Britain.

1832
Parliament extends voting rights with passage of the Reform Bill.

1848
Marx and Engels publish *The Communist Manifesto.*

1875
British unions win right to strike.

Human and Physical Geography

The **Industrial Revolution** refers to the greatly increased output of machine-made goods that began in England in the middle 1700s. There are several reasons why the Industrial Revolution began in England. In addition to political stability and a large population of workers, England had the extensive natural resources required for **industrialization**—the process of developing machine production of goods. These natural resources included 1) water power and coal to fuel the new machines; 2) iron ore to construct machines, tools, and buildings; 3) rivers for inland transportation; and 4) harbors from which merchant ships set sail. Britain's highly developed banking system also contributed to industrialization by providing bank loans that allowed people to invest in new machinery and expand their operations. Growing overseas trade, economic prosperity, and a climate of progress led to the increased demand for goods. Other countries had some of these advantages. But Britain had all the **factors of production**—the land, labor, and capital (or wealth) needed to produce goods and services—that the Industrial Revolution required. It did not take long, however, for the Industrial Revolution to spread to Continental Europe and North America.

Agrarian Revolution

A revolution in farming also helped pave the way for the Industrial Revolution. In 1700, wealthy landowners, began buying up much of the land that village farmers had once worked. They combined the land into larger fields, which were called **enclosures** because they were enclosed by fences or hedges. The enclosure movement had two important results. First, landowners tried new agricultural methods developed by scientific farmers. Second, large landowners forced small farmers to become tenant farmers or to give up farming and move to the cities.

Farmers took advantage of Jethro Tull's seed drill, which allowed them to sow seeds in well-spaced rows at specific depths. A larger share of the seeds took root, boosting crop yields. They also adopted a new process of **crop rotation**. One year, for example, a farmer might plant a field with wheat, which exhausted soil nutrients. The next year he planted a root crop, such as turnips, to restore nutrients. This might be followed in turn by barley and then clover.

Livestock breeders also improved their methods, which resulted in increased output. As food supplies increased and living conditions improved, England's population mushroomed. An increasing population boosted the demand for food and goods such as cloth. As farmers lost their land to large enclosed farms, many became factory workers.

The British Industrial Revolution

In an explosion of creativity, inventions now revolutionized industry. Britain's textile industry clothed the world in wool, linen, and cotton. This industry was the first to be transformed. Cloth merchants boosted their profits by speeding up the process by which spinners and weavers made cloth.

Changes in the Textile Industry By 1800, several major inventions had modernized the cotton industry. In 1733, John Kay invented the flying shuttle, a boat-shaped piece of wood to which yarn was attached. The shuttle, which sped back and forth on wheels, doubled the work a weaver could do in a day. Around 1764, James Hargreaves invented a faster

TAKING NOTES

Following Chronological Order On a time line, note important events in Britain's industrialization.

1700   1830

5.39 Preparing for the Regents

Human and Physical Geography What effects did advances in agricultural techniques and practices have on the Industrial Revolution?

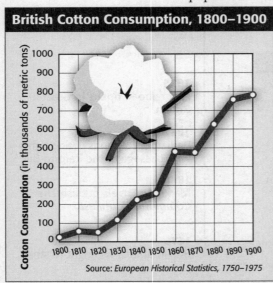

British Cotton Consumption, 1800–1900

Cotton Consumption (in thousands of metric tons)

1000 / 900 / 800 / 700 / 600 / 500 / 400 / 300 / 200 / 100 / 0

1800 1810 1820 1830 1840 1850 1860 1870 1880 1890 1900

Source: *European Historical Statistics, 1750–1975*

spinning wheel—the spinning jenny (named after his daughter)—which allowed one spinner to work eight threads at a time. At first, textile workers operated the flying shuttle and the spinning jenny by hand. Then, in 1769, Richard Arkwright invented the water frame, which used the waterpower from rapid streams to drive spinning wheels. In 1779, Samuel Crompton combined features of the spinning jenny and the water frame to produce the spinning mule. The spinning mule made thread that was stronger, finer, and more consistent than earlier spinning machines. Run by waterpower, Edmund Cartwright's power loom sped up weaving after its invention in 1787.

Growth of the Factory System The new spinning machinery was bulky and expensive. Wealthy textile merchants set up the machines in large buildings called **factories**. This marked the shift from cottage industries, in which spinning and weaving were done in people's homes, to the **factory system**, where the manufacturing of goods was concentrated in a central location.

By the late 1700s, steam-driven machinery powered English factories. The development of the steam engine stemmed from the search for a cheap, convenient source of power. As early as 1705, coal miners were using steam-powered pumps to remove water from deep mine shafts. But pumps gobbled great quantities of fuel, making them expensive to run. In 1765, James Watt figured out a way to make the steam engine work faster and more efficiently while burning less fuel.

Improvements in Transportation Transportation also underwent improvements in the 1800s. An American inventor named Robert Fulton used a steam engine to build a steamboat called the *Clermont*, which made its first successful trip in 1807. In England, water transportation improved with the creation of a network of canals, or human-made waterways, that slashed the cost of transporting both raw materials and finished goods. British roads also improved. Private investors formed companies that built roads and then operated them for profit. People called the new roads turnpikes because travelers had to stop at tollgates (turnstiles or turnpikes) to pay tolls before traveling farther.

Even more important was the development of a steam engine on wheels— the railroad locomotive. In 1821, George Stephenson began work on the world's first railroad line. It was to run 27 miles from the Yorkshire coal fields to the port of Stockton on the North Sea. In 1825, the railroad opened. It used four locomotives that Stephenson had designed and built. The invention and perfection of the locomotive had at least four major effects. First, railroads spurred industrial growth by giving manufacturers a cheap way to transport materials and finished products. Second, the railroad boom created hundreds of thousands of new jobs for both railroad workers and the miners who provided iron for the tracks and coal for the steam engines. Third, the railroads boosted England's agricultural and fishing industries, which could transport their products to distant cities. Finally, by making travel easier, railroads encouraged country people to take distant city jobs and lured city dwellers to resorts in the countryside.

Consequences of Industrialization

The Industrial Revolution affected every part of life in Great Britain, but proved to be a mixed blessing. Eventually, industrialization led to a better quality of life for most people. But the change to machine production initially caused human suffering. Rapid industrialization brought plentiful jobs, but it also caused unhealthy working conditions, air and water pollution, the ills of child labor, and rising class tensions.

5.40 Preparing for the Regents

Science and Technology
How did new technologies contribute to the Industrial Revolution?

5.41 Preparing for the Regents

Economic Systems How did the shift from cottage industries to the factory system change where people worked?

5.42 Preparing for the Regents

Movement of People and Goods How did improvements in transportation contribute to the Industrial Revolution?

TAKING NOTES
Outlining Organize main ideas and details.

I. Industrialization Changes Life
   A.
   B.
II. Class Tensions Grow

Urbanization

Urbanization For centuries, most Europeans had lived in rural areas. After 1800, the balance shifted toward cities. This shift was caused by the growth of the factory system. Factories developed in clusters because **entrepreneurs** (AHN•truh•pruh•NURS)—people who organize, manage, and take on the risks of a business—built them near sources of energy, such as water and coal. Between 1800 and 1850, the number of European cities boasting more than 100,000 inhabitants rose from 22 to 47. Most of Europe's urban areas at least doubled in population; some even quadrupled. This period was one of **urbanization**—city building and the movement of people to cities.

Because England's cities grew rapidly, they had no development plans, sanitary codes, or building codes. Moreover, they lacked adequate housing, education, and police protection for the people who poured in from the countryside to seek jobs. Workers lived in dark, dirty shelters, with whole families crowding into one bedroom. Sickness was widespread. Epidemics of the deadly disease cholera regularly swept through the slums of Great Britain's industrial cities. In 1842, a British government study showed an average life span to be 17 years for working-class people in one large city, compared with 38 years in a nearby rural area. But not everyone in urban areas lived miserably. Well-to-do merchants and factory owners often built luxurious homes in the suburbs.

Working Conditions

To increase production, factory owners wanted to keep their machines running as many hours as possible. As a result, the average worker spent 14 hours a day at the job, 6 days a week. Workers faced many dangers. Factories were seldom well lit or clean. Machines injured workers. And there was no government program to provide aid in case of injury. The most dangerous conditions of all were found in coal mines. Frequent accidents, damp conditions, and the constant breathing of coal dust made the average miner's life span ten years shorter than that of other workers. Many women and children were employed in the mining industry because they were the cheapest source of labor.

Social Classes and Changing Roles

Though poverty gripped Britain's working classes, the Industrial Revolution created enormous wealth in the nation. Most of this new money belonged to factory owners, shippers, and merchants. These people were part of a growing **middle class**, a social class made up of skilled workers, professionals, businesspeople, and wealthy farmers.

The new middle class transformed the social structure of Great Britain. In the past, landowners and aristocrats had occupied the top position in British society. With most of the wealth, they wielded the social and political power. Now some factory owners, merchants, and bankers grew wealthier than the landowners and aristocrats. Yet important social distinctions divided the two wealthy classes. Landowners looked down on those who had made their fortunes in the "vulgar" business world. Not until late in the 1800s were rich entrepreneurs considered the social equals of the lords of the countryside.

Gradually, a larger middle class—neither rich nor poor—emerged. The upper middle class consisted of government employees, doctors, lawyers, and managers of factories, mines, and shops. The lower middle class included factory overseers and such skilled workers as toolmakers, mechanical drafters, and printers. These people enjoyed a comfortable standard of living.

During the years 1800 to 1850, however, laborers, or the working class, saw little improvement in their living and working conditions. They watched their livelihoods disappear as machines replaced them. In frustration, some smashed the machines they thought were putting them out of work.

5.43 Preparing for the Regents

Urbanization What were cities like during the Industrial Revolution?

5.44 Preparing for the Regents

Environment and Society What effect did the Industrial Revolution have on social classes and social roles in Great Britain?

5.45 Preparing for the Regents

Economic Systems Why can it be said that some laborers fell victim to technological unemployment during the Industrial Revolution?

Effects of the Industrial Revolution Despite the problems that followed industrialization, the Industrial Revolution had a number of positive effects. It created jobs for workers. It contributed to the wealth of the nation. It fostered technological progress and invention. It greatly increased the production of goods and raised the standard of living. Perhaps most important, it provided the hope of improvement in people's lives.

The Industrial Revolution produced a number of other benefits as well. These included healthier diets, better housing, and cheaper, mass-produced clothing. Because the Industrial Revolution created a demand for engineers as well as clerical and professional workers, it expanded educational opportunities. The middle and upper classes prospered immediately from the Industrial Revolution. For the workers it took longer, but their lives gradually improved during the 1800s. Laborers eventually won higher wages, shorter hours, and better working conditions after they joined together to form labor unions.

Responses to Industrialization

In industrialized countries in the 19th century, the Industrial Revolution opened a wide gap between the rich and the poor. This gap inspired many writers of the era. The English realist novelist Charles Dickens created unforgettable characters and scenes of London's working poor. Many of the scenes showed the despair of London's poor. In his book *Little Dorrit*, Dickens described the life of a working-class person as sheer monotony set in a gloomy neighborhood. The novels of the French writer Émile Zola exposed the miseries of French workers in small shops, factories, and coal mines. His revelations shocked readers and spurred reforms of labor laws and working conditions in France.

Business leaders believed that governments should stay out of business and economic affairs. Reformers, however, felt that governments needed to play an active role to improve conditions for the poor. Workers also demanded more rights and protection. They formed labor unions to increase their influence.

Philosophers of Industrialization The term **laissez faire** (LEHS•ay•FAIR) refers to the economic policy of letting owners of industry and business set working conditions without interference. This policy favors a free market unregulated by the government. The term is French for "let do," and by extension, "let people do as they please." Laissez-faire economics stemmed from French economic philosophers of the Enlightenment. They criticized the idea that nations grow wealthy by placing heavy tariffs on foreign goods. They believed that if government allowed free trade—the flow of commerce in the world market without government regulation—the economy would prosper.

Adam Smith, a professor at the University of Glasgow, Scotland, defended the idea of a free economy, or free markets, in his 1776 book *The Wealth of Nations*. According to Smith, economic liberty guaranteed economic progress. As a result, government should not interfere. Smith's arguments rested on what he called the three natural laws of economics: 1) the law of self-interest—people work for their own good; 2) the law of competition—competition forces people to make a better product; and 3) the law of supply and demand—enough goods would be produced at the lowest possible price to meet demand in a market economy.

Smith's basic ideas were supported by British economists Thomas Malthus and David Ricardo. Like Smith, they believed that natural laws governed economic life. Their important ideas were the foundation of laissez-faire capitalism. **Capitalism** is an economic system in which the factors of production are

5.46 Preparing for the Regents
Economic Systems What were some of the positive effects of the Industrial Revolution?

5.47 Preparing for the Regents
Economic System How were the writings of Charles Dickens and Émile Zola influenced by the Industrial Revolution?

5.48 Preparing for the Regents
Economic Systems According to laissez-faire capitalism, what role should the government play in shaping the economy?

TAKING NOTES
Summarizing Use a chart to summarize the characteristics of capitalism and socialism.

Capitalism	Socialism
1.	1.
2.	2.
3.	3.

privately owned and money is invested in business ventures to make a profit. These ideas also helped bring about the Industrial Revolution.

In *An Essay on the Principle of Population*, written in 1798, Thomas Malthus argued that population tended to increase more rapidly than the food supply. Without wars and epidemics to kill off the extra people, most were destined to be poor and miserable. The predictions of Malthus seemed to be coming true in the 1840s.

David Ricardo, a wealthy stockbroker, took Malthus's theory one step further in his book, *Principles of Political Economy and Taxation* (1817). Like Malthus, Ricardo believed that a permanent underclass would always be poor. In a market system, if there are many workers and abundant resources, then labor and resources are cheap. If there are few workers and scarce resources, then they are expensive. Ricardo believed that wages would be forced down as population increased.

Laissez-faire thinkers such as Smith, Malthus, and Ricardo opposed government efforts to help poor workers. They thought that creating minimum wage laws and better working conditions would upset the market system, lower profits, and undermine the production of wealth in society.

Rise of Socialism In contrast to laissez-faire philosophy, which advised governments to leave business alone, other theorists believed that governments should intervene. These thinkers believed that wealthy people or the government must take action to improve people's lives.

In the late 1700s, English philosopher Jeremy Bentham introduced the philosophy of **utilitarianism**. According to Bentham's theory, people should judge ideas, institutions, and actions on the basis of their utility, or usefulness. He argued that the government should try to promote the greatest good for the greatest number of people. John Stuart Mill, a philosopher and economist, led the utilitarian movement in the 1800s. Mill wished to help ordinary working people with policies that would lead to a more equal division of profits. He also favored a cooperative system of agriculture and women's rights, including the right to vote. Mill called for the government to do away with great differences in wealth. Utilitarians also pushed for reforms in the legal and prison systems and in education.

French reformers such as Charles Fourier (FUR•ee•AY), Saint-Simon (san see•MOHN), and others sought to offset the ill effects of industrialization with a new economic system called **socialism**. In socialism, the factors of production are owned by the public and operate for the welfare of all. Socialists argued that the government should plan the economy rather than depend on free-market capitalism to do the job. Today, this would be called a command economy. Socialists believed that government control of factories, mines, railroads, and other key industries would end poverty and promote equality, thereby helping workers.

The writings of a German journalist named **Karl Marx** introduced the world to a radical type of socialism called Marxism. Marx and Friedrich Engels, a German whose father owned a textile mill in Manchester, outlined their ideas in a 23-page pamphlet called *The Communist Manifesto*. In their manifesto, Marx and Engels argued that human societies have always been divided into warring classes. In their own time, these were the middle class "haves" or employers, called the bourgeoisie (BUR•zhwah•ZEE), and the "have-nots" or workers, called the proletariat (PROH•lih•TAIR•ee•iht). While the wealthy controlled the means of producing goods, the poor performed backbreaking labor under terrible conditions. This situation resulted in conflict.

Marx believed that the capitalist system, which produced the Industrial Revolution, would eventually destroy itself in the following way. Factories would

⚓ 5.49 Preparing for the Regents

Human and Physical Geography How might scientific advances in farming make Malthus's prediction wrong?

⚓ 5.50 Preparing for the Regents

Political Systems According to utilitarianism and socialism, what roles should government play in shaping the economy?

⚓ 5.51 Preparing for the Regents

Economic Systems Based on the following excerpt from *Communist Manifesto*, what view do you think Marx and Engels held of the Industrial Revolution?

"Let the ruling class tremble at the Communist revolution. The proletarians have nothing to lose but their chains. They have a world to win. Workingmen of all countries, unite."

drive small artisans out of business, leaving a small number of manufacturers to control all the wealth. The large proletariat would revolt, seize the factories and mills from the capitalists, and produce what society needed. Workers, sharing in the profits, would bring about economic equality for all people. The workers would control the government in a "dictatorship of the proletariat." After a period of cooperative living and education, the state or government would wither away as a classless society developed.

Marx called this final phase pure communism. He described **communism** as a form of complete socialism in which the means of production—all land, mines, factories, railroads, and businesses—would be owned by the people. Private property would in effect cease to exist. All goods and services would be shared equally.

Labor Unions and Labor Laws Factory workers faced long hours, dirty and dangerous working conditions, and the threat of being laid off. By the 1800s, working people became more active in politics. To press for reforms, workers joined together in voluntary labor associations called **unions**. A union spoke for all the workers in a particular trade. Unions engaged in collective bargaining, negotiations between workers and their employers. They bargained for better working conditions and higher pay. If factory owners refused these demands, union members could **strike**, or refuse to work.

Eventually, reformers and unions forced political leaders to look into the abuses caused by industrialization. In both Great Britain and the United States, new laws reformed some of the worst abuses of industrialization. In Britain, for example, a Parliamentary committee headed by Michael Sadler began investigating child labor and working conditions in factories and mines. They published their report in 1833. As a result of the committee's findings, Parliament passed the Factory Act of 1833. The new law made it illegal to hire children under 9 years old. Children from the ages of 9 to 12 could not work more than 8 hours a day. Young people from 13 to 17 could not work more than 12 hours. In 1842, the Mines Act prevented women and children from working underground. The Ten Hours Act of 1847 limited the work-day to ten hours for women and children who worked in factories.

Industrialization and Suffrage In addition to better working conditions. many people also began to call for political reforms. They demanded that more people be given a greater voice in government. Many different groups, including the middle class, workers, and women, argued that the right to vote be extended to groups that were excluded. The first group to demand a greater voice in politics was the wealthy middle class—factory owners, bankers, and merchants. Beginning in 1830, protests took place around England in favor of a bill in Parliament that would extend **suffrage**, or the right to vote. Parliament responded by passing the Reform Bill of 1832. This law eased the property requirements so that well-to-do men in the middle class could vote. It also gave the thriving new industrial cities more representation in Parliament.

Although the Reform Bill increased the number of British voters, only a small percentage of men were eligible to vote. A popular movement arose among workers and other groups who still could not vote to press for more rights. It was called the **Chartist movement** because the group first presented its demands to Parliament in a petition called The People's Charter of 1838. The People's Charter called for suffrage for all men, annual Parliamentary elections, a secret ballot, an end to property ownership as a requirement to serve in Parliament, and pay for members of Parliament.

5.52 Preparing for the Regents

Political and Economic Systems What did Karl Marx and Friedrich Engels believe would be the result when communism finally emerged as the dominate political and economic system?

5.53 Preparing for the Regents

Environment and Society Why did workers form labor unions?

5.54 Preparing for the Regents

Citizenship What impact did the Industrial Revolution have on suffrage in the 19th and early 20th centuries?

Parliament rejected the Chartists' demands. However, over the years, workers continued to press for political reform, and Parliament responded. It gave the vote to working-class men in 1867 and to male rural workers in 1884. After 1884, most adult males in Britain had the right to vote. By the early 1900s, all the demands of the Chartists, except for annual elections, became law. Although women also campaigned for the vote, both in Great Britain and the United States, they would have to wait until after World War I to achieve their goal.

Industrialization and Global Migrations

The Industrial Revolution that began in Britain spread to United States, continental Europe, and eventually to other parts of the world. As industrialization took hold, it led to a global migration of labor and capital. To keep factories running and workers fed, industrialized countries required a steady supply of raw materials from less-developed lands. In turn, industrialized countries viewed poor countries as markets for their manufactured products. People were also part of this global migration, as millions were drawn to large urban areas and industrial centers in search of work.

Not all migrations of people during the period were spurred by industrialization. In the 1840s, Ireland experienced one of the worst famines of modern history. For many years, Irish peasants had depended on potatoes as virtually their sole source of food. From 1845 to 1848, a plant fungus ruined nearly all of Ireland's potato crop. Out of a population of 8 million, about a million people died from starvation and disease over the next few years.

During the famine years, about a million and a half people fled from Ireland. Most went to the United States; others went to Britain, Canada, and Australia. At home, in Ireland, the British government enforced the demands of the English landowners that the Irish peasants pay their rent. Many Irish lost their land and fell hopelessly in debt, while large landowners profited from higher food prices. This helped fuel a growing nationalism among the Irish. Opposition to British rule over Ireland took two forms. Some Irish wanted independence for Ireland. A greater number of Irish preferred home rule, local control over internal matters only. The British, fearful of Irish moves toward independence, refused to consider either option.

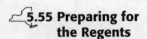

5.55 Preparing for the Regents

Human and Physical Geography What was the main cause of mass starvation in Ireland during the 19th century? What effect did this have on Irish migration?

PREPARING THE REGENTS

On a separate sheet of paper, write a well-organized essay that includes an introduction, several paragraphs addressing the task below, and a conclusion. Before beginning, check the Score the Essay box for pointers.

Theme: Economic Change
Since the 19th century, industrialization has had positive and negative effects on the lives of workers.

Task:
- Define the term *industrialization*.
- Discuss *two* specific examples of the ways in which industrialization changed the lives of workers in Great Britain in the 19th century
- Discuss the response of the workers, reformers, and government to these changes

SCORE THE ESSAY To receive a score of 5 on your essay, you will need to:
- show a thorough understanding of the theme
- thoroughly develop all aspects of the task evenly and in depth by describing both the positive and negative effects of industrialization.
- be more analytical than descriptive.
- richly support the theme with relevant facts, examples, and details.
- demonstrate a logical and clear plan of organization.
- introduce the theme by establishing a framework that goes beyond a simple restatement of the task and concludes with a summation of the theme

Imperialism, 1850–1914

Section Overview

Industrialization stirred ambitions in many European nations. They wanted more resources to fuel their industrial production. They competed for new markets for their goods. Many nations looked to Africa as a source of raw materials and as a market for industrial products. As a result, colonial powers seized vast areas of Africa during the 19th and early 20th centuries. In carving up the continent, the European countries paid little or no attention to historical political divisions or to the many ethnic and language groupings in Africa. Uppermost in the minds of the Europeans was the ability to control Africa's land, its people, and its resources.

Britain also took colonial control of India. British economic interest in India began in the 1600s, when the British East India Company set up trading posts at Bombay, Madras, and Calcutta. By 1850, the British controlled most of the Indian subcontinent.

European powers also made their presence felt in China. During the 1800s, a series of conflicts with foreign powers resulted in treaties that allowed foreign nations to take increasing control of China's economy.

The Ethiopian Emperor Menelik II
(1844–1913)

MAIN IDEAS

EMPIRE BUILDING   During the 19th and early 20th centuries, Western powers divided Africa and colonized large areas of Asia.

POWER AND AUTHORITY   At the Berlin Conference in 1884–1885, European nations established rules for the division of Africa with little concern about how their actions would affect the African people.

ECONOMICS   Industrialization increased the need for raw materials and new markets. Western imperialists were driven by this need as they looked for new colonies to acquire.

CULTURAL INTERACTION   Western economic pressure forced China to open to foreign trade and influence.

TERMS AND NAMES

- imperialism
- Social Darwinism
- racism
- sphere of influence
- paternalism
- Berlin Conference
- Boers
- Boer War
- Menelik II
- sepoy
- "jewel in the crown"
- Sepoy Mutiny
- Raj
- Opium War
- extraterritorial rights
- Boxer Rebellion
- Kuomintang
- Sun Yixian

PREPARING FOR THE REGENTS

As you read this section, consider
- what relationship there is between industrialization, nationalism, and imperialism.

TIME LINE

1839
China and Britain clash in Opium War.

1857
Indians stage Sepoy Mutiny.

1884–1885
Berlin Conference sets rules for African colonization.

1899
Boer War begins in Africa.

1900
Boxer Rebellion occurs in China.

1911
Chinese Nationalists oust the last Qing emperor.

1914
Most of Africa is under European control.

Forces Driving Imperialism

The seizure of a country or territory by a stronger country is called **imperialism**. Many motives drove European imperialism during the 18th and 19th centuries. One of the chief motives was the Industrial Revolution. As European nations industrialized, they searched for new markets and raw materials to improve their economies. The race for colonies also grew out of a strong sense of national pride. Europeans viewed an empire as a measure of national greatness.

Social Darwinism, a theory that applied Charles Darwin's ideas about evolution and "survival of the fittest" to human society, also drove imperialism. This theory stated that those who were fittest for survival enjoyed wealth and success and were considered superior to others. The belief that one race is superior to others is called **racism**. Since non-Europeans had not made the scientific and technological progress that Europeans had, Social Darwinism considered them to be on a lower level of cultural and physical development. Consequently, Europeans had the right and the duty to bring the results of their progress to non-Europeans— what the poet Rudyard Kipling called "The White Man's Burden." This belief was supported by people like Cecil Rhodes, a successful businessman, who argued that the more land Britain inhabited, the better it was for the human race.

The push for expansion also came from missionaries who worked to convert the peoples of Asia, Africa, and the Pacific Islands to Christianity. Many missionaries wanted to "civilize," that is, to "Westernize," the peoples of the foreign land. They also believed that European rule was the best way to end evil practices such as the slave trade.

Britain was the first to end the slave trade. William Wilberforce led the fight in Parliament. In 1807, Parliament passed a bill to end the slave trade in the British West Indies. After he retired from Parliament in 1825, Wilberforce continued his fight to free the slaves. Britain finally abolished slavery in its empire in 1833. Other European nations and the United States also eventually outlawed slavery.

The New Imperialism

The imperialism of the 18th and 19th centuries was conducted differently from that of the 15th and 16th centuries. In the earlier period, imperial powers often did not penetrate far into the conquered areas in Asia and Africa. Nor did they always have a substantial influence on the lives of the people. Now Europeans demanded more influence over the economic, political, and social lives of the people.

Over time, four forms of colonial control emerged: 1) colony—a country or a territory governed internally by a foreign power; 2) protectorate—a country or a territory with its own internal government but under the control of an outside power; 3) **sphere of influence**—an area in which an outside power claims exclusive investment or trading privileges; and 4) economic imperialism—an independent but less developed country controlled by private business interests.

European rulers also developed two basic methods of day-to-day management: indirect control and direct control. Britain favored indirect control, which relied on local officials to handle the daily management of the colony. In addition, each colony had a legislative council that included colonial officials as well as local merchants and professionals nominated by the colonial governor. The goal was to train local leaders in the British method of government so that eventually the local population could govern itself. The French and other European powers preferred more direct control of their colonies. They developed a policy called **paternalism**, in which Europeans governed people in a parental way.

5.56 Preparing for the Regents

Factors of Production What is the relationship between the Industrial Revolution and imperialism?

5.57 Preparing for the Regents

Imperialism In what ways did Europeans attempt to justify imperialism?

5.58 Preparing for the Regents

Imperialism What is a sphere of influence?

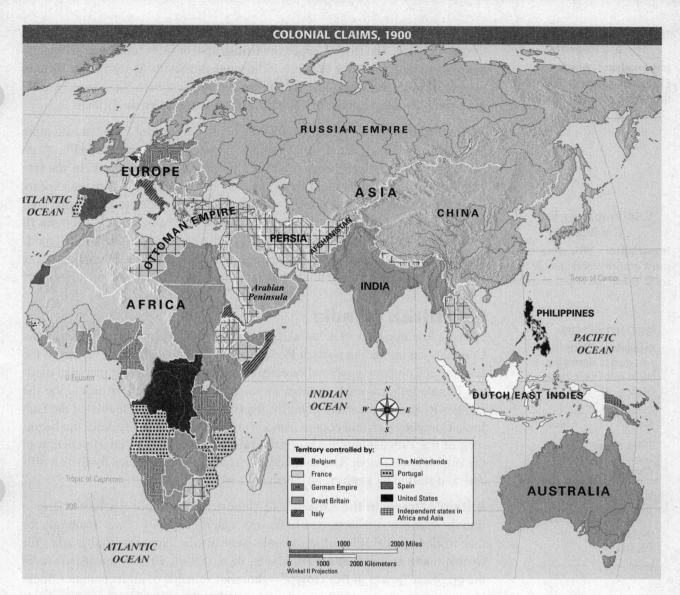

Territory controlled by:

- Belgium
- France
- German Empire
- Great Britain
- Italy
- The Netherlands
- Portugal
- Spain
- United States
- Independent states in Africa and Asia

0   1000   2000 Miles
0   1000   2000 Kilometers
Winkel II Projection

The Scramble for Africa

The European scramble for African territory began in earnest about 1880, when the French began to expand from the West African coast toward western Sudan. With interest heightened by the discoveries of diamonds in 1867 and gold in 1886 in South Africa, no European power wanted to be left out of the race.

The Berlin Conference Competition was so fierce that Europeans feared war among themselves. Thus, 14 European nations met at the **Berlin Conference** in 1884–85 to lay down rules for the division of Africa. They agreed that any European country could claim land in Africa by notifying other nations of its claims and showing it could control the area. The European nations divided the continent with little thought about how African ethnic or linguistic groups were distributed. By 1914, only Liberia and Ethiopia remained free from European control.

The Boer War The Berlin Conference did not completely eliminate conflict between the European powers. The first Europeans to settle in South Africa were the Dutch. These settlers were known as **Boers**, which is Dutch for "farmers." (The Boers are also known as Afrikaners.) When diamonds and gold were discovered in southern Africa in the 1860s and 1880s, adventurers from all parts of the world rushed in to make their fortunes. The Boers tried to keep these

TAKING NOTES

Summarizing Use a web to record the forms and methods of European imperialism in Africa, the resistance it met with, and its impact.

5.59 Preparing for the Regents

Imperialism Which European nation controlled the Union of South Africa?

"outsiders" from gaining political rights. An attempt to start a rebellion against the Boers failed. The Boers blamed the British and, in 1899, took up arms against them, launching the **Boer War** (also known as the South African War). Britain eventually won the war. In 1910, the Boer republics were joined into a self-governing Union of South Africa, which was controlled by the British.

African Resistance Africans across the continent resisted European attempts to colonize their lands. However, the contest between African states and European powers was never equal because of the Europeans' superior arms. In the late 1800s, for instance, the Zulus lost their kingdom to the British when their spears proved no match to British guns. Ethiopia was the only African nation that successfully resisted the Europeans. Its victory was due to one man—**Menelik II**, who became emperor of Ethiopia in 1889. 1896, armed with a stockpile of modern weapons purchased from France and Russia, Menelik's Ethiopian forces successfully defeated the Italians and kept their nation independent.

5.60 Preparing for the Regents

Imperialism Why were most African states unable to resist European imperialism?

The British in India

British economic interest in India began in the 1600s, when the British East India Company set up trading posts at Bombay, Madras, and Calcutta. Eventually, the East India Company governed directly or indirectly an area that included modern Bangladesh, most of southern India, and nearly all the territory along the Ganges River in the north. Officially, the British government regulated the East India Company's efforts both in London and in India. In reality, until the beginning of the 19th century, the company ruled India with little interference from the British government. The company even had its own army, led by British officers and staffed by **sepoys**, or Indian soldiers.

TAKING NOTES

Recognizing Effects Use a diagram to identify the effects of the three causes listed.

Cause	Effect
1. The East India Company	
2. Colonial policies	
3. Sepoy Mutiny	

Britain's "Jewel in the Crown" The Industrial Revolution had turned Britain into the world's workshop, and India was a major supplier of raw materials for that workshop. Its 300 million people were also a large potential market for British-made goods. It is not surprising, then, that the British considered India the brightest **"jewel in the crown"**—the most valuable of all its colonies. India became increasingly valuable to the British after they established a railroad network there. Railroads transported raw products from the interior to the ports and manufactured goods back again. Most of the raw materials were agricultural products produced on plantations. Plantation crops included tea, indigo, coffee, cotton, and jute. Another crop was opium. The British shipped opium to China and exchanged it for tea, which they then sold in England.

The Sepoy Mutiny By 1850, the British controlled most of the Indian subcontinent. However, there were many pockets of discontent. Many Indians believed that in addition to controlling their land, the British were trying to convert them to Christianity. The Indian people also resented the constant racism that the British expressed toward them. In addition, India faced mounting economic problems brought on by British control of Indian industries and the emphasis on cash crops.

As economic problems increased for Indians, so did their feelings of resentment and nationalism. In 1857, gossip spread among the sepoys that the cartridges of their new Enfield rifles were greased with beef and pork fat. To use the cartridges, soldiers had to bite off the ends. Both Hindus, who consider the cow sacred, and Muslims, who do not eat pork, were outraged by the news. A garrison commander was shocked when 85 of the 90 sepoys refused to accept the

5.62 Preparing for the Regents

Imperialism What were the causes and the consequences of the Sepoy Mutiny?

cartridges. The British handled the crisis badly. The soldiers who had disobeyed were jailed. The next day, on May 10, 1857, the sepoys rebelled. They marched to Delhi, where they were joined by Indian soldiers stationed there. They captured the city of Delhi. From Delhi, the rebellion spread to northern and central India. Some historians have called this outbreak the **Sepoy Mutiny**. The East India Company took more than a year to regain control of the country.

The mutiny marked a turning point in Indian history. As a result of the mutiny, in 1858 the British government took direct command of India. The part of India that was under direct British rule was called the Raj. The term **Raj** referred to British rule over India from 1757 until 1947. A cabinet minister in London directed policy, and a British governor-general in India carried out the government's orders. After 1877, this official held the title of viceroy.

China

China under the Qing dynasty presented a different kind of challenge for Europeans. Out of pride for their ancient culture, the Chinese looked down on all foreigners. In addition, China was economically self-sufficient, and thus had little interest in trading with the West. For decades, the only place they would allow foreigners to do business was at the southern port of Guangzhou (gwahng•joh). And the balance of trade at Guangzhou was clearly in China's favor. This means that China earned much more for its exports than it spent on imports. European merchants were determined to find a product the Chinese would buy in large quantities. Eventually they found one—opium.

Opium War Opium is a habit-forming narcotic made from the poppy plant. Chinese doctors had been using it to relieve pain for hundreds of years. In the late 18th century, however, British merchants smuggled opium into China for nonmedical use. It took a few decades for opium smoking to catch on, but by 1835, as many as 12 million Chinese people were addicted to the drug.

When China's pleas to the British to stop trading in opium went unanswered, the result was the **Opium War** of 1839. The battles took place mostly at sea. China's outdated ships were no match for Britain's steam-powered gunboats. As a result, the Chinese suffered a humiliating defeat. In 1842, they signed the Treaty of Nanjing. This peace treaty gave Britain the island of Hong Kong. After signing another treaty in 1844, U.S. and other foreign citizens also gained extraterritorial rights. Under **extraterritorial rights**, foreigners were not subject to Chinese law at Guangzhou and four other Chinese ports. This allowed foreign powers such as Britain, France, Germany, Russian, and Japan to develop spheres of influence in China. Many Chinese greatly resented the foreigners and the bustling trade in opium they conducted.

Boxer Rebellion China faced growing internal problems during the second half of the 1800s. Food production could not keep up with population growth. As a result, hunger was widespread. Many people became discouraged, and opium addiction rose steadily. As their problems mounted, the Chinese began to rebel against their Qing rulers. Throughout this period, many foreign nations took advantage of the situation and attacked China. Treaty negotiations after each conflict gave these nations increasing control over China's economy. Many of Europe's major powers and Japan gained a strong foothold in China.

Widespread frustration among the Chinese finally erupted into violence. Poor peasants and workers resented the special privileges granted to foreigners. They also resented Chinese Christians, who had adopted a foreign faith. To

Identifying Problems
Use a chart to identify the internal and external problems faced by China in the 1800s and early 1900s.

China's Problems	
Internal	External

5.63 Preparing for the Regents

Conflict What were the causes and consequences of the Opium War?

5.64 Preparing for the Regents

Imperialism What factors caused the Boxer Rebellion?

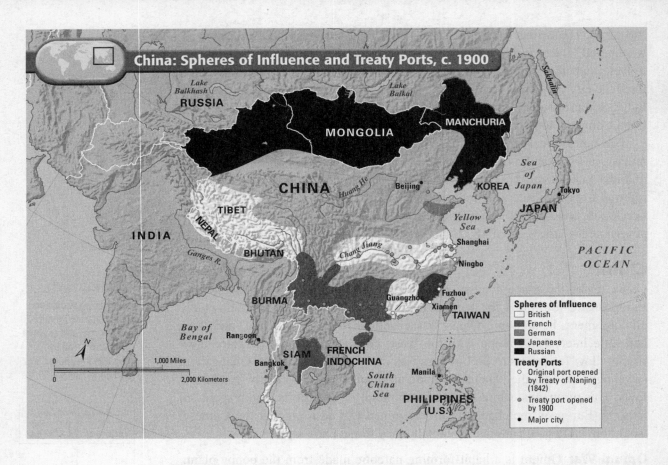

China: Spheres of Influence and Treaty Ports, c. 1900

Spheres of Influence
- British
- French
- German
- Japanese
- Russian

Treaty Ports
- ○ Original port opened by Treaty of Nanjing (1842)
- ◉ Treaty port opened by 1900
- ● Major city

demonstrate their discontent, they formed a secret organization called the Society of Righteous and Harmonious Fists. They soon came to be known as the Boxers. Their campaign against the rule of China's Dowager Empress Cixi (tsoo•shee) and foreigner privilege was called the **Boxer Rebellion**. In the spring of 1900, the Boxers descended on Beijing. Shouting "Death to the foreign devils," the Boxers surrounded the European section of the city. They kept it under siege for several months. The Dowager Empress expressed support for the Boxers but did not back her words with military aid. In August, a multinational force of 19,000 troops marched on Beijing and quickly defeated the Boxers.

✐**5.65 Preparing for the Regents**

Nationalism Who led the nationalist movement in China?

Sun Yixian and the Revolutionary Alliance Despite the failure of the Boxer Rebellion, a strong sense of nationalism had emerged in China. The Chinese people realized that their country must resist more foreign intervention and modernize. Among the groups pushing for modernization and nationalization was the **Kuomintang** (KWOH•mihn•TANG), or the Nationalist Party. Its first great leader was **Sun Yixian** (soon yee•shyahn). In 1911, the Revolutionary Alliance, a forerunner of the Kuomintang, succeeded in overthrowing the last Qing emperor.

In 1912, Sun became president of the new Republic of China. Sun hoped to establish a modern government based on the "Three Principles of the People": 1) nationalism—an end to foreign control, 2) people's rights—democracy, and 3) people's livelihood—economic security for all Chinese. Sun Yixian considered nationalism vital. Despite his lasting influence as a revolutionary leader, Sun lacked the authority and military support to secure national unity. Sun turned over the presidency to a powerful general, Yuan Shikai, who quickly betrayed the democratic ideals of the revolution. His actions sparked local revolts. After the general died in 1916, civil war broke out. Real authority fell into the hands of provincial warlords or powerful military leaders.

Perspectives on Imperialism

The patterns of behavior of imperialist powers were similar, no matter where their colonies were located. In some cases, the European colonial rule brought benefits, but for the most part, the effects were negative. On the negative side, Africans lost control of their land and their independence, as Europeans exploited their natural resources. Many died of new diseases such as smallpox. They also lost thousands of their people in resisting the Europeans. Famines resulted from the change to cash crops in place of subsistence agriculture. Similarly, British restrictions on Indian-owned industries such as cotton textiles damaged these businesses. The emphasis on cash crops resulted in a loss of self-sufficiency for many villagers. As in Africa, the conversion to cash crops reduced food production, causing famines in the late 1800s. In addition, the increased presence of missionaries and the racist attitude of most British officials threatened traditional Indian life.

On the positive side, colonialism reduced local warfare in Africa. Humanitarian efforts in some colonies improved sanitation and provided hospitals and schools. As a result, lifespans increased and literacy rates improved. Also positive was the economic expansion. African products came to be valued on the international market. To aid the economic growth, railroads, dams, and telephone and telegraph lines were built in African colonies. But for the most part, these benefited only European business interests, not Africans' lives. In India, the laying of the world's third largest railroad network was a major British achievement. When completed, the railroads enabled India to develop a modern economy and brought unity to the connected regions. Along with the railroads, a modern road network, telephone and telegraph lines, dams, bridges, and irrigation canals enabled India to modernize. Sanitation and public health improved. Schools and colleges were founded, and literacy increased. Also, British troops cleared central India of bandits and put an end to local warfare among competing local rulers.

For Europeans, imperialism helped lay the foundations for World War I. The quest for colonies in Africa and Asia sometimes pushed Europeans to the brink of war. As European countries continued to compete for overseas empires, their sense of rivalry and mistrust on one another deepened.

5.66 Preparing for the Regents

Imperialism What effect did European imperialism have on Africa's natural resources?

5.67 Preparing for the Regents

Imperialism What were some of the positive and negative consequences of imperialism?

PREPARING FOR THE REGENTS

Answer the following question. Use the Analyze the Question hints to help you answer the question.

1 Which statement best expresses the motive for 19th-century European imperialism?

(1) Living space was needed for the excess population in Western Europe.

(2) European leaders believed imperialism was an effective method of reducing the number of wars.

(3) European nations would benefit from some aspect of the nation's culture.

(4) Imperialism would benefit the economies of the colonial powers.

ANALYZE THE QUESTION
- Read the question stem. You are being asked to determine why Europeans engaged in imperialism in the 19th century.
- Think about the main motives for imperialism as you read each alternative.
- Rule out the alternatives that contradict or are not directly linked to one of the motives.
- If more than one motive seems to remain, select the one that most closely matches the main reason for European imperialism.

Japan and the Meiji Restoration

Section Overview

In the early 17th century, Japan had shut itself off from almost all contact with other nations. Under the rule of the Tokugawa shoguns, Japanese society was very tightly ordered. The shogun parceled out land to the daimyo, or lords. The peasants worked for and lived under the protection of their daimyo and his small army of samurai, or warriors. This rigid feudal system managed to keep the country free of civil war. Peace and relative prosperity reigned in Japan for two centuries.

Although they continued to trade with China and with Dutch merchants from Indonesia, the Japanese had almost no contact with the industrialized world during this time of isolation. Beginning in the early 19th century, however, Western powers pushed Japan to open its ports to foreign trade. In 1854, Japan signed the Treaty of Kanagawa, which opened two ports to U.S. ships. Agreements with other nations soon followed.

Alarmed that Western nations might try to colonize the island, Japan began a rapid program of modernization and industrialization. By the early 20th century, Japan's economy had become as modern as any in the world, and the island was actively engaged in foreign trade.

Japan's industrialization and economic growth spurred imperialist plans. Lacking the abundant supply of natural resources enjoyed by Britain and other European industrial powers, Japan needed sources for raw materials. Thus, Japan built up its military and turned its attention to gaining access to Korea and other neighboring countries.

The Meiji Emperor
Mutsuhito (1867–1912)

MAIN IDEAS

CULTURAL INTERACTION   Japan followed the model of Western powers by industrializing and expanding its foreign influence.

TERMS AND NAMES

- Treaty of Kanagawa
- Meiji era
- Sino-Japanese War
- Russo-Japanese War
- annexation

PREPARING FOR THE REGENTS

As you read this section, consider
- why the Industrial Revolution occurred in Japan before it occurred in other Asian or African nations.
- why Japan turned to imperialism and militarism in the late 19th and early 20th centuries.
- what caused conflicts between China, Japan, and Russia.
- why Japan annexed Korea.

TIME LINE

1853
Commodore Perry enters Tokyo harbor.

1872
Japan builds its first railroad line.

1904
Russo-Japanese War begins.

1910
Japan annexes Korea.

Human and Physical Geography

In the early 17th century, the Tokugawa shoguns had shut Japan off from almost all contact with other nations. The Japanese continued, however, to trade with China and with Dutch merchants from Indonesia. They also had diplomatic contact with Korea. Beginning in the early 19th century, Westerners tried to convince the Japanese to open their ports to trade. British, French, Russian, and American officials occasionally anchored off the Japanese coast. Like China, however, Japan repeatedly refused to receive them.

The Opening of Japan

In 1853, U.S. Commodore Matthew Perry took four ships into what is now Tokyo Harbor. These massive black wooden ships, with their cannons and steam power, astounded and shocked the Japanese. The Tokugawa shogun realized he had no choice but to receive Perry and the letter Perry had brought from U.S. president Millard Fillmore. Fillmore's letter politely asked the shogun to allow free trade between the United States and Japan. Perry delivered it with a threat, however. He would come back with a larger fleet in a year to receive Japan's reply. That reply was the **Treaty of Kanagawa** of 1854. Under its terms, Japan opened two ports at which U.S. ships could take on supplies. After the United States had pushed open the door, other Western powers soon followed. By 1860, Japan, like China, had granted foreigners permission to trade at several treaty ports. It had also extended extraterritorial rights to many foreign nations.

5.68 Preparing for the Regents

Power How did Commodore Perry's actions contribute to the Meiji Restoration?

Modernization and Industrialization

The Japanese were angry that the shogun had given in to the foreigners' demands. They turned to Japan's young emperor, Mutsuhito (moot•soo•HEE•toh), who seemed to symbolize the country's sense of pride and nationalism. In 1867, the Tokugawa shogun stepped down, ending the military dictatorships that had lasted since the 12th century. Mutsuhito's reign, which lasted 45 years, is known as the **Meiji era**. *Meiji* means "enlightened rule."

The Meiji emperor realized that the best way to counter Western influence was to modernize. He sent diplomats to Europe and North America to study Western ways. The Japanese then chose what they believed to be the best that Western civilization had to offer and adapted it to their own country. They used Germany's constitution, with its strong central government, as a model for their own. They attempted to imitate the discipline of the German army and the skill of the British navy as they modernized their military. They adopted the U.S. system of universal public education and required that all Japanese children attend school.

The emperor also energetically supported following the Western path of industrialization. By the early 20th century, the Japanese economy was modern and competitive. The country built its first railroad line in 1872. By 1914, Japan had more than 7,000 miles of railroad. Coal production grew from half a million tons in 1875 to more than 21 million tons in 1913. Large, state-supported companies built thousands of factories. Traditional Japanese industries, such as silk production, expanded to give the country unique products to trade.

As its strength grew, Japan sought to eliminate the extraterritorial rights of foreigners. The Japanese foreign minister assured foreigners that they could rely on fair treatment in Japan, since its constitution and legal codes were similar to those of European nations. His reasoning was convincing, and in 1894, foreign powers accepted the abolition of their extraterritorial rights.

TAKING NOTES

Analyzing Causes List the steps that Japan took toward modernization and the events that contributed to its growth as an imperialistic power.

Modernization
Imperialism

5.69 Preparing for the Regents

Economic Systems What economic changes took place in Japan during the Meiji Restoration?

Imperial Japan

By 1890, Japan had become the strongest military power in Asia. As Japan's sense of power grew, the nation also became more imperialistic. As in Europe, national pride motivated imperialist plans. Lacking in natural resources, Japan also needed raw materials to fuel industrialization and food to feed its people. The Japanese were also determined to show the world that they were powerful.

Sino-Japanese War In 1876, Japan forced Korea to open three ports to Japanese trade. China also considered Korea important, both as a trading partner and a military outpost. In 1885, Japan and China pledged that they would not send their armies into Korea. In June 1894, however, China broke that agreement when rebellions broke out against Korea's king. Chinese troops marched into Korea to help the king. Japan protested and sent its troops to Korea to fight the Chinese. This **Sino-Japanese War** lasted just a few months. In that time, Japan drove the Chinese out of Korea, destroyed the Chinese navy, and gained a foothold in Manchuria. In 1895, China and Japan signed a peace treaty. This treaty gave Japan its first colonies, Taiwan and the neighboring Pescadores Islands.

Russo-Japanese War Japan's victory over China changed the world's balance of power. Russia and Japan emerged as the major powers—and enemies—in East Asia. The two countries soon went to war over Manchuria. In 1903, Japan offered to recognize Russia's rights in Manchuria if the Russians would agree to stay out of Korea. But the Russians refused. In February 1904, Japan launched a surprise attack on Russian ships anchored off the coast of Manchuria. In the resulting **Russo-Japanese War**, Japan drove Russian troops out of Korea and destroyed most of Russia's fleet. The peace treaty ending the war gave Japan the captured territories. It also forced Russia to withdraw from Manchuria and to stay out of Korea.

Annexation of Korea After defeating Russia, Japan attacked Korea with a vengeance. In 1905, it made Korea a protectorate. Japan sent in "advisers," who grabbed more and more power from the Korean government. The Korean king was unable to rally international support for his regime. In 1907, he gave up control of the country. Within two years the Korean Imperial Army was disbanded. In 1910, Japan officially imposed **annexation** on Korea, or brought that country under Japan's control. The Japanese were harsh rulers. They shut down Korean newspapers and took over Korean schools, where they replaced Korean subjects with Japanese subjects. They took land away from Korean farmers and gave it to Japanese settlers. They encouraged Japanese businessmen to start industries in Korea, but forbade Koreans from going into business. Resentment of Japan's repressive rule grew, helping to create a strong Korean nationalist movement.

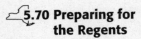
5.70 Preparing for the Regents

Imperialism What factors motivated Japanese imperialism?

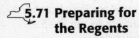
5.71 Preparing for the Regents

Conflict What effect did the Sino-Japanese War and the Russo-Japanese War have on Japan as a world power?

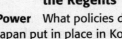
5.72 Preparing for the Regents

Power What policies did Japan put in place in Korea?

PREPARING FOR THE REGENTS

Answer the following question. Use the Analyze the Question hints to help you answer the question.

1 Japan's increased foreign trade during the Meiji Restoration was closely related to its

    (1) need to maintain a traditional society
    (2) desire for a modern industrial society
    (3) colonization by Western nations
    (4) encouragement of foreign investment

ANALYZE THE QUESTION
- Read the question stem. You are being asked to determine which alternative is related to Japan's increased foreign trade during the Meiji Restoration.
- Think about what factors would lead to increased trade, and select the alternative that is most closely associated with those factors.

An Age of Revolution (1450–1914)

Part I: MULTIPLE-CHOICE QUESTIONS

Directions (1–10): For each statement or question, write on a separate answer sheet the *number* of the word or expression that, of those given, best completes the statement or answers the questions.

Base your answers to questions 1 and 2 on the quotation below and on your knowledge of social studies.

"We hold these truths to be self-evident, that all men are created equal, that they are endowed by their Creator with certain unalienable Rights, that among these are Life, Liberty, and the pursuit of Happiness. . . ."

1 This statement best expresses the philosophy of

(1) Adam Smith   (3) Thomas Hobbes
(2) Karl Marx   (4) John Locke

2 The statement best represents the values of

(1) the Enlightenment   (3) feudalism
(2) Social Darwinism   (4) communism

3 Which statement best describes the effects of the works of Nicolaus Copernicus, Galileo Galilei, Sir Isaac Newton, and René Descartes?

(1) The acceptance of traditional authority was strengthened.
(2) The scientific methods was used to solve problems.
(3) Funding to education was increased by the English government.
(4) Interest in Greek and Roman drama was renewed.

4 What event had the greatest influence on the development of laissez-faire capitalism?

(1) fall of the Roman Empire
(2) invention of the printing press
(3) Industrial Revolution
(4) Green Revolution

5 Which event was an example of Asian reaction to imperialism?

(1) Boxer Rebellion
(2) Glorious Revolution
(3) Boer War
(4) Congress of Berlin

6 Simón Bolívar, José de San Martín, and Toussaint L'Ouverture are important in Latin American history because they were

(1) 20th-century caudillos
(2) leaders of liberation movement
(3) members of the Organization of American States (OAS)
(4) winners of the Nobel Peace Prize

7 Which 19th-century ideology led to the unification of Germany and Italy and to the eventual breakup of Austria-Hungary and the Ottoman Empire?

(1) imperialism   (3) liberalism
(2) nationalism   (4) socialism

8 A key principle of the economic theory of communism is?

(1) restoration of a bartering system
(2) organization of workers' unions
(3) government ownership of property
(4) privatization of business

9 Which statement best describes events in Japan during the period of the Meiji Restoration?

(1) Japan sought to isolate itself from world affairs.
(2) Rapid industrialization and economic growth occurred.
(3) Local lords increased their power over the Japanese emperor.
(4) Agriculture was taken over by the government.

10 The theory of Social Darwinism was sometimes used to justify

(1) the establishment of communist governments in Asia
(2) Latin American revolutions in the early 19th century
(3) the independence movement in India
(4) European imperialism in the late 19th century

In developing your answers to Parts II and III, be sure to keep these general definitions in mind:

(a) *discuss* means "to make observations about something using facts, reasoning, and argument; to present in some detail"

(b) *describe* means "to illustrate something in words or tell about it"

(c) *evaluate* means "to examine and judge the significance, worth, or condition of; to determine the value of"

Part II: THEMATIC ESSAY

Directions: Write a well-organized essay that includes an introduction, several paragraphs addressing the task below, and a conclusion.

Theme: Economic Systems

Societies have developed different economic systems for many reasons. Some of these economic systems include manorialism, capitalism, and communism.

Task:

- Discuss the historical circumstances surrounding the development of capitalism in Western Europe during the Industrial Revolution
- Describe *two* features of capitalism during the Industrial Revolution
- Evaluate the impact of capitalism on Western Europe during the Industrial Revolution

Guidelines:

In your essay, be sure to

- Address all aspects of the *Task*
- Support the theme with relevant facts, examples, and details
- Use a logical and clear plan of organization
- Include an introduction and a conclusion that are beyond the simple restatement of the *Theme*

Part III: DOCUMENT-BASED QUESTION

This question is based on the accompanying documents (1–3). The question is designed to test your ability to work with historic documents. Some of these documents have been edited for the purpose of this question. As you analyze the documents, take into account both the source of each document and any point of view that may be presented in the document.

Historical Context:

During the 1800s, Great Britain's empire expanded to include India, other parts of Asia, and parts of Africa. Great Britain's colonial rule had both positive and negative effects on the colonial empire.

Task:

Using information from the documents and your knowledge of global history, answer the question that follows each document in Part A. Your answers to the questions will help you write the Part B essay, in which you will be asked to:

> • Discuss the political, social, and/or economic causes of British imperialism
> • Discuss the positive effects and the negative effects of British colonial rule

Part A: Short Answer

Directions: Analyze the documents and answer the short-answer questions that follow in the space provided.

Document 1

THE DEVILFISH IN EGYPTIAN WATERS.

Document 2

To sum up the whole, the British rule has been—morally, a great blessing; politically peace and order on one hand, blunders on the other, materially, impoverishment. . . . The natives call the British system "Sakar ki Churi," the knife of sugar. That is to say there is no oppression, it is all smooth and sweet, but it is a knife, notwithstanding. I mention this that you should know these feelings. Our greatest misfortune is that you do not know our wants. When you will know our real wishes, I have not the least doubt that you would do justice. The genius and the spirit of the British people is fair play and justice.

—Dadabhai Naoroji, the first Indian elected to the British Parliament, 1871

1 In Document 1, what does the representation of England suggest about the cartoonist's view of British imperialism?

_____

2 According to the author in Document 2, what is India's greatest misfortune in relation to British rule?

_____

Document 3

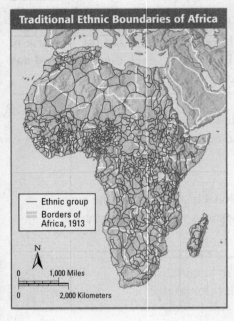

Traditional Ethnic Boundaries of Africa

— Ethnic group

▦ Borders of Africa, 1913

N

0   1,000 Miles

0   2,000 Kilometers

3 Examine the Document 3 map of traditional ethnic boundaries in Africa. What effect might the difference in ethnic boundaries and political borders have on social and political relations in Africa?

_____

_____

_____

_____

_____

_____

Part B: Essay

Directions: Write a well-organized essay that includes an introduction, several paragraphs, and a conclusion. Use evidence from at least *two* documents to support your response.

Historical Context: During the 1800s, Great Britain's empire expanded to include India, other parts of Asia, and parts of Africa. Great Britain's colonial rule had both positive and negative effects on the colonial empire.

Task: Using information from the documents and your knowledge of global history, answer the question that follows each document in Part A. Your answers to the questions will help you write the Part B essay, in which you will be asked to:

- Discuss the political, social, *and/or* economic causes of British imperialism
- Discuss the positive effects *and* the negative effects of British colonial rule

Guidelines:

In your essay, be sure to

- Address all aspects of the *Task* by accurately analyzing and interpreting at least **two** documents
- Incorporate information from the documents
- Incorporate relevant outside information
- Support the theme with relevant facts, examples, and details
- Use a logical and clear plan of organization
- Introduce the theme by establishing a framework that is beyond a simple statement of the *Task* or *Historical Context* and conclude with a summation of the theme

UNIT 6

A Half Century of Crisis and Achievement 1900–1945

Unit Overview

This unit examines the period in global history framed by the two World Wars. The unit begins by looking at World War I. It then looks at the social change set in motion by the war, focusing on revolution in Russia, nationalist movements, the Great Depression, the rise of totalitarian governments, and the growing aggression of Germany, Italy, and Japan. It closes by tracing the course of World War II.

Concepts and Themes

Among the concepts and themes explored in this unit are

- Change
- Conflict
- Economic Systems
- Human and Physical Geography
- Imperialism

- Justice and Human Rights
- Nationalism
- Political Systems
- Power
- Science and Technology

PREPARING FOR THE REGENTS: Building Thematic Essay Skills

Throughout history, groups of people have faced violations of their basic human rights. Christians in the Roman Empire, native peoples in Spain's American colonies, and Africans under the slave system are three examples. As you read about the World Wars and the time between the wars, look for examples of human rights violations. Use the following web diagram to organize information about groups you encounter that have suffered human rights violations, the factors that led to the violations, and the efforts, if any, to deal with the violations. You can add additional boxes as needed.

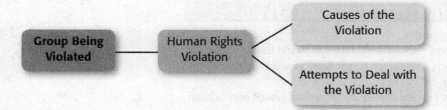

Group Being Violated — Human Rights Violation — Causes of the Violation / Attempts to Deal with the Violation

World War I, 1914–1918

Section Overview

By 1914, Europe was divided into two rival camps. One alliance, the Triple Entente, included Great Britain, France, and Russia. The other, known as the Triple Alliance, included Germany, Austria-Hungary, and Italy. Austria-Hungary's declaration of war against Serbia, an ally of Russia, set off a chain reaction within the alliance system. The countries of Europe followed through on their pledges to support one another. As a result, nearly all of Europe soon joined World War I—the largest, most destructive war the world had yet seen.

World War I was much more than a European conflict, however. Australia, Japan, and the United States, for example, entered the war on the Allies side. India supplied troops to fight alongside their British rulers. Meanwhile, the Ottoman Turks and, later, Bulgaria allied themselves with Germany and the Central Powers.

World War I soldiers wearing gas masks and using a machine gun

MAIN IDEAS

POWER AND AUTHORITY   The quest among European nations for greater power played a role in causing World War I. By the turn of the 20th century, relations among these countries had grown increasingly tense.

SCIENCE AND TECHNOLOGY   Advances in weaponry, from improvements to the machine gun and airplane, to the invention of the tank, led to mass devastation during World War I.

ECONOMICS   The war affected many European economies. Desperate for resources, the warring governments converted many industries to munitions factories. They also took greater control of the production of goods.

TERMS AND NAMES

- militarism
- Triple Alliance
- Triple Entente
- Central Powers
- Allies

- Western Front
- trench warfare
- Eastern Front
- unrestricted submarine warfare

- total war
- rationing
- propaganda
- armistice

PREPARING FOR THE REGENTS

As you read this section, consider
- what role nationalism and imperialism played in World War I.
- why the Germans, French, and British might have viewed the causes of World War I differently.
- in what ways World War I raised questions regarding justice and human rights.
- to what extent World War I was a turning point in history.

TIME LINE

1914
World War I begins as Austria-Hungary declares war on Serbia.

1917
United States enters World War I.

1918
Russia and Germany sign Treaty of Brest-Litovsk.

1918
Armistice signed as Allies defeat Central Powers.

Europe: The Physical Setting

While peace and harmony characterized much of Europe at the beginning of the 1900s, there were less visible—and darker—forces at work as well. One such force was the growth of nationalism. By the turn of the 20th century, a fierce rivalry had developed among Europe's Great Powers—Germany, Austria-Hungary, Great Britain, Russia, Italy, and France. This rivalry stemmed from several sources, including competition for materials and markets, territorial disputes, and mistrust born of imperialism. Added to these factors was the rise of a dangerous European arms race. The nations of Europe believed that to be truly great, they needed to have a powerful military that could quickly mobilize for war. The policy of glorifying military power and keeping an army prepared for war was known as **militarism**.

Growing rivalries and mutual mistrust had led to the creation of several military alliances among the Great Powers as early as the 1870s. By 1907, two rival camps existed in Europe. On one side was the **Triple Alliance**—Germany, Austria-Hungary, and Italy. On the other side was the **Triple Entente**—Great Britain, France, and Russia. A dispute between two rival powers could draw all the nations of Europe into war.

TAKING NOTES

Summarizing Create a time line of major events that led to the start of World War I.

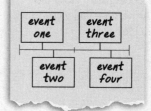

6.1 Preparing for the Regents

Conflict Why did the Great Powers enter into alliances?

Crisis in the Balkans

Nowhere was that dispute more likely to occur than on the Balkan Peninsula. With a long history of nationalist uprisings and ethnic clashes, the Balkans was known as the "powder keg" of Europe. The situation between Serbia, which had broken away from the Ottoman Empire, and its neighbor to the north, Austria-Hungary, was particularly tense. In 1908, Austria had annexed Bosnia and Herzegovina—two Balkan areas that the Serbians sought to rule. The Serbs were outraged and vowed to take Bosnia and Herzegovina away from Austria. Austria-Hungary responded by vowing to crush any Serbian attempt to undermine its authority in the Balkans.

Into this poisoned atmosphere stepped the heir to the Austro-Hungarian throne, Archduke Franz Ferdinand, and his wife, Sophie. On June 28, 1914, the couple paid a state visit to Bosnia's capital, Sarajevo. The royal pair was shot at point-blank range as they rode through the streets of Sarajevo in an open car. The killer was Gavrilo Princip, a 19-year-old Serbian and member of the Black Hand, a secret society committed to ridding Bosnia of Austrian rule.

Because the assassin was a Serbian, Austria decided to use the murders as an excuse to punish Serbia. On July 28, Austria declared war on Serbia. That same day, Russia, an ally of Serbia, ordered the mobilization of troops toward the Austrian border. Leaders all over Europe suddenly took notice.

6.2 Preparing for the Regents

Conflict Why were the Balkans considered a "powder keg" of Europe?

Europe Plunges into War

Expecting Germany to join Austria, Russia also mobilized along the German border. On August 1, the German government responded by declaring war on Russia. Russia looked to its ally France for help. Not waiting for France to react, Germany declared war on France. Soon afterward, Great Britain declared war on Germany. Much of Europe was now locked in battle.

By mid-August 1914, the battle lines were clearly drawn. On one side were Germany and Austria-Hungary, known as the **Central Powers** because of their location in the heart of Europe. Bulgaria and the Ottoman Empire would later join the Central Powers in the hopes of regaining lost territories.

TAKING NOTES

Outlining Use an outline to organize main ideas and details.

I. The Great War Begins
  A.
  B.
II. A Bloody Stalemate

On the other side were Great Britain, France, and Russia. Together, they were known as the Allied Powers or the **Allies**. Japan joined the Allies within weeks. Italy, which had been a member of the Triple Alliance with Germany and Austria-Hungary, later joined the Allies after accusing their former partners of unjustly starting the war. The Armenians also sided with the Allies, for which they paid a heavy price. The Ottoman Turks responded by deporting nearly 2 million Armenians. Along the way, more than 600,000 died of starvation or were killed by Turkish soldiers.

The War Fronts In the late summer of 1914, millions of soldiers marched happily off to battle, convinced that the war would be short. As the summer of 1914 turned to fall, the war turned into a long and bloody stalemate, or deadlock, along the battlefields of France. This deadlocked region in northern France became known as the **Western Front**. By early 1915, opposing armies on the Western Front had dug miles of parallel trenches to protect themselves from enemy fire. This set the stage for what became known as **trench warfare**. In this type of warfare, soldiers fought each other from trenches. Armies traded huge losses of human life for pitifully small land gains.

Military strategists were at a loss. New tools of war—machine guns, poison gas, armored tanks, larger artillery, airplanes—had not delivered the fast-moving war they had expected. All this new technology did was kill greater numbers of people more effectively.

Even as the war on the Western Front claimed thousands of lives, both sides were sending millions more men to fight on the **Eastern Front**. This area was a stretch of battlefield along the German and Russian border. Here, Russians and Serbs battled Germans and Austro-Hungarians. The war in the east was a more mobile war than that in the west. Here too, however, slaughter and stalemate were common.

✐ **6.3 Preparing for the Regents**

Human Rights How did the Armenians fall victim to genocide?

✐ **6.4 Preparing for the Regents**

Science and Technology What role did technology play in World War I?

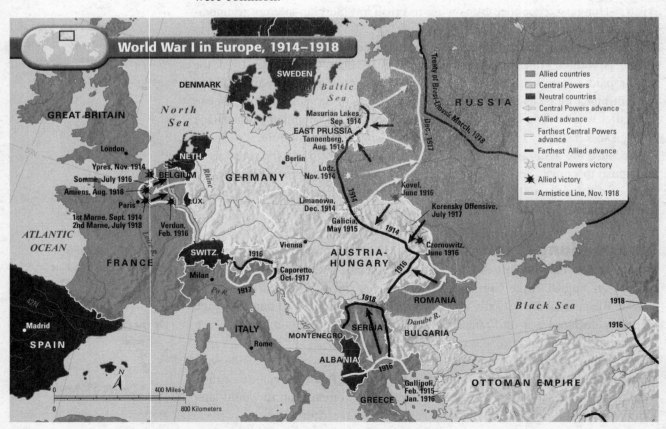

World War I in Europe, 1914–1918

As the war raged on, fighting spread beyond Europe to Africa, as well as to Southwest and Southeast Asia. The Gallipoli campaign in 1915—an Allied attempt to capture the Dardanelles strait as a step toward taking the Ottoman capital, Constantinople, ended in an Allied defeat. The Allies had better luck in their assaults against German colonial possessions in Asia and Africa. Japan quickly overran German outposts in China and captured Germany's Pacific island colonies. The English and French seized control of three of Germany's four African possessions. Elsewhere in Asia and Africa, the British and French recruited subjects in their colonies for the struggle. India, South Africa, Senegal, Egypt, Algeria, and Indochina provided fighting troops and laborers.

In 1917, the focus of the war shifted to the high seas. In January 1917, the Germans announced that their submarines would sink without warning any ship in the waters around Britain—a policy known as **unrestricted submarine warfare**. Ignoring warnings by President Woodrow Wilson, German U-boats sank three American ships.

Then, in February 1917, officials intercepted a telegram written by Germany's foreign secretary, Arthur Zimmermann, stating that Germany would help Mexico "reconquer" the land it had lost to the United States if Mexico would ally itself with Germany. The Zimmermann note simply proved to be the last straw. On April 2, 1917, President Wilson asked Congress to declare war on Germany. The United States entered the war on the side of the Allies.

The Home Front World War I soon became a **total war**. This meant that countries devoted all their resources to the war effort. In Britain, Germany, Austria, Russia, and France, the wartime government took control of the economy. Governments told factories what to produce and how much. Numerous facilities were converted to munitions factories. Nearly every able-bodied civilian was put to work. Unemployment in many European countries all but disappeared. So many goods were in short supply that governments turned to **rationing**. Under this system, people could buy only small amounts of those items that were also needed for the war effort.

Governments also suppressed antiwar activity, sometimes forcibly. In addition, they censored news about the war, fearing that honest reporting of the war would turn people against it. Governments also used **propaganda**, one-sided information designed to persuade, to keep up morale and support for the war.

Total war meant that governments turned to help from women as never before. Thousands of women replaced men in factories, offices, and shops. Women built tanks and munitions, plowed fields, paved streets, and ran hospitals. They also kept troops supplied with food, clothing, and weapons. Some women saw the horrors of war firsthand, working on or near the front lines as nurses. Although most women left the work force when the war ended, their war efforts were decisive in helping them win the right to vote. After the war, women's suffrage became law in many countries, including the United States, Britain, Germany, Sweden, and Austria.

The Allies Win the War In March 1917, civil unrest in Russia—due in large part to war-related shortages of food and fuel—forced Czar Nicholas to step down. In his place a provisional government was established. Although the new government pledged to continue the war, the war-weary Russian army refused to fight any longer. Eight months after the new government took over, a revolution shook Russia. In November 1917, the Communists seized power. They quickly ended their country's involvement in the war. In March 1918, Germany and Russia signed the Treaty of Brest-Litovsk.

6.5 Preparing for the Regents

Human and Physical Geography Why did the Allies want to capture the Dardanelles strait?

6.6 Preparing for the Regents

Political and Economic Systems What actions did governments take on the home front during World War I? What effect did World War I have on unemployment?

6.7 Preparing for the Regents

Culture and Intellectual Life What role did women play in the war?

6.8 Preparing for the Regents

Conflict Why did Russia leave the war?

Germany turned its attention to the Western Front. In March 1918, the Germans mounted one final, massive attack on the Allies in France. By late May 1918, the Germans had reached the Marne River. Paris was less than 40 miles away. Victory seemed within reach. However, the effort to reach the Marne had exhausted German men and supplies alike. Sensing this weakness, the Allies— with the aid of nearly 140,000 fresh U.S. troops—launched a counterattack. In July 1918, the Allies and Germans clashed at the Second Battle of the Marne. Leading the Allied attack were some 350 tanks that rumbled slowly forward, smashing through the German lines. With the arrival of 2 million more American troops, the Allied forces began to advance steadily toward Germany.

Soon, the Central Powers began to crumble. First the Bulgarians and then the Ottoman Turks surrendered. In October, revolution swept through Austria-Hungary. On November 9, 1918, Germany's Kaiser Wilhelm II stepped down. Germany declared itself a republic. On November 11, Germany and France signed an **armistice**, or an agreement to stop fighting. World War I came to an end.

Impact of the War

World War I was, in many ways, a new kind of war. It involved the use of new technologies. It ushered in the notion of war on a grand and global scale. It also left behind a landscape of death and destruction such as was never before seen. Both sides in World War I paid a tremendous price in terms of human life. About 8.5 million soldiers died as a result of the war. Another 21 million were wounded. In addition, the war led to the death of countless civilians by way of starvation, disease, and slaughter. Taken together, these figures spelled tragedy— an entire generation of Europeans wiped out.

The war also had a devastating economic impact on Europe. The great conflict drained the treasuries of European countries. One account put the total cost of the war at $338 billion, a staggering amount for that time. The war also destroyed acres of farmland, as well as homes, villages, and towns.

The enormous suffering that resulted from the Great War left a deep mark on Western society as well. A sense of disillusionment settled over the survivors. The insecurity and despair that many people experienced are reflected in the art and literature of the time.

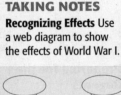

TAKING NOTES
Recognizing Effects Use a web diagram to show the effects of World War I.

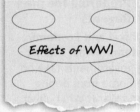

Effects of WWI

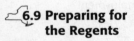

6.9 Preparing for the Regents

Change What impact did World War I have on European society?

PREPARING FOR THE REGENTS

On a separate sheet of paper, write a well-organized essay that includes an introduction, several paragraphs addressing the task below, and a conclusion. Before beginning, check the Score the Essay box for pointers.

Theme: Turning Points
Turning points are major events in history that have led to lasting change. World War I is one of those turning points.

Task:
- Describe the historical circumstances surrounding World War I.
- Explain how the World War I changed the course of history.

Be sure to include specific examples in your essay.

SCORE THE ESSAY To receive a score of 5 on your essay, you will need to:
- thoroughly develop all aspects of the task evenly and in depth by describing the historical circumstances surrounding World War I and explaining how the World War I changed the course of history.
- be more analytical than descriptive.
- richly support the theme with relevant facts, examples, and details.
- demonstrate a logical and clear plan of organization.

Revolution and Change in Russia

Section Overview

The Russian Revolution was like a firecracker with a very long fuse. The explosion came in 1917, yet the fuse had been burning for nearly a century. The fuse got much shorter under Alexander III, who succeeded his reform-minded father, Alexander II, in 1881. Like his grandfather Nicholas I, Alexander III clung to the principles of autocracy, a form of government in which he had total power. To wipe out revolutionaries, Alexander III imposed strict censorship codes on published materials and written documents, had his secret police carefully watch both secondary schools and universities, and sent political prisoners to Siberia, a remote region of eastern Russia. He also intensified the policy of **Russification**—*the forcing of Russian culture on all the ethnic groups in the empire.*

When Nicholas II became czar in 1894, he continued the tradition of Russian autocracy. Soon Russia was heading toward a full-scale revolution. In March 1917, the Russians revolted, forcing Nicholas II to abdicate. Then in November 1917, Lenin led the Bolsheviks in a revolution that seized the government and established the Soviet Union.

Determined to make the Soviet Union one of the most powerful nations in the world, Joseph Stalin, Lenin's successor, dramatically transformed the government. Using tactics designed to rid himself of opposition, Stalin worked to establish total control of all aspects of life in the Soviet Union. He controlled not only the government, but also the economy and many aspects of citizens' private lives.

Lenin (1870–1924),
leader of the Bolshevik Revolution

MAIN IDEAS

REVOLUTION   Long-term social unrest in Russia exploded in revolution, and ushered in the first Communist government.
POWER   After Lenin died, Stalin seized power and transformed the Soviet Union into a totalitarian state.

TERMS AND NAMES

- Russification
- proletariat
- Bolsheviks
- Lenin

- provisional government
- soviet
- Communist Party
- Joseph Stalin

- totalitarianism
- Great Purge
- command economy
- Five-Year Plan
- collective farm

PREPARING FOR THE REGENTS

As you read this section, consider
- the causes of the revolution in Russia.
- what human rights conditions were like under Joseph Stalin.

TIME LINE

1905
Russian workers protest for better conditions.

1917
Lenin leads Bolshevik Revolution.

1920
Stalin becomes dictator of Soviet Union.

1928
Stalin launches the first Five-Year Plan.

1937
Stalin launches the Great Purge.

The Revolutionary Movement Grows

When Nicholas II became czar in 1894, he continued the tradition of Russian autocracy. Unfortunately, it blinded him to the changing conditions of his times. Russia was undergoing rapid industrialization. The number of factories more than doubled between 1863 and 1900. The grueling working conditions, low wages, and child labor that accompanied industrialization stirred discontent. The government outlawed trade unions. Unhappy workers organized strikes.

Revolutionary movements began to grow and compete for power. A group that followed the views of Karl Marx successfully established a following in Russia. The Marxists believed that industrial workers would overthrow the czar. These workers would then form "a dictatorship of the proletariat." This meant that the **proletariat**—the workers—would rule the country. In 1903, Russian Marxists split into two groups over revolutionary tactics. The more moderate Mensheviks (MEHN•shuh•vihks) wanted a broad base of popular support for the revolution. The **Bolsheviks** (BOHL•shuh•vihks), who were more radical, supported a small number of committed revolutionaries willing to sacrifice everything for change. The major leader of the Bolsheviks was Vladimir Ilyich Ulyanov (ool•YAH•nuhf), who adopted the name of **Lenin**. In the early 1900s, Lenin fled to Western Europe to avoid arrest by the czarist regime.

The Revolution of 1905

Tensions continued to mount. On January 22, 1905, about 200,000 workers and their families approached the czar's Winter Palace in St. Petersburg. They carried a petition asking for better working conditions, more personal freedom, and an elected national legislature. Nicholas II's generals ordered soldiers to fire on the crowd. More than 1,000 were wounded and several hundred were killed. Russians quickly named the event "Bloody Sunday." Bloody Sunday provoked a wave of strikes and violence that spread across the country. In October 1905, Nicholas reluctantly promised more freedom and approved the creation of the Duma (DOO•muh)—Russia's first parliament. The first Duma met in May 1906. Its leaders were moderates who wanted Russia to become a constitutional monarchy similar to Britain. Hesitant to share his power, the czar dissolved the Duma after ten weeks.

The March Revolution

In March 1917, women textile workers in Petrograd led a citywide strike. Riots flared up over shortages of bread and fuel brought on by World War I. Nearly 200,000 workers swarmed the streets shouting, "Down with the autocracy!" and "Down with the war!" At first the soldiers obeyed orders to shoot the rioters but later sided with them. The local protest exploded into a general uprising—the March Revolution. It forced Czar Nicholas II to abdicate his throne. A year later revolutionaries executed Nicholas and his family.

The Duma established a **provisional government**, or temporary government, headed by Alexander Kerensky. Kerensky's decision to continue fighting in World War I cost him the support of both soldiers and civilians. Angry peasants demanded land. City workers grew more radical. Competing for power, socialist revolutionaries formed **soviets**—local councils consisting of workers, peasants, and soldiers. In many cities, the soviets had more influence than the government.

The Bolshevik Revolution and Civil War

Lenin returned from exile in April 1917. He and the Bolsheviks soon gained control of the Petrograd soviet, as well as the soviets in other major Russian cities. By the fall of 1917, people in the cities were rallying to the call, "All power to the soviets." Lenin's slogan—"Peace, Land, and Bread"—gained widespread appeal.

TAKING NOTES

Following Chronological Order Create a time line to show major events in the changing of Russian government.

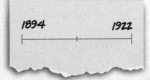

1894   1922

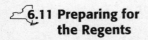

6.10 Preparing for the Regents

Change According to the Marxist, how would the "dictatorship of the proletariat" come to power?

6.11 Preparing for the Regents

Conflict How did Nicholas II contribute to revolution in Russia? What relationship is there between World War I and revolution in Russia?

6.12 Preparing for the Regents

Conflict Why do you think Lenin promised "peace, land, and bread?"

Lenin decided to take action. In November 1917, without warning, armed factory workers stormed the Winter Palace in Petrograd. Calling themselves the Bolshevik Red Guards, they took over government offices and arrested the leaders of the provisional government.

Within days after the Bolshevik takeover, Lenin ordered that all farmland be distributed among the peasants and that control of the factories be given to workers. The Bolshevik government also ended Russia's involvement in World War I. The treaty of Brest-Litvosk, which Russia and Germany signed in March 1918, surrendered a large part of Russia's territory to Germany and its allies. The humiliating terms of the treaty triggered widespread anger among many Russians. They objected to the Bolsheviks and their policies and to the murder of the royal family.

The Bolsheviks' opponents formed the White Army, which was made up of a variety of groups united only by their desire to defeat the Bolsheviks. The revolutionary leader, Leon Trotsky, expertly commanded the Bolshevik Red Army. From 1918 to 1920, civil war raged in Russia. In the end, the Red Army crushed all opposition. The victory showed that the Bolsheviks were able both to seize power and to maintain it. But the cost was heavy. Around 14 million Russians died in the struggle and in the famine that followed.

Lenin Rules Russia

War and revolution destroyed the Russian economy. Trade was at a standstill, industrial production dropped, and many skilled workers fled to other countries. Lenin turned to reviving the economy and restructuring the government. In March 1921, he temporarily put aside his plan for a state-controlled economy and launched the New Economic Policy (NEP), a small-scale version of capitalism. NEP reforms allowed peasants to sell their surplus crops instead of turning them over to the government. The government kept control of major industries, banks, and means of communication, but it let some small factories, businesses, and farms operate under private ownership. The government also encouraged foreign investment. The country slowly recovered. By 1928, Russia's farms and factories were producing as much as they had before World War I.

Bolshevik leaders saw nationalism as a threat to unity and party loyalty. To keep nationalism in check, Lenin organized Russia into several self-governing republics under the central government. In 1922, the country was named the Union of Soviet Socialist Republics (USSR), in honor of the councils that helped launch the revolution. The Bolsheviks renamed their party the **Communist Party**. The name came from the writings of Karl Marx. In 1924, the Communists created a constitution based on socialist and democratic principles. In reality, the Communist Party held all the power. Lenin had established a dictatorship of the party, not "a dictatorship of the proletariat," as Marx had promoted.

Stalin and the Rise of Totalitarianism

Lenin suffered a stroke in 1922. He survived, but the incident set in motion competition for heading up the Communist Party. By 1928, **Joseph Stalin** was in total command of the Communist Party. Stalin now stood poised to wield absolute power as a dictator.

Stalin and Human Rights Stalin aimed to create a perfect Communist state in Russia. To realize his vision, he planned to transform the Soviet Union into a totalitarian state. The term **totalitarianism** describes a government that takes total, centralized, state control over every aspect of public and private life.

6.13 Preparing for the Regents

Conflict   What factors led to the Bolshevik Revolution?

6.14 Preparing for the Regents

Change   Why was the Bolshevik Revolution of 1917 a major turning point in history?

6.15 Preparing for the Regents

Economic Systems   What steps did Lenin take to improve the Soviet economy following the revolution?

6.16 Preparing for the Regents

Political Systems   What type of political system did Joseph Stalin establish?

TAKING NOTES

Categorizing Create a chart listing examples of methods of control used in the Soviet Union.

Methods of control	Example
1.	
2.	
3.	
4.	

Stalin built a police state to maintain his power. His secret police monitored telephone lines, read mail, planted informers everywhere, and used tanks and armored cars to stop riots. In 1937, he launched the **Great Purge**, a campaign of terror designed to eliminate anyone who threatened his power, including Communist Party members. By the time the purge ended in 1938, millions had died.

Stalin's government controlled all newspapers, motion pictures, radio, and other sources of information. Many Soviet writers, composers, and other artists faced official censorship. The government also controlled all education, from nursery schools through the universities. Party leaders lectured workers and peasants on the ideals of communism. Communists also worked to replace religious teachings with the ideals of communism. The Russian Orthodox Church was the main target of persecution.

Stalin and the Economy Stalin also worked to overhaul the economy. His plan called for a **command economy**, a system in which the government made all economic decisions. Under this system, political leaders identify the country's economic needs and determine how to fulfill them. In 1928, Stalin outlined the first of several **Five-Year Plans** for economic development. The Five-Year Plans set impossibly high targets for the output of steel, coal, oil, and electricity. To reach these targets, the government limited production of consumer goods. As a result, people faced severe shortages of housing, food, clothing, and other necessary goods. Stalin's tough methods produced impressive economic results. Although most of the targets of the first Five-Year Plan fell short, the Soviets made substantial gains. A second plan, launched in 1933, proved equally successful.

Stalin also worked to reform agriculture. In 1928, the government began to seize over 25 million privately owned farms in the USSR. It combined them into large, government-owned farms, called **collective farms**, or collectives. Hundreds of families worked on these collectives, producing food for the state. The government expected that the collectives' modern machinery would boost food production and reduce the number of workers. Resistance was strong, especially among Ukrainian kulaks, a class of wealthy peasants. The government decided to eliminate them. More than 3 million Ukrainians were shot, exiled, or imprisoned. Some 6 million people died in the government-engineered famine that resulted from the destruction of crops and animals. By 1935, the kulaks had been eliminated, and by 1938, more than 90 percent of all peasants lived on collective farms.

By the mid-1930s, Stalin had forcibly transformed the Soviet Union into a totalitarian regime and an industrial and political power. He stood unopposed as dictator and maintained his authority over the Communist Party.

6.17 Preparing for the Regents

Economic Systems What were the economic accomplishments of the Soviet Union under Joseph Stalin?

6.18 Preparing for the Regents

Human Rights What led to the forced famine in the Ukraine?

PREPARING FOR THE REGENTS

Answer the following question. Use the Analyze the Question hints to help you answer the question.

1 Under Joseph Stalin, peasants in the Soviet Union were forced to

(1) become members of the ruling party
(2) support the Russian Orthodox Church
(3) join collective farms
(4) move to large cities

ANALYZE THE QUESTION
- Read the stem. You are being asked to indicate what Stalin forced the peasants to do.
- Think about Stalin's policies and the role of peasants in Soviet before reading the alternatives.
- Select the alternative that matches Stalin's policies.

Between the Wars, 1919–1939

Section Overview

World War I was over. The terms of peace, however, still had to be worked out. On January 18, 1919, delegates representing 32 countries met at the Paris Peace Conference held at the Palace of Versailles, outside Paris. Russia, in the grip of civil war, was not represented. Neither were Germany and its allies. Out of this conference came the Treaty of Versailles, which severely punished Germany and established the League of Nations, an international organization whose goal was to maintain peace.

The Treaty of Versailles and the other treaties signed following the war led to land losses for the Central Powers and even some of the Allies. New nations were created in Europe. Germany's colonial possessions fell under the control of League of Nations, as did former Ottoman lands in Southwest Asia. The bitterness that grew out of these treaties helped spur independence movements in Southwest Asia and contributed to the rise of totalitarian governments in Germany and Italy. In less than two decades, aggressions by Germany, Italy, and Japan threatened to plunge the world into another catastrophic war.

Mohandas K. Gandhi (1869–1948), leader of the Indian independence movement

MAIN IDEAS

POWER AND AUTHORITY   After winning World War I, the Allies dictated a harsh peace settlement that left many nations feeling betrayed.

EMPIRE BUILDING   Nationalism triggered independence movements in Southwest Asia to overthrow colonial powers.

ECONOMICS   An economics depression in the United States spread throughout the world.

POWER AND AUTHORITY   In response to political turmoil and economic crisis, Italy and Germany turned to totalitarian dictators.

POWER AND AUTHORITY   As Germany, Italy, and Japan conquered other countries, the rest of the world did nothing to stop them.

TERMS AND NAMES

- Fourteen Points
- self-determination
- Treaty of Versailles
- League of Nations
- Rowlatt Acts
- Amritsar Massacre
- Mohandas K. Gandhi
- civil disobedience
- Salt March
- Mustafa Kemal
- Great Depression
- fascism
- Benito Mussolini
- Adolf Hitler
- Nazism
- *Mein Kampf*
- Weimar Republic
- appeasement
- Axis Powers
- Third Reich
- Munich Conference

PREPARING FOR THE REGENTS

As you read this section, consider
- to what extent fascism challenged liberal democratic traditions.

TIME LINE

1919
Treaty of Versailles signed.

1920
Gandhi leads Indian campaign of civil disobedience.

1922
Mussolini comes to power in Italy.

1923
Mustafa Kemal transforms Turkey into a republic.

1929
U.S. stock market crashes.

1931
Hirohito's Japan seizes Manchuria.

1933
Hitler is named chancellor of Germany.

The Treaty of Versailles and the League of Nations

In January 1918, while World War I was still raging, President Woodrow Wilson had drawn up a series of peace proposals known as the **Fourteen Points**. The first four points included an end to secret treaties, freedom of the seas, free trade, and reduced national armies and navies. The fifth point was the adjustment of colonial claims with fairness toward colonial peoples. The sixth through thirteenth points were specific suggestions for changing borders and creating new nations. The guiding idea behind these points was **self-determination**—the right of people to decide for themselves under what government they wished to live. The fourteenth point proposed a "general association of nations" that would protect "great and small states alike."

The war now over, Wilson and the other delegates met at the Paris Peace Conference to work out the terms of peace. Britain and France showed little sign of agreeing to Wilson's proposals. However, after heated argument, a compromise was reached. The **Treaty of Versailles** between Germany and the Allied powers was signed on June 28, 1919. Adopting Wilson's fourteenth point, the treaty also created a **League of Nations**, an international association whose goal would be to keep peace among nations.

Human and Physical Geography

The treaty punished Germany. The defeated nation lost substantial territory and had severe restrictions placed on its military operations. The harshest provision was Article 231—the "war guilt" clause—which placed sole responsibility for the war on Germany. As a result, Germany had to pay reparations to the Allies. All of Germany's Africa and the Pacific territories were declared mandates, or

TAKING NOTES

Clarifying Use a chart to record the reaction by various groups to the Treaty of Versailles.

Reaction to Treaty
Germany
Africans & Asians
Italy & Japan

6.19 Preparing for the Regents

Conflict How did the Treaty of Versailles punish Germany for its role in World War I?

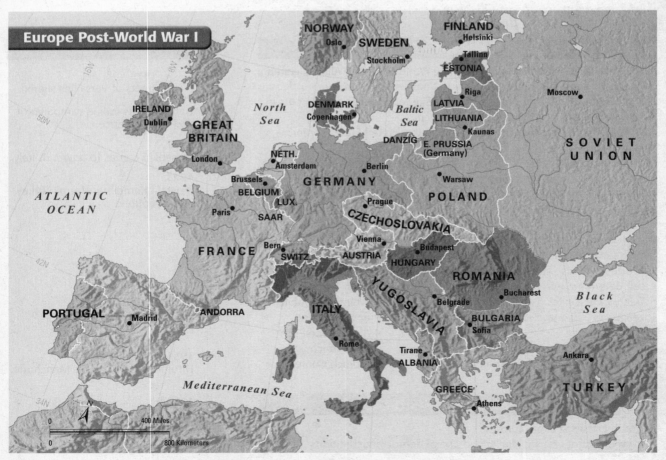

Europe Post-World War I

territories to be administered by the League of Nations. The Allies would govern the mandates until they were judged ready for independence.

The Western powers signed separate peace treaties in 1919 and 1920 with each of the other defeated nations: Austria-Hungary, Bulgaria, and the Ottoman Empire. These treaties, too, led to huge land losses for the Central Powers. The independent nations of Austria, Hungary, Czechoslovakia, and Yugoslavia were carved out of the Austro-Hungarian Empire. The Ottoman Turks were forced to give up all of their former empire except the territory that is today the country of Turkey. The Allies carved up the lands that the Ottomans lost in Southwest Asia into mandates rather than independent nations. Palestine, Iraq, and Transjordan came under British control; Syria and Lebanon went to France. Russia, which had left the war early, also lost land. Romania and Poland both gained Russian territory. Finland, Estonia, Latvia, and Lithuania, formerly part of Russia, became independent nations.

Nationalism and Reform

People in the mandated territories were angry at the way the Allies disregarded their desire for independence. The European powers, it seemed to them, merely talked about the principle of national self-determination. European colonialism, disguised as the mandate system, continued.

India Until World War I, most Indians had little interest in nationalism. This changed when the British government promised reforms that would eventually lead to self-government if Indians would enlist in the British army during World War I. When Indian troops returned home from the war, they expected Britain to fulfill its promise. Instead, they were once again treated as second-class citizens. In protest, radical nationalists carried out acts of violence. To curb dissent, the British passed the **Rowlatt Acts** in 1919. These acts allowed the government to jail protesters without trial for as long as two years.

To protest the Rowlatt Acts, around 10,000 Hindus and Muslims flocked to Amritsar, a major city in the Punjab, in the spring of 1919 for a political festival. Believing that the people were openly defying a British ban on public meetings, the British commander at Amritsar ordered his troops to fire on the crowd without warning. Nearly 400 Indians died and about 1,200 were wounded. News of the slaughter, called the **Amritsar Massacre**, sparked an explosion of anger across India. Almost overnight, millions of Indians demanded independence.

The massacre set the stage for **Mohandas K. Gandhi** (GAHN•dee) to emerge as the leader of the independence movement. A moral person, Gandhi urged the Indian National Congress to follow a policy of noncooperation with the British. In 1920, the Congress Party endorsed **civil disobedience**—the deliberate and public refusal to obey an unjust law—and nonviolence as the means to achieve independence. Gandhi then launched his campaign of civil disobedience. Gandhi called on Indians to refuse to buy British goods, attend government schools, pay British taxes, or vote in elections. Gandhi also staged a successful boycott of British cloth, a source of wealth for the British.

In 1930, Gandhi organized a demonstration to defy the hated Salt Acts—British laws that required Indians to buy salt from the government and to pay a salt tax. Gandhi and his followers walked about 240 miles to the seacoast, where they made their own salt by evaporating seawater. This peaceful protest was called the **Salt March**. Soon afterward, some demonstrators planned a march to a British saltworks. Police officers with steel-tipped clubs attacked the peaceful demonstrator, who refused to defend themselves. An American

6.20 Preparing for the Regents

Nationalism Why did the peace treaties following World War I change European boundaries? Which nations lost territory?

TAKING NOTES

Categorizing Create a web diagram identifying the styles of government adopted by nations in this section.

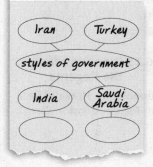

6.21 Preparing for the Regents

Nationalism What is civil disobedience? How did Gandhi use civil disobedience in his quest for Indian independence?

journalist was an eyewitness to the event. Newspapers across the globe carried the journalist's story, which won worldwide support for Gandhi's independence movement. More demonstrations against the salt tax took place throughout India. Eventually, about 60,000 people, including Gandhi, were arrested. Progress was being made, however. In 1935, the British Parliament passed the Government of India Act. It provided local self-government and limited democratic elections, but not total independence.

Turkey At the end of World War I, the Ottoman Empire was forced to give up all its territories except Turkey—the old Turkish homeland of Anatolia and a small strip of land around Istanbul. In 1919, Greek soldiers invaded Turkey. The Turkish sultan was powerless to stop the Greeks. However, in 1922, a brilliant commander, **Mustafa Kemal** (keh•MAHL), successfully led Turkish nationalists in fighting back the Greeks and their British backers. After winning a peace, the nationalists overthrew the last Ottoman sultan.

In 1923, Kemal became the president of the new Republic of Turkey. To achieve his goal of transforming Turkey into a modern nation, Kemal separated the laws of Islam from the laws of the nation, abolished religious courts and created a new legal system based on European law, granted women the right to vote and to hold public office, and launched government-funded programs to industrialize Turkey and to spur economic growth. His influence was so strong that the Turkish people gave him the name Ataturk—"father of the Turks."

Iran Before World War I, Britain and Russia had established spheres of influence in Persia. After the war, when Russia was still reeling from the Bolshevik Revolution, the British tried to take over all of Persia. This triggered a nationalist revolt. In 1921, Reza Shah Pahlavi (PAL•uh•vee), a Persian army officer, seized power. In 1925, he deposed the ruling shah. Persia's new leader, like Kemal in Turkey, set out to modernize his country. He established public schools, built roads and railroads, promoted industrial growth, and extended women's rights. Unlike Kemal, Reza Shah Pahlavi kept all power in his own hands. In 1935, he changed the name of the country from the Greek name Persia to the traditional name Iran.

Saudi Arabia While Turkey broke with many Islamic traditions, another new country held strictly to Islamic law. In 1902, Abd al-Aziz Ibn Saud (sah•OOD) began a successful campaign to unify Arabia. In 1932, he renamed the new kingdom Saudi Arabia after his family. Ibn Saud carried on Arab and Islamic traditions. Loyalty to the Saudi government was based on custom, religion, and family ties. Ibn Saud brought some modern technology, such as telephones and radios, to his country. However, modernization in Saudi Arabia was limited to religiously acceptable areas. There also were no efforts to begin to practice democracy.

Zionist Nationalism During the late 19th and early 20th centuries, Jewish Zionists began returning to Palestine, the region their ancestors had fled so long ago. At the time, Palestine was still ruled by Islamic Turks. After the defeat of the Ottomans in World War I, the League of Nations asked Britain to oversee Palestine until it was ready for independence. The Zionists were pressing for their own nation in the territory. The Palestinians living in the region strongly opposed such a move. In a 1917 letter to Zionist leaders, British Foreign Secretary Sir Arthur Balfour promoted the idea of creating a Jewish homeland in Palestine while protecting the "rights of existing non-Jewish communities." Despite the Balfour Declaration, however, efforts to create a Jewish state failed—and hostility between Palestinians and Jews continued to grow.

6.22 Preparing for the Regents

Nationalism How did Kemal Ataturk transform Turkey? Why might religious forces have opposed some of his efforts?

6.23 Preparing for the Regents

Nationalism How did Reza Shah Pahlavi transform Iran?

6.24 Preparing for the Regents

Nationalism How did Ibn Saud transform Saudi Arabia?

6.25 Preparing for the Regents

Nationalism What idea did Sir Arthur Balfour promote in his letter to the Zionist leaders?

The Great Depression

By the late 1920s, European nations were rebuilding war-torn economies. They were aided by loans from the more prosperous United States. Only the United States and Japan came out of the war in better financial shape than before. In the late 1920s, American economic prosperity largely sustained the world economy. If the U.S. economy weakened, the whole world's economic system might collapse. In 1929, it did.

The Stock Market Crash Despite prosperity, several weaknesses in the U.S. economy caused serious problems. These included an uneven distribution of wealth (the richest 5 percent of the population received 33 percent of all personal income in 1929), overproduction by businesses and farms, and the fact that many Americans could not afford to buy the goods being produced. These factors set off a downward economic spiral. Factories cut production and laid off workers. Farmers, unable to sell their crops at a profit, defaulted on their bank loans.

The danger signs of overproduction by factories and farms should have warned people against gambling on the stock market. Yet few heeded the warning. Stock prices soared. Then, in September 1929, some investors started selling their stocks, believing the prices would soon go down. By Thursday, October 24, the gradual lowering of stock prices had become an all-out slide downward. A panic resulted. Everyone wanted to sell stocks, and no one wanted to buy. Prices plunged to a new low on Tuesday, October 29. Then the market collapsed.

A Global Depression A long business slump, which would come to be called the **Great Depression**, followed. The stock market crash alone did not cause the Great Depression, but it quickened the collapse of the U.S. economy. The collapse of the American economy sent shock waves around the world. Worried American bankers demanded repayment of their overseas loans, and American investors withdrew their money from Europe. The American market for European goods dropped sharply as the U.S. Congress placed high tariffs on imported goods to encourage Americans to buy U.S. goods. This policy backfired. Other nations imposed their own higher tariffs. World trade dropped by 65 percent. This contributed further to the economic downturn.

Because of war debts and dependence on American loans and investments, Germany and Austria were particularly hard hit. In 1931, Austria's largest bank failed. In Asia, both farmers and urban workers suffered as the value of exports fell by half between 1929 and 1931. The crash was felt heavily in Latin America as well. As European and U.S. demand for such Latin American products as sugar, beef, and copper dropped, prices collapsed.

The Rise of Fascism

Many democracies, including the United States, Britain, and France, remained strong despite the economic crisis caused by the Great Depression. However, millions of people lost faith in democratic government. In response, they turned to an extreme system of government called fascism. **Fascism** (FASH•IHZ•uhm) was a new, militant political movement that emphasized loyalty to the state and obedience to its leader. Unlike communism, fascism had no clearly defined theory or program. Nevertheless, most Fascists shared several ideas. They preached an extreme form of nationalism. Fascists believed that nations must struggle—peaceful states were doomed to be conquered. They pledged loyalty to an authoritarian leader who guided and brought order to the state. In each nation, Fascists wore uniforms of a certain color, used special salutes, and held mass rallies.

TAKING NOTES
Recognizing Effects
Use a diagram to show the effects of the Great Depression in the world.

6.26 Preparing for the Regents
Economic Systems What effect did the collapse of the U.S. economy have on Europe? Why were Germany and Austria hit particularly hard by the Great Depression?

TAKING NOTES
Comparing and Contrasting Use a chart to compare Mussolini's rise to power and his goals with Hitler's.

Hitler	Mussolini
Rise:	Rise:
Goals:	Goals:

6.27 Preparing for the Regents

Political Systems In what ways are fascism and communism similar?

In some ways, fascism was similar to communism. Both systems were ruled by dictators who allowed only their own political party (one-party rule). Both denied individual rights. In both, the state was supreme. Neither practiced any kind of democracy. However, unlike Communists, Fascists did not seek a classless society. Rather, they believed that each class had its place and function. Most Fascist parties were made up of aristocrats and industrialists, war veterans, and the lower middle class. Also, Fascists were nationalists, and Communists were internationalists, hoping to unite workers worldwide.

6.28 Preparing for the Regents

Political Systems Why would a Benito Mussolini be likely to agree with the following quotation?

"Why should freedom of speech and freedom of the press be allowed? Why should a government, doing what it believes is right, allow itself to be criticized? It would not allow opposition by lethal weapons. Ideas are much more fatal things than guns.'"

Italy Fascism's rise in Italy was fueled by bitter disappointment over the failure to win large territorial gains at the 1919 Paris Peace Conference. Rising inflation and unemployment also contributed to widespread social unrest. To growing numbers of Italians, their democratic government seemed helpless to deal with the country's problems. A newspaper editor and politician named **Benito Mussolini** boldly promised to rescue Italy by reviving its economy and rebuilding its armed forces. Mussolini had founded the Fascist Party in 1919.

As economic conditions worsened, Mussolini's popularity rapidly increased. Because he played on the fear of a workers' revolt, he began to win support from the middle classes, the aristocracy, and industrial leaders. In October 1922, the Fascists demanded that King Victor Emmanuel III put Mussolini in charge of the government. Once he abolished democracy, outlawed all political parties except the Fascists, jailed his opponents, instituted censorship, and outlawed strikes. He sought to control the economy by allying the Fascists with the industrialists and large landowners.

6.29 Preparing for the Regents

Power How did the Treaty of Versailles contribute to the rise of Nazism?

Germany When Mussolini became dictator of Italy, **Adolf Hitler** was a little-known political leader. In 1919, he joined a tiny right-wing political group that believed that Germany had to overturn the Treaty of Versailles. The group later named itself the National Socialist German Workers' Party, or Nazi for short. Its policies formed the German brand of fascism known as **Nazism**. The party adopted the swastika, or hooked cross, as its symbol. The Nazis also set up a private militia called the storm troopers or Brown Shirts.

Hitler was soon chosen *der Führer* (duhr FYUR•uhr), or the leader, of the Nazi party. Inspired by Mussolini, Hitler and the Nazis plotted to seize power in 1923. The attempt failed, and Hitler was arrested. He was tried for treason but was sentenced to only five years in prison. He served less than nine months.

While in jail, Hitler wrote ***Mein Kampf*** (*My Struggle*). In the book, Hitler asserted that the Germans, whom he incorrectly called "Aryans," were a "master race." He declared that non-Aryan "races," such as Jews, Slavs, and Gypsies, were inferior. He called the Versailles Treaty an outrage and vowed to regain German lands. Hitler also promised to get more living space for Germany by conquering eastern Europe and Russia.

6.30 Preparing for the Regents

Economic Systems How did the Treaty of Versailles contribute to Germany's economic problems? How did these economic problems contribute to the rise of fascism?

Throughout much of the 1920s, most Germans ignored Hitler. The inflation that had plagued Germany following the war had finally ended. The nation was enjoying a brief economic recovery, fueled in part by American loans. Then the Great Depression hit. When American loans stopped, the German economy collapsed. Civil unrest broke out. Frightened and confused, Germans now turned to Hitler, hoping for security and firm leadership. The Nazis had become the largest political party by 1932. Conservative leaders mistakenly believed they could control Hitler and use him for their purposes. In January 1933, they advised Paul von Hindenburg, president of the **Weimar Republic**, Germany's democratic government, to name Hitler chancellor.

Hitler used his new power to turn Germany into a totalitarian state. He banned all other political parties and created an elite, black-uniformed unit called the SS (*Schutzstaffel*, or protection squad). It was loyal only to Hitler. In 1934, the SS arrested and murdered hundreds of Hitler's enemies. This brutal action and the terror applied by the Gestapo, the Nazi secret police, shocked most Germans into total obedience. Hitler also turned the press, radio, literature, painting, and film into propaganda tools. Books that did not conform to Nazi beliefs were burned in huge bonfires. Churches were forbidden to criticize the Nazis or the government. Schoolchildren had to join the Hitler youth groups.

The Nazis quickly took command of the economy. New laws banned strikes, dissolved independent labor unions, and gave the government authority over business and labor. Hitler put millions of Germans to work constructing factories, building highways, manufacturing weapons, and serving in the military. As a result, the number of unemployed dropped from about 6 to 1.5 million in 1936.

Japanese Militarism and Imperialism

As fascism spread in Europe, Japan fell under military rule. During the 1920s, the Japanese government became more democratic. In 1922, Japan signed an international treaty agreeing to respect China's borders. In 1928, it signed the Kellogg-Briand Pact renouncing war. Japan's parliamentary system had several weaknesses, however. Most importantly, civilian leaders had little control over the armed forces. Military leaders reported only to the emperor. When the Great Depression struck in 1929, many Japanese blamed the government. Military leaders gained support and soon won control of the country. Unlike the Fascists in Europe, the militarists did not try to establish a new system of government. Instead of a forceful leader like Mussolini or Hitler, the militarists made the Emperor Hirohito the symbol of state power.

Like Hitler and Mussolini, Japan's militarists were extreme nationalists. They wanted to solve the country's economic problems through foreign expansion. Japanese businesses had invested heavily in China's northeast province, Manchuria. It was an area rich in iron and coal, raw materials that Japan needed. In 1931, the Japanese army seized Manchuria, despite objections from the Japanese parliament. The army then set up a puppet government. Japanese engineers and technicians began arriving in large numbers to build mines and factories. When Japan seized Manchuria, many League of Nations members vigorously protested. Japan ignored the protests and withdrew from the League in 1933. Four years later, a border incident touched off a full-scale war between Japan and China. Japanese forces swept into northern China. Despite having a million soldiers, China's army was no match for the better equipped and trained Japanese. Beijing and other northern cities, as well as the capital, Nanjing, fell to the Japanese in 1937. Japanese troops killed tens of thousands of captured soldiers and civilians in Nanjing.

The Policy of Appeasement

The League's failure to stop the Japanese encouraged European Fascists to plan aggression of their own. The Italian leader Mussolini dreamed of building a colonial empire in Africa like those of Britain and France. The Ethiopians had successfully resisted an Italian attempt at conquest during the 1890s. To avenge that defeat, Mussolini ordered a massive invasion of Ethiopia in October 1935. The Ethiopian emperor urgently appealed to the League for help. Hoping to keep peace in Europe, the League condemned the attack, but did nothing.

6.31 Preparing for the Regents

Political Systems What are some examples of totalitarianism in Germany during the 1930s?

TAKING NOTES
Following Chronological Order Use a time line to trace the movement of Japan from democratic reform to military aggression.

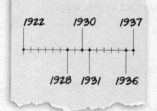

1922   1930   1937

1928   1931   1936

6.32 Preparing for the Regents

Imperialism When and why did Japan invade Manchuria?

6.33 Preparing for the Regents

Conflict Why might critics suggest that the League of Nations failed in its intended goals?

Hitler also took bold steps. In March 1935, he announced that Germany would not obey the Versailles Treaty's restriction on the size of the German army. The League issued only a mild condemnation. Hitler took even greater risks. On March 7, 1936, German troops moved into the Rhineland, a 30-mile zone on either side of the Rhine River that the treaty had set as a buffer between Germany and France. Stunned, the French were unwilling to risk war. The British urged **appeasement**, giving into an aggressor to keep peace.

6.34 Preparing for the Regents

Conflict   What is appeasement?

Hitler's growing strength convinced Mussolini to seek an alliance with Germany. In October 1936, the two dictators reached an agreement that became known as the Rome-Berlin Axis. A month later, Germany also made an agreement with Japan. Germany, Italy, and Japan came to be called the **Axis Powers**.

On November 5, 1937, Hitler announced to his advisers his plans to absorb Austria and Czechoslovakia into the **Third Reich** (ryk), or German Empire. In March 1938, Hitler sent his army into Austria and annexed it. France and Britain ignored their pledge to protect Austrian independence. In September 1938, Hitler demanded that Czechoslovakia give Germany its western border regions called the Sudetenland. The Czechs refused and asked France for help.

6.35 Preparing for the Regents

Conflict   How did Britain and France respond to Germany's actions in Czechoslovakia? Why did they react in this way?

France and Britain were preparing for war when Mussolini proposed a meeting of Germany, France, Britain, and Italy in Munich, Germany. The **Munich Conference** was held on September 29, 1938. The Czechs were not invited. British prime minister Neville Chamberlain believed that he could preserve peace by giving in to Hitler's demand. Britain and France agreed that Hitler could take the Sudetenland. In exchange, Hitler pledged to respect Czechoslovakia's new borders. Less than six months after the Munich meeting, Hitler took Czechoslovakia. Soon after, Mussolini seized Albania. Then Hitler demanded that Poland return the former German port of Danzig. The Poles refused and turned to Britain and France for aid. But appeasement had convinced Hitler that neither nation would risk war.

Britain and France asked the Soviet Union to join them in stopping Hitler's aggression. As Stalin talked with Britain and France, he also bargained with Hitler. The two dictators reached an agreement. Once bitter enemies, Fascist Germany and Communist Russia now publicly pledged never to attack one another. On August 23, 1939, their leaders signed a nonaggression pact. As the Axis Powers moved unchecked at the end of the decade, war appeared inevitable.

PREPARING FOR THE REGENTS

On a separate sheet of paper, write a well-organized essay that includes an introduction, several paragraphs addressing the task below, and a conclusion. Before beginning, check the Score the Essay box for pointers.

Theme: Nationalism
Nationalism is a powerful force that can have positive and negative effects.

Task:
- Discuss how nationalism had positive *and/or* negative effects in the nations and regions you studied in this section.
- Evaluate whether nationalism in general had a more or less positive *or* a more or less negative impact during this period.

SCORE THE ESSAY   To receive a score of 5 on your essay, you will need to:
- thoroughly develop all aspects of the task evenly and in depth by describing both the positive and negative effects of nationalism in the years between World War I and World War II.
- be more analytical than descriptive.
- richly support the theme with relevant facts, examples, and details.
- demonstrate a logical and clear plan of organization.

World War II, 1939–1945

Japanese attack on Pearl Harbor, December 7, 1941

Section Overview

On September 1, 1939, German tanks rolled across the Polish border. Within days, France and Great Britain declared war on Germany. Soon war would engulf Europe, North Africa, Asia, and the Pacific as the Allies squared off against the Axis Powers. A Japanese attack on Pearl Harbor on December 7, 1941, brought the United States into the war. By the time the war ended in 1945, close to 40 million Europeans had died, two-thirds of them civilians. Constant bombing and shelling had reduced hundreds of cities to rubble. Japan was in equally grim shape. Two atomic bombs had turned Hiroshima and Nagasaki into blackened wastelands.

MAIN IDEAS

EMPIRE BUILDING   Germany, Italy, and Japan tried to build empires. They began their expansion by conquering other nations and dominating them politically and economically.

SCIENCE AND TECHNOLOGY   Far-reaching developments in science and technology changed the course of World War II. Improvements in aircraft, tanks, and submarines and the development of radar and the atomic bomb drastically altered the way wars were fought.

ECONOMICS   Fighting the Axis terror weakened the economies of Great Britain, the Soviet Union, and other European countries. In contrast, when the United States entered the war, its economy grew sharply. The strength of the American economy bolstered the Allied war effort.

TERMS AND NAMES

- nonaggression pact
- blitzkrieg
- Winston Churchill
- Battle of Britain
- Franklin D. Roosevelt
- Pearl Harbor
- Holocaust

- *Kristallnacht*
- ghetto
- "Final Solution"
- genocide
- Dwight D. Eisenhower
- Battle of Stalingrad
- D-Day

- Battle of the Bulge
- Battle of Midway
- Battle of Guadalcanal
- kamikaze
- Nuremberg Trials

PREPARING FOR THE REGENTS

As you read this section, consider
- what roles Churchill, Roosevelt, Stalin, Hitler, and Mussolini played in World War II.
- how geography affected the conduct of World War II.

TIME LINE

Sept. 1939
Germany invades Poland; France and Great Britain declare war on Germany.

June 1940
France surrenders to Germany; Battle of Britain begins.

June 1941
Germans invade Soviet Union.

Dec. 1941
Japan attacks Pearl Harbor.

June 1942
Allies defeat Japan at Battle of Midway.

Feb. 1943
Germans surrender at Stalingrad; Allies defeat Japan at Guadalcanal.

June 1944
D-Day invasion takes place.

May 1945
Germany surrenders.

Aug.–Sept. 1945
Allies use atomic bombs; Japan surrenders.

Human and Physical Geography: The War Begins

During the 1930s, Hitler played on the hopes and fears of the Western democracies. Each time he grabbed new territory, he would declare an end to his demands. Peace seemed guaranteed—until Hitler moved again. In 1939, Hitler demanded the return of the Polish Corridor, German territory that had been transferred to Poland following World War I. At this point, Soviet dictator Joseph Stalin signed a ten-year **nonaggression pact** with Hitler. In a secret part of the pact, Germany and the Soviet Union agreed to divide Poland between them. They also agreed that the USSR could take over Finland, Lithuania, Latvia, and Estonia.

After signing this nonaggression pact, Hitler quickly moved to conquer Poland. His surprise attack took place at dawn on September 1, 1939. German tanks and troop trucks rumbled across the Polish border. At the same time, German aircraft and artillery began a merciless bombing of Poland's capital, Warsaw. France and Great Britain declared war on Germany on September 3. But Poland fell some time before those nations could make any military response. After his victory, Hitler annexed the western half of Poland, which had a large German population. The German invasion of Poland was the first test of Germany's newest military strategy—the **blitzkrieg** (BLIHTS•kreeg), or "lightning war." It involved using fast-moving airplanes and tanks, followed by massive infantry forces, to take enemy defenders by surprise and quickly overwhelm them. In the case of Poland, the strategy worked.

On September 17, Stalin sent Soviet troops to occupy the eastern half of Poland. Stalin then moved to annex countries to the north of Poland. Lithuania, Latvia, and Estonia fell without a struggle, but Finland resisted. In November, Stalin sent nearly one million Soviet troops into Finland. The Soviets suffered heavy losses, but by March 1940, Stalin had forced the Finns to surrender.

The Early War in Europe and the Mediterranean

After they declared war on Germany, the French and British mobilized their armies. They stationed their troops along the Maginot (MAZH•uh•NOH) Line, a system of fortifications along France's border with Germany. There they waited for the Germans to attack—but nothing happened. Suddenly, on April 9, 1940, Hitler launched a surprise invasion of Denmark and Norway. In just four hours after the attack, Denmark fell. Two months later, Norway surrendered as well.

Dunkirk and the Fall of France In May 1940, Hitler began a dramatic sweep through the Netherlands, Belgium, and Luxembourg as part of his strategy to strike at France. Keeping the Allies' attention on those countries, Hitler sent an even larger force toward France's northern coast. After reaching the French coast, the Germans swung north again and joined with German troops in Belgium. By the end of May 1940, the Germans had trapped the Allied forces around the northern French city of Lille (leel). The Allies retreated to the beaches of Dunkirk, a French port city near the Belgian border. In one of the most heroic acts of the war, Great Britain sent a fleet of about 850 military and civilian ships across the English Channel to Dunkirk to rescue the army. From May 26 to June 4, this amateur armada, under heavy fire from German bombers, sailed back and forth from Britain to Dunkirk. The boats carried some 338,000 soldiers to safety.

Following Dunkirk, French resistance crumbled. By June 14, the Germans had taken Paris. French leaders surrendered on June 22, 1940. The Germans took control of the northern part of the country. They left the southern part to a French puppet government headquartered in the city of Vichy (VEESH•ee).

6.36 Preparing for the Regents

Conflict On what date did Hitler invade Poland?

6.37 Preparing for the Regents

Conflict Why did France and Great Britain declare war on Germany?

TAKING NOTES

Recognizing Effects
Use a chart to identify the effects of some of the early events of World War II.

Cause	Effect
First blitzkrieg	
Allies stranded at Dunkirk	
Lend-Lease Act	

The Battle of Britain Hitler now turned to an invasion of Great Britain. In the summer of 1940, the Luftwaffe (LOOFT•VAHF•uh), Germany's air force, began bombing Britain's airfields, aircraft factories, and eventually its cities, especially London. True to the promise of <u>Winston Churchill</u>, Britain's prime minister, the British did not surrender.

The Royal Air Force (RAF) began to hit back hard. Two technological devices helped turn the tide in the RAF's favor. One was an electronic tracking system known as radar. Developed in the late 1930s, radar could tell the number, speed, and direction of incoming warplanes. The other device was a German code-making machine named Enigma, which had been smuggled into Britain in the late 1930s. Enigma enabled the British to decode German secret messages and quickly launch attacks on the enemy. To avoid the RAF's attacks, the Germans gave up daylight raids in October 1940 in favor of night bombing. The <u>Battle of Britain</u> continued until May 10, 1941. Stunned by British resistance, Hitler decided to call off his attacks.

6.38 Preparing for the Regents

Nationalism Why can the following quotation by Winston Churchill be seen as an expression of nationalism?

"We shall defend our island, whatever the cost shall be. We shall fight on the beaches, we shall fight on the landing grounds, we shall fight in the fields and in the streets. . . . We shall never surrender."

European and African Battles, 1939–1945

Leningrad (Sept. 8, 1941–Jan. 27, 1944)

FINLAND
NORWAY
SWEDEN
ESTONIA
LATVIA
LITHUANIA
SOVIET UNION

UNITED KINGDOM
IRELAND
DENMARK

Battle of Britain (July, 1940–Oct., 1940)
NETH.
Berlin (Apr. 16, 1945–Apr. 30, 1945)
EAST PRUSSIA (Ger.)
Warsaw (Sept. 8, 1939–Sept. 27, 1939)

Normandy (D-day) (June 6, 1944)
BELGIUM
GERMANY
Dresden (Feb. 13, 1945–Apr. 17, 1945)
POLAND

ATLANTIC OCEAN

Battle of Stalingrad (Aug 23, 1942–Feb. 2, 1943)

Paris (Aug. 19, 1944–Aug. 25, 1944)
LUX.
Battle of the Bulge (Dec. 16, 1944–Jan. 16, 1945)
CZECHOSLOVAKIA
LIECH.
FRANCE
SWITZ.
AUSTRIA
HUNGARY
ROMANIA

Caucasus Mts.

PORTUGAL
SPAIN
ITALY
YUGOSLAVIA
BULGARIA
Black Sea

ALBANIA
GREECE
TURKEY

Sicily (July 10, 1943–Aug. 17, 1943)
Mediterranean Sea

MOROCCO
ALGERIA
TUNISIA

Tobruk (June 20, 1942–June 21, 1942)

El Alamein (Oct. 23, 1942–Nov. 4, 1942)

Al-Agheila (Mar. 24, 1941)
LIBYA
EGYPT

Allied control
Axis nation
Farthest extent of Axis control
Neutral nation
Major Battle

0   250   500 Miles
0   250   500 Kilometers
Conic Projection

The Eastern Front Hitler, instead, turned his attention to Eastern Europe. He quickly secured the Balkans in preparation for invading the Soviet Union. Early in the morning of June 22, 1941, the Germans launched the invasion. The Soviet Union was not prepared. The Germans pushed 500 miles inside the Soviet Union. As the Soviet troops retreated, they burned and destroyed everything in the enemy's path. The Russians had successfully used this scorched-earth strategy against Napoleon. On September 8, German forces put Leningrad under siege. By early November, the city was completely cut off from the rest of the Soviet Union. To force a surrender, Hitler was ready to starve the city's more than 2.5 million inhabitants. German bombs destroyed warehouses where food was stored. Nearly one million people died in Leningrad during the winter of 1941–1942. Yet the city refused to fall.

Impatient with the progress in Leningrad, Hitler looked to Moscow, the capital and heart of the Soviet Union. A Nazi drive on the capital began on October 2, 1941. By December, the Germans had advanced to the outskirts of Moscow. The Soviets counterattacked. As temperatures fell, the Germans, in summer uniforms, retreated. Ignoring Napoleon's winter defeat 130 years before, Hitler ordered his generals to keep fighting. German troops dug in about 125 miles west of Moscow. They held on until March 1943. Hitler's advance on the Soviet Union gained nothing but cost the Germans 500,000 lives.

The United States Aids Its Allies Most Americans felt that the United States should not get involved in the war. But President <u>**Franklin D. Roosevelt**</u> knew that if the Allies fell, the United States would be drawn into the war. Under the Lend-Lease Act, passed in March 1941, the president could lend or lease arms and other supplies to any country vital to the United States. By the summer of 1941, the U.S. Navy was escorting British ships carrying U.S. arms. On September 4, a German U-boat fired on a U.S. destroyer in the Atlantic. In response, Roosevelt ordered navy commanders to shoot German submarines on sight. The United States was now involved in an undeclared naval war with Hitler.

The War in the Pacific

To almost everyone's surprise the attack that actually drew the United States into the war did not come from Germany. It came from Japan. Early in the morning of December 7, 1941, American sailors at <u>**Pearl Harbor**</u> in Hawaii awoke to the roar of explosives. A Japanese attack was underway! U.S. military leaders had known that a Japanese attack might come, but not where. Within two hours, the Japanese had sunk or damaged 19 ships, including 8 battleships, moored in Pearl Harbor. More than 2,300 Americans were killed—with over 1,100 wounded. News of the attack stunned the American people. The next day, President Roosevelt addressed Congress. December 7, 1941, he declared, was "a date which will live in infamy." Congress quickly accepted his request for a declaration of war on Japan and its allies.

Japanese Victories The Japanese drive for a Pacific empire was under way. Lightly defended, Guam and Wake Island quickly fell to Japanese forces. The Japanese then turned their attention to the Philippines. In January 1942, they marched into the Philippine capital of Manila. American and Filipino forces took up a defensive position on the Bataan (buh•TAN) Peninsula on the northwestern edge of Manila Bay. The Japanese took the Bataan Peninsula in April.

The Japanese also continued their strikes against British possessions in Asia. After seizing Hong Kong, they invaded Malaya. By February 1942, the

✎ **6.39 Preparing for the Regents**

Human and Physical Geography In what ways did Hitler and Napoleon make similar military mistakes?

✎ **6.40 Preparing for the Regents**

Conflict On what date was Pearl Harbor attacked?

TAKING NOTES

Recognizing Effects Use a chart to identify the effects of the major events of the war in the Pacific between 1941 and 1943.

Event	Effect

Japanese had reached Singapore, which surrendered after a fierce pounding. Within a month, the Japanese had conquered the resource-rich Dutch East Indies (now Indonesia), including the islands of Java, Sumatra, Borneo, and Celebes (SEHL•uh•BEEZ). The Japanese also moved westward, taking Burma.

By the time Burma fell, Japan had taken control of more than 1 million square miles of Asian land. They often treated the people of their new colonies with extreme cruelty. However, the Japanese reserved the most brutal treatment for Allied prisoners of war. The Japanese considered it dishonorable to surrender, and they had contempt for the prisoners of war in their charge. On the Bataan Death March—a forced march of more than 50 miles up the peninsula—the Japanese subjected their captives to terrible cruelties. Of the approximately 70,000 prisoners who started the Bataan Death March, only 54,000 survived.

The Allies Strike Back Slowly, the Allies began to turn the tide of war. Early in May 1942, an American fleet with Australian support intercepted a Japanese strike force headed for Port Moresby in New Guinea, the site of a critical Allied air base. Control of the air base would put the Japanese in easy striking distance of Australia. In the battle that followed—the Battle of the Coral Sea—both sides used a new kind of naval warfare. The opposing ships did not fire a single shot. Instead, airplanes taking off from huge aircraft carriers attacked the ships. The Allies suffered more losses in ships and troops than did the Japanese. However, the Battle of the Coral Sea was something of a victory, for the Allies had stopped Japan's southward advance.

6.41 Preparing for the Regents

Human and Physical Geography How might the need for oil, rubber, and other raw materials have contributed to Japan's war strategy in the Pacific?

6.42 Preparing for the Regents

Science and Technology What new kind of naval warfare was used in the Battle of the Coral Sea?

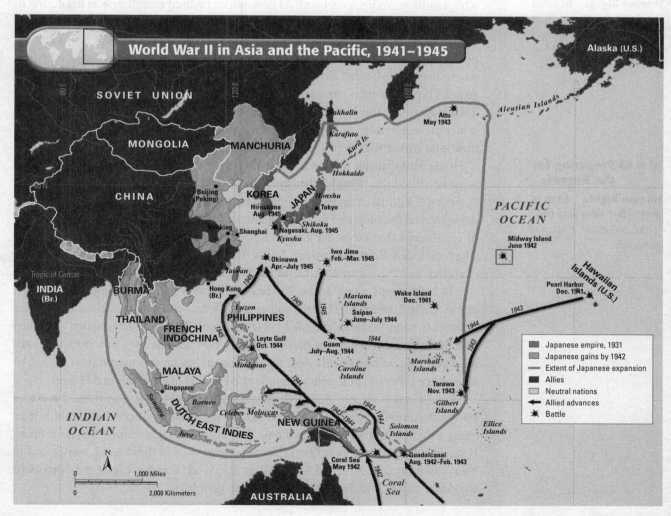

World War II in Asia and the Pacific, 1941–1945

The Holocaust

As Japan worked to establish a new world order in Southeast Asia and the Pacific, the Nazis moved ahead with Hitler's design for a new world order in Europe. The racist message that Hitler had outlined in *Mein Kampf* eventually lead to the **Holocaust**, the systematic mass slaughter of Jews and other groups judged inferior by the Nazis. To gain support for his racist ideas, Hitler knowingly tapped into a hatred for Jews that had deep roots in European history. In Russia, for example, Alexander III had used pogroms (puh•GRAHMS)—organized campaigns of violence—against Jews. Nazis made the targeting of Jews a government policy. The Nuremberg Laws, passed in 1935, deprived Jews of their rights to German citizenship and forbade marriages between Jews and non-Jews. Laws passed later also limited the kinds of work that Jews could do.

Worse was yet to come. Early in November 1938, 17-year-old Herschel Grynszpan (GRIHN•shpahn), a German Jew, was visiting his uncle in Paris. Angered over news that his father was being deported to Poland, Grynszpan shot a German diplomat living in Paris. In response, Nazi leaders launched a violent attack on the Jewish community. On November 9, Nazi storm troopers attacked Jewish homes, businesses, and synagogues across Germany, murdering close to 100 Jews and systematically smashing shop windows. The night became known as *Kristallnacht* (krih•STAHL•NAHKT), or "Night of Broken Glass."

By the end of 1939, a number of German Jews had fled to other countries. Many, however, remained in Germany. Later, Hitler conquered territories in which millions more Jews lived. At first, Hitler favored emigration as a solution to what he called "the Jewish problem." Getting other countries to continue admitting Germany's Jews became an issue, however. Hitler developed a new plan. He ordered Jews in all countries under his control to be moved to designated cities, where they were herded into dismal, overcrowded **ghettos**, or segregated Jewish areas. The Nazis then sealed off the ghettos with barbed wire and stone walls. They hoped that the Jews inside would starve to death or die from disease. Even under these horrible conditions, the Jews hung on. Some formed resistance organizations within the ghettos. They also struggled to keep their traditions.

Impatient waiting for Jews to die from starvation or disease, Hitler launched what he called the "**Final Solution**." It was actually a program of **genocide**, the systematic killing of an entire people. Hitler believed that his plan of conquest depended on the purity of the German race. To protect racial purity, the Nazis had to eliminate other races, nationalities, or groups they viewed as "subhumans." They included Roma (gypsies), Poles, Russians, homosexuals, the insane, the disabled, and the incurably ill. But the Nazis focused especially on the Jews.

As Nazi troops swept across Eastern Europe and the Soviet Union, the killings began. Units from the SS (Hitler's elite security force) and their collaborators rounded up men, women, children, and even babies and took them to isolated spots. They then shot their prisoners in pits that became the prisoners' graves. Jews in communities not reached by the killing squads were rounded up and taken to concentration camps, or slave-labor prisons. These camps were located mainly in Germany and Poland.

The "Final Solution" reached its last stage in 1942. At that time, the Nazis built extermination camps equipped with huge gas chambers that could kill as many as 6,000 human beings in a day. The largest of these camps was Auschwitz (OUSH•vihts). Some six million European Jews died in these death camps and in Nazi massacres. Fewer than four million survived. Some escaped the horrors of the death camps with help from non-Jewish people.

TAKING NOTES

Analyzing Bias Use a web diagram to identify examples of Nazi persecution.

Nazi persecution

6.43 Preparing for the Regents

Human Rights In what ways did the Nazis violate people's human rights during the Holocaust?

6.44 Preparing for the Regents

Human Rights What is genocide? Why was the "Final Solution" a form of genocide.

The War Comes to an End

On December 22, 1941, just after Pearl Harbor, Winston Churchill and President Roosevelt met at the White House to develop a joint war policy. Stalin had asked his allies to relieve German pressure on his armies in the east. He wanted them to open a second front in the west. This would split the Germans' strength by forcing them to fight major battles in two regions instead of one. Churchill agreed with Stalin's strategy. The Allies would weaken Germany on two fronts before dealing a deathblow. Roosevelt ultimately agreed. Stalin wanted the second front to be in France, but Churchill wanted to strike first at North Africa and southern Europe.

The Tide Turns When German general Erwin Rommel took the key Libyan port city of Tobruk in June 1942, London sent General Bernard Montgomery—"Monty" to his troops—to take control of British forces in North Africa. By the time Montgomery arrived, however, the Germans had advanced to an Egyptian village called El Alamein (AL•uh•MAYN), west of Alexandria. Montgomery decided his only option was a massive frontal attack. The Battle of El Alamein began on the night of October 23. By November 4, Rommel's army had been beaten. He and his forces fell back. Then on November 8, an Allied force of more than 100,000 troops led by American general **Dwight D. Eisenhower** landed in Morocco and Algeria. Caught between Montgomery's and Eisenhower's armies, Rommel was finally crushed in May 1943.

German armies also met their match in the Soviet Union. The German advance had stalled at Leningrad and Moscow late in 1941. When the summer of 1942 arrived, Hitler sent his Sixth Army to seize the oil fields in the Caucasus Mountains and capture Stalingrad (now Volgograd), a major industrial center on the Volga River. The **Battle of Stalingrad** began on August 23, 1942. By early November 1942, Germans controlled 90 percent of the city. Then another Russian winter set in. On November 19, Soviet troops outside the city launched a counterattack. Closing in around Stalingrad, they trapped the Germans inside and cut off their supplies. Once again, Hitler would not let his army retreat. On February 2, 1943, some 90,000 frostbitten, half-starved German troops—all that remained of an army of 330,000—surrendered to the Soviets. Stalingrad's defense had cost the Soviets over one million soldiers. The city was 99 percent destroyed. However, the Germans were now on the defensive.

As the Battle of Stalingrad raged, Stalin continued to urge the British and Americans to invade France. However, Roosevelt and Churchill decided to attack Italy first. On July 10, 1943, Allied forces landed on Sicily and captured it from Italian and German troops about a month later. On July 25, King Victor Emmanuel III had Mussolini arrested. On September 3, Italy surrendered. But the Germans seized control of northern Italy and put Mussolini back in charge. Finally, the Germans retreated northward, and the victorious Allies entered Rome on June 4, 1944. Fighting in Italy, continued, however, until Germany fell in May 1945. On April 27, 1945, Italian resistance fighters ambushed some German trucks near the northern Italian city of Milan. Inside one of the trucks, they found Mussolini disguised as a German soldier. They shot him the next day and later hung his body in downtown Milan for all to see.

Victory in Europe In 1943, Stalin finally got his wish. The Allies began secretly building an invasion force in Great Britain. Their plan was to launch an attack on German-held France across the English Channel. By May 1944, the invasion force was ready. Thousands of planes, ships, tanks, and landing craft and more than three million troops awaited the order to attack. General Dwight

TAKING NOTES
Recognizing Effects
Use a chart to identify the outcomes of several major World War II battles.

Battle	Outcome
Battle of El Alamein	
Battle of Stalingrad	
D-Day Invasion	

6.45 Preparing for the Regents

Conflict On what date did the Battle of Stalingrad begin?

6.46 Preparing for the Regents

Human and Physical Geography How did the Soviet Union's size and its climate help the Soviets defend themselves against the Germans?

6.47 Preparing for the Regents

Conflict Why was the invasion of France on D-Day significant? On what date did D-Day begin?

D. Eisenhower, the commander of this enormous force, planned to strike on the coast of Normandy, in northwestern France. Code-named Operation Overlord, the invasion of Normandy was the largest land and sea attack in history. The invasion began on June 6, 1944—known as **D-Day**. At dawn on this day, British, American, French, and Canadian troops fought their way onto a 60-mile stretch of beach in Normandy. The Allies took heavy casualties. Among the American forces alone, more than 2,700 men died on the beaches that day.

Despite heavy losses, the Allies held the beachheads. On July 25, the Allies punched a hole in the German defenses near Saint-Lô (san•LOH), and the United States Third Army, led by General George Patton, broke out. A month later, the Allies marched triumphantly into Paris. By September, they had liberated France, Belgium, and Luxembourg. They then set their sights on Germany.

As the Allied forces moved toward Germany from the west, the Soviet army was advancing toward Germany from the east. Hitler now faced a war on two fronts. In a desperate gamble, he decided to counterattack in the west. On December 16, German tanks broke through weak American defenses along a 75-mile front in northern France. The push into Allied lines gave the campaign its name—the **Battle of the Bulge**. Although caught off guard, the Allies eventually pushed the Germans back. The Germans had little choice but retreat, since there were no reinforcements available.

After the Battle of the Bulge, the war in Europe rapidly drew to a close. By the middle of April, a noose was closing around Berlin. Hitler prepared for his end in an underground headquarters beneath the crumbling city. On April 29, he married his longtime companion, Eva Braun. The next day, Hitler and Eva Braun committed suicide. Their bodies were then carried outside and burned.

On May 7, 1945, General Eisenhower accepted the unconditional surrender of the Third Reich from the German military. President Roosevelt, however, did not live to witness the long-awaited victory. He had died suddenly on April 12. Roosevelt's successor, Harry Truman, received the news of the Nazi surrender. On May 9, the surrender was officially signed in Berlin. The United States and other Allied powers celebrated V-E Day—Victory in Europe Day.

Victory in the Pacific Although the war in Europe was over, the Allies were still fighting the Japanese in the Pacific. With the Allied victories in the **Battle of Midway** in June 1942 and the **Battle of Guadalcanal** in February 1943, however, the Japanese advances in the Pacific had been stopped. By the fall of 1944, the Allies were moving in on Japan. In October, Allied forces defeated the Japanese navy in the Battle of Leyte (LAY•tee) Gulf in the Philippines. Now, only the Japanese army and its feared kamikazes stood between the Allies and Japan. The **kamikazes** were Japanese suicide pilots.

In March 1945, after a month of bitter fighting and heavy losses, American Marines took Iwo Jima (EE•wuh JEE•muh), an island 760 miles from Tokyo. On April 1, U.S. troops moved onto the island of Okinawa, only about 350 miles from southern Japan. The Japanese put up a desperate fight. Nevertheless, on June 21, one of the bloodiest land battles of the war ended. The Japanese lost over 100,000 troops, and the Americans 12,000.

After Okinawa, the next stop for the Allies had to be Japan. President Truman's advisers had informed him that an invasion of the Japanese homeland might cost the Allies half a million lives. Truman had to decide whether to use a powerful new weapon called the atomic bomb, or A-bomb. Most of his advisers felt that using it would bring the war to the quickest possible end.

6.48 Preparing for the Regents

Science and Technology What role did new weapons play in ending the war in the Pacific?

President Truman then warned the Japanese that unless they surrendered, they could expect a "rain of ruin from the air." The Japanese did not reply. So, on August 6, the United States dropped an atomic bomb on Hiroshima, a Japanese city of nearly 350,000 people. Between 70,000 and 80,000 people died in the attack. Three days later, on August 9, a second bomb was dropped on Nagasaki, a city of 270,000. More than 70,000 people were killed immediately. Radiation fallout from the two explosions killed many more.

The Japanese finally surrendered on September 2. The ceremony took place aboard the United States battleship *Missouri* in Tokyo Bay. With Japan's surrender, the war had ended. Now, countries faced the task of rebuilding a war-torn world.

The War's Aftermath

After six long years of war, the Allies finally were victorious. However, their victory had been achieved at a very high price. World War II had caused more death and destruction than any other conflict in history. It left 60 million dead. About one-third of these deaths occurred in one country, the Soviet Union. Another 50 million people had been uprooted from their homes and wandered the countryside in search of somewhere to live. Property damage ran into billions of U.S. dollars.

While nations were struggling to recover, they also tried to deal with the issue of war crimes. During 1945 and 1946, an International Military Tribunal representing 23 nations put Nazi war criminals on trial in Nuremberg, Germany. In the first of these **Nuremberg Trials**, 22 Nazi leaders were charged with waging a war of aggression. They were also accused of committing "crimes against humanity"—the murder of 11 million people. Hitler and several of his top staff had committed suicide long before the trials began. However, Hermann Göring, the commander of the Luftwaffe; Rudolf Hess, Hitler's former deputy; and other high-ranking Nazi leaders remained to face the charges. Hess was found guilty and was sentenced to life in prison. Göring received a death sentence, but cheated the executioner by committing suicide. Ten other Nazi leaders were hanged on October 16, 1946. The bodies of those executed were burned at the concentration camp of Dachau (DAHK•ow). They were cremated in the same ovens that had burned so many of their victims.

6.49 Preparing for the Regents

Conflict On what dates were the bombs dropped on Hiroshima and Nagasaki?

6.50 Preparing for the Regents

Justice What were the Nuremberg Trials? What did they accomplish?

PREPARING FOR THE REGENTS

Answer the following question. Use the Analyze the Question hints to help you answer the question.

1 A. **Atomic bombs dropped on Hiroshima and Nagasaki.**
   B. **Allies invade Europe on D-Day.**
   C. **Germany invades Poland.**
   D. **Japanese attack Pearl Harbor.**

Which sequence shows the correct chronological order of these World War II events, from earliest to latest?

(1) A ➔ B ➔ C ➔ D
(2) B ➔ A ➔ D ➔ C
(3) C ➔ D ➔ B ➔ A
(4) D ➔ C ➔ A ➔ B

ANALYZE THE QUESTION
• Read the question stem. You are being asked to list the events in the order they occurred.
• Think about the date of each event.
• Select the alternative that places the events in the correct order.

UNIT 6 A Half Century of Crisis and Achievement (1900–1945)

Part I: MULTIPLE-CHOICE QUESTIONS

Directions (1–10): For each statement or question, write on a separate answer sheet the *number* of the word or expression that, of those given, best completes the statement or answers the questions.

Unemployment Rate, 1928–1938

Percent of Work Force

□ Great Britain ■ Germany ■ United States

Sources: *European Historical Statistics: 1750–1970;
Historical Statistics of the United States: Colonial Times to 1970.*

1 According to the graph above, in what year was the difference between British and German unemployment levels the greatest?

  (1) 1928   (3) 1934
  (2) 1930   (4) 1938

2 The process that France, Britain, and Italy chose to follow at the Munich Conference is known as

  (1) appeasement   (3) self-determination
  (2) liberation   (4) pacification

3 One similarity between the pogroms in Russia and the Nazi Holocaust is that both

  (1) expanded the power of labor unions
  (2) limited the power of European rulers
  (3) prohibited government censorship
  (4) violated the human rights of Jews

4 Kemal Ataturk's efforts to modernize Turkish culture were most strongly opposed by?

  (1) Indian nationalists (3) industrialists
  (2) republicans   (4) religious forces

5 The early 20th-century Zionist movement calling for a Jewish homeland was an example of

  (1) imperialism   (3) capitalism
  (2) nationalism   (4) isolationism

"Archduke Franz Ferdinand Assassinated!"
"Germany Declares War on Russia and France!"
"Peace Treaty Signed at Versailles!"

6 Which event is referred to in these headlines?

  (1) Franco-Prussian War
  (2) Crimean War
  (3) World War I
  (4) Cold War

7 During World War II, which event occurred last?

  (1) German invasion of Poland
  (2) Russian defense of Stalingrad
  (3) United States bombing of Hiroshima and Nagasaki
  (4) Japanese invasion of Manchuria

8 Nazi Germany, Fascist Italy, and Communist Russia were similar in that each

  (1) protected individual rights
  (2) elected their leaders through popular vote
  (3) supported market-based economies
  (4) established totalitarian governments

9 Which statement best describes a relationship between World War I and the Bolshevik Revolution?

  (1) World War I created conditions in Russia that helped trigger a revolution.
  (2) World War I postponed the revolution in Russia by restoring confidence in the czar.
  (3) Opposing Russian forces cooperated to fight the foreign invaders.
  (4) World War I gave the czar's army the needed experience to suppress the revolution.

10 What was the major goal of Joseph Stalin's five-year plans in the Soviet Union?

  (1) encouraging rapid industrialization
  (2) supporting capitalism
  (3) improving literacy rates
  (4) including peasants in the decision-making process

In developing your answers to Parts II and III, be sure to keep these general definitions in mind:

(a) *discuss* means "to make observations about something using facts, reasoning, and argument; to present in some detail"

(b) *describe* means "to illustrate something in words or tell about it"

(c) *evaluate* means "to examine and judge the significance, worth, or condition of; to determine the value of"

Part II: THEMATIC ESSAY

Directions: Write a well-organized essay that includes an introduction, several paragraphs addressing the task below, and a conclusion.

Theme: Justice and Human Rights

Throughout history, the human rights of certain groups of people have been violated. Efforts have been made to address these violations.

Task:

- Define the term "human rights"
- Identify *two* examples of human rights violations that have occurred in a specific time and place
- Describe the causes of these human rights violations
- For *one* of the violations identified, discuss one specific effort that was made or is being made to deal with the violation

You may use any example from your study of Unit Six. Some suggestions you might wish to consider include the Armenian Massacre, human rights under Stalin, and the Jews in Nazi Germany.

You are not limited to these suggestions.

Guidelines:

In your essay, be sure to
- Address all aspects of the *Task*
- Support the theme with relevant facts, examples, and details
- Use a logical and clear plan of organization, including an introduction and a conclusion that are beyond the simple restatement of the *Theme*

Part III: DOCUMENT-BASED QUESTION

This question is based on the accompanying documents (1–3). The question is designed to test your ability to work with historic documents. Some of these documents have been edited for the purpose of this question. As you analyze the documents, take into account both the source of each document and any point of view that may be presented in the document.

Historical Context:

Throughout history, many nations have attempted to change their economic systems with mixed results.

Task:

Using information from the documents and your knowledge of global history, answer the question that follows each document in Part A. Your answers to the questions will help you write the Part B essay, in which you will be asked to:

- Discuss how the Soviet Union under Lenin and Stalin attempted to bring about economic reform and describe the economic system that was in place before the change
- Evaluate the impact of the economic reform

Part A: Short Answer

Directions: Analyze the documents and answer the short-answer questions that follow in the space provided.

Document 1

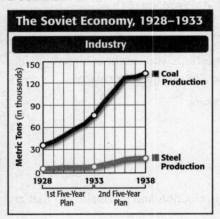

Document 2

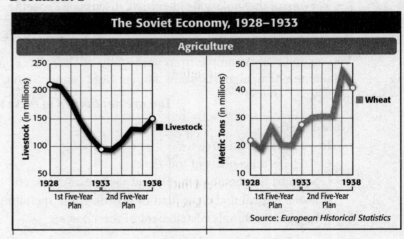

1 According to Document 1, how much did coal production increase between 1928 and 1933?

_____

2 According to Document 2, which Five-Year Plan produced the greatest increase in wheat production?

_____

Document 3 a and b

Stalin's first Five-Tear Plan, adopted in 1928, called for rapid industrialization of the economy, with an emphasis on heavy industry. It set goals that were unrealistic—a 250 percent increase in overall industrial development and a 330 percent expansion in heavy industry alone. All industry and services were nationalized, managers were given predetermined output quotas by central planners, and trade unions were converted into mechanisms for increasing worker productivity.

The Socialist way . . . is to set up collective farms and state farms which leads to the joining together of the small peasant farms into large collective farms, technically and scientifically equipped, and to the squeezing out of the capitalist elements of Agriculture . . .

3 What were Stalin's economic policies toward industry and agriculture?

_____

_____

_____

_____

Part B: Essay

Directions: Write a well-organized essay that includes an introduction, several paragraphs, and a conclusion. Use evidence from at least *two* documents to support your response.

Historical Context: Throughout history, many nations have attempted to change their economic systems with mixed results.

Task: Using information from the documents and your knowledge of global history, answer the question that follows each document in Part A. Your answers to the questions will help you write the Part B essay, in which you will be asked to:

- Discuss how the Soviet Union under Lenin and Stalin attempted to bring about economic reform and describe the economic system that was in place before the change
- Evaluate the impact of the economic reform

Guidelines:

In your essay, be sure to

- Address all aspects of the *Task* by accurately analyzing and interpreting at least **two** documents
- Incorporate information from the documents
- Incorporate relevant outside information
- Support the theme with relevant facts, examples, and details
- Use a logical and clear plan of organization
- Introduce the theme by establishing a framework that is beyond a simple statement of the *Task* or *Historical Context* and conclude with a summation of the theme

UNIT 7

The Twentieth Century Since 1945

Unit Overview

This unit examines the period in global history from World War II to the present. The unit begins by looking at the causes and consequences of the Cold War and the rise of communism in China. It then focuses on the collapse of European imperialism that led to the birth of new nations in Africa and Asia. Next, it looks at the breakup of the Soviet Union that followed the collapse of its Communist system. The unit closes by examining conditions in the Middle East and Latin America .

Concepts and Themes

Among the concepts and themes explored in this unit are

- Change
- Conflict
- Decision Making
- Economic Systems
- Human and Physical Geography

- Human Rights
- Nationalism
- Political Systems
- Power
- Science and Technology

PREPARING FOR THE REGENTS: Building Thematic Essay Skills

Turning points are major events in history that have led to lasting change. Since World War II, the world has experienced many major turning points. The Communist Revolution in China, the collapse of European imperialism, and the collapse of the Soviet Union are just three notable examples. As you read this unit, think about how these and the other events you encounter produced lasting changes. Use the following chart to organize information about these events. You can add additional rows as needed.

Turning Point	Circumstances Surrounding the Turning Point	Changes Produced by the Turning Point

The Cold War Balance of Power

Section Overview

During World War II, the United States and the Soviet Union had joined forces to fight against the Germans. The Soviet army marched west; the Americans marched east. When the Allied soldiers met at the Elbe River in Germany in 1945, they embraced each other warmly because they had defeated the Nazis. Their leaders, however, regarded each other much more coolly. The United States' coolness turned to alarm when the Soviet Union installed or secured Communist governments in Albania, Bulgaria, Hungary, Czechoslovakia, Romania, Poland, and Yugoslavia following the war.

As the "iron curtain" of communism dropped on Eastern Europe, the United States and the Soviet Union entered a nearly half-century of hostility called the Cold War. The Cold War dictated U.S. and Soviet foreign policy, as each side tried to stop the other from extending its power. It also influenced world alliances. The United States, Canada, and ten western European nations formed a defensive military alliance called the North Atlantic Treaty Organization (NATO). The Soviet Union and its satellite nations formed the Warsaw Pact. Other nations of the world struggled to remain independent, or nonaligned.

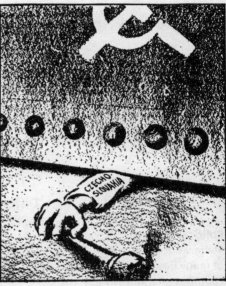

The iron curtain drops on Czechoslovakia, 1948

MAIN IDEAS

ECONOMICS Two conflicting economic systems, capitalism and communism, competed for influence and power after World War II. The superpowers in this struggle were the United States and the Soviet Union.

EMPIRE BUILDING The United States and the Soviet Union used military, economic, and humanitarian aid to extend their control over other countries. Each also tried to prevent the other superpower from gaining influence.

TERMS AND NAMES

- United Nations
- iron curtain
- demilitarization
- democratization
- Marshall Plan
- containment
- Truman Doctrine
- Cold War
- NATO
- Warsaw Pact
- nonaligned nations
- Third World
- brinkmanship
- Nikita Khrushchev
- Leonid Brezhnev

PREPARING FOR THE REGENTS

As you read this section, consider
- what impact the Cold War conflict between the superpowers had on other nations of the world.
- why nations like Greece and Turkey were important in the struggle.

TIME LINE

1945
United Nations formed.

1948
United States launches the Marshall Plan.

1948
Soviets begin the Berlin blockage.

1949
NATO is formed.

1955
Warsaw Pact is formed.

1958
Hungarian Revolt begins.

1959
Soviets launch *Sputnik*.

1968
Soviets invade Czechoslovakia to end revolt.

The World in 1945: The Physical and Human Setting

The war was not yet over in February 1945. But the leaders of the United States, Britain, and the Soviet Union met at the Soviet Black Sea resort of Yalta. There, they agreed to divide Germany into zones of occupation controlled by the Allied military forces. Germany also would have to pay the Soviet Union to compensate for its loss of life and property. Stalin promised that Eastern Europeans would have free elections.

Creation of the United Nations In June 1945, the United States, Britain, and the Soviet Union joined 47 other countries in forming the **United Nations** (UN). This international peacekeeping organization, which was to be based in New York, was intended to protect the members against aggression. The charter established a large body called the General Assembly. There, each UN member nation could cast its vote on a broad range of issues. An 11-member body called the Security Council had the real power to investigate and settle disputes, though. Its five permanent members were Britain, China, France, the United States, and the Soviet Union. Each could veto any Security Council action. This provision was intended to prevent any members from voting as a bloc to override the others.

Differing U.S. and Soviet Goals Despite agreement at Yalta and their presence on the UN Security Council, the United States and the Soviet Union had very different goals following the war. A major goal of the Soviet Union was to shield itself from another invasion from the west. After they had pushed the Nazis back across Eastern Europe at the end of the war, Soviet troops had occupied a strip of countries along the Soviet Union's western border. Stalin regarded these countries as a necessary buffer, or wall of protection. Ignoring his Yalta promise, he extended communism's power by installing or securing Communist governments in Albania, Bulgaria, Hungary, Czechoslovakia, Romania, Poland, and Yugoslavia.

TAKING NOTES

Following Chronological Order Organize important early Cold War events in a time line.

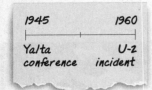

1945	1960
Yalta conference	U-2 incident

📐 7.1 Preparing for the Regents

Conflict Why was the United Nations formed?

📐 7.2 Preparing for the Regents

Political Systems Why did Stalin want keep control of many Eastern European countries after the World War II?

Superpower Aims in Europe

- ▨ Communist countries, 1948
- ▢ Non-Communist countries, 1948
- ▬ Iron curtain

N

0　　500 Miles
0　　1,000 Kilometers

NORWAY, SWEDEN, FINLAND, DENMARK, *North Sea*, *Baltic Sea*, IRELAND, GREAT BRITAIN, NETH., BELG., LUX., WEST GERMANY, E. GER., POLAND, SOVIET UNION, CZECHOSLOVAKIA, FRANCE, SWITZ., AUSTRIA, HUNGARY, ROMANIA, YUGOSLAVIA, ITALY, BULGARIA, *Black Sea*, ALBANIA, GREECE, TURKEY, PORTUGAL, SPAIN, *ATLANTIC OCEAN*, *Mediterranean Sea*

Superpower Aims in Europe

American president Harry S. Truman believed that Stalin's reluctance to allow free elections in Eastern European nations was a clear violation of those countries' rights. Truman, Stalin, and Churchill met at Potsdam, Germany, in July 1945. There, Truman pressed Stalin to permit free elections in Eastern Europe. The Soviet leader refused. In a speech in early 1946, Stalin declared that communism and capitalism could not exist in the same world.

A Divided Europe Europe now lay divided between East and West. Winston Churchill described the division of Europe: "From Stettin in the Baltic to Trieste in the Adriatic, an iron curtain has descended across the continent. Behind that line lie all the capitals of the ancient states of Central and Eastern Europe." Churchill's phrase "**iron curtain**" came to represent Europe's division into mostly democratic Western Europe and communist Eastern Europe.

Rebuilding Europe and Japan

Japan and much of Western Europe lay in ruins after World War II. There was also economic turmoil—a scarcity of jobs and food. In addition, the Allies needed to deal with the defeated nations of Germany and Japan.

The Occupation of Germany At the Yalta Conference, the Allies had divided Germany into four military occupation zones. France, Britain, the United States, and the Soviet Union each oversaw one zone. The rise of the iron curtain effectively split Germany into two sections. The Soviets controlled the eastern part. France, Britain, and the United States controlled the western part.

The United States and its allies clashed with the Soviet Union over Germany. The Soviets wanted to keep Germany weak and divided. But in 1948, France, Britain, and the United States decided to withdraw their forces from Germany and allow their occupation zones to form one nation. The Soviet Union responded by holding West Berlin hostage. Although Berlin lay well within the Soviet occupation zone, it too had been divided into four zones. The Soviet Union cut off highway, water, and rail traffic into Berlin's western zones. The city faced starvation. Stalin gambled that the Allies would surrender West Berlin or give up their idea of reunifying Germany. But American and British officials flew food and supplies into West Berlin for nearly 11 months. In May 1949, the Soviet Union admitted defeat and lifted the blockade. That same year, the western zones became the Federal Republic of Germany, and Communist East Germany was named the German Democratic Republic.

The Occupation of Japan The United States also took charge of the occupation of postwar Japan. General Douglas MacArthur led the efforts. MacArthur began a process of **demilitarization**, or disbanding the Japanese armed forces, and launched war-crimes trials. He then turned his attention to **democratization**, the process of creating a government elected by the people. In February 1946, he and his American political advisers drew up a new constitution that changed the empire into a constitutional monarchy like that of Great Britain. Like the ruler of Great Britain, the emperor became largely a figurehead—a symbol of Japan. The new constitution, which went into effect on May 3, 1947, guaranteed that real political power rested with the people. The people elected a two-house parliament, called the Diet. All citizens over the age of 20, including women, had the right to vote. The government was led by a prime minister chosen by a majority of the Diet. In addition, Article 9 of the constitution stated that the Japanese could no longer make war. They could fight only if attacked.

MacArthur's objectives included broadening land ownership and increasing the participation of workers and farmers in the new democracy. Thus, he put forward a plan that required absentee landlords with huge estates to sell land to the government. The government then sold the land to tenant farmers at reasonable prices. Other reforms gave workers the right to create independent labor unions.

The Marshall Plan The United States also took steps to help rebuild Europe. In 1947, U.S. Secretary of State George Marshall proposed that the United States give aid to needy European countries. This assistance program, called the **Marshall Plan**, would provide food, machinery, and other materials to rebuild Western Europe. As Congress debated the $12.5 billion program in 1948, the Communists seized power in Czechoslovakia. Congress immediately voted approval. Under the Marshall Plan, nations like West Germany, Turkey, and Greece that were under threats from communism received financial aid.

TAKING NOTES

Comparing and Contrasting Use a Venn diagram to compare and contrast the aftermath of World War II in Europe and Japan.

Europe only

both

Japan only

7.3 Preparing for the Regents

Conflict Why did the Soviets blockade Berlin?

7.4 Preparing for the Regents

Political and Economic Systems What reforms did General Douglas MacArthur undertake during the U.S. occupation of Japan?

7.5 Preparing for the Regents

Political and Economic Systems What was the Marshall Plan? How did it help promote political stability in Europe?

The Political Climate of the Cold War

The Marshall Plan was part of President Truman's foreign policy of **containment**. The policy aimed to block Soviet influence and stop the expansion of communism. Containment policies included forming alliances and helping weak countries resist Soviet advances. As part of this strategy, Congress authorized more than $400 million in aid to Turkey and Greece prior to the Marshall Plan. This support for countries that rejected communism was called the **Truman Doctrine**.

The United States and the Soviet Union—the world's superpowers—were soon locked in the **Cold War**. A cold war is a struggle over political differences carried on by means short of military action or war. Beginning in 1949, the superpowers used spying, propaganda, diplomacy, and secret organizations in their dealings with each other. Much of the world allied with one side or the other.

NATO and the Warsaw Pact The Berlin blockade had heightened Western Europe's fears of Soviet aggression. As a result, in 1949, ten Western European nations joined the United States and Canada to form a defensive military alliance called the North Atlantic Treaty Organization (**NATO**). An attack on any NATO member would be met with armed force by all members. In 1955, the Soviets responded by forming their own alliance, the **Warsaw Pact**. It included the Soviet Union, East Germany, Czechoslovakia, Poland, Hungary, Romania, Bulgaria, and Albania. In 1961, the East Germans built a wall to separate East and West Berlin. The Berlin Wall symbolized a world divided into rival camps.

The Role of Nonaligned Nations Not every country joined the new alliances. Some, like India, chose not to align with either side. And China, the largest Communist country, remained unaligned out of distrust of the Soviet Union. In 1955, Indonesia, a populous island nation in Southeast Asia, hosted many leaders from Asia and Africa at the Bandung Conference. They met to form what they called a "third force" of independent countries, or **nonaligned nations**.

Many of the nonaligned countries were developing nations, often newly independent, in Latin America, Africa, and Asia. They came to be called the **Third World**. (The first world was the United States and the capitalist nations allied with it. The second world was the Communist nations led by the Soviet Union.) To gain influence in the Third World, the superpowers backed wars of revolution, liberation, or counterrevolution. Although the superpowers did not fight each other directly, they fought indirectly by backing opposing sides in these surrogate wars. (Surrogate means substitute.) Their intelligence agencies engaged in covert, or secret, activities, ranging from spying to assassination attempts. The United States also gave military aid, built schools, set up programs to fight poverty, and sent volunteers to many developing nations. The Soviets offered military and technical assistance, mainly to India and Egypt.

Nuclear Weapons and Space As the alliances were forming, the Cold War threatened to heat up enough to destroy the world. The United States already had atomic bombs. In 1949, the Soviet Union exploded its own atomic weapon. President Truman responded by authorizing work on the hydrogen or H-bomb, a weapon thousands of times more powerful than the A-bomb. In 1952, the United States tested the first H-bomb. The Soviets exploded their own in 1953.

When Dwight D. Eisenhower became the U.S. president in 1953, he appointed the firmly anti-Communist John Foster Dulles as his secretary of state. Dulles issued a warning—if the Soviet Union or its supporters attacked U.S. interests, the United States would "retaliate instantly, by means and at places of our own

7.6 Preparing for the Regents

Political Systems What was the Truman Doctrine? What was its purpose?

7.7 Preparing for the Regents

Conflict Why were NATO and the Warsaw Pact formed?

7.8 Preparing for the Regents

Conflict What was the goal of the nonaligned nations?

7.9 Preparing for the Regents

Economic and Political Systems What is meant by the Third World? How did the superpowers try to gain influence in the Third World?

7.10 Preparing for the Regents

Science and Technology What factors led to the arms race and the space race?

choosing." This willingness to go to the brink, or edge, of war became known as **brinkmanship**. Brinkmanship required a reliable source of nuclear weapons and airplanes to deliver them. The arms race was on as both sides began strengthening their air force and stockpiling nuclear weapons.

The Cold War also affected space. In August 1957, the Soviets announced the development of a rocket that could travel great distances—an intercontinental ballistic missile, or ICBM. On October 4, the Soviets used an ICBM to push *Sputnik*, the first unmanned satellite, above the earth's atmosphere. In 1958, the United States launched its own satellite, *Explorer I*. The space race had begun.

In 1960, the skies again provided the arena for a superpower conflict. In May 1960, the Soviets shot down a high-altitude U.S. spy plane called a U-2. The plane's pilot, Francis Gary Powers, was captured. This U-2 incident heightened Cold War tensions.

Soviet Policy in Eastern Europe Joseph Stalin died in 1953. **Nikita Khrushchev** became the dominant Soviet leader. In 1956, Khrushchev denounced Stalin for jailing and killing loyal Soviet citizens. His speech signaled the start of a policy called destalinization, or purging the country of Stalin's memory. Khrushchev called for "peaceful competition" with capitalist states.

But this new Soviet outlook did not change life in satellite countries. In October 1956, the Hungarian army joined protesters to overthrow Hungary's Soviet-controlled government. A popular and liberal Hungarian Communist leader named Imre Nagy (IHM•ray nahj) formed a new government. Nagy promised free elections and demanded Soviet troops leave. In response, Soviet tanks and infantry entered Budapest in November, overwhelming the freedom fighters. A pro-Soviet government was installed, and Nagy was eventually executed.

In 1964, Khrushchev was replaced by **Leonid Brezhnev**. Brezhnev quickly made clear that he would not tolerate dissent in Eastern Europe. His policy was put to the test in early 1968 when Czech Communist leader Alexander Dubček (DOOB•chehk) loosened controls on censorship to offer his country socialism with "a human face." This period of reform, when Czechoslovakia's capital bloomed with new ideas, became known as Prague Spring. However, it did not survive the summer. On August 20, armed forces from the Warsaw Pact nations invaded Czechoslovakia. Brezhnev justified this invasion by claiming the Soviet Union had the right to prevent its satellites from rejecting communism, a policy known as the Brezhnev Doctrine.

7.11 Preparing for the Regents

Conflict   What is brinkmanship?

7.12 Preparing for the Regents

Power   How did the Soviet Union respond to revolts in Hungary and Czechoslovakia?

PREPARING FOR THE REGENTS

On a separate sheet of paper, write a well-organized essay that includes an introduction, several paragraphs addressing the task below, and a conclusion. Before beginning, check the Score the Essay box for pointers.

Theme: Conflict
Differences among groups have often led to conflict.

Task:
- Discuss the historical circumstances that led to the Cold War
- Analyze the effect of the Cold War on *two* groups involved

Be sure to include specific examples in your essay.

SCORE THE ESSAY   To receive a score of 5 on your essay, you will need to:
- thoroughly develop all aspects of the task evenly and in depth by discussing the historical circumstances surrounding the Cold War and the effects on two of the groups involved.
- be more analytical than descriptive.
- richly support the theme with relevant facts, examples, and details.
- demonstrate a logical and clear plan of organization.

The Chinese Communist Revolution

Section Overview

After the Communists came to power in China in 1949, Mao Zedong set out to transform China. Mao believed that peasant equality, revolutionary spirit, and hard work were all that was needed to improve the Chinese economy. However, lack of modern technology damaged Chinese efforts to increase agricultural and industrial output. In addition, Mao's policies stifled economic growth. He eliminated incentives for higher production and he tried to replace family life with life in the communes. These policies took away the peasants' motive to work for the good of themselves and their families.

Facing economic disaster, some Chinese Communists talked of modernizing the economy. Accusing them of "taking the capitalist road," Mao began the Cultural Revolution in 1966 to cleanse China of antirevolutionary influences. Instead of saving radical communism, however, the Cultural Revolution turned many people against it. When Deng Xiaoping came to power in 1980, he instituted many economic reforms that increased China's economic growth and dramatically reduced poverty. These economic reforms, however, did not lead to political reforms. A prodemocracy movement in 1989 led to bloodshed in Beijing's Tiananmen Square, as Chinese soldiers fired on crowds of student protesters.

Chinese Communist leader
Mao Zedong (1893–1976)

MAIN IDEAS

REVOLUTION   After World War II, Chinese Communists defeated Nationalist forces and two separate Chinas emerged.

CULTURAL INTERACTION   In response to contact with the West, China's government has experimented with capitalism but has rejected calls for democracy.

TERMS AND NAMES

- Mao Zedong
- Jiang Jieshi
- Long March
- commune
- Red Guards
- Cultural Revolution
- Zhou Enlai
- Deng Xiaoping
- Four Modernizations
- Tiananmen Square
- Hong Kong

PREPARING FOR THE REGENTS

As you read this section, consider
- how the Communist Revolution in China was similar to other revolutions.
- how successful Mao was in meeting the needs of the Chinese.
- why Communists under Deng Xiaoping were willing to adopt elements of the West's market economies but not the West's concept of human rights.

TIME LINE

1949
Communists take control of China.

1958
Mao Zedong begins the Great Leap Forward.

1966
Mao Zedong launches the Cultural Revolution.

1978
Deng Xiaoping begins economic reforms in China.

1989
Chinese soldiers attack prodemocracy protesters in Tiananmen Square.

1997
Hong Kong is returned to Chinese control.

Human and Physical Geography: The Communist Rise to Power

When the Japanese invaded China in 1937, a bitter civil war was raging between the Nationalists and the Communists. The Chinese Communist Party had been founded in 1921 by **Mao Zedong** (MOW dzuh•dahng) and others. Mao believed that he could bring Soviet-style communism to China by mobilizing the peasants. The Nationalists under Sun Yixian had allied with the new Communist Party. However, when Sun Yixian died in 1925, **Jiang Jieshi** (jee•ahng jee•shee), formerly called Chiang Kai-shek, took over leadership of the Nationalists. Jiang was the son of a middle-class merchant, and most of his followers were middle class. They feared the Communists' goal of creating a socialist economy modeled after the Soviet Union's. In 1927, Nationalist troops and armed gangs attacked and killed many Communist leaders and trade union members in Shanghai and other cities. They nearly wiped out the Chinese Communist Party. Then, in 1928, Jiang became president of the Nationalist Republic of China. By 1930, the Nationalists and the Communists were fighting a bloody civil war.

The Chinese Civil War Mao and other Communist leaders established themselves in the hills of south-central China, where they trained peasants in guerrilla warfare. In 1933, Jiang surrounded the Communists' mountain stronghold with an army of at least 700,000 men. Outnumbered, 100,000 Communist forces fled in what came to be called the **Long March**, a hazardous, 6,000-mile-long journey. Thousands died from hunger, cold, exposure, and battle wounds. Finally, after a little more than a year, Mao and the seven or eight thousand Communist survivors settled in caves in northwestern China.

The Japanese invasion of China in 1937 forced an uneasy truce between Jiang's and Mao's forces. From his stronghold in northwestern China, Mao fought a guerrilla war against the Japanese. By 1945, the Communists controlled much of northern China. The Nationalist forces under Jiang dominated southwestern China. Jiang gathered an army of 2.5 million men.

After Japan surrendered, the Nationalists and the Communists resumed fighting. The renewed civil war lasted from 1946 to 1949. At first, a large and well-funded army gave the Nationalists the advantage. The Nationalist forces, however, did little to win popular support. With China's economy collapsing, thousands of Nationalist soldiers deserted to the Communists. In spring 1949, China's major cities fell to the Communists. The remnants of Jiang's shattered army fled south. In October 1949, Mao Zedong gained control of the country. He proclaimed it the People's Republic of China. Jiang and other Nationalist leaders retreated to the island of Taiwan, which Westerners called Formosa.

Two Chinas China had split into two nations. The island of Taiwan, or Nationalist China, had an area of 13,000 square miles. With the aid of the United States, Jiang set up a government and named the nation the Republic of China. The mainland, or People's Republic of China, had an area of more than 3.5 million square miles. The Soviets gave financial, military, and technical aid to Communist China. In addition, the Chinese and the Soviets pledged to come to each other's defense if either was attacked. (This bond would break by the late 1950s, as each sought to lead the worldwide Communist movement.) In the early years of Mao's reign, Chinese troops expanded into Tibet, India, and southern, or Inner, Mongolia. Northern, or Outer, Mongolia, which bordered the Soviet Union, remained in the Soviet sphere.

TAKING NOTES

Recognizing Effects
Use a chart to identify the causes and effects of the Communist Revolution in China.

Cause	Effect
1.	1.
2.	2.
3.	3.

7.13 Preparing for the Regents

Conflict What was the Long March?

7.14 Preparing for the Regents

Political and Economic Systems Why might the splitting of China into two nations have contributed to Cold War tensions?

Communism Under Mao Zedong

After taking control of China, the Communists began to tighten their hold. Like the Soviets, the Chinese Communists set up two parallel organizations, the Communist Party and the national government. Mao headed both until 1959.

7.15 Preparing for the Regents

Economic Systems What did Mao hope to accomplish with his first five-year plan? How were his goals similar to those of Joseph Stalin in the Soviet Union?

Mao's Brand of Marxist Socialism Mao was determined to reshape China's economy based on Marxist socialism. Although 80 percent of the people lived in rural areas, 10 percent of the rural population controlled 70 percent of the farmland. Under the Agrarian Reform Law of 1950, Mao seized the holdings of these landlords and divided the land among the peasants. Later, to further Mao's socialist principles, the government forced peasants to join collective farms. Each of these farms was comprised of 200 to 300 households. Mao's changes also transformed industry and business. Gradually, private companies were nationalized, or brought under government ownership. In 1953, Mao launched a five-year plan that set high production goals for industry. By 1957, China's output of coal, cement, steel, and electricity had increased dramatically.

7.16 Preparing for the Regents

Economic Systems What was Mao's "Great Leap Forward"? How successful was his plan?

"The Great Leap Forward" To expand the success of the first five-year plan, Mao proclaimed the "Great Leap Forward" in early 1958. This plan called for still larger collective farms, or **communes**. By the end of 1958, about 26,000 communes had been created. The average commune sprawled over 15,000 acres and supported over 25,000 people. In the strictly controlled life of the communes, peasants worked the land together. They ate in communal dining rooms, slept in communal dormitories, and raised children in communal nurseries. And they owned nothing. The peasants had no incentive to work hard when only the state profited from their labor. The Great Leap Forward was a giant step backward. Poor planning and inefficient "backyard," or home, industries hampered growth. The program was ended in 1961 after crop failures caused a famine that killed about 20 million people.

The Red Guards and the Cultural Revolution After the failure of the Great Leap Forward, Mao reduced his role in government. Other leaders moved away from Mao's strict socialist ideas. For example, farm families could live in their own homes and could sell crops they grew on small private plots. Factory workers could compete for wage increases and promotions.

Mao thought China's new economic policies weakened the Communist goal of social equality. In 1966, he urged China's young people to "learn revolution by making revolution." Millions of high school and college students responded. They left their classrooms and formed militia units called **Red Guards**.

7.17 Preparing for the Regents

Change Who were the Red Guards?

Mao's Attempts to Change China	
Mao's Programs	**Program Results**
First Five-Year Plan 1953–1957	• Industry grew 15 percent a year. • Agricultural output grew very slowly.
Great Leap Forward 1958–1961	• China suffered economic disaster—industrial declines and food shortages. • Mao lost influence.
Cultural Revolution 1966–1976	• Mao regained influence by backing radicals. • Purges and conflicts among leaders created economic, social, and political chaos.

The Red Guards led a major uprising known as the **Cultural Revolution**. Its goal was to establish a society of peasants and workers in which all were equal. The new hero was the peasant who worked with his hands. Intellectual and artistic activities were considered useless and dangerous. Red Guards shut down colleges and schools and targeted anyone who resisted the regime. Intellectuals had to "purify" themselves by doing hard labor in remote villages. Thousands were executed or imprisoned. Chaos threatened farm production and closed down factories. Civil war seemed possible. The army was ordered to put down the Red Guards.

Communism Under Deng Xiaoping

Throughout the Cultural Revolution, China played almost no role in world affairs. China's isolation worried **Zhou Enlai** (joh ehn•leye), Chinese Communist Party founder and premier since 1949. He began to send out signals that he was willing to form ties to the West. In 1971, the United States reversed its policy and endorsed UN membership for the People's Republic of China. The next year, President Nixon made a state visit to China to meet with Mao and Zhou. The three leaders agreed to begin cultural exchanges and a limited amount of trade. In 1979, the United States and China established diplomatic relations.

Both Mao and Zhou died in 1976. By 1980, **Deng Xiaoping** (duhng show•pihng) had emerged as the most powerful leader in China. He was the last of the "old revolutionaries" who had ruled China since 1949.

Economic Reforms Unlike Mao, Deng Xiaoping was willing to use capitalist ideas to help China's economy. He embraced a set of goals known as the **Four Modernizations**, which called for progress in agriculture, industry, defense, and science and technology. To accomplish these goals, Deng eliminated Mao's communes and leased the land to individual farmers. The farmers paid rent by delivering a fixed quota of food to the government. They could then grow crops and sell them for a profit. Under this system, food production increased by 50 percent in the years 1978 to 1984. Deng extended his program to industry. The government permitted private businesses to operate. It gave the managers of state-owned industries more freedom to set production goals. Deng also welcomed foreign technology and investment.

Deng's economic policies produced striking changes in Chinese life. As incomes increased, people began to buy appliances and televisions. Gleaming hotels filled with foreign tourists symbolized China's new openness.

The Prodemocracy Movement Deng's economic reforms produced a number of unexpected problems. As living standards improved, the gap between the rich and poor widened. Increasingly, the public believed that party officials profited from their positions. Furthermore, the new policies admitted not only Western investments and tourists but also Western political ideas. Increasing numbers of Chinese students studied abroad and learned about the West. In Deng's view, the benefits of opening the economy exceeded the risks. Nevertheless, as Chinese students learned more about democracy, they began to question China's lack of political freedom.

In 1989, students sparked a popular uprising that stunned China's leaders. Beginning in April of that year, more than 100,000 students occupied **Tiananmen** (tyahn•ahn•mehn) **Square**, a huge public space in the heart of Beijing. The students mounted a protest for democracy. When thousands of students began a hunger strike to highlight their cause, people poured into Tiananmen Square to support them. Many students called for Deng Xiaoping to resign.

7.18 Preparing for the Regents

Power What was the goal of the Cultural Revolution? What was its outcome?

TAKING NOTES
Following Chronological Order Use a diagram to show events leading up to the demonstration in Tiananmen Square.

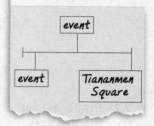

7.19 Preparing for the Regents

Economic Systems How did Deng Xiaoping attempt to improve China's economy? What effects did his changes have?

7.20 Preparing for the Regents

Human Rights What effect did economic reform have on political reform and human rights in China under Deng?

Deng responded by declaring martial law and surrounding Beijing with about 100,000 troops. About 5,000 students remained in the square. These students revived their spirits by defiantly erecting a 33-foot statue that they named the "Goddess of Democracy." On June 4, 1989, the standoff came to an end as thousands of heavily armed soldiers stormed Tiananmen Square. Tanks smashed through barricades and crushed the Goddess of Democracy. Soldiers sprayed gunfire into crowds of frightened students. They also attacked protesters elsewhere in Beijing. The assault killed hundreds and wounded thousands.

The attack on Tiananmen Square marked the beginning of a massive government campaign to stamp out protest. Police arrested thousands of people. The state used the media to announce that reports of a massacre were untrue. Officials claimed that a small group of criminals had plotted against the government. Television news, however, had already broadcast the truth to the world.

China Enters the New Millennium

🗽 **7.21 Preparing for the Regents**

Economic Systems What did China agree to when it took control of Hong Kong?

Deng died in February 1997. Communist Party General Secretary Jiang Zemin (jee•ahng zeh•meen) assumed the presidency. One issue he faced was the status of **Hong Kong**, a thriving business center and British colony on the southeastern coast of China. On July 1, 1997, Great Britain handed Hong Kong over to China, ending 155 years of colonial rule. As part of the transfer, China promised to respect Hong Kong's economic system and political liberties for 50 years. Nevertheless, in the first four or five years after the transfer, the control of mainland China over Hong Kong tightened. After Jiang announced his retirement in late 2002, Hu Jintao became president of the country and general secretary of the Communist Party.

The case of China demonstrates that the creation of democracy can be a slow, fitful, and incomplete process. Liberal economic reforms have not led immediately to political reforms. However, as economic and social conditions improve, the prospects for democracy also may improve. International trade may also help the process. In 2000, the U.S. Congress voted to normalize trade with China. Supporters of such a move argue that the best way to prompt political change in China is through greater engagement rather than isolation.

PREPARING FOR THE REGENTS

On a separate sheet of paper, write a well-organized essay that includes an introduction, several paragraphs addressing the task below, and a conclusion. Before beginning, check the Score the Essay box for pointers.

Theme: Change

Individuals have brought about great change in history. These individuals have had positive and/or negative effects on nations or regions.

Task:

Choose *two* individuals from this section and for *each* individual chosen:

- Discuss *two* specific changes made by the individual in China
- Evaluate whether these changes have had a positive or negative effect on China

SCORE THE ESSAY To receive a score of 5 on your essay, you will need to:
- thoroughly develop all aspects of the task evenly and in depth by discussing the changes made by the individuals and evaluating the effects.
- be more analytical than descriptive.
- richly support the theme with relevant facts, examples, and details.
- demonstrate a logical and clear plan of organization.

The Collapse of European Imperialism

Section Overview

*After World War II, people in Asia and Africa were unwilling to
return to colonial domination. The ways in which these nations
achieved independence varied widely. In some cases, the colonial
powers readily gave up control. Britain, for instance, heavily in debt
following the war, moved quickly to grant independence to India.
In other cases, such as Kenya, nationalists had to fight to win their
freedom. Regardless of the methods through which independence
was achieved, the newly formed nations faced many challenges.
Diverse populations and weak economies often made it difficult to
achieve political and economic stability.*

*Blacks in South Africa faced special challenges. Following
the war, the white minority government instituted a strict policy
of racial segregation. Political activists such as Nelson Mandela
struggled to gain rights for the black majority population. Their
long struggle finally paid off in 1994 when South Africa held its first
multiracial election. Korea and Vietnam also faced challenges, as
they found themselves locked in wars backed by the superpowers.*

Nelson Mandela (1918–)
of South Africa

MAIN IDEAS

REVOLUTION   Independence movements swept Africa and Asia as World
War II ended. Through both nonviolent and violent means, revolutionaries
overthrew existing political systems to create their own nations.

POWER AND AUTHORITY   Systems of government shifted for one
billion people when colonies in Africa and Asia gained their freedom.
New nations struggled to unify their diverse populations. In many cases,
authoritarian rule and military dictatorships emerged.

REVOLUTION   In Asia, the Cold War flared into actual wars supported
mainly by the superpowers.

TERMS AND NAMES

- Congress Party
- Muslim League
- partition
- Jawaharlal Nehru
- Indira Gandhi
- Negritude
  Movement
- Kwame Nkrumah

- Jomo Kenyatta
- Mobutu Sese Seko
- federal system
- martial law
- dissident
- apartheid
- Nelson Mandela
- 38th parallel

- Ho Chi Minh
- domino theory
- Ngo Dinh Diem
- Vietcong
- Khmer Rouge
- Aung San Suu Kyi

PREPARING FOR THE REGENTS

As you read this section, consider
- what forces brought about the collapse of European imperialism.
- what role non-Western nationalism played in the collapse of European
  imperialism.

TIME LINE

1947
India gains independence
from Britain.

1948
South Africa establishes
apartheid system.

1950
Korean War begins.

1957
Ghana wins independence.

1975
Vietnam War ends.

1994
South Africa holds its first
multiracial election.

1997
Mobutu dictatorship in Zaire falls.

Human and Physical Geography

After World War II, dramatic political changes began to take place across the world. This was especially the case with regard to the policy of colonialism. Countries that held colonies began to question the practice. After the world struggle against dictatorship, many leaders argued that no country should control another nation. Others questioned the high cost and commitment of holding colonies. Meanwhile, people in India, Southeast Asia, and Africa continued to press for their freedom.

Indian Independence

World War II left Britain with enormous war debts. This set the stage for granting India independence. However, the British faced a key problem: Who should receive the power—Hindus or Muslims?

In the 1940s, India had approximately 350 million Hindus and about 100 million Muslims. The Indian National Congress, or the **Congress Party**, was India's national political party. Most members of the Congress Party were Hindus. In competition with the Congress Party was the **Muslim League**, an organization founded in 1906 in India to protect Muslim interests. Members of the league felt that the mainly Hindu Congress Party looked out primarily for Hindu interests. The Muslim League stated that it would never accept Indian independence if it meant rule by the Hindu-dominated Congress Party.

7.22 Preparing for the Regents

Conflict Why did the British decide to partition India?

The Partition of India As rioting between Muslims and Hindus broke out in several cities, British officials became convinced that **partition**—the division of India into separate Hindu and Muslim nations—was the only way to ensure a safe and secure region. The northwest and eastern regions of India, where most Muslims lived, would become the new nation of Pakistan. (Pakistan, as the map shows, comprised two separate states in 1947: West Pakistan and East Pakistan.)

On July 16, 1947, the British House of Commons passed an act that granted two nations, India and Pakistan, independence in one month's time. In that short period, more than 500 independent native princes had to decide which nation they would join. The administration of the courts, the military, the railways, and the police—the whole of the civil service—had to be divided. Most difficult of all, millions of Indian Hindus, Muslims, and Sikhs had to decide where to go.

During the summer of 1947, 10 million people were on the move in the Indian subcontinent. As people scrambled to relocate, violence among the different

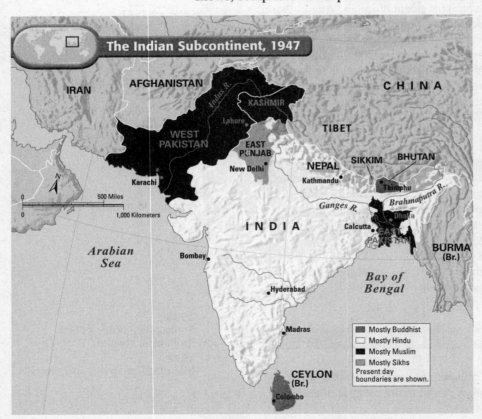

The Indian Subcontinent, 1947

Mostly Buddhist
Mostly Hindu
Mostly Muslim
Mostly Sikhs
Present day boundaries are shown.

religious groups erupted. In all, an estimated 1 million died. Gandhi personally went to the Indian capital of Delhi to plead for fair treatment of Muslim refugees. While there, he himself became a victim of the nation's violence. A Hindu extremist who thought Gandhi too protective of Muslims shot and killed him on January 30, 1948.

The Battle for Kashmir   Shortly after independence, India and Pakistan began battling each other for control of Kashmir, a small region at the northern point of India next to Pakistan. Although its ruler was Hindu, Kashmir had a majority Muslim population. The fighting continued until the United Nations arranged a cease-fire in 1949. The cease-fire left a third of Kashmir under Pakistani control and the rest under Indian control. The two countries continue to fight over the region today.

Modern India   With the granting of its independence on August 15, 1947, India became the world's largest democracy. <u>Jawaharlal Nehru</u>, India's first prime minister, led the nation for its first 17 years of independence. Educated in Britain, Nehru won popularity among all groups in India. He emphasized democracy, unity, and economic modernization. Nehru called for a reorganization of the states by language. He also pushed for industrialization and sponsored social reforms. He tried to elevate the status of the lower castes, or those at the bottom of society, and expand the rights of women.

Nehru's death in 1964 left the Congress Party with no leader strong enough to hold together the nation's many political factions. Then, in 1966, Nehru's daughter, <u>Indira Gandhi</u>, was chosen prime minister. After a short spell out of office, she was reelected in 1980. Gandhi faced many challenges, including the growing threat from Sikh extremists who themselves wanted an independent state. The Golden Temple at Amritsar stood as the religious center for the Sikhs. From there, Sikh nationalists ventured out to attack symbols of Indian authority. In June 1984, Indian army troops overran the Golden Temple, killing about 500 Sikhs and destroying sacred property. In retaliation, Indira Gandhi's Sikh bodyguards gunned her down.

In the wake of the murder of Indira Gandhi, her son, Rajiv (rah•JEEV) Gandhi, took over as prime minister. His party, however, lost its power in 1989 because of accusations of widespread corruption. In 1991, while campaigning again for prime minister near the town of Madras, Rajiv was killed by a bomb. Members of a group opposed to his policies claimed responsibility.

Since winning election as prime minister in 1998, Atal Bihari Vajpayee, leader of the Hindu nationalist party, has ruled over a vibrant but often unstable nation. He faces challenges brought on by an increasing population that is expected to push India past China as the world's most populous nation by 2035. In addition, the country is racked with social inequality and constantly threatened by religious strife. Even more troubling are India's tense relations with its neighbor Pakistan, and the fact that both have become nuclear powers. In 1974, India exploded a "peaceful" nuclear device. For the next 24 years, the nation quietly worked on building up its nuclear capability. In 1998, Indian officials conducted five underground nuclear tests. Meanwhile, the Pakistanis had been building their own nuclear program. Shortly after India conducted its nuclear tests, Pakistan demonstrated that it, too, had nuclear weapons. The presence of these weapons in the hands of such bitter enemies and neighbors has become a matter of great international concern, especially in light of the continuing struggle over Kashmir.

7.23 Preparing for the Regents

Conflict   What role does Kashmir play in relations between India and Pakistan?

TAKING NOTES

Following Chronological Order Create a time line of prominent Indian prime ministers from independence through the current day.

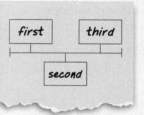

7.24 Preparing for the Regents

Diversity   Why has it been a challenge for India to achieve political stability and a sense of national unity?

Ghana	
Kenya	
Congo	
Rwanda	
Nigeria	

7.25 Preparing for the Regents

Nationalism What roles did Kwame Nkrumah, Jomo Kenyatta, and the Mau Mau play in ending colonial rule in their countries?

African Independence

The African push for independence began before World War II. French-speaking Africans and West Indians formed the **Negritude movement**, a movement to celebrate African culture, heritage, and values. When World War II erupted, African soldiers fought alongside Europeans to "defend freedom." This experience made them unwilling to accept colonial domination when they returned home.

Ghana and Kenya The Gold Coast was the first sub-Saharan colony to achieve independence. **Kwame Nkrumah** (KWAH•mee uhn•KROO•muh) was the leader of the largely nonviolent movement to free the colony from British rule. Starting in 1947, Nkrumah organized strikes and boycotts and was often imprisoned by the British government. Ultimately, his efforts were successful.

On receiving its independence in 1957, the Gold Coast took the name Ghana, in honor of a famous West African kingdom of the past. Nkrumah became the nation's first prime minister and later its president-for-life. He pushed through programs for industrialization and built new roads, schools, and health facilities. Nkrumah's programs showed good intentions. However, their expense undermined the economy and strengthened his opposition.

Nkrumah was also criticized for spending too much time on Pan-African efforts. He dreamed of a "United States of Africa." In 1966, while Nkrumah was in China, the army and police in Ghana seized power. Since then, the country has shifted back and forth between civilian and military rule and has struggled for economic stability. In 2000, Ghana held its first open elections.

In contrast, the British colony of Kenya had to take up arms to win its freedom. Many British settlers resisted independence, especially those who had taken over prize farmland in Kenya's northern highlands. Two factors forced them to accept the change: the strong leadership of Kenyan nationalist **Jomo Kenyatta** and the rise of a secret society known as the Mau Mau (MOW mow).

The Mau Mau, made up mostly of native Kenyan farmers forced out of the highlands by the British, used guerrilla war tactics to push white farmers into leaving the highlands. By the time the British granted Kenya independence in 1963, more than 10,000 Africans and 100 settlers had been killed.

Kenyatta became president of the new nation. He worked hard to unite the country's various ethnic and language groups. Daniel arap Moi, Kenyatta's successor, was less successful. In 2002, he stepped down, and a new party gained power through free elections.

Africa, 1975

TUNISIA 1956
MOROCCO 1956
ALGERIA 1962
LIBYA
EGYPT
SPANISH SAHARA
MAURITANIA 1960
MALI 1960
NIGER 1960
CHAD 1960
SUDAN 1956
SENEGAL 1960
GAMBIA 1965
GUINEA-BISSAU 1974
GUINEA 1958
UPPER VOLTA 1960
NIGERIA 1960
AFARS AND ISSAS TERR. (FR.)
SIERRA LEONE 1961
IVORY COAST 1960
CAMEROON 1960
CENTRAL AFRICAN REP. 1960
ETHIOPIA
LIBERIA
DAHOMEY 1960
SOMALIA 1960
GHANA 1957
TOGO 1960
CONGO 1960
ZAIRE 1960
UGANDA 1962
KENYA 1963
SÃO TOMÉ AND PRÍNCIPE 1975
EQ. GUINEA 1968
RWANDA 1962
GABON 1960
BURUNDI 1962
TANZANIA 1961
ANGOLA 1975
ZAMBIA 1964
MALAWI 1964
COMOROS 1975
MOZAMBIQUE 1975
MAURITIUS 1968
RHODESIA (BR.)
MALAGASY REPUBLIC 1960
SOUTH-WEST AFRICA (NAMIBIA)
BOTSWANA 1966
SWAZILAND 1968
SOUTH AFRICA
LESOTHO 1966

Mediterranean Sea
ATLANTIC OCEAN
INDIAN OCEAN

☐ Colonies
■ Independent countries
1951 Date of independence

N

1,000 Miles
2,000 Kilometers

Congo The Belgian Congo was one of the most exploited European possessions in Africa. Belgium ruthlessly plundered the colony's rich resources of rubber and copper, ruled its people with a harsh hand, and provided no social services. Belgian officials also made no attempt to prepare the people for independence. Not surprisingly, Belgium's granting of independence in 1960 to the Congo (known as Zaire from 1971 to 1997) resulted in upheaval.

After years of civil war, an army officer, Colonel Joseph Mobutu, later known as **Mobutu Sese Seko** (moh•BOO•too SAY•say SAY•koh), seized power in 1965. For 32 years, Mobutu ruled the country that he renamed Zaire through a combination of force, one-party rule, and gifts to supporters. He was finally overthrown in 1997 by rebel leader Laurent Kabila after months of civil war. Shortly thereafter, the country was renamed the Democratic Republic of the Congo. On becoming president, Kabila promised a transition to democracy and free elections by April 1999. Such elections never came. By 2000 the nation endured another round of civil war, as three separate rebel groups sought to overthrow Kabila's autocratic rule. In January 2001, a bodyguard assassinated Kabila. His son, Joseph Kabila, took power and began a quest for peace.

Rwanda Perhaps no African nation has seen more blood spilled than Rwanda. The tiny nation in East Africa gained its independence in 1962. Over the next 30 years, its main ethnic groups, the Hutus and Tutsis, often clashed. In the spring of 1994, the Rwandan president, a Hutu, died in a suspicious plane crash. In the months that followed, Hutus slaughtered about 1 million Tutsis before Tutsis rebels put an end to the killings. The United Nations set up a tribunal to punish those responsible for the worst acts of genocide.

Nigeria The former British colony of Nigeria won its independence peacefully in 1960. Nigeria is Africa's most populous country and one of its richest. Three major ethnic groups live within its borders—the Hausa, the Yoruba, and the Igbo (also called Ibo). After independence, Nigeria organized the country into regions based on dominant ethnic groups and adopted a **federal system** of government. In a federal system, power is shared between state governments and a central authority.

Ethnic differences soon led to conflict. In 1963, ethnic minorities living in the Yoruba-controlled Western Region tried to break away and form their own region. This led to fighting. In January 1966, a group of army officers, most of them Igbo, seized power in the capital city of Lagos. These officers abolished the regional governments and declared **martial law**, or temporary military rule. The Hausa-Fulani, who did not trust the Igbo, launched an attack from the north. They persecuted and killed many Igbo. The survivors fled east. In 1967, the Eastern Region seceded from Nigeria, declaring itself the new nation of Biafra (bee•AF•ruh). The Nigerian government then went to war to reunite the country. In 1970, Biafra surrendered and Nigeria was reunited, but perhaps more than a million Igbo died, most from starvation.

The military governed Nigeria for most of the 1970s. During this time, Nigerian leaders tried to create a more stable federal system and build a more modern economy based on oil income. In 1979, the military handed power back to civilian rulers. However, Nigerian democracy was short-lived. In 1983, the military overthrew the civilian government, charging it with corruption. A new military regime, dominated by the Hausa-Fulani, took charge. The army held elections in 1993, but officers declared the results invalid, and a dictator, General Sani Abacha, took control. General Abacha banned political activity

7.26 Preparing for the Regents

Political Systems What are some of the challenges that the Congo has faced since independence?

7.27 Preparing for the Regents

Human Rights How did the United Nations attempt to deal with genocide in Rwanda?

TAKING NOTES

Comparing Use a Venn diagram to compare political events in Nigeria and South Africa.

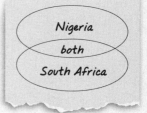

Nigeria

both

South Africa

7.28 Preparing for the Regents

Political Systems What are some of the challenges that Nigeria has faced since independence?

and jailed **dissidents**, or government opponents. Upon Abacha's death in 1998, General Abdulsalami Abubakar seized power and ended military rule. In 1999, Nigerians elected their first civilian president, Olusegun Obasanjo, in nearly 20 years. Obasanjo was reelected in 2003.

South Africa In South Africa, racial conflict was the result of colonial rule. Under both the Dutch and the British, a small white minority ruled a large black majority. The policy continued when South Africa became an independent member of the British Commonwealth in 1931. Although South Africa had a constitutional government, the constitution gave whites power and denied the black majority its rights.

In 1948, the National Party came to power in South Africa. This party promoted Afrikaner, or Dutch South African, nationalism. It also instituted a policy of **apartheid**, the complete separation of the races. The minority government established segregated schools, hospitals, and neighborhoods and banned social contacts between whites and blacks. In 1959, it set up reserves, called homelands, for the country's major black groups. Blacks were forbidden to live in white areas unless they worked as servants or laborers for whites. The homelands policy was totally unbalanced. Although blacks made up about 75 percent of the population, the government set aside only 13 percent of the land for them.

The blacks of South Africa resisted the controls imposed by the white minority. In 1912, they formed the African National Congress (ANC) to fight for their rights. The ANC organized strikes and boycotts to protest racist policies. The government banned the ANC and imprisoned many of its members. One was ANC leader **Nelson Mandela** (man•DEHL•uh).

The troubles continued. In 1976, riots over school policies broke out in the black township of Soweto, leaving about 600 students dead. In 1977, police beat popular protest leader Stephen Biko to death while he was in custody. As protests mounted, the government declared a nationwide state of emergency in 1986. By the late 1980s, South Africa was under great pressure to change. For years, a black South African bishop, Desmond Tutu, had led an economic campaign against apartheid. He asked foreign nations not to do business with South Africa. In response, many nations imposed trade restrictions. (In 1984, Tutu won the Nobel Peace Prize for his nonviolent methods.)

In 1989, white South Africans elected a new president, F. W. de Klerk. His goal was to transform South Africa and end its isolation. In February 1990, he legalized the ANC and also released Nelson Mandela from prison. These dramatic actions marked the beginning of a new era in South Africa. Over the next 18 months, the South African parliament repealed apartheid laws that had segregated public facilities and restricted land ownership by blacks. World leaders welcomed these changes and began to ease restrictions on South Africa.

After lengthy negotiations, President de Klerk agreed to hold South Africa's first universal elections, in which people of all races could vote, in April 1994. Among the candidates for president were F. W. de Klerk and Nelson Mandela. To no one's surprise, the ANC won 63 percent of the vote and 252 of 400 seats in the National Assembly (the larger of the two houses in Parliament). Mandela was elected president. In 1999, ANC official Thabo Mbeki won election as president in a peaceful transition of power.

In 1996, after much debate, South African lawmakers passed a new, more democratic constitution. It guaranteed equal rights for all citizens. The constitution included a bill of rights modeled on the U.S. Bill of Rights.

7.29 Preparing for the Regents
Human Rights   What is apartheid?

7.30 Preparing for the Regents
Human Rights   What people and tactics contributed to the downfall of apartheid in South Africa?

Korea and Southeast Asia

World War II had a significant impact on the colonized groups of Southeast Asia. During the war, the Japanese seized much of Southeast Asia from the European nations that had controlled the region for many years. The Japanese conquest helped the people see that the Europeans were far from invincible. When the war ended and the Japanese themselves were forced out, many Southeast Asians refused to live again under European rule. They called for and won their independence. Adding to the turmoil in the region were Cold War tensions between the United States and the Soviet Union. These tensions played a leading role in the United States' involvement in the Korean and Vietnam Wars.

The Korean War When World War II ended, Korea became a divided nation. North of the **38th parallel**, a line that crosses Korea at 38 degrees north latitude, Japanese troops surrendered to the Soviets. South of this line, the Japanese surrendered to the Americans. As in Germany, two nations developed. One was the Communist industrial north, whose government had been set up by the Soviets. The other was the non-Communist rural south, supported by the Western powers.

Gambling that the United States would not defend South Korea, the Soviets supplied North Korea with tanks, airplanes, and money in an attempt to take over the peninsula. On June 25, 1950, North Koreans swept across the 38th parallel in a surprise attack on South Korea. Within days, North Korean troops had penetrated deep into the south. President Truman's policy of containment was being put to the test. He resolved to help South Korea resist communism.

South Korea asked the United Nations to intervene. When the matter came to a vote in the Security Council, the Soviets were absent. They had refused to take part in the Council to protest admission of Nationalist China (Taiwan), rather than Communist China, into the UN. As a result, the Soviet Union could not veto the UN's plan to send an international force to Korea to stop the invasion. A total of 15 nations, including the United States and Britain, participated. The Communist Chinese soon sent troops to aid the North Koreans.

Fighting raged for several years. Finally, in July 1953, the UN forces and North Korea signed a cease-fire agreement. The border between the two Koreas was set near the 38th parallel, almost where it had been before the war. In the meantime, 4 million soldiers and civilians had died.

The Vietnam War In the early 1900s, France controlled most of resource-rich Southeast Asia. (French Indochina included what are now Vietnam, Laos, and Cambodia.) But nationalist independence movements had begun to develop. A young Vietnamese nationalist, **Ho Chi Minh**, turned to the Communists for help in his struggle. During the 1930s, Ho's Indochinese Communist party led revolts and strikes against the French. The French responded by jailing Vietnamese protesters. They also sentenced Ho to death. He fled into exile, but returned to Vietnam in 1941, a year after the Japanese seized control of his country during World War II. Ho and other nationalists founded the Vietminh (Independence) League. The Japanese were forced out of Vietnam after their defeat in 1945. Ho Chi Minh believed that independence would follow, but France intended to regain its colony.

Vietnamese Nationalists and Communists joined to fight the French armies. The French held most major cities, but the Vietminh had widespread support in the countryside. The Vietminh used hit-and-run tactics to confine the French to the cities. In France the people began to doubt that their colony was worth the lives and money the struggle cost. In 1954, after a major military defeat at Dien Bien Phu, the French surrendered to Ho.

TAKING NOTES

Comparing and Contrasting Use a diagram to compare and contrast the Korean and Vietnam Wars.

Korean War

both

Vietnam War

7.31 Preparing for the Regents

Conflict What role did the Cold War play in the Korean War?

7.32 Preparing for the Regents

Nationalism Who was Ho Chi Minh?

7.33 Preparing for the Regents

Imperialism In what way can the fighting in Vietnam be seen as an anti-imperialist revolt?

7.34 Preparing for the Regents

Conflict What role did the Cold War play in the Vietnam War?

With the defeat of the French, the United States saw a rising threat to the rest of Asia. President Eisenhower described this threat in terms of the **domino theory**. Asian nations were like a row of dominos, he said. The fall of one to communism would lead to the fall of its neighbors. This theory became a major justification for U.S. foreign policy during the Cold War era.

After France's defeat, an international peace conference divided Vietnam at the 17° north latitude. North of that line, Ho Chi Minh's Communist forces governed. To the south, the United States and France set up an anti-Communist government under the leadership of **Ngo Dinh Diem** (NOH dihn D'YEM). Diem ruled the south as a dictator. As opposition to his government grew, Communist guerrillas, called **Vietcong**, began to gain strength in the south. In 1963, a group of South Vietnamese generals had Diem assassinated. But the new leaders were no more popular than he had been. It appeared that a takeover by the Communist Vietcong, backed by North Vietnam, was inevitable.

Faced with the possibility of a Communist victory, the United States decided to escalate, or increase, its involvement in Vietnam. By late 1965, more than 185,000 U.S. soldiers were in combat on Vietnamese soil. U.S. planes had also begun to bomb North Vietnam. By 1968, more than half a million U.S. soldiers were in combat there. During the late 1960s, the war grew increasingly unpopular in the United States. Dissatisfied young people began to protest the tremendous loss of life in a conflict on the other side of the world. Bowing to intense public pressure, President Richard Nixon began withdrawing U.S. troops from Vietnam in 1969. The last left in 1973. Two years later, the North Vietnamese overran South Vietnam. The war ended, but more than 1.5 million Vietnamese and 58,000 Americans lost their lives.

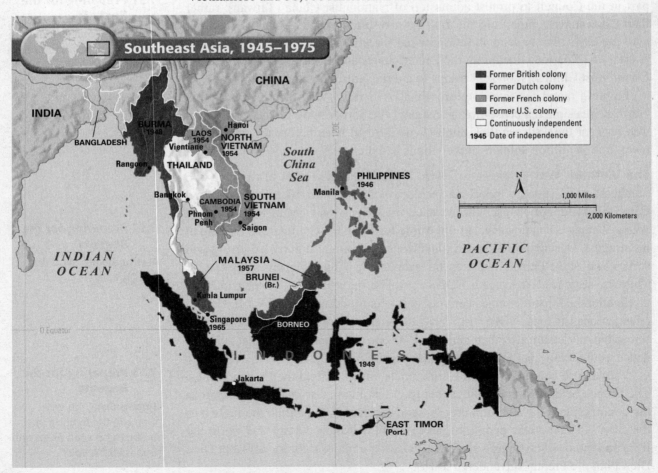

Southeast Asia, 1945–1975

- Former British colony
- Former Dutch colony
- Former French colony
- Former U.S. colony
- Continuously independent
- **1945** Date of independence

Cambodia War's end did not bring an immediate halt to bloodshed and chaos in Southeast Asia. Cambodia (also known as Kampuchea) was under siege by Communist rebels known as the **Khmer Rouge**. In 1975, the Khmer Rouge set up a brutal Communist government under the leadership of Pol Pot. In a ruthless attempt to transform Cambodia into a Communist society, Pol Pot's followers slaughtered 2 million people. This was almost one quarter of the nation's population. The Vietnamese invaded in 1978. They overthrew the Khmer Rouge and installed a less repressive government. But fighting continued. The Vietnamese withdrew in 1989. In 1993, under the supervision of UN peacekeepers, Cambodia adopted a democratic constitution and held free elections.

Burma (Myanmar) Britain's timetable for granting independence to its Southeast Asian colonies depended on local circumstances. Burma had been pressing for independence from Britain for decades. It became a sovereign republic in 1948. In 1989, Burma was officially named Myanmar (myahn•MAH), its name in the Burmese language. After gaining freedom, Burma's people struggled between repressive military governments and prodemocracy forces. Conflict among Communists and ethnic minorities also disrupted the nation. In 1962, General Ne Win set up a military government, with the goal of making Burma a socialist state. Although Ne Win stepped down in 1988, the military continued to rule repressively.

In 1988, **Aung San Suu Kyi** (owng sahn soo chee) returned to Burma after many years abroad. Aung San Suu Kyi became active in the newly formed National League for Democracy. For her prodemocracy activities, she was placed under house arrest for six years by the government. In the 1990 election—the country's first multiparty election in 30 years—the National League for Democracy won 80 percent of the seats. The military government refused to recognize the election, and it kept Aung San Suu Kyi under house arrest. She was finally released in 1995, only to be placed under house arrest again in 2000. Freed in 2002, she was detained again in 2003, leaving many residents to doubt whether Burma will embrace democracy anytime soon.

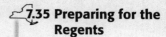

7.35 Preparing for the Regents

Human Rights What role did Pol Pot and the Khmer Rouge play in Cambodian history?

7.36 Preparing for the Regents

Political Systems What are some of the challenges that Burma has faced since independence?

7.37 Preparing for the Regents

Human Rights Who is Aung San Suu Kyi?

PREPARING FOR THE REGENTS

On a separate sheet of paper, write a well-organized essay that includes an introduction, several paragraphs addressing the task below, and a conclusion. Before beginning, check the Score the Essay box for pointers.

Theme: Change
Individuals have brought about great change in history. These individuals have had positive and/or negative effects on nations or regions.

Task:
Choose *two* individuals from this section and for *each* individual chosen:
- Discuss *two* specific changes made by the individual in a specific nation or region
- Evaluate whether these changes have had a positive or negative effect on that nation or region

SCORE THE ESSAY To receive a score of 5 on your essay, you will need to:
- thoroughly develop all aspects of the task evenly and in depth by discussing the changes made by the individuals and evaluating the effects.
- be more analytical than descriptive.
- richly support the theme with relevant facts, examples, and details.
- demonstrate a logical and clear plan of organization.

The Collapse of Communism and the Soviet Union

Section Overview

When the Communist Party leaders chose Mikhail Gorbachev as the party's new general secretary in 1985, they did not realize they were unleashing another Russian Revolution. The Soviet people welcomed Gorbachev's election. At 54, he was the youngest Soviet leader since Stalin. Gorbachev was only a child during Stalin's ruthless purge of independent-minded party members.

Unlike other Soviet leaders, Gorbachev decided to pursue new ideas. His new thinking led him to support movements for change in both the economic and political systems within the Soviet Union. Powerful forces for democracy were building in the country, and Gorbachev decided not to oppose reform. Glasnost, perestroika, and democratization were all means to reform the system. However, the move to reform the Soviet Union ultimately led to its breakup and to the collapse of Communist Party control, as people in the Soviet Union and Central and Eastern Europe demanded and won their independence. In 1991, the Soviet Union ceased to exist.

Former Soviet leader
Mikhail Gorbachev (1931–)

MAIN IDEAS

REVOLUTION   Democratic reforms brought important changes to the Soviet Union.

REVOLUTION   In 1989, revolutions overthrew Communist governments in the Soviet Union and Central and Eastern Europe.

CULTURAL INTERACTION   Changes in the Soviet Union led to changes throughout Central and Eastern Europe.

TERMS AND NAMES

- John F. Kennedy
- Richard M. Nixon
- détente
- Ronald Reagan
- Politburo

- Mikhail Gorbachev
- glasnost
- perestroika
- Boris Yeltsin
- CIS

- "shock therapy"
- Solidarity
- Lech Walesa
- reunification
- ethnic cleansing

PREPARING FOR THE REGENTS

As you read this section, consider
- how the collapse of the Soviet Union can be compared to the fall of the Roman Empire and the Han Dynasty.
- why the collapse of communism in the Soviet Union was a major turning point in global history.

TIME LINE

1985
Mikhail Gorbachev announces policies of glasnost and perestroika.

1989
Berlin Wall comes down.

1990
Germany officially reunites.

1991
Mikhail Gorbachev announces his resignation as president of the Soviet Union; the Soviet Union breaks up.

Human and Physical Geography: Communism's Road to Collapse

In the postwar years, the Soviet Union kept a firm grip on its satellite countries in Eastern Europe. These policies greatly hampered Eastern Europe's economic recovery. Nevertheless, by the 1960s, it appeared that communism was permanently established in the region.

U.S.–Soviet Relations The early 1960s were troubling times for U.S.–Soviet relations. In 1962, for example, secret attempts by Nikita Khrushchev to build Soviet missile sites in Cuba sparked the Cuban Missile Crisis. When President **John F. Kennedy** demanded the removal of the missiles, people around the world feared nuclear war. Fortunately, Khrushchev agreed to removal. Tensions eased in early 1970s. Under **Richard M. Nixon**, brinkmanship was replaced by **détente**, a policy of lessening Cold War tensions. However, détente cooled during Jimmy Carter's administration in the late 1970s, and even more so when **Ronald Reagan** took office in 1981. Fiercely anti-Communist, Reagan dramatically increased defense spending, putting both economic and military pressure on the Soviets.

Reforms Under Gorbachev During the 1960s and 1970s, Leonid Brezhnev and the **Politburo**—the ruling committee of the Communist Party—crushed all political disagreement and restricted freedom of speech and worship. After Brezhnev's death in 1982, the aging leadership of the Soviet Union tried to hold on to power. However, each of Brezhnev's two successors died after only about a year in office. Eventually, the Politburo chose **Mikhail Gorbachev** (mih•KYL GAWR•buh•chawf) as the party's new general secretary.

Past Soviet leaders had created a totalitarian state that rewarded silence and discouraged individual action. Gorbachev realized that economic and social reforms could not occur without a free flow of ideas and information. In 1985, he announced a policy known as **glasnost** (GLAHS•nuhst), or openness. Glasnost brought remarkable changes. The government allowed churches to open. It released dissidents from prison and allowed the publication of books by previously banned authors. Reporters investigated problems and criticized officials.

The new openness allowed Soviet citizens to complain about economic problems. Gorbachev blamed these problems on the Soviet Union's inefficient system of central planning. In this system, party officials told farm and factory managers how much to produce and what wages to pay. To remedy these problems, Gorbachev introduced the idea of **perestroika** (PEHR•ih•STROY•kuh), or economic restructuring, in 1985. In 1986, he made changes to revive the Soviet economy. Local managers gained greater authority over their farms and factories, and people were allowed to open small private businesses.

Gorbachev also knew that for the economy to improve, the Communist Party would have to loosen its grip on Soviet society and politics. In 1987, he unveiled a third new policy, called democratization. The plan called for the election of a new legislative body. In the past, voters had merely approved candidates who were handpicked by the Communist Party. Now, voters could choose from a list of candidates for each office.

Soviet foreign policy also changed. Gorbachev realized that the Soviet economy could not afford the costly arms race that Ronald Reagan had launched. Arms control became one of Gorbachev's top priorities. In December 1987, he and Reagan signed the Intermediate-Range Nuclear Forces (INF) Treaty. This treaty banned nuclear missiles with ranges of 300 to 3,400 miles.

TAKING NOTES
Following Chronological Order Use a time line to record significant events in the Soviet Union and Russia.

1985   2002

7.38 Preparing for the Regents
Political and Economic Systems What political and economic reforms did Gorbachev institute?

7.39 Preparing for the Regents
Economic Systems Why did the Soviet's command economy fail?

The Breakup of the Soviet Union

Ethnic tensions brewed beneath the surface of Soviet society. Non-Russians formed a majority in all the republics except Russia. As reforms loosened central controls, nationalist in Georgia, Ukraine, and Moldavia (now Moldova) demanded self-rule. Muslims in Soviet Central Asia called for religious freedom.

The first challenge came from the Baltic nations of Lithuania, Estonia, and Latvia. In March 1990, Lithuania declared its independence. Fearing that Lithuania's example might encourage other republics to secede, Gorbachev tried to force the republic back into the Soviet Union. In January 1991, Soviet troops attacked unarmed civilians in Lithuania's capital, killing 14 and wounding hundreds. The assault and the lack of economic progress hurt Gorbachev's popularity. Looking for leadership, in June 1991, voters chose the reform-minded **Boris Yeltsin** as the first directly elected president of the Russian Federation.

The Communist Party hard-liners—the conservatives who opposed reform—were furious with Gorbachev. On August 18, 1991, they detained Gorbachev at his vacation home on the Black Sea and demanded that he resign as Soviet president. Early the next day, hundreds of tanks and armored vehicles rolled into Moscow. Protesters quickly gathered at the Russian parliament building, where Yeltsin had his office. On August 20, the hardliners ordered troops to attack the parliament building, but they refused. Their refusal turned the tide. On August 21, the military withdrew its forces from Moscow.

The coup attempt sparked anger against the Communist Party. Gorbachev resigned as general secretary of the party. The Soviet parliament voted to stop all party activities. Having first seized power in 1917 in a coup that succeeded, the Communist Party now collapsed because of a coup that failed. Estonia and Latvia quickly declared their independence. Other republics soon followed. By early December, all 15 republics had declared independence.

✒7.40 Preparing for the Regents

Nationalism What role did nationalism play in the breakup of the Soviet Union?

✒7.41 Preparing for the Regents

Political Systems What led to the collapse of the Communist Party in the Soviet Union?

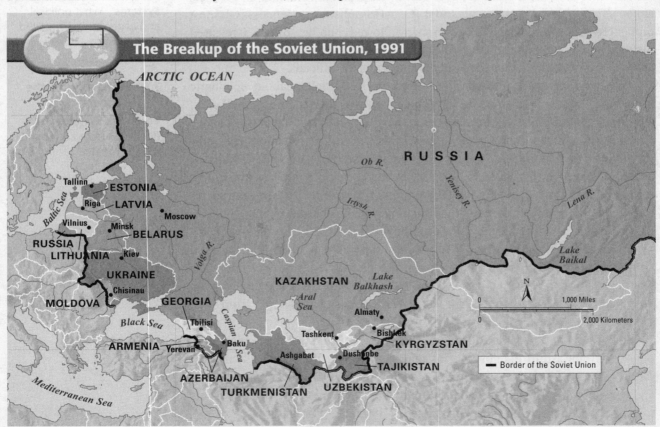

The Breakup of the Soviet Union, 1991

Yeltsin met with the leaders of other republics to chart a new course. They agreed to form the Commonwealth of Independent States, or **CIS**, a loose federation of former Soviet territories. Only the Baltic republics and Georgia declined to join. The formation of the CIS meant the death of the Soviet Union. On Christmas Day 1991, Gorbachev announced his resignation as president of the Soviet Union, a country that ceased to exist.

Russia Under Yeltsin and Putin

One of Yeltsin's goals as president of the Russian Federation was to reform the economy. He adopted a bold plan known as "**shock therapy**," an abrupt shift to free-market economics. Yeltsin lowered trade barriers, removed price controls, and ended subsidies to state-owned industries.

In addition to economic problems, Yeltsin also faced war in Chechnya (CHEHCH•nee•uh), a largely Muslim area in southwestern Russia. In 1991, Chechnya declared its independence, but Yeltsin denied the region's right to secede. In 1994, he ordered 40,000 Russian troops into the breakaway republic. Russian forces reduced the capital city of Grozny (GROHZ•nee) to rubble. In 1999, as fighting raged, Yeltsin resigned from his second term and named Vladimir Putin as acting president.

Putin dealt forcefully with the rebellion in Chechnya—a popular move that helped him win the presidential election in 2000. Nonetheless, the fighting in the region dragged on for years. In July 2002, Russia said it would begin pulling some of its 80,000 troops out of Chechnya, but Russia had made and broken such a promise before. Then, in October 2002, Chechen rebels seized a theater in Moscow, and more than 150 people died in the rescue attempt.

The nation's economic problems continued, and some observers wondered whether democracy could survive. Experts estimated that there were between 30,000 and 50,000 homeless children on the streets of Moscow—about half younger than 13. Other indications of a society experiencing severe stress included high rates of domestic violence and unemployment, a steep population decline, and declines in the standard of living and the average life expectancy.

Poland—Solidarity and Beyond

Even before Gorbachev, Poland pushed for reforms. In 1980, Polish workers at the Gdansk shipyard went on strike, demanding government recognition of their union, **Solidarity**. When millions of Poles supported the action, the government gave in to the union's demands. Union leader **Lech Walesa** (lehk vah•WEHN•sah) became a national hero. The next year, however, the Polish government banned Solidarity again and declared martial law.

In the 1980s, public discontent deepened as the economic crisis worsened. In August 1988, defiant workers walked off their jobs. They demanded raises and the legalization of Solidarity. In April 1988, the military leader, General Jaruzelski (YAH•roo•ZEHL•skee), legalized Solidarity and agreed to hold Poland's first free election since the Communists took power. In elections during 1989 and 1990, Polish voters voted against Communists and overwhelmingly chose Solidarity candidates. They elected Lech Walesa president. Like Yeltsin, Walesa adopted a strategy of shock therapy to move Poland toward a free-market economy. Inflation and unemployment shot up. By the mid-1990s, the economy was improving. Nevertheless, in the elections of 1995, voters turned Walesa out of office in favor of a former Communist, Aleksander Kwasniewski (kfahs•N'YEHF•skee).

7.42 Preparing for the Regents

Political and Economic Systems What problems did Yeltsin face as president of Russia?

7.43 Preparing for the Regents

Conflict How did Putin deal with Chechnya?

7.44 Preparing for the Regents

Political and Economic Systems What role did Solidarity play in reforming Polish society?

Germany Reunites

7.45 Preparing for the Regents

Political Systems
What factors led to the reunification of Germany?

Inspired by Poland, Hungary launched sweeping reforms. East Germany's 77-year-old party boss, Erich Honecker, dismissed reforms as unnecessary. Then, in 1989, Hungary allowed vacationing East German tourists to cross the border into Austria. From there they could travel to West Germany. Thousands of East Germans took this new escape route to the west. In response, the East German government closed its borders entirely. Protests broke out across East Germany. Honecker lost his authority with the party and resigned on October 18, 1989.

In June 1987, President Reagan had stood before the Berlin Wall and demanded: "Mr. Gorbachev, tear down this wall!" Two years later, the new East German leader, Egon Krenz, opened the Berlin Wall on November 9, 1989. By the end of 1989, the East German Communist Party had ceased to exist.

7.46 Preparing for the Regents

Economic Systems What economic challenges does the united Germany face?

With the fall of Communism in East Germany, many Germans began to speak of **reunification**—the merging of the two Germanys. Germany was officially reunited on October 3, 1990, under the leadership of Chancellor Helmut Kohl. The newly created Germany faced serious problems. Eastern Germany's railroads, highways, and telephone system had not been modernized since World War II. Its industries produced goods that could not compete in the global market. As inefficient factories closed, millions of workers lost their jobs. In 1998, voters elected a new chancellor, Gerhard Schroeder, of the Socialist Democratic Party. Schroeder started out as a market reformer, but the slow growth of the German economy made the task of reform difficult. Although Germany had the world's third largest economy, it was the slowest-growing economy in Europe in the early years of the 21st century. Germany's unemployment rate was among the highest in Europe, and rising inflation was also a continuing problem. Nonetheless, Schroeder won reelection in 2002.

Changing Political Boundaries—Czechoslovakia

In Czechoslovakia, a conservative government led by Milos Jakes resisted all change. On October 28, 1989, about 10,000 people gathered in Wenceslas Square in the center of Prague. They demanded democracy and freedom. Hundreds were arrested. Three weeks later, about 25,000 students inspired by the fall of the Berlin Wall gathered in Prague to demand reform. Following orders from the government, the police brutally attacked the demonstrators and injured hundreds.

TAKING NOTES

Analyzing Causes
Use a chart to record reasons that nations in Central and Eastern Europe broke apart.

Former nations	Reasons for breakup
Yugoslavia	
Czecho-slovakia	

The government crackdown angered the Czech people. Huge crowds gathered in Wenceslas Square. They demanded an end to Communist rule. On November 25, about 500,000 protesters crowded into downtown Prague. Within hours, Milos Jakes and his entire Politburo resigned. One month later, a new parliament elected Czech playwright Václav Havel (VAH•tslahv HAH•vehl), a popular critic of the Communist government, president of Czechoslovakia.

7.47 Preparing for the Regents

Economic Systems What problems did Czechoslovakia face following the collapse of communism?

Reformers launched an economic program based on shock therapy. The program caused a sharp rise in unemployment. It especially hurt Slovakia, the republic occupying the eastern third of Czechoslovakia. Unable to agree on economic policy, the country's two parts—Slovakia and the Czech Republic—split into two countries on January 1, 1993. Havel, who had resigned because of the split, was elected president of the Czech Republic. After winning reelection in 1998, Havel stepped down as president in 2003, in part because of ill health. The Czech parliament chose Vaclav Klaus, a right-wing economist and former prime minister, to succeed him. The economy of the Czech Republic slowly improved in the face of some serious problems.

Ethnic Conflicts and Challenges—Yugoslavia

Yugoslavia, a federation of six republics, was plagued by conflict among its eight major ethnic groups—Serbs, Croats, Muslims, Slovenes, Macedonians, Albanians, Hungarians, and Montenegrins. Ethnic and religious differences dating back centuries caused these groups to view one another with suspicion. At the time of the breakup of the Soviet Union, Serbian leader Slobodan Milosevic (mee•LOH•sheh•vihch) asserted leadership over Yugoslavia.

In June 1991, the Serbian-led Yugoslav army invaded Slovenia and Croatia, after both republics declared independence from the federation. After months of bloody fighting, both republics freed themselves from Serbian rule. Then, in early 1992, Bosnia-Herzegovina declared its independence. (In April, Serbia and Montenegro formed a new Yugoslavia.) Bosnia's population included Muslims (44 percent), Serbs (31 percent), and Croats (17 percent). While Bosnia's Muslims and Croats backed independence, Bosnian Serbs strongly opposed it. Supported by Serbia, the Bosnian Serbs launched a war in March 1992. During the war, Serbian military forces used violence and forced emigration against Bosnian Muslims living in Serb-held lands. Called **ethnic cleansing**, this policy was intended to rid Bosnia of Muslims. In December 1995, leaders of the three factions involved in the war signed a UN- and U.S.-brokered peace treaty. In September 1996, Bosnians elected a three-person presidency, one leader from each ethnic group.

The Balkan region descended into violence again in 1998. Serbian military forces invaded Kosovo, a province in southern Serbia made up almost entirely of ethnic Albanians, as an independence movement grew increasingly violent. In response to reports of atrocities—and the failure of diplomacy to bring peace—NATO began a bombing campaign against Yugoslavia in the spring of 1999. This caused Yugoslav leaders to finally withdraw their troops from Kosovo.

In the early years of the 21st century, there were conflicting signs in Yugoslavia. Slobodan Milosevic was extradited to stand trial for war crimes. A large portion of the country's foreign debt was erased. Despite an independence movement in Kosovo, parliamentary elections under UN supervision took place in November 2001 without violence. Nonetheless, in February 2003, Yugoslavia's parliament voted to replace what remained of the federation with a loose union of Serbia and Montenegro. Outright independence for each could come as early as 2006.

7.48 Preparing for the Regents

Nationalism Why did the United Nations and NATO intervene in the conflicts in the Balkans?

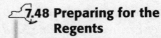

PREPARING FOR THE REGENTS

On a separate sheet of paper, write a well-organized essay that includes an introduction, several paragraphs addressing the task below, and a conclusion. Before beginning, check the Score the Essay box for pointers.

Theme: Conflict

Differences among groups have often led to conflict.

Task:

- Discuss the historical circumstances that led to the breakup of the Soviet Union
- Analyze the effect of the breakup on *two* groups involved

Be sure to include specific examples in your essay.

SCORE THE ESSAY To receive a score of 5 on your essay, you will need to:

- thoroughly develop all aspects of the task evenly and in depth by discussing the historical circumstances surrounding the breakup and the effects on two of the groups involved.
- be more analytical than descriptive.
- richly support the theme with relevant facts, examples, and details.
- demonstrate a logical and clear plan of organization.

Conflict and Change in the Middle East and Latin America

Section Overview

In the aftermath of World War II, the United Nations took up the issue of establishing a Jewish homeland in the Middle East. In 1947, the UN Security Council voted to partition Palestine into a Palestinian state and a Jewish state. The state of Israel was created on May 14, 1948. Thanks in part to the violence that Israel's formation sparked in the Arab world, the Palestinian state was never created. Today, the land called Palestine consists of Israel, the West Bank, and the Gaza Strip. To Jews, their claim to the land dates back 3,000 years, when Jewish kings ruled the region from Jerusalem. To Palestinians (both Muslim and Christian), the land has belonged to them since the Jews were driven out around A.D. 135. To Arabs, the land has belonged to them since their conquest of the area in the 7th century. These competing claims and the rise of Islamic fundamentalism have brought much conflict to the region.

Latin America has also faced many challenges since World War II. During the Cold War, Cuba and Nicaragua found themselves caught up in the power struggle between the United States and the Soviet Union. Today, the people of Cuba, in particular, suffer the effects of the loss of financial aid that resulted from the breakup of the Soviet Union. Argentina and many other Latin American nations face the challenges of building strong economies and democratic governments.

Israel's Golda Meir
(1898–1978)

MAIN IDEAS

POWER AND AUTHORITY   Division of Palestine after World War II made the Middle East a hotbed of competing nationalist movements.
ECONOMICS   In Latin America, economic problems and authoritarian rule delayed democracy.

TERMS AND NAMES

- Anwar Sadat
- Golda Meir
- Camp David Accords
- PLO
- Yasir Arafat
- intifada
- Oslo Peace Accords
- Ayatollah Ruholla Khomeini
- mujahideen
- Taliban
- Fidel Castro
- Anastasio Somoza
- Daniel Ortega
- Panama Canal

PREPARING FOR THE REGENTS

As you read this section, consider
- why it has proved so difficult to resolve conflict in the Middle East.
- the future of Latin America in the post-Cold War.

TIME LINE

1948
Israel is founded.

1959
Cuba becomes Communist.

1967
Israel wins Six Day War.

1973
Arab forces attack Israel in the Yom Kippur War.

1990
Communists are voted out of power in Nicaragua.

1991
Iraq loses the Persian Gulf War.

2001
Taliban are driven from power in Afghanistan.

Israel and Its Neighbors

Following World War II, the Jewish people won what for so long had eluded them: their own state. Their homeland along the eastern coast of the Mediterranean Sea came at a heavy price, however. A Jewish state was unwelcome in this mostly Arab region, and the resulting hostility led to conflict.

Human and Physical Geography—Israel Becomes a State In 1947, the United Nations General Assembly voted to partition Palestine into a Palestinian state and a Jewish state. Jerusalem was to be an international city owned by neither side. The terms of the partition gave Jews 55 percent of the area even though they made up only 34 percent of the population. In the wake of the war and the Holocaust, the United States and many European nations felt great sympathy for the Jews. All of the Islamic countries voted against partition, and the Palestinians rejected it outright. They argued that the UN did not have the right to partition a country without considering the wishes of the majority of its people. Nonetheless, the date was set for the formation of Israel—May 14, 1948.

The Arab–Israeli Conflict The new nation of Israel got a hostile greeting from its neighbors. The day after it proclaimed itself a state, six Islamic states—Egypt, Iraq, Jordan, Lebanon, Saudi Arabia, and Syria—invaded Israel. This first of many Arab-Israeli wars ended within months in a victory for Israel.

A second Arab-Israeli war followed in 1956. That year, Egypt seized control of the Suez Canal, which ran along Egypt's eastern border between the Gulf of Suez and the Mediterranean Sea. With air support provided by their European allies, the Israelis marched on the Suez Canal and quickly defeated the Egyptians. However, world pressure forced the victors to withdraw from Egypt. This left Egypt in charge of the canal and thus ended the Suez Crisis.

By early 1967, Egyptian president Gamal Abdel Nasser and his Arab allies felt ready to confront Israel. Convinced that the Arabs were about to attack, the Israelis struck airfields in Egypt, Iran, Jordan, and Syria. Safe from air attack, Israeli ground forces struck like lightning on three fronts. Israel quickly defeated the Arab states in what became known as the Six-Day War. Israel lost 800 troops, while Arab losses exceeded 15,000. Israel gained control of the old city of Jerusalem, the Sinai Peninsula, the Golan Heights, and the West Bank.

A fourth Arab-Israeli conflict erupted in October 1973. Nasser's successor, Egyptian president **Anwar Sadat** (AHN•wahr suh•DAT), planned a joint Arab attack on Yom Kippur, the holiest of Jewish holidays. This time the Israelis were caught by surprise. Arab forces inflicted heavy casualties and recaptured some of the territory lost in 1967. The Israelis, under their prime minister, **Golda Meir** (MY•uhr), launched a counterattack and regained most of the lost territory. Both sides agreed to a truce after several weeks of fighting.

TAKING NOTES

Following Chronological Order Use a graphic to fill in some important political and military events that occurred following the Suez Crisis.

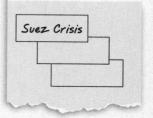

Suez Crisis

7.49 Preparing for the Regents

Nationalism When was the state of Israel created? How did the Arab world react?

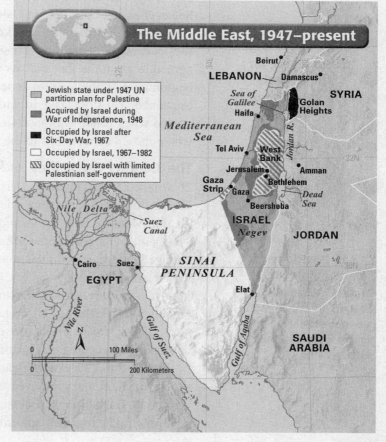

The Middle East, 1947–present

- Jewish state under 1947 UN partition plan for Palestine
- Acquired by Israel during War of Independence, 1948
- Occupied by Israel after Six-Day War, 1967
- Occupied by Israel, 1967–1982
- Occupied by Israel with limited Palestinian self-government

Beirut
LEBANON Damascus
Sea of Galilee
Haifa
SYRIA
Golan Heights
Mediterranean Sea
Tel Aviv
West Bank
Jerusalem
Amman
Gaza Strip
Bethlehem
Gaza
Dead Sea
Beersheba
Nile Delta
Suez Canal
ISRAEL
Negev
JORDAN
Cairo Suez
EGYPT
SINAI PENINSULA
Elat
Nile River
Gulf of Suez
Gulf of Aqaba
SAUDI ARABIA

0   100 Miles
0   200 Kilometers

7.50 Preparing for the Regents

Conflict What roles did Egypt and the United States play in the Arab-Israeli peace process in the 1970s?

Camp David Accords In November 1977, Anwar Sadat stunned the world by inviting his one-time enemies to join him in a quest for peace. In 1978, U.S. president Jimmy Carter invited Sadat and Israeli prime minister Menachem Begin (mehn•AHK•hehm BAY•gihn) to meet at Camp David, the presidential retreat in rural Maryland. After 13 days of negotiations, Carter triumphantly announced that Egypt recognized Israel as a legitimate state. In exchange, Israel agreed to return the Sinai Peninsula to Egypt. Signed in 1979, the **Camp David Accords** ended 30 years of hostilities between Egypt and Israel and became the first signed agreement between Israel and an Arab country. Enraged by the agreement, a group of Muslim extremists assassinated Sadat in 1981. However, Egypt has worked to maintain peace with Israel.

The Palestine Liberation Organization The Palestinians, a large number of whom lived in the West Bank and Gaza Strip, lands occupied by Israel, continued to clash with the Israelis. During the 1970s and 1980s, the military wing of the **PLO**—the Palestine Liberation Organization—intensified its armed struggle against Israel. (The PLO was formed in 1964. In 1969 **Yasir Arafat** (YAH•sur AR•uh•FAT) became its chairman.) Israel responded forcefully, bombing suspected rebel bases in Palestinian towns.

7.51 Preparing for the Regents

Conflict What tactics did the Palestinians use in the first intifada?

In 1987, Palestinians began to express their frustrations in a widespread campaign of civil disobedience called the **intifada**, or "uprising." The intifada took the form of boycotts, demonstrations, attacks on Israeli soldiers, and rock throwing by unarmed teenagers. The intifada continued into the 1990s, with little progress made toward a solution. However, the civil disobedience affected world opinion, which, in turn, put pressure on Israel to negotiate with the Palestinians. In October 1991, Israeli and Palestinian delegates met for a series of peace talks.

The Oslo Peace Accords Little progress was made in the 1991 talks. In 1993, however, secret talks held in Oslo, Norway, produced a surprise agreement: the Declaration of Principles, also known as the **Oslo Peace Accords**. Israel, under the leadership of Prime Minister Yitzhak Rabin (YIHTS•hahk rah•BEEN), agreed to grant the Palestinians self-rule in the Gaza Strip and the West Bank, beginning with the town of Jericho. Rabin and Arafat signed the agreement on September 13, 1993. The difficulty of making the agreement work was demonstrated when Rabin was assassinated in 1995 by a right-wing Jewish extremist who opposed concessions to the Palestinians.

7.52 Preparing for the Regents

Conflict Why was Yitzhak Rubin assassinated? What does this point out about the peace process?

The Conflict Intensifies Attempts at reviving the peace plan in 1997 and 2000 failed. Then, in 2000, a visit by Israeli political leader Ariel Sharon to the Temple Mount in Jerusalem, a Jewish holy place, sparked a second intifada. The Temple Mount is also the location of one of the most holy places for Muslims, The Dome of the Rock. Sharon's visit to the vicinity of such a revered Muslim site outraged Palestinians. In the second intifada, Palestinian militants began using a new weapon—suicide bombers. In response to the uprising, Israeli forces moved into Palestinian refugee camps and clamped down on militants. Troops destroyed buildings in which they suspected extremists were hiding and bulldozed entire areas of Palestinian towns and camps. The Israeli army even bombed Arafat's headquarters, trapping him inside his compound for many days.

7.53 Preparing for the Regents

Conflict What new weapon did the Palestinians use against Israel in the second intifada? How did Israel respond?

In early 2003, Palestinian leaders appointed Mahmoud Abbas, a high-ranking PLO official, as their first-ever prime minister. Shortly afterward, U.S. president George W. Bush brought together Sharon and Abbas to begin working on a new peace plan. The two men appeared committed to reaching an agreement. .

Islamic Fundamentalism

Religious differences are not the only source of conflict in the Middle East. The clash between traditional Islamic values and modern Western materialism also has a long history.

Iranian Revolution After World War II, Iran's leader, Shah Mohammed Reza Pahlavi (pah•luh•vee), embraced Western governments and wealthy Western oil companies. Iranian nationalists resented these foreign alliances. In 1953, they forced the shah to flee. Fearing Iran might turn to the Soviets for support, the United States helped restore the shah to power. With U.S. support, the shah westernized his country. He also tried to weaken the political influence of Iran's conservative Muslim leaders, known as ayatollahs (eye•uh•TOH•luhz), who opposed westernization. The leader of this religious opposition, **Ayatollah Ruholla Khomeini** (koh•MAY•nee), was living in exile. Spurred by his tape-recorded messages, Iranians rioted in every major city in late 1978. Faced with overwhelming opposition, the shah fled Iran in 1979. A triumphant Khomeini returned to establish an Islamic state and to export Iran's militant form of Islam.

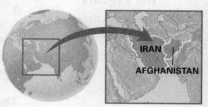

7.54 Preparing for the Regents

Belief Systems What role did Islamic fundamentalism play in the Iranian Revolution?

Afghanistan In the late 1970s, a Muslim revolt threatened to topple Afghanistan's Communist regime. This led to a Soviet invasion in 1979. The Afghan rebels, called **mujahideen** (moo•JAH•heh•DEEN), or holy warriors, fought back, finally pushing the Soviets out in 1989. Islamic religious students, or taliban, were among the mujahideen rebels who fought the Soviets. Various groups of students loosely organized themselves during a civil war among mujahideen factions that followed the Soviet withdrawal. In 1996, one of these groups, called the **Taliban**, seized power and established an Islamic government based on an extreme interpretation of Islamic law. Taliban leaders restricted women's lives by forbidding them to go to school or hold jobs. They banned everything from television and movies to modern music. Punishment for violating the rules included severe beatings, amputation, and even execution. They also gave sanctuary to international Islamic terrorists. In 2001, an anti-terrorist coalition led by the United States drove them from power.

7.55 Preparing for the Regents

Belief Systems What restrictions did the Taliban place on Afghan society in the 1990s?

Turkey Although Turkey is predominately Muslim, Islamic fundamentalists have had difficulty gaining political power in the country. The Turkish constitution strictly enforces a secular state. When the Islamic Welfare Party formed a coalition government with a secular party in 1996, people protested the government's attempt to enforce Islamic law. In 1998, Turkey's highest court declared that the Welfare Party violated the constitution. The party was disbanded.

7.56 Preparing for the Regents

Political Systems Why was the Islamic Welfare Party disbanded in Turkey?

Iraq and Its Neighbors

Iraq under Saddam Hussein (hoo•SAYN) has a history of aggression in the region. In the 1980s, secular Iraq went to war with fundamentalist Iran. By the time the UN secured a cease-fire, a million Iranians and Iraqis had died. Then in 1990, Iraq invaded Kuwait in an attempt to seize its oil fields.

The Persian Gulf War When Iraq invaded Kuwait, fears began to mount that it would also invade Saudi Arabia, another major source of oil. This would have put most of the world's petroleum supplies under Iraqi control. Economic sanctions imposed by the UN failed to persuade Iraq to withdraw from Kuwait. Then, in early 1991, a coalition of some 39 nations declared war on Iraq. After several weeks of fighting, the Iraqis left Kuwait and accepted a cease-fire.

7.57 Preparing for the Regents

Conflict What sparked the Persian Gulf War?

7.58 Preparing for the Regents

Conflict Why did the coalition forces overthrow Saddam Hussein?

Disarming Iraq As part of the cease-fire arrangements in the Persian Gulf War, Iraq agreed to destroy its weapons of mass destruction. However, in 2002, Saddam Hussein once again came under suspicion of developing such weapons. The UN Security Council issued a resolution threatening Iraq with "severe consequences" unless weapons inspectors were allowed into the country. Iraq complied, but some UN members suspected that the Iraqis were not fully cooperating with the inspectors. So, in March 2003, a coalition led by the United States and Great Britain sent troops to disarm Iraq by force. After four weeks of fighting, Saddam Hussein's government fell.

7.59 Preparing for the Regents

Human Rights What human rights violations have the Kurds faced?

The Kurds Fear of Iraq's weapons of mass destruction rested in part on the experience of the Kurds. For decades, Kurds have wanted their own separate country. But their traditional lands cross the borders of three nations—Turkey, Iran, and Iraq. In the past, the Turks responded to Kurdish nationalism by forbidding Kurds to speak their native language. The Iranians also persecuted the Kurds, attacking them over religious issues. In the late 1980s, however, the Iraqis took persecution to new level when they dropped poison gas on the Kurds, killing 5,000. Several international organizations, including the UN, are working to end the human rights abuses inflicted upon the Kurds.

Terrorism in the Middle East

7.60 Preparing for the Regents

Conflict What role does terrorism play in the Middle East?

Many Middle Eastern terrorist organizations have roots in the Israeli-Palestinian conflict. Groups such as the Palestine Islamic Jihad, Hamas, and Hizballah have sought to prevent a peace settlement between Israel and the Palestinians. They want a homeland for the Palestinians on their own terms, with the most extreme among them denying Israel's right to exist. Afghanistan became a haven for international terrorists when Osama bin Laden, a Saudi Arabian millionaire involved in terrorist activities, moved to Afghanistan in 1996. There he began using mountain hideouts as a base of operations for his global network of Muslim terrorists known as al-Qaeda.

Political and Economic Change in Latin America

After World War II, rapid industrialization, population growth, and a lingering gap between the rich and the poor led Latin American nations to seek aid from both superpowers. At the same time, many of these countries struggled to move from dictatorships and military control to democracies.

Cuba In the 1950s, Cuba was ruled by an unpopular dictator, Fulgencio Batista, who had U.S. support. Cuban resentment led to a popular revolution, which overthrew Batista in January 1959. A young lawyer named **Fidel Castro** led that revolution. At first, many people praised Castro for bringing social reforms to Cuba, improving the economy, and raising the standard of living for many Cubans. Yet Castro was a harsh dictator. He suspended elections, jailed or executed his opponents, and tightly controlled the press. When Castro took over U.S.-owned sugar mills and refineries, the United States ordered an embargo on all trade with Cuba. Castro then turned to the Soviets for economic and military aid. In exchange for Soviet support, he backed Communist revolutions in Latin America and Africa. Soviet aid to Cuba ended abruptly with the breakup of the Soviet Union in 1991. This loss dealt a crippling blow to the Cuban economy. But the aging Castro refused to adopt economic reforms or to give up power.

7.61 Preparing for the Regents

Interdependence How was Cuba affected by the breakup of the Soviet Union?

Nicaragua Just as the United States had supported Batista in Cuba, it had funded the Nicaraguan dictatorship of **Anastasio Somoza** and his family since 1933. In 1979, Communist Sandinista rebels toppled Somoza's son. Both the United States and the Soviet Union initially gave aid to the Sandinistas and their leader, **Daniel Ortega** (awr•TAY•guh). The Sandinistas, however, gave assistance to other Marxist rebels in nearby El Salvador. To help the El Salvadoran government fight those rebels, the United States supported Nicaraguan anti-Communist forces called the Contras or *contrarevolucionarios*. The civil war in Nicaragua lasted more than a decade and seriously weakened the country's economy. In 1990, President Ortega agreed to hold free elections, the first in the nation's history. Violeta Chamorro, a reform candidate, defeated him.

Argentina Argentina had struggled to establish a democracy. In 1946, Argentine workers supported an army officer, Juan Perón, who won the presidency and then established a dictatorship. In 1955, the military ousted Perón and drove him into exile. Perón returned to power in 1973, but ruled for only a year before dying in office. In 1976, the generals seized power again. They established a brutal dictatorship and hunted down political opponents. For several years, torture and murder were everyday events. By the early 1980s, several thousand Argentines had simply disappeared, kidnapped by their own government. Groups like the *Abuelas de Plaza de Mayo* (Grandmothers of the Plaza de Mayo) demanded to know the fate of their relatives.

In 1983, Argentines elected Raúl Alfonsín (ahl•fohn•SEEN) president in the country's first free election in 37 years. During the 1980s, Alfonsín worked to rebuild democracy and the economy. Carlos Menem gained the presidency in 1989 and continued the process. He attempted to stabilize the currency and privatize industry. By the late 1990s, however, economic problems intensified. In December 2001, the International Monetary Fund (IMF) refused to provide financial aid to Argentina. Then President Fernando de la Rua resigned in the face of protests over the economy. He was succeeded by Eduardo Duhalde, who tried to deal with the economic and social crisis. In 2002, Argentina had an unemployment rate of about 24 percent. The country defaulted on $132 billion in debt, the largest debt default in history, and devalued its currency. In 2003, Argentina struggled to regain its political and economic footing. In elections that year, Nestor Kirchner became the new president of Argentina.

> **7.62 Preparing for the Regents**
> **Power** How was Nicaragua affected by Cold War rivalries?

> **7.63 Preparing for the Regents**
> **Human Rights** What human rights violations have occurred in Argentina?

> **7.64 Preparing for the Regents**
> **Economic Systems** What economic challenges does Argentina face?

PREPARING FOR THE REGENTS

On a separate sheet of paper, write a well-organized essay that includes an introduction, several paragraphs addressing the task below, and a conclusion. Before beginning, check the Score the Essay box for pointers.

Theme: Political Events
Twentieth-century political events have had positive and negative effects on global history.

Task:
Identify *two* 20th-century political events in the Middle East or Latin America and for *each*
- Discuss the historical circumstances surrounding the event
- Evaluate the extent to which this event has had a positive *or* negative effect on the Middle East or Latin America

SCORE THE ESSAY To receive a score of 5 on your essay, you will need to:
- thoroughly develop all aspects of the task evenly and in depth by discussing the historical circumstances surrounding the events and the effects of the events on the country or region.
- be more analytical than descriptive.
- richly support the theme with relevant facts, examples, and details.
- demonstrate a logical and clear plan of organization.

The Twentieth Century Since 1945

Part I: MULTIPLE-CHOICE QUESTIONS

Directions (1–10): For each statement or question, write on a separate answer sheet the *number* of the word or expression that, of those given, best completes the statement or answers the questions.

1 One similarity in the actions of Ho Chi Minh and Jomo Kenyatta was that both leaders

(1) introduced Western ideas to their societies
(2) established democratic government
(3) led nationalists movements
(4) supported separation of church and state

2 Which statement is accurate about the Hungarian Revolution of 1956 and the Tiananmen Square demonstrations in 1989?

(1) These events led to democratic reforms.
(2) Repressive action was taken to end both protests.
(3) Strong action was taken by the United Nations.
(4) Both events brought Communist governments to power.

3 A major source of the dispute between the Israelis and the Palestinians is that each side

(1) wants to control oil reserves in the area
(2) has historic ties to the same land
(3) believes in different interpretations of the same religion
(4) has close military alliances with neighboring countries

4 The United Nations was created primarily to

(1) prosecute persons accused of war crimes
(2) contain the spread of communism
(3) channel relief aid to war-torn nations
(4) provide a means of solving international problems

5 The formation of the North Atlantic Treaty Organization (NATO), the division of Germany into East Germany and West Germany, and the Korean War were immediate reactions to

(1) Japanese military aggression in the 1930s
(2) the rise of German nationalism after World War I
(3) ethnic conflict in the 1950s
(4) Communist expansion after World War II

6 Mikhail Gorbachev instituted the policies of glasnost and perestroika to

(1) reinforce the basic economic principles of communism
(2) bring the Soviet Union into the European Economic Community
(3) reform the Soviet Union politically and economically
(4) gain acceptance for free political elections

7 Since the 1980s, Chinese leaders have tried to improve China's economy by implementing a policy of

(1) isolation
(2) collectivization
(3) limited free-enterprise
(4) representative government

8 Although Cuba has lost support from many nations, one reason Fidel Castro has remained in power is that he has

(1) established free trade with the United States
(2) opposed communism
(3) prohibited the practice of Catholicism
(4) raised the standard of living for many Cubans

9 The partition of India and the division of Yugoslavia were similar in that both were divided

(1) as a result of the Berlin Conference
(2) because of religious and ethnic differences
(3) to form Communist and non-Communist states
(4) to conform to United Nations guidelines

10 The Truman Doctrine and the Marshall Plan were designed to

(1) promote economic and political stability in Europe
(2) end German demands for Sudetenland
(3) restore democratic rule in Haiti
(4) prevent Iraq's takeover of Kuwait

In developing your answers to Part II, be sure to keep these general definitions in mind:

(a) *describe* means "to illustrate something in words or tell about it"

(b) *explain* means "to make plain or understandable; to give reasons for or causes of; to show the logical development or relationship of"

(c) *compare and contrast* means "to express similarities and differences"

(d) *discuss* means "to make observations about something using facts, reasoning, and argument; to present in some detail"

Part II: THEMATIC ESSAY

Directions: Write a well-organized essay that includes an introduction, several paragraphs addressing the task below, and a conclusion.

Theme: Change—Turning Points

> Political, economic, and social conditions have often led to turning points that have changed the course of history for nations and peoples.

Task:

> Identify *two* turning points from your study of this unit and for each
> - Describe the causes and key events that led to the turning point
> - Explain how each turning point changed the course of history for nations and peoples

You may use any example from your study of Unit Seven. Some suggestions you might wish to consider include the establishment of the state of Israel, the Chinese Communist Revolution, the collapse of European imperialism, Nelson Mandela's election as president of South Africa, or the fall of the Berlin Wall/collapse of Soviet Union.

You are not limited to these suggestions.

Guidelines:

In your essay, be sure to
- Address all aspects of the *Task*
- Support the theme with relevant facts, examples, and details
- Use a logical and clear plan of organization, including an introduction and a conclusion that are beyond the simple restatement of the *Theme*

Part III: DOCUMENT-BASED QUESTION

This question is based on the accompanying documents (1–3). The question is designed to test your ability to work with historic documents. Some of these documents have been edited for the purpose of this question. As you analyze the documents, take into account both the source of each document and any point of view that may be presented in the document.

Historical Context:

Despite the horrors of the Holocaust, abuses of human rights have continued in the post–World War II era.

Task:

Using information from the documents and your knowledge of global history, answer the question that follows each document in Part A. Your answers to the questions will help you write the Part B essay, in which you will be asked to:

> • Describe examples of human rights abuses in the post–World War II era
> • Discuss efforts that the world community has made to eliminate these human rights abuses

Part A: Short Answer

Directions: Analyze the documents and answer the short-answer questions that follow in the space provided.

Document 1

> From the middle of 1975 to the end of 1978, between one million and 3 million Cambodians, out of a population of about seven million, died at the hands of Pol Pot's Khmer Rouge. Former government employees, army personnel, and "intellectuals" were executed in the hundreds of thousands. Others were killed by disease, exhaustion, and malnutrition during forced urban evacuations, migrations, and compulsory labor. Families were broken apart and communal living established; men and women were compelled to marry partners selected by the state.

—David Hawk, "The Killing of Cambodia," *The New Republic,* 1982

Document 2

Ending Apartheid in South Africa	
1973:	United Nations General Assembly declares apartheid a crime against humanity.
1977:	United Nations Security Council embargoes arms exported to South Africa.
1983:	New Constitution gives limited political rights to coloured and Asian minorities.
1986:	United States imposes broad economic sanctions.
1990:	Mandela released from prison. Legal end of segregation in public places.
1991–93:	Dismantling apartheid and enfranchising black majority.
1994:	First all-race election.

1 Identify *two* human rights violations by the Khmer Rouge mentioned in Document 1.

_____

_____

2 Based on Document 2, identify *two* actions taken to end apartheid.

_____

_____

Document 3

Universal Declaration of Human Rights

Article 1 — All human beings are born free and equal in dignity and rights.

Article 3 — Everyone has the right to life, liberty and security of person.

Article 4 — No one shall be held in slavery or servitude; slavery and the slave trade shall be prohibited in all their forms.

Article 5 — No one shall be subjected to torture or to cruel, inhumane or degrading treatment or punishment.

Article 9 — No one shall be subjected to arbitrary arrest, detention, or exile.

Article 13 — 1. Everyone has the right to freedom of movement and residence within the borders of each State.
2. Everyone has the right to leave any country, including his own, and to return to his country.

Article 14 — Everyone has the right to seek and to enjoy in other countries asylum from persecution.

3 State *two* human rights listed in this document.

_____

_____

_____

_____

Part B: Essay

Directions: Write a well-organized essay that includes an introduction, several paragraphs, and a conclusion. Use evidence from at least **two** documents to support your response.

Historical Context: Despite the horrors of the Holocaust, abuses of human rights have continued in the post–World War II era

Task: Using information from the documents and your knowledge of global history, answer the question that follows each document in Part A. Your answers to the questions will help you write the Part B essay, in which you will be asked to:

> • Describe examples of human rights abuses in the post–World War II era
> • Discuss efforts that the world community has made to eliminate these human rights abuses

Guidelines:

In your essay, be sure to
- Address all aspects of the *Task* by accurately analyzing and interpreting at least **two** documents
- Incorporate information from the documents
- Incorporate relevant outside information
- Support the theme with relevant facts, examples, and details
- Use a logical and clear plan of organization
- Introduce the theme by establishing a framework that is beyond a simple statement of the *Task* or *Historical Context* and conclude with a summation of the theme

Global Connections and Interactions

Section 1   Social, Political, and Economic Patterns
Section 2   Science, Technology, and the Environment

Unit Overview

This unit examines the increasingly global nature of the world since World War II. It begins by looking at a variety of social, political, and economic issues. These issues include migration and urbanization, the effects of rapid population growth and other population pressures, human rights, world peace, and economic interdependence and globalization. It then looks at how people and society have been affected by advances in science and technology. The unit closes by examining the environmental effects of economic development and globalization.

Concepts and Themes

Among the concepts and themes explored in this unit are

- Change
- Conflict
- Economic Systems
- Environment and Society
- Human and Physical Geography

- Human Rights
- Interdependence
- Movement of People and Goods
- Science and Technology
- Wants and Needs

PREPARING FOR THE REGENTS: Building Thematic Essay Skills

Science and technology have played critical roles in altering the course of human history. In modern times, the computer and the Internet, for instance, have revolutionized the way many people and businesses interact with the world. As you read this unit, think about how the scientific and technological advances you encounter have produced lasting changes. Use the following chart to organize information about these advances. You can add additional rows as needed.

Scientific or Technological Advance	Short-Term Effects	Long-Term Effects

Social, Political, and Economic Patterns

Section Overview

The world's story since World War II has been the continuing march toward globalization. Globalization can be described in broad terms as a process that makes something worldwide. Globalization is most often used in reference to the spread and diffusion of economic or cultural influences. But the process of globalization also includes the movement of people. In recent decades, this has increasingly meant the movement of people from less developed to more developed nations as they seek economic opportunity or try to escape from political oppression or natural disasters. Not all immigrants have a place to go. Millions end up in crowded refugee camps.

Population levels in many developing regions of the world continue to grow. This places additional pressures on scarce resources and makes the establishment of stable democracies and sound economies more difficult. In attempts to develop their economies, many nations in Latin America and Africa have built up crushing foreign debts, only adding to their economic problems.

The situation is much different for nations like Japan and Korea, who have built strong economies based on industry and foreign trade. These nations can take full advantage of the positive effects of economic globalization.

Afghan refugees

MAIN IDEAS

POWER AND AUTHORITY Since 1945, nations have used collective security efforts to solve problems.

ECONOMICS The economies of the world's nations are so tightly linked that the actions of one nation affect others.

TERMS AND NAMES

- refugee
- emerging nation
- standard of living
- AIDS
- Universal Declaration of Human Rights
- gender inequality
- proliferation
- SALT
- global economy
- free trade
- developed nation

PREPARING FOR THE REGENTS

As you read this section, consider
- the factors that influence the global patterns of modern migration.
- why urbanization and population pressures are issues facing all nations.
- how the global economy has changed since 1945.
- how globalization has different effects in developed and emerging nations.

TIME LINE

1968
Many nations sign the Nuclear Non-Proliferation Treaty.

1975
The Helsinki Accords support human rights.

1983
French research scientists isolate the AIDS virus.

1992
The European Economic Community becomes the European Union.

1994
NAFTA goes into effect.

Human and Physical Geography: Migration and Urbanization

8.1 Preparing for the Regents

Movement of People and Goods Why do people migrate from their homelands to other places?

The global movement of people has increased dramatically in recent years. Most people move from less developed nations to more developed nations in hope of a better life. Many people move because they feel pushed out of their homelands by such factors as a lack of food, natural disasters, or political oppression. In 2001 alone, the number of **refugees**—people who leave their country to move to another to find safety—stood at 12 million. Because of the huge volume of people migrating from war-torn, famine-stricken, and politically unstable regions, millions of immigrants have no place to go. Crowded into refugee camps, these migrants face a very uncertain future.

Everyone has the right to leave his or her country. However, the country to which a migrant wants to move may not accept that person. The receiving country might have one acceptance policy for political refugees, and another for migrants coming for economic reasons. This can lead to illegal immigration, as it has in the case of poor Mexicans seeking work in the United States. Concern over the fate of such workers has led the Mexican government to urge the U.S. government to legalize the status of millions of illegal Mexican immigrants living within U.S. borders.

8.2 Preparing for the Regents

Movement of People and Goods What issues exist between Mexico and the United States concerning immigration?

There also has been an increase in migration within countries, as industrialization has caused people to move from rural areas to cities in search of employment. In 1960, only New York City had a population of over 10 million. By 2000, the number of cities with more than 10 million people had climbed to 19. The United Nations estimates that by 2015, the five largest cities in the world will each have populations of over 20 million people.

Population Pressures

Most of the world's largest and fastest-growing cities are in **emerging nations**, those in the process of becoming industrialized. In 1975, Bombay (Mumbai), India, for instance, had a population of about 6.9 million people. By 2000, the city's population had jumped to about 17.8 million. India is expected to push past China as the world's most populous nation by 2035. In 1979, China introduced a "one-child family" policy. The policy, although controversial, has helped slow China's population growth. While the Indian government has also spent considerable money and effort promoting family planning measures, it has had only limited success.

8.3 Preparing for the Regents

Culture and Intellectual Life How has China attempted to deal with its population growth?

Poverty Experts disagree about what constitutes overpopulation. Some experts measure overpopulation in relation to a county's **standard of living**, or level of material comfort. A country is considered overpopulated, if having fewer people would raise the standard of living to an adequate level. Others hold that overpopulation occurs when the number of people outpaces the available resources. This is referred to as an area's carrying capacity. Regardless of the definition, large populations in emerging nations are often associated with high rates of poverty and disease. This is true in many nations in Latin America and Asia. Troubled by the poverty,

Poverty Levels in Asia, 2002

Country	% of population in poverty
Philippines	41%
Bangladesh	35.6%
Pakistan	35%
India	25%
Myanmar	25%
United States	12.7%

% of population in poverty

Source: The CIA World Factbook, 2002

disease, and homelessness that she saw on the streets of Calcutta (Kolkata), India, Mother Teresa (1910–1997) founded the Order of the Missionaries of Charity in Calcutta to help the needy.

The AIDS Epidemic Disease also takes its toll on populations. Perhaps the greatest global health issue is a disease known as **AIDS**, or acquired immune deficiency syndrome. It attacks the immune system, leaving sufferers open to deadly infections. Since the disease was first detected in the early 1980s, AIDS has claimed the lives of nearly 25 million people. By the end of 2002, there were 42 million people across the world living with HIV (the virus that causes AIDS) or AIDS. About 70 percent of those people were living in Sub-Saharan Africa. In 2002, on average, more than 6,500 people died of AIDS each day in this region. Most of those dying were between the ages of 15 and 49—the years at which people are most productive economically.

Human Rights

In 1948, the UN issued the **Universal Declaration of Human Rights**, which set human rights standards for all nations. It stated that "All human beings are born free and equal in dignity and rights. . . . Everyone has the right to life, liberty, and security of person." The declaration further listed specific rights that all human beings should have. Later, in the Helsinki Accords of 1975, the UN addressed the issues of freedom of movement and freedom to publish and exchange information. Both the declaration and the accords are nonbinding. However, the sentiments in these documents inspired many people around the world. They made a commitment to ensuring that basic human rights are respected.

The Status of Women and Children In 1975, the United Nations held the first of several international conferences on the status of women in the world. In 2000, the UN reviewed the status of women. Its report, titled *Progress of the World's Women 2000*, found that women had made notable gains during the 1990s, especially in the areas of education and work. Even so, the report concluded that **gender inequality**—the difference between men and women in terms of wealth and status—still very much existed.

The rights of children is also a growing concern. To save on labor costs in the 1990s and 2000s, many corporations moved their manufacturing operations overseas to emerging countries. There, in sweatshops, young children work long hours under wretched conditions, unprotected by labor laws. For mere pennies per hour, children weave carpets, sort vegetables, or assemble expensive athletic shoes. Several organizations are working to end child labor, including the Child Welfare League of America and the International Labor Rights Fund.

Ethnic and Religious Tensions Ethnic or religious violence is a problem in some countries. In Guatemala, for instance, tens of thousands of Guatemalan peasants, mostly Native Americans, were killed before the country's 36-year civil war ended in 1996. The people of East Timor, a primarily Roman Catholic nation in Southeast Asian, suffered decades of human rights violations in their quest for independence from the predominately Muslim Indonesia. In August 1999, after the East Timorese voted overwhelmingly for independence in a UN-sponsored referendum, pro-Indonesian forces went on a bloody rampage. They killed hundreds of East Timorese and forced thousands into refugee camps in West Timor, which is a part of Indonesia. UN intervention forces eventually brought peace to the area. In 2002 East Timor celebrated independence.

8.4 Preparing for the Regents

Human and Physical Geography What is AIDS? What effect has it had in Africa?

8.5 Preparing for the Regents

Human Rights How has the UN attempted to promote and protect human rights?

8.6 Preparing for the Regents

Human Rights What are some of the human rights issues that children face?

8.7 Preparing for the Regents

Human Rights What role did the UN play in the conflict in East Timor?

8.8 Preparing for the Regents

Human Rights Why do you think the UN views education and literacy as human rights issues?

Literacy and Education Citing literacy and education as basic human rights, the United Nations proclaimed 2003–2012 as the United Nations Literacy Decade. According to the UN, over 113 million children do not attend school, and more than 861 million adults are unable to read or write. The UN believes that literacy is an essential tool in ending poverty, reducing infant death rates, curbing population growth, achieving gender equality, and ensuring economic development, peace, and democracy.

Issues of War and Peace

One of the major aims of the UN is to promote world peace. The UN provides a public forum, private meeting places, and skilled mediators to help nations try to resolve conflicts at any stage of their development. At the invitation of the warring parties, the UN also provides peacekeeping forces. These forces are made up of soldiers from different nations. As of the end of 2002, the UN had close to 40,000 soldiers and police in 13 peacekeeping forces around the world.

Nations also work to keep peace by forging treaties to limit the manufacturing, testing, and trade of weapons. The weapons of most concern are those that cause mass destruction. These include nuclear, chemical, and biological weapons that can kill thousands, even millions, of people. In 1968, many nations signed a Nuclear Non-Proliferation Treaty to help prevent the **proliferation**, or spread, of nuclear weapons to other nations. In the 1970s, the United States and the Soviet Union signed the Strategic Arms Limitation Treaties (**SALT**), and in the 1980s, both countries talked about deactivating some of their nuclear weapons.

Economic Interdependence and Globalization

TAKING NOTES

Categorizing Use a web diagram to identify the forces that have shaped the global economy.

Forces that shape a global economy

One of the hallmarks of the modern world is the rise of the true global economy. The **global economy** includes all the financial interactions—among people, businesses, and governments—that cross international borders. A major goal of globalization is **free trade**, or the elimination of trade barriers, such as tariffs, among nations. As early as 1947, nations began discussing ways to open trade. The result was the General Agreement on Tariffs and Trade (GATT).

Multinational Corporations Companies that operate in a number of different countries are called multinational or transnational corporations. U.S. companies such as Exxon Mobil, General Motors, and Ford; European companies such as BP, DaimlerChrysler, and Royal Dutch/Shell; and Japanese companies such as Toyota, Mitsubishi, and Mitsui all became multinational giants. All of these companies have established manufacturing plants, offices, or stores in many countries. For their manufacturing plants, they select spots where the raw materials or labor are cheapest. This enables them to produce components of their products on different continents. They ship the various components to another location to be assembled. This level of economic integration allows such companies to view the whole world as the market for their goods. Goods or services are distributed throughout the world as if there were no national boundaries.

8.10 Preparing for the Regents

Interdependence What role do trading blocs play in the global economy?

Trading Blocs In 1951, a group of European countries established an organization to promote tariff-free trade among member countries. The success of this experiment led to formation of the European Economic Community (EEC) six years later. Over time, most Western European countries joined the organization, which has been known as the European Union (EU) since 1992. Several of the former Communist nations of Eastern Europe also have applied to become EU members.

The economic success of the EU inspired countries in other regions to make trade agreements with each other. The North American Free Trade Agreement (NAFTA), put into effect in 1994, called for the gradual elimination of tariffs and trade restrictions among Canada, the United States, and Mexico. Organizations in Asia, Africa, Latin America, and the South Pacific have also created regional trade policies. The Organization of Petroleum Exporting Countries (OPEC), for instance, establishes oil production and pricing policies for its members.

8.11 Preparing for the Regents

Interdependence Why is OPEC an important player in the global economy?

Economic Development in Latin America and Africa

There is considerable debate on the impact of globalization. Supporters suggest that open, competitive markets and the free flow of goods, services, technology, and investments benefit all nations. Some opponents agree that most nations gain some benefit from globalization. However, they note that **developed nations**—those nations with the industrialization, transportation, and business facilities for advanced production of manufactured goods—have benefited the most. Other opponents charge that globalization has been a disaster for the poorest countries.

Critics of globalization often cite conditions in Latin America and Africa to make their point. Three centuries of European rule left Latin American economies too dependent on a single crop. While Latin America has made progress in establishing industries, many regions remain underdeveloped and many countries suffer from soaring foreign debt. The colonial powers also encouraged the export of one or two cash crops in Africa, rather than the production of a range of products to serve local needs. They also developed few factories. Instead, manufactured goods were imported from European countries. As a result, most African nations still have unbalanced economies and a small middle class.

8.12 Preparing for the Regents

Economic Systems What economic challenges do Latin America and Africa face? How are these challenges influenced by the fact that many of the nations are former colonies?

Economic Development in Japan and South Korea

Supporters of globalization often cite the economic success of Japan and South Korea. Following World War II, Japan created a strong economy based on participation in global markets. It poured money into industrial development, focusing on shipbuilding and on the manufacture of automobiles, cameras, and electronic goods. By the 1970s, Japan was the third-largest industrial nation in the world. South Korea followed Japan's example in the 1960s. During the 1980s and 1990s, South Korea had one of the highest economic growth rates in the world. Today, South Korea is a major producer of such manufactured goods as automobiles and electronics.

8.13 Preparing for the Regents

Economic Systems How did Japan and Korea build their economic success after World War II?

PREPARING FOR THE REGENTS

Answer the following question. Use the Analyze the Question hints to help you answer the question.

1 The main purpose of the European Union (EU) and the North American Free Trade Agreement (NAFTA) is to

(1) reduce the spread of nuclear weapons

(2) address the problem of international political corruption

(3) increase educational opportunities for underdeveloped nations

(4) stimulate economic growth for participating countries

ANALYZE THE QUESTION
- Read the question stem. You are being asked to indicate the purpose of the EU and NAFTA.
- Think about what you know about each organization and determine what purpose they both share.
- Eliminate any alternative that does not relate to the main purpose of both organizations. The remaining alternative will be the correct answer.

Science, Technology, and the Environment

Section Overview

The space race that began in the late 1950s helped change the world. The heavy emphasis on science and technology that the space race required led to the development of products that changed life for people across the globe. New technologies changed how many people lived and where and how they worked. The computer and the silicone chip created new industries and changed the way old ones operated. The revolution in global communications that computers and the Internet sparked helped turn the world into a global village. And for many, advances in medicine improved their prospects for a healthy life. Scientific efforts also improved crop yields and helped lessen famine and hunger in the world.

These advances in science and technology and the economic growth they helped generate did not come without an environmental cost, however. Deforestation, desertification, pollution, and the loss of plant and animal species were unintended consequences. This has led scientists and economists to work together to develop methods for sustainable growth—growth that meets current economic needs while still protecting the environment and natural resources.

Handheld computer

MAIN IDEAS

SCIENCE AND TECHNOLOGY   Advances in technology after World War II led to increased global interaction and improved quality of life.

TERMS AND NAMES

- International Space Station
- Internet
- genetic engineering
- cloning
- green revolution
- ozone layer
- sustainable growth

PREPARING FOR THE REGENTS

As you read this section, consider
- what Thomas Malthus would have thought about the impact of science and technology on life spans and health.
- how societies balance the desire for economic development with the pressures such development places on the environment.

TIME LINE

1972
U.S. and Soviets agree to a joint space venture.

1990
U.S. launches *Magellan* probe to study Venus.

1998
Construction begins on the International Space Station.

Breakthroughs in Science, Technology, and Medicine

Beginning in the late 1950s, the United States and the Soviet Union competed in the exploration of space. The heavy emphasis on science and technology that the space race required led to the development of products that changed life for people across the globe.

Space Exploration Although it started out as a race, space exploration eventually became an arena for cooperation. On July 17, 1975, years before the end of the Cold War, the United States and the Soviet Union docked their spacecraft some 140 miles above Earth. While this event was isolated, people from different countries continued to work together to explore space. The crew of the Soviet *Soyuz 28*, which orbited Earth in 1978, included a Czech cosmonaut. Since the mid-1980s, United States space shuttle crews have included astronauts from Saudi Arabia, France, Germany, Canada, Italy, Japan, Israel, and Mexico. The space shuttle is being used in the most ambitious cooperative space venture—the **International Space Station** (ISS), sponsored by the United States, Russia, and 14 other nations. Since 1998, U.S. shuttles and Russian spacecraft have transported sections of the ISS to be assembled in space. Once completed, the ISS will cover an area the size of a football field and house a crew of six.

Unmanned space probes have been used to study the farther reaches of the solar system. The Soviet *Venera* spacecraft in the 1970s and the *Magellan* probe launched by the United States in 1990 have provided in-depth information about Venus. The U.S. *Voyager 2*, launched in 1977, sent dazzling pictures of Jupiter, Saturn, Uranus, and Neptune back to Earth during its 12-year journey. The U.S. probe *Pathfinder*, which landed on Mars in 1997, provided spectacular results.

In 1990, the U.S. space agency, NASA, and the European space agency, ESA, worked together to develop and launch the Hubble Space Telescope. This orbiting telescope continues to observe and send back images of objects in the most remote regions of the universe.

Global Communications Since the 1960s, artificial satellites launched into orbit around Earth have aided worldwide communications. This linking of the globe through worldwide communications is made possible by the miniaturization of the computer, which, in turn, was made possible by the development of the silicon chip. Smaller than contact lenses, silicon chips hold millions of microscopic circuits. Today a variety of consumer products such as microwave ovens, telephones, keyboard instruments, and cars use computers and chips. Computers have become essential in most offices, and millions of people around the globe have computers in their homes.

Starting in the 1990s, businesses and individuals began using the **Internet**. The Internet is the voluntary linkage of computer networks around the world. It began in the late 1960s as a method of linking scientists so they could exchange information about research. Between 1995 and late 2002, the number of worldwide Internet users soared from 26 million to more than 600 million. Conducting business on the Internet has become a way of life for many. The Internet, along with fax machines, transmits information electronically to remote locations. Both paved the way for home offices and telecommuting—working at home using a computer connected to a business network. Once again, technology has changed how and where people work.

TAKING NOTES
Recognizing Effects Use a chart to list the effects of scientific and technological developments.

Developments	Effects
Communications	
Health and Medicine	
Green Revolution	

8.14 Preparing for the Regents

Science and Technology What general conclusion can you draw about global Internet usage from the chart below?

Internet Users Worldwide	
Africa	6.31 million
Asia and the Pacific	187.24 million
Europe	190.91 million
Middle East	5.12 million
Canada and U.S.	182.67 million
Latin America	33.35 million
Worldwide	**605.60 million**

Source: Nua Internet Surveys

⚜ **8.15 Preparing for the Regents**

Science and Technology
How did technology change the way people worked, what they produced, and how they processed information?

Technology and the Economy In both Asia and the Western world, an explosion in scientific knowledge prompted great progress that quickly led to new industries. A prime example was plastics. In the 1950s, a process to develop plastics from petroleum at low pressures and low temperatures was perfected. Within a few years, industries made a host of products easily and cheaply out of plastics. Other technological advances have also changed industrial processes, lowered costs, and increased the quality or the speed of production. For example, robotic arms on automobile assembly lines made possible the fast and safe manufacture of high-quality cars.

Technological advances in manufacturing reduced the need for factory workers. But in other areas of the economy, new demands were emerging. Computerization and communications advances changed the processing of information. By the 1980s, people could transmit information quickly and cheaply. Information industries such as financial services, insurance, market research, and communications services boomed. Those industries depended on "knowledge workers"—people who work with information.

⚜ **8.16 Preparing for the Regents**

Science and Technology
How have advances in health and medicine improved life?

Health and Medicine Advances with computers and communications networks have transformed not only the ways in which people work but their health as well. In the 1960s and 1970s, new technologies, such as more powerful microscopes, the laser, and ultrasound, were developed. Many of these technologies advanced surgical techniques. Advances in medical imaging also helped to improve health care. Using data provided by CAT scans and MRI techniques, doctors can build three-dimensional images of different organs or regions of the body to use in diagnosing injuries, detecting tumors, or collecting other medical information.

In the 1980s, genetics, the study of heredity through research on genes, became a fast-growing field of science. Found in the cells of all organisms, genes are hereditary units that cause specific traits, such as eye color. Technology allowed scientists to isolate and examine individual genes that are responsible for different traits. Through **genetic engineering**, scientists were able to introduce new genes into an organism to give that organism new traits. Another aspect of genetic engineering is **cloning**—the creation of identical copies of DNA, the chemical chains of genes that determine heredity. Cloning allows scientists to reproduce plants and animals that are identical to existing plants and animals. The application of genetics research to everyday life has led to many breakthroughs, especially in agriculture.

⚜ **8.17 Preparing for the Regents**

Wants and Needs What were some of the positive and negative consequences of the green revolution?

The Green Revolution and World Hunger In the 1960s, agricultural scientists started a campaign known as the **green revolution**. It was an attempt to increase food production worldwide. Scientists promoted the use of fertilizers, pesticides, and high-yield, disease-resistant strains of a variety crops. The green revolution helped avert famine and increase crop yields in many parts of the world. There were drawbacks, however. The cost of the chemicals and the equipment to harvest more crops was far too expensive for an average peasant farmer. Some farmers were even forced off their land by agricultural businesses. In addition, fertilizers and pesticides often contain dangerous chemicals that may cause cancer and pollute the environment. Advances in genetics research seem to be helping to fulfill some of the goals of the green revolution. By breeding pest resistance and tolerance to poor soils into plants, scientists are able to reduce the need for pesticides and fertilizers. This "gene revolution" involves some risks, however, including the accidental creation of disease-causing organisms. Nonetheless, the revolution holds great promise for increasing food production in a world with an expanding population.

The Environment

Economic development and advances in science and technology have improved the lives of many. Such advances have not been without environmental costs, however. The deforestation that occurs when trees are cut down for timber, fuel, mining, agriculture, or other purposes and not replanted has long been an environmental problem. The World Bank estimates that about 54,000 square miles are deforested each year around the world. Much of this deforestation occurs in the Amazon Basin, the Congo, and other tropical rainforests. Desertification—the spread of deserts that results from such factors as climate changes, overgrazing, poor farming techniques, and deforestation—is particularly a problem in parts of Africa and the Indian subcontinent. It is estimated that about 135 million people are directly affected by desertification. Sometimes societies fall victim to accidents. On April 26, 1986, the nuclear power plant in Chernobyl, a town in northern Ukraine, exploded, immediately killing 32 people. The area was permanently evacuated, as a fallout cloud drifted west across Europe.

Pollution Economic development has had a major impact on pollution levels. The burning of coal and oil as an energy source releases carbon dioxide into the atmosphere, causing health-damaging air pollution and acid rain. Some scientists believe that the buildup of carbon dioxide in the atmosphere also has contributed to global warming. The release of chemicals called chlorofluorocarbons (CFCs), used in refrigerators, air conditioners, and manufacturing processes, has destroyed ozone in Earth's upper atmosphere. The **ozone layer** is our main protection against the Sun's damaging ultraviolet rays. With the increase in ultraviolet radiation reaching Earth's surface, the incidence of skin cancer continues to rise in many parts of the world. Increased ultraviolet radiation also may result in damage to populations of plants and plankton at the bases of the food chains, which sustain all life on Earth.

Endangered Species Economic development has also led to problems with the land. Large-scale soil erosion is a worldwide problem due to damaging farming techniques. The habitat destruction that comes from land development has also led to shrinking numbers of wildlife around the world. At present, the extinction rate of plants and animals is about a thousand times greater than it would naturally be, and appears to be increasing. This high extinction rate means that certain species can no longer serve as an economic resource. The resulting loss of wildlife could endanger complex and life-sustaining processes that keep Earth in balance.

Sustainable Growth

Working together, economists and scientists are looking for ways to reduce the negative environmental effects of development. This concept is sometimes called "green growth," or **sustainable growth**. Sustainable growth involves two goals: meeting current economic needs, while ensuring the preservation of the environment and the conservation of resources for future generations. Making such plans and putting them into practice have proved to be difficult. But many scientists believe that meeting both goals is essential for the health of the planet

8.18 Preparing for the Regents
Environment and Society
What is deforestation and desertification, and in what regions are they most severe?

8.19 Preparing for the Regents
Environment and Society
Why can Chernobyl be considered a global disaster?

8.20 Preparing for the Regents
Environment and Society
What are some of the negative environmental consequences of economic development?

8.21 Preparing for the Regents
Environment and Society
What is sustainable growth?

in the future. Because the economies of nations are tied to their political climates, such development plans will depend on the efforts of nations in both economic and political areas.

Answer the following questions. Use the Analyze the Question hints to help you answer the questions.

1 The main goal of the green revolution was to

(1) prevent further destruction of the world's rainforests
(2) solve chronic food shortages through the use of technology
(3) expand the economies of developing nations with foreign investment
(4) insure that foreign aid was received by people with the greatest need

ANALYZE THE QUESTION
- Read the question stem. You are being asked to indicate the main goal of the green revolution.
- Think about what you know about the green revolution.
- Eliminate any alternative that does not relate to the general purposes of the campaign. The remaining alternative will be the correct answer.

2 What is the most severe threat to the physical environment of Brazil, Costa Rica, and the democratic Republic of the Congo (Zaire)?

(1) spread of urban centers
(2) nuclear waste disposal
(3) increased immigration
(4) destruction of the rainforest

ANALYZE THE QUESTION
- Read the question stem. You are being asked to indicate the most serious environmental threat the three countries faced.
- Think about what features the three countries share in terms of their physical environment.
- Read each alternative with those shared features in mind.
- Eliminate any alternatives that are not true for each of the three countries. The remaining alternative will be the correct answer.

3 • **Nuclear accident at Chernobyl in the former Soviet Union**
• **Dumping toxic waste in the ocean**
• **Cutting down the rainforest in Africa and South America**

Which conclusion can be drawn from these situations?

(1) Environmental problems need global solutions.
(2) The fall of the Soviet Union has caused severe environmental hazards.
(3) Technology has helped the world stop polluting the environment.
(4) Only nations that create environmental problems will suffer from them.

ANALYZE THE QUESTION
- Read the question stem. You are being asked to draw a conclusion based on the list of situations.
- Look for clues in the list, such as whether the situations are from the same geographic regions.
- Eliminate any alternative that contradicts or does not fit with each situation. The remaining alternative will be the correct answer.

4 A negative impact of the use of modern technology is that

(1) levels of air and water pollution often increase
(2) economic opportunities are frequently limited
(3) contacts with other cultures decrease
(4) international trade is limited

ANALYZE THE QUESTION
- Read the question stem. You are being asked to indicate a drawback of modern technology.
- Read each alternative carefully. Think about whether technology relates to the proposed impact in a positive way, negative way, or not at all.
- Eliminate all alternative that would benefit from technology or not be significantly affected. The remaining alternative will be the correct answer.

Global Connections and Interactions

UNIT 8

Part I: MULTIPLE-CHOICE QUESTIONS

Directions (1–10): For each statement or question, write on a separate answer sheet the *number* of the word or expression that, of those given, best completes the statement or answers the questions.

1 Since the late 1970s, which measure has the Chinese government taken to reduce the effects of overpopulation?

   (1) supported a policy of forced migration to other nations
   (2) reduced food production
   (3) emphasized the teachings of Confucius
   (4) imposed a one-child policy that limits family size

2 • **The United Nations Declaration of Human Rights**

This documents is considered a

   (1) secondary source
   (2) example of oral tradition
   (3) primary source
   (4) statement of different religious beliefs

3 The United Nations was created primarily to

   (1) prosecute persons accused of war crimes
   (2) contain the spread of communism
   (3) channel relief aid to war-torn nations
   (4) provide a means of solving international problems

4 The reason that the Organization of Petroleum Exporting Countries (OPEC) greatly influences the world today is that it

   (1) commands the loyalty of the worldwide Islamic community
   (2) develops and exports important technology
   (3) controls access to trade routes between East and West
   (4) manages the oil supply that affects the global economy

5 Since the 1960s, famine in many parts of the world has been reduced by

   (1) increased urbanization
   (2) global warming
   (3) laissez-faire capitalism
   (4) the green revolution

6 Which statement about the spread of nuclear weapons is a fact rather than an opinion?

   (1) Nations possessing nuclear weapons should not have to limit the production of weapons.
   (2) The spread of nuclear weapons was s smaller problem in the 1990s than in the 1970s.
   (3) The United States and Russia signed the Strategic Arms Limitation Treaties during the 1970s.
   (4) Only developing nations are concerned about the spread of nuclear weapons.

7 A main goal of the European Union is to strengthen European

   (1) isolationism   (3) interdependence
   (2) socialism   (4) colonialization

8 What is the primary reason that increasing numbers of Latin American citizens have immigrated to the United States over the last three decades?

   (1) escape from the threat of communism
   (2) desire for religious freedom
   (3) fear of natural disasters
   (4) hope for economic opportunities

9 Which statement describes the economic history of Japan since World War II?

   (1) Japan has been limited in industrial development by the occupation of the United States,
   (2) Japan has built a strong economy based on the export of manufactured goods.
   (3) Japan has withdrawn from the world economic community and has practiced economic self-sufficiency
   (4) Japan has concentrated on rebuilding its defense industry.

10 In Latin America, the deforestation of the Amazon rainforest has led to

   (1) the maintenance of a traditional way of life
   (2) the discovery of new medicines
   (3) overpopulation in rural regions
   (4) environmental dangers

In developing your answers to Parts II and III, be sure to keep these general definitions in mind:

(a) *discuss* means "to make observations about something using facts, reasoning, and argument; to present in some detail"

(b) *explain* means "to make plain or understandable; to give reasons for or causes of; to show the logical development or relationship of"

(c) *evaluate* means "to examine and judge the significance, worth, or condition of; to determine the value of"

(d) *analyze* means "to determine the nature and relationship of the component elements"

Part II: THEMATIC ESSAY

Directions: Write a well-organized essay that includes an introduction, several paragraphs addressing the task below, and a conclusion.

Theme: Science and Technology

Science and technology have played a critical role in altering the course of human history.

Task:

- Identify *two* scientific or technological advances that have had a major impact on global history since World War II
- Explain the relationship between the scientific or technological advance and a specific historical event during this period
- Analyze how these advances changed the course of history

You may use any example from your study of Unit Eight. Some suggestions you might wish to consider include space exploration, computers, the Internet, CAT scans and MRI techniques, genetic engineering, cloning, and the green revolution.

You are not limited to these suggestions.

Guidelines:

In your essay, be sure to
- Address all aspects of the *Task*
- Support the theme with relevant facts, examples, and details
- Use a logical and clear plan of organization, including an introduction and a conclusion that are beyond the simple restatement of the *Theme*

Part III: DOCUMENT-BASED QUESTION

This question is based on the accompanying documents (1–3). The question is designed to test your ability to work with historic documents. Some of these documents have been edited for the purpose of this question. As you analyze the documents, take into account both the source of each document and any point of view that may be presented in the document.

Historical Context:

The success of industrialization has led to environmental problems throughout the world. As the 21st century begins, many nations are trying to deal with the environmental effects of industrialization.

Task:

Using information from the documents and your knowledge of global history, answer the question that follows each document in Part A. Your answers to the questions will help you write the Part B essay, in which you will be asked to:

- Discuss the problems that industrialization has caused in the nations of the world
- Explain how nations are responding to the problems created by industrialization

Part A: Short Answer

Directions: Analyze the documents and answer the short-answer questions that follow in the space provided.

Document 1

The average . . . Japanese consumes 10 times as much of the world's resources as the average Bangladeshi. Japan and Bangladesh have the same [number of people] but [these people] have a vastly different effect on their ecosystems [envi-ronments].

—The *"Living Planet"* Report

Document 2

Rich nations point out that developing coun-tries, while responsible for just 26 percent of the carbon emissions since 1950, are quickly becoming major emitters in their own right. And, as industrial countries emphasize, booming populations and economic growth are fueling an explosive increase in carbon emissions. The United States Department of Energy projects that carbon output from de-veloping nations will, in the absence of any new policies, outgrow that of their neighbors as early as 2020, with China eclipsing the United States as the world's leading emitter by 2015.

—*World Watch*, 1998

1 According to Document 1, how does Japan's use of resources differ from Bangladesh's use of resources?

_____

_____

2 What concern about the future of the environment is being expressed in Document 2?

_____

_____

Document 3

The United States and 34 other industrial countries met in Rio de Janeiro, Brazil, to discuss world environmental concerns.

> **Rio Pact 1992**
> **Agenda 21**
> The Agenda establishes the following priorities for international environmental action:
> - achieving sustainable growth, as through integrating environment and development in decision making;
> - making the world habitable by addressing issues of urban water supply, solid waste management, and urban pollution
> - encouraging efficient resource use, a category which includes management of energy resources, care and use of fresh water, forest development, management of fragile ecosystems, conservation of biological diversity, and management of land resources;
> - protecting global and regional resources, including the atmosphere, oceans and seas, and living marine resources;
> - managing chemicals and hazardous and nuclear waste.

3 Identify *two* environmental issues discussed at the Rio Conference.

_____

_____

_____

_____

Part B: Essay

Directions: Write a well-organized essay that includes an introduction, several paragraphs, and a conclusion. Use evidence from at least *two* documents to support your response.

Historical Context: The success of industrialization has led to environmental problems throughout the world. As the 21st century begins, many nations are trying to deal with the environmental effects of industrialization.

Task: Using information from the documents and your knowledge of global history, answer the question that follows each document in Part A. Your answers to the questions will help you write the Part B essay, in which you will be asked to:

> - Discuss the problems that industrialization has caused in the nations of the world
> - Explain how nations are responding to the problems created by industrialization

Guidelines:

In your essay, be sure to
- Address all aspects of the *Task* by accurately analyzing and interpreting at least **two** documents
- Incorporate information from the documents
- Incorporate relevant outside information
- Support the theme with relevant facts, examples, and details
- Use a logical and clear plan of organization
- Introduce the theme by establishing a framework that is beyond a simple statement of the *Task* or *Historical Context* and conclude with a summation of the theme

SAMPLE

REGENTS HIGH SCHOOL EXAMINATION

GLOBAL HISTORY
AND GEOGRAPHY

Student Name_____

School Name _____

Print your name and the name of your school on the lines above. Then turn to the last page of this booklet, which is the answer sheet for Part I. Fold the last page along the perforations and, slowly and carefully, tear off the answer sheet. Then fill in the heading of your answer sheet. Now print your name and the name of your school in the heading of each page of your essay booklet.

This examination has three parts. You are to answer **all** questions in all parts. Use black or dark-blue ink to write your answers.

Part I contains 50 multiple-choice questions. Record your answers to these questions on the separate answer sheet.

Part II contains one thematic essay question. Write your answer to this question in the essay booklet, beginning on page 1.

Part III is based on several documents:

> **Part III A** contains the documents. Each document is followed by one or more questions. In the test booklet, write your answer to each question on the lines following that question. Be sure to enter your name and the name of your school on the first page of this section.

> **Part III B** contains one essay question based on the documents. Write your answer to this question in the essay booklet, beginning on page 7.

When you have completed the examination, you must sign the statement printed on the Part I answer sheet, indicating that you had no unlawful knowledge of the questions or answers prior to the examination and that you have neither given nor received assistance in answering any of the questions during the examination. Your answer sheet cannot be accepted if you fail to sign this declaration.

DO NOT OPEN THIS EXAMINATION BOOKLET UNTIL THE SIGNAL IS GIVEN.

Part I
Answer all questions on this part.

Directions (1– 50): For each statement or question, write on the separate answer sheet the *number* of the word or expression that, of those given, best completes the statement or answers the question.

1 **"Archaeologists Revise Historical Interpretations After New Discovery"**
"New Research Sheds Light on Causes of World War I"
"Computer Technology Helps Reconstruct Ancient Languages"

These headlines indicate that the understanding of historical facts

(1) remains the same over time
(2) is passed down from one generation to another
(3) reflects a variety of personal opinions
(4) is shaped by the available evidence

2 What was an important result of the Neolithic Revolution?

(1) Food supplies became more reliable.
(2) New sources of energy became available.
(3) People became more nomadic.
(4) Populations declined.

3 The growth of maritime and overland trading routes led to

(1) decreased interest in inventions and technology
(2) the limited migration of peoples
(3) increased cultural diffusion
(4) the development of subsistence agriculture

4 Before the use of the Silk Road, how did geography affect early China?

(1) The mountains and deserts in western and southwestern China slowed the exchange of ideas.
(2) The northwestern region provided many fertile areas suitable for farming.
(3) The three major river systems provided barriers against invasion.
(4) The lack of deep-water ports on the eastern coast prevented China from developing trade with other nations.

5 Which heading best completes this partial outline?

I. _____
   A. Natural boundaries of desert, mountains, and the sea
   B. Yearly flooding to enrich farmlands
   C. Old and Middle Kingdoms
   D. Production of papyrus plant

(1) Egypt—Gift of the Nile
(2) Mesopotamia—Land Between the Rivers
(3) China's Sorrow—Huang He River
(4) Harappa—City on the Indus

6 • Roman women could own property.
  • Roman women could make wills leaving their property to whomever they chose.

A valid conclusion drawn from these facts is that Roman women

(1) had the right to vote
(2) enjoyed some legal rights
(3) were equal to men
(4) could hold political offices

7 Which belief is most closely associated with the teachings of Siddhartha Gautama (Buddha)?

(1) People are born into a specific caste.
(2) Believers must follow the Ten Commandments.
(3) Followers must fast during Ramadan.
(4) People can overcome their desires by following the Eight-Fold Path.

8 Which empire had the greatest influence on the development of early Russia?

(1) Roman
(2) Byzantine
(3) Egyptian
(4) British

9 • Showing respect for parents
  • Maintaining family honor
  • Honoring all elders

Which term is most closely related to these three actions?

(1) nirvana
(2) animism
(3) filial piety
(4) hadj (hajj)

Base your answer to question 10 on the passage below and on your knowledge of social studies.

. . . And we cannot reckon how great the damage is, since the mentioned merchants are taking every day our natives, sons of the land and the sons of our noblemen and vassals and our relatives, because the thieves and men of bad conscience grab them wishing to have the things and wares of this Kingdom which they are ambitious of; they grab them and get them to be sold; and so great, Sir, is the corruption and licentiousness [lack of restraint] that our country is being completely depopulated, and Your Highness should not agree with this nor accept it as in your service. . . .

—Nzinga Mbemba (King Affonso),
Letters to the King of Portugal, 1526

10 Which event in African history is described in this passage?

(1) exploration of the African interior
(2) discovery of gold mines in Nigeria
(3) Belgium's takeover of the Congo
(4) Atlantic slave trade

11 The feudal systems in both medieval Europe and early Japan were characterized by

(1) a decentralized political system
(2) religious diversity
(3) an increased emphasis on education
(4) the development of a wealthy middle class

12 The travels of Marco Polo and of Ibn Battuta were similar in that these travels

(1) led to nationalistic movements
(2) helped to spread the ideas of religious leaders
(3) stimulated the expansion of trade
(4) supported democratic forms of government

13 In the early 1500s, Martin Luther's "Ninety-five Theses," Henry VIII's "Act of Supremacy," and John Calvin's *Institutes of the Christian Religion* contributed to

(1) a decline in the power of the Catholic Church
(2) an increased sense of nationalism in Tudor England
(3) the growing power of the feudal nobility in Europe
(4) a major conflict among Eastern Orthodox Christians

Base your answer to question 14 on the information below and on your knowledge of social studies.

Edict of 1635 Ordering the Closing of Japan
• Japanese ships are strictly forbidden to leave for foreign countries.
• No Japanese is permitted to go abroad. If there is anyone who attempts to do so secretly, he must be executed. . . . The ship so involved must be impounded and its owner arrested, and the matter must be reported to the higher authority.
• If any Japanese returns from overseas after residing there, he must be put to death. . . .
• Any informer revealing the whereabouts of the followers of the priests must be rewarded accordingly. If anyone reveals the whereabouts of a high ranking priest, he must be given one hundred pieces of silver. For those of lower ranks, depending on the deed, the reward must be set accordingly. . . .

14 These rules reflect the Japanese policy of

(1) totalitarianism
(2) appeasement
(3) interdependence
(4) isolationism

15 During the Commercial Revolution, where did trading centers most often develop?

(1) in the mountains
(2) near grasslands
(3) along waterways
(4) on the tundra

Base your answer to question 16 on the map below and on your knowledge of social studies.

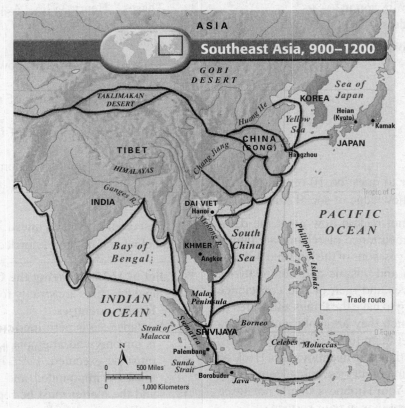

16 According to the map, which conclusion about China during the Song dynasty is accurate?

(1) Most trade routes began on the Haung He.
(2) China's overland trade routes connected China to Japan.
(3) China's ocean trade routes connected China to the Philippine Islands.
(4) China traded extensively with other nations and regions.

17 In England, the Magna Carta, the Puritan Revolution, the Glorious Revolution, and the English Bill of Rights led to the development of

(1) a dictatorship
(2) an absolute monarchy
(3) a theocracy
(4) a limited monarchy

18 A study of Aztec, Maya, and Inca agricultural systems would show that these civilizations

(1) relied on mechanized agricultural techniques
(2) carried on extensive food trade with each other
(3) adapted to their environments with creative farming techniques
(4) relied on a single-crop economy

19 Many European monarchs of the 1600s maintained that they should have absolute power to rule because they

(1) needed to defend their nations against threats from the Western Hemisphere
(2) thought that all people should have the right to a good ruler
(3) had been given their power to govern from God
(4) thought that communism was the superior political system

20 The heliocentric model, the development of inductive reasoning, and the work of Descartes are all associated with which revolution?

(1) Neolithic
(2) Agricultural
(3) Green
(4) Scientific

21 Which idea became a central belief of the Enlightenment?

(1) The use of reason would lead to human progress.
(2) Mathematics could be used to solve all human problems.
(3) The ancient Romans had the best form of government.
(4) People should give up their natural rights to their rulers.

Base your answer to question 22 on the statements below and on your knowledge of social studies.

Statement A: We worked in a place that was noisy and dangerous. We did the same work over and over again. Many workers, often children, lost fingers, limbs, and even their lives.

Statement B: Government should not interfere in business. To do so would disrupt the balance of supply and demand.

Statement C: Government has a duty to interfere in order to best provide its people with a happy and safe life.

Statement D: Advances in agricultural techniques and practices resulted in an increased supply of food and raw materials, causing a movement of the farmers from the countryside to the city.

22 All of these statements describe events or viewpoints that relate to the

(1) Protestant Reformation
(2) Commercial Revolution
(3) Industrial Revolution
(4) Berlin Conference

23 What is a key principle of a market economy?

(1) The means of production are controlled by the state.
(2) Supply and demand determine production and price.
(3) Employment opportunities are determined by social class.
(4) Businesses are owned by the people collectively.

Base your answer to question 24 on the graphs below and on your knowledge of social studies.

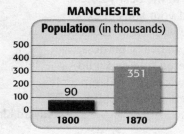

MANCHESTER

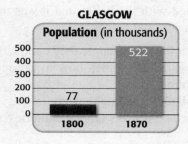

GLASGOW

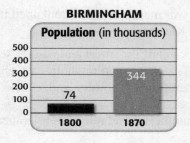

BIRMINGHAM

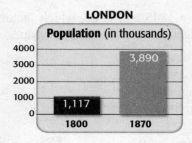

LONDON

24 Which conclusion about Great Britain's population between 1800 and 1870 is best supported by these graphs?

(1) Political unrest caused rural people to move to the towns.
(2) Many people moved out of the London area to the area around Liverpool and Birmingham.
(3) The size of most urban areas decreased.
(4) The population of some cities and towns increased dramatically.

25 **The White Man's Burden.**

"Take up the White Man's burden—
Send forth the best ye breed—
Go, bind your sons to exile
To serve your captives' need;
To wait, in heavy harness,
On fluttered folk and wild—
Your new-caught sullen peoples,
Half devil and half child. . . ."

—Rudyard Kipling, 1899

This stanza from Kipling's poem is most closely associated with the belief that it was the duty of Western colonial powers to

(1) learn from the people they conquered
(2) teach their colonies how to produce manufactured goods
(3) civilize the people they controlled
(4) welcome less developed countries as equals

26 Which two major ideas are contained in the writings of Karl Marx?

(1) survival of the fittest and natural selection
(2) class struggle and revolutionary change
(3) separation of powers and checks and balances
(4) monotheism and religious tolerance

27 Between 1845 and 1860, which factor caused a large decline in Ireland's population?

(1) famine
(2) civil war
(3) plague
(4) war against Spain

28 The ability of the Ottoman Empire to expand its borders depended on

(1) military assistance from western Europe
(2) extensive trade with the Americas
(3) alliances formed during World War I
(4) strategic location between Europe and Asia

29 One action that many governments took during World War I was to

(1) encourage political dissent and freedom of the press
(2) regulate their economic systems to increase production
(3) prevent women from seeking employment in factories
(4) raise tariffs to encourage trade

30 The Treaty of Versailles angered many Germans after World War I because the treaty

(1) divided Germany into Communist and non-Communist zones
(2) made Germany restore its emperor
(3) required all German-speaking Europeans to return to Germany
(4) forced Germany to pay large war reparations

31 ". . . The key-stone of the Fascist doctrine is its conception of the State, of its essence, its functions, and its aims. For Fascism the State is absolute, individuals and groups relative. Individuals and groups are admissable in so far as they come within the State. Instead of directing the game and guiding the material and moral progress of the community, the liberal State restricts its activities to recording results. The Fascist State is wide awake and has a will of its own. For this reason it can be described as 'ethical'. . . ."

—Benito Mussolini, *Fascism: Doctrine and Institutions,* Howard Fertig, 1932

Which statement expresses the main idea of the passage?

(1) The people have a right to overthrow ineffective governments.
(2) The state is more important than the individuals within it.
(3) The state gets its authority from the power of individuals.
(4) The establishment of an empire will cause division and chaos.

32 Which event is most closely associated with the start of World War II in Europe?

(1) invasion of Poland by Nazi forces
(2) signing of the Munich Agreement
(3) building of the Berlin Wall
(4) assassination of Archduke Franz Ferdinand

33 Although Cuba has lost support from many nations, one reason Fidel Castro has remained in power is that he has

(1) established free trade with the United States
(2) opposed communism
(3) prohibited the practice of Catholicism
(4) raised the standard of living for many Cubans

Base your answer to question 34 on the statement below and on your knowledge of social studies.

. . . The Parties agree that an armed attack against one or more of them in Europe or North America shall be considered an attack against them all and consequently they agree that, if such an armed attack occurs, each of them, in exercise of the right of individual or collective self-defence . . . will assist the Party or Parties so attacked by taking forthwith, individually and in concert with the other Parties, such action as it deems necessary, including the use of armed force, to restore and maintain the security of the . . . area. . . .

34 Which organization includes this statement in its charter?

(1) Warsaw Pact
(2) United Nations
(3) Organization of American States
(4) North Atlantic Treaty Organization

---

35 A similarity between Peter the Great of Russia and Deng Xiaoping of the People's Republic of China was that each

(1) resisted economic and social reforms in his country
(2) rejected the culture of his country in favor of a foreign culture
(3) promoted economic and technological modernization of his country
(4) experienced foreign invasions of his country that almost succeeded

36 ". . . The Communist party of the Soviet Union has been and remains a natural and inalienable part of social forces.

Their cooperation will make it possible to attain the ultimate goal of Perestroika: to renew our society within the framework of the socialist choice, along the lines of advance to a humane democratic socialism. . . ."

Which leader would most likely have made this statement?

(1) Kwame Nkrumah
(2) Mohandas Gandhi
(3) Benito Mussolini
(4) Mikhail Gorbachev

Base your answer to question 37 on the graphic organizer below and on your knowledge of social studies.

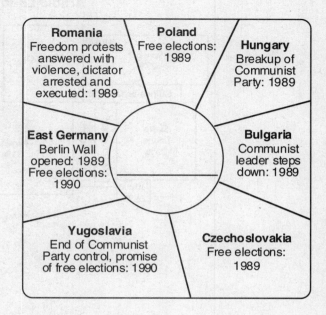

37 Which title would best fit this graphic organizer?

(1) Capitalism in Full Retreat
(2) Collapse of the Soviet Union
(3) Formation of the Warsaw Pact
(4) Buildup of the Cold War

---

38 In the late 20th century, what was a problem common to the Balkans, Rwanda, and Indonesia?

(1) disposal of nuclear waste
(2) ethnic or religious conflicts
(3) drought and famine
(4) overcrowding of urban centers

Base your answer to question 39 on the cartogram below and on your knowledge of social studies.

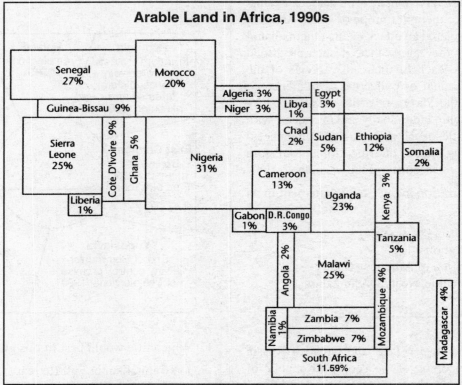

Arable Land in Africa, 1990s

Source: *The 1998 Information Please Almanac*, Houghton Mifflin (adapted)

39 Based on the information in this cartogram, what is a valid conclusion about arable land in Africa in the 1990s?

(1) The distribution of arable land in Africa is unequal.
(2) Most of the arable land in Africa is located in South Africa.
(3) The arable land in Africa has increased in the 1990s.
(4) Tanzania has a greater percentage of arable land than Senegal has.

40 Deforestation, acid rain, and the greenhouse effect are major world problems that indicate a need for

(1) cooperation between nations to reduce pollution and environmental destruction
(2) the development of mass transit systems in developing nations
(3) an increase in the worldwide production of oil
(4) a reduction in crop production in some areas of the world

41 The Gupta civilization (4th–6th centuries) and the Maya civilization (4th–10th centuries) were similar in that both

(1) built temple complexes and developed the concept of zero
(2) eliminated standing armies and introduced an aristocracy
(3) developed early democratic systems
(4) were conquered by European imperialists

Base your answer to question 42 on the graph below and on your knowledge of social studies.

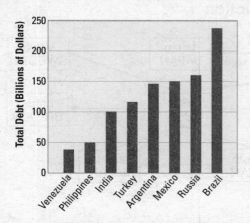

42 According to information provided by the graph, which nation had the highest foreign debt in billions of U.S. dollars in 2000?

(1) Brazil
(2) Argentina
(3) Mexico
(4) Venezuela

43 The terms *cottage industries, mercantilism, guilds,* and *laissez-faire* are most closely associated with

(1) political systems
(2) social systems
(3) economic systems
(4) belief systems

44 In the years following the Meiji Restoration in Japan and the unification of Germany in the 19th century, both nations experienced

(1) an increase in military production and strengthened military forces
(2) a reduction in tensions with neighboring nations
(3) a restructuring of government that included popularly elected monarchs
(4) a decrease in the reliance on industrialization and trade

Base your answer to questions 45 and 46 on the graph below and on your knowledge of social studies.

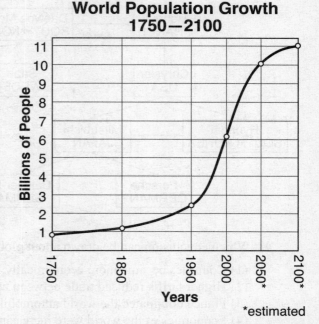

*estimated

Source: United Nations (adapted)

45 The graph shows that between 1950 and 2000 the world's population increased by approximately

(1) 1 billion
(2) 4 billion
(3) 6 billion
(4) 8 billion

46 What is one explanation for the great change in the world's population between 1950 and 2000?

(1) Family planning was successful.
(2) There was an absence of war and conflict.
(3) New medicines and technology were discovered and applied.
(4) Famine and other natural disasters increased.

47 One way in which Alexander II, Catherine the Great, and Boris Yeltsin played similar roles in Russian history was that they

(1) led communist revolutions
(2) encouraged reforms
(3) were subjects of Stalinist purges
(4) supported territorial expansion

Base your answer to question 48 on the diagram below and on your knowledge of social studies.

Automobile Production

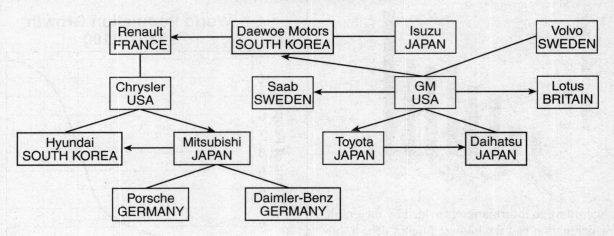

48 Which conclusion can be drawn about global economics in the 1990s?

(1) Countries became more economically isolated.
(2) Higher tariffs reduced trade between nations.
(3) France dominated the world automobile industry.
(4) Economies of the world were increasingly interdependent.

49 • Berlin airlift
   • Cuban missile crisis
   • Nuclear arms race

These events were part of an era known as the

(1) Age of Imperialism
(2) Scientific Revolution
(3) Enlightenment
(4) Cold War

50 Conflicts between Hutu and Tutsi, Ottoman Turks and Armenians, and Soviets and Ukrainian kulaks all resulted in

(1) establishment of new governments
(2) international intervention
(3) massacres or genocide
(4) cultural interdependence

When you have finished Part 1, go right on to Part 2.

Answers to essay questions are to be written in a separate essay booklet.

In developing your answers to Part II, be sure to keep these general definitions in mind:

(a) *discuss* **means "to make observations about something using facts, reasoning, and argument; to present in some detail"**

(b) *evaluate* **means "to examine and judge the significance, worth, or condition of; to determine the value of"**

Part II
THEMATIC ESSAY QUESTION

Directions: Write a well-organized essay that includes an introduction, several paragraphs addressing the task below, and a conclusion.

Theme: Change [Political Events]

> Twentieth-century political events have had positive and negative effects on global history.

Task:

> Identify *two* 20th-century political events and for *each*
> - Discuss the historical circumstances surrounding the event
> - Evaluate the extent to which this event has had a positive or a negative effect on global history

You may use any major political event from your study of global history. Some suggestions you might wish to consider include Lenin's establishment of a Communist government in Russia, rise of totalitarian governments in Europe, Ho Chi Minh's unification of Vietnam against imperialism, increasing support for Islamic fundamentalism in the Middle East, Mao Zedong's Cultural Revolution in China, the dismantling of the Berlin Wall, development of nuclear weapons in India and Pakistan, and Nelson Mandela's opposition to apartheid in South Africa.

You are not limited to these suggestions.

Do *not* use United States events in your answer, although the discussion of positive or negative effects may involve the role of the United States.

Guidelines:

In your essay, be sure to
- Address all aspects of the *Task*
- Support the theme with relevant facts, examples, and details
- Use a logical and clear plan of organization, including an introduction and a conclusion that are beyond the simple restatement of the *Theme*

In developing your answer to Part III, be sure to keep this general definition in mind:

discuss means "to make observations about something using facts, reasoning, and argument; to present in some detail"

Part III
DOCUMENT-BASED QUESTION

This question is based on the accompanying documents. The question is designed to test your ability to work with historical documents. Some of these documents have been edited for the purpose of the question. As you analyze the documents, take into account both the source of each document and any point of view that may be presented in the document.

Historical Context:
Throughout history, conquests have led to political, economic, and social changes in specific societies. Groups such as the **Mongols**, the **Spanish**, and the **French** have brought many changes to conquered areas.

Task:
Using information from the documents and your knowledge of global history, answer the question that follows each document in Part A. Your answers to the questions will help you write the Part B essay, in which you will be asked to:

> Select *two* of the groups mentioned in the historical context and for *each*
> • Discuss the political, economic, *and/or* social changes that resulted from the conquest

Part A: Short Answer Questions

Directions: Analyze the documents and answer the short-answer questions that follow in the space provided.

Document 1

> . . . The wholesale looting and destruction of property and life in Russia during the Mongol invasion of 1237– 40 was a staggering blow which left the Russian people stunned, and for a time disrupted the normal course of economic and political life. It is hard to estimate the Russian casualties but they must have been tremendous, and if we include the vast throngs of civilians, both men and women, who were enslaved by the Mongols they can hardly have been less than 10 per cent of the total population.
>
> The cities suffered most in the debacle [disastrous defeat]. Such old centers of Russian civilization as Kiev, Chernigov, Pereiaslav, Riazan, Suzdal, and the somewhat younger Vladimir-in-Suzdalia, as well as a number of other towns, were thoroughly destroyed, and the first three named above lost their former importance for several centuries. Only a few major cities in West and North Russia such as Smolensk, Novgorod, Pskov, and Galich (Halicz) escaped devastation at that time. The Mongol policy of conscripting [drafting] master craftsmen and skilled artisans for the khan's service added a new burden even for those cities which had been spared physical destruction during the first period of the conquest. A quota of the best Russian jewelers and craftsmen was sent to the great khan. As we have seen, Friar John of Plano Carpini met one of them, the goldsmith Kuzma, in Guyuk's camp. Many others were requisitioned by the khan of the Golden Horde for his personal service as well as to build and embellish [decorate] his capital, Saray. Artisans of various kinds — smiths, armorers, saddlers, and so on — were also assigned to the ordus [palaces] of the members of the house of Juchi as well as to those of the major commanders of the Mongol armies in South Russia. . . .

Source: George Vernadsky, *The Mongols and Russia*, Yale University Press

1 According to this document, what are *two* ways the Mongol conquest changed Russia? [2]

(1)_____

_____

Score ☐

(2)_____

_____

Score ☐

Document 2

. . . The Mongol impact, assert the Eurasian historians, proved highly beneficial to the Russians. "The Tatars [Mongols] defended Russia from Europe," sparing it from conquest by the West. After the conquest Mongols and the people of Rus [Russia] coexisted in harmony and peace. From their conquerors the Rus adopted typical Turanian [Asian] character traits: steadiness, conviction, strength, and religiosity, all of which promoted the development of the Muscovite state. The Mongols assured to Rus secure commercial and cultural relations with the Orient; they enhanced the position of the Orthodox church. In the mid-13th century Alexander Nevskii, prince of Novgorod, faced with a fateful choice, wisely chose the East over the West: "Alexander saw in the Mongols a friendly force in a cultural sense that could assist him to preserve and consolidate Russian cultural identity from the Latin West." . . .

Source: MacKenzie and Curran, *A History of Russia, the Soviet Union, and Beyond,*
Wadsworth/Thomson Learning

2 Based on this document, state *two* changes that occurred in Russia as a result of Mongol rule. [2]

(1)_____

_____

Score [ ]

(2)_____

_____

Score [ ]

Document 3

. . . By the time of his death in 1227, Genghis Khan controlled most of northern China, but the swampy lands to the south stopped his cavalry from further advances. His sons expanded Mongol control farther by conquering lands to the east and west. They divided the empire into four large khanates, in Persia, Central Asia, Russia, and East Asia. . . .

Kublai Khan was a vigorous and capable ruler. He carried on large warlike hunts to show that he kept Mongol tradition, but he also showed some appreciation for Chinese culture. He acted to restore some of the devastation in North China. He began a vast renovation of the Grand Canal, which was so important to the wealth and unity of the country. He directed the building of water-control projects, such as dams and dikes, along the Yellow River. . . .

During the Mongol rule, trade revived with Central Asia and the Middle East. Both of these areas were ruled by relatives of the khan. The vast lands controlled by the Mongols experienced general peace, called the *Pax Mongolica*. It was said that "a maiden bearing a nugget of gold on her head could wander safely throughout the realm." Camel caravans once more carried Chinese products such as porcelain, tea, medicines, silk, and playing cards to the Middle East and into Europe. . . .

Source: Dorothy Hoobler et al., *China*, Globe Book

3 Based on this document, identify *two* ways China was changed by Mongol rule. [2]

(1)_____

_____

Score ☐

(2)_____

_____

Score ☐

Aztec drawing of an encounter between Spanish soldiers and Aztec warriors

4 Based on what is shown in this drawing, state *one* impact the Spanish had on the lives of the native peoples in Mexico. [1]

_____

_____

Score

Document 5

Life in colonial New Spain [Spanish colonies] was complex—the dominant institutions and cultural patterns were Spanish in origin, but they were modified in their New World setting. Society was not static; evolution marked the political and religious systems; and change was a feature of the economic, social, and intellectual life. These adaptations generally mirrored developments in Europe, the source of basic decisions and control. During its three centuries as a colony, New Spain was kept subservient to the mother country in a number of ways, beginning with an enforced loyalty to the crown. . . .

In New Spain itself the viceroy [governor] was the ranking officer and agent of royal absolutism. As a personal representative of the king he was armed with considerable authority and enjoyed high honors and deference [respect]. He received a handsome salary (twenty thousand pesos in the seventeenth century, triple that amount in the eighteenth), lived in a splendid palace surrounded by liveried [uniformed] servants, and maintained a court like a petty European monarch. During the colonial era there were sixty-one viceroys. Most of them belonged to the titled nobility or at least were of high birth; eleven were from the Church hierarchy [church leaders], and only three holders of this exalted [high] office were *criollos* [Creoles], two of them being sons of viceroys.

The viceroy functioned as chief executive, captain-general of military forces, governor, supervisor of the royal treasury (*real hacienda*), and president of the *audiencia* (administrative court) of Mexico. He enforced royal laws and decrees, issued ordinances dealing with local matters, nominated minor colonial officials, distributed land and titles, promoted colonization and settlement, and protected the Indians. He was vice-patron of most religious endeavors, and his ecclesiastical [church] powers included the right to determine boundaries of bishoprics [districts] and to nominate some Church officers. . . .

Source: Robert Ryal Miller, *Mexico: A History,* University of Oklahoma Press

5 According to this document, what effect did the Spanish have on their colonies in New Spain? [1]

_____

_____

Score ☐

Document 6

Social Classes in Spanish America

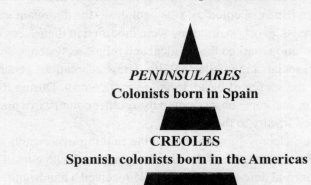

PENINSULARES
Colonists born in Spain

CREOLES
Spanish colonists born in the Americas

MESTIZOS
People of mixed Spanish and Native American Ancestry

MULATTOES
People of mixed European and African ancestry

AFRICAN SLAVES

NATIVE AMERICAN INDIANS

6 Based on this chart, identify *one* change that resulted from the Spanish conquest of Latin America. [1]

_____

_____

Score ☐

Document 7

Napoleon's Empire, 1810

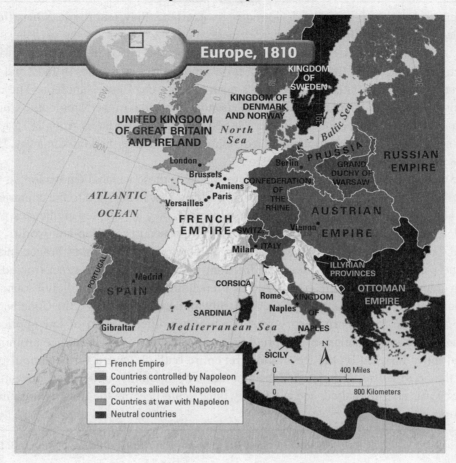

7 Based on this map, state *one* political impact of Napoleon's conquests in Europe. [1]]

_____

_____

Score ☐

Document 8

> . . . Even in places such as Holland, Germany, Switzerland, Italy, and Illyria, where the Code [Napoléon] did not outlive the Empire, it made a strong imprint on the civil laws of the region. Abolition of the Code brought such confusion and chaos in certain countries that they returned to it. In the Italian peninsula, for example, the Two Sicilies in 1812 and Parma, Modena, and Sardinia later adopted codes derived from the Code Napoléon. The code of the Kingdom of Italy, adopted in 1864, likewise had its source in the Napoleonic Code. The Belgians, who were incorporated in the Kingdom of the Netherlands from 1815 to 1830, fought so strongly for the Napoleonic Code that, even after they had broken away, Holland in 1838 adopted a code based on Napoleon's.
>
> The Code Napoléon so impressed governments, even those which did not adopt it, that the 19th century became the great century of legal codification. In addition to the countries mentioned above, Austria, Portugal, Spain, Germany, and Turkey all adopted civil codes. But that of Napoleon easily predominates in the civil-law, as opposed to common-law, world. . . .
>
> The Code contributed greatly to Napoleon's achievement of helping France turn away from the past. It cemented the ideas of freedom of person and of contract (including the right to enter any occupation), equality of all Frenchmen, and freedom of civil society from ecclesiastical [religious] control. As the first truly modern code of laws, the Code Napoléon for the first time in modern history gave a nation a unified system of law applicable to all citizens without distinction. By providing uniformity of laws it further promoted the national unity fostered by the Revolution. Its entire outlook gave a further impulse to the rise of the *bourgeoisie*. A threatened disintegration of the family under the Convention and Directory was sharply halted, and the family once again became the most important social institution. . . .

Source: Robert B. Holtman, *The Napoleonic Revolution*, J.B. Lippincott

8 Based on this document, identify *two* changes brought about by the Code Napoléon. [2]

(1)_____

_____

Score ☐

(2)_____

_____

Score ☐

Document 9

> . . . The plans and ambitions of Napoleon Bonaparte, however, did inspire the Latin Americans, although hardly in a way Napoleon expected. The French dictator invaded Spain in 1808, forced the king to abdicate [give up the throne], and presented the Spanish crown to his brother Joseph. At a stroke, Spanish America became part of the Bonaparte family empire. (A few months earlier, Napoleon had invaded Portugal, and the Portuguese royal family had fled to its colony of Brazil.)
>
> Spanish Americans reacted sharply against this French usurper. They refused to accept Joseph Bonaparte as their king, affirmed [declared] their loyalty to the Spanish House of Bourbon, and seized control of their local governments. But almost from the beginning, the rebellion against Napoleon turned into a revolution for complete independence. There could be no turning back to the old system. . . .

Source: Robert J. Alexander, *Latin America*, Scholastic Book Services

9 According to this document, what effect did Napoleon's invasion of Spain have on Latin America? [1]

_____

_____

Score ☐

Part B: Essay

Directions: Write a well-organized essay that includes an introduction, several paragraphs, and a conclusion. Use evidence from at least *four* documents in your essay. Support your response with relevant facts, examples, and details. Include additional outside information..

Historical Context:

Throughout history, conquests have led to political, economic, and social changes in specific societies. Groups such as the **Mongols**, the **Spanish**, and the **French** have brought many changes to conquered areas.

Task:

Using information from the documents and your knowledge of global history, answer the question that follows each document in Part A. Your answers to the questions will help you write the Part B essay, in which you will be asked to:

> Select *two* of the groups mentioned in the historical context and for *each*
> • Discuss the political, economic, *and/or* social changes that resulted from the conquest

Guidelines:

In your essay, be sure to
- Develop all aspects of the *Task*
- Incorporate information from *at least four* documents
- Incorporate relevant outside information
- Support the theme with relevant facts, examples, and details
- Use a logical and clear plan of organization, including an introduction and conclusion that are beyond a restatement of the theme

GLOBAL HISTORY AND GEOGRAPHY

Part I

ANSWER SHEET

☐ Male

Sex: ☐ Female

Student ....

Teacher ....

School ....

Write your answers for Part I on this answer sheet, write your answers to Part III A in the test booklet, and write your answers for Parts II and III B in the separate essay booklet.

FOR TEACHER USE ONLY	
Part I Score	_____
Part III A Score	_____
Total Part I and III A Score	☐
Part II Essay Score	_____
Part III B Essay Score	_____
Total Essay Score	☐
Final Score (obtained from conversion chart)	☐

1.........	26.........
2.........	27.........
3.........	28.........
4.........	29.........
5.........	30.........
6.........	31.........
7.........	32.........
8.........	33.........
9.........	34.........
10.........	35.........
11.........	36.........
12.........	37.........
13.........	38.........
14.........	39.........
15.........	40.........
16.........	41.........
17.........	42.........
18.........	43.........
19.........	44.........
20.........	45.........
21.........	46.........
22.........	47.........
23.........	48.........
24.........	49.........
25.........	50.........

No.
Right ☐

The declaration below should be signed when you have completed the examination.

I do hereby affirm, at the close of this examination, that I had no unlawful knowledge of the questions or answers prior to the examination and that I have neither given nor received assistance in answering any of the questions during the examination.

_____

Signature

ANSWER KEY

Use the following rubrics to evaluate whether your essays will achieve a score of 5.

THEMATIC ESSAY GENERIC SCORING RUBRIC

Score of 5:
- Shows a thorough understanding of the theme or problem
- Addresses all aspects of the task
- Shows an ability to analyze, evaluate, compare and/or contrast issues and events
- Richly supports the theme or problem with relevant facts, examples, and details
- Is a well-developed essay, consistently demonstrating a logical and clear plan of organization
- Introduces the theme or problem by establishing a framework that is beyond a simple restatement of the task and concludes with a summation of the theme or problem

---

DOCUMENT-BASED QUESTION GENERIC SCORING RUBRIC

Score of 5:
- Thoroughly addresses all aspects of the *Task* by accurately analyzing and interpreting at least *two* documents
- Incorporates information from the documents in the body of the essay
- Incorporates relevant outside information
- Richly supports the theme or problem with relevant facts, examples, and details
- Is a well-developed essay, consistently demonstrating a logical and clear plan of organization
- Introduces the theme or problem by establishing a framework that is beyond a simple restatement of the *Task* or *Historical Context* and concludes with a summation of the theme or problem

---

Unit 1: Ancient World–Civilizations and Religions
Preparing for the Regents Margin Questions

1.1 anthropology

1.2 nomads whose food supply depends on hunting animals and gathering edible plants; invented tools such as digging sticks, spears, knives, fish hooks, harpoons, chisel cutters, needles for sewing

1.3 more reliable food sources due to farming and herding

1.4 organized into city-states, each with own government; rulers passed power to sons, creating dynasties; polytheistic; several social classes; women had rights

1.5 allowed history to be recorded and passed to future generations

1.6 first recorded system of laws; reinforced government's role as head of society; subjected everyone to same rules

1.7 Similar—Polytheistic, built temples to honor gods; Different—Egyptians believed kings were gods and ruled even after death; Mesopotamians believed kings were representatives of gods and did not believe in an afterlife

1.8 Indus and Ganges rivers, which formed fertile river valley; mountains that separated the region from the rest of Asia

1.9 North China Plain between the Huang He and Chang Jiang rivers; fertile deposited by Huang He

1.10 polytheistic like Mesopotamia and Egypt, though had one supreme god; believed in afterlife like Egypt; ruled by king and warrior-nobles

1.11 gave a just ruler divine approval; losing mandate meant losing right to rule; used to explain rebellions, civil wars, and new dynasties

1.12 highly structured centralized government; included a bureaucracy and civil service jobs requiring an exam

1.13 faced economic imbalance where rich got richer at expense of poor; government didn't tax large landowners, pressing small farmers for more money

1.14 Aegean, Ionian, and Black seas provided trade and transportation; mountains created numerous regions so small, independent communities developed instead of a single unified government

1.15 Debt slavery (debtors working as slaves until the debt is repaid) existed until it was outlawed by Solon.

1.16 Sparta was a military state governed by an oligarchy; Athens was a democracy ruled by the people.

1.17 universe worked according to absolute, unchanging laws understood through logic and reasoning

1.18 built cities where Greek culture blended with that of the conquered, creating Hellenistic culture and a common language

1.19 Both were recorded laws that governed society and were displayed so people could see them.

1.20 two consuls, with power to overrule each other, directed the army and government; senate served legislative and administrative duties; assemblies represented democratic side of republic

1.21 period of Roman peace and prosperity; united territories as a single state with efficient and sound rulers; set of roads linked the empire

1.22 Greco-Roman culture; Latin language; architecture, some of which still remains; Roman law

1.23 Guaranteed fair and humane treatment, preached nonviolence, and urged religious tolerance

1.24 3400 B.C.

1.25 allowed exchange of goods, ideas, religious beliefs, arts, and ways of living; connected people with products not found in their native lands

1.26 religion that believes that ancestors and other spirits inhabit animals, plants, and other natural forces; spirits regulate daily life

1.27 religion liberates souls from mistakes of everyday life; liberation achieved through *moksha*; souls, and their karma, reincarnate until *moksha* is achieved

1.28 Jainism is based on the belief that everything has a soul and should not be harmed. Followers adhere to doctrines of nonviolence and religious tolerance.

1.29 personal suffering ends when desire is overcome and enlightenment achieved; nirvana reached by following the Eightfold Path, or Middle Way

1.30 spread by trade and by missionaries; spread from India to China, China to Korea, Korea to Japan

1.31 by organizing society around five basic relationships that are each governed by a code of proper conduct

1.32 by devoting oneself to one's parents during their lifetime and by honoring them after death

1.33 highly efficient and powerful government was key to restoring order; believed in controlling ideas and actions, rewarding compliance, punishing defiance

1.34 worshipping the spirits of nature and ancestors

1.35 belief in a single god.

1.36 all three established rules that governed people's behavior in an effort to create a more stable society

1.37 people should treat others as one wants to be treated

1.38 both represent codes of behavior

Unit 1: Section Review Questions
1: Early People and the Rise of Civilization   **1** (2)   **3** (1)
                                                    2 (4)   **4** (1)

2: Early River Valley Civilizations
See the Thematic Essay Rubric on p. 318

3: Classical Civilizations and Empires
See the Thematic Essay Rubric on p. 318

4: Emergence and Spread of Belief Systems   **1** (4)

Unit 1: Practice Regents Exam
PART I: Multiple-Choice Questions

1 (3)	**3** (4)	**5** (1)	**7** (4)	**9** (1)
2 (2)	**4** (1)	**6** (1)	**8** (2)	**10** (2)

PART II: Thematic Essay Question
See the Thematic Essay Rubric on p. 318

PART III : Document-Based Question
Part A: Short Answer

1 A wife should be treated with love and tact. A husband should consider her aims and wishes.

2 The home is the wife's domain and she should run it according to established rules. In all other capacities, a wife should obey her husband.

3 Women should stay in the background, be modest and respectful, never speak of their own goodness or flinch away from duty, and be able to endure humiliation.

PART B: Essay
See the Document-Based Question rubric on p. 318

Unit 2: Expanding Zones of Exchange and Encounter
Preparing for the Regents Margin Questions

2.1 rigid caste system; most lived in small villages; farmers walked from their homes to the outlying fields; merchants lived in homes above their shops

2.2 continued to embrace hundreds of gods, but began to believe that only one divine force existed in the universe and these various gods were all a part of it; many people devoted themselves to Vishnu and Shiva; Guptas created temples to honor gods

2.3 plays, poems, drama, and dance; expanded trade; astronomy; banking; modern numerals, the decimal system, pi, and the length of the year; medical guides

2.4 reinstated and expanded civil service exam; created an intelligent and capable governing class

2.5 taxes failed to cover the rising costs of government, like military expansion; Muslim armies, border attacks, and internal rebellions diminished power

2.6 The status of Chinese women declined. A sign was the custom of women's binding the feet.

2.7 movable type, paper money, gunpowder, porcelain, mechanical clock, magnetic compass, advances in arithmetic and algebra, use of negative numbers, beautiful poetry and painting, advances in farming

2.8 capital located on trade route; relied on ocean trade when lost control of the Silk Roads

2.9 Spread through trade, travel, and migration; Koreans passed influences onto Japan

2.10 created a single, uniform code of laws that included relevant Roman laws; similar to Twelve Tables and Hammurabi's Code in that it set rules for behavior

2.11 located on the Bosporus Strait so goods from Asia, Africa, and Europe passed through it

2.12 preserved Greco-Roman culture, including writings by Homer, Euclid, Herotodus, and Galen

2.13 empire faced riots, religious quarrels, and palace intrigues; shrank under foreign attacks; bubonic plague destroyed population

2.14 differences within Christianity due to distance and lack of communication; after split, Eastern and Western branches competed for converts

2.15 missionaries invented a Slavic alphabet; traded with Slavs; Slavs absorbed many Greek Byzantine ways, eventually producing Russian culture.

2.16 rivers let Vikings come from the north and sail to Constantinople to trade for foreign products

2.17 Vladimir expanded Kiev and fought off nomads; Yaroslav created trading alliances and a legal code

2.18 close link between Church and state; emperor served as supreme ruler of the Church

2.19 much of Arabian Peninsula was desert; towns near the coast became markets for trade; a small, fertile strip of land and several oases had water for farming

2.20 spread 6,000 miles, from Atlantic Ocean to Indus River

2.21 Muhammed died without naming successor or leaving followers with a way to choose; Umayyads came to power, moved Muslim capital to Damascus, and abandoned the simple life

2.22 located on key trade routes with access to goods and information

2.23 engaged in sea and land trade; set up banks where merchants could exchange money

2.24 Shari'a is a Muslim system of law composed of the Qur'an and Sunna, a model of Islamic life based on Muhammed's teachings and life.

2.25 Shari'a required religious tolerance for Christians and Jews because they are considered "people of the book." The Qur'an also forbids forced conversion.

2.26 gave Muslim women legal rights concerning marriage, family, and property, but still expected to submit to men

2.27 Muslims entered areas with rich artistic traditions and adapted them to suit Islam. Architecture often reflected culture of the people living in the area.

2.28 was a prosperous period of Muslim history in which riches flowed in, rulers built luxurious cities and supported scholars, and scholars preserved and produced enormous bodies of knowledge

2.29 disrupted trade; led to the downfall of cities as people fled to the countryside; affected the economy, government, and culture; literacy decreased and different dialects of Latin evolved

2.30 extended authority of Church into politics

2.31 both systems created hierarchical social structure that determined work and status in society

2.32 economic arrangement in which lord provided housing, farmland, and protection to the serfs who maintained lord's land, animals, and estate

2.33 Serfs' lives revolved around work, but despite hardships, like child labor and a life expectancy of 35 years, serfs accepted position as God's will.

2.34 Most women were powerless and considered inferior to men, but they played an important familial role. Noblewomen could inherit estates from their husbands, but their lives were still limited.

2.35 provided sense of order and stability, performed rites that paved way for salvation, village church served as social and religious center

2.36 Gothic cathedrals inspired majesty of God, while literature idealized castle life

2.37 reclaim the Holy Land—Palestine—from the Muslims

2.38 Some wanted adventure. Younger sons without a property or inheritance wanted land and a position in society. Others wanted freedom from feudal obligations or forgiveness from God.

2.39 Jerusalem remained under Muslim control, but unarmed Christian pilgrims could visit its holy places.

2.40 Reconquista—Long effort by the Spanish to drive Muslims out of Spain; Inquisition—Church court used to suppress heresy; many Jews and Muslims converted, but were still suspected of heresy; all Jews and Muslims expelled in 1492

2.41 increased trade between Europe and Southwest Asia

Unit 2: Section Review Questions
1: The Gupta Empire of India 1 (2)
2: The Tang and Song Dynasties of China 1 (2)
3: The Byzantine Empire and Early Russia 1 (3) 2 (1)
4: The Spread of Islam 1 (4)
5: Medieval Europe
  See the Thematic Essay Rubric on p. 318
6: The Crusades 1 (4)

Unit 2: Practice Regents Exam
PART I: Multiple-Choice Questions

1 (2) 3 (4) 5 (2) 7 (4) 9 (4)
2 (2) 4 (2) 6 (1) 8 (4) 10 (1)

PART II: Thematic Essay Question
See the Thematic Essay Rubric on p. 318

PART III : Document-Based Question
Part A: Short Answer
1   300,000

2   900,000
3   Vikings, Muslims, and Magyar
PART B: Essay
See the Document-Based Question Rubric on p. 318

Unit 3: Global Interactions
Preparing for the Regents Margin Questions

3.1 Advantages—Mild climate, plentiful rainfall in the south. Disadvantages—Mountains, few natural resources, natural disasters.

3.2 Korean travelers brought Buddhism to Japan.

3.3 Buddhism; calligraphy; landscape painting; Chinese styles in cooking, gardening, drinking tea, and hairdressing

3.4 Samurai were supposed to show courage, respect for gods, and generosity towards the weak and poor. This is similar to the code of chivalry.

3.5 In both Japan and Europe, feudalism was formed during a time of violence and disorder. Society in both places had a pyramid structure.

3.6 noh dramas, haiku, kabuki theater

3.7 They were eager to expand their markets and buy European weapons.

3.8 The missionaries actively converted the Japanese to Christianity. This upset the shogun, who feared their influence. His desire to end their influence led to the persecution of Christians and contributed to the closing of Japan.

3.9 The Japanese did not want European ideas in Japan, but they still wanted foreign goods. By closing Japan's borders, the Japanese kept out missionaries and gained control of foreign trade.

3.10 dry, windswept plain stretching across Europe and Asia; short, hardy grasses; dramatic temperature differences, little rain, particularly in east

3.11 People of the steppe were nomadic, following weather patterns. They herded animals and depended on them for food, clothing, and housing.

3.12 vast empire included many different geographic areas and cultures

3.13 Russians could follow their own customs as long as they obeyed the Mongols and paid them tribute. They were isolated from their neighbors, however.

3.14 united China for first time in more than 300 years

3.15 typhoon destroyed their fleet

3.16 The Pax Mongolica made Central Asia safe for missionaries, travelers, and traders. Kublai Khan also invited foreign merchants to China.

3.17 a Venetian trader at Kublai Khan's court

3.18 family members argued over who would rule; Chinese rebellions fueled by resentment and years of famine, flood, disease, economic problems, and corruption

3.19 Large deserts and tsetse flies prevented human migration across the continent and the development of thriving cities in Africa's interior. Africa has few navigable rivers, harbors, ports, or inlets, which would limit trade. The northern and southern tips of the country have more welcoming climates, however, so they were more developed.

3.20 located along caravan routes to Egypt and Meroë; access to the Mediterranean Sea and Indian Ocean sea trades

3.21 spread Islam through conquest

3.22 through the gold-salt trade

3.23 empire expanded during his rule; Timbuktu attracted Muslim scholars, doctors, judges, and religious leaders to its outstanding mosques and universities

3.24 traveler and historian from Tangier

3.25 access to trade routes; efficient tax system; able officials

3.26 West African city-states benefited from supplying the needs of trading caravans. East African city-states entered the Indian Ocean trade.

3.27 harness that allowed horses to plow fields and three-field system increased food production

3.28 rise in capitalism, increase in foreign trade, use of banking and bills of exchange

3.29 at ports and crossroads, on hilltops, and along rivers

3.30 caused city-states to grow and wealthy merchant class to develop in Italy

3.31 protecting the trading interests of its member towns

3.32 caravels, new sails, astrolabe, magnetic compass

3.33 sailed around Africa to reach Calicut in India

3.34 traveled the trade routes

3.35 killed almost 25 million Europeans; prestige of Church suffered; wages increased because there were so few laborers; manorial system crumbled as serfs left the manor in search of higher wages; conflict between nobles and serfs over wages led to peasant revolts; trade declined; Jews were blamed for plague

3.36 William the Conqueror unified control of England

3.37 decreased the power of nobles

3.38 Possible Answer: The feelings of unity produced by nationalism would make people more willing to accept a strong centralized government.

3.39 no taxation without representation, a jury trial, and the protection of the law

3.40 The growth of royal power under the Capetian kings unified France.

3.41 The pope didn't want priests to have to pay taxes to the French king, Philip IV. In turn, Philip refused to obey the pope.

3.42 caused people to think of the king as a national leader fighting for their country

3.43 had large cities and towns were ideas could be exchanged; the bubonic plague had slowed business expansion, thus merchants had money to invest in the arts; artists, architects, and scholars could draw inspiration from the ruins of Rome and had access to Latin and Greek manuscripts

3.44 intellectual movement that focused on human potential and achievements; influenced by Greek values in history, literature, and philosophy

3.45 depicted religious subjects but with a realistic style, including the use of perspective

3.46 showed very realistic details and the personality of its subjects, often showed daily life

3.47 one's native language; Possible Answer: to reach a wider audience

3.48 might have to trick people for the good of the state

3.49 Unlike medieval Christians, the Christian humanists were willing to examine traditional teachings of the Church. They wanted to reform society, promote education, and inspire people to live a Christian life.

3.50 the period from 1558–1603 when Elizabeth I ruled England

3.51 maps presented a more realistic view of the known world than medieval maps

3.52 allowed printers to produce hundreds of copies of the same book; made books cheap enough for most people to afford

3.53 thought Church leaders were corrupt, extravagant, and too involved in worldly affairs; troubled by fact that many priests and monks were poorly educated and broke vows

3.54 It is a turning point because it led to the Reformation, when churches that did not follow the pope's authority were founded.

3.55 Holy Roman Emperor Charles V, a Catholic, went to war against Protestant princes in Germany.

3.56 declared Henry, the king of England, the official head of England's Church

3.57 set up the Church of England, or Anglican Church, as the only legal church in England

3.58 The book argued that people could not earn salvation. God had already chosen who would be saved. This was a very different view of salvation than the one held by the Catholic Church. Calvinism attracted many followers.

3.59 reforming the Catholic Church, converting non-Christians, stopping the spread of Protestantism; seeking out heresy, establishing Church doctrines

3.60 decreased the Catholic Church's power and increased the power of European monarchies

Unit 3: Section Review Questions

1: Feudal Japan	**1 (2)**
2: The Mongols	**1 (3)**
3: African Civilizations	**1 (2)**
4: Global Trade and Interactions	**1 (4)**

5: European Nation-States
See the Thematic Essay Rubric on p. 318

6: Renaissance and Humanism
See the Thematic Essay Rubric on p. 318

7: Protestant and Catholic Reformations
See the Thematic Essay Rubric on p. 318

Unit 3: Practice Regents Exam

PART I: Multiple-Choice Questions

1 (4)	**3** (2)	**5** (1)	**7** (4)	**9** (3)
2 (3)	**4** (2)	**6** (1)	**8** (4)	**10** (3)

PART II: Thematic Essay Question
See the Thematic Essay Rubric on p. 318

PART III : Document-Based Question

Part A: Short Answer

1 96 million people

2 Possible Answers: Great palaces stood empty; families were left without heirs; young, healthy people died suddenly.

3 Mongols probably carried the disease across Asia, where merchants on the trade routes picked it up and carried it back to Europe.

PART B: Essay
See the Document-Based Question Rubric on p. 318

Unit 4: The First Global Age

Preparing for the Regents Margin Questions

4.1 impress the world with the power of Ming China; expand China's tribute system.

4.2 Possible Answer: They generated interest in trade with China.

4.3 Possible Answer: China's concept of the Middle Kingdom made it less interested in contact with other nations, since it considered these nations inferior.

4.4 By making regular payments, a vassal state was acknowledging submission to China's power.

4.5 the construction of the Forbidden City, the rebuilding of the Great Wall, flourishing of the arts

4.6 The Ottomans created their empire by purchasing land, forming alliances, and conquering territory. Possible Answer: Their location in the northwest corner of Asia Minor gave them easy access to Europe and Asia.

4.7 find a sea route to the East.

4.8 because he created a law code

4.9 Possible Answer: It put the Ottomans in a position to control the trade routes.

4.10 caravel, astrolabe, magnetic compass, Mercator map projection, printing press

4.11 Prince Henry established a navigation school; Portuguese sailors were the first Europeans to explore the African coastline, round the tip of Africa, and reach India by sailing across the Indian Ocean from Africa.

4.12 Possible Answer: Columbus's landing in the Americas opened North and South America to European exploration, conquest, and colonization.

4.13 Thinking that Columbus had reached Asia, Portugal suspected that Spain was claiming lands that Portugal had reached first.

4.14 led fleet that sailed around the world; claimed the Philippines for Spain

4.15 emperor at top of social pyramid, followed by noble class, commoners, and enslaved persons

4.16 major role; capital city of Tenochtitlán had hundreds of temples and religious structures; rituals included human sacrifice

4.17 *chinampas* were an adaptation to Tenochtitlán's island location on Lake Texcoco

4.18 Montezuma II's call for more tribute and sacrifice

4.19 steep and rocky land; poor soil; ice and snow at highest elevations year-round; hot days, cold nights; difficult travel; harsh desert

4.20 Terrace farming was an adaptation to the mountainous environment.

4.21 architecture, road systems, postal service, and data-recording device

4.22 important to society; reinforced the power of the state

4.23 Huayna Capac left unequal amounts of the empire to his sons. It led to civil war and tore apart the empire.

4.24 laid claim to large areas of North and South America

4.25 superior technology (muskets and cannons), foreign diseases, the help of natives

4.26 His forces ambushed the Incan forces and kidnapped their ruler. The Incans gave up without a struggle.

4.27 people of mixed Spanish and Native American ancestry

4.28 little to no power

4.29 The abolition of the *encomienda* system resulted in a need for cheap labor. The Spanish filled that need with enslaved Africans.

4.30 Slaves were exported from African in exchange for rum, tobacco, and manufactured goods.

4.31 the middle passage

4.32 global transfer of food, plants, and animals during the colonization of the Americas; food exchanges

improved health and led to population growth, European diseases killed millions of Native Americans

4.33 provided money and structure for colonization and other business ventures

4.34 Mercantilism held that a nation's power came mainly from wealth. A nation could increase its wealth by obtaining gold and silver and by establishing a favorable balance of trade. The triangular trade provided gold, silver, and raw materials from a nation's colonies and offered a colonial market for a nation's goods.

4.35 created class of wealthy merchants, contributed to the creation of a national identity, and expanded the power of monarchs

4.36 to maintain order in their kingdoms

4.37 as God's representatives on earth, answerable only to God

4.38 both believed in strong, powerful rulers

4.39 He controlled every aspect of society in his empire.

4.40 He believed that he and the state were one and the same, and he controlled all aspects of his society.

4.41 He controlled every aspect of society in his empire.

4.42 He increased the power of the monarchy by taking control of the Russian Orthodox Church and by reducing the power of the landowners.

4.43 raising the status of women, improving education, building a new seaport city, ordering nobles to wear western clothes, starting the first Russian newspaper, introducing potatoes into the Russian diet

4.44 dissolved Parliament; signed, but ignored, the Petition of Right

4.45 Charles I offended Puritans by trying to force both of his kingdoms to follow one religion; he also attempted to arrest the leaders of Parliament.

4.46 *Habeas corpus* was passed during the reign of Charles II. Possible Answer: It contributed to the development of a constitutional monarchy by giving prisoners the right to obtain writs outlining the charges against them. This meant that monarchs could not hold people indefinitely for simply opposing them.

4.47 bought Protestants William and Mary to the throne, thereby protecting Protestantism in Britain; contributed to constitutional monarchy because William and Mary agreed to rule in partnership with Parliament

4.48 made clear the things a ruler could not do; paved way for development of the cabinet, further limiting the power of monarchs

Unit 4: Section Review Questions

1: The Ming Dynasty	1 (4)	
2: The Ottoman Empire	1 (3)	
3: Spain and Portugal on the Eve of Encounter	1 (4)	
4: Mesoamerican and South American Empires	1 (2)	2 (1)
5: Europe Encounters the World	1 (4)	2 (4)
6: Absolutism	1 (2)	2 (4)

Unit 4: Practice Regents Exam
PART I: Multiple-Choice Questions

1 (4)	3 (4)	5 (2)	7 (3)	9 (1)
2 (1)	4 (4)	6 (2)	8 (3)	10 (1)

PART II: Thematic Essay Question
See the Thematic Essay Rubric on p. 318

PART III : Document-Based Question
Part A: Short Answer

1   From the Americas—Tobacco, pumpkins, squash, sweet potato, turkey, quinine, avocado, pineapple, peppers, cassava, cacao bean, peanut, beans, potato, tomato, vanilla, corn. To the Americas—Onion, olive, coffee bean, peach, bear, citrus fruits, grape, banana, sugar cane, honeybee, grain, livestock, disease

2   24.3

3   The author is describing a journey on a slave ship.

PART B: Essay
See the Document-Based Question Rubric on p. 318

Unit 5: An Age of Revolution
Preparing for the Regents Margin Questions

5.1   The Scientific Revolution was based on a new way of thinking about the natural world and a willingness to question accepted beliefs. For example, Copernicus, Kepler, and Galileo challenged the Church-supported geocentric theory.

5.2   theory that stars, earth, and other planets revolve around sun; Copernicus

5.3   Galileo's findings went against Church teachings and authority. Religious leaders feared that if they admitted being wrong about this, people would start questioning other teachings of the Church.

5.4   logical procedure for gathering and testing ideas; Galileo—Developed theory based on observation. Newton—Combined breakthroughs of others into a single theory. Descartes—Used logic and mathematics to test theories.

5.5   Hobbes believed that the contract was between the people and their ruler. This put the power in the hands of the ruler.

5.6   because it would keep any individual or group from gaining total control of the government

5.7   When enlightened writers used reason and logic to examine principles like the divine right of monarchs, the union of church and state, and the existence of unequal social classes, they found a need to reform such beliefs. Faith in science and progress led to emphasis on individualism and inspired revolutions in America and France that led to major governmental, social, and economic changes.

5.8   because they made reforms that reflected Enlightenment ideas, such as those held by Voltaire, Rousseau, and Diderot

5.9   Britain started taxing the colonies after the French and Indian War to help pay off the huge debt. The colonists argued that this was taxation without representation, since colonists were not represented in Parliament.

5.10 Since Locke believed that people had the right to rebel against an unjust ruler, Jefferson included a long list of George III's abuses.

5.11 The American Revolution resulted in the Constitution and Bill of Rights, which put Enlightenment ideas into practice and spread optimism that reason, reform, and progress were attainable. It inspired the French people who were also seeking reform.

5.12 economic decline of France, high taxes, rising cost of living, grain shortages due to crop failures, high government debt, lack of strong leadership

5.13 marked the end of the absolute monarchy and the beginning of representative government in France

5.14 stated that men were born free and equal and had the right to liberty, prosperity, security, resistance to oppression, justice, freedom of speech, and freedom of religion—all Enlightenment ideals

5.15 guillotine

5.16 period during which Maximilien Robespierre ruled; ended with his death on July 28, 1789

5.17 Britain, Portugal, Sweden, and Ottoman Empire

5.18 Bolívar is suggesting that people in the Spanish colonies lacked freedom and power, just as medieval serfs had.

5.19 many colonies gained their independence; Simón Bolívar and José de San Martín

5.20 Three schools of thought arose—conservatives, who wanted to protect traditional monarchies; liberals, who wanted to give more power to elected parliaments; and radicals, who wanted to carry on the ideals of the revolution. It also helped fuel the revolutions of the 1830s and 1848.

5.21 They both wanted to reform Russia.

5.22 Positive—Tied to the spread of democratic ideas and the growth of an educated middle class, fueled efforts to build nation-states and unify places like Germany. Negative—Created conflict within empires as groups tried to break free, some rulers used nationalist feelings to maintain power.

5.23 because he is stating Italy's desire to rid itself of foreign rulers

5.24 Possible Answer: Without national unity, it would have been difficult to achieve the economic or military power to control colonies.

5.25 Otto von Bismarck used "blood and iron"—military conquest—to unify Germany.

5.26 early 1900s

5.27 Positive—Pushed for a liberal constitution, many reforms, parliamentary elections, end of censorship and the secret police, and improvements in women's rights. Negative—Ruled like dictators.

5.28 Austria-Hungary was afraid it would stir rebellion among its own Slavic population.

5.29 Because the Ottoman Empire had become weak militarily, European powers like Russia started wars to take its lands in Europe and Africa.

5.30 A long history of exile and persecution convinced Jews to work for a homeland in Palestine. Zionism reflects this goal for a Jewish nation-state.

5.31 The caudillos were military dictators. Wealthy landowners supported them because they opposed giving power to lower classes. Also, Latin Americans had little experience with democracy, so dictators did not seem unusual.

5.32 *peninsulares*, creoles, mestizos, mulattos, enslaved Africans; *peninsulares*

5.33 In both systems, peasants worked the land for rich landowners.

5.34 the United States and Britain

5.35 did not industrialize; did not build schools, roads, and hospitals; borrowed foreign money at high interest rates to fund export industries

5.36 Mexico was plagued by the effects of colonialism and by political instability. Political parties formed in opposition to Porfirio Díaz's harsh rule; Francisco Madero called for an armed revolution.

5.37 Revolutionary leaders Francisco "Pancho" Villa and Emiliano Zapata were from poor peasant families.

5.38 During revolution--Mexicans united to fight for new leadership and a revised constitution. After—Constitutional reforms and public education united regions and people.

5.39 New farming methods increased the food supply. As food supplies increased, living conditions improved, and England's population boomed, demand for food and goods skyrocketed. Small farmers, now without land, went to work in factories.

5.40 New technologies simplified and sped up industrial work, which helped satisfy growing demands. In the textile industry, for example, new machinery doubled the amount of work weavers did daily.

5.41 shifted from working at home to working in factories

5.42 gave manufacturers cheap ways to transport materials and finished products, created new jobs, boosted industries that depended on export to distant cities, and made travel easier

5.43 Cities grew quickly and lacked development plans, sanitation laws, building codes, adequate housing, education, and police protection. While the wealthy built luxurious suburban homes, diseases and epidemics regularly swept across England's slums.

5.44 The Industrial Revolution created a middle class that included wealthy farmers, professionals, skilled workers, and businesspeople. Many people in this new class grew wealthier than landowners and aristocrats.

5.45 because their jobs were replaced by machines

5.46 created jobs, contributed to Britain's wealth, fostered technological progress, increased the production of goods, raised the standard of living, gave people hope for improvement, improved diets and housing, lowered cost of clothing, expanded educational opportunities.

5.47 dealt with miserable lives of workers

5.48 should not interfere

5.49 Possible Answer: by increasing food production so that it keeps pace with population growth

5.50 Utilitarianism—Government should try to promote the greatest good for the greatest number of people by judging ideas on the basis of their utility. Socialism—Government should plan the economy and control all key industries.

5.51 that it was bad for workers

5.52 After a period of cooperative living, a classless society would replace government. With no private property and all goods and services shared equally, the people would own all means of production.

5.53 to help workers deal with long hours, dangerous working conditions, and the threat of termination and to push for reform

5.54 The Industrial Revolution created the middle class, which was the first group to demand the right to vote. Middle class and worker protests forced Parliament to lessen restrictions on voter eligibility.

5.55 plant fungus ruined Ireland's potato crop; people fled Ireland

5.56 The Industrial Revolution was a chief motive of imperialism. As European countries industrialized, they needed new markets and materials to further improve their economies.

5.57 Social Darwinism, duty to pass on European progress to the less advanced non-Europeans, chance to "Westernize" people and convert them to Christianity, best way to end slavery

5.58 type of colonial control in which an outside power claims exclusive investment or trading privileges in a specific area

5.59 Britain

5.60 African weaponry, like spears, couldn't compete with Europe's superior arms, like guns.

5.61 supplied raw materials, valuable market for British goods

5.62 Cause—Began when Indian soldiers were jailed for refusing to accept rifle cartridges that they believed were greased with beef and pork fat. Consequence—Britain took direct command of India.

5.63 Cause—British merchants ignored China's requests to stop trading opium. Consequence—China suffered a humiliating defeat that included giving Hong Kong to Britain; other foreign countries developed spheres of influence in China.

5.64 population growth outpaced food production, leading to widespread hunger; resentment by poor peasants and workers over special privileges given to foreigners; resentment toward Chinese Christians

5.65 Sun Yixian (Sun-Yatsen)

5.66 Europeans exploited the natural resources of Africa.

5.67 Positive—Reduced local warfare; humanitarian efforts improved sanitation, hospitals, schools, and public health; lifespans and literacy rates increased; economies expanded through construction of railroads, roads, dams, bridges, irrigation, telephone and telegraph lines. Negative—Loss of land and independence, exploitation of natural resources, lives lost to new diseases like smallpox and to resisting European advances, famines and a loss of self-sufficiency resulted from the change to cash crops, racism.

5.68 The Japanese resented that the shogun had given into foreign demands, a trend Commodore Perry started. The Japanese turned to Emperor Mutsuhito, a symbol of Japan's nationalism. When the shogun stepped down and Matsuhito began his reign, it became known as the Meiji era.

5.69 industrialized, railroads and factories were built, coal production grew, and traditional Japanese industries expanded for trade

5.70 Japan became the strongest military power in Asia, which fueled the country's sense of power, pride, and imperialism. Japan also lacked natural resources that they needed for industrialization.

5.71 As a result of the Sino-Japanese War, the world's balance of power changed. Japan destroyed China's navy and got its first colonies. Russia and Japan then went to war over Manchuria in the Russo-Japanese War. Japan forced Russia to withdraw from Manchuria and stay out of Korea.

5.72 Japan shut down Korea's newspapers, took over Korean schools, took land from Korean farmers for Japanese settlers, and only allowed Japanese businessmen to start industries in Korea.

Unit 5: Section Review Questions

**1: The Scientific Revolution and the
Enlightenment**   **1** (3)   **2** (4)

2: Political Revolutions and Reactions
See the Thematic Essay Rubric on p. 318

3: Global Nationalism
See the Thematic Essay Rubric on p. 318

4: Latin America After Independence   **1** (2)

5: Economic and Social Revolutions
See the Thematic Essay Rubric on p. 318

6: Imperialism   **1** (4)

7: Japan and the Meiji Restoration   **1** (2)

Unit 5: Practice Regents Exam

PART I: Multiple-Choice Questions

1 (4)   **3** (2)   **5** (1)   **7** (2)   **9** (2)
2 (1)   **4** (3)   **6** (2)   **8** (3)   **10** (4)

PART II: Thematic Essay Question
See the Thematic Essay Rubric on p. 318

PART III : Document-Based Question
Part A: Short Answer

1   The octopus suggests that the author holds a negative view of British imperialism. The author shows Britain ready to grab Egypt.

2   India's greatest misfortune is that the British do not understand, or consider, the wants of the Indian people.

3   Political borders that differ from ethnic boundaries means tribes are split apart and regrouped in a way that doesn't account for cultural, political, and linguistic differences. These ideological differences could lead to fighting within and across political borders.

PART B: Essay
See the Document-Based Question Rubric on p. 318

Unit 6: A Half Century of Crisis and Achievement
Preparing for the Regents Margin Questions

6.1   for protection due to growing rivalries and mistrust among the countries

6.2   The Balkans was a "powder keg" because of its history of nationalist uprisings and ethnic clashes.

6.3   When the Armenians sided with the Allies, the Turks deported 2 million Armenians; 600,000 of them died of starvation or were killed.

6.4   Machine guns, armored tanks, larger artillery, and airplanes killed greater numbers of people more effectively, but they did not lead to a fast-moving war, as hoped.

6.5   to gain access to Constantinople

6.6   took control of the economy, telling factories what to produce and how much; rationed items; nearly ended unemployment.

6.7   Women replaced men in factories, offices, and shops, and worked as nurses at or near front lines.

6.8   Russian army refused to fight any longer; the new Communist government ended involvement

6.9   millions killed; drained the treasuries of European countries; destroyed farmland, homes, towns, and villages; left a sense of disillusionment

6.10 by the industrial workers overthrowing the czar

6.11 He approved the Duma, and then quickly dissolved it so he wouldn't have to share his power. Russian workers opposed the war and other conditions in Russia. Their protests led to revolution. The new Communist leaders pulled out of the war.

6.12 Possible Answer: The slogan addressed the concerns of the Russian people.

6.13 The provisional government was unable to address the concerns of the people. In response, Lenin and his Red Guards stormed the Winter Palace and arrested the government's leaders.

6.14 It changed the government and structure of life in Russia forever.

6.15 allowed some factories, businesses, and farms to operate under private ownership; encouraged foreign investment, allowed peasants to sell their surplus crops; kept government control of major industries

6.16 totalitarian

6.17 The Five-Year Plans increased the output of steel, coal, oil, and electricity, and they limited production of consumer goods, leading to a stronger economy.

6.18 Ukrainian kulaks resisted establishment of collective farms

6.19 required that Germany pay reparations to the Allies.

6.20 As part of the agreement in the treaties, various countries had to give up land. Germany, the Austro-Hungarian Empire, the Ottoman Turks, and Russia lost territory.

6.21 the deliberate and public refusal to obey an unjust law using nonviolence to achieve a goal; called on Indians to refuse to buy British goods, attend government schools, pay British taxes, or vote in elections; organized Salt March

6.22 He separated the laws of the nation from the law of Islam, created a new legal system, granted women rights. Possible Answer: They many have wanted to keep religion involved in the legal system.

6.23 modernized country, established public schools, built roads and railroads, promoted industrial growth, and extended women's rights

6.24 carried on Islamic and Arab traditions; introduced some new technologies, such as telephones, but limited modernization to religiously acceptable areas

6.25 creating Jewish homeland in Palestine while honoring the rights of the Palestinians

6.26 hurt European economies; American bankers demanded repayment of European loans, American investors withdrew money from Europe; U.S. demand for European goods dropped; Austria and Germany particularly hard hit because of war debts and dependence on American loans and investment

6.27 the state is supreme, one-party system headed by a dictator

6.28 Possible Answer: Because the state is supreme under fascism.

6.29 The terms of the treaty regarding German territory enraged some Germans enough to form their own brand of fascism called Nazism.

6.30 The reparations placed a financial burden on Germany. When the Great Depression worsened the economic situation, Germans turned to Hitler and his fascist party for security and firm leadership.

6.31 banned other political parties, used the media and arts for propaganda, banned strikes, dissolved labor unions, gave the government authority over business and labor

6.32 Japan invaded Manchuria in 1931 as a way to try to solve the country's economic problems.

6.33 Possible Answer: It did not respond to Ethiopia's plea for help against an Italian invasion.

6.34 giving in to an aggressor in order to keep peace

6.35 gave in to Hitler in hope of avoiding war

6.36 September 1, 1939

6.37 Germany launched a surprise attack on Poland.

6.38 Possible Answer: It shows that the British were willing to do whatever it took to defend Britain.

6.39 They both lost to the Soviets during the winter because they weren't prepared for the conditions.

6.40 December 7, 1941

6.41 Possible Answer: Japan had few natural resources of their own. The needed to expand into other territories to acquire natural resources.

6.42 fighter planes launched from aircraft carriers

6.43 The Nazis used a series of increasingly harsh measures against Jews, Roma, Poles, Russians, homosexuals, the insane, the disabled, and the incurably ill. Early measures included the Nuremberg Laws, which deprived Jews of the rights of German citizenship; forced emigration; and the creation of Jewish ghettos. The "Final Solution" involved confining Jews and others in concentration and death camps, where millions of people died.

6.44 Genocide is the systematic killing of an entire people. The "Final Solution" attempted to eliminate certain races, groups, and nationalities.

6.45 August 23, 1942

6.46 The Soviet Union's size made It difficult for the Germans to maintain their supply lines. The cold winters took a harsh toll on the German soldiers.

6.47 The Allies were able to advance and hold the beaches, eventually liberating France. It began on June 6, 1944.

6.48 The atomic bomb was used against Japan to end the war in the Pacific.

6.49 Hiroshima—August 6, 1945. Nagasaki—August 9, 1945

6.50 They were the trials at which Nazi leaders were tried for war crimes. They punished many of the Nazi leaders for crimes against humanity.

Unit 6: Section Review Questions

1: World War I
See the Thematic Essay Rubric on p. 318

2: Revolution and Change in Russia 1 (3)

3: Between the Wars
See the Thematic Essay Rubric on p. 318

4: World War II 1 (3)

Unit 6: Practice Regents Exam

PART I: Multiple-Choice Questions

1 (4)	3 (4)	5 (2)	7 (3)	9 (1)
2 (1)	4 (4)	6 (3)	8 (4)	10 (1)

PART II: Thematic Essay Question
See the Thematic Essay Rubric on p. 318

PART III : Document-Based Question
Part A: Short Answer

1 It increased by about 45,000 metric tons.

2 Second Five-Year Plan

PART B: Essay
See the Document-Based Question Rubric on p. 318

Unit 7: The Twentieth Century Since 1945
Preparing for the Regents Margin Questions

7.1 to protect its members against aggression

7.2 as a buffer against another invasion

7.3 They hoped the Allies would surrender West Berlin or give up the idea of reunifying Germany.

7.4 established constitutional monarchy, disbanded the Japanese armed forces (demilitarization), broadened land ownership, and increased participation of workers and farmers in democracy

7.5 assistance program for Western Europe; helped countries that were threatened by communism

7.6 Truman's policy of giving aid to countries that rejected communism; to contain the spread of communism

7.7 to form alliances among countries that supported different sides of the Cold War

7.8 to remain neutral in the struggle between the superpowers

7.9 developing nations; superpowers backed surrogate wars and provided assistance

7.10 Arms race—Development of the A-bomb and H-bomb, brinkmanship. Space race—Development of the ICBM rocket and the launching of *Sputnik*.

7.11 willingness to go to the edge of war

7.12 Armed forces ended the revolts, and a pro-Soviet government was installed in Hungary.

7.13 dangerous 6,000-mile-long journey Chinese Communists took to flee the Nationalists

7.14 Possible Answer: The United States aided the Republic of China, while the Soviet Union aided the People's Republic of China.

7.15 reshape China's economy based on Marxist socialism and increase industrial output; both set high production goals

7.16 plan for even bigger communes; poor planning and low motivation caused the program to fail

7.17 Militia units formed by former students at Mao's urging

7.18 to establish a completely equal society; the Red Guards shut down schools and targeted anyone who resisted the regime, leading to chaos

7.19 eliminated communes, allowed private businesses, welcomed foreign technology and investment; a dramatic increase in production and income

7.20 Economic reform did not lead to political reform or to the protection of human rights.

7.21 to respect Hong Kong's economic and political freedom for 50 years

7.22 to control violence between Hindus and Muslims

7.23 Both countries want to control Kashmir.

7.24 Possible Answer: India's large and diverse population, social inequality, religious strife, and tensions with Pakistan make unity difficult.

7.25 Nkruhmah—Organized strikes and boycotts to gain independence. Kenyatta—Provided strong leadership. Mau Mau—Used guerilla war tactics against the British.

7.26 autocratic rule, corrupt officials, and civil war

7.27 set up a tribunal to punish the criminals

7.28 fighting among ethnic groups, martial law, civil war, persecution

7.29 complete separation of the races

7.30 Nelson Mandela and the ANC—Organized strikes and boycotts. Desmond Tutu—Convinced foreign countries to not do business with South Africa. F.W. de Klerk—Helped repeal apartheid laws.

7.31 Soviets set up a Communist government in the north, while the U.S. aided the south. The Communist Chinese and North Koreans invaded South Korea; the South Koreans and UN forces tried to stop them.

7.32 Vietnamese nationalist who asked the Communists for help in fighting the French

7.33 Possible Answer: The Vietminh wanted independence from the French.

7.34 The United States became involved because Eisenhower believed that if one Asian nation fell to communism, the others would fall like dominos (domino theory).

7.35 They killed 2 million people in an attempt to transform Cambodia into a Communist society.

7.36 fighting between the military government and prodemocracy forces, conflict among Communists and ethnic minorities

7.37 Burmese activist

7.38 Glasnost—policy of openness that allowed for the free exchange of information. Perestroika—Economic restructuring that gave local managers greater authority over farms and factories and allowed people to open small private businesses. Democratization—Allowed people to elect members to a new legislative body.

7.39 because it was an inefficient system in which party officials controlled decision making

7.40 As reforms loosened government control, non-Russians, who formed the majority in all republics except Russia, demanded self-rule.

7.41 failed coup in Moscow in August 1991 after reform-minded Boris Yeltsin was elected president

7. 42 economic problems like ending trade barriers, price controls and subsidies to state-owned industries; war in Chechnya after it declared independence

7.43 forcefully, which made Putin popular and helped him win the 2000 presidential election

7.44 went on strike until the Polish government recognized the union and raised wages; Solidarity leader Lech Walesa was eventually elected president of Poland

7.45 Hungary allowed East Germans to cross the border and escape to the West; Communism fell in East German when the Berlin Wall opened

7.46 East German industries couldn't compete globally and needed modernizing; slow-growing economy, high unemployment rates, and rising inflation

7.47 economic problems and rise in unemployment; country split into Slovakia and Czech Republic over economic policy

7.48 increasing violence and atrocities like the Serbs' attempt at ethnic cleansing against Muslims and their invasion of Kosovo; the failure of diplomacy to bring peace

7.49 May 14, 1948; six Islamic states invaded the next day, leading to the first of many Arab-Israeli wars

7.50 Egypt was the first Arab country to recognize Israel as a legitimate state; Egypt and Israel signed a peace treaty at Camp David in the U.S.

7.51 boycotts, demonstrations, attacks on Israeli soldiers, rock throwing, and other acts of civil disobedience

7.52 A right-wing Jewish extremist assassinated Rabin because he had made concessions to the Palestinians. Possible Answer: The peace process is difficult because both sides are unwilling to make concessions.

7.53 suicide bombers; Israeli troops destroyed buildings and bulldozed entire towns where extremists were suspected of hiding

7.54 rioters forced the shah to flee, enabled Khomeini to establish fundamentalist Islamic state

7.55 restricted women from education and employment; banned television, movies, and modern music

7.56 declared unconstitutional

7.57 Iraq invaded Kuwait to seize its oil fields

7.58 believed he had weapons of mass destruction

7.59 forbidden to speak their language, religious persecution, attacked with poison gas

7.60 used by Palestinians and other Middle Eastern groups to push for Palestinian homeland

7.61 crippled economy by ending Soviet economic aid

7.62 The United States supported Nicaragua's anti-Communist forces.

7.63 torture, murders, kidnappings

7.64 high unemployment rate, failure to repay its $132 billion debt, devalued currency

Unit 7: Section Review Questions
1: The Cold War Balance of Power
See the Thematic Essay Rubric on p. 318
2: The Chinese Communist Revolution
See the Thematic Essay Rubric on p. 318
3: The Collapse of European Imperialism
See the Thematic Essay Rubric on p. 318
4: The Collapse of Communism and the Soviet Union
See the Thematic Essay Rubric on p. 318
5: Conflict and Change in the Middle East and Latin America
See the Thematic Essay Rubric on p. 318

Unit 7: Practice Regents Exam
PART I: Multiple-Choice Questions

1 (3)	**3** (2)	**5** (4)	**7** (3)	**9** (2)
2 (2)	**4** (4)	**6** (3)	**8** (4)	**10** (1)

PART II: Thematic Essay Question
See the Thematic Essay Rubric on p. 318
PART III : Document-Based Question
Part A: Short Answer
1 Possible Answers: executions, forced urban evacuations and migrations, compulsory labor, forced communal living, marriages selected by state

2 Possible Answers: apartheid declared a crime and later dismantled; Constitution gave limited rights to minorities; legal end of segregation in public places; enfranchised black majority

3 Possible Answers: all humans equal and free; right to life, liberty, security of person; slavery, torture, cruel treatment outlawed; arbitrary arrests prohibited; freedom of movement; right to seek asylum

PART B: Essay
See the Document-Based Question rubric on p. 318

Unit 8: Global Connections and Interactions
Preparing for the Regents Margin Questions

8.1 hope for a better life, lack of food, natural disasters, political oppression

8.2 Many poor Mexicans come to the U.S. illegally.

8.3 "one-child family" policy

8.4 disease that attacks the immune system; large numbers of working-age Africans are dying from it

8.5 issued the Universal Declaration of Human Rights and the Helsinki Accords

8.6 sweatshops, low pay, bad working conditions

8.7 supported East Timorese independence and brought peace to the area after pro-Indonesian forces clashed with the East Timorese

8.8 Possible Answer: Literacy helps a society end poverty, reduce infant death rates, curb population growth, achieve gender equality, and ensure economic development and peace.

8.9 Helps nations resolve conflicts and provides peacekeeping forces

8.10 allow tariff-free trade among members

8.11 establishes oil production and pricing policies

8.12 dependent on a single crop, underdeveloped areas, foreign debts, few factories, too many imports; colonial powers encouraged the development of only one or two cash crops and also built few factories.

8.13 put money into industrial development

8.14 Possible Answer: in developed nations

8.15 led to home offices and telecommuting; new industrial processes lowered costs, and increased quality and speed of production; information moved quickly and cheaply

8.16 Improved surgical techniques, advances in medical imaging, and breakthroughs in genetic research have improved lives.

8.17 Positive—Helped avert famine and increase crop yields worldwide. Negative—Expensive and dangerous chemicals and equipment; pollution.

8.18 Deforestation—when trees are cut down and not replanted—mostly occurs in the Amazon Basin, the Congo, and other tropical rainforests. Desertification—the spread of deserts due to climate changes, poor farming, and deforestation—is most severe Africa and India.

8.19 Possible Answer: because the fallout drifted westward over Europe

8.20 increase in atmospheric carbon dioxide, pollution, acid rain, global warming, depleted ozone, increased ultraviolet radiation, higher rates of skin cancer, soil erosion, habitat destruction, loss of plant and animal species

8.21 reducing the negative environmental effects of development while meeting current economic needs.

Unit 8: Section Review Questions
1: Social, Political, and Economic Patterns   **1** (4)
2: Science, Technology, and the
   Environment   **1** (2)   **3** (1)
                                      2 (4)   **4** (1)

Unit 8: Practice Regents Exam
PART I: Multiple-Choice Questions

1 (4)	**3** (4)	**5** (4)	**7** (3)	**9** (2)
2 (3)	**4** (4)	**6** (3)	**8** (4)	**10** (4)

PART II: Thematic Essay Question
See the Thematic Essay Rubric on p. 318

PART III : Document-Based Question
Part A: Short Answer

1 Japan exploits more of the world's resources than Bangladesh.

2 Developing nations are becoming major carbon emitters and may eventually contribute more than industrialized nations.

3 Possible Answers: achieving sustainable growth; world habitability issues like water supply, solid waste management, and pollution; efficient resource usage; protecting global and regional resources; managing chemical, hazardous, and nuclear wastes

PART B: Essay
See the Document-Based Question Rubric on p. 318

Sample Regents Exam
PART I: Multiple-Choice Questions

1 (4)	**11** (1)	**21** (1)	**31** (2)	**41** (1)
2 (1)	**12** (3)	**22** (3)	**32** (1)	**42** (2)
3 (3)	**13** (1)	**23** (2)	**33** (4)	**43** (3)
4 (1)	**14** (4)	**24** (3)	**34** (4)	**44** (1)
5 (1)	**15** (3)	**25** (3)	**35** (3)	**45** (2)
6 (2)	**16** (4)	**26** (2)	**36** (4)	**46** (3)
7 (4)	**17** (4)	**27** (1)	**37** (2)	**47** (2)
8 (2)	**18** (3)	**28** (4)	**38** (2)	**48** (1)
9 (3)	**19** (3)	**29** (2)	**39** (1)	**49** (4)
10 (4)	**20** (4)	**30** (4)	**40** (1)	**50** (3)

PART II: Thematic Essay Question
See the Thematic Essay Rubric on p. 318

PART III : Document-Based Question
Part A: Short Answer

1 Possible Answers: destroyed cities and property, enslaved Russians, drafted craftsmen and artisans

2 Possible Answers: peace and protection from invasion, development of state and church

3 Possible Answers: renovation of Grand Canal, built water-control projects, established Pax Mongolica

4 Possible Answer: led to conflict

5 Possible Answers: enforced loyalty to the crown; viceroy's ruled colonies in king's name

6 Possible Answer: introduction of new social classes

7 Possible Answers: many countries under French control; some nations allied with Napoléon, others went to war.

8 Possible Answers: influenced region's civil laws; cemented idea of freedom of civil society from religious control; unified system of laws promoted national unity

9 Possible Answer: led to revolution in Latin America

PART B: Essay
See the Document-Based Question Rubric on p. 318

GLOSSARY

The Glossary is an alphabetical listing of many key terms from the chapters, along with their meanings. The definitions listed in the Glossary apply to the way the words are used in this textbook. The Glossary gives the part of speech of each word. The following abbreviations are used:

adj. adjective   *n.* noun   *v.* verb

Pronunciation Key

Some of the words in this book are followed by respellings that show how the words are pronounced. The following key will help you understand what sounds are represented by the letters used in the respellings.

Symbol	Examples	Symbol	Examples
a	apple [AP•uhl], catch [kach]	oh	road, [rohd], know [noh]
ah	barn [bahrn], pot [paht]	oo	school [skool], glue [gloo]
air	bear [bair], dare [dair]	ow	out [owt], cow [kow]
aw	bought [bawt], horse [hawrs]	oy	coin [koyn], boys [boyz]
ay	ape [ayp], mail [mayl]	p	pig [pihg], top [tahp]
b	bell [behl], table [TAY•buhl]	r	rose [rohz], star [stahr]
ch	chain [chayn], ditch [dihch]	s	soap [sohp], icy [EYE•see]
d	dog [dawg], rained [raynd]	sh	share [shair], nation [NAY•shuhn]
ee	even [EE•vuhn], meal [meel]	t	tired [tyrd], boat [boht]
eh	egg [ehg], ten [tehn]	th	thin [thihn], mother [MUH•thuhr]
eye	iron [EYE•uhrn]	u	pull [pul], look [luk]
f	fall [fawl], laugh [laf]	uh	bump [buhmp], awake [uh•WAYK],
g	gold [gohld], big [bihg]		happen [HAP•uhn], pencil [PEHN•suhl],
h	hot [haht], exhale [ehks•HAYL]		pilot [PY•luht]
hw	white [hwyt]	ur	earth [urth], bird [burd], worm [wurm]
ih	into [IHN•too], sick [sihk]	v	vase [vays], love [luhv]
j	jar [jahr], badge [baj]	w	web [wehb], twin [twihn]
k	cat [kat], luck [luhk]	y	As a consonant: yard [yahrd], mule [myool]
l	load [lohd], ball [bawl]		As a vowel: ice [ys], tried [tryd], sigh [sy]
m	make [mayk], gem [jehm]	z	zone [zohn], reason [REE•zuhn]
n	night [nyt], win [wihn]	zh	treasure [TREHZH•uhr], garage [guh•RAHZH]
ng	song [sawng], anger [ANG•guhr]		

Syllables that are stressed when the words are spoken appear in CAPITAL LETTERS in the respellings. For example, the respelling of *patterns* (PAT•uhrnz) shows that the first syllable of the word is stressed.

Syllables that appear in SMALL CAPITAL LETTERS are also stressed, but not as strongly as those that appear in capital letters. For example, the respelling of *interaction* (IHN•tuhr•AK•shuhn) shows that the third syllable receives the main stress and the first syllable receives a secondary stress.

A

Abbasids [uh•BAS•IHDZ] *n.* a dynasty that ruled much of the Muslim Empire from A.D. 750 to 1258. (p. 68)

absolute monarch [MAHN•uhrk] *n.* a king or queen who has unlimited power and seeks to control all aspects of society. (p. 157)

Aksum [AHK•SOOM] *n.* an African kingdom, in what is now Ethiopia and Eritrea, that reached the height of its power n the fourth century A.D. (p. 99)

al-Andalus [al•AN•duh•LUS] *n.* a Muslim-ruled region in what is now Spain, established in the eighth century A.D. (p. 68)

Allah [AL•uh] *n.* God (an Arabic word, used mainly in Islam) (p. 45)

Allies [uh•LYZ] *n.* in World War I, the nations of Great Britain, France, and Russia, along with the other nations that fought on their side; also, the group of nations including Great Britain, the Soviet Union, and the United States that opposed the Axis Powers in World War II. (p. 216)

Almohads [AL•moh•HADZ] *n.* a group of Islamic reformers who overthrew the Almoravid dynasty and established an empire in North Africa and southern Spain in the 12th century A.D. (p. 100)

Almoravids [AL•muh•RAHV•uhdz] *n.* an Islamic religious brotherhood that established an empire in North Africa and southern Spain in the 11th century A.D. (p. 100)

Amritsar Massacre *n.* killing by British troops of nearly 400 Indians gathered at Amritsar to protest the Rowlatt Acts (p. 225)

Anabaptists [AN•uh•BAP•tihsts] *n.* in the Reformation, a Protestant group that believed in baptizing only those persons who were old enough to decide to be Christian and believed in the separation of church and state. (p. 124)

Anatolia [AN•uh•TOH•lee•uh] *n.* the Southwest Asian peninsula now occupied by the Asian part of Turkey— also called Asia Minor. (p. 136)

Anglican [ANG•glih•kuhn] *adj.* relating to the Church of England. (p. 123)

animism [AN•uh•MIHZ•uhm] *n.* the belief that spirits are present in animals, plants, and other natural objects. (p. 40)

annexation [AN•ihk•SAY•shuhn] *n.* the adding of a region to the territory of an existing political unit. (p. 208)

annul [uh•NUHL] *v.* to cancel or set aside. (p. 122)

apartheid [uh•PAHRT•hyt] *n.* a South African policy of complete legal separation of the races, including the banning of all social contacts between blacks and whites. (p. 260)

apostle [uh•PAHS•uhl] *n.* one of the followers of Jesus who preached and spread his teachings. (p. 45)

appeasement *n.* the making of concessions to an aggressor in order to avoid war. (p. 230)

aqueduct [AK•wih•DUHKT] *n.* a pipeline or channel built to carry water to populated areas. (p. 36)

aristocracy [AR•ih•STAHK•ruh•see] *n.* a government in which power is in the hands of a hereditary ruling class or nobility. (p. 32)

armistice [AHR•mih•stihs] *n.* an agreement to stop fighting. (p. 218)

artifact *n.* a human-made object, such as a tool, weapon, or piece of jewelry. (p. 19)

artisan [AHR•tih•zuhn] *n.* a skilled worker, such as a weaver or a potter, who makes goods by hand. (p. 21)

Aryans [AIR•ee•uhnz] *n.* **1.** an Indo-European people who, about 1500 B.C., began to migrate into the Indian subcontinent (p. 40). **2.** to the Nazis, the Germanic peoples who formed a "master race." (p. 228)

Atlantic slave trade *n.* the buying, transporting, and selling of Africans for work in the Americas. (p. 152)

Axis Powers *n.* in World War II, the nations of Germany, Italy, and Japan, which had formed an alliance in 1936. (p. 230)

ayllu [EYE•loo] *n.* in Incan society, a small community or clan whose members worked together for the common good. (p. 147)

B

balance of power *n.* a political situation in which no one nation is powerful enough to pose a threat to others. (p. 180)

the Balkans [BAWL•kuhnz] *n.* the region of southeastern Europe now occupied by Greece, Albania, Bulgaria, Romania, the European part of Turkey, and the former republics of Yugoslavia. (p. 185)

Bantu-speaking peoples *n.* the speakers of a related group of languages who, beginning about 2,000 years ago, migrated from West Africa into most of the southern half of Africa. (p. 21)

barter *n.* a form of trade in which people exchange goods and services without the use of money. (p. 23)

Battle of Britain *n.* a series of battles between German and British air forces, fought over Britain in 1940–1941. (p. 233)

Battle of Guadalcanal [GWAHD•uhl•kuh•NAL] *n.* a 1942–1943 battle of World War II, in which Allied troops drove Japanese forces from the Pacific island of Guadalcanal. (p. 238)

Battle of Midway *n.* a 1942 sea and air battle of World War II, in which American forces defeated Japanese forces in the central Pacific. (p. 238)

Battle of Stalingrad [STAH•lihn•GRAD] *n.* a 1942–1943 battle of World War II, in which German forces were defeated in their attempt to capture the city of Stalingrad in the Soviet Union. (p. 237)

Battle of the Bulge *n.* a 1944–1945 battle in which Allied forces turned back the last major German offensive of World War II. (p. 238)

Benin [buh•NIHN] *n.* a kingdom that arose near the Niger River delta in the 1300s and became a major West African state in the 1400s. (p. 103)

Berlin Conference of 1884–85 *n.* a meeting at which representatives of European nations agreed upon rules for the European colonization of Africa. (p. 201)

Bill of Rights *n.* the first ten amendments to the U.S. Constitution, which protect citizens' basic rights and freedoms. (p. 174)

blitzkrieg [BLIHTS•KREEG] *n.* "lightning war"—a form of warfare in which surprise attacks with fast-moving airplanes are followed by massive attacks with infantry forces. (p. 232)

Boer [bohr] *n.* a Dutch colonist in South Africa. (p. 201)

Boer War *n.* a conflict, lasting from 1899 to 1902, in which the Boers and the British fought for control of territory in South Africa. (p. 202)

Bolsheviks [BOHL•shuh•VIHKS] *n.* a group of revolutionary Russian Marxists who took control of Russia's government in November 1917. (p. 220)

Boxer Rebellion *n.* a 1900 revolt in China, aimed at ending foreign influence in the country. (p. 204)

boyars [boh•YAHRZ] *n.* landowning nobles of Russia. (p. 158)

Brahma [BRAH•muh] *n.* a Hindu god considered the creator of the world. (p. 40)

Brahmin [BRAH•mihn] *n.* in Aryan society, a member of the social class made up of priests. (p. 52)

brinkmanship *n.* a policy of threatening to go to war in response to any enemy aggression. (p. 249)

bubonic plague [boo•BAHN•ihk PLAYG] *n.* a deadly disease that spread across Asia and Europe in the mid-14th century, killing millions of people. (p. 109)

bureaucracy [byu•RAHK•ruh•see] *n.* a system of departments and agencies formed to carry out the work of government. (p. 30)

burgher [BUR•guhr] *n.* a medieval town dweller. (p. 107)

Bushido [BUSH•ih•DOH] *n.* the strict code of behavior followed by samurai warriors in Japan. (p. 89)

C

cabinet *n.* a group of advisors or ministers chosen by the head of a country to help make government decisions. (p. 161)

caliph [KAY•lihf] *n.* a supreme political and religious leader in a Muslim government. (p. 67)

calligraphy [kuh•LIHG•ruh•fee] *n.* the art of beautiful handwriting. (p. 71)

Calvinism [KAL•vih•NIHZ•uhm] *n.* a body of religious teachings based on the ideas of the reformer John Calvin. (p. 123)

Camp David Accords *n.* the first signed agreement between Israel and an Arab country, in which Egyptian president Anwar Sadat recognized Israel as a legitimate state and Israeli prime minister Menachem Begin agreed to return the Sinai Peninsula to Egypt. (p. 272)

canon law *n.* the body of laws governing the religious practices of a Christian church. (p. 76)

capitalism *n.* an economic system based on private ownership and on the investment of money in business ventures in order to make a profit. (p. 105, 195)

Carolingian [KAR•uh•LIHN•juhn] **Dynasty** *n.* a dynasty of Frankish rulers, lasting from A.D. 751 to 987. (p. 74)

caste [kast] *n.* one of the four classes of people in the social system of the Aryans who settled in India—priests, warriors, peasants or traders, and non-Aryan laborers or craftsmen. (p. 52)

Catholic Reformation [REHF•uhr•MAY•shuhn] *n.* a 16th century movement in which the Roman Catholic Church sought to make changes in response to the Protestant Reformation. (p. 124)

caudillo [kaw•DEEL•yoh] *n.* a military dictator of a Latin American country. (p. 188)

centralized government *n.* a government in which power is concentrated in a central authority to which local governments are subject. (p. 30)

Central Powers *n.* in World War I, the nations of Germany and Austria-Hungary, along with the other nations that fought on their side. (p. 215)

Chartist movement *n.* in 19th-century Britain, members of the working class who demanded reforms in Parliament and in elections, including suffrage for all men. (p. 197)

checks and balances *n.* measures designed to prevent any one branch of government from dominating the others. (p. 174)

chivalry [SHIHV•uhl•ree] *n.* a code of behavior for knights in medieval Europe, stressing ideals such as courage, loyalty, and devotion. (p. 75)

CIS *n.* the Commonwealth of Independent States—a loose association of former Soviet republics that was formed after the breakup of the Soviet Union. (p. 267)

city-state *n.* a city and its surrounding lands functioning as an independent political unit. (p. 24)

civil disobedience *n.* a deliberate and public refusal to obey a law considered unjust. (p. 225)

civilization *n.* a form of culture characterized by cities, specialized workers, complex institutions, record keeping, and advanced technology. (p. 21)

civil service *n.* the administrative departments of a government—especially those in which employees are hired on the basis of their scores on examinations. (p. 30)

classical art *n.* the art of ancient Greece and Rome, in which harmony, order, and balance were emphasized. (p. 33)

clergy [KLUR•jee] *n.* a body of officials who perform religious services—such as priests, ministers, or rabbis. (p. 76)

cloning [KLOH•nihng] *n.* the creation of plants or animals that are genetically identical to an existing plant or animal. (p. 288)

Cold War *n.* the state of diplomatic hostility between the United States and the Soviet Union in the decades following World War II. (p. 248)

collective farm *n.* a large government-controlled farm formed by combining many small farms. (p. 222)

colony *n.* a land controlled by a distant nation. (p. 141)

Columbian Exchange *n.* the global transfer of plants, animals, and diseases that occurred during the European colonization of the Americas. (p. 154)

comedy *n.* a humorous form of drama that often includes slapstick and satire. (p. 33)

command economy *n.* an economic system in which the government makes all economic decisions. (pp. 33, 222)

Commercial Revolution *n.* the expansion of trade and business that transformed European economies during the 16th and 17th centuries. (p. 105)

common law *n.* a unified body of law formed from rulings of England's royal judges that serves as the basis for law in many English-speaking countries today, including the United States. (p. 111)

commune [KAHM•YOON] *n.* in Communist China, a collective farm on which a great number of people work and live together. (p. 252)

Communist Party *n.* a political party practicing the ideas of Karl Marx and V.I. Lenin; originally the Russian Bolshevik Party. (p. 221)

communism *n.* an economic system in which all means of production—land, mines, factories, railroads, and businesses—are owned by the people, private property does not exist, and all goods and services are shared equally. (p. 197)

Congress of Vienna [vee•EHN•uh] *n.* a series of meetings in 1814–1815, during which the European leaders sought to establish long-lasting peace and security after the defeat of Napoleon. (p. 180)

Congress Party *n.* a major national political party in India—also known as the Indian National Congress. (p. 256)

conquistadors [kahng•KEE•stuh•DAWRZ] *n.* the Spanish soldiers, explorers, and fortune hunters who took part in the conquest of the Americas in the 16th century. (p. 151)

conservatives *n.* in the first half of the 19th century, those Europeans—mainly wealthy landowners and nobles—who wanted to preserve the traditional monarchies of Europe. (p. 180)

constitutional monarchy [MAHN•uhr•kee] *n.* a system of governing in which the ruler's power is limited by law. (p. 161)

consul [KAHN•suhl] *n.* in the Roman republic, one of the two powerful officials elected each year to command the army and direct the government. (p. 34)

containment *n.* a U.S. foreign policy adopted by President Harry Truman in the late 1940s, in which the United States tried to stop the spread of communism by creating alliances and helping weak countries to resist Soviet advances. (p. 248)

Continental System *n.* Napoleon's policy of preventing trade between Great Britain and continental Europe, intended to destroy Great Britain's economy. (p. 177)

Council of Trent *n.* a meeting of Roman Catholic leaders, called by Pope Paul III to rule on doctrines criticized by the Protestant reformers. (p. 125)

covenant [KUHV•uh•nuhnt] *n.* a mutual promise or agreement—especially an agreement between God and the Hebrew people as recorded in the Bible. (p. 43)

creoles [KREE•OHLZ] *n.* in Spanish colonial society, colonists who were born in Latin America to Spanish parents. (p. 178)

Crimean [kry•MEE•uhn] **War** *n.* a conflict, lasting from 1853 to 1856, in which the Ottoman Empire, with the aid of Britain and France, halted Russian expansion in the region of the Black Sea. (p. 186)

crop rotation *n.* the system of growing a different crop in a field each year to preserve the fertility of the land. (p. 192)

Crusade *n.* one of the expeditions in which medieval Christian warriors sought to recover control of the Holy Land from the Muslims. (p. 79)

cultural diffusion *n.* the spreading of ideas or products from one culture to another. (p. 24)

Cultural Revolution *n.* a 1966–1976 uprising in China led by the Red Guards, with the goal of establishing a society of peasants and workers in which all were equal. (p. 253)

culture *n.* a people's unique way of life, as shown by its tools, customs, arts, and ideas. (p. 19)

cuneiform [KYOO•nee•uh•FAWRM] *n.* a system of writing with wedge-shaped symbols, invented by the Sumerians around 3000 B.C. (p. 25)

Cyrillic [suh•RIHL•ihk] **alphabet** *n.* an alphabet for the writing of Slavic languages, devised in the ninth century A.D. by Saints Cyril and Methodius. (p. 63)

D

daimyo [DY•mee•OH] *n.* a Japanese feudal lord who commanded a private army of samurai. (p. 90)

Daoism [DOW•IHZ•uhm] *n.* a philosophy based on the ideas of the Chinese thinker Laozi, who taught that people should be guided by a universal force called the Dao (Way). (p. 42)

D-Day *n.* June 6, 1944—the day on which the Allies began their invasion of the European mainland during World War II. (p. 238)

Declaration of Independence *n.* a statement of the reasons for the American colonies' break with Britain, approved by the Second Continental Congress in 1776. (p. 173)

delta *n.* a marshy region formed by deposits of silt at the mouth of a river. (p. 25)

demilitarization [dee•MIHL•ih•tuhr•ih•ZAY•shuhn] *n.* a reduction in a country's ability to wage war, achieved by disbanding its armed forces and prohibiting it from acquiring weapons. (p. 247)

democracy *n.* a government controlled by its citizens, either directly or through representatives. (p. 32)

democratization *n.* the process of creating a government elected by the people. (p. 247)

détente [day•TAHNT] *n.* a policy of reducing Cold War tensions that was adopted by the United States during the presidency of Richard Nixon. (p. 265)

developed nation *n.* a nation with all the facilities needed for the advanced production of manufactured goods. (p. 285)

devshirme [dehv•SHEER•meh] *n.* in the Ottoman Empire, the policy of taking children from conquered Christian peoples to be trained as Muslim soldiers. (p. 137)

Diaspora [dy•AS•puhr•uh] *n.* the dispersal of the Jews from their homeland in Palestine—especially during the period of more than 1,800 years that followed the Romans' destruction of the Temple in Jerusalem in A.D. 70. (p. 186)

dictator *n.* in ancient Rome, a political leader given absolute power to make laws and command the army for a limited time. (p. 34)

direct democracy *n.* a government in which citizens rule directly rather than through representatives. (p. 33)

dissident [DIHS•ih•duhnt] *n.* an opponent of a government's policies or actions. (p. 260)

divine right *n.* the idea that monarchs are God's representatives on earth and are therefore answerable only to God. (p. 157)

domestication *n.* the taming of animals for human use. (p. 20)

domino theory *n.* the idea that if a nation falls under Communist control, nearby nations will also fall under Communist control. (p. 262)

Dutch East India Company *n.* a company founded by the Dutch in the early 17th century to establish and direct trade throughout Asia. (p. 150)

dynastic [dy•NAS•tihk] **cycle** *n.* the historical pattern of the rise, decline, and replacement of dynasties in ancient China. (p. 30)

dynasty [DY•nuh•stee] *n.* a series of rulers from a single family. (p. 24)

E

Eastern Front *n.* in World War I, the region along the German-Russian border where Russians and Serbs battled Germans, Austrians, and Turks. (p. 216)

emerging nation *n.* a nation in which the process of industrialization is not yet complete. (p. 282)

empire *n.* a political unit in which a number of peoples or countries are controlled by a single ruler. (p. 25)

enclosure *n.* one of the fenced-in or hedged-in fields created by wealthy British landowners on land that was formerly worked by village farmers. (p. 192)

encomienda [ehng•kaw•MYEHN•dah] *n.* a grant of land made by Spain to a settler in the Americas, including the right to use Native Americans as laborers on it. (p. 152)

English Civil War *n.* a conflict, lasting from 1642 to 1649, in which Puritan supporters of Parliament battled supporters of England's monarchy. (p. 160)

enlightened despot [DEHS•puht] *n.* one of the 18th century European monarchs who was inspired by Enlightenment ideas to rule justly and respect the rights of subjects. (p. 171)

enlightenment [ehn•LYT•uhn•muhnt] *n.* in Buddhism, a state of perfect wisdom in which one understands basic truths about the universe. (p. 41)

Enlightenment *n.* an 18th-century European movement in which thinkers attempted to apply the principles of reason and the scientific method to all aspects of society. (p. 169)

entrepreneur [AHN•truh•pruh•NUR] *n.* a person who organizes, manages, and takes on the risks of a business. (p. 194)

estate [ih•STAYT] *n.* one of the three social classes in France before the French Revolution—the First Estate consisting of the clergy; the Second Estate, of the nobility; and the Third Estate, of the rest of the population. (p. 174)

Estates-General [ih•STAYTS•JEHN•uhr•uhl] *n.* an assembly of representatives from all three of the estates, or social classes, in France. (p. 113)

"ethnic cleansing" *n.* a policy of murder and other acts of brutality by which Serbs hoped to eliminate Bosnia's Muslim population after the breakup of Yugoslavia. (p. 269)

excommunication [EHKS•kuh•MYOO•nih•KAY•shuhn] *n.* the taking away of a person's right of membership in a Christian church. (p. 63)

extraterritorial [EHK•struh•TEHR•ih•TAWR•ee•uhl] **rights** *n.* an exemption of foreign residents from the laws of a country. (p. 203)

F

factors of production *n.* the resources—including land, labor, and capital—that are needed to produce goods and services. (p. 105)

factory *n.* a large building in which machinery is used to manufacture goods. (p. 193)

factory system *n.* manufacturing of products concentrated in a central location. (p. 193)

fascism [FASH•IHZ•uhm] *n.* a political movement that promotes an extreme form of nationalism, a denial of individual rights, and a dictatorial one-party rule. (p. 227)

Fatimid [FAT•uh•MIHD] *n.* a member of a Muslim dynasty that traced its ancestry to Muhammad's daughter Fatima and that built an empire in North Africa, Arabia, and Syria in the 10th–12th centuries. (p. 69)

favorable balance of trade *n.* an economic situation in which a country sells more goods abroad than it buys from abroad. (p. 155)

federal system *n.* a system of government in which power is divided between a central authority and a number of individual states. (p. 259)

Fertile Crescent [FUHR•tuhl KREHS•uhnt] *n.* an arc of rich farmland in Southwest Asia, between the Persian Gulf and the Mediterranean Sea. (p. 24)

feudalism [FYOOD•uhl•IHZ•uhm] *n.* a political system in which nobles are granted the use of lands that legally belong to their king, in exchange for their loyalty, military service, and protection of the people who live on the land. (p. 30)

fief [feef] *n.* an estate granted to a vassal by a lord under the feudal system in medieval Europe. (p. 74)

filial piety [FIHL•ee•uhl PY•ih•tee] *n.* respect shown by children for their parents and elders. (p. 42)

"Final Solution" *n.* Hitler's program of systematically killing the entire Jewish people. (p. 236)

Five-Year Plans *n.* plans outlined by Joseph Stalin in 1928 for the development of the Soviet Union's economy. (p. 222)

Four Modernizations *n.* a set of goals adopted by the Chinese leader Deng Xiaoping in the late 20th century, involving progress in agriculture, industry, defense, and science and technology. (p. 253)

Fourteen Points *n.* a series of proposals in which U.S. president Woodrow Wilson outlined a plan for achieving a lasting peace after World War I. (p. 224)

Franks *n.* a Germanic people who settled in the Roman province of Gaul (roughly the area now occupied by France) and established a great empire during the Middle Ages. (p. 73)

free trade *n.* commerce between nations without economic restrictions or barriers (such as tariffs). (p. 284)

G

gender inequality *n.* the difference between men and women in terms of wealth and status. (p. 283)

genetic [juh•NEHT•ihk] **engineering** *n.* the transferring of genes from one living thing to another in order to produce an organism with new traits. (p. 288)

genocide [JEHN•uh•SYD] *n.* the systematic killing of an entire people. (p. 236)

gentry *n.* a class of powerful, well-to-do people who enjoy a high social status. (p. 58)

geocentric theory *n.* in the Middle Ages, the earth-centered view of the universe in which scholars believed that the earth was an immovable object located at the center of the universe. (p. 168)

geopolitics [JEE•oh•PAHL•ih•tihks] *n.* a foreign policy based on a consideration of the strategic locations or products of other lands. (p. 186)

Ghana [GAH•nuh] *n.* a West African kingdom that grew rich from taxing and controlling trade and that established an empire in the 9th–11th centuries A.D. (p. 101)

ghazi [GAH•zee] *n.* a warrior for Islam. (p. 136)

ghettos [GEHT•ohz] *n.* city neighborhoods in which European Jews were forced to live. (p. 236)

glasnost [GLAHS•nuhst] *n.* a Soviet policy of openness to the free flow of ideas and information, introduced in 1985 by Mikhail Gorbachev. (p. 265)

global economy *n.* all the financial interactions—involving people, businesses, and governments—that cross international boundaries. (p. 284)

Glorious Revolution *n.* the bloodless overthrow of the English king James II and his replacement by William and Mary. (p. 161)

glyph [glihf] *n.* a symbolic picture—especially one used as part of a writing system for carving messages in stone. (p. 38)

Gothic [GAHTH•ihk] *adj.* relating to a style of church architecture that developed in medieval Europe, featuring ribbed vaults, stained glass windows, flying buttresses, pointed arches, and tall spires. (p. 77)

Great Depression *n.* the severe economic slump that followed the collapse of the U.S. stock market in 1929. (p. 227)

Great Fear *n.* a wave of senseless panic that spread through the French countryside after the storming of the Bastille in 1789. (p. 175)

Great Purge *n.* a campaign of terror in the Soviet Union during the 1930s, in which Joseph Stalin sought to eliminate all Communist Party members and other citizens who threatened his power. (p. 222)

Great Schism [SIHZ•uhm] *n.* a division in the medieval Roman Catholic Church, during which rival popes were established in Avignon and in Rome. (p. 120)

Greco-Roman culture *n.* an ancient culture that developed from a blending of Greek, Hellenistic, and Roman cultures. (p. 36)

green revolution *n.* a 20th-century attempt to increase food resources worldwide, involving the use of fertilizers and pesticides and the development of disease-resistant crops. (p. 288)

guild [gihld] *n.* a medieval association of people working at the same occupation, which controlled its members' wages and prices. (p. 105)

guillotine [GIHL•uh•teen] *n.* a machine for beheading people, used as a means of execution during the French Revolution. (p. 176)

Gupta [GUP•tuh] **Empire** *n.* the second empire in India, founded by Chandra Gupta I in A.D. 320. (p. 53)

H

habeas corpus [HAY•bee•uhs KAWR•puhs] *n.* a document requiring that a prisoner be brought before a court or judge so that it can be decided whether his or her imprisonment is legal. (p. 160)

Hagia Sophia [HAY•ee•uh soh•FEE•uh] *n.* the Cathedral of Holy Wisdom in Constantinople, built by order of the Byzantine emperor Justinian. (p. 61)

haiku [HY•koo] *n.* a Japanese form of poetry, consisting of three unrhymed lines of five, seven, and five syllables. (p. 91)

hajj [haj] *n.* a pilgrimage to Mecca, performed as a duty by Muslims. (p. 46)

Han [hahn] **dynasty** *n.* a Chinese dynasty that ruled from 202 B.C. to A.D. 9 and again from A.D. 23 to 220. (p. 30)

Harappan civilization *n.* another name for the Indus Valley civilization that arose along the Indus River, possibly as early as 7000 B.C.; characterized by sophisticated city planning. (p. 27)

Hausa [HOW•suh] *n.* a West African people who lived in several city-states in what is now northern Nigeria. (p. 103)

heliocentric [HEE•lee•oh•SEHN•trihk] **theory** *n.* the idea that the earth and the other planets revolve around the sun. (p. 168)

Hellenistic [HEHL•uh•NIHS•tihk] *adj.* relating to the civilization, language, art, science, and literature of the Greek world from the reign of Alexander the Great to the late second century B.C. (p. 34)

hieroglyphics [HY•uhr•uh•GLIHF•ihks] *n.* an ancient Egyptian writing system in which pictures were used to represent ideas and sounds. (p. 26)

Hijrah [HIHJ•ruh] *n.* Muhammad's migration from Mecca to Yathrib (Medina) in A.D. 622. (p. 46)

Holocaust [HAHL•uh•KAWST] *n.* a mass slaughter of Jews and other civilians, carried out by the Nazi government of Germany before and during World War II. (p. 236)

Holy Roman Empire *n.* an empire established in Europe in the 10th century A.D., originally consisting mainly of lands in what is now Germany and Italy. (p. 77)

hominid [HAHM•uh•nihd] *n.* a member of a biological group including human beings and related species that walk upright. (p. 19)

Homo sapiens [HOH•moh SAY•pee•uhnz] *n.* the biological species to which modern human beings belong. (p. 19)

House of Wisdom *n.* a center of learning established in Baghdad in the 800s. (p. 70)

humanism [HYOO•muh•NIHZ•uhm] *n.* a Renaissance intellectual movement in which thinkers studied classical texts and focused on human potential and achievements. (p. 115)

Hundred Days *n.* the brief period during 1815 when Napoleon made his last bid for power, deposing the French king and again becoming emperor of France. (p. 178)

Hundred Years' War *n.* a conflict in which England and France battled on French soil on and off from 1337 to 1453. (p. 113)

hunter-gatherer *n.* a member of a nomadic group whose food supply depends on hunting animals and collecting plant foods. (p. 19)

I

icon [EYE•KAHN] *n.* a religious image used by eastern Christians. (p. 63)

imperialism [ihm•PEER•ee•uh•LIHZ•uhm] *n.* a policy in which a strong nation seeks to dominate other countries politically, economically, or socially. (p. 200)

indulgence [ihn•DUHL•juhns] *n.* a pardon releasing a person from punishments due for a sin. (p. 121)

industrialization [ihn•DUHS•tree•uh•lih•ZAY•shuhn] *n.* the development of industries for the machine production of goods. (p. 192)

Industrial Revolution *n.* the shift, beginning in England during the 18th century, from making goods by hand to making them by machine. (p. 192)

inflation *n.* a decline in the value of money, accompanied by a rise in the prices of goods and services. (p. 35)

Inquisition [IHN•kwih•ZIHSH•uhn] *n.* a Roman Catholic tribunal for investigating and prosecuting charges of heresy—especially the one active in Spain during the 1400s. (p. 81)

institution *n.* a long-lasting pattern of organization in a community. (p. 21)

intendant [ihn•TEHN•duhnt] *n.* a French government official appointed by the monarch to collect taxes and administer justice. (p. 158)

International Space Station *n.* cooperative venture sponsored by the United States, Russia, and 14 other nations to establish and maintain a working laboratory for scientific experimentation in space. (p. 287)

Internet *n.* a linkage of computer networks that enables people around the world to exchange information and communicate with one another. (p. 287)

intifada *n.* Palestinian campaign of civil disobedience against Israeli occupation of the West Bank and Gaza Strip, which continued into the 1990s. (p. 272)

iron curtain *n.* during the Cold War, the figurative boundary separating the Communist nations of Eastern Europe from the mostly democratic nations of Western Europe. (p. 246)

Islam [ihs•LAHM] *n.* a monotheistic religion that developed in Arabia in the seventh century A.D. (p. 45)

J

Jainism [JY•nihz•uhm] *n.* a religion founded in India in the sixth century B.C., whose members believe that everything in the universe has a soul and therefore should not be harmed. (p. 40)

janissary [JAN•ih•SEHR•ee] *n.* a member of an elite force of soldiers in the Ottoman Empire. (p. 137)

Jesuits [JEHZH•oo•ihts] *n.* members of the Society of Jesus, a Roman Catholic religious order founded by Ignatius of Loyola. (p. 124)

"jewel in the crown" *n.* the British colony of India—so called because of its importance in the British Empire, both as a supplier of raw materials and as a market for British trade goods. (p. 202)

joint-stock company *n.* a business in which investors pool their wealth for a common purpose, then share the profits. (p. 154)

Junkers [YUNG·kuhrz] *n.* strongly conservative members of Prussia's wealthy landowning class. (p. 184)

Justinian [juh·STIHN·ee·uhn] **Code** *n.* the body of Roman civil law collected and organized by order of the Byzantine emperor Justinian around A.D. 534. (p. 61)

K

kabuki [kuh·BOO·kee] *n.* a type of Japanese drama in which music, dance, and mime are used to present stories. (p. 91)

kaiser [KY·zuhr] *n.* a German emperor (from the Roman title Caesar). (p. 185)

kamikaze [KAH·mih·KAH·zee] *n.* during World War II, Japanese suicide pilots trained to sink Allied ships by crashing bomb-filled planes into them. (p. 238)

karma [KAHR·muh] *n.* in Hinduism and Buddhism, the totality of the good and bad deeds performed by a person, which is believed to determine his or her fate after rebirth. (p. 40)

Khmer Rouge [kmair roozh] *n.* a group of Communist rebels who seized power in Cambodia in 1975. (p. 263)

knight *n.* in medieval Europe, an armored warrior who fought on horseback. (p. 75)

Kristallnacht [krih·STAHL·NAHKT] *n.* "Night of Broken Glass"—the night of November 9, 1938, on which Nazi storm troopers attacked Jewish homes, businesses, and synagogues throughout Germany. (p. 236)

Kuomintang [KWOH·mihn·TANG] *n.* the Chinese Nationalist Party, formed after the fall of the Qing dynasty in 1912. (p. 204)

L

laissez faire [LEHS·ay·FAIR] *n.* the idea that government should not interfere with or regulate industries and businesses. (p. 195)

lay investiture [ihn·VEHS·tuh·chur] *n.* the appointment of religious officials by kings or nobles. (p. 77)

League of Nations *n.* an international association formed after World War I with the goal of keeping peace among nations. (p. 224)

Legalism *n.* a Chinese political philosophy based on the idea that a highly efficient and powerful government is the key to social order. (p. 43)

Legislative [LEHJ·ih·SLAY·tihv] **Assembly** *n.* a French congress with the power to create laws and approve declarations of war, established by the Constitution of 1791. (p. 175)

legitimacy [luh·JIHT·uh·muh·see] *n.* the hereditary right of a monarch to rule. (p. 180)

liberals *n.* in the first half of the 19th century, those Europeans—mainly middle-class business leaders and merchants—who wanted to give more political power to elected parliaments. (p. 180)

loess [LOH·uhs] *n.* a fertile deposit of windblown soil. (p. 27)

Long March *n.* a 6,000-mile journey made in 1934–1935 by Chinese Communists fleeing from Jiang Jieshi's Nationalist forces. (p. 251)

lord *n.* in feudal Europe, a person who controlled land and could therefore grant estates to vassals. (p. 74)

Lutheran [LOO·thuhr·uhn] *n.* a member of a Protestant church founded on the teachings of Martin Luther. (p. 122)

M

Macedonia [MAS·ih·DOH·nee·uh] *n.* an ancient kingdom north of Greece, whose ruler Philip II conquered Greece in 338 B.C. (p. 33)

Maghrib [MUHG·ruhb] *n.* a region of western North Africa, consisting of the Mediterranean coastlands of what is now Morocco, Tunisia, and Algeria. (p. 98)

Magna Carta [MAG·nuh KAHR·tuh] *n.* "Great Charter"— a document guaranteeing basic political rights in England, drawn up by nobles and approved by King John in A.D. 1215. (p. 111)

Mahayana [MAH·huh·YAH·nuh] *n.* a sect of Buddhism that offers salvation to all and allows popular worship. (p. 42)

maize [mayz] *n.* a cultivated cereal grain that bears its kernels on large ears—usually called corn in the United States. (p. 37)

Mali [MAH·lee] *n.* a West African empire that flourished from 1235 to the 1400s and grew rich from trade. (p. 101)

Manchus [MAN·chooz] *n.* a people, native to Manchuria, who ruled China during the Qing dynasty (1644–1912). (p. 133)

Mandate of Heaven *n.* in Chinese history, the divine approval thought to be the basis of royal authority. (p. 30)

manor *n.* a lord's estate in feudal Europe. (p. 75)

Marshall Plan *n.* a U.S. program of economic aid to European countries to help them rebuild after World War II. (p. 247)

martial [MAHR·shuhl] **law** *n.* a temporary rule by military authorities over a civilian population, usually imposed in times of war or civil unrest. (p. 259)

matriarchal [MAY·tree·AHR·kuhl] *adj.* relating to a social system in which the mother is head of the family. (p. 54)

Mauryan [MAH·ur·yuhn] **Empire** *n.* the first empire in India, founded by Chandragupta Maurya in 321 B.C. (p. 36)

Meiji [MAY·JEE] **era** *n.* the period of Japanese history from 1867 to 1912, during which the country was ruled by Emperor Mutsuhito. (p. 207)

Mein Kampf [MYN KAHMPF] *n.* "My Struggle"—a book written by Adolf Hitler during his imprisonment in 1923–1924, in which he set forth his beliefs and his goals for Germany. (p. 228)

mercantilism [MUR·kuhn·tee·LIHZ·uhm] *n.* an economic policy under which nations sought to increase their wealth and power by obtaining large amounts of gold and silver and by selling more goods than they bought. (p. 155)

Mesoamerica [MEHZ·oh·uh·MEHR·ih·kuh] *n.* an area extending from central Mexico to Honduras, where several of the ancient complex societies of the Americas developed. (p. 37)

mestizo [mehs·TEE·zoh] *n.* a person of mixed Spanish and Native American ancestry. (p. 151)

Middle Ages *n.* the era in European history that followed the fall of the Roman Empire, lasting from about 500 to 1500—also called the medieval period. (p. 72)

middle class *n.* a social class made up of skilled workers, professionals, businesspeople, and wealthy farmers. (p. 194)

middle passage *n.* the voyage that brought captured Africans to the West Indies, and later to North and South America, to be sold as slaves—so called because it was considered the middle leg of the triangular trade. (p. 153)

militarism [MIHL•ih•tuh•RIHZ•uhm] *n.* a policy of glorifying military power and keeping a standing army always prepared for war. (p. 215)

Ming dynasty *n.* a Chinese dynasty that ruled from 1368 to 1644. (p. 132)

mita [MEE•tuh] *n.* in the Inca Empire, the requirement that all able-bodied subjects work for the state a certain number of days each year. (p. 147)

monarchy [MAHN•uhr•kee] *n.* a government in which power is in the hands of a single person. (p. 32)

monastery [MAHN•uh•STEHR•ee] *n.* a religious community of men (called monks) who have given up their possessions to devote themselves to a life of prayer and worship. (p. 76)

monotheism [MAHN•uh•thee•IHZ•uhm] *n.* a belief in a single god. (p. 43)

monsoon [mahn•SOON] *n.* a wind that shifts in direction at certain times of each year. (p. 27)

mosque [mahsk] *n.* an Islamic place of worship. (p. 46)

movable type *n.* blocks of metal or wood, each bearing a single character, that can be arranged to make up a page for printing. (p. 58)

mujahideen [moo•JAH•heh•DEEN] *n.* in Afghanistan, holy warriors who banded together to fight the Soviet-supported government in the late 1970s. (p. 273)

mummification [MUHM•uh•fih•KAY•shuhn] *n.* a process of embalming and drying corpses to prevent them from decaying. (p. 26)

Munich [MYOO•nihk] **Conference** *n.* a 1938 meeting of representatives from Britain, France, Italy, and Germany, at which Britain and France agreed to allow Nazi Germany to annex part of Czechoslovakia in return for Adolf Hitler's pledge to respect Czechoslovakia's new borders. (p. 230)

Muslim [MUHZ•luhm] *n.* a follower of Islam. (p. 45)

Muslim League *n.* an organization formed in 1906 to protect the interests of India's Muslims, which later proposed that India be divided into separate Muslim and Hindu nations. (p. 256)

Mutapa [moo•TAHP•uh] *adj.* relating to a southern African empire established by Mutota in the 15th century A.D. (p. 103)

N

Napoleonic [nuh•POH•lee•AHN•ihk] **Code** *n.* a comprehensive and uniform system of laws established for France by Napoleon. (p. 177)

National Assembly *n.* a French congress established by representatives of the Third Estate on June 17, 1789, to enact laws and reforms in the name of the French people. (p. 175)

nationalism *n.* the belief that people should be loyal mainly to their nation—that is, to the people with whom they share a culture and history—rather than to a king or empire. (p. 110)

nation-state *n.* an independent geopolitical unit of people having a common culture and identity. (p. 110)

NATO [NAY•toh] *n.* the North Atlantic Treaty Organization—a defensive military alliance formed in 1949 by ten Western European nations, the United States, and Canada. (p. 248)

Nazism [NAHT•SIHZ•uhm] *n.* the fascist policies of the National Socialist German Workers' party, based on totalitarianism, a belief in racial superiority, and state control of industry. (p. 228)

Negritude [NEE•grih•TOOD] **movement** *n.* a movement in which French-speaking Africans and West Indians celebrated their heritage of traditional African culture and values. (p. 258)

Neolithic [NEE•uh•LIHTH•ihk] **Age** *n.* a prehistoric period that began about 8000 B.C. and in some areas ended as early as 3000 B.C., during which people learned to polish stone tools, make pottery, grow crops, and raise animals—also called the New Stone Age. (p. 19)

Neolithic Revolution *n.* the major change in human life caused by the beginnings of farming—that is, by people's shift from food gathering to food producing. (p. 20)

nirvana [neer•VAH•nuh] *n.* in Buddhism, the release from pain and suffering achieved after enlightenment. (p. 41)

nomad *n.* a member of a group that has no permanent home, wandering from place to place in search of food and water. (p. 19)

nonaggression [NAHN•uh•GRESHS•uhn] **pact** *n.* an agreement in which nations promise not to attack one another. (p. 232)

nonaligned nations *n.* the independent countries that remained neutral in the Cold War competition between the United States and the Soviet Union. (p. 248)

Nuremberg [NUR•uhm•BURG] **Trials** *n.* a series of court proceedings held in Nuremberg, Germany, after World War II, in which Nazi leaders were tried for aggression, violations of the rules of war, and crimes against humanity. (p. 239)

O

Old Regime [ray•ZHEEM] *n.* the political and social system that existed in France before the French Revolution. (p. 174)

oligarchy [AHL•ih•GAHR•kee] *n.* a government in which power is in the hands of a few people—especially one in which rule is based upon wealth. (p. 32)

Opium War *n.* a conflict between Britain and China, lasting from 1839 to 1842, over Britain's opium trade in China. (p. 203)

Oslo Peace Accords *n.* an agreement in 1993 in which Israeli prime minister Rabin granted Palestinian self-rule in the Gaza Strip and the West Bank. (p. 272)

ozone layer *n.* a layer of the earth's upper atmosphere, which protects living things from the sun's damaging ultraviolet rays. (p. 289)

P

Paleolithic [PAY•lee•uh•LIHTH•ihk] **Age** *n.* a prehistoric period that lasted from about 2,500,000 to 8000 B.C., during which people made use of crude stone tools and weapons—also called the Old Stone Age. (p. 19)

papyrus [puh•PY•ruhs] *n.* a tall reed that grows in the Nile delta, used by the ancient Egyptians to make a paperlike material for writing on. (p. 26)

parliament [PAHR•luh•muhnt] *n.* a body of representatives that makes laws for a nation. (p. 112)

partition *n.* a division into parts, like the 1947 division of the British colony of India into the two nations of India and Pakistan. (p. 256)

pastoralist [PAS•tuhr•uh•lihst] *n.* a member of a nomadic group that herds domesticated animals. (p. 94)

paternalism [puh•TUR•nuh•LIHZ•uhm] *n.* a policy of treating subject people as if they were children, providing for their needs but not giving them rights. (p. 200)

patriarch [PAY•tree•AHRK] *n.* a principal bishop in the eastern branch of Christianity. (p. 63)

patriarchal [PAY•tree•AHR•kuhl] *adj.* relating to a social system in which the father is head of the family. (p. 54)

patrician [puh•TRIHSH•uhn] *n.* in ancient Rome, a member of the wealthy, privileged upper class. (p. 34)

patron [PAY•truhn] *n.* a person who supports artists, especially financially. (p. 115)

Pax Mongolica [paks mahng•GAHL•ih•kuh] *n.* the "Mongol Peace"—the period from the mid-1200s to the mid-1300s when the Mongols imposed stability and law and order across much of Eurasia. (p. 96)

Pax Romana [PAHKS roh•MAH•nah] *n.* a period of peace and prosperity throughout the Roman Empire, lasting from 27 B.C. to A.D. 180. (p. 35)

Peace of Augsburg [AWGZ•BURG] *n.* a 1555 agreement declaring that the religion of each German state would be decided by its ruler. (p. 122)

Pearl Harbor *n.* Naval base where, on December 7th, 1941, American sailors awoke to a Japanese attack that led to the American involvement in World War II. (p. 234)

Peloponnesian [PEHL•uh•puh•NEE•zhuhn] **War** *n.* a war, lasting from 431 to 404 B.C., in which Athens and its allies were defeated by Sparta and its allies. (p. 33)

perestroika [PEHR•ih•STROY•kuh] *n.* a restructuring of the Soviet economy to permit more local decision making, begun by Mikhail Gorbachev in 1985. (p. 265)

perspective [puhr•SPEHK•tihv] *n.* an artistic technique that creates the appearance of three dimensions on a flat surface. (p. 116)

pharaoh [FAIR•oh] *n.* a king of ancient Egypt, considered a god as well as a political and military leader. (p. 26)

philosophe [FIHL•uh•SAHF] *n.* one of a group of social thinkers in France during the Enlightenment. (p. 170)

philosophers *n.* thinkers who use logic and reason to investigate the nature of the universe, human society, and morality. (p. 33)

plebeian [plih•BEE•uhn] *n.* in ancient Rome, one of the common farmers, artisans, and merchants who made up most of the population. (p. 34)

PLO *n.* the Palestine Liberation Organization—an organization dedicated to the establishment of an independent state for Palestinians in the Middle East. (p. 272)

polis [POH•lihs] *n.* a Greek city-state—the fundamental political unit of ancient Greece after about 750 B.C. (p. 32)

Politburo [PAHL•iht•BYOOR•oh] *n.* the ruling committee of the Communist Party in the Soviet Union. (p. 265)

polytheism [PAHL•ee•thee•IHZ•uhm] *n.* a belief in many gods. (p. 24)

pope *n.* the bishop of Rome, head of the Roman Catholic Church. (p. 63)

predestination [pree•DEHS•tuh•NAY•shuhn] *n.* the doctrine that God has decided all things beforehand, including which people will be eternally saved. (p. 123)

Presbyterian [PREHZ•bih•TEER•ee•uhn] *n.* a member of a Protestant church governed by presbyters (elders) and founded on the teachings of John Knox. (p. 124)

proletariat [PROH•lih•TAIR•ee•iht] *n.* in Marxist theory, the group of workers who would overthrow the czar and come to rule Russia. (p. 220)

proliferation [pruh•LIHF•uh•RAY•shuhn] *n.* a growth or spread—especially the spread of nuclear weapons to nations that do not currently have them. (p. 284)

propaganda [PRAHP•uh•GAN•duh] *n.* information or material spread to advance a cause or to damage an opponent's cause. (p. 217)

Protestant [PRAHT•ih•stuhnt] *n.* a member of a Christian church founded on the principles of the Reformation. (p. 122)

provisional government *n.* a temporary government. (p. 220)

pyramid [PIHR•uh•mihd] *n.* a structure with a rectangular base and four triangular sides, like those that were built in Egypt as burial places for Old Kingdom pharaohs. (p. 26)

Q

Qin [chihn] **Dynasty** *n.* a short-lived Chinese dynasty that replaced the Zhou dynasty in the third century B.C. (p. 30)

Qing [chihng] **Dynasty** *n.* China's last dynasty, which ruled from 1644 to 1912. (p. 133)

Quetzalcoatl [keht•SAHL•koh•AHT•uhl] *n.* "the Feathered Serpent"—a god of the Toltecs and other Mesoamerican peoples. (p. 145)

quipu [KEE•poo] *n.* an arrangement of knotted strings on a cord, used by the Inca to record numerical information. (p. 147)

Qur'an [kuh•RAN] *n.* the holy book of Islam. (p. 46)

R

racism [RAY•SIHZ•uhm] *n.* the belief that one race is superior to others. (p. 200)

radicals *n.* in the first half of the 19th century, those Europeans who favored drastic change to extend democracy to all people. (p. 180)

Raj [rahj] *n.* the British-controlled portions of India in the years 1757–1947. (p. 203)

rationing [RASH•uh•nihng] *n.* the limiting of the amounts of goods people can buy—often imposed by governments during wartime, when goods are in short supply. (p. 217)

realpolitik [ray•AHL•POH•lih•TEEK] *n.* "the politics of reality"—the practice of tough power politics without room for idealism. (p. 184)

Reconquista [reh•kawn•KEES•tah] *n.* the effort by Christian leaders to drive the Muslims out of Spain, lasting from the 1100s until 1492. (p. 81)

Red Guards *n.* militia units formed by young Chinese people in 1966 in response to Mao Zedong's call for a social and cultural revolution. (p. 252)

Reformation [REHF•uhr•MAY•shuhn] *n.* a 16th-century movement for religious reform, leading to the founding of Christian churches that rejected the pope's authority. (p. 121)

refugee *n.* a person who leaves his or her country to move to another to find safety. (p. 282)

Reign [rayn] **of Terror** *n.* the period, from mid-1793 to mid-1794, when Maximilien Robespierre ruled France nearly as a dictator and thousands of political figures and ordinary citizens were executed. (p. 176)

reincarnation [REE•ihn•kahr•NAY•shuhn] *n.* in Hinduism and Buddhism, the process by which a soul is reborn continuously until it achieves perfect understanding. (p. 40)

religious toleration *n.* a recognition of people's right to hold differing religious beliefs. (p. 37)

Renaissance [REHN•ih•SAHNS] *n.* a period of European history, lasting from about 1300 to 1600, during which renewed interest in classical culture led to far-reaching changes in art, learning, and views of the world. (p. 115)

republic *n.* a form of government in which power is in the hands of representatives, and leaders are elected by the people. (p. 34)

Restoration [REHS•tuh•RAY•shuhn] *n.* the period of Charles II's rule over England, after the collapse of Oliver Cromwell's government. (p. 160)

reunification [ree•YOO•nuh•fih•KAY•shuhn] *n.* a bringing together again of things that have been separated, like the reuniting of East Germany and West Germany in 1990. (p. 268)

Rowlatt Acts *n.* laws passed in 1919 that allowed the British government in India to jail anti-British protesters without trial for as long as two years. (p. 225)

Royal Road *n.* a road in the Persian Empire, stretching over 1,600 miles from Susa in Persia to Sardis in Anatolia. (p. 225)

Russification [RUHS•uh•fih•KAY•shuhn] *n.* the process of forcing Russian culture on all ethnic groups in the Russian Empire. (p. 219)

Russo-Japanese War *n.* a 1904–1905 conflict between Russia and Japan, sparked by the two countries' efforts to dominate Manchuria and Korea. (p. 208)

S

sacrament [SAK•ruh•muhnt] *n.* one of the Christian ceremonies in which Christians believe that God's grace is transmitted to believers. (p. 76)

Sahel [suh•HAYL] *n.* the African region along the southern border of the Sahara. (p. 99)

SALT *n.* the Strategic Arms Limitation Talks—a series of meetings in the 1970s, in which leaders of the United States and the Soviet Union agreed to limit their nations' stocks of nuclear weapons. (p. 284)

Salt March *n.* a peaceful protest against the Salt Acts in 1930 in India in which Mohandas Gandhi led his followers on a 240-mile walk to the sea, where they made their own salt from evaporated seawater. (p. 225)

samurai [SAM•uh•RY] *n.* one of the professional warriors who served Japanese feudal lords. (p. 89)

savanna [suh•VAN•uh] *n.* a flat, grassy plain. (p. 99)

scientific method *n.* a logical procedure for gathering information about the natural world, in which experimentation and observation are used to test hypotheses. (p. 169)

Scientific Revolution *n.* a major change in European thought, starting in the mid-1500s, in which the study of the natural world began to be characterized by careful observation and the questioning of accepted beliefs. (p. 168)

scribe *n.* one of the professional record keepers in early civilizations. (p. 25)

secular [SEHK•yuh•luhr] *adj.* concerned with worldly rather than spiritual matters. (p. 73)

self-determination [SEHLF•dih•TUR•muh•NAY•shuhn] *n.* the freedom of a people to decide under what form of government they wish to live. (p. 224)

senate *n.* in ancient Rome, the supreme governing body, originally made up only of aristocrats. (p. 34)

sepoy [SEE•POY] *n.* an Indian soldier serving under British command. (p. 202)

Sepoy Mutiny [MYOOT•uh•nee] *n.* an 1857 rebellion of Hindu and Muslim soldiers against the British in India. (p. 203)

serf *n.* a medieval peasant legally bound to live on a lord's estate. (p. 75)

shari'a [shah•REE•ah] *n.* a body of law governing the lives of Muslims. (p. 69)

Shi'a [SHEE•uh] *n.* the branch of Islam whose members acknowledge Ali and his descendants as the rightful successors of Muhammad. (p. 68)

Shinto [SHIHN•toh] *n.* the native religion of Japan. (p. 43)

Shiva [SHEE•vuh] *n.* a Hindu god considered the destroyer of the world. (p. 40)

"shock therapy" *n.* an economic program implemented in Russia by Boris Yeltsin in the 1990s, involving an abrupt shift from a command economy to a free-market economy. (p. 267)

shogun [SHOH•guhn] *n.* in feudal Japan, a supreme military commander who ruled in the name of the emperor. (p. 89)

Silk Roads *n.* a system of ancient caravan routes across Central Asia, along which traders carried silk and other trade goods. (p. 38)

Sino-Japanese War *n.* in 1894, a conflict between China and Japan, sparked by the two countries' efforts to dominate Korea. (p. 208)

slash-and-burn farming *n.* a farming method in which people clear fields by cutting and burning trees and grasses, the ashes of which serve to fertilize the soil. (p. 21)

Slavs [slahvz] *n.* a people from the forests north of the Black Sea, ancestors of many peoples in Eastern Europe today. (p. 63)

social contract *n.* the agreement by which people define and limit their individual rights, thus creating an organized society or government. (p. 157)

Social Darwinism [DAHR•wih•NIHZ•uhm] *n.* the application of Charles Darwin's ideas about evolution and "survival of the fittest" to human societies—particularly as justification for imperialist expansion. (p. 200)

socialism *n.* an economic system in which the factors of production are owned by the public and operate for the welfare of all. (p. 196)

Solidarity [SAHL•ih•DAR•ih•tee] *n.* a Polish labor union that during the 1980s became the main force of opposition to Communist rule in Poland. (p. 267)

Songhai [SAWNG•HY] *n.* a West African empire that conquered Mali and controlled trade from the 1400s to 1591. (p. 102)

soviet [SOH•vee•EHT] *n.* one of the local representative councils formed in Russia after the downfall of Czar Nicholas II. (p. 220)

specialization *n.* the development of skills in a particular kind of work, such as trading or record keeping. (p. 21)

sphere of influence *n.* a foreign region in which a nation has control over trade and other economic activities. (p. 200)

standard of living *n.* the quality of life of a person or a population, as indicated by the goods, services, and luxuries available to the person or people. (p. 282)

strike *v.* to refuse to work in order to force an employer to meet certain demands. (p. 197)

stupa [STOO-puh] *n.* mounded stone structures built over Buddhist holy relics. (p. 42)

subcontinent *n.* a large landmass that forms a distinct part of a continent. (p. 26)

suffrage [SUHF•rihj] *n.* the right to vote. (p. 197)

Sufi [SOO•fee] *n.* a Muslim who seeks to achieve direct contact with God through mystical means. (p. 68)

sultan *n.* "overlord," or "one with power"; title for Ottoman rulers during the rise of the Ottoman Empire. (p. 136)

Sunna [SUN•uh] *n.* an Islamic model for living, based on the life and teachings of Muhammad. (p. 69)

Sunni [SUN•ee] *n.* the branch of Islam whose members acknowledge the first four caliphs as the rightful successors of Muhammad. (p. 68)

sustainable growth *n.* economic development that meets people's needs but preserves the environment and conserves resources for future generations. (p. 289)

Swahili [swah•HEE•lee] *n.* an Arabic-influenced Bantu language that is spoken widely in eastern and central Africa. (p. 103)

T

Taliban *n.* conservative Islamic group that took control of Afghanistan after the Soviet Union withdrew its troops; driven from power by U.S. forces in December, 2001, because of its harboring of suspected terrorists. (p. 273)

Tamil [TAM•uhl] *n.* a language of southern India; also, the people who speak that language. (p. 53)

technology *n.* the ways in which people apply knowledge, tools, and inventions to meet their needs. (p. 19)

terraces *n.* a form of agriculture invented in Aksum, in which stepped ridges constructed on mountain slopes helped retain water and reduced erosion. (p. 100)

theocracy [thee•AHK•ruh•see] *n.* **1.** a government in which the ruler is viewed as a divine figure. (p. 26). **2.** a government controlled by religious leaders. (p. 124)

Theravada [THEHR•uh•VAH•duh] *n.* a sect of Buddhism focusing on the strict spiritual discipline originally advocated by the Buddha. (p. 42)

Third Reich [ryk] *n.* the Third German Empire, established by Adolf Hitler in the 1930s. (p. 230)

Third World *n.* during the Cold War, the developing nations not allied with either the United States or the Soviet Union. (p. 248)

three-field system *n.* a system of farming developed in medieval Europe, in which farmland was divided into three fields of equal size and each of these was successively planted with a winter crop, planted with a spring crop, and left unplanted. (p. 105)

Tiananmen [tyahn•ahn•mehn] **Square** *n.* a huge public space in Beijing, China; in 1989, the site of a student uprising in support of democratic reforms. (p. 253)

tithe [tyth] *n.* a family's payment of one-tenth of its income to a church. (p. 75)

Tokugawa Shogunate [TOH•koo•GAH•wah SHOH•guh•niht] *n.* a dynasty of shoguns that ruled a unified Japan from 1603 to 1867. (p. 90)

Torah [TAWR•uh] *n.* the first five books of the Hebrew Bible—the most sacred writings in the Jewish tradition. (p. 43)

totalitarianism [toh•TAL•ih•TAIR•ee•uh•NIHZ•uhm] *n.* government control over every aspect of public and private life. (p. 221)

total war *n.* a conflict in which the participating countries devote all their resources to the war effort. (p. 217)

tournaments *n.* mock battles that combined recreation with combat training. (p. 76)

traditional economy *n.* based on agriculture, with some people working at simple crafts, such as manufacturing cloth or pottery; economic decisions are based on customs, beliefs, religion, and habits. (p. 23)

tragedy *n.* a serious form of drama dealing with the downfall of a heroic or noble character. (p. 33)

Treaty of Kanagawa [kah•NAH•gah•wah] *n.* an 1854 agreement between the United States and Japan, which opened two Japanese ports to U.S. ships and allowed the United States to set up an embassy in Japan. (p. 207)

Treaty of Tordesillas [TAWR•day•SEEL•yahs] *n.* a 1494 agreement between Portugal and Spain, declaring that newly discovered lands to the west of an imaginary line in the Atlantic Ocean would belong to Spain and newly discovered lands to the east of the line would belong to Portugal. (p. 142)

Treaty of Versailles [vuhr•SY] *n.* the peace treaty signed by Germany and the Allied powers after World War I. (p. 224)

trench warfare *n.* a form of warfare in which opposing armies fight each other from trenches dug in the battlefield. (p. 216)

triangular trade *n.* the transatlantic trading network along which slaves and other goods were carried between Africa, England, Europe, the West Indies, and the colonies in North America. (p. 152)

tribune [TRIHB•YOON] *n.* in ancient Rome, an official elected by the plebeians to protect their rights. (p. 34)

Triple Alliance *n.* **1.** an association of the city-states of Tenochtitlán, Texcoco, and Tlacopan, which led to the formation of the Aztec Empire (p. 144). **2.** a military alliance between Germany, Austria-Hungary, and Italy in the years preceding World War I. (p. 215)

Triple Entente [ahn•TAHNT] *n.* a military alliance between Great Britain, France, and Russia in the years preceding World War I. (p. 215)

troubadour [TROO•buh•DAWR] *n.* a medieval poet and musician who traveled from place to place, entertaining people with songs of courtly love. (p. 77)

Truman Doctrine *n.* announced by President Harry Truman in 1947, a U.S. policy of giving economic and military aid to free nations threatened by internal or external opponents. (p. 248)

tyrant [TY•ruhnt] *n.* in ancient Greece, a powerful individual who gained control of a city-state's government by appealing to the poor for support. (p. 32)

U

Umayyads [oo•MY•adz] *n.* a dynasty that ruled the Muslim Empire from A.D. 661 to 750 and later established a kingdom in al-Andalus. (p. 68)

union *n.* an association of workers, formed to bargain for better working conditions and higher wages. (p. 197)

United Nations *n.* an international peacekeeping organization founded in 1945 to provide security to the nations of the world. (p. 246)

Universal Declaration of Human Rights *n.* a 1948 statement in which the United Nations declared that all human beings have rights to life, liberty, and security. (p. 283)

unrestricted submarine warfare *n.* the use of submarines to sink without warning any ship (including neutral ships and unarmed passenger liners) found in an enemy's waters. (p. 217)

urbanization [UR•buh•nih•ZAY•shuhn] *n.* the growth of cities and the migration of people into them. (p. 194)

utilitarianism [yoo•TIHL•ih•TAIR•ee•uh•NIHZ•uhm] *n.* the theory, proposed by Jeremy Bentham in the late 1700s, that government actions are useful only if they promote the greatest good for the greatest number of people. (p. 196)

utopia [yoo•TOH•pee•uh] *n.* an imaginary land described by Thomas More in his book *Utopia*—hence, an ideal place. (p. 118)

V

vassal [VAS•uhl] *n.* in feudal Europe, a person who received a grant of land from a lord in exchange for a pledge of loyalty and services. (p. 74)

Vedas [VAY•duhz] *n.* four collections of sacred writings produced by the Aryans during an early stage of their settlement in India. (p. 40)

vernacular [vuhr•NAK•yuh•luhr] *n.* the everyday language of people in a region or country. (p. 117)

Vietcong [vee•EHT•KAHNG] *n.* a group of Communist guerrillas who, with the help of North Vietnam, fought against the South Vietnamese government in the Vietnam War. (p. 262)

Vishnu [VIHSH•noo] *n.* a Hindu god considered the preserver of the world. (p. 40)

W

Warsaw Pact *n.* a military alliance formed in 1955 by the Soviet Union and seven Eastern European countries. (p. 248)

Weimar [WY•MAHR] **Republic** *n.* the republic that was established in Germany in 1919 and ended in 1933. (p. 228)

Western Front *n.* in World War I, the region of northern France where the forces of the Allies and the Central Powers battled each other. (p. 216)

westernization *n.* an adoption of the social, political, or economic institutions of Western—especially European or American—countries. (p. 159)

Y

Yoruba [YAWR•uh•buh] *n.* a West African people who formed several kingdoms in what is now Benin and southern Nigeria. (p. 103)

Z

ziggurat [ZIHG•uh•RAT] *n.* a tiered, pyramid-shaped structure that formed part of a Sumerian temple. (p. 24)

Zionism [ZY•uh•NIHZ•uhm] *n.* a movement founded in the 1890s to promote the establishment of a Jewish homeland in Palestine. (p. 186)

INDEX

An *i* preceding an italic page reference indicates that there is an illustration, and usually text information as well, on that page. An *m* or a *c* preceding an italic page reference indicates a map or chart, as well as text information on that page.

A

Abbasids, 68–69, 70–71
Abbas, Mahmoud, 272
absolute monarchs, 157–161, 169, 171, 173, 175, 176, 181
absolutism, 156–161, 181
Abu-Bakr (caliph), 66, 67–68
Afghanistan, 273, *m273,* 274
Africa. *See also* East Africa; North Africa; South Africa; West Africa
  AIDS in, 283
  animism in, 40
  Christianity in, 99–100
  civilizations of, 99–100
  economic development in, 285
  geographic contrasts, 99
  imperialism in, 200, 201–202, 205, 285
  independence, 258–260
  maps
    1975, *m258*
    agriculture's emergence, *m20*
    arable land, *m302*
    colonial claims, 1900, *m201*
    empires, *m101, m102*
    exploration of, *m134*
    Islam in, 1200, *m67*
    movement of people, *m47*
    Nile River, *m25*
    Ottomans in, *m137*
    plague in, *m129*
    triangular trade, *m153*
    trade routes, 1500, *m107*
    traditional ethnic boundaries, *m212*
  Muslim states, 100
  nomads, 100
  political developments in 258–260
  Portuguese in, 108, 140–141
  resistance movements in, 202
  role of slavery in, 103, 141, 152–153, *m153*
  Sahara, 99, 100
  Sahel, 99
  trade in, 99–103, 140–141, 152, 154
  in World War I, 217
  in World War II, *m233, 237*
African National Congress (ANC), 260
Afrikaners, 260
Age of Exploration. *See* European Exploration.
Age of Faith, 78, 113
Agrarian Revolution, 192
agriculture, 24, 25, 26, 27, 35, 67, 88, 192, 221, 222, 227
  in Africa, 21, 99, 205, 285
  in the Americas, 37, 145, 149, 147, 153, 285
  in China, 59, 132, 252, 253
  beginnings, 20, *m20*
  in the Middle Ages, 75, 105
  modern advances, 288
  and slavery, 153
AIDS, 283
Akbar, 157
Aksum, 99–100
Alexander the Great, 33–34, 36
Alexander II (Russian czar), 181, 219
Allah, 45, 46, 67, 71
Allies, 216
  World War I, 216, *m216,* 217–218
  World War II, *m233,* 234, 235, 237–239
Almohads, 100
Almoravids, 100
al-Qaeda, 274
American Revolution, 173–174
Americas, the, *See also* Aztec civilization; Inca civilization; Maya civilization; North America.

African influence on, 153
Columbian Exchange, 154, *i164*
colonization of, 150, *m150,* 154–155, *c165,* 173, 185, 188, *c312*
early societies, 144, *m144,* 146, *m146*
economic development, 189, 274–275, 285
empires in, 37–38, 143–148, *m144, m146*
European conquest of, 151–152
European exploration, 141–142, 150
independence, 173–174, 178–179
maps
  agriculture's emergence, *m20*
  European claims, 1700, *m150*
  Latin America, 1800, *m179*
  Latin America, 1830, *m179*
  Mesoamerican civilizations, *m144*
  triangular trade, *m153*
  South American culture areas, *m146*
slavery in, 152–153, *c153*
Amorites, 25
Amritsar Massacre, 225
Anabaptists, 124
Anatolia, *m35,* 36, 135, 136
Andhra Dynasty, 53
Anglican Church, 123, 124, 159, 160
animism, 40, 101
annul, 122
anthropologists, 19
Antoinette, Marie, 175, 176
Anyang, 28
apartheid, 260, 278
apostles, 45
appeasement, 229–230
aqueducts, 36, 62
Arabian Peninsula, 45, 46, 66, 67, 68, 99, 131
Arafat, Yasir, 272
archaeologists, 19
architecture, 27, 34, 71, 77, 117, 138, 147
Argentina, 178, 188, 275
Arkwright, Richard, 193
aristocracy, 32, 34, 228
Aristotle, 33, 49, 70, 168
armistice, 218
art, 33, 36, 42, 54, 58–59, 70, 77, 89, 101, 103, 115, 116–117, 133–134, 138, 153, 218, 222, 253. *See also* drama.
Articles of Confederation, 173
artifacts, 19, 27
artisans, 21, 24, 26, 31, 34, 58, *i90,* 91, 105, 144, 197
Aryabhata, 55
Aryans, 40, 228
Asia, 36, 149, 154
  economic development in, 285
  imperialism in, 202–204, *m204,* 205, 208, 229
  independence, 261–262
  maps,
    agriculture's emergence, *m20*
    colonial claims in, 1900, *m201*
    exploration of, *m134*
    Mongols in, *m97*
    plague in, *m129*
    Southeast Asia, 900–1200, *m298*
    Southeast Asia, 1945–1975, *m262*
    spheres of influence in, *m204*
    trade routes, 1500, *m107*
    treaty ports in, *m204*
  poverty in, *c282,* 282–283
  in World War II, 234–235, *m234,* 238–239
Asoka, 37, 53
astrolabe, 108, 119, 140
Atahualpa, 148, 151
Ataturk, Kemal (Mustafa), 226
Athens, 32–33
  Golden Age of Athens, 33

Atlantic slave trade, 152–153
Attila the Hun, 36
Augustus, 35
Auschwitz, 236
Australia, 198, *m201,* 235
Axis Powers, 230, 231, *m233*
ayllu, 147
Aztec civilization, *m144*
  conquest of, 151
  empire of, 143, 144–145, 148

B

Babylonian Empire, 25
Bacon, Francis, 169
balance of power, 180, 182, 208
Balboa, Vasco Núñez de, 142
Balfour, Arthur, 226
Balkans, 63, 136, 185–186, 215, 234, 269
Bantu-speaking peoples, 21–22, *m47,* 103
barter, 23
Bartolomeu Dias, 108
Bataan Death March, 235
Begin, Menachem, 272
Belgium, 109, 178, *m201, m224,* 232, 238, 259
Benin, 98, *m101, m102,* 103
Bentham, Jeremy, 196
Berlin, *m184,* 184, 238
  blockade, 247, 248
  Conference, 201
  division, 247
  Wall, 248, 268
Bible, 43, 44–45, 63, 118, 119, 121, 124, 125
Bill of Rights
  English, 161
  South African, 260
  United States, 174
Bin Laden, Osama, 274
Bismarck, Otto von, 184–185
Black Death. *See* bubonic plague
blitzkrieg, 232
"Bloody Sunday," 220
bodhisattvas, 42
Boers, 201
Boer War, The, 201–202
Bolívar, Simón, 178, 179, *m179*
Boleyn, Anne, 122–123
Bolshevik Revolution, 219, 220–221, 226
Bolsheviks, 219, 220–221
Bonaparte, Napoleon (French Emperor), 176, 177–178, 180
Bosnia, 215
Bosnia-Herzegovina, 269
Bossuet, Jacques, 157, 161
bourgeoisie, 174, 196
Boxer Rebellion, 203–204
boyars, 158
Brahma, 40, 54
Brahman, 40
Brahmin, 52, 55
Braun, Eva, 238
Brezhnev, Leonid, 249, 265
brinkmanship, 249
Britain, 108, 109, 116, 121, 152, 157, 169, 170, 183
  absolutism in, 159–161
  Anglo-Saxons, 111
  colonies of, 149, 154, 173, 185, 199, *m201,* 202–203, *i211,* 225–226, 256, 258, 259, 260, *m262,* 263
  English Civil War, 160
  Glorious Revolution, 161
  in Hundred Years' War, 113
  Industrial Revolution in, *c192,* 192–195, 197, 198
  Magna Carta, 111–112

Munich Conference, 230
as nation-state, 110, 111–112
Parliament, 112, 113, 122, 123, 156, 157, 159–161, 170, 173, 197, 198, 200, 211, 226
Reformation in, 122–123, *m123*
Renaissance in, 118
Restoration, 160
slave trade, 200
suffrage in, 197–198
and triangular trade, 152, *m153*
urban growth in, 194, *c299*
in World War I, 216, 217
in World War II, 231, 232, 233, *m233*, 237–238, 246
bubonic plague, 62, 109, 104, *i104*, *c109*, 114, 115, 116,117, *m128, m129*
Buddha, 41, 42
Buddhism, 40, *c41*, 41–42, 54, 59, 88, 92
Eightfold Path, 41
Four Noble Truths, 41
Siddhartha Gautama, 41
bureaucracy, 30, 37, 57, 68, 137, 147, 156, 157
burghers, 107
Burma, 42, 235, *m235, m262,* 263
Bush, George W., 272
Bushido, 89
Byzantine Empire, 60–65
Byzantium, 36

C

cabinet, 161
Cabral, Pedro Álvares, 142
caliph(s), 67–69, 70
calligraphy, 71, 89
Calvinism, 123–124
Calvin, John, 123–124
Cambodia, 261, *m262,* 263, 278
Camp David Accords, 272
canon law, 76
Capet, Hugh, 112
Capetian dynasty, 112, 113
capitalism, 105, 154, 195–196, 221, 253
caravel, 108, 119, 140
Caribbean, 139, 141, 151, *m153, c153,* 177, 178
Carolingian Dynasty, 74
Carranza, Venustiano, 190
Carter, Jimmy, 272
Cartwright, Edmund, 193
castes, 36, 52, 54, *i55,* 257
Castiglione, Baldassare, 116
Catherine the Great (Russian empress), 171
Catholic Reformation, 124–125
Catholicism. *See* Inquisition, Roman Catholic Church.
caudillos, 188, 189
Cavour, Camillo di, 183, 184
centralized government, 30, 59, 90, 110, 111–113
Central Powers, 215, *m216,* 218,223, 225
Chandra Gupta I (Indian king), 52, 53
Chandra Gupta II (Indian emperor), 52, 54
Chandragupta Maurya (Indian emperor), 36–37, 53
Chang Jiang, 27, 28, 30, *m32,* 57
Charlemagne, 74, *m74,* 77, 112
Charles I (English king), 160
Charles II (English king), 160
Charles V, 138, 157
Chartist movement, 197–198
Chavín, 146
Chechnya, 267
checks and balances, 170, 174
children, 35, 42, 54, 70, 75, 76, 80, 91, 105, 124, 194, 197, 207, 229, 236, 252, 267, 283, 284
Children's Crusade, 80
Chimú, 146
China, *m298. See also* names of dynasties.
agriculture, 59, 132, 252, 253
Chinese philosophies, 42–43
communes, 251
communism in, 250–254, *c252*
and democracy, 253–254
economic developments, 252, *c252,* 253, 254

foot-binding, 58
and Hong Kong, transfer to, 254
imperialism in, 203–204, *m204*
industrialization, 133, 253
inventions, 31, 58, 96, 108
isolationism in, 132–133
Japanese invasion, 229, 251
Mongol rule, 95–97, *m97,* 131, 132, 133, 139
Nationalists in, 204, 251
North China Plain, 28
"one-child family" policy, 282
People's Republic of China (mainland China), 151, 253
Republic of China, 204, 251
Taiwan, 133, *m204,* 208, 251, 261
Tiananmen Square, 253–254
Yellow River civilization, 27–28
chinampas, 145
chivalry, 75, 77, 113
Christian humanists, 118, 121
Christianity, 44–45, *c45,* 144, 120, 123, 139, 140, 141, 168, 200
in Africa, 99–100
in China, 133, 203
in India, 202
in Japan, 92
and Ottomans, 136
Jesus, 44, 45
in Roman Empire, 45
Christians, 45, 63, 69, 70, 72, 75, 76, 78, 81, 92, 100, 106, 114, 122, 124, 125, 203
missionaries, 92, 133
Churchill, Winston, 233, 237, 246
CIS. *See* Commonwealth of Independent States.
cities, 24, 27, 28, 34, 36, 37, 38, 59, 66, 68, 69, 73, *c84,* 101, 102, 103, 115, 197, 282, *c299*
growth of, 91, 104, 106–108, 116, 137, 145, 147, 148, 155, 157, 194
and rise of civilization, 18, 21, *c21,* 22
city-states, 23, 24, 25, 32
African, 98, 103
Aztec, 144
Egypt, 25
Greek, 32–33
Italian, 107, 108, 115
Maya, 37
polis, 32
Sumerian, 24, 25
civil disobedience, 225, 272
civilization
characteristics of, 21, *c21*
civil service, 30, 35, 57, 89, 132, 185, 256
Cixi (Chinese Dowager Empress), 204
classical art, 33
Cleisthenes, 32
clergy, 63, 76, 107, 121, 174, 175
Clermont, 193
cloning, 288
Clovis, 73
Code of Hammurabi, *See* Hammurabi's code.
Cold War, 248–249, 261, 262, 265, 270, 287
collective farms, 222, 243, 252
colonialism, 139, 141–142, 149, 150, *m150,* 151, 154–155, 173, 178, 185, 187, 188, 189, 199, 200, 201–202, 205, 206, 217, 223, 224, 235, 254, 255, 256, 258, 260, 261, 285, *c312. See also* colonies; imperialism.
colonies, 34, 59, 99, 141, 149, 152, 150, 151, 152, 153, 154, 155, 157, 173, 177, 178, 179, *m179,* 180, 200, 202, 205, 208, 217, 256, *m258,* 263
Columbian Exchange, 154, *i164*
Columbus, Christopher, 139, 141, 142, 149
comedy, 33, 118
command economy, 196, 222
Commercial Revolution, 104, 106, *c106*
common law, 110, 111
Commonwealth of Independent States, 267
communism, 197, 217, 222, 227, 228, 245, 246, *m246,* 247, 248, 249, 250–254, *c252,* 261, 262, 264–267, 268
Communist Manifesto, The (Marx and Engels), 191, 196
compass, magnetic, 58, 59, 108, 119, 140
Confucianism, 42, 59
Confucius, 42, 43, 91

Analects, 42
Congo, *m258,* 259
Democratic Republic of, 259
Congress of Vienna, 180, 181, 182
Congress Party, 225, 256, 257
conquistadors, 151
conservatives, 172, 176, 180, 181, 185, 228, 266, 252
Constantine, 36, 60
Constantinople, *m35, m61,* 60, 61–63, 64, 65, 78, 79, 80, 81, *c84,* 106, 115, 136, *m137,* 159, 217
constitutional monarchy, 156, 161, 175, 220
consul(s), 34, 177
containment, 248, 261
Continental System, 177
Contras, 275
Copernicus, Nicolaus, 168, 169
Cortés, Hernando, 151
Council of Trent, 124
covenant, 43, 44
creoles, 178, 179, 188
Crimean War, 181, 186
Cro-Magnons, 19
Crompton, Samuel, 193
Cromwell, Oliver, 160
crop rotation, 192
Crusades, 78–81, *m80,* 106, 107, 139, 140
Cuba, *m179,* 265, 270, *m274,* 274, 275
Cuban Missile Crisis, 265
cultural diffusion, 24, 38
Cultural Revolution (China), 251–252, *c252*
culture
definition of, 19
complex, 21
Cyrillic alphabet, 63
czar(s). *See* individual names of czars.
Czechoslovakia, *m224,* 225, 230, 245, *i245,* 246, *m246,* 247, 248, 249, 268

D

da Gama, Vasco, 108, 139 141
daimyo, 90, *i90,* 91, 206
Damascus, 68
Dao De Jing (The Way of Virtue), 42
Daoism, 42–43, 59
Darius (Persian king), 157
Darwin, Charles, 200
da Vinci, Leonardo, 114, 116
Declaration of Independence, 173, 174, 175
D-Day invasion, *m233,* 238
deforestation, 286, 289
delta, 25, 57, *m271*
demilitarization, 247
democracy, 32, 33, 34, 170, 180, 188, 189, 204, 226, 228, 247, 250, 253–254, 257, 259, 260, 263, 264, 267, 268, 275, 284
democratization, 247, 264, 265
Deng Xiaoping, 250, 253–254
Depression, the, 227, 228, 229, *c240*
Descartes, René, 169
desertification, 286, 289
Dessalines, Jean-Jacques, 178
destalinization, 249
détente, 265
developed nations, 281, 282, 285
developing nations, 248
devshirme, 137
dharma, 41
Diaspora, 186
Díaz, Porfirio, 187, *i187,* 189–190
Dickens, Charles, 195
dictator(s), 34, 35, 89, 160, 176, 177, 185, 188, 190, 221, 222, 228, 230, 232, 256, 259, 262, 274, 275
"dictatorship of the proletariat," 197, 220, 221
Diderot, Denis, 170
Encyclopedia, 170
direct democracy, 33, 170
disease, 55, 97, 105, 142, 153, 194, 198, 205218, 236, 278, 282, 283, 283. *See also* AIDS; bubonic plague.
in native Americans, 148, 149, 151, 154
divine right, 157, 159, 170
Dome of the Rock, 272
Donatello, 116

Tours, Battle of, 68, 73
trade, 69, 103, 106, 108, 140, 141
Mussolini, Benito, 228, 229, 230, 237, 300
Mutapa Empire, 98, 103
Mutsuhito, *i206,* 207
Myanmar. *See* Burma.

N

NAFTA (North American Free Trade Agreement), 285
Nagy, Imre, 249
Napoleonic Code, 177
NASA, 287
National Assembly, 175
nationalism, 110, 173, 182–186, 190, 198, 202, 204, 207, 221, 225–226, 227
nation-state, 110–113, 125, 183
Native Americans, 141, 149, 151, 152, 154, 179, 188, 189, 283. *See also* individual cultures.
Nazca culture, 146
Nazis, 228–229, 234, 236, 238, 239
Nazism, 228–229, 236
Negritude movement, 258
Nehru, Jawaharlal, 257
nemontemi, 145
Neolithic Age, 19, 20
Neolithic Revolution, 20, *m20*
Netherlands, *m180*
French annexation, 177
German invasion of in World War II, 232
Kingdom of Netherlands, 180
Spanish Netherlands, 157, 158
United Provinces of, 158, 161
New Economic Policy (NEP), 221
Newton, Isaac, 169, 170
Nicaragua, 270, *m274,* 275
Nicholas II (Russian Czar), 217, 219
Nigeria, 21, *m258*
civil war in, 259
democracy in, 259
dissidents, 260
economy of, 259
government of, 259
independence of, 259
martial law, 259
Nile River, 25, *m25,* 26, *m271*
nirvana, 41, 42
Nixon, Richard (U.S. president)
détente, 265
and Vietnam, 262
Nkrumah, Kwame, 258
nomads, 19, 30, 36, 38, 52, 53, 64, 67, 94, 100
nonaligned nations, 248
North Atlantic Treaty Organization (NATO), 248
North China Plain, 28
North Korea, 261
Nuclear Non-Proliferation Treaty, 284
nuclear weapons
during Cold War, 248–249
in India and Pakistan, 257
reduction of, 265, 284
Nuremburg Trials, 239

O

Obregón, Alvaro, 190
Oda Nobunaga, 90
oil, 150, 237, 259, 273, 285
Old Regime, 174, 175
oligarchy, 32, 33
Olympic Games, 33
OPEC (Organization of Petroleum Exporting Countries), 285
Opium War, 203
Orkhan I, 136
Ortega, Daniel, 275
Oslo Peace Accords, 272
Osman, 135, 136
Orthodox Christian Church, *c45,* 63, 65
Ottoman Empire, 135–138, *m137,* 158, 177, 186, 215, 226, 223
Ankara, Battle of, 136
Chaldiran, Battle of, 137
Constantinople, 63, 136, 217

Crimean War, 186
cultural developments of, 137–138
decline of, 138, 185, 186, 226
defeated by Spanish, 158
devshirme system, 137
geopolitics, 186
government, 137
nationalism in, 185, 186
social organization, 137
Suleyman, *i135,* 137–138, 157
in World War I, 214, 215, *m216,* 218, 225
ozone layer, 289

P

Pachacuti (Inca ruler), 146
Pahlavi, Reza Shah (Iranian shah), 226, 273
painting
perspective in, *i116,* 116
Renaissance, 114, 116–117
of Song dynasty, 58–59
Pakistan, 26, 256, *m256,* 257
independence of, 256
Paleolithic Age, 19
paleontologists, 19
Palestine
conflicts with Israel, 271, 272
intifada, 272
Palestine Liberation Organization (PLO), 272
papyrus, 26
Paris Peace Conference, 223, 224, 228
parliament, 112, 113, 122, 123, 156, 157, 159–161, 164, 170, 173, 184, 185, 197, 198, 200, 211, 220, 226, 229, 247, 260, 266, 268, 269
Parthenon, 33
partition
India, 256–257
Palestine, 271
pastoralists, 94
paternalism, 200
Pathfinder, 287
patriarch, 63, 159
patriarchal, 54
patrician, 34
patrons (of the arts), 70, 115
Patton, General George, 238
Pax Mongolica, 96
Pax Romana, 35, 45
Peace of Augsburg, 122
Pearl Harbor, *i231,* 231, 234, *m235*
Peloponnesian War, 33
peninsulares, 151, 188
peonage, 188
Pepin the Short, 74
Pericles, 33
Perón, Juan, 275
Perry, Commodore Matthew, 207
Persia, 33, 34, 53, 62, 67, 70, 71, 93, 95, 96, 97, 99, 137, 138, 157, 226
Persian Empire, 33
Persian Gulf, *m24*
Persian Gulf War, 273
Peru, 143, 146, 178, 179, *m179*
Peter I, "Peter the Great" (Russian czar), 159
Petition of Right, 160
Petrarch, Francesco, 117
Philip II (French king), 79, , 80, *i110,* 112, 157–158
Philip II (Macedonian king), 33
Philip II (Spanish king), 157–158
Philip IV (French king), 113
Philippine Islands, 142, 150, *m204,* 234, 235, *m235,* 238, *m262,* *c282*
philosophes, 170, *c170,* 171
philosophers, 33, 36, 42, 66, 70, 167, 168, 169, 170, 195, 196
Pizarro, Francisco, 151
plague. *See* bubonic plague.
Plato, 33, 70
plebeian, 34
Poland, 64, 124, 181, 225, 230, 232, 245, 246
Solidarity, 267
in World War II, 231, 232, *m233,* 236
polis, 32
Politburo, 265, 268
pollution, 193, 286, 288, 289, 294

Polo, Marco, 96, *m97,* 139
Pol Pot, 263, 278
polytheism, 24, 26, 43, 45
pope(s), 63, 72, *i72,* 73, 74, 76, 77, 121, 122, 123, 184
Alexander VI, 142
Boniface VIII, 113
Great Schism, 120
Gregory I, 73
Gregory VII, 77
Leo III, 72, 74
Leo X, 121
Otto I, 77
Paul III, 124–125
Paul IV, 125
Urban II, 78, 79, 80, 81
Portugal, 157, 177, *m180*
colonies of, 141, 149, *m150, m179,* 179
exploration, 108, 136, 139, 140–141, 142, 150
rivalry with Spain, 141–142
trade, 108, 136, 139, 140–141, 150
predestination, 123
Presbyterians, 124, 160
Princip, Gavrilo, 215
printing, 58, 96, 119
printing press, 98, 119, 121, 140, 167
proletariat, 196, 197, 220, 221
proliferation (nuclear), 284
propaganda, 217, 229, 248
Protestantism, 120, 123, *m123,* 124, 125, 158, 161
Protestants, *c45,* 122, 123, 124, 125, 158, 161, 168, 185
provisional government, 220
Ptolemy, 119, 168
Puritans, 160
Putin, Vladimir, 267
pyramids
Egyptian, 26
Maya, 37

Q

Qin Dynasty, 30, 43
Qing dynasty, 133, 203–204
queens. *See* individual names.
quipu, 147, 148
Quetzalcoatl, *i143,* 145
Qur'an, 46, 67, 69, 70, 102

R

Rabin, Yitzhak, 272
racism, 200, 202
radicals, 124, 176, 180, 183
railroad locomotive, 193
railroads, 189, 193, 196, 197, 202, 205, 207, 268
Raj, 203
Raphael, 116
rationing, 217
Reagan, Ronald (U.S. president), 265, 268
realpolitik, 184
Reconquista, 81, 141, 151
Red Guards
Bolshevik, 221
Chinese, 252–253
Reformation, the, 120–125, 158
Catholic, 124–125
English, 122–123
legacy, 125
Protestant, 120, 121–124, *m123,* 125
women in, 123, 125
Reform Bill, 197
refugees, *i281,* 282
Reign of Terror, 176
religion, 21, 23, 26, 28, 37, 39–46, 65, 69, 95, 136, 145, 148, 153, 161, 167, 169, 174, 175. *See also* individual religions.
religious conflict, 256–257, *m256,* 271–272, 274, 283
religious toleration, 37, 171
Renaissance, 114–119, 121, 138, 140, 159
architecture, 117
art, 116–117
causes of, 115–116